Counseling and Psychotherapy
Theories in Context and Practice

SECOND EDITION

Counseling and Psychotherapy Theories in Context and Practice
Skills, Strategies, and Techniques

John Sommers-Flanagan
Rita Sommers-Flanagan

WILEY

John Wiley & Sons, Inc.

Published by John Wiley & Sons, Inc., Hoboken, New Jersey.
Published simultaneously in Canada.

For general information on our other products and services please contact our Customer Care Department within the U.S. at (800) 762-2974, outside the United States at (317) 572-3993 or fax (317) 572-4002.

Wiley publishes in a variety of print and electronic formats and by print-on-demand. Some material included with standard print versions of this book may not be included in e-books or in print-on-demand. If this book refers to media such as a CD or DVD that is not included in the version you purchased, you may download this material at http://booksupport.wiley.com. For more information about Wiley products, visit www.wiley.com.

Library of Congress Cataloging-in-Publication Data:
Sommers-Flanagan, John, 1957–
   Counseling and psychotherapy theories in context and practice : skills, strategies, and techniques /
John Sommers-Flanagan, Rita Sommers-Flanagan. — 2nd ed.
      p. cm.
   Includes bibliographical references and index.
   ISBN 978-1-119-08420-4 (hardback : acid-free paper)
   ISBN 978-1-119-08789-2 (ePDF)
   ISBN 978-1-119-08791-5 (ePub)
   1. Counseling. 2. Psychotherapy. I. Sommers-Flanagan, Rita, 1953– II. Title.
   BF637.C6S69 2012
   158.3—dc23
                                                        2011038810

Printed in the United States of America

10 9 8

Contents

Preface

One morning, long ago, John woke up in the midst of a dream about having written a theories book. Over breakfast, John shared his dream with Rita. Rita said, "John go sit down, relax, and I'll sit behind you as you free associate to the dream" (see Chapter 2, Psychoanalytic Approaches).

As John was free-associating, Rita tried to gently share her perspective using a two-person, relational psychotherapy model. She noted that it had been her lived experience that, in fact, they had already written a theories text together and that he must have been dreaming of a second edition. John jumped out of his seat and shouted, "You're right! I *am* dreaming about a second edition."

This profound insight led to further therapeutic exploration. Rita had John look at the purpose of his dream (see Chapter 3, Individual Psychology); then he acted out the dream, playing the role of each object and character (see Chapter 6; Gestalt Therapy). When he acted out the role of Rita, he became exceedingly enthusiastic about the second edition. She, of course, accused him of projection while he suggested that perhaps he had absorbed her thoughts in a psychic process related to Jung's idea of the collective unconscious. Rita noted that was a possibility, but then suggested we leave Jung and the collective unconscious online where it belongs (see the Jungian chapter in the big contemporary collective unconscious of the Internet online at www.wiley.com/go/counselingtheories).

For the next week, Rita listened to and resonated with John as he talked about the second edition. She provided an environment characterized by congruence, unconditional positive regard, and empathic understanding (see Chapter 5, Person-Centered Theory and Therapy). John flourished in that environment, but sneakily decided to play

a little behavioral trick on Rita. Every time she mentioned the word *theories* he would say "Yesss!," pat her affectionately on the shoulder and offer her a piece of dark chocolate (see Chapter 7, Behavioral Theory and Therapy). Later he took a big risk and allowed a little cognition into the scenario, asking her: "Hey, what are you thinking?" (see Chapter 8, Cognitive-Behavioral Theory and Therapy).

Rita *was* still thinking it was too much work and not enough play. John responded by offering to update his feminist views and involvement if she would only reconsider (see Chapter 10, Feminist Theory and Therapy); he also emphasized to Rita that writing a second edition would help them discover more meaning in life and perhaps they would experience the splendor of awe (see Chapter 4, Existential Theory and Therapy). Rita still seemed ambivalent and so John asked himself the four questions of choice theory (see Chapter 9, Choice Theory and Reality Therapy):

1. What do you want?

2. What are you doing?

3. Is it working?

4. Should you make a new plan?

It was time for a new plan, which led John to develop a new narrative (see Chapter 11, Constructive Theory and Therapy). He had a sparkling moment where he brought in and articulated many different minority voices whose discourse had been neglected (see Chapter 13, Developing Your Multicultural Orientation and Skills). He also got his daughters to support him and conducted a short family intervention (see Chapter 12, Family Systems Theory and Therapy).

Something in the mix seemed to work: Rita came to him and said, "I've got the solution, we need to do something different while we're doing something the same and approach this whole thing with a new attitude of mindful acceptance" (see Chapter 11, Constructive Theory and Therapy and Chapter 14, Integrative and Evidence-Based New Generation Therapies). To this John responded with his own version of radical acceptance saying: "That's a perfect idea and you know, I think it will get even better over a nice dinner." It was at that nice dinner that they began to articulate their main goals for the second edition of *Counseling and Psychotherapy Theories in Context and Practice*.

OUR GOALS

We have five main goals for this book.

1. To provide a theories textbook that is comprehensive enough and practical enough to serve as a solid foundation for building additional knowledge and skills you'll need to become an excellent mental health professional.

2. To situate the theories that guide the work of all professional helpers within the gender, cultural, and other contexts associated with their development. We believe understanding context is essential to ethical and wise mental health practice.

3. To write about a challenging topic (counseling and psychotherapy theories) in a way that's clear, stimulating, engaging, and occasionally funny. (We firmly believe that if you're able to stay awake while reading you'll have a better learning experience.)

4. To include information that's more practical and applied than is typically included in introductory theories textbooks. We think theories are best learned in a hands-on, practical, and experiential format.

5. To provide faculty with an introductory theories text that will make their teaching experience more pleasant and prepare students for practicing professional skills in the real world

WHAT'S NEW ABOUT THE SECOND EDITION?

There are too many changes from the first to the second editions for us to name them all here. The biggest changes include:

There are **three new chapters**. In the first edition existential and Gestalt theories shared a chapter. To provide greater breadth and depth to our coverage of these important areas we followed our reviewers' recommendations and split them into two chapters. As a consequence you'll find much greater depth in terms of history, theoretical concepts, and application in the new existential and Gestalt chapters. Additionally, we added a chapter on family systems, co-written by Kirsten Murray.

To get the space needed for adding two chapters, after great teeth gnashing and hair pulling, we decided to pull the Jungian chapter out of the text. However, because we didn't want instructors to lose access to the content, **we revised the Jungian chapter and placed it online**. This will enable instructors and students to access the Jungian chapter through the John Wiley & Sons website www.wiley.com/go/counselingtheories.

We expanded coverage of material we consider vital to the helping professions. Specifically, we (a) provide **a stronger definition of counseling and psychotherapy**; (b) include **two brief vignettes** in the 12 theories chapters; (c) review an **extended case example** in each of the 12 theories chapters; (d) **integrate treatment planning information** into the extended case examples. Overall, these expansions and improvements make the text more practical than ever.

There's a stronger focus on three critical issues within the helping professions. Specifically, there's **a deeper and more continuous examination of gender and cultural issues** in Chapter 1 and throughout the text. Additionally, although there's **a stronger emphasis on evidence-based practice**, this emphasis is balanced with a critical and questioning attitude toward the nature of scientific evidence. The section previously titled Therapy Outcomes is expanded and now titled Evidence-Based Status.

Additional changes include:

- A new section on Outcome Measures helps students to see how they might track client outcomes by collecting **practice-based evidence**.

- A **sample informed consent** is included in each theory chapter. These informed consents simultaneously provide a taste of what it might be like to seek therapy from each theoretical perspective and functions as a short summary of each approach.

- A chapter summary and **list of key terms** at the end of each chapter. These terms are italicized when you initially encounter them in each chapter.

- Every chapter has been updated using the latest research and practice literature.

ORGANIZATIONAL FEATURES AND MORE TEXTBOOK HIGHLIGHTS

This textbook has a foundational introductory chapter followed by 13 chapters focusing on specific counseling and psychotherapy theories and applications. The introductory chapter is substantially revised to include and emphasize the following:

- A comprehensive definition of counseling and psychotherapy that will knock your socks off.

- A stronger emphasis on integrating multicultural diversity perspectives and feminist thought into counseling and psychotherapy theory development and application.

- Extended coverage of the scientific context of counseling and psychotherapy—including information and distinctions that help students develop a foundation for critically analyzing contemporary therapy research.

- Crucial coverage of how counseling and psychotherapy can cause harm and positive guidelines to help new practitioners increase positive therapy outcomes while minimizing potential negative effects.

After reading the first edition of this book, the renowned behavioral and constructive theorist and therapist Michael Mahoney commented: **"This is a wonderful text that will both inform and inspire."** In keeping with that description, our goal for each of the 13 theory chapters is to capture the excitement linked to learning and applying specific theoretical ideas and to pass that excitement on to readers. To accomplish this, each chapter includes many essential components in a consistent sequence. These components and the rationale behind them are listed below:

Opening Chapter Objectives: Readers can see the roadmap for their learning at the beginning of their journey.

Biographical Information and Historical Context: To help readers understand the historical and personal context of each theory, every chapter opens with this intriguing information. Depending on chapter content, this information may be covered in a single, integrated section or two separate sections.

Theoretical Principles: Core theoretical principles are described and explained. As much as possible, **concrete and real-life examples are included** to help bring abstract theoretical principles to life.

The Practice of (each therapy approach): Beginning with a **sample informed consent**, each therapy approach is articulated and illustrated. At the end of this section **two vignettes are provided** to help readers see how these approaches are applied in the real world.

Case Analysis and Treatment Planning: Although contemporary counseling and psychotherapy practice typically includes treatment planning—not all historical therapy models fit perfectly into a modern empirically oriented treatment-planning model. Nevertheless, we take the unusual step of providing an extensive case analysis that describes the implementation of theory-based procedures while identifying **a problem list, problem formulation, specific interventions**, and potential **outcomes assessment**. We should note here that most theories texts apply 10 to 14 different theory-based approaches to the same case across all chapters. In this text we decided to illustrate an ethical and evidence-based practice wherein therapy approaches vary based on clients and their particular problem. Consequently, similar to the real world, **you'll never see the same case repeated in this text**.

Cultural and Gender Considerations: Extending this textbook's integrated orientation toward culture and gender, this section includes **a reflection on culture and gender issues** raised in the preceding case analysis as well as more general culture and gender issues associated with each theoretical perspective.

Evidence-Based Status: For the most part, clinicians or practitioners are required to **understand the theory and evidence-base** that supports their treatment approach. Again, although the contemporary scientific paradigm doesn't fit perfectly for each approach, we do our best to review evidence supporting (or not supporting) each theory.

Concluding Comments: At the close of each chapter the authors provide brief comments that help **highlight key issues or integrate key concepts**.

Chapter Summary: New to this edition is a **concisely worded chapter summary keyed to each chapter section**. This summary can be used to provide readers with an initial overview (by reading it first) or to provide a systematic review (by reading it last).

Key Terms: **Key terms are italicized** when first used in each chapter and then included in a comprehensive list at the end of each chapter.

Recommended Readings and Resources: Learning never ends. As a consequence, each chapter concludes with several lists designed **to facilitate future learning**. These lists include: (a) specific theory-based professional journals; (b) theory-based readings; (c) training organizations and websites; and (d) videos/DVDs that show the specific therapy approaches in action.

Questions for Reflection: Questions for reflections are included throughout each chapter. These questions **help readers pause and engage in focused reflection**. Because there's so much material included in each chapter, both students and professors have told us that having specific places to pause and reflect enhances their learning.

Putting It Into Practice: The goal of every theories textbook is to teach readers how to implement various psychotherapy and counseling approaches. To extend our practical application emphasis, we include separate "boxed" information scattered throughout each chapter to help develop and maintain links between theory and practice. These Putting It Into Practice features range from **practitioner commentaries** to **sample informed consents**, to **specific practice activities**. In every case, our goal is to establish clear connections between dense or abstract theoretical material and concrete clinical practice.

BEYOND THIS TEXTBOOK

After publishing the first edition of this text we realized how important it is to develop even better aids to enhance student learning and faculty teaching. The following resources are now available:

A new *Student Manual and Study Guide* for students. This supplementary resource provides students with more of what they need to learn and master the theories of counseling and psychotherapy. The *Student Manual and Study Guide* offers:

- A **theories beliefs pre- and post-test** in each chapter to orient students to key theoretical principles and evaluate how well those principles fit with student values and beliefs.

- An **opening professional development essay** written by a student, practitioner, or faculty member who is active within the counseling or psychology professions.

- A **theory review** section that includes a **glossary of key terms, theories crossword puzzle,** and **critical reflections** on each theory.

- A section on **practice activities** designed to help students experience and practice implementation of each theory.

- A section for each chapter titled **Testing Yourself** that includes a **25-item multiple choice practice test** and a comprehensive **short-answer question review**; these materials will help students succeed on even the most difficult examinations.

- **A closing essay** by another student or practitioner who has applied theory-based knowledge in a practice setting.

A revised online *Instructor's Resource Manual* available to qualified adopters that includes the following teaching aids:

- Sample course syllabi.

- Supplementary lecture outlines and ideas.

- A test bank with 50 multiple choice questions for each chapter.

- Generic PowerPoint slides that can be downloaded and adapted for instructor needs.

ABOUT THE VIDEO RESOURCE CENTER

If a picture is worth a thousand words, then a website full of moving pictures and audio should be worth a million words. We're not certain about exactly how to do the mathematical calculations for this, but we are very certain—along with our editorial team at Wiley—that a "theories" Video Resource Center (VRC) provides an unmatched supplement to this textbook; it also can provide an excellent stand-alone learning experience.

Because there are other theories videos on the market, we should address the question of: Why produce another one? Our goal was create a set of theories videos that were different . . . and hopefully better than the existing options. To accomplish this goal we emphasized

Spontaneity—The videos are not scripted.

Real Life—The volunteer clients in these sessions are talking about real issues.

Ethnic Diversity—The therapists in these videos include a Latina woman, a Vietnamese man, and a Native American woman. Among the clients are a Pakistani woman and an Asian man. This emphasis on diversity gives viewers a glimpse of how different theoretical orientations can fit therapists and clients from differing cultural backgrounds.

Gender Diversity—Both females and males function as therapists as well as clients in the videos.

Diversity of Problems—Without scripting, it was inevitable that the clients in these videos would bring unique problems into the room.

The VRC accompanying this textbook features videos of 11 different therapy approaches in action. These approaches include:

1. Psychoanalytic

2. Adlerian

3. Existential

4. Gestalt

5. Person-Centered

6. Behavioral

7. Cognitive-Behavioral

8. Reality Therapy

9. Feminist

10. Solution-Focused

11. Family Systems

Whether you're watching these videos within the context of a Counseling and Psychotherapy course or on your own, you may use the VRC in any of several different ways. How you choose to use it will depend on your own individual teaching and learning needs. Here are a few ideas:

You can watch the clip in its entirety and just focus on absorbing what you see as an example of a particular therapy prototype.

You can watch the chapter in segments, as each chapter includes an introduction to the specific approach, followed by a video clip of the therapy session, followed by a brief discussion, followed by a final clip from the therapy session.

You can also watch these chapters or segments with a critical eye. Because the therapy sessions are spontaneous and non-scripted, you may notice points during which the therapist struggles (as John does while trying to illustrate the psychoanalytic approach during a 20 minute clip). These struggles may involve the challenges of adhering to a single theoretical model or, quite simple, the struggle of what to say at any given point in a therapy session. In fact, as we've watched these videos ourselves (and with students), some of our best learning has come when our students notice (a) a missed therapeutic opportunity, (b) a theoretical inconsistency, or (c) spontaneously begin discussing how they might have behaved differently (and more effectively!) had they been the therapist in the video.

No matter how you decide to use the VRC, we strongly recommend that you be sure to press the pause button (at least occasionally). We recommend this even if you're choosing to watch it in its entirety.

This is because, as with all therapy sessions, the interactions are rich and nuanced and therefore deserve thought, reflection, and, whenever possible, a lively discussion (you can even do the discussion with yourself if you're feeling in a Gestalt sort of mood). We hope you learn and enjoy the videos available on the VRC and that you find it helpful in your growth and development as a professional counselor or psychotherapist.

In conclusion, although our next true confession is likely no surprise, we feel compelled to admit that the set of videos accompanying this textbook is our personal favorite. However we recognize that you may or may not agree with our highly biased opinion about this. Therefore, we encourage you to not only view our videos, but to also view others and to come to your own conclusion. Even though we think you'll like ours best, we'd love to hear from you either way and so please feel free to email John at john.sf@mso.umt.edu to share your perspective and offer your compliments or your constructive feedback.

ACKNOWLEDGMENTS

Like raising children, writing books always seems to require involving a small village of support people if you ever hope to get a well-developed child (or book) out of your house. We have many people to thank and will undoubtedly miss a few and then need several years of therapy to get over our guilt. Oh well. We've never let the fear of additional therapy scare us out of trying to do the right thing ... which in this case means thanking as many people as we can think of to thank.

Bunched in a small group at the first of the thank-you line is the Wiley team. In particular, we thank Rachel Livsey, Sweta Gupta, Judi Knott, Amanda Orenstein, and Leigh Camp. You all should get gold stars for your patience. Writers are notoriously eccentric and although we've worked to keep our neurotic, absent-minded professor-ness out of our other book-writing activities with John Wiley & Sons, somehow everything leaked out in this one. After four editions of *Clinical Interviewing*, who would guess that John would somehow be unable to correctly read the not-so-fine print involving the manuscript deadline date? You also get additional gold stars for helping us with last-minute details. Thank you again and again.

The next group in the thank-you line is the manuscript reviewer team. Somehow Sweta recruited 10 of you and you each provided us with fantastic chapter-by-chapter feedback on the first edition and excellent guidance for the second. We honor you below in alphabetical order:

Steven L. Berman, PhD, Associate Professor, Department of Psychology, University of Central Florida

Kurt L. Kraus, EdD, Professor, Department of Counseling and College Student Personnel, Shippensburg University

Brandy Liebscher, PsyD, Chair, Department of Psychology, Simpson University

Kurt D. Michael, PhD, Professor, Department of Psychology, Appalachian State University

Jeffrey Parsons, PhD, Director of Program Evaluation and Technology, School of Professional Counseling, Lindsey Wilson College

John Joseph Pietrofesa, Professor, College of Education, Wayne State University

Brent Richardson, EdD, Associate Professor, Department of School and Community Counseling, Xavier University

Lisa B. Spanierman, PhD, Associate Professor, McGill University

Alan C. Tjeltveit, PhD, Professor, Department of Psychology, Muhlenberg College

Donald Ward, PhD, Professor, Department of Psychology and Counseling, Pittsburgh State University—Kansas

Next, we have a list of individuals who were especially helpful with particular chapters—either through a direct contribution of writing, by reading drafts and providing chapter feedback, or by providing helpful information. These honorees are also listed alphabetically by first name.

Alan Tjeltveit, Muhlenberg University

Arthur Nezu, Drexel University

Carl Leguez, University of Maryland

Giorgio Nardone, Direttore del Centro di Terapia Strategica

Jonathon Shedler, University of Colorado—Denver

Judith Beck, Beck Institute for Cognitive Therapy and Research

Jyoti Nanda, Regent's College, United Kingdom

K. Michelle Hunnicutt Hollenbaugh, Texas A&M University—Corpus Christi

Kirk Schneider, Saybrook Graduate School

Kirsten Murray, University of Montana

Kurt Kraus, Shippensburg University

Laura M. Schmuldt, Lindsey Wilson College

Leslie Greenberg, York University

Luis Vargas, University of New Mexico

Marianne Spitzform, Independent Practice

Maryl Baldridge, Independent Practice

Michele P. Manion, Salve Regina University

Natalie Rogers, California Institute of Integral Studies

Nick Heck, University of Montana

Nicki Nance, Webster University

Richard E. Watts, Sam Houston State University

Robbie Dunton, EMDR Institute

Robert Elliott, University of Strathclyde, Scotland

Robert Wubbolding, International Center for Reality Therapy

Scott T. Meier, State University of New York—Buffalo

Sherry Cormier, West Virginia University

Susan Simons, Washington State University

Thomas Burdenski, Tarleton State University

Troyann I. Gentile, Lindsey Wilson College

Veronica I. Johnson, Winona State University

Our next auspicious group includes a few students from our program and one daughter for helping with an (it-will-not-be-named) citation program. Thanks to:

Megan Bagley, MA

Olin Martin, MA

Rylee Sommers-Flanagan, BA

We also have numerous additional students who provided feedback, rated our textbook online, and listened as we tried out new material now and again.

And finally, since authors typically thank their lovely spouses for support and patience, we'd like to finish by thanking each other for being the super-glue that helps everything stick together.

John Sommers-Flanagan
Rita Sommers-Flanagan
Absarokee and Missoula, Montana

About the Authors

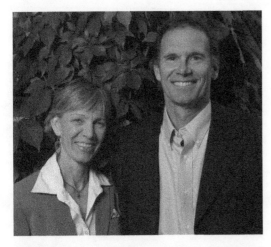

John Sommers-Flanagan, PhD, is a clinical psychologist and professor of counselor education at the University of Montana. He has been a columnist for the *Missoulian* newspaper, a local public radio show co-host of "What Is It with Men?," and is coauthor of over 40 professional publications. John is a long-time member of both the American Counseling Association and the American Psychological Association and regularly presents professional workshops at the annual conferences of both these organizations.

Rita Sommers-Flanagan, PhD, has been a professor of counselor education at the University of Montana for the past 21 years. Her favorite teaching and research areas are ethics and women's issues, and she served as the director of Women's Studies at the University of Montana, as well as the acting director of the Practical Ethics Center. She is the author or co-author of over 40 articles and book chapters, and most recently authored a chapter titled "Boundaries, Multiple Roles, and Professional Relationships" in the new *APA Handbook on Ethics in Psychology*. She is also a clinical psychologist, and has worked with youth, families, and women for many years.

John and Rita work together as the mental health consultants for Trapper Creek Job Corps. They also enjoy providing seminars and professional presentations nationally and internationally.

Together, John and Rita have coauthored seven books, including books aimed at helping mental health professionals work more effectively with their clients:

- *How to Listen so Parents Will Talk and Talk so Parents Will Listen* (Wiley)

- *Tough Kids, Cool Counseling* (American Counseling Association)

- *Problem Child or Quirky Kid* (Free Spirit Press)

- *The Last Best Divorce Book* (Families First)

- *Don't Divorce Us!* (American Counseling Association; also available in Turkish, co-authored with Senel Poyralzi),

John and Rita have also written two other textbooks with John Wiley & Sons. These include:

- *Clinical Interviewing*, 4th edition

- *Becoming an Ethical Helping Professional*

John and Rita have two daughters, one son-in-law, twin grandbabies, and can hardly believe their good fortune. They are deeply rooted in Montana, and in the summers, alternate writing with irrigating and haying on the family ranch. Both John and Rita enjoy professional speaking, exercising, gardening, exploring alternative energy technologies, and restoring old log cabins, old sheds, and any other old thing that crosses their path—which, given the passage of time, is now starting to include each other.

CHAPTER 1

Psychotherapy and Counseling Essentials
An Introduction

My first act of free will shall be to believe in free will. . . .

—William James

A theory is not built on observation. In fact, the opposite is true. What we observe follows from our theory.

—Albert Einstein

For most of history, Anonymous was a woman.

—Virginia Woolf

THIS CHAPTER

- Places the development of counseling and psychotherapy in historical context
- Defines counseling and psychotherapy
- Reviews and describes scientific factors contributing to the development of counseling and psychotherapy procedures
- Outlines essential ethical issues within the mental health and helping professions
- Discusses issues pertaining to the development or emergence of your personal theory of counseling and psychotherapy
- Describes the authors' personal and professional biases
- Offers resources for further learning and professional development

BACKGROUND AND OVERVIEW

The drama imbedded in theories of human pain, suffering, change, and development rivals anything Hollywood has to offer. These theories are revealed in great literature, in myth, in religion, and in our dominant political and social systems. They can explain and predict ways we treat each other, including how we define mental health and mental illness, our ideas about helping, rehabilitation, and personal responsibility. They also help us answer big questions like:

- What motivates people to do what they do?

- What disturbs thinking processes, triggers unmanageable anger, lowers individual productivity, and destroys relationships?

- What makes or breaks an individual?

- What causes one person to be satisfied with a simple and cheerful life, while another claws his or her way ruthlessly to the top?

- What makes some people come out stronger after facing tragedy or hardship, while others are weakened or deeply damaged?

If you've come this far in your studies of psychology and counseling, you know there's no single answer to these questions. It's common for mental health professionals to strongly disagree with each other on just about every topic under the sun. Therefore, it should be no surprise that this book—a book about the major theories and techniques of psychotherapy and counseling—will contain stunning controversies and conflict. In the following pages, we do our best to bring you more than just the theoretical basics; we also bring you the excitement and conflicts linked to these theories of human motivation, functioning, and change.

Human Suffering and Hope

Many years ago, a young man named Philip came for therapy. He was plagued by his own thoughts. When he left the kitchen, he couldn't be sure he'd turned off the stove. When he got out of his car, he repeatedly re-entered it to double- and triple- and quadruple-check to see if the emergency brake was properly engaged . . . even when he was parked on absolutely level ground. He had repeated thoughts about being contaminated. "Have I been infected by worms and germs?" he would wonder. These obsessive thoughts were nearly always followed by a cascade of compulsive behavior; he washed his hands 100 times a day and so his hands were red and chapped.

One day, in the midst of a therapy session, Philip couldn't stop thinking about whether a client in the waiting room had placed his foot on Philip's soda pop bottle, thereby contaminating it. Philip expressed his desire to go out and check to see if this contamination had occurred.

The therapist gently asked about the probability that Philip's pop bottle had been contaminated. Philip acknowledged that, in fact, the bottle had been in his own hands and that the other client had been seated across the room.

Based on this factual information, Philip was asked to engage in behaviors designed to help him break free from his debilitating cycle of obsessive thoughts and compulsive behaviors. The therapist guided him through a relaxation activity, including deep breathing. This approach emphasized response prevention. Philip's compulsion to repeatedly engage in checking behaviors when feeling anxiety was maladaptive or unhelpful. Breaking the link between his anxiety-ridden thoughts and his maladaptive checking behaviors was crucial.

After 20 minutes of relaxation and therapeutic conversation, Philip reported feeling better. A few minutes later, he asked to use the restroom. As he left, the therapist wondered if Philip might be slipping away to perform a checking ritual. She sat for a minute and then walked to the waiting room. There, she saw Philip seated about 15 feet away from a pop bottle, leg stretched out as far as possible, in an effort to see if he could reach the bottle with his foot. His foot was still at least 10 feet from the bottle. The therapist gently intervened and escorted Philip back to the counseling office.

Although there's a psychiatric diagnosis for Philip's condition (obsessive-compulsive disorder) and evidence-based therapies available, there's no guarantee he can successfully change. Psychotherapy is an imperfect science, at least partly because every human is unique with his or her idiosyncratic ways of being. There's much we don't know about human behavior, the brain, emotions, and interpersonal relationships. But hope remains. Many individuals like Philip seek help, overcome many of their debilitating behaviors, and go on to lead happy and meaningful lives.

Understanding why people suffer, how they change, and how to help them live more satisfying and gratifying lives is a fascinating, huge, and important undertaking . . . and the reason this book exists.

Context

Context is a small word with big implications. It's defined as the particular set of circumstances or facts surrounding a specific event or situation. Nothing happens without being influenced by the context in which it happens.

In this text we recognize that theories of counseling and psychotherapy do not represent isolated "truths" and did not suddenly appear devoid of any connection to the time, place, and people involved.

Instead, there were politics, beliefs, wars, scientific discoveries, incidents and circumstances and people and facts and everything else operating together to create and sustain the theories we write about, and the professional activity that we've come to know as counseling and psychotherapy. Context will also cast its long shadow into the future to define and redefine what we mean by counseling and psychotherapy. As a consequence, when describing the theory and practice of psychotherapy, we also weave in a discussion of many contextual factors.

HISTORICAL CONTEXT

Every human practice or set of beliefs has its own particular historical context. This is also the case for psychotherapy and its close relatives: counseling, therapy, mental health consultation, clinical social work, and other human service activities. Unfortunately, history is an imperfect, subjective account of the past. As the old African proverb states, "Until lions have their historians, tales of the hunt shall always glorify the hunter."

Modern psychology originated in Western Europe and the United States in the late 1800s. During that time, women and other minorities were generally excluded from higher education. Consequently, much of psychotherapy's history is written from the perspective of privileged white men advocating a particular theory. This tendency, so dominant in psychology over the years, has inspired several book and chapter titles such as: "Even the rats were white and male" (Guthrie, 2004; Mays, 1988).

Despite these limitations, and recognizing there are neglected feminist and multicultural voices within traditional historical accounts, we begin our exploration of contemporary theories and techniques of counseling and psychotherapy with a look back in time to the possible origins of psychotherapy.

The Father of Psychotherapy?

Theories textbooks often make the metaphoric claim that Sigmund Freud is the father of modern psychotherapy. Although there's truth to this claim, it's impossible to give a single individual the credit—or blame—for an enterprise as huge as psychotherapy. We also can't help but wonder how modern psychotherapy could have been birthed without a mother.

If it were possible or appropriate to bestow a fatherhood title, Freud would be a leading candidate. But Freud had professional forebears as well. For example, back in the late 1890s, the Frenchman Pierre Janet claimed that some of Freud's early work was not original but, instead, supported his (Janet's) previous findings:

> We are glad to find that several authors, particularly M. M. Breuer and Freud, have recently verified our interpretation already somewhat old, of subconscious fixed ideas with hystericals. (Janet, 1901, p. 290, italics added)

Clearly, as we can see from this and other information, Janet believed *he* was developing a new theory about human functioning, a theory that Freud was simply helping validate. Not surprisingly, Janet had conflicts with Freud, and he wasn't alone. Freud's interest in inner conflict was outpaced perhaps only by his propensity, as we will see in later chapters, for interpersonal conflict. With regard to Janet and Freud, Bowers and Meichenbaum (1984) stated: "It is clear from their writings that Freud and Janet had a barely concealed mutual animosity" (p. 11).

Questions remain regarding who, in the late 19th century, initially led the psychotherapy and counseling movements in Western Europe and, later, the United States. However, we should note that even to seek to crown one individual as the first, or greatest originator of psychotherapy is a highly masculinized and Western endeavor. (J. V. Jordan, Walker, & Hartling, 2004; J. V. Jordan, 2010). It's also inappropriate to singularly credit white, Western European males with the origins of counseling and psychotherapy theory and practice. It's unlikely any theory exists that doesn't draw truths and tenets from earlier human practices and beliefs.

Bankart (1997) articulated this point about historic discovery:

> My best friend has a bumper sticker on his truck that reads, "Indians Discovered Columbus." Let's heed the warning. Nineteenth-century European physicians no more discovered the unconscious than John Rogers Clark "discovered" Indiana. Indeed, a stronger argument could be made for the reverse, as the bumper sticker states so elegantly. (p. 21)

Of course, 19th century European physicians didn't discover the unconscious (Ellenberger, 1970). Nevertheless, we're intrigued by the implications of Bankart's comment. Could it be that European physicians, Russian feminists, the Senoi Indians, and many other individuals and cultural groups were "discovered" by the human unconscious? Of all the theorists discussed in this book, we think Carl Jung would most appreciate the concept of an active unconscious seeking to emerge into the awareness of humans (see the online Jungian chapter at www.wiley.com/go/counselingtheories).

Alternative Historical–Cultural Realities: Four Perspectives

Early treatments for human distress and disturbance typically consisted of a combination of biomedical, spiritual, psychosocial, and feminist-indigenous procedures. As you may already know, there's a tendency for old explanations and treatments of mental disturbance and distress to be discovered, rediscovered, and recycled through the ages—which is one reason why a quick historical review is useful.

The Biomedical Perspective

An extreme example of this recycling and rediscovery includes trephining and lobotomies. Early archaeological finds provide evidence of a treatment procedure now called **trephining**. This procedure involved using a stone tool to chip away at a human skull until a circular opening was created. It's believed, in the absence of written documentation, that this opening was a treatment by a shaman or healer to release an evil spirit from the afflicted individual's brain. Although the goal was to address the patient's "evil spirit issues," consistent with the **biomedical perspective**, trephining involved a physical intervention. Interestingly, evidence indicates that some patients survived this crude procedure, living for many years afterward (Selling, 1943).

About a half million years later, a similar procedure, the prefrontal lobotomy, emerged as a popular medical treatment for patients with "mental problems" in the United States. This medical procedure was hailed as a great step forward in the treatment of mental disorders. It was described in *Time* magazine in 1942 (Dawes, 1994):

> After drilling a small hole in the temple on each side of the skull, the surgeon then inserts a dull knife into the brain, makes a fan-shaped incision through the prefrontal lobe, then downward a few minutes later. He then repeats the incision on the other side of the brain. (p. 42, as cited in Dawes, 1994, p. 48)

Although neither lobotomies nor trephining is currently in vogue, many scientists and practitioners are currently investigating and applying physical or biomedical interventions that directly target brain functioning. Examples include psychotropic medications, electroconvulsive therapy (ECT), transcranial magnetic stimulation, vagus nerve stimulation, and deep brain stimulation (Dell'Osso, Priori, & Altamura, 2011; Holtzheimer & Mayberg, 2010; Rasmussen, 2011). The biological perspective is an important area for research and treatment. Although responsible counselors and psychotherapists keep abreast of developments from the biomedical perspective, the focus of this text is on nonbiological (aka psychosocial) explanations for human behavior and on non–biologically based interventions.

The Religious/Spiritual Perspective

Clergy, shamans, mystics, monks, elders, and other religious and spiritual leaders have been sought for advice and counsel over the centuries. It was reported that Hild of Whitby (an abbess of a double monastery in the seventh century) possessed prudence of such magnitude that not only ordinary folk, but even kings and princes, would come to ask her advice about their difficulties (Petroff, 1986). For many Native American tribes, spiritual authority and spiritual practices still hold as much or more salience for healing than most forms of counseling or psychotherapy (Hodge & Limb, 2009; Salois, Holkup, Tripp-Reimer, & Weinert, 2006). The same is true for other indigenous people, as well as those of Western European descent who have strongly held religious commitments. Many Asian and African cultures also believe spiritual concerns and practices are intricately related to psychological health (D. W. Sue & D. Sue, 2008).

Contemporary psychosocial interventions sometimes include components linked to spirituality. In fact, two prominent approaches with scientific support, dialectical behavior therapy (DBT) and acceptance and commitment therapy (ACT), use Buddhist mindfulness approaches to facilitate emotional regulation (Hayes, 2002; Hayes, Strosahl, & Wilson, 1999; Linehan, 2000; Powers et al., 2009; Waltz, 2003). Most practitioners readily acknowledge the emotional healing potential of many spiritual practices and beliefs. Religious and spiritual leaders often have great wisdom, compassion, and insight into the human condition. However, once again, due to this text's focus, we don't directly address spiritual strategies for emotional healing (other than in cases, like DBT and ACT, when the spiritually based practice is integrated into a psychosocial approach; see Chapters 13 and 14).

The Psychosocial Perspective
Just as trephining dates back about 500,000 years, humans have probably also understood, from a time prior to recorded history, that verbal interactions and relationship alterations can change thinking patterns, mood, and behavior. At the very least, we know that for centuries wise healers from many cultures and traditions used psychological and relational techniques that, upon close inspection, look very familiar to current theoretically driven strategies for helping people with psychological change and healing. Typical examples include Siddhartha Gautama (563–483 b.c.), better known as the Buddha and the Roman philosopher Epictetus (50–138

a.d.), both of whom are considered forebears to contemporary cognitive theory and therapy.

A less cited example, from the 10th and 11th centuries, is Avicenna (980–1037 a.d.), a great figure in Islamic medicine. The following case description illustrates Avicenna's distinctly psychological approach to treating mental and emotional disorders:

> A certain prince . . . was afflicted with melancholia, and suffered from the delusion that he was a cow . . . he would low like a cow, causing annoyance to everyone, crying "Kill me so that a good stew may be made of my flesh," [and] . . . he would eat nothing. . . . Avicenna was persuaded to take the case. . . . First of all he sent a message to the patient bidding him be of good cheer because the butcher was coming to slaughter him. Whereas . . . the sick man rejoiced. Some time afterwards, Avicenna, holding a knife in his hand, entered the sickroom saying, "Where is this cow that I may kill it?" The patient lowed like a cow to indicate where he was. By Avicenna's orders he was laid on the ground bound hand and foot. Avicenna then felt him all over and said, "He is too lean, and not ready to be killed; he must be fattened." Then they offered him suitable food of which he now partook eagerly, and gradually he gained strength, got rid of his delusion, and was completely cured. (Browne, 1921, pp. 88–89)

Based on this description, Avicenna appears to have been an early strategic or constructive theorist-practitioner (see Chapter 11).

The Feminist-Multicultural Perspective
It's possible to make a case for including or excluding the **feminist-multicultural perspective** from this set of historical-cultural realities. As an organized, academic discipline, feminist and multicultural pedagogy is rather young. However, because these perspectives have likely simmered in the background and operated in indigenous cultures, we've decided to include it here as a way of articulating its long-term existence.

As discussed previously, traditional historical voices have been predominately white and male. The fact that much of what we read and digest as history has the sound and look of whiteness and maleness is an example of context. Human history and knowledge can't help but be influenced by those who write and tell the history. Nevertheless, as human service providers, mental health professionals must be aware of alternative perspectives that include minority voices (D. W. Sue & D. Sue, 2008; Taylor, 2002).

Brown (2010) illustrates one way in which the feminist mind set differs from traditional male perspectives.

> Feminist therapy, unlike many other theories of therapy, does not have an identifiable founding parent or parents who created it. It is a paradigm developed from the grassroots of many different feminists practicing psychotherapy, and its beginnings occurred in the context of many people's experiences and interactions in personal, political, and professional settings. Because there is no central authority, accrediting body, or founder, those who identify as its practitioners do not always agree on the boundaries of what constitutes feminist therapy. (p. 7)

If historical and contemporary therapeutic processes are viewed through a feminist lens, we might expect a more interconnected, female-oriented, grass-roots design. In fact, feminist influences have quietly (and sometimes less quietly) had progressively more explicit influence on therapy process. Over the past 40-plus years, many feminist concepts and procedures have been integrated into all counseling and psychotherapy approaches. For example, mutuality, mutual empathy, client empowerment, and informed consent all give psychotherapy a more feminist look and feel (Brown, 2010; Jordan, 2010). Similarly, as the United States has become more culturally diverse and the dominant culture has begun to open itself to alternative cultural paradigms, new therapeutic possibilities have emerged and been woven into the fabric of therapy. Most notably, we now know that cultural sensitivity and cultural humility (and therefore multicultural training) are crucial to positive therapy outcomes with diverse client populations (Constantine, Fuertes, Roysircar, & Kindaichi, 2008; Griner & Smith, 2006).

Additionally, distinctly Eastern therapy techniques and strategies such as mindfulness now hold prominent positions within several contemporary and evidence-based therapeutic modalities (Linehan, 1993).

Historically, counseling and psychotherapy focused on helping individuals move toward individuation, independence, and rational thinking. Behaviors associated with dependence and powerful emotional expression have generally been viewed as pathological. In contrast, feminist and multicultural perspectives emphasize relationship and community over individuality. These are human values that counseling and psychotherapy professionals are beginning to recognize and appreciate as different ways of being and not as pathological. Going forward, feminist and multicultural values will continue to influence and be integrated into traditional psychotherapy systems. Watching how the field of counseling and psychotherapy deals with conflicts and challenges inherent in this process will be fascinating.

DEFINITIONS OF COUNSELING AND PSYCHOTHERAPY

Over the years, because many students want to work with people and learn to do counseling, they've asked us: "Should I get a PhD in psychology, a master's degree in counseling, or a master's in social work?"

This question usually brings forth a lengthy response, during which we not only explain the differences between these various degrees, but also discuss additional career information pertaining to the PsyD degree, psychiatry, school counseling, school psychology, and the psychiatric nurse practitioner credential. Generally, this discussion leads to the confusing topic of the differences between counseling and psychotherapy. If time permits during these discussions, we also offer up our thoughts about the meaning of life.

Sorting out differences between mental health disciplines can be difficult. When responding to the question "In relation to being a successful therapist, what are the differences between psychiatrists, social workers, and psychologists?" Jay Haley wrote: "Except for ideology, salary, status, and power the differences are irrelevant" (Haley, 1977, p. 165). This response accurately captures the fact that many professional tracks can lead you toward becoming a successful therapist, despite a few ideological, salary, status, and power differences.

In this section we explore three confusing and sometimes conflict-ridden questions: What is psychotherapy? What is counseling? And what are the differences between the two?

What Is Psychotherapy?

Anna O., an early psychoanalytic patient of Breuer, referred to the treatment she received as **"the talking cure."** This is an elegant, albeit vague description of psychotherapy. Technically, it tells us very little, but at the intuitive level, it explains psychotherapy very well. Anna is proclaiming something most people readily admit: Talking, expressing, verbalizing, or somehow sharing one's pain is, in and of itself, potentially healing. Of course, this definition doesn't and shouldn't satisfy contemporary psychotherapy researchers, but it provides an elegant historic and foundational frame.

As we write today, a heated debate about how psychotherapy should be practiced is flaring (Baker, McFall, & Shoham, 2008; Littell, 2010; Rakovshik & McManus, 2010; Shedler, 2010). This debate won't soon end and is directly relevant to how psychotherapy is defined (Wampold, 2010). We explore dimensions of this debate in the pages to come. For now, keep in mind that although historically Anna O. viewed and experienced *talking as her cure* (an expressive process), many contemporary evidence-based researchers and writers emphasize that the opposite is more important—that a future Anna O. would benefit even more from *listening to and learning from her therapist* (a receptive process). Based on this perspective, some factions in the **great psychotherapy debate** believe therapists are more effective when they actively and expertly teach their

clients cognitive and behavioral principles and skills (aka psychoeducation).

QUESTIONS FOR REFLECTION

Think about where you stand on this issue. Is listening to clients more important than teaching them? Or should therapists actively teach their clients specific skills? Or perhaps you can see around this dichotomy. Are there other possibilities?

Despite the great debates over what constitutes effective psychotherapy, we have four favorite psychotherapy definitions we'd like to share:

1. "A conversation with a therapeutic purpose" (Korchin, 1976).

2. "The purchase of friendship" (Schofield, 1964).

3. "[A] situation in which two people interact and try to come to an understanding of one another, with the specific goal of accomplishing something beneficial for the complaining person" (Bruch, 1981).

4. "When one person with an emotional disorder gets help from another person who has a little less of an emotional disorder" (J. Watkins, personal communication, October 13, 1983).

What Is Counseling?

In some settings, an evaluative or judgmental distinction is made between counseling and psychotherapy. In fact, Alfred Adler, whom we'll get to know more intimately in Chapter 3, might claim that counseling has an inferiority complex with respect to its older sibling, psychotherapy (Adler, 1958). Or, perhaps more accurately, it could be claimed that psychotherapy has a superiority complex with respect to its younger rival, counseling. Either way, at some point you may notice or experience a judgmental-sounding side to the distinction between psychotherapy and counseling.

Overall, counselors have struggled with the definition of their craft in ways similar to psychotherapists. Consider, for example, this quotation:

Counseling is indeed an ambiguous enterprise. It is done by persons who can't agree on what to call themselves, what credentials are necessary to practice, or even what the best way is to practice—whether to deal with feelings, thoughts, or behaviors; whether to be primarily supportive or confrontational; whether to focus on the past or the present. Further, the consumers of counseling services can't exactly articulate what their concerns are, what counseling can and can't do for them, or what they want when it's over. (Kottler & Brown, 2008, pp. 16–17)

As with the term *psychotherapy*, a good definition of *counseling* is hard to find. Here's a sampling:

• "Counseling is the artful application of scientifically derived psychological knowledge and techniques for the purpose of changing human behavior" (Burke, 1989, p. 12).

• "Counseling consists of whatever ethical activities a counselor undertakes in an effort to help the client engage in those types of behavior that will lead to a resolution of the client's problems" (Krumboltz, 1965, p. 3).

• "[Counseling is] an activity . . . for working with relatively normal-functioning individuals who are experiencing developmental or adjustment problems" (Kottler & Brown, 1996, p. 7).

With both lists of definitions in mind, we turn now to the question of the differences between counseling and psychotherapy.

What Are the Differences Between Psychotherapy and Counseling?

Years ago, Patterson (1973) answered this question directly by claiming: "There are no essential differences between counseling and psychotherapy" (p. xiv). Of course, Patterson's comment could be taken to mean that although there are no essential

differences between counseling and psychotherapy, there are *unessential* differences. On this issue, we find ourselves in step with Corsini and Wedding (2000), who stated:

Counseling and psychotherapy are the same qualitatively; they differ only quantitatively; there is nothing that a psychotherapist does that a counselor does not do. (p. 2)

This suggests that both counselors and psychotherapists engage in the same behaviors—listening, questioning, interpreting, explaining, advising, and so on, but may do so in different proportions.

Generally, psychotherapists are less directive, go a little deeper, work a little longer, and charge a higher fee. In contrast, counselors are slightly more directive, work more on developmentally normal—but troubling—issues, work more overtly on practical client problems, work more briefly, and charge a bit less for their services. Of course, in the case of individual counselors and psychotherapists, each of these rules may be reversed. For example, some counselors work longer with clients and charge more, whereas some psychotherapists work more briefly with clients and charge less. Additionally, although it used to be that counselors worked with less disturbed clients and psychotherapists worked with more disturbed patients, now, perhaps because obtaining services from master's-level counselors or social workers is less expensive, counselors often work more with lower income clients whose financial stress interacts with and complicates their personal and family problems.

QUESTIONS FOR REFLECTION

In your community and at your university are counseling and psychotherapy considered with equal (or unequal) reverence? What sorts of people go see a counselor vs. a psychotherapist? How do professional training programs in counseling, social work, psychology, and psychiatry distinguish themselves from one another on your campus or within your community?

A Working Definition of Counseling and Psychotherapy

At the very least, there are strong similarities between counseling and psychotherapy. At the most, they may be considered identical. Because the similarities vastly outweigh the differences we use the words *counseling* and *psychotherapy* interchangeably. And sometimes we insert the word *therapy* as a third, perhaps less divisive, alternative.

For the purposes of this text and to keep things simple, we offer a 12-part general definition of counseling and psychotherapy (in case you weren't sure, this reference to keeping things "simple" is an example of sarcasm). Counseling or psychotherapy is:

(a) a process that involves (b) a trained professional who abides by (c) accepted ethical guidelines and has (d) skills and competencies for working with (e) diverse individuals who are in distress or have life problems that led them to (f) seek help (possibly at the insistence of others) or they may be (g) choosing to seek personal growth, but either way, these parties (h) establish an explicit agreement (informed consent) to (i) work together (more or less collaboratively) toward (j) mutually agreed on or acceptable goals (k) using theoretically-based or evidence-based procedures that, in the broadest sense have been shown to (l) facilitate human learning or human development or effectively reduce disturbing symptoms.

We should note that, although this definition is long and multifaceted, it's still probably insufficient. For example, it wouldn't fit for any self-administered forms of therapy, such as self-analysis or self-hypnosis—although we're quite certain if you read through this definition several times you're likely to experience a self-induced hypnotic trance-state.

WHAT IS A THEORY?

As long as we're making our way through elusive definitions, we should attempt to define the word *theory*.

Basically, a theory involves a gathering together and organizing of knowledge about a particular object or phenomenon. In psychology, theories are used to generate hypotheses about human thinking, emotions, and behavior. Most of us, as a function of being social creatures, build our own personalized theories about human behavior. These personal theories guide our observations and evaluations of others. This makes all of us theorists (or potential theorists) even though our thinking isn't as explicit (or as detailed) as most famous psychological theorists.

A theory needs to accurately describe, explain, and predict a wide range of therapist and client behaviors. A theory also needs to have relevance to its domain. For example, a good theory should clearly explain what causes client problems (or psychopathology) and offer specific strategies for how to alleviate these problems. Think back to the case of Philip from earlier in this chapter: A good theory would (a) explain how he developed his obsessive and compulsive symptoms, (b) provide strategies for change, and (c) predict how Philip would respond to various therapy techniques. These predictions should help us know what techniques to use, how long therapy will last, and how a particular technique is likely to affect a particular client.

A great task of theory is to provide therapists with a clear model or foundation from which they conduct their professional service. To be without a theory, to be a "vulnerable, directionless creature" (Prochaska & Norcross, 2003, p. 4), is something most of us would just as soon avoid.

Some psychological theorists have claimed their particular theory can and should be used to predict and control human behavior (Skinner, 1971; Watson, 1913, 1924). As British psychologist David Smail writes, we should be concerned when prediction and control become the goal of psychological theory:

[T]he prediction and control of human behavior is, as an aim of human inquiry, no new phenomenon: it expresses an intellectual aspiration as old as magic, and restates a practical interest dear to the hearts of tyrants ever since time began. (Smail, 1984, p. 47)

Smail's concerns are important. Although the theories in this book were designed to explain and address suffering and to facilitate human healing, growth and development, they should still be examined with a critical eye to whether they're being implemented in ways that respect human dignity and freedom.

THE SCIENTIFIC CONTEXT OF COUNSELING AND PSYCHOTHERAPY

All treatments that address human suffering should be rigorously evaluated to determine their effectiveness. This section reviews historical and contemporary developments in the evaluation of counseling and psychotherapy.

Major Historical Developments: Eysenck's Review

In 1952, Hans Eysenck published a bold and controversial article titled "The Effects of Psychotherapy: An Evaluation." In the article, he claimed that after over 50 years of therapy, research, and practice, no evidence existed attesting to its beneficial effects. He stated that "roughly 2/3 of a group of neurotic patients will recover or improve to a marked extent within about two years of the onset of their illness [in the absence of treatment]" (Eysenck, 1952, p. 322). Further, he compared this natural recovery rate with rates produced by traditional psychotherapy and reported that,

> patients treated by means of psychoanalysis improved to the extent of 44%; patients treated eclectically improved to the extent of 64%; patients treated only custodially or by general practitioners improved to the extent of 72%. There thus appears to be an inverse correlation between recovery and psychotherapy. (p. 322)

As you can imagine, Eysenck's article sparked strong reactions among psychotherapy researchers and practitioners. Supporters of psychotherapy complained that Eysenck's conclusions were based on poorly controlled studies; they clamored that he didn't address severity of diagnosis issues; and they moaned that the measures of improvement used in the studies he reviewed were generally poor and crude. Overall, Eysenck's critics were correct—his review was flawed. Of course, a primary reason for this was because many existing studies of counseling and psychotherapy effectiveness were also flawed. The truth is, despite the fact that psychotherapy researchers and practitioners in the 1950s believed psychotherapy was more effective than no treatment, they hadn't adequately gathered scientific evidence to support their beliefs.

A Psychotherapy Research Boom

Along with other factors, Eysenck's psychotherapy critique motivated researchers to evaluate psychotherapy efficacy with greater scientific scrutiny. As a consequence, many treatment outcomes studies were conducted on many different therapeutic approaches. For the most part, Eysenck's critique was laid to rest in the 1970s and early 1980s when several substantial and positive literature reviews focusing on psychotherapy efficacy were published.

Two highly influential reviews were conducted by Mary Smith and Gene Glass who developed a new statistical method for combining information across different treatment outcomes studies (Smith & Glass, 1977; Smith, Glass, & Miller, 1980). Smith and Glass's method, **meta-analysis**, is now a household name in research and statistics. As applied to psychotherapy treatment outcomes, meta-analysis pools together and obtains an overall average effect size from outcome measures across different therapy research studies. **Effect size** (ES) is a statistic used to estimate how much change is produced by a particular intervention. ES is reported as the statistic d and represents the difference in efficacy between evaluated interventions (e.g., psychoanalytic psychotherapy or cognitive therapy) and no-treatment control groups. Additional

Table 1.1   A Closer Look at Effect Sizes

Descriptive Terms	ES or d	Percentile rank magnitude of ES
Humongous	+2.00	97.7
Very large	+1.00	84.0
Large	+0.80	79.0
Smith, Glass, & Miller, 1977	+0.68	75.0
Medium	+0.50	69.0
Small	+0.20	58.0
None	+0.00	50.0
Adverse effects	−0.20	42.0

Note: This Table places the Smith & Glass (1977) meta-analysis results in context of Cohen's (1977) traditional descriptive terms of small, medium, and large effect sizes. These effect sizes are also listed in terms of their percentile rank. When researchers, like Smith and colleagues, state: "the average client treated with psychotherapy was better off than 75% of clients who received no treatment" they're using percentile rankings. As you can see from the table, if there is no effect size ($d = +0.00$), then "the average person receiving the intervention would be better off than 50% of people not receiving treatment." In other words, on average, there would be no effect.

information about meta-analytic effect size (ES or d) is in Table 1.1.

In 1977, Smith and Glass published their landmark review, titled, "Meta-analysis of psychotherapy outcome studies." They evaluated 375 outcome studies and reported that the average study "showed a .68 standard deviation superiority [ES or d] of the treated group over the control group" (Smith & Glass, 1977, p. 756). They concluded that the average client treated with psychotherapy was better off than 75% of clients who received no treatment. Later, upon expanding their study to 475 outcome studies and publishing the results in a book, they concluded that the average treated person was better off than 80% of the untreated sample (Smith et al., 1980).

Although Smith and her colleagues helped settle the issue of whether psychotherapy is generally efficacious, they didn't clear up the big debate over whether one form of therapy was more effective than others. This is because Smith and colleagues generally found that different therapist theoretical orientations and different techniques didn't produce

significantly different outcomes. Their findings, consistent with previous and later research, lent support to the conclusion that, "Everybody has won and all must have prizes" (a quotation from *Alice in Wonderland's* Dodo Bird). Consequently, the relative equivalent efficacy of various therapy approaches is now often referred to as the **Dodo bird effect** (Luborsky, Singer, & Luborsky, 1975).

Overall, despite initial outrage over Eysenck's article, it's now easy to see that he provided the entire field of psychotherapy with a much-needed reality check. Perhaps the most important and enduring consequence of the Eysenck effect was a greater emphasis on the need for scientific evidence to support counseling and psychotherapy practice.

The Great Psychotherapy Debate

At the close of the 20th century, Hubble, Duncan, and Miller (1999) reflected on psychotherapy outcomes research with undaunted optimism:

> The uncertainties loosed on the clinical and counseling disciplines by Eysenck and like-minded critics have now been set aside. Therapy works. . . . More than 40 years of outcome research make clear that therapists are not witch doctors, snake oil peddlers, or over-achieving do-gooders. . . . Study after study, meta-analyses, and scholarly reviews have legitimized psychologically based or informed interventions. Regarding at least its general efficacy, few believe that therapy need be put to the test any longer. (1999, pp. 1–2)

Hubble et al. weren't alone in their positive evaluation of therapy. As they implied, nearly everyone agreed (and still does) that psychotherapy is generally more effective than no treatment (Miller, 2010; Norcross & Lambert, 2011; Weiner & Bornstein, 2009).

Given the celebratory language about psychotherapy effectiveness, you might be thinking the big debate is over. After all, if there's agreement that therapy is significantly better than no treatment, what's left to argue about? Well, as is typically the case with humans, there's plenty to keep arguing about. The deepest of these arguments focuses on the following point and counterpoint:

- *Point*: Research has demonstrated the superiority of a few select psychotherapy techniques over other specific techniques; these techniques should be identified as "empirically supported" or "evidence-based" and should constitute the primary techniques or methods employed by mental health practitioners.

- *Counterpoint*: Research doesn't show that some specific techniques are better than others; instead, research shows there are common therapeutic factors operating across different therapy techniques, rendering them all, more or less, equivalent. Therefore, psychotherapists should be trained to deliver therapy in ways that emphasize these common factors.

Wampold (1997, 2001) labeled this conflict: "The Great Psychotherapy Debate."

Like all good arguments, the great psychotherapy debate is multidimensional. These dimensions include (but are not limited to) questions like: (a) What constitutes scientific evidence? and (b) Can we take scientifically based therapy techniques and procedures, generalize them to real-world clinical settings, and expect them to work the same as they do in research settings? In this section we dive headlong into the great psychotherapy debate and then later step back to examine the questions about what constitutes science and whether we can directly apply scientific research findings to clinical practice.

For now, let's pretend the preceding counterpoint is true or mostly true. That is, if positive treatment outcomes are mostly produced by a few common therapeutic factors, what are those factors?

Common Therapeutic Factors

Many researchers have conducted theoretical and empirical analyses of **common therapeutic factors** (Frank, 1961; J. D. Frank & J. B. Frank, 1991; Lambert, 1992; Wampold, 2001). The following discussion focuses on Lambert's (1992) four-factor model.

In his review, Lambert (1992) identified the following four common factors and estimated how much each factor typically accounts for therapeutic change.

1. Extratherapeutic factors (40%).
2. Therapeutic relationship (30%).
3. Expectancy (placebo effects; 15%).
4. Techniques (15%).

Lambert's estimates are, of course, simply estimates and not designed to be perfectly precise (Beutler, 2009). However, his conceptual frame is strong and meaningful and has become a popular way of thinking about how therapy works—especially within the common factors camp.

Extratherapeutic Factors

Lambert (1992) defines **extratherapeutic factors** broadly. They include client factors such as severity of disturbance, motivation, capacity to relate to others, ego strength, psychological-mindedness, and the ability to identify a single problem to work on in counseling, as well as "sources of help and support within [client] environments" (Asay & Lambert, 1999, p. 33). For example, many clients who experience spontaneous remission (sudden improvement without therapy) do so because of positive support from important people in their lives. Lambert contends that extratherapeutic change factors account for about 40% of client success.

Therapeutic Relationship

There are at least two ways the **therapeutic relationship** seems to generate positive therapy results. First, as Rogers (1942) posited, when therapists connect with clients using the core conditions of unconditional positive regard, empathy, and congruence, positive therapeutic outcomes are facilitated (see Chapter 6). Rogers referred to these conditions as therapist attitudes.

Second, as Freud originally implied, the therapeutic alliance, characterized by an attachment between therapist and client working together, also seems to be a relationship ingredient that fosters client improvement. This alliance or bond between therapist and client has been identified as an important therapeutic component in many studies (Barber, Connolly, Crits-Christoph, Gladis, & Siqueland, 2009; Byrd, Patterson, & Turchik, 2010; Crits-Christoph, Gibbons, & Hearon, 2006; Kendall et al., 2009; Meissner, 2007). A specific interaction that's both an example of the therapeutic alliance and that likely facilitates or deepens the therapy alliance occurs when therapist and client collaborate on goal setting. Overall, Lambert estimates that therapeutic relationship factors account for about 30% of the variation in therapy outcomes.

Expectancy

Frank (1961) defined this therapeutic variable as hope. Vastly different procedures can all be viewed as including positive **expectancy** or hope as an active therapeutic ingredient. Obviously, as a potential positive change factor, hope is complex and can be used and abused. Interestingly, controlled research studies indicate that clients treated with placebos (an inert substance with no inherent therapeutic value) are usually better off than clients who receive no treatment and often do just as well as clients who take antidepressant medications for depressive symptoms (Overholser, 2006; Turner, Matthews, Linardatos, Tell, & Rosenthal, 2008). Overall, Lambert estimated that expectation, hope, and placebo factors account for 15% of the variation in therapy outcomes.

Techniques

In the 1870s, Anton Mesmer, then famous for "mesmerizing" or hypnotizing patients would have claimed that his particular technique—involving purple robes, rods of iron, and magnetic baths—produced therapeutic change due to shifting magnetic fields or "animal magnetism." More recently, psychoanalysts would say helping clients develop insight into repeating destructive relationship patterns is essential; in contrast, behaviorists would claim exposure and response prevention techniques are powerful change ingredients.

For better or worse, common factors proponents would point out that Mesmer, as well as the psychoanalysts and behaviorists, are generally incorrect (Duncan, Miller, Wampold, & Hubble, 2010; Norcross & Lambert, 2011). Instead, although their techniques appear invaluable, research indicates

that extratherapeutic factors, the therapy relationship, and expectation are even more powerful psychotherapeutic factors. Recently, Duncan and colleagues (2010) stated:

> To be frank, any assertion for the superiority of special treatments for specific disorders should be regarded, at best, as misplaced enthusiasm, far removed from the best interests of consumers. (p. 422)

This isn't to say that technique is unimportant to therapeutic success. In most cases, the preceding three factors are all activated while therapists employ specific therapy techniques. Consequently, although it's difficult to show different efficacy rates based on different techniques, doing counseling or psychotherapy without a theoretical model and techniques is difficult to imagine.

With all this in mind, Lambert estimated that 15% of treatment outcomes variation is due to the specific techniques employed. Wampold (2001) has suggested it may be as low as 4%.

What Constitutes Evidence? Efficacy, Effectiveness, and Other Research Models

To some extent, all contemporary helping interventions should have at least some supportive scientific evidence. This statement, as bland and general as it may seem, would generate substantial controversy among academics, scientists, and people on the street. One man or one woman's evidence may or may not stand up to another man or woman's scrutiny. That being the case, we should state up front that we understand and embrace the ultimate subjectivity of human experience. We also recognize that because humans design scientific studies and construct and administer all assessment instruments, evaluation processes associated with measuring treatment outcomes always include error and subjectivity. At the same time, lest we arouse the ghost of B. F. Skinner or be required to give back our dusty diplomas, we should state with equal emphasis that we support and respect the scientific method and appreciate efforts to objectively measure psychotherapy outcomes. Understanding the ubiquity of subjectivity, while engaging in scientific pursuits, is a paradox or dialectic that can help improve research quality.

There are two primary approaches to counseling and psychotherapy outcomes research: (1) efficacy research and (2) effectiveness research. These terms flow from the well-known experimental design concepts of internal and external validity (Campbell, Stanley, & Gage, 1963). **Efficacy research** employs experimental designs that maximize **internal validity**, allowing researchers to comment on causal mechanisms; **effectiveness research** uses experimental designs that maximize **external validity**, allowing researchers to comment on generalizability of their findings.

Efficacy Research

Efficacy research involves tightly controlled experimental trials with high internal validity. Within medicine, psychology, counseling, and social work, **randomized controlled trials (RCTs)** are considered the scientific research gold standard for determining treatment efficacy. An RCT statistically compares outcomes between a randomly assigned treatment group and a control group. In medicine and psychiatry, the control group is usually administered an inert placebo (i.e., placebo pill). Consequently, treatment is considered efficacious if the active medication relieves symptoms, on average, at a rate significantly higher than placebo. In psychology, counseling, and social work, treatment groups are generally compared with a waiting list or attention-placebo control group. To maximize researcher control over independent variables, RCTs require that participants meet specific inclusion and exclusion criteria prior to being randomly assigned to a treatment or comparison group. This allows researchers to statistically determine with a greater degree of certainty whether the treatment itself had a direct or causal effect on treatment outcomes. To give you a better feel for the extensive experimental controls involved in an RCT, see Putting it in Practice 1.1.

Before discussing effectiveness research, it's important to examine historical context as it relates to efficacy research.

In 1986, Gerald Klerman, then head of the National Institute of Mental Health, gave a keynote address to the Society for Psychotherapy Research. During his speech, he emphasized that psychotherapy should be evaluated systematically through randomized controlled trials (RCTs). Further, he claimed:

> We must come to view psychotherapy as we do aspirin. That is, each form of psychotherapy must have known ingredients, we must know what these ingredients are, they must be trainable and replicable across therapists, and they must be administered in a uniform and consistent way within a given study. (Quoted in Beutler, 2009, p. 308)

Klerman's declaration involves the medicalization of psychotherapy. Most likely, Klerman's motivation for medicalizing psychotherapy went beyond his love for science; he was also aware of increasing health care costs and heated competition for health care dollars. This is an important contextual factor. In many ways, the events that ensued constituted an effort to place psychological interventions on par with medical interventions

The strategy of using science to compete for health care dollars eventually coalesced into a movement within professional psychology. In 1993, Division 12 (the Society of Clinical Psychology) of the American Psychological Association (APA) formed a "Task Force on Promotion and Dissemination of Psychological Procedures" This task force published an initial set of **empirically validated treatments**. To be considered empirically validated, treatments were required to be (a) manualized, and (b) shown to be superior to a placebo or other treatment, or equivalent to an already established treatment in at least two "good" group design studies or in a series of single case design experiments conducted by different investigators (Chambless et al., 1998).

Not surprisingly, Division 12's proclamations were extremely controversial. Many critics complained the process favored behavioral and cognitive-behavioral treatments over all others.

PUTTING IT IN PRACTICE 1.1

TADS: A Sample Randomized Controlled Trial of Psychotherapy Efficacy

The Treatment of Adolescents With Depression Study (Treatment for Adolescents With Depression Study [TADS] Team, U.S., 2004) provides a clear example of how RCTs are designed and implemented. Take special note of the extensive inclusion/exclusion criteria, the structured nature of the treatments implemented, and standardized measurement protocols. All information below is adapted from the original TADS Team report (2004, pp. 808–809).

TADS inclusion criteria: Participants were included in the study if they: (a) were 12 to 17 years old; (b) were able to receive outpatient care; (c) had a *DSM-IV* diagnosis of major depressive disorder at consent and again at baseline; (d) had a depressive mood for at least 6 weeks prior to consent in at least two or three settings (i.e., home, school, among peers); (e) obtained a Children's Depression Rating Scale-Revised total score of 45 or higher at baseline; (f) had a full-scale IQ of 80 or higher.

TADS exclusion criteria: Participants were excluded from the study if they: (a) were taking antidepressant medications prior to consent; (b) had a current or past diagnosis of bipolar disorder, conduct disorder, substance abuse or dependence, pervasive developmental disorder, or a thought disorder; (c) were receiving concurrent treatment with psychotropic medication or psychotherapy outside the study; (d) had two failed selective serotonin reuptake inhibitor (SSRI) trials or a poor response to clinical treatment containing CBT for depression; (e) showed an intolerance to fluoxetine; (f) had a confounding medical condition; (g) were a non-English–speaking patient or parent; (h) were currently pregnant or refusing to use birth control; (i) displayed, upon evaluation, dangerousness to self or others; (j) had been hospitalized for dangerousness within 3 months of consent or were deemed by a cross-site panel to be "high risk" because of a suicide attempt requiring medical attention within 6 months; (k) reported a clear intent or an active plan to commit suicide; or (l) reported suicidal ideation and had a disorganized family unable to guarantee adequate safety monitoring.

The TADS CBT Intervention: Treatment included 15 sessions, which lasted between 50 and 60 minutes. Treatment was manualized and included psychoeducation about depression, goal setting with the adolescent, mood monitoring, homework to increase pleasant activities, social problem solving, and cognitive restructuring. Optional content included: social engagement, communication, negotiation, compromise, or assertiveness training. Two parent-only sessions and one to three conjoint parent and adolescent sessions were provided.

> **TADS outcome measures:** These included the Schedule for Affective Disorders and Schizophrenia for School-Age Children-Present and Lifetime Version, the scalar Child Depression Rating Scale-Revised, total score. Outcome measures were assessed by the independent evaluator at baseline, week 6, and week 12. Additional measures included the Reynolds Adolescent Depression Scale (RADS) and the Suicidal Ideation Questionnaire-Junior High School Version (SIQ-Jr).

Others criticized the idea of forgoing clinical sensitivity and intuition in favor of using manualized treatment protocols (Silverman, 1996). Division 12 held to their procedures for identifying efficacious treatments, but changed the name of empirically validated treatments to *empirically supported treatments* (ESTs). Nevertheless, the controversy over which therapies to include as ESTs and what criteria that should be used to evaluate therapy approaches continues today.

Overall, the efficacy and EST perspective is partly about using scientifically-based treatment performance to compete for health care dollars. In late 2008, Baker and colleagues issued a call for clinical psychology to embrace the efficacy and EST perspective.

> Our view is that if an EST performs well relative to other competitors for the healthcare dollar (e.g., pharmacotherapy), this finding retains public health and clinical significance. If there are other interventions that produce similar effects, then it would be important to learn how clinicians can achieve those effects reliably, cheaply, and quickly—so that these interventions can also be designated as ESTs. These might also become strong competitors for the nation's health care dollars. (Baker et al., 2008, p. 82)

Baker et al. (2008) also cited evidence suggesting that treatments based on efficacy research (or RCTs) generally remain highly efficacious when directly "exported" to clinical settings (Fiore et al., 2008; Franklin, DeRubeis, & Westen, 2006). Their position is deeply entrenched in the medical model and strongly emphasizes efficacy research as the road to developing valid psychological procedures for treating medical conditions. Other researchers have been less optimistic about generalizing efficacy research into real-world clinical settings (Beutler, 2009; Luborsky, Barrett, Antonuccio, Shoenberger, & Stricker, 2006; Norcross, Beutler, & Levant, 2006).

Effectiveness Research

Sternberg, Roediger, and Halpern (2007) described effectiveness studies:

> An effectiveness study is one that considers the outcome of psychological treatment, as it is delivered in real-world settings. Effectiveness studies can be methodologically rigorous in the sense that careful procedures are employed to identify the nature of the client's problems and to measure changes in their adjustment during the course of treatment, but they do not include random assignment to treatment conditions or placebo control groups. (p. 208)

As can be seen, in contrast to efficacy research, effectiveness research focuses on collecting data with strong external validity. For example, if the goal were to evaluate the effectiveness of solution-focused therapists at a mental health center, therapists who identify themselves as solution-focused might provide treatment as usual (TAU), while other therapists continue to provide therapy from an eclectic perspective. These treatments would be provided to whoever seeks counseling at the mental health center, without random assignment. As possible, some clients might be assigned to a waiting list control condition and the mental health center would try to provide the same assessment protocol for all clients. In the end, outcomes for the solution-focused therapists could be directly compared with outcomes for eclectic therapists as well as the waiting-list control. Results from this effectiveness study could be used to determine whether more therapists should receive training in solution-focused therapy or whether the solution-focused therapists should begin using eclectic approaches.

Other Research Models

There are, of course, other research models that inform researchers and clinical practitioners about therapy process and outcomes. These models include survey research, single-participant designs, qualitative data collection, and so on. However, based on current health care and mental health care reimbursement practices and future trends, providers are increasingly expected to provide services consistent with findings from efficacy and effectiveness research—and the medical model (Baker et al., 2008).

Techniques or Common Factors? The Wrong Question

Wampold (2001, 2010) and others claim that a common factors model provides a better empirical explanation for treatment success than specific treatment models. In contrast, Baker et al. (2008) and like-minded researchers contend that common or **nonspecific factors** contribute little to the understanding and application of counseling and psychotherapy interventions (Chambless et al., 2006). Although this leaves us with a dilemma, typically, when prestigious scientists and practitioners wholeheartedly disagree, important lessons can be learned from both sides of the argument. Perhaps the question is not, "Techniques or common factors?" but instead, "How do techniques *and* common factors operate together to produce positive therapy outcomes?"

Some days when we find ourselves boggled by the abundance of ESTs and worried that some excellent approaches just haven't yet accumulated enough evidence to qualify as an EST, we wonder if perhaps we should abandon theory and technique and focus instead on teaching students how best to employ the common factors. Although a case might be made for doing just that, it's probably impossible

to separate common factors from technique (Safran, Muran, & Eubanks-Carter, 2011). In fact, Norcross and Lambert (2011) stated:

> The relationship does not exist apart from what the therapist does in terms of method, and we cannot imagine any treatment methods that would not have some relational impact. Put differently, treatment methods are relational acts. (p. 5)

This comment suggests that each theory-based approach, when practiced well, includes or activates common factors. In fact, it's often the case that, when employed sensitively and competently, the specific techniques are what instill hope, strengthen the therapeutic relationship, and activate extratherapeutic factors. In summary, embracing a reasonable and scientifically supported theoretical perspective and using it faithfully is one of the best ways to:

- Help clients activate their extratherapeutic factors.
- Develop a positive working relationship.
- Create expectancy or placebo effects.
- Know how to use a healthy number of techniques that fit within your theoretical frame.

As Baker et al. (2008) described, even though it's a research-based fact that physicians with a better bedside manner produce better outcomes, medicine involves much more than a bedside manner—it also involves specific medical procedures. The EST movement is an effort to establish psychological procedures as efficacious as medical procedures. As we move into the future, we need to embrace both an understanding of psychological procedures and common factors; this might also be framed as the science and art of psychotherapy.

Each theory chapter in this text has a section summarizing what's known about its efficacy. You'll notice that more straightforward theories have more outcomes research than the richer, more complex theories. We revisit this issue and the issue of ESTs throughout this text. For now, we take a detour to a central issue in counseling and psychotherapy—essential ethical principles and practice.

> **QUESTIONS FOR REFLECTION**
>
> Which of the common factors do you personally think is most important? Do you agree with the point about common factors approaches to therapy being activated by specific techniques?

ETHICAL ESSENTIALS

Here's some unsettling news. Reading this book and pursuing your studies will contribute to your loss of innocence. For example, in many states, "Good Samaritan" laws allow untrained bystanders to help accident victims without fear of being sued for doing something wrong. But these laws don't cover trained medical personnel. If bystanders trained in medical procedures help someone at an accident, they're practicing medicine and expected to use their professional judgment wisely. If they don't, they can be held liable for their mistakes.

Similarly, you'll soon no longer be an armchair philosopher, a good friend, a kind co-worker, or an understanding son or daughter. If you're reading this book, you're likely on your way to obtaining credentials in the wonderful world of mental health professionals. Soon you'll be a professional helper, change-agent, listener, and diagnostician. Even when off duty, you'll be accountable to certain ethical guidelines. This should motivate you to engage in a careful reading of the ethical codes of the profession you're aspiring toward. In fact, you should be so motivated that you might even postpone reading the rest of this chapter until you've obtained and read your professional code (although tearing yourself away from this book will undoubtedly require extraordinary self-discipline).

A good ethics code defines the professional knowledge base, describes the activities sanctioned in the profession, and provides a clear picture of the boundaries of professional activity. A good code has three main dimensions: It is educational, aspirational, and judicial (Elliott-Boyle, 1985). As you read the code for your profession, see if you can discern these three components.

Because this is a theories book, what follows is a bare-bones consideration of basic ethical issues. Your professional training should include a whole class or seminar in applied ethics; ethical issues should be a common discussion topic in your classes and supervision.

Competence and Informed Consent

A central tenet of any professional code is competence: The practitioner must have adequate knowledge to perform whatever service the profession offers (R. Sommers-Flanagan & J. Sommers-Flanagan, 2007). As a student, you're not expected to be completely competent yet. However, you are expected to strive toward competency by obtaining training and supervision from knowledgeable instructors and supervisors. Providing effective therapy is both art and science. You learn the science by reading, studying, thinking, and doing good literature-based and applied research. This learning never ends. Most ethics codes and state licensing boards encourage or mandate continuing professional education; the ethical practitioner is a lifelong learner (Welfel, 2006).

Research on training in counseling and psychotherapy suggests that therapy competence is developed through three primary strategies (Hill, 2009; Woodside, Oberman, Cole, & Carruth, 2007).

1. *Working out your own issues*: This involves a journey of improving yourself—a journey that includes a focus on self-awareness and other growth-related activities—possibly including personal therapy, balanced and healthy life activities, and being as honest as you can possibly be about your needs, shortcomings, fears, and failures. Your purpose in providing therapy should be to help others and not as a means of meeting your own personal needs.

2. *Working within a learning community*: A learning community not only increases your access to cutting-edge knowledge and information, it also provides unmatched opportunity to observe

practicing therapists through video, audio, and role-playing modalities. Learning communities also facilitate critical analysis and critical thinking processes.

3. *Skills practice and feedback*: As Allen Ivey recently stated, therapy skill development requires, "Practice, practice, practice, feedback, feedback, feedback" (J. Sommers-Flanagan & Heck, 2012, p. 152). Whether learning to ride a bicycle, navigate the Internet, or develop therapy skills, there's really nothing quite like focused personal experiences to facilitate learning.

Closely related to competence is an important ethical concept referred to as **informed consent**. Informed consent refers to clients' rights to know about and consent to ways you intend to work with them. Clients have the right to know your training status and the supervision arrangements you have. They also should have some idea about the techniques you use and why you've chosen them, and they should have some indication about the length of time counseling might last. Involving your client in these topics, both in dialogue and by providing a written statement, is an empowering act for both of you (Goddard, Murray, & Simpson, 2008; Pomerantz & Handelsman, 2004).

Multicultural Competence

Thinking about therapy from a multicultural view is challenging because counseling and psychotherapy were conceived of and developed within a Western cultural frame. From a different cultural perspective even the most basic components of therapy (e.g., the 50-minute hour and the talking cure) can seem odd or unnecessary. D. Sue and D. W. Sue (2008) noted that all too often traditional counseling and psychotherapy have reinforced cultural stereotypes and forced minority clients to fit into a dominant, White American frame.

Despite historical cultural insensitivity, for the past 20-plus years, psychology, counseling, and social work have worked hard to promote multicultural knowledge and competence. In particular,

both the American Psychological Association (APA) and the American Counseling Association (ACA) have adopted **multicultural competencies** (see Chapter 13). Even further, multicultural competencies have been integrated into professional training programs and are now present within the ethical standards for counselors and psychologists. For example, the latest revision of the ACA ethical standards includes multicultural guidelines in the areas of confidentiality, assessment, supervision (American Counseling Association, 2005). Additionally, when it comes to teaching or training individuals to become professional counselors, ACA Standard F.11.c. states:

> Counselor educators actively infuse multicultural/diversity competency in their training and supervision practices. They actively train students to gain awareness, knowledge, and skills in the competencies of multicultural practice. Counselor educators include case examples, role-plays, discussion questions, and other classroom activities that promote and represent various cultural perspectives. (p. 16)

Multicultural competencies outlined by the APA and ACA (as articulated by the Association for Multicultural Counseling and Development) are very similar. The focus is on competency within three general areas (these areas are listed below and described in greater detail in Chapter 13; see also Putting it in Practice 1.2 for comments on evidence-based practice and cultural competence):

1. Self-awareness.

2. Multicultural knowledge.

3. Culturally specific techniques.

Confidentiality

Confidentiality implies trust. When clients come to counseling, they'll wonder if they can trust that what they share will be kept private. If you work as a mental health professional, you'll be expected to hold what your client says to you in strict confidence.

PUTTING IT IN PRACTICE 1.2

Reflections of a Process-Oriented Contextualist

The following comments were contributed by Luis Vargas, associate professor and director of the clinical psychology predoctoral internship program in the Department of Psychiatry at the University of New Mexico School of Medicine.

I have always considered myself a scientist-practitioner. I am a strong believer in evidence-based practice. I have always strived to be culturally responsive in my work. However, I have been bothered by psychology's increasing emphasis on empirically supported treatments and on the current focus on cultural competence. I don't say this to be provocative or iconoclastic. I say this out of concern about what we are endeavoring to do as psychologists involved in carrying out interventions.

The emphasis on "empirical support" troubles me for three major reasons. One, it seems to assume that support of an intervention must come from one epistemology, empiricism, and, I believe, epistemologies are, to use Hallowell's term from anthropology, culturally constituted. Second, the term excludes other forms of evidence, which, I believe are potential sources of important contributions to the area of mental health (e.g., contextualist, social constructionist, and narrative perspectives), particularly in working with culturally diverse groups. Third, empiricists' efforts to "manualize" treatment has, I believe, unintentionally de-emphasized the critical aspect of the interaction between therapist and client. Over the years, my focus in the process of conducting culturally responsive psychotherapeutic interventions has been much more on who the psychologist is and less on who the clients are. You see, as psychologists involved in intervention, we inevitably transmit culture—for example, sometimes imperialistically (as in, "let me teach these African American parents proper parenting skills or practices") or sometimes in a dominant-culture-centric way (as in, "this Mexican mother and son are enmeshed and they need to learn to relate appropriately" or "this American Indian father needs to assume a more appropriately paternal role in the limit-setting with his children"). What is proper or appropriate is determined by cultural context. When we, as psychologists, interact with our clients, we become part of that context. The effects of these interactions are multidirectional—we are changed as much as we may facilitate change. Because of this, we must appreciate how we ourselves are culturally constituted before we embark in an endeavor to intervene with others.

The focus on cultural competence also worries me. I very much try to be culturally responsive to my clients. But can I say that I am "culturally competent"? Absolutely not! I am still, despite my many and genuine efforts, "a toro (bull) in a China shop" with all the cultural implications of this altered adage intended. I do not believe that "cultural competence" is the best way to think about what we want to do or teach. I believe that thinking in terms of "cultural competence" often leads to an emphasis on teaching to cultural content and, therefore, running the risk of teaching to stereotypes or of making static overgeneralizations about local cultures. It can lead to a patronizing sense of complacency and a misguided sense of expertise that may further alienate us from those with whom we intend to work. Culture is not about outcome. Culture is an ever-changing process. One cannot get a firm grip of it just as one cannot get a good grasp of water. As an educator, what I try to do is to teach about the process of culture—how we will never obtain enough cultural content, how important it is to understand the cultural context in which we are working, and how crucial it is to understand our role in the interactions with the people with whom we want to work or the communities in which we seek to intervene. I try to emphasize the need to appreciate our values, beliefs, and attitudes in interaction with those of our clients, the need to appreciate issues of power and privilege, the need to understand and appreciate our clients' worldviews, and the need to work in collaboration with our clients. I do not want to enter the intervention arena (whether in family therapy or in implementing a community-based intervention) as an "expert" who has the answers and knows what needs to be done. I am not a conquistador, intent on supplanting my culture on others. I have a certain expertise that, when connected with the knowledge and experience of my clients, can be helpful and meaningful to my clients.

Many professions assume client confidentiality. In fact, honoring confidentiality boundaries is often seen as part of the definition of what it means to be a professional, in fields ranging from architecture to law to business consulting (R. Sommers-Flanagan, Elliott, & Sommers-Flanagan, 1998).

Confidentiality is central to counseling and psychotherapy. Mental health professionals create safe environments where clients can disclose and work on their deepest and most vexing issues. Of course, there are limits to confidentiality, and these limits should be clearly spelled out to the client before counseling begins. Within those limits, the counselor is expected to keep the contents of the counseling relationship–even the fact that there *is* a counseling relationship—absolutely confidential.

Why is confidentiality so important? The theories in this book vary in their claims regarding why things go wrong for people and what should be done to fix them. They also vary in the degree to which they value the confidential setting and the relationship between client and practitioner. But all theoretical perspectives involve an interpersonal enterprise in which the professional relationship

is foundational. If the therapist doesn't have the client's confidence, trust is impaired. All the fancy theories and techniques in the world won't compensate for an absence of trust.

Practically speaking, you need to keep the identity of your client confidential, you need to keep therapy notes and videos secure, and you can't discuss the content of therapy sessions in ways that identify your client. You also need to research the limits of confidentiality legally and ethically in your state, province, or region, and in the context of the clinic or lab in which you work. You should provide a list of these limits to clients and go over them verbally as well.

Multiple Roles

Although it may be neither wise nor easy for teachers to have their own sons and daughters in class, or for physicians to treat their own children, these activities are not considered unethical. In contrast, because psychotherapy involves a relationship with strict boundaries and expectations, mental health professionals generally avoid **multiple roles**, working only with people they don't know from other contexts. Further, once you're someone's therapist, that's the dominant relationship, and you typically shouldn't allow other relationships with the client to develop—including friendship, romance, or business (Barnett, Lazarus, Vasquez, Johnson, & Moorehead-Slaughter, 2007; Hartl et al., 2007).

Why is this ethical guideline in place? There are several reasons:

- There's always a power differential between client and therapist. Counseling is sometimes called a one-way intimacy. The client is in need and has sought help from a trained, ethical professional. In offering help, the professional implicitly or explicitly acknowledges expertise or authority. Therefore, the professional holds power and could use this power (consciously or unconsciously) to inappropriately meet personal needs, especially if another type of relationship is formed.

- Offering professional counseling to family members and friends imperils relationships at many levels. Imagine the following scenario: A friend of yours wants to quit smoking. When you tell him hypnosis sometimes works for smoking, he asks if you'll hypnotize him. You agree. Unfortunately, you're now in a no-win situation. If the hypnosis works, then your relationship is forever changed. Maybe he'll start asking you for more help, or maybe he'll feel indebted to you. On the other hand, if it doesn't work, then your relationship will be transformed in different ways. And worst of all, while under hypnosis he may share intimate details of childhood abuse or other trauma that would place you in an uncomfortable position.

- If you have a social or familial relationship with someone before or after you have a therapy relationship, the client will know more about you than when the relationship was strictly therapeutic. This new knowledge can make both clients and therapists uncomfortable.

Understanding these power and influence dynamics is important for professional counselors

and psychotherapists. However, in the latest version of the ACA guidelines there's an acknowledgement that sometimes multiple relationships can be beneficial to clients. In some ways this complicates things. It's always difficult to sort out your own best interests from the best interests of your clients. Our best advice in this area is to seek supervision and consultation to make sure you manage multiple relationships in sensitive and ethical ways.

There are many examples of boundary breaks that lead to inappropriate or unacceptable client-therapist relationships. It's especially hard to find a good therapist in film or on television. Year after year, we've come to dread watching films that include a therapist character. If you watch therapists on the screen, you're likely to assume that all therapists are reckless, unprofessional risk-takers who establish multiple roles and violate relationship boundaries. You're also likely to assume that therapists can't resist their sexual impulses and therefore often end up in bed with their clients (or their client's husband, wife, sibling, etc.). In truth, therapist-client sexual relations occur in a vast minority of therapy cases (see Putting it in Practice 1.3). Even so, therapist-client sex occurs far too often in the real world (Barnett et al., 2007; Gottlieb & Younggren, 2009; Graham & Liddle, 2009; Hartl et al., 2007).

On a lighter note, as you begin learning about theories and techniques associated with mental health work, it will be natural for you to try out minor therapy–like things with friends or family members. We certainly did, and we're happy to report that we didn't do any lasting damage (that we're aware of). But there are dangers. Engaging in nondirective, active listening with someone who's accustomed to having lively, interactive exchanges with you will not go unnoticed (see Chapter 5). One of our friends told us that she was very relieved when we finally got over our "exclusively Carl Rogers" stage, and she could hear a direct, bossy opinion from us again.

Overall, it's best to restrain your impulse to practice therapy techniques on innocent bystanders—with the possible exception of trying out various listening strategies.

PUTTING IT IN PRACTICE 1.3

Client Harm: The Sexual Abuse of Therapy Clients

Believe it or not, in the 1960s and 1970s, some mental health professionals claimed that sexual contact between therapist and client could be therapeutic (McCartney, 1966; Shepard, 1972). Even worse, prior to the landmark legal case *Roy v. Hartogs* (*Roy v. Hartogs*, 1975) the courts generally avoided psychotherapy-sex cases, in part because of the belief that mentally unbalanced women were merely fantasizing sexual relations with their esteemed psychotherapists. As late as 1978, the highly regarded author and psychotherapist M. Scott Peck wrote, "Were I ever to have a case in which I concluded after careful and judicious consideration that my patient's spiritual growth would be substantially furthered by our having sexual relations, I would proceed to have them" (Peck, 1978, p. 176). Despite the fact that Peck concludes his commentary on this issue with the statement "I find it difficult to imagine that such a case could really exist" (Peck), he leaves open the possibility of sexual contact between therapist and client as being beneficial.

In more recent years, hundreds of substantiated and successful legal proceedings against therapists have led all mental health professional groups to establish crystal-clear ethical guidelines prohibiting sexual contact between mental health practitioners and clients (R. Sommers-Flanagan & Sommers-Flanagan, 2007; R. Sommers-Flanagan, Sommers-Flanagan, & Welfel, 2009). For example, the American Counseling Association (2005) ethical guidelines state that "Counselors do not have any type of sexual intimacies with clients and do not counsel persons with whom they have had a sexual relationship," and prohibition of sexual relations is unequivocal in the American Psychological Association (APA) ethical guidelines: "Sexual activity with a current or former client is unethical" (APA, 2002).

Based on research, legal precedent, and anecdotal information, the bottom line is that sexual contact between therapist and client is harmful. Unfortunately, over the years, too many therapists have *imagined* or rationalized that their sexual touch was healing. It wasn't until the 1980s that Kenneth Pope began referring to sexual contact between therapist and client as what it is: sexual abuse of clients (Pope, 1988).

Sexual contact between therapist and client constitutes sexual abuse for two main reasons. First, the relationship between therapist and client is characterized by a power imbalance. The therapist has more power and prestige and charges clients for services. Second, research has shown that sexual contact between therapist and client causes clients significant psychological and emotional damage (Gottlieb & Younggren, 2009; Herlihy et al., 2006).

> Despite new and strict ethical guidelines and evidence attesting to its harmfulness, sexual abuse of clients continues, albeit at lower rates (Anderson & Handelsman, 2010). However it's difficult to know if the decrease is real or due to decreased reporting.
>
> In conclusion, the following question is directly relevant to potential client harm: If we as therapists are prone to exploiting and abusing clients sexually, might we also be prone to exploiting clients in other ways? Of course, the answer to this question is affirmative. There is always the potential for therapists to exploit clients. From our perspective, exploiting clients is not only a disservice, but the royal road to client harm.

Doing No Harm: A Convergence of Ethics and Science

As described in Putting it in Practice 1.4, the Latin phrase, primum non nocere ("**first, do no harm**") is a primary ethical mandate for medical and mental health professionals. Unfortunately, despite this mandate, research shows that psychotherapy can and does produce **negative outcomes**; estimates indicate that approximately 3% to 10% of psychotherapy cases result in client deterioration (Boisvert & Faust, 2003; Harmon et al., 2007; M. J. Lambert & M. J. Lambert, 2010; M. Lambert, 2007). Negative effects may even climb as high as 15% with substance abuse treatments (Ilgen & Moos, 2005; Moos, 2005).

Client deterioration (aka negative outcome) is usually linked to at least one of three sources: (1) therapist factors; (2) client factors; or (3) specific psychological interventions.

Therapist Factors

If you experienced a serious knee injury you'd want surgery from the best surgeon possible. This might inspire you to conduct a survey on local surgeon quality. No doubt, asking a few individuals about their surgery experiences would provide you with information about surgeons to avoid and surgeons to trust. This is because it's perfectly natural for some professionals to be more or less skilled or talented, based on experience and other factors.

As a consequence, it should be no surprise to find differential effectiveness exists among counselors and psychotherapists. In a study of 71 therapists who provided counseling services for clients

with roughly equivalent problem severity, Lambert (2007) reported "One therapist who saw more than 160 patients had a 19% deterioration rate, whereas another saw more than 300 patients, with less than 1% deteriorating" (p. 11). In this situation, your choice of which therapist to see would be obvious. Unfortunately, the therapists in Lambert's study were anonymous and therefore no conclusions could be made regarding specific qualities associated with high success and failure rates. However, other research suggests that the following four therapist factors or behaviors may be linked with negative outcomes:

1. Therapists who show little empathy or warmth in their interactions with clients (Greenberg, Watson, Elliot, & Bohart, 2001; Lafferty, Beutler, & Crago, 1989).

2. Therapists who employ overly confrontational or intrusive therapy approaches (Castonguay, Boswell, Constantino, Goldfried, & Hill, 2010; Mohr, 1995).

3. Therapists using inadequate or inaccurate assessment procedures (including culturally biased assessments).

4. Therapists whose personality or approach is a poor fit for a given client (Beutler, 2009).

The general tendency is for therapists to be unaware of both their own negative behaviors and negative treatment outcomes (Hannan et al., 2005). One strong take-away message from this research is that therapists need to scrutinize themselves and make efforts to systematically evaluate their outcomes.

Client Factors

As discussed previously, extratherapeutic factors linked to individual clients likely account for the greatest proportion of positive therapy outcomes (Lambert, 1992). Not surprisingly, it makes sense that client characteristics (including a lack of personal resources) might similarly contribute to negative treatment outcomes.

Research supports several client factors as potentially contributing to negative treatment outcomes:

- Low client motivation (Clarkin, Levy, Lenzenweger, & Kernberg, 2004).

- High client psychopathology (e.g., paranoia, psychosis, antisocial behavior).

- Limited client personal resources (e.g., limited intelligence, insight, family, or social support).

It's often difficult to change or modify the "client or extratherapeutic factors" that clients bring into the therapy office. And it's typically impossible to know what strengths or limitations clients have before they arrive for treatment.

The best solution to this conundrum is for practicing therapists to modify their approaches based on each individual client. In particular, Beutler's (2009) review shows that one of the most significant contributors to positive treatment outcomes is goodness of fit—both the fit between therapist and client and the fit between technique and client. Beutler stated: "The fit of the treatment to the particular patient accounted for the strongest effects on outcomes of all variable classes at one year after treatment" (p. 313).

Psychological Intervention Factors

Lilienfeld (Lilienfeld, 2007; Lilienfeld, Lynn, & Lohr, 2003) systematically reviewed psychotherapy outcomes literature and identified specific therapy approaches that consistently produce unacceptable negative effects. He refers to these therapy approaches as **potentially harmful therapies**

Table 1.2 Potentially Harmful Therapies

Critical incident stress debriefing.
Scared Straight interventions.
Facilitated communication.
Attachment therapies (e.g., rebirthing).
Recovered-memory techniques.
DID-oriented therapy.
Induction of "alter" personalities.
Grief counseling for individuals with normal
 bereavement reactions.
Expressive-experiential therapies.
Boot-camp interventions for conduct disorder.
DARE (Drug Abuse Resistance Education) programs.

Note: As several authors have noted, these are not harmful therapies, but are potentially harmful therapies. Although some are more clearly dangerous and sometimes lethal, others can be implemented appropriately (see Chapter 6). For detailed information about these PHTs, see Lilienfeld, S. O. (2007). Psychological treatments that cause harm. *Perspectives on Psychological Science, 2,* 53–70.

(PHTs). In developing his PHT list, Lilienfeld (2007) relied on (a) at least one replicated RCT showing potential harm; (b) meta-analytic reviews of multiple RCTs; and (c) research reports linking sudden adverse events to the initiation of therapy (p. 58).

It should be noted that potential negative psychotherapy effects are not minor. In many situations charismatic therapists can have a powerfully positive or negative influence on clients. As Beutler (2009, p. 307) stated: "In some cases, such as rebirthing therapy, the result has been death; in others, such as reprogramming therapy, it has been the psychological destruction of lives and families."

The serious negative PHT effects are a reminder of psychotherapy potency. It's also a reminder of how important it is for ethical therapists to stay attuned not only to efficacy and effectiveness studies, but also to do research that explores and identifies treatment approaches that carry with them risks of harming clients. Lilienfeld's list of PHTs are included in Table 1.2.

Going Forward and Getting Positive

After focusing on negative therapy outcomes, negative therapist characteristics, and potentially harmful therapies (PHTs), you might be feeling a bit of negativity yourself. After all, even though you're studying this field because you want to help distressed individuals improve their lives, the fact that some negative outcomes are inevitable may feel worrisome. Nevertheless, there's reason for hope. As an ethical clinician you can address this issue by building a plan for minimizing negative outcomes and maximizing positive ones.

A Plan for Maximizing Positive Outcomes

There's nothing like a good plan to help with goal attainment (see Chapter 9). Using the following plan can help you minimize negative outcomes and maximize positive ones.

1. As appropriate, integrate empirically supported treatments (ESTs) or **evidence-based principles (EBPs)** into your therapy practice: There are many ESTs, but to use them, you'll need advanced training, supervision, and it's impossible to become proficient in the vast array of ESTs available. Therefore, you should learn a few that serve you well as you work with specific populations (e.g., if you want to work with individuals suffering from trauma, learning both Trauma-Focused Cognitive Behavioral Therapy [TF-CBT] and/or Eye Movement Desensitization Reprocessing [EMDR] would be useful). However, there will always be situations where clients don't perfectly fit a diagnostic category with a specific EST or you don't think a manualized approach is best, or the client will not want to work using certain approaches. In those cases you should follow EBPs. For example, using Beutler's systematic treatment selection model, you can systematically select both general and specific approaches that are a good fit for the client and consistent with empirical knowledge about how to address particular problems (Beutler, 2011; Beutler, Harwood, Bertoni, & Thomann, 2006; Beutler, Moleiro, & Talebi, 2002).

2. Understand and capitalize on evidence-based (or empirically supported) relationships and other common factors: As the common factors advocates have articulated so well, evidence exists for much more than psychological interventions or procedures (Norcross & Lambert, 2011). For better or worse, psychological procedures tend to be implemented within the crucible of interpersonal relationships. Consequently, the ethical therapist intentionally attends to the therapeutic relationship in ways consistent with the research base (e.g., by collaboratively setting goals and obtaining consistent feedback from clients about their perceptions of therapy process and content).

3. Avoid pitfalls and procedures associated with negative outcomes: To address potential negative outcomes, ethical therapists should: (a) engage in activities to facilitate awareness including, but not limited to individual supervision, peer supervision, and consistent client feedback; (b) individualize therapy approaches to fit clients—rather than expecting all clients to benefit from a single approach; and (c) avoid using high risk approaches by knowing (and avoiding) potentially harmful therapy (PHT) approaches (Lilienfeld, 2007).

4. Use flexible, but systematic assessment approaches to tailor the treatment to the client and the client's problem: Much like good mechanics assess the engine before initiating change, ethical therapists conduct some form of assessment prior to using specific therapy interventions. As discussed in each chapter, the particular assessment process you use will likely be more simple or more complex, depending on your theoretical orientation. Nevertheless, empathic, culturally sensitive, and ongoing collaborative assessment helps guide therapeutic processes (Finn, 2009).

5. Use practice-based evidence to monitor your personal therapy outcomes: **Practice-based evidence** is a term used to describe when clinicians collect data, sometimes every session, pertaining to client symptoms and/or client satisfaction. Duncan, Miller, and Sparks (2004) refer to this process as client informed therapy. Regardless of the terminology, this is a process wherein clients are empowered to directly share their treatment progress (or lack thereof) with their therapists. This allows therapists to make modifications in their approach to facilitate more positive outcomes (Lambert, 2010a; Lambert, 2010b).

PUTTING IT IN PRACTICE 1.4

Beneficence: Helping Not Hurting

While writing this book we asked professional therapists and scholars to contribute their insights on issues ranging from ethics, to theory, to technique, to multiculturalism. We've sprinkled the comments of these wise colleagues throughout the text within these Putting it in Practice features. In this installment, Dr. Alan C. Tjeltveit of the Department of Psychology at Muhlenberg College shares his thoughts on the ethical principle of **beneficence**:

"I want to help people," many people reply when asked, "Why do you want to go into psychology or counseling?" That desire to benefit others is essential to being a good psychotherapist or counselor. However, that desire to help may also be very dangerous.

Beneficence, the American Psychological Association (APA, 2002) ethics code notes, means striving "to benefit those with whom [psychologists] work" (Principle A, p. 1062). Similarly, Principle A1a of the American Counseling Association (ACA, 2005) ethics code begins, "The primary responsibility of counselors is to respect the dignity and to promote the welfare of clients" (p. 4). This fits with what "profession" has historically meant. The "defining characteristic" of the professional, Pope and Vasquez (2007) note, is "an ethic of placing the client's welfare foremost and not allowing professional judgment or services to be drawn off course by one's own needs" (p. 39).

So, how can wanting to help people be problematic, or even dangerous?

Suppose a 23-year-old client enters counseling to alleviate the distress he is experiencing because of ongoing tension with his parents, with whom he is living. Motivated to help the client, the counselor advises him to move out and become more independent. The client complies, breaking off family ties, but then becomes very depressed because he and his culture deeply value close family relationships. That intervention, though well-intended, harmed that client, in whose culture family relationships are very important and who was problematically subservient to authority figures.

In addition to a motivation to benefit others, excellent clinical work and optimally ethical practice thus requires:

- Competence. We must possess or obtain relevant knowledge and skills so we can, in fact, help people.
- Recognizing diverse ideas about what "benefit" means. Determining what will benefit a particular client is often challenging. "Benefit"—which is tied to the goals

of psychotherapy—has to do with ideas about the good life, obligations, and what is right and wrong (Tjeltveit, 2006), about which deep cultural and philosophical differences exist. One's ideas about benefit may also be tied to client and therapist religiousness, spirituality, religiousness and spirituality, or neither. It is crucial that psychotherapists don't assume that their ideas about a good life ("benefit") are the only or only correct ideas, in part so they don't impose their views on clients.

- Openness to relevant empirical evidence. Our intuitions about what will help a person may be mistaken. Obtaining relevant empirical evidence about what actually benefits people in general is thus essential. Where relevant empirical evidence about the benefits and risks of treatment options is not available, or pertinent characteristics of a client indicate that an intervention that is generally effective may not help (or even harm) a particular client, we need to make the best possible judgment. Taking client views and choices very seriously and substantial humility are, however, essential, so we exhibit the respect for clients addressed in the APA (2002) and ACA (2005) ethics codes.

- Cultural sensitivity. Insensitivity and imposing ideas about the good life and well-being (Christopher, 1999) that are foreign to client may result in harm to them, despite our wanting to help them. Sensitivity benefits clients and avoids harming them.

- Avoiding harm. The ethical principle of beneficence is often yoked with the ethical principle of nonmaleficence or harmavoidance (don't harm clients). Expressed in medical ethics as Primum non nocere, or "First, do no harm" (Beauchamp & Childress, 2001, p. 113), its relevance to psychotherapy and counseling is this: Any intervention that has the power to benefit also has the power to harm. Mental health professionals need to be aware of the potential negative consequences of the services they provide, and avoid such harm. The goal, of course, is to benefit clients in ways that don't harm them. How to do so, of course, is one of the great challenges of clinical practice.

- Self-care. Professionals are not obligated to harm or impoverish themselves in order to benefit others. Neglecting oneself is, however, an occupational hazard of the mental health professions. Care for others thus needs to be matched with self-care. We need to be able to sustain ourselves in order to continue to benefit others. Psychotherapists who don't do so get burned out, provide substandard care, develop their own psychological problems, and/or act unethically. A variety of self-care strategies exist, with each professional needing to develop a repertoire that works, including interpersonal support, the right balance of work and relaxation, and so forth.

Drawing on ethical and psychological sources that sustain a commitment to help others. Entering a field with a desire to help others is relatively easy. Far more difficult is identifying rich, sustaining sources that enable us to continue to be motivated to help others across the span of a career. Doing so is difficult, but mental health professionals face few more crucial tasks.

Those factors all help structure, channel, and empower professionals' commitment to beneficence, to helping others. Technical knowledge and training is not enough if a professional is not committed to helping those with whom he or she works.

When we draw on sustaining psychological, social, and ethical resources, avoid harming clients, exhibit humility about what we know, attend to relevant empirical evidence, respect client views on the meaning of benefit, and exhibit cultural sensitivity, then we can best benefit our clients. And that is what the mental health professions are, at core, all about.

Additional Ethical Issues

There are, of course, many more ethical issues to grapple with as you develop professionally. Most authors in this area adamantly point out that ethics codes are just a rudimentary attempt to hold practitioners to high standards of care (Anderson & Handelsman, 2010; R. Sommers-Flanagan & Sommers-Flanagan, 2007). Unfortunately, ethics codes have become increasingly legal in orientation, and sometimes serve protective rather than proactive functions. Being an ethical practitioner requires ongoing attention to the heart of the profession. It will require trusted colleagues, a good problem-solving model, ongoing reading and education, and a willingness to ask painfully hard questions.

EMERGENCE OF PERSONAL THEORY

If you want to become an excellent mental health professional, then it makes sense to closely study the thinking of some of the greatest minds and models in the field. This text covers 12 of the most comprehensive and practical theories in existence. We hope you absorb each theory as thoroughly as possible and try to experience it from the inside out. As you proceed through each chapter, suspend doubt, and try thinking like a practitioner from each theoretical orientation.

Another goal we have is for you to discover which theory or theories fit best for you. We also want you to do the thinking and exploration necessary to understand and further develop your own theory of

human functioning and change. In some ways, we want you to develop a 13th theory.

Some of you reading this book may already have considerable knowledge and experience about counseling and psychotherapy theories. You may already have your favorite theory. However, even if you have very little knowledge and experience, you undoubtedly have at least some theoretical or philosophical perspectives about what helps people change. Therefore, before you explore the theories put forth by the experts, we encourage you to take at least a brief look at your own implicit or natural psychological theories about people.

Your First Client and Your First Theory

Pretend this is the first day of your career as a mental health professional. You have all the amenities: a tastefully decorated office, two comfortable chairs, a graduate degree, and a client.

You also have everything that any scarecrow, tin man, or lion might yearn for: a brain full of knowledge about how to provide therapy, a heart full of compassion for a diverse range of clients, and courage for facing the challenge of providing therapy services. But do you have what it takes to help a fellow human being climb out of the pit of despair? Do you have the judgment to apply your knowledge in an effective way?

You walk to the waiting room. She's there. She's your first client ever. You greet her. The two of you walk back to the office.

In the first 20 minutes of your interview, you learn quite a lot about your client: She's a 21-year-old college student experiencing apathy, insomnia, no romantic interest, carbohydrate cravings, an absence of hobbies, and extremely poor grades. She reports she isn't using drugs or alcohol. Based on this information, you decide to classify her as depressed and proceed with treatment. But the question is: How do you proceed? Do you focus on her automatic thoughts and deep beliefs about herself and how they might be contributing to her depressive symptoms? Do you help her get a tutor in hope that improving her grades might improve her overall condition? Do you recommend she begin an exercise routine? Do you explore her history on the assumption that some childhood trauma needs to be understood and worked through? Do you teach her about mindfulness principles and have her practice meditation? Do you have her role play and rehearse possible solutions to her problems? Do you focus on listening, based on the assumption that if you provide her a positive therapy environment she will gain insight into herself and move toward greater psychological health? Do you help her recast herself and her life into a story with a positive ending to help her construct a more adaptive identity? Do you ask her to alternate sitting in different chairs—speaking from different perspectives to explore her here and now feelings of success and failure? (See Table 1.3 for a brief review of theoretical perspectives included in this book).

Obviously, you have many choices for how to proceed with therapy, depending upon your theoretical orientation. Here's our advice: Don't get stuck too soon with a single theoretical orientation. It's unlikely that all humans will respond to a single approach. As suggested in Putting it in Practice 1.5, experiment and reflect before choosing your preferred theory.

QUESTIONS FOR REFLECTION

At first glance, which theoretical approaches do you find most appealing? Are you more inclined toward the scientific security of behaviorism or more attracted to the relationship emphasis of person-centered therapy?

OUR BIASES

Good qualitative researchers try to acknowledge their personal biases when reporting their research results. We think the same should be true for textbook authors. As a consequence, we provide you with a brief overview of some of our main biases.

Our Theoretical Roots

At this point, we've been eclectic so long it seems we were both born that way. However, because telling you that we're eclectic doesn't tell you much about our deeper preferences, tendencies, and biases, we decided to look deeper and explore our biases.

In a sense, it's true that we were born and raised eclectic. Our clinical psychology faculty at the University of Montana in the 1980s included a psychoanalytic/hypnoanalytic professor, a cognitively oriented professor, a person-centered professor, and two behaviorists. John went to a strictly psychoanalytic predoctoral internship at a medical center in New York in 1985, and Rita went to a family systems child and family clinic in Oregon in 1988. After licensure, John spent time teaching, working as a health psychologist in an industrial setting, in private practice, and as director of a nonprofit organization dedicated to parent education. Rita has consulted with two different Veteran's Centers, established a part-time private practice, and taught the past 21 years as a professor of counselor education. During this time period, we lived in Montana, New York, Washington, Oregon, Belize, Central America, and Northampton, England.

John's favorite theoretical figures are Carl Rogers, Alfred Adler, and Irvin Yalom. Rita's are Jean Baker Miller and the feminists, Alfred Adler, and Viktor Frankl. John loves to quote Freud and Rita loves to dethrone Freud, considering him overrated and antithetical to her feminist beliefs.

Our generalist background makes us slow to jump on contemporary bandwagons. For example, we're especially cautious about new theories or techniques that claim remarkable recovery rates for psychologically distressed individuals. Hopefully,

PUTTING IT IN PRACTICE 1.5

Your Emerging Personal Theory

Dr. Kurt Kraus of the Department of Counseling and College Student Personnel at Shippensburg State University shares his thoughts on theories:

> I am afraid that students are encouraged to identify their emerging theoretical identity way too early. Students write papers for professors of Introduction to Counseling and Survey of Theoretical Approaches espousing their growing theoretical identities. Nonsense! Take time to learn about mental health professionals who have practiced for many years, study their contributions, write about them and their experiences, their beliefs, their skills, the benefits and liabilities inherent in their practices. Only after you have explored the journeys of many others can you really begin to make a decision about your own. Heck, you are only beginning; how dare we imply that you should know where you want to be? (K. Kraus, personal communication, August, 2002)

Another colleague who teaches theories of counseling and psychotherapy to graduate students, Janice DeLucia-Waack of the State University of New York, Buffalo, gives the following advice to her students:

> I tell my students that I don't expect or even want them to marry any particular theory while they're taking my course. However, I *do* tell them that I expect them to spend at least a week dating each theory before the semester ends. (J. DeLucia-Waack, personal communication, April, 2002)

this doesn't mean we're not open to new ideas. We're just reluctant to believe that having clients pop a pill or hum a few tunes will cure their longstanding personal problems.

Balance and Uncertainty

We have a strong bias against certainty. Several years ago we attended a workshop conducted by the great structural family therapist and theorist Salvador Minuchin. The subtitle of his presentation was "Don't be too sure." We agree. No theory holds the key to all problems. No theory entirely

explains what it means to be human. When we get too sure about our theory, we close ourselves off to different perspectives; even worse, being too sure places us in danger of forcing the client to fit our theory, rather than the other way around.

We also tend to be skeptical about empirical research. The biggest problem with research is that it's tremendously difficult to conduct studies that truly reflect what happens in the real therapy offices of practitioners around the world. As W. Silverman (1996) stated, "Efficacy studies do not reflect models and they do not represent psychotherapy as practiced in the field" (p. 210).

Table 1.3   A Summary of 13 Major Theoretical Perspectives

1. **Psychoanalytic/psychodynamic/object relations theory.**   Freud was mostly neutral or pessimistic about the nature of humans. Therapies derived from psychoanalytic theory hold the common belief that human personality and behavior are powerfully shaped by early childhood relationships. Classical Freudians believe humans are primarily pleasure-seeking creatures dominated by sexual and aggressive impulses.

    Contemporary object relations theorists emphasize that humans are driven by human relationship and attachment needs, rather than instinctual drives. Psychopathology develops from conflicted, maladaptive, or inadequate parent-child interactions. The overriding goal of therapy is to bring maladaptive unconscious relationship dynamics into consciousness. Therapy process involves an exploration of past relationships, development of insights into current relationship dynamics, and an application of this growing insight to contemporary relationships. Therapy is effective because the therapist accurately interprets or gives the client feedback about conflicted issues outside the client's awareness and relationship patterns, including transference reactions and dreams.

2. **Adlerian theory (individual psychology).**   In contrast to Freud, Adler was an optimist. Individual psychology considers each client to be a unique, whole individual who strives toward completion and toward achieving his or her idiosyncratic, fictional personal goals. Psychopathology develops when clients construct a belief system or lifestyle that is maladaptive, inaccurate, and dysfunctional. The goal of therapy is to help clients develop a more adaptive lifestyle. This is accomplished when the therapist helps clients have insight into the "basic mistakes" imbedded in their lifestyle. Once this insight is attained, clients are naturally motivated to change in positive ways, and therefore more directive techniques, including guidance and advice, can be used. Therapy is effective because of a friendly, collaborative relationship, insight into maladaptive aspects of the lifestyle, and education about how to remediate the maladaptive lifestyle.

3. **Existential theory.**   Existential approaches to therapy are derived primarily from existential philosophy. Overall, existentialists have a wide range of different views of the nature of humans and the nature of reality. Some existentialists are optimistic, whereas others focus on nihilism and meaninglessness. Some are very religious, and others are atheists. The existential approach emphasizes that individuals must grapple with core life issues such as death, freedom, isolation, and meaninglessness. Anxiety is viewed as a part of normal human experience. Psychopathology arises when the individual avoids, rather than confronting and coping with, life's core issues. Existential therapists can be alternatively gentle and confrontational as they strive to develop a deep and authentic relationship with clients. Existential interventions emerge in the relational space between client and therapist; prescriptive pre-planned techniques are generally not used. Therapy is effective because, within the context of an authentic relationship, clients are able to begin facing their ultimate concerns and constructively embrace anxiety in ways that enhance personal meaning.

4. **Person-centered theory.**   Developed by Carl Rogers, person-centered therapy is an optimistic, humanistic, and phenomenological approach to therapy. Person-centered

Table 1.3   *continued*

theory posits that each individual has within him- or herself a capacity for dramatic and positive growth. This growth is stymied and psychopathology arises when clients, usually in childhood relationships, begin to believe they are not worthwhile or lovable unless they meet specific behavioral conditions (i.e., conditions of worth). In person-centered therapy, clients can talk about the past, present, or future, because it's basically a nondirective therapy wherein therapists trust the client's capacity for growth and therefore follows his or her lead, discussing whatever he or she believes is important. Person-centered therapy is effective when therapists help clients recapture their natural propensity for growth by establishing a therapy relationship characterized by therapist congruence or genuineness, unconditional positive regard or prizing of the client, and accurate empathy.

5. **Gestalt theory.**   Fritz and Laura Perls were the dominant forces in creating Gestalt theory and therapy. Gestalt theory is an amalgamation of psychoanalysis, developmental psychology, existential philosophy, Gestalt psychology, field theory, and Reichian muscular defensiveness, all within an anarchical framework. Humans are viewed as having both natural growth potential and natural defensiveness from experiential contact. Gestalt therapy focuses on developing an I-Thou relationship between client and therapist and then works in the here-and-now to deal with unfinished emotional and behavioral experiences from the past. Intellectualization is discouraged and action within the session is encouraged. Gestalt therapists don't engage in authoritative interpretation, but instead stimulate clients to come to their senses and make their own interpretation via Gestalt experiments.

6. **Behavioral theory.**   In the tradition of John B. Watson, behaviorists believe deeply in the importance of basing all therapeutic approaches on scientific research. Behaviorists view humans as neither inherently positive or negative, but simply a function of their environment. Psychopathology is directly caused by maladaptive learning, either from the classical or operant conditioning model. Behavior therapy essentially consists of relearning, so the focus of therapy is primarily on the present. The past may be discussed briefly to enhance motivation and the future may be discussed in order to establish goals, but the therapy process and work occur in the present. Therapy is effective because the therapist teaches the client to apply basic behavioral learning principles both within and outside of therapy.

7. **Cognitive-behavioral theory.**   Cognitive theory and therapy are usually used in combination with behavioral approaches and also have a neutral perspective on the nature of humans. Two main cognitive theoretical perspectives are integrated into cognitive-behavioral therapy—social learning theory and cognitive appraisal theory. Generally, social learning theory focuses on vicarious learning and cognitive theory emphasizes that it's not what happens to individuals that causes them distress, but what they think or believe about what happens to them that causes distress. Maladaptive or irrational thinking styles and beliefs about the self and maladaptive inner speech is what produces psychopathology. Cognitive therapy primarily uses teaching or psychoeducational approaches with clients. Therapy is effective because clients learn new and more adaptive or rational ways of thinking about themselves and their lives.

Table 1.3 *continued*

8. **Reality therapy/choice theory.** Choice theory, as developed by William Glasser, holds that individuals are responsible for choosing their thoughts and behavior, which directly influence their feelings and physiology. All humans are viewed as being motivated to satisfy one or more of their five basic needs: survival, love and belonging, power, freedom, and fun. Psychopathology develops because clients choose to restrain anger, want to receive help from others, or are choosing to avoid important issues. Reality therapy focuses exclusively on the present. Therapy is effective because the therapist forms a positive therapy relationship with the client and then teaches the client choice theory from within the context of that relationship.

9. **Feminist theory.** Feminist theory was developed by women to address the social and cultural oppression and unequal treatment of women. Implied in the feminist perspective is the tendency for humans who wield more power to use that power to oppress and suppress those with less power. Feminists view psychopathology as arising from social, cultural, and masculine-based power inequities. Recognition of these inequities and the empowerment of women and minorities are the major focus of feminist therapy. Effective therapy is based on a strong, mutual, supportive, and empowering relationship between therapist and client. When therapy is effective, clients are empowered to use their strength and inner resources to further and deepen mutual relations in their lives.

10. **Constructive theory.** Constructive theory emphasizes the power of language, information processing, and cybernetics in influencing human behavior and change. This theory takes no position regarding the innate goodness or badness of humans. Humans are shaped by the way they construct reality, which directly influences human behavior, problem-solving strategies, and human emotions. Psychopathology is a function of each individual client's construction of reality. Both direct and indirect strategies are used to help clients change. The focus is on the future, solutions, and reshaping the narrative or story the client is living. Therapy is effective when therapist and client have a conversation or dialogue and co-create a reality wherein the client engages in positive, solution-focused strategies for constructing and maintaining his or her world.

11. **Family systems theory.** Practitioners who use family systems theory to guide their work, generally view problems as emanating from dysfunctional family processes, rather than being owned by individuals. Psychopathology is viewed as a function of interpersonal transactions and interactions within the family context. As a consequence, interventions focus on changing family dynamics or behaviors within the family, rather than focusing on changing individuals. In some ways, because family systems theorists may adopt any one of a number of "other theoretical orientations" family systems work might be viewed as less of a formal theory and more of an approach to therapeutic intervention. Specifically, therapy strategies range from being strategic and paradoxical to straightforward and behavioral.

12. **Multicultural theory of therapy.** Multicultural theory focuses on the power of culture in influencing human behavior, emotions, and values. This theory takes no position on the innate goodness or badness of humans and generally accepts and

Table 1.3   *continued*

tolerates diverse culturally sanctioned behaviors. Psychopathology varies depending upon cultural experiences and beliefs. Multiculturalists tailor their approaches to clients' cultural orientation. Many multicultural approaches acknowledge and embrace religious and spiritual perspectives. There are no clear explanations for why clients benefit from therapy and spiritual counseling approaches are distinctly non-empirical in their orientation.

13. **Integration/eclectic theory.**   Psychotherapy and counseling integration acknowledges the potential positive contributions of all theoretical orientations to effective therapy. No single theory is viewed as more correct or inherently better than any other. Three approaches to weaving together diverse theoretical perspectives are emphasized. First, a common factors approach to therapy is used to develop therapy approaches based on what active ingredients work across a wide range of theoretical approaches. Second, technical eclecticism emphasizes using the best treatment technique available, given a particular client and a particular problem. Third, theoretical integration seeks to weave together two or more therapy systems to create a more effective hybrid system. There are several evidence-based, new generation integrative approaches to counseling and psychotherapy. The nature of humans, psychopathology, and theoretical constructs shifts, depending upon the specific approaches employed. Effective therapy is characterized by positive outcomes.

On the other hand, we deeply value counseling and psychotherapy research. Good research is essential to guiding mental health professionals. When a particular form of treatment makes great claims of effectiveness in the absence of empirical research, we become very suspicious.

THE ZEITGEIST, THE ORTGEIST, AND THE POLTERGEIST

The **Zeitgeist** is defined as "the spirit of the time." It refers to the fact that more often than would be predicted by chance, several individuals will make a significant discovery at around the same time. This spirit of the time explains why Pierre Janet and Sigmund Freud, in France and Austria, could both independently begin suspecting that efforts to work directly with client unconscious processes might help resolve longstanding and troublesome symptoms. In other words, in the late 1890s, the time was right to begin working more explicitly with the unconscious.

The **Ortgeist** refers to the "spirit of the place." It explains why people in close proximity often move toward similar discoveries. Perhaps the Ortgeist spirit was operating in Europe in the late 1890s. Bankart (1997) speaks of the Zeitgeist and Ortgeist in relation to Freud: "A genuine understanding of Freud's psychoanalysis, for example, requires (and at the same time provides) a reasonably deep understanding of middle-class life in turn-of-the-century Europe" (Bankart, p. 8).

Similarly, on the National Public Radio show "The Writer's Almanac," Garrison Keillor quoted the plainspoken philosopher Eric Hoffer's perspective on Freud:

Ah, don't talk to me about Freud. Freud lived in a tight little circle in Vienna, and inside that tight little circle was another tight little circle, and inside that tight little circle was still *another* tight little circle. What applies to that poor man, Freud, does not necessarily apply to me. (Keillor, 2002)

A **Poltergeist** is a mischievous spirit or ghost. We include reference to it here because, in our experience, conducting psychotherapy or counseling sometimes includes mysterious and mischievous surprises. An example of a poltergeist is given in the famous Harry Potter book series:

> Peeves the Poltergeist was worth two locked doors and a trick staircase if you met him when you were late for class. He would drop wastepaper baskets on your head, pull rugs from under your feet, pelt you with bits of chalk, or sneak up behind you, invisible, grab your nose, and screech, "GOT YOUR CONK!" (Rowling, 1997, p. 132)

We reference poltergeists not because we're big believers in ghosts, but because it's a nice way to bring your attention to the fact that, as a therapist, you should be prepared for the unexpected. Sometimes your clients will say and do outrageous things. At other times, you'll suddenly feel the urge to say or do something inappropriate. For whatever reason, sitting privately with another individual for long periods of time can produce unusual and profound experiences. Just when you least suspect it, your video-recording equipment will malfunction or you'll feel like crying or you'll want to fidget and want to leave the room or the clock hanging on the wall in your office will stop or your client will tell you something shocking. Our point is: Be ready for surprises.

Overall, we hope as you explore the theories in this book and as you come to know contemporary perspectives in counseling and psychotherapy, that you'll keep the Zeitgeist, Ortgeist, and Poltergeist in mind. What spirits of time, place, and mischief are operating right now? What will be the next big discovery and next big scandal in the field of counseling and psychotherapy?

CONCLUDING COMMENTS

In this chapter we've taken you on a quick tour of major issues in counseling and psychotherapy. From historical context to contemporary research to ethical essentials, the field of counseling and psychotherapy is filled with amazing and interesting information. We wish you the best as you begin

to explore the main theories of therapy in greater depth.

CHAPTER SUMMARY

This book is about how to apply the many different theories and approaches to counseling and psychotherapy to alleviate human suffering. To understand these varying approaches it's important to consider the contexts, both historical and cultural, that shaped their development.

Freud is often considered the father of psychotherapy, but this narrow formulation of how the talking cure developed ignores many other contributors. For example, Janet, one of Freud's contemporaries, claimed that he and his colleagues were already working on the ideas Freud was developing. Additionally, focusing on a "White father" of psychotherapy can be seen as having racist and sexist overtones.

At least four different cultural and historical realities or perspectives have shaped the development of counseling and psychotherapy. These included: (1) biomedical; (2) religious/spiritual; (3) psychosocial; and (4) feminist/multicultural.

Many different definitions for counseling and psychotherapy have been offered over the years. Psychotherapy tends to be seen as a longer, deeper, and more expensive process as compared to counseling. A 12-part comprehensive definition of counseling and psychotherapy was provided.

A theory is organized of knowledge about a particular object or phenomenon. In psychology, theories are used to generate hypotheses about human thinking, emotions, and behavior. All of the theories of counseling and psychotherapy in this book should be evaluated using modern (and postmodern) research principles and procedures.

In 1952, Hans Eysenck conducted a review of psychotherapy outcomes and concluded psychotherapy was less effective than no treatment whatsoever. This finding was controversial and stimulated substantial research on psychotherapy outcomes. Currently, most researchers and practitioners agree that counseling and psychotherapy are very effective, but there are still heated arguments over which approaches are more effective with which problems.

There are two main positions constituting the great psychotherapy debate. One position claims that specific therapy procedures are superior to other procedures and therefore should constitute most of what therapists provide. The other position claims there are common factors within all approaches that account for the fact that research generally shows all therapy approaches have equal efficacy or effectiveness.

Counseling and psychotherapy approaches are evaluated in either highly controlled research protocols (randomized controlled trials) or real world settings. Research protocols provide evidence to support treatment efficacy and research in real world settings are considered as providing evidence to support treatment effectiveness.

Counselors and psychotherapists are required to abide by professional ethics. Essential ethical topics include: (a) competence and informed consent; (b) multicultural competence; (c) confidentiality; (d) multiple roles; and (e) beneficence. It's important for counseling and psychotherapy professionals to be aware that some treatment approaches are potentially harmful.

As you read this book you will have a chance to explore your own ideas about counseling, psychotherapy, and human change. This will help you develop a personal theory of how to work effectively with clients that's based on your own ideas, combined with the 13 theoretical perspectives you study in this book.

INTRODUCTORY KEY TERMS

Beneficence

Biomedical perspective

Common therapeutic factors

Confidentiality

Context

Dodo bird effect

Effect size

Effectiveness research

Efficacy research

Empirically supported treatment (EST)

Empirically validated treatment

Evidence-based principles

Expectancy

External validity

Extratherapeutic factors

Feminist/multicultural perspective

First, do no harm

Great psychotherapy debate

Informed consent

Internal validity

Meta-analysis

Multicultural competencies

Multiple roles

Negative outcomes

Nonspecific factors

Ortgeist

Poltergeist

Potentially harmful therapies

Practice-based evidence

Psychosocial perspective

Randomized controlled trials (RCTs)

Religious-spiritual perspective

The talking cure

The working definition of counseling and psychotherapy

Therapeutic relationship

Trephining

Zeitgeist

RECOMMENDED READINGS AND RESOURCES

If you'd like to explore topics covered in this chapter in greater detail, the following resources may be helpful.

PROFESSIONAL ASSOCIATIONS

Websites for several professional associations are listed below. Each website has a wide array of information, including (a) professional ethical codes, (b) lead journals, (c) annual conventions/conferences, (d) association magazines, and (e) additional professional publications.

American Association for Marriage and Family Therapy (AAMFT; www.aamft.org)

American Counseling Association (ACA; www.counseling .org)

American Psychological Association (APA; www.apa .org)

American School Counselor Association (ASCA; www .schoolcounselor.org)

Association for Addiction Professionals (NAADAC; www .naadac.org)

National Association of Social Workers (NASW; www .socialworkers.org)

READINGS ON ETHICS, THEORIES, AND RESEARCH

Beutler, L. E. (2009). Making science matter in clinical practice: Redefining psychotherapy. *Clinical Psychology: Science and Practice, 16*(3), 301–317.

Duncan, B. L., Miller, S. D., Wampold, B. E., & Hubble, M. A. (Eds.). (2010). *The heart and soul of change: Delivering what works in therapy* (2nd ed.). Washington, DC: American Psychological Association.

Herlihy, B., & Corey, G. (2006). *Boundaries issues in counseling* (2nd ed.). Alexandria, VA: American Counseling Association

Lambert, M. J. (2010b). *Prevention of treatment failure: The use of measuring, monitoring, and feedback in clinical practice.* Washington, DC: American Psychological Association.

Luborsky, L., Singer, B., & Luborsky, L. (1975). Comparative studies of psychotherapies: Is it true that "Everybody has won so all shall have prizes"? *Archives of General Psychiatry, 32,* 995–1008.

Norcross, J. C., Beutler, L. E., & Levant, R. F. (Eds.). (2006). *Evidence-based practices in mental health: Debate and dialogue on the fundamental questions.* Washington, DC: American Psychological Association.

Pope, K. S., & Vasquez, M. J. T. (2011). *Ethics in psychotherapy and counseling: A practical guide* (4th ed.). Hoboken, NJ: John Wiley & Sons.

Smith, M. L., Glass, G. V., & Miller, T. I. (1980). *The benefits of psychotherapy.* Baltimore, MD: Johns Hopkins University Press.

Sommers-Flanagan, R., & Sommers-Flanagan, J. (2007). *Becoming an ethical helping professional: Cultural and philosophical foundations.* Hoboken, NJ: John Wiley & Sons.

Wampold, B. E. (2010). *The basics of psychotherapy: An introduction to theory and practice.* Washington, DC: American Psychological Association.

GOING FARTHER AND DEEPER

Additional general counseling and psychotherapy resources are available at johnsommersflanagan.com.

CHAPTER 2

Psychoanalytic Approaches

A man like me cannot live without a hobby-horse, a consuming passion—in Schiller's words a tyrant. I have found my tyrant, and in his service I know no limits. My tyrant is psychology.

—Sigmund Freud, 1895, in a letter to W. Fliess

THIS CHAPTER

- Reviews key figures and contextual factors contributing to the development and evolution of psychoanalytically oriented psychotherapy and counseling
- Outlines and describes traditional Freudian psychoanalytic theoretical principles as well as more contemporary psychoanalytic or psychodynamic modifications
- Describes and discusses principles and techniques associated with psychoanalytic therapy practice, including
  - Assessment procedures
  - Free association, interpretation, transference, countertransference, insight, and dream interpretation
- Offers short vignettes to demonstrate psychoanalytic therapy principles and techniques in action
- Illustrates how treatment planning, outcomes assessment, and gender and cultural issues can be integrated into a psychoanalytic therapy case
- Reviews the evidence-based status of psychoanalytic or psychodynamic therapies
- Offers resources for further study

Sigmund Freud has maintained his place as the central figure in psychoanalysis since the early 1900s. For some psychoanalytic and psychodynamic practitioners, he remains a source of inspiration and brilliance. For others, he is an object of disdain, frequently viewed as a symbol of much that is wrong with psychology, psychiatry, psychotherapy, and counseling. The fact that speaking his name in public still produces strong emotional and intellectual reactions is a testament to his widespread influence. Let us begin with a brief examination of his childhood and personal history, because, frankly, Freud himself wouldn't have it any other way.

BIOGRAPHICAL INFORMATION: SIGMUND FREUD

Sigmund Freud

Sigmund Freud was born in Freiberg, Moravia, in 1856. He was the first-born of the union between his father, Jakob and his mother Amalie (Jakob's second wife). Although Jakob had two children from a previous marriage, Sigmund held the favored position of eldest son in a family with three boys and five girls. Jakob, a wool merchant, has been described as very authoritarian and Amalie as protective and nurturing. Due to financial limitations, the family lived together in a small apartment.

Freud's intellectual potential was obvious early on. For example, he and a friend taught themselves Spanish because they wanted to read *Don Quixote* in its original language. His parents supported his intellectual appetite as much as they could. Freud obtained his medical degree from the University of Vienna with the goal of becoming a research scientist. Given his later fascination with psychosexual development and the unconscious sexual meaning of many behaviors, it seems especially interesting that he spent time searching for the testes of the eel in his first major research project.

Freud was unable to continue his research career due to financial needs. Consequently, he went into the private practice of neurology.

As a neurologist, Freud was exposed to the disorder "hysteria," which affected a significant number of European women in the late nineteenth century. This disorder included unexplained symptoms of numbness, paralysis, and tremors. During a visit to France, he became familiar with the work of Jean Charcot, who was using hypnosis to *produce* hysterical symptoms. This convinced Freud that the same procedure might be used to treat hysteria. Subsequently, Freud found he could use hypnosis to get his patients to talk about important incidents that they didn't recall when awake. After experimenting with hypnosis and reporting that it made him feel like "a miracle worker," Freud began working with Viennese physician Josef Breuer. Breuer was successfully treating hysteria symptoms by having patients talk about emotionally laden childhood experiences. In the early 1880s Breuer worked extensively with Anna O., discussing her hysteria symptoms and treatment in great detail with Freud. Together, they published *Studies in Hysteria* (Breuer & Freud, 1895). Eventually, Freud became even more impressed with this "talking cure" than he had been with hypnosis. And the rest, as they say, is history.

HISTORICAL CONTEXT

As we suggested toward the end of Chapter 1, psychological theories are generally a product of the prevailing Zeitgeist and Ortgeist. Bankart (1997) stated:

> To fathom Freud's near-obsession with the sexual foundations of emotional distress is also to come to a fuller awareness of the sexual repression and hypocrisy in the lives of the Austrian middle class at the turn of the . . . [nineteenth] century and the effect of this repression on the mental health of adolescents and young adults during the time when Freud derived his theories. (p. 8)

A good illustration of psychoanalytic historical context and of Freud's dominant persuasive powers is the dramatic story of Freud's development and subsequent recanting of **the seduction hypothesis**. This story captures his psychoanalytic thinking along with the social dynamics of his time. Interestingly, there is conflict over the truth of this story—which further illustrates the divisive nature of Freud and his legacy. As you read through the drama of the seduction hypothesis, keep in mind that certain points have been contested . . . but the general unfolding of a spectacular drama around sexuality, sexual fantasy, and sexual abuse in a sexually repressed society is likely accurate.

The Seduction Hypothesis

In 1885, Freud went to France to study under the famous neurologist Jean Charcot. According to Jeffrey Masson, former projects director of the Freud Archives, it's likely that during his time in France, Freud visited the Paris Morgue, observing autopsies of young children who had been brutally physically and sexually abused (Masson, 1984). Masson speculated that Freud's exposure to the grisly reality of child abuse combined with stories of abuse he heard from his patients, led him to believe that hysteria was caused by child sexual abuse.

Eventually, Freud presented a paper titled **"The Aetiology of Hysteria"** at the Society for Psychiatry and Neurology in Vienna (Freud,

1896). In this paper, he outlined his controversial hypothesis:

> I therefore put forward the thesis that at the bottom of every case of hysteria there are one or more occurrences of premature sexual experience, occurrences which belong to the earliest years of childhood, but which can be reproduced through the work of psychoanalysis in spite of the intervening decades. (Freud, 1896, cited in Masson, 1984, p. 263)

Note that Freud stated, "at the bottom of every case of hysteria." This shows that during his professional presentation he was emphasizing a clear causal connection between childhood sexual abuse and hysteria. This presentation was based on 18 cases (12 women and 6 men), all of which included childhood sexual abuse. At least three key points are important in this presentation: (1) Freud's idea about the connection between childhood sexual abuse and subsequent psychopathology may represent an early formulation of the contemporary diagnosis of Posttraumatic Stress Disorder and/or Dissociative Identity Disorder (American Psychiatric Association, 2000); (2) critics contend that in Freud's paper, "the 'facts' of specific case histories are never provided" (Wilcocks, 1994); and (3) more recent critiques suggest that Freud may have been constructing sexual memories both through a direct pressure technique and by distorting what he heard to fit with his ideas—rather than modifying his ideas to fit what his clients were saying (Esterson, 2001).

Despite a lack of supporting detail in his presentation and the possibility that he was building evidence to support his theory, Freud goes on to suggest that hysterical symptoms don't arise immediately, but instead develop later:

> Our view then is that infantile sexual experiences . . . create the hysterical symptoms, but . . . they do not do so immediately, but remain without effect to begin with and only exercise a pathogenic action later, when they have been aroused after puberty in the form of unconscious memories. (Freud, 1896, cited in Masson, 1984, p. 272)

It appears that Freud continued to believe his clients' sexual abuse stories (or perhaps he believed his own constructed version of his client's sexual abuse stories) until the late 1800s or early 1900s.

Recanting the Seduction Hypothesis

Imagine yourself alone with a great and horrible insight. In Masson's version of the seduction hypothesis story, this was Freud's situation. Masson (1984) describes the reception Freud received after presenting his hypothesis (and this part of the seduction hypothesis story is not disputed):

> The paper . . . met with total silence. Afterwards, he was urged never to publish it, lest his reputation be damaged beyond repair. The silence around him deepened, as did the loneliness. But he defied his colleagues and published "The Aietology of Hysteria." (pp. xviii–xix)

Five days after presenting his paper, Freud wrote about the experience to Fliess. Freud's anger is obvious:

> [My] lecture on the aetiology of hysteria at the Psychiatric Society met with an icy reception from the asses, and from Kraft-Ebing [the distinguished professor and head of the Department of Psychiatry at the University of Vienna] the strange comment: "It sounds like a scientific fairy tale." And this after one has demonstrated to them a solution to a more than thousand-year-old problem, a "source of the Nile!" They can all go to hell. (Schur, 1972, p. 104)

Although it's clear that Freud's lecture received "an icy reception" it's less clear why the audience was unimpressed. According to Masson, the reception is icy because Freud is bringing up sex and sexual abuse and that psychiatry (and most professionals and citizens at the time) were uncomfortable with facts linked to high sexual abuse rates. Alternatively, others have suggested that Freud's style, perhaps a combination of arrogance along with an absence of scientific rigor or detail, moved the audience to rebuke him. For example, Wilcocks (1994) wrote:

> The inferential support offered—without detail, of course—is that in eighteen cases out of eighteen,

Freud has "discovered" the same etiological factors. But since neither we nor his audience are/were privy to the circumstances of any of his cases, this claim—whatever it's other inferential mistakes—is simply useless. (p. 129)

It may never be clear whether Freud's initial motives in presenting the seduction hypothesis were noble or manipulative. However, regardless of his motives, the ensuing years following his "Aetiology of Hysteria" lecture were difficult. Reportedly, his private practice was in decline and his professional life in shambles. It was at this time that Freud began what has been described as "his lonely and painful self-analysis" (Prochaska & Norcross, 2003, p. 29). His 2-year self-analysis included uncovering memories of yearning for his mother and equally powerful feelings of resentment toward his father (Bankart, 1997).

Eventually, Freud abandoned his seduction hypothesis in favor of Oedipal theory and its associated seduction and power fantasies. Some suggest this was because he began noticing seductive patterns in so many parent-child interactions that it was unrealistic to assume that child sexual abuse occurred at such a ubiquitous rate. Others believe Freud was ahead of his time in discovering child sexual abuse, but buckled under the social and psychological pressure and abandoned his belief in the truths his patients shared with him. Still others contend that while Freud was constructing his theoretical principles, he was projecting and mixing his own fantasies into his clients' stories. The following statement illustrates the highly personalized nature of some of Freud's theorizing:

I found in myself a constant love for my mother, and jealousy of my father. I now consider this to be a universal event in childhood. (R. A. Paul, 1991)

Eventually, in 1925, long after he recanted the seduction hypothesis, he reflected on his struggle:

I believed these stories, and consequently supposed that I had discovered the roots of the subsequent neurosis in these experiences of sexual seduction in childhood.... If the reader feels inclined to shake his head at my credulity, I cannot altogether blame him.... I was at last obliged to recognize that these scenes of seduction had never taken place, and that they were only fantasies which my patients had made up. (Freud, 1925, cited in Masson, 1984, p. 11)

In the creation and recanting of the seduction hypothesis, it's difficult to sort out fact from fantasy. Perhaps this is as it should be, as it illustrates at least one formidable lesson about psychology. That is, when diving headlong into the deep psychological processes of humans, it's possible to elicit confused and confusing storylines and to knowingly or unknowingly (unconsciously) mix (or project) our own personal issues into the plot. In the end, it may be that we create Kraft-Ebing's "Scientific fairy tale" or, alternatively, something with lasting and meaningful significance. More likely, we create a combination of the two. (See Table 2.1 for three possible conclusions about Freud's dabbling with the seduction hypothesis.)

PSYCHOANALYTIC THEORETICAL PRINCIPLES

Freud's theory is one of what P. Miller (2010) refers to as the "giant theories" of developmental psychology (p. 108). If you've studied basic psychology, you've undoubtedly read about Freudian theory. One of our psychoanalytic colleagues refers to classical Freudian theory as a *museum theory*, not so much because it belongs in a museum (although a case can be made for that as well), but because classical Freudian theory is a one-person intrapsychic model that treats clients as separate, individual artifacts to be objectively examined. In contrast, modern analytic theory treats therapy as a two-person field, where the therapist's and client's intrapsychic and relationship interactions help shed light on patterns that may be troubling the client (Renik, 1993; Wachtel, 2008; Wachtel, 2010).

Given the museum nature of classical Freudian theory, our coverage of this material is brief. Resources on classical Freudian and contemporary psychoanalytic theories are listed at the end of this chapter.

Table 2.1   Freud's Seduction Hypothesis: Three Conclusions

The official Freudian storyline goes something like this: Sigmund Freud was an astute observer who had to abandon his earlier views about child seduction and sexual abuse to discover the more basic truth of the power of internal fantasy and of spontaneous childhood sexuality. Although he initially believed his clients' sexual abuse reports, he later discovered that it was not actual abuse, but imagined sexualized relationships (fantasies) between children and caretakers—aka: the Oedipal complex—that caused psychopathology.	Masson's (1984) version, subsequently labeled "a new fable based on old myths" by Esterson (1998), suggests that Freud was ahead of his time in recognizing child sexual abuse. These abuses were real and it was correct of Freud to identify them and to develop his seduction hypothesis. However—and unfortunately—Freud abandoned his sexually abused clients by recanting the seduction theory. He abandoned them because of pressure from medical and scientific colleagues and because society was not ready to face the reality of rampant child sexual abuse.	Freudian critics suggest that Freud was an exceptionally bright, persuasive, and powerful speaker and writer, but he was practicing bad science. He was more interested in building his theory than psychological reality. Consequently, he twisted his clients' stories, mixing them with his own issues and fantasies, and created an elaborate theory initially around sexual abuse and later around sexual fantasy. His theories, although fascinating and capturing much about the projective potential in human thinking, are more about Freud than they are about his clients.

The Dynamic Approach

Freud's **dynamic approach** to human psychology is known as drive theory or instinct theory. He believed that humans are filled with mental or psychic energy. This energy comes from two essential sources: **Eros** (energy associated with life and sex) and **Thanatos** (energy associated with death and aggression).

In constructing his theory, Freud used physical models to describe how psychic energy is built up, transformed, connected to certain images, distributed, and discharged. But, as Brenner (1973) pointed out, "Psychic energy is a term for a psychological concept, not a physical one" (p. 20). Parallel physical processes may exist, but they have yet to be pinpointed.

The hypothesis of **psychic determinism** underlies the dynamic approach. Brenner (1973) stated: "in the mind, as in physical nature . . . nothing happens by chance, or in a random way. Each psychic event is determined by the ones which preceded it" (p. 2).

Psychic determinism proposes an underlying psychological explanation for every emotion, thought, impulse, and behavior. There are no accidents. If you oversleep, you're probably avoiding something or someone. If you party too hard, maybe

you're expressing antagonism toward your parents' demands for responsible behavior. If you forget your professor's name, perhaps you have an unconscious aggressive impulse toward her. Or she may remind you, in some unconscious way, of someone you felt sexual feelings for and so you defend against your sexual impulse by not recalling her name.

The concept of psychic determinism is one reason some people feel uncomfortable talking to psychology or counseling majors. If you go to a party and someone asks, "Are you analyzing me?" you can at least partially blame Freud and his concept of psychic determinism.

Eros and thanatos are the two basic drives that energize behavior. Freud referred to eros-related energy as **libido**, whereas thanatos- or destructive-related energy was unnamed. Based on Freudian drive (dynamic) theory, every impulse has an *origin*, *aim*, *object*, and *intensity*. An impulse always *originates* from some place in the body. For example, in very young children, most pleasure (or libidinal) impulses arise from the oral region. This is why young children put everything into their mouths. Their *aim* (or goal) is oral gratification.

If we stay with a small child example, the dynamic approach might look like this:

- Origin of impulse: Baby experiences physical hunger sensations.

- Aim of impulse: Get food! (Gratification).

- Object of impulse: Breast or bottle (Caregiver).

- Intensity of impulse: Strength of hunger sensation varies.

Most importantly, this impulse-gratification cycle involving an object (person) is often repeated in a baby's life. As a consequence, a process or pattern occurs over and over and is eventually internalized. Some may refer to this as the caregiver-child *dance*. This internalized interaction pattern becomes an **internal working model**. If this internalized cycle is dysfunctional due to parental overindulgence or withholding, a **repetition compulsion** of the pathological cycle may occur and continue during adulthood. Psychoanalytic therapy brings automatic, dysfunctional impulse-gratification cycles into awareness so they can be replaced with more adaptive and intentional behavior patterns.

The Topographic Approach

The psychoanalytic mind is divided into three interrelated regions: the **unconscious**, the **preconscious**, and the **conscious**. Freud described the scene:

> Let us . . . compare the system of the unconscious to a large entrance hall, in which the mental impulses jostle one another like separate individuals. Adjoining this entrance hall there is a second, narrower, room—a kind of drawing-room—in which consciousness, too, resides. But on the threshold between these two rooms a watch-man performs his function: he examines the different mental impulses, acts as a censor, and will not admit them into the drawing-room if they displease him. (Freud, 1963, p. 295)

Freud believed human consciousness is an "exceptional rather than a regular attribute" (Brenner, 1973, p. 2). In other words, there's much more going on at the unconscious level than at the conscious.

Because awareness of primitive sexual and aggressive impulses might disrupt our daily lives, our brain protects us from them. As we will see later, the main purpose of psychoanalytic therapy is to help us slowly become aware of unconscious impulses or maladaptive internal working models. By bringing unconscious impulses to awareness, we're better able to manage them, because even when existing outside awareness, primitive impulses still influence us in indirect and destructive ways.

For example, if a young man has an unresolved **Oedipal conflict** with his father, he may be overly aggressive and competitive. His lack of awareness of the origin, aim, intensity, and object of these impulses allows for their escalation. As a consequence, one night while out with friends, he becomes belligerent toward a police officer and ends up in jail. Alternatively, if the young man had received psychoanalytic therapy, he might recognize this pattern, manage his competitive and combative impulses, and avoid jail time. Note: Consistent with the Greek myth, the Oedipal conflict involves a male child's sexual attraction and wish to possess or marry his mother. This conflict emerges at the phallic stage (see below) and is resolved when the boy identifies with his father. Freud thought that resolution of this conflict led to development of the superego. A similar dynamic involving female development is referred to as the Electra complex.

The Developmental Stage Approach

In recent years early brain development has been emphasized in the popular press and in the schools (Badenoch, 2008; Begley, 2007; Siegel, 2007). For many, this emphasis seems like common sense, but in the early 1900s, the idea that adult functioning is shaped by early childhood experiences was groundbreaking. Freud was the first to outline an extensive developmental theory explaining how early childhood experiences influence later adult functioning.

P. Miller (1983) described Freud's developmental stages:

> Each stage is defined in terms of the part of the body around which drives are centered. The eye of the storm shifts from the oral to the anal to the

phallic area during the first five years. Then a period of latency in middle childhood is followed by the genital stage of adolescence. Each stage presents new needs that must be handled by the mental structures. The way in which these needs are met (or not met) determines not only how sexual satisfaction is achieved, but also how the child relates to other people and how he [sic] feels about himself. He develops characteristic attitudes, defenses, and fantasies. Unresolved conflicts in any stage may haunt the person throughout his lifetime. (pp. 125–126)

Freud's developmental theory is relatively straightforward. Children move through four developmental stages and a latency period. Progress through stages is driven by biological maturation—which forces individuals to confront demands inherent to each stage. At each stage, if parents are overly indulgent or withholding, the child can end up with fixations or complexes. A fixation or complex is an unresolved unconscious conflict (aka dysfunctional internal working model). Freud's developmental stages include:

- *Oral*: birth to 1 year old.
- *Anal*: 1 to 3 years old.
- *Phallic*: 3 to 5 years old.
- *Latency*: 5 to 12 years old.
- *Genital*: adolescence to adulthood.

Most contemporary psychoanalysts don't find much value in Freud's original developmental stages. As one of our psychoanalytic colleagues put it, "Freud's stages don't really match up with reality; they're not really taken seriously any more" (Spitzform, personal communication, February, 2003).

On the other hand, Freud's general premise that individuals have developmentally based dysfunctions that can be treated via analysis remains alive and well within psychoanalytic circles. Contemporary analysts consider a variety of developmental theories when working with clients (Erikson, 1963; Mahler & Bergman, 1975; Stern, 1985).

The Structural Approach

Freud's **structural approach** involves interrelationships of the well-known concepts of id, ego, and superego. As discussed previously, powerful, unconscious forces flow through the body and mind. If not for the system's structural components, human behavior would be completely dictated by sexual and aggressive forces or drives. However, because these primal forces flow through the id, ego, and superego, humans learn to constructively manage their urges; we learn to wait, to watch, and to control ourselves.

The **id** is the seat of biological desires. As a structural entity within the human personality, it functions on the *pleasure principle* and *primary-process thought*. Freud described the id as "a chaos, a cauldron full of seething excitations" (Freud, 1964, p. 73).

For the most part, id impulses are outside awareness or unconscious. However, it's possible to glimpse these impulses in society—as in cases when individuals seek immediate sexual or aggressive gratification. Additionally, we can view id impulses within ourselves via dreams, fantasies, flashes of instinctual desire, and powerful pleasure-seeking urges. Primary process thought, another facet of id functioning, is characterized by hallucination-like images of fulfilled sexual or aggressive desires.

In many ways, the id is mother of the ego. Because it's impossible to continuously have one's desires gratified, you must learn to wait for what you want. Although the id is a powerful seething cauldron of desire, the ego has potent resources of its own. Ego functions include memory, problem-solving abilities, and logical thought. These functions are considered *secondary thought processes* and help us cope with primary sexual and aggressive drives.

The **superego** develops when children resolve their Oedipal (or Electra) issues and begin more strongly identifying with same-sex parents and parental demands or expectations. There are two parts of the superego: First, there is the **conscience**. The conscience develops as a function of parental prohibitions. When mom, dad, or another adult authority figure says, "No!" or "Stop that!" or administers punishment, these admonitions are internalized within the child's psyche and later used by the child (and, in later years, by the adult) to self-punish or prohibit unacceptable impulses. The conscience becomes the inner source of punishment, which may be why children of strict and punitive parents often end up with neurotic guilt as adults.

The superego also includes the **ego-ideal**. In contrast to the negative, punishing conscience, the ego-ideal is a positive desire to emulate adult standards. For example, when parents model healthy, rational, and functional behavior, the child strives to behave similarly. Using the language of behavioral psychology, the conscience is an inner presence that uses a "stick" or punishment as a motivator, while the ego-ideal uses a "carrot" or reinforcement as a primary motivator.

Overall, the **ego** acts as a mediator within the human personality. It must contend not only with the id's primitive impulses, but also with admonitions and expectations of the superego, as well as realities of the external world. This is no easy task, and therefore the ego often must use defense mechanisms as a means of dealing with battling forces.

Defense mechanisms are designed to ward off unacceptable id impulses that are at odds with superego standards or that would result in problems within the real world. They have four primary characteristics:

1. They are automatic: Individuals reflexively use their defense mechanisms.

2. They are unconscious.

3. They ward off unacceptable impulses.

4. They distort reality (to a greater or lesser extent, depending upon the defense mechanism employed).

From an applied perspective, most therapies are ego supportive; they aim to help the ego—a rational and logical thinking entity—deal more effectively with primitive desires, internalized parental and societal standards, and the real world. Brief descriptions of eight common ego defense mechanisms are in Table 2.2.

Psychopathology and Human Change

Based on psychoanalytic theory, psychopathology arises from early childhood experiences. Further, Freud believed psychopathology existed on a continuum, with even healthy individuals showing occasional signs of pathology. This portion of his theory has been referred to as the **normal-abnormal continuum**:

> In an abnormal personality, psychological processes are exaggerated or distorted. A melancholic patient has an overly strong superego. A sadistic killer has a strong, uncontrolled aggressive drive. An amnesiac must repress all of a painful past. Yet every normal personality has traces of melancholia, sadism, and unaccountable forgetting. (P. Miller, 1983, p. 128)

The building blocks of psychopathology were described in the preceding sections. To summarize, there are several key issues pertaining to psychopathology and human change that have remained relatively constant in psychoanalytic theory and therapy. First, therapy focuses primarily on internalized, dysfunctional childhood experiences as the origin of psychopathology. Second, pathological childhood experiences are not completely understood, recalled, or dealt with consciously. Consequently, repetitive and dissatisfying behavior and thinking patterns exist and changing these patterns feels beyond the client's control. Third, a cornerstone of human change involves an insightful or consciousness-raising experience. Fourth, human change isn't instantaneous; it requires a working through process where consistent practicing of new ways of understanding and dealing with inner impulses and human relationships occurs.

Table 2.2   Ego Defense Mechanisms

Defense mechanism descriptions and examples

Repression involves forgetting an emotionally painful memory. When a client has repressed a memory, there may be behavioral evidence that it exists, but the client genuinely has an absence of recall: "Hmm. Nope. I don't remember anything unusual about my childhood. In fact, I don't recall much at all."

In contrast to repression, *denial* is usually expressed with more force. Its essence is captured by Shakespeare's famous line about protest[ing] too much. Clients using denial often say, "No way, that's not true" and repeat their denial forcefully.

Projection occurs when clients push their unacceptable thoughts, feelings, or impulses outward, onto another person. A client may accuse someone else of anger, while denying his or her own: "I'm not mad about anything; you're the one who's pissed off!"

If it's too dangerous to directly express aggression toward someone, the individual may behave in an excessively loving way. This is *reaction formation*. The inverse example occurs when it's not acceptable to express sexual attraction; therefore, the individual behaves in ways suggestive of hatred or distaste toward the person toward whom he or she really feels an attraction.

Displacement occurs when the aim of sexual or aggressive impulses is shifted from a more dangerous person or activity to a less dangerous person or activity. Aggressive displacement is characterized by the colloquialism of "kicking the dog." Sexual displacement occurs when sexual feelings are aroused by a forbidden object (person) and displaced onto a more acceptable object.

Humans are notorious for rationalizing or intellectualizing away primitive impulses.

Rationalization occurs when clients use excessive explanations to account for their behavior. For example, if a student makes an impulsive, hostile comment to someone in class, he or she might extensively explain and justify the comment.

Regression involves going back to old, less sophisticated methods of doing things. Traumatized children may regress to wetting the bed or pooping their pants rather than using more advanced toileting skills. Adults who are skillful communicators may regress to shouting and aggression rather than controlling their impulses.

Sublimation is one of the most constructive defense mechanisms. It occurs when primal sexual or aggressive energy is channeled into positive loving or vocational activities. For example, sexual energy is often sublimated into creative tasks and aggression into hard work (e.g., house cleaning, yard work).

EVOLUTION AND DEVELOPMENT IN PSYCHOANALYTIC THEORY AND PRACTICE

As we've seen, Freudian theory originally focused on biological or somatic instinctual sexual and aggressive drives as the primary motivational factor influencing behavior. Despite Freud's dynamic appeal, two of his inner circle split away, personally and theoretically, going on to develop their own approaches—first Alfred Adler stepped away

(Chapter 3) and later Carl Jung (see Putting it in Practice 2.1 and online at www.wiley.com/go/counselingtheories). This makes the evolution and development of psychoanalysis complex and multifaceted. One way of reducing confusion is to follow Pine's (1990) four primary stages of development in psychoanalytic thinking:

1. Drive
2. Ego
3. Object
4. Self

PUTTING IT IN PRACTICE 2.1

The Former Heir Apparent: Carl Gustav Jung

Carl Gustav Jung was born in Kesswil, Switzerland, in 1875 and died in Zurich in 1961. For a period of time, Freud, Adler, and Jung were all close associates. In fact, Freud considered Jung to be his heir apparent for a short time, but this was before Jung had the audacity to begin questioning some of Freud's practices and began distinguishing himself by formulating new concepts and alternative ways to think about the old ones.

For instance, Jung began redefining libido as creative life energy, rather than simply sexual energy. He also didn't see the unconscious as a bubbling cauldron of primitive impulses, but rather, a source of both peril and wisdom. Jung believed our psyches are self-regulating systems, seeking balance between opposing forces and impulses.

Jung divided the unconscious into two entities, the personal unconscious and the collective unconscious, with the personal being unique to an individual, and the collective being a shared pool of motives, urges, fears, and potentialities that we inherit by being human. Jung believed that this part of the unconscious was far larger than the personal unconscious and that it was universally shared by all members of the human race.

Although Jungian therapy and analysis are highly specialized and less common than most, many of Jung's concepts have become part of our popular lexicon. Though perhaps not correctly understood, many people speak of archetypes, complexes, and their shadows.

Jung also believed that our personalities are organized by certain mental functions and attitudes that determine how we habitually or preferentially orient ourselves. Along with the defining attitudes of Introversion and Extraversion, Jung identified four functions: The perceptional functions, Sensation or Intuition, and the rational functions, Thinking or Feeling. These concepts were used in developing the popular psychological questionnaire—The Myers-Briggs Type Indicator (Myers, 1955).

Sensation is the function that notices the real world around us and establishes the fact that something exists. Intuition is the function that guesses or surmises the origins and direction of things and ideas. People tend to trust one or the other of these functions more fully as their source of information. Thinking and Feeling are the judging functions, influenced not by perception, but by reflection. People who have a Thinking preference apply specific, logical, linear principles in their analyses of the information they've taken in via their perception functions—either sensing or intuiting. Feeling judgments are informed by an assessment of values and the potential impact of choices on individuals and groups of people.

Again, these concepts are widely known but perhaps not fully appreciated nor understood as Jung may have intended. This short box cannot do justice to Jung's ideas or their potential applications. We encourage you to go online and read our online Jungian chapter to further expand your understanding of this unique and important early figure.

Interestingly, one of the most important psychoanalytic expansionists was also named Freud. We now turn to the story of Anna Freud (Sigmund's youngest daughter) and her influence on ego psychology.

Anna and the Ego: Psychoanalytic Ego Psychology

Anna Freud

One way Sigmund Freud controlled psychoanalytic theory and therapy was to insist that his disciples submit to a course of psychoanalysis by the master. During this early period of psychoanalysis, there were no state licensing boards or professional ethics codes. Thus, Freud was able to take what we would now consider the most unusual, and most likely unethical, step of accepting his youngest daughter, Anna, into analysis. As Bankart (1997) stated, Anna was barely out of her teens when she began analysis, and "From those days until the end of her life, Anna had room for only one man in her life, and that man was her father" (p. 183).

Anna was one of the few practicing psychoanalysts ever to be without an official professional degree. Essentially, she was "home schooled."

Anna Freud ushered in a new generation of psychoanalysis. As you may recall, Sigmund Freud based his theoretical propositions about child development on his intensive study of adults through psychoanalysis. In contrast, Anna Freud studied children directly. She listened as children told about their dreams and fantasies. Perhaps more importantly, she discovered how to observe children's unconscious mental processes through play. Although she never directly disputed her father's belief in the dominance of id impulses in human development and functioning, she helped shift the psychoanalytic focus from the study of instinctual drives to a study of ego development. She's best known for her work with children and her theoretical writing on ego defense mechanisms.

Beginning in about the 1930s, **ego psychology** began claiming a portion of the psychoanalytic landscape. These theorists didn't completely break with Freud; rather, following Anna Freud's lead, they extended his ideas, eventually emphasizing that certain ego functions were inborn and autonomous of biological drives (Hartmann, 1958; Rapaport, 1951). These ego functions include memory, thinking, intelligence, and motor control. As Wolitzky and Eagle (1997) stated, "Following . . . ego psychology, there was now room in psychoanalytic theory for behavior and functions relatively autonomous of the vicissitudes of drive" (p. 44). In addition, the greater emphasis on ego functioning as apart from and interacting with id impulses brought the interpretation of ego defenses to the forefront.

The new focus on ego had ramifications for both psychoanalytic theory and practice. A profound development during this period came from one of Anna Freud's analysands and followers, Erik Erikson.

Like Anna Freud, Erik Erikson had little formal academic training. Nonetheless, perhaps because he was an artist with exceptional observational skills, he managed to outline and describe a highly regarded theory of human development. In his **eight-stage epigenetic psychosocial theory of development**, Erikson (1963) deviated from Freudian developmental theory in two key ways: He emphasized psychosocial development instead of psychosexual development, and he emphasized the continuous nature of development into old age, rather than ending his theorizing, like Freud, in early adulthood. Erikson's eight stages of development are summarized in most introductory and developmental psychology textbooks. For a glimpse into the ever-evolving nature of developmental theories, we recommend viewing Joan Erikson's (Erik's wife) video on the ninth stage of human development (F. Davidson, 1995).

Object Relations

In the 1950s, **object relations** theorists began conceptually reformulating traditional psychoanalytic theory. Specifically, whereas traditional Freudian theory focused primarily on parent-child dynamics during the Oedipal crisis, **object relations theory** focused on the dynamics and motivation captured within the context of earlier parent-child relationships. These dynamics are referred to as *pre-oedipal*. Also, objects are not things; objects are internalized versions of people.

The most profound shift in psychoanalytic thinking brought about by object relations theorists is captured by Fairbairn's (1952) renowned statement:

Libido is object seeking, not pleasure seeking.
(p. 82)

Fairbairn was emphasizing that human behavior is not fueled by instinctual (libidinal) drives for sexual and aggressive gratification; instead, behavior is influenced and motivated by desire for human connection. Wolitzky and Eagle (1997) commented, "In contrast to Freud's psychic world which is populated by unconscious wishes and defenses against those wishes, Fairbairn's psychic world is populated by internalized objects and internalized object relations" (p. 56).

Object relations theorists believe that humans mentally internalize both a representation of self and a representation of early caretaker figures (St. Clair & Wigren, 2004). These internalized self and other representations are then carried within the

individual into adulthood. If during early childhood an interpersonal relationship was characterized by trauma or destructive patterns, remnants of these early self-other relationship patterns can continue dominating contemporary relationships. A major goal of object relations therapy is to "exorcise" the old maladaptive internalized representations and replace them with healthier representations (Fairbairn, 1952). Essentially, object relations therapy attempts to "replace the 'bad object' with a 'good object'" (Wolitzky & Eagle, 1997, p. 59). In some ways, this process is similar to Alexander and French's (1946) concept of the **corrective emotional experience**. The therapist acts as a good object, and through this experience the client is able to replace the original bad internalized object.

The different theoretical foundation of object relations makes the focus of interpretive work in object relations therapy different from traditional Freudian analysis. In particular, whereas Freudian analysis focused on Oedipal conflicts and sexual and aggressive wishes and drives, object relations therapy focuses on relationship wishes and pre-Oedipal interpersonal dynamics as played out in the regressive analytic situation. As a "good object," the therapist makes distinct efforts to respond empathically to client struggles. Althea Horner (1998) stated,

Once we have ascertained the core relationship conflict as it is manifest in the treatment relationship, it is important that it be laid out in a manner that communicates empathy. (p. 14)

Self–Psychology

Pine's (1990) fourth phase of psychoanalytic evolution centers on the theoretical writings of Heinz Kohut (1971, 1977, 1984). In contrast to the preceding theoretical perspectives, Kohut considers needs for self-cohesiveness and self-esteem to be the overarching motivations that fuel human behavior. His focus is not on instincts, ego, or even object relations, but instead on the development of healthy narcissism within individuals. This approach is termed **self-psychology**.

Along with his focus on the development of a healthy or cohesive self, Kohut focused on self-defects and the noncohesive self. He believed self-defects and noncohesion stemmed from early childhood experiences. In particular, he emphasized that the development of a "cohesive self requires the parental provision of empathic mirroring and the later availability of a parental figure permitting idealization" (Wolitzky & Eagle, 1997, p. 67).

Practically speaking, Kohutian self-psychological psychotherapy proceeds on the basis of the following process:

- Due to early childhood developmental defects, the client quickly establishes a mirroring and idealizing transference within the therapy situation.

- This mirroring and idealizing transference is both regressive and progressive; it seeks to reengage a mirroring and ideal object in order to repair and build up its psychic structure.

- The major fear of the client is retraumatization by the therapist; this fear produces resistance.

- The therapist interprets the resistance.

- The therapist is imperfect and therefore will inevitably fail at providing for the client's wish and need for perfect empathy and will not be a perfect figure for idealizing.

- The client will then retreat from intimacy with the therapist.

- If the therapist's deficiencies and failures are not of traumatic proportions, then this retreat can be interpreted in conjunction with the therapist's acknowledgment of his or her failures.

- These failures, if handled well, will be "optimal failures," and then "new self structure will be acquired and existing ones will be firmed" (Kohut, 1984, p. 69).

Wolitzky and Eagle (1997) summarize the Kohutian therapeutic unit: "For Kohut, empathic understanding and the repeated working through of optimal failures in empathy constitute 'the basic therapeutic unit' of treatment" (p. 69).

Contemporary Movements

To this point in our discussion, the evolution of psychoanalytic thinking might be described, following Pine (1990), as a progression of focus from drive to ego to object to self. Unfortunately, although Pine's distinctions are helpful, the evolution of psychoanalytic thought hasn't been so simple and linear. In fact, Gedo (1979) described the progression as "piecemeal patching" rather than an organized effort at theoretical evolution (p. 9).

Around the time of ego psychology and its development, Karen Horney's work, similar to Alfred Adler (see Chapter 3), focused on how social and cultural factors can powerfully affect personality development (Horney, 1950). In particular, Horney articulated many early feminist critiques of Freudian theory. (See Putting it in Practice 2.2 for a taste of her opposition to Freudian views of female sexuality.) Horney's work has generally been labeled *neo-Freudian*.

Alternative theoretical developments have often resisted theoretical purity, striving instead for integration. For example, Margaret Mahler's formulations are something of an amalgamation of different theoretical perspectives. She includes components of drive, ego, object relations, and self-psychology within her writings. Her observations of mother-child interactions, in combination with the attachment research and writings of John Bowlby and Mary Ainsworth as well as Donald Winnicott's object relations work, provided the foundation for contemporary attachment-based psychotherapy models (Ainsworth, 1969; Bowlby, 1978; Bowlby, 1988; Hughes, 1998; Winnicott, 1965; Winnicott, 1975).

The Relational Psychoanalytic Movement

Psychoanalysis, in the classical sense, reflects Freud's original image of a thoroughly analyzed, dispassionate, objective psychoanalyst expertly interpreting derivatives from the client's unconscious mind in order to eradicate maladaptive childhood fixations and neuroses. Renik (1993) describes the classical Freudian position in these terms: "The image of the analyst as detached psychic surgeon,

PUTTING IT IN PRACTICE 2.2

Karen Horney Versus Freudian Orthodoxy: The Battle of the Sexes

Karen Horney grew up in an era when both men and women feared female emancipation. As Otto Weininger wrote in *The Emancipated Woman*, "All women who really strive for emancipation are sexual intermediate forms.... [A]ll the so-called important women are either strongly masculine or imprinted by man or overestimated" (Quinn, 1987, p. 103).

Despite the odds, Karen Horney obtained her medical degree in 1911. This was the same year she gave birth to her first child, Brigitte.

Alfred Adler may have been the first Freudian disciple with feminist leanings (see Chapter 3), but as a woman herself, Horney took the battle of the sexes to new and exciting depths.

She did not believe in Freud's penis envy, and she did not believe that women were naturally inferior beings. Despite her traditional psychoanalytic training, she found her voice and began strong arguments against masculine formulations of female sexuality and development. She wrote:

> How far has the evolution of women, as depicted to us today by analysis, been measured by masculine standards and how far therefore does this picture fail to present quite accurately the real nature of women?

And further:

> [I]f we try to free our minds from masculine mode of thought, nearly all the problems of feminine psychology take on a different appearance.

She then turns the tables on penis envy:

> When one begins, as I did, to analyze men only after a fairly long experience of analyzing women, one receives a most surprising impression of the intensity of this envy of pregnancy, childbirth, and motherhood, as well as of breasts and of the act of suckling.

Finally, she interprets male behavior from a new, feminine perspective:

> Is not the tremendous strength in man of the impulse to creative work in every field precisely due to their feeling of playing a relatively small part in the creation of living beings, which constantly impels them to an overcompensation in achievement?

Later in her career, she focused even more on male inferiority.

> One of the exigencies of the biological differences between the sexes is this: that the man is actually obliged to go on proving his manhood to the woman. There is no analogous necessity for her. Even if she is frigid, she can engage in sexual intercourse and conceive and bear a child. She performs her part by merely *being*, without any doing—a fact that has always filled men with admiration and resentment. (Horney, 1932, pp. 348–360)
>
> Whether you're a woman or a man, Karen Horney is worth reading. She was steady and forthright in her views. She accepted some of what psychoanalysis offered, but rejected erroneous assumptions about the nature of women. She's a role model for us all, at least with regard to the need to look long and hard at the perspectives of both women and men before formulating a more complete psychology of humanity.

dissecting the patient's mental operations in an antiseptic field" (p. 553).

For many psychoanalysts, the analyst as detached psychic surgeon is gone. This paradigm shift began in the 1980s. The new paradigm is usually referred to as **relational psychoanalysis** (Mitchell, 1988), although **two-person psychology** and *intersubjectivity* are other commonly used terms (E. Balint, 1950; Ghent, 1989). Two-person psychology emphasizes that the psychoanalyst is always subjective:

> Instead of saying that it is *difficult* for an analyst to maintain a position in which his or her analytic activity objectively focuses on a patient's inner reality, I would say that it is impossible for an analyst to be in that position even for an instant: since we are constantly acting in the analytic situation on the basis of personal motivations of which we cannot be aware until after the fact, our technique, listening included, is *inescapably* subjective. (Renik, 1993, p. 560)

Many psychoanalysts, including French psychoanalyst Jacques Lacan, view relational psychoanalysis as "the most fertile line of thought traced out since Freud's death" (Lacan, 1988, p. 11). In relational psychoanalysis the analyst is viewed as participant-observer. Renik provides an articulate summary:

> Consider an analogy from physics. Let us say that we want to ascertain the exact temperature of a glass of water. As soon as we introduce a thermometer into the water, we alter the

temperature we want to measure. (Renik, 1993, pp. 561–562)

This line of thinking parallels the paradigm shift from Newtonian physics to Einsteinian physics. Consequently, the inherent relativity and subjectivity of the psychoanalyst is now an important focus of study in and of itself.

This new perspective has dramatic implications for psychoanalysis and psychoanalytic psychotherapy. The therapist and client are now considered the psychoanalytic couple. This means the analyst no longer has the authority to make "interpretations" of his client's unconscious derivatives. Instead, interpretations are cast as an alternative viewpoint for the client to consciously consider while making up his or her own mind. Moreover, not only is the client's enactment of transference considered important therapeutic information, but so is the analyst's enactment of countertransference. In fact, many writers strongly recommend greater psychoanalyst spontaneity, countertransference enactment, and emotional involvement (Benjamin, 1990; Boesky, 1990; Ringstrom, 2001; Wachtel, 2008).

QUESTIONS FOR REFLECTION

Relational psychoanalysis changes much of traditional psychoanalytic thinking. Do you think the two-person psychology model makes psychoanalytic approaches more or less acceptable?

Attachment-Informed Psychotherapy

Attachment, both as a model for healthy child development and as a template for understanding human behavior is immensely popular within the United States (Cassidy & Shaver, 2008; Wallin, 2007). This is especially ironic because attachment theory's rise to glory parallels decreasing interest in psychoanalytic models. If you were to ask a sample of mental health professionals their thoughts on attachment theory, you'd elicit primarily positive responses—despite the fact that attachment theory is a psychoanalytically oriented approach.

John Bowlby, who was raised primarily by a nanny and sent to boarding school at age seven, began writing about the importance of parent-child interactions in the 1950s. He was a psychoanalyst. Similar to other neo-Freudians, Bowlby's thinking deviated from Freud's. Instead of focusing on infant or child parental fantasies, Bowlby emphasized real and observable interactions between parent and child. He believed actual caretaker-infant interactions were foundational to personality formation (aka the internal working model).

In 1970, Mary Ainsworth, a student of Bowlby's and scholar in her own right, published a study focusing on children's attachment styles using a research paradigm called the **strange situation** (Ainsworth & Bell, 1970). Ainsworth brought individual mother-child (6 to 18 months) pairs into her lab and observed them in a series of seven 3-minute episodes or interactions.

1. Parent and infant spending time alone.

2. A stranger joins parent and infant.

3. The parent leaves infant and stranger alone.

4. Parent returns and stranger leaves.

5. Parent leaves; infant left completely alone.

6. Stranger returns.

7. Parent returns and stranger leaves.

During this event sequence, Ainsworth observed the infant's:

• Exploration behavior.

• Behavioral reaction to being separated from parent.

• Behavioral reaction to the stranger.

• Behavior when reunited with parent.

Based on this experimental paradigm, Ainsworth identified three primary attachment styles. These styles included:

1. **Secure attachment**.

2. **Anxious-resistant insecure attachment**.

3. **Anxious-avoidant insecure attachment**.

In 1986, Ainsworth's student and colleague Mary Main (1986, 1990), identified a fourth attachment style labeled **disorganized/disoriented attachment**.

Many contemporary therapists view attachment theory in general, and Ainsworth and Main's attachment style formulations in particular, as having powerful implications for human relationships and the therapy process (Eagle, 2003; Wallin, 2007). For example, one of the most popular approaches to couple counseling relies heavily on attachment theory principles (Johnson, 2010). In addition, attachment theory has profoundly influenced child development and parent training programs (J. Sommers-Flanagan & R. Sommers-Flanagan, 2011).

At its core, attachment theory involves an effort to understand how early child-caretaker interactions have been internalized and subsequently serve as a model for interpersonal relationships. This is, of course, the internal working model—with an emphasis on how real (and not fantasized) early relationships have become a guide or template for all later relationships. Byrd, Patterson, and Turchik (2010) describe how attachment theory can help with selecting appropriate and effective interventions:

> Therapists may be better able to select effective interventions by taking the client's attachment pattern into consideration. For instance, a client who is comfortable with closeness may be able to make good use of the therapeutic relationship to

correct dysfunctions in his or her working models of self and others. On the other hand, a client who is not comfortable with closeness may find it difficult to change internal working models through the therapeutic relationship. Finally, knowing that a client is not comfortable with closeness would allow the therapist to anticipate a relatively impoverished alliance, and therefore avoid interventions such as insight oriented or object relations therapies that rely heavily on the alliance. (p. 635)

As an internal working model, attachment theory also has implications for how therapists handle within-session interpersonal process. Later in this chapter we provide an attachment-informed psychoanalytic case example (see the Treatment Planning section).

It should be emphasized that many criticisms of attachment theory exist. Some critiques have similarities to criticisms of psychoanalytic theory. Perhaps the greatest criticism is the tendency for individuals to take Mary Ainsworth's 21 minutes of behavioral observations with one primary caregiver and generalize it to the entire global population. In this sense, the theory is not especially multiculturally sensitive. It seems obvious that there are many divergent ways to raise children and not all cultures subscribe to the "American" overemphasis and perhaps preoccupation with the infant's relationship with a single caregiver (usually the mother).

Although scientific critiques have sought to reign in attachment theory as it has galloped its way into pop psychology and the media (Rutter, 1995), its popularity continues to escalate and the consequences seem to magnify the importance of an overly dramatized dance of love between a child and his or her mother. In the following excerpt from *A general theory of love* (2001), you can see the language is absolute and, interestingly, rather sexist—in that children are typically portrayed as male and parents as female.

One of a parent's most important jobs is to remain in tune with her child, because she will focus the eyes he turns toward inner and outer worlds. He faithfully receives whatever deficiencies her own vision contains. A parent who is a poor resonator

cannot impart clarity. Her inexactness smears his developing precision in reading the emotional world. If she does not or cannot teach him, in adult-hood he will be unable to sense the inner states of others or himself. Deprived of the limbic compass that orients a person to his internal landscape, he will slip through his life without understanding it. (Lewis, Amini, & Lannon, 2001, p. 156)

Take a moment to imagine how Karen Horney or Mary Ainsworth might respond to this overgeneralization of attachment concepts and blaming of mothers for their children's emotional deficiencies.

Practical Modifications: Short-Term and Time-Limited Psychoanalytic Psychotherapy

Early in the psychoanalytic movement, discussion began on how to shorten treatment duration. The first psychoanalyst to push for more active and directive therapy was probably Sandor Ferenczi (1920, 1950), one of Freud's closest friends. Ferenczi claimed that because all therapy techniques were more or less suggestive, his proposal to be more active was an acceptable option.

Over the years, many other analysts recommended modifying the psychoanalytic procedure to speed the therapeutic process. Notably, Alexander and French (1946) experimented with methods of time-limited psychoanalysis at the Chicago Institute of Psychoanalysis. They developed a procedure called the corrective emotional experience, designed to speed the curative therapeutic process. Alexander and French recommended that analysts adopt a compensatory role toward clients. If the client suffered from an overly critical parent and therefore, due to the transference phenomenon, expected criticism from the analyst, then the analyst would instead adopt a very positive and supportive role. This manner of interacting was supposed to produce a corrective emotional experience, thereby reducing the time required for a complete analysis.

In contrast, other theorists have advocated role playing by the analyst wherein he or she purposely acts in ways to further the transference. This might involve an analyst's behaving in a cold and critical manner toward the patient who had cold and critical parents. Horowitz and colleagues (1984) stated,

> The technique of "seeding," or manipulating, the transference has the apparent advantage of accelerating its development and the possible disadvantage of traumatizing the patient, causing him to feel manipulated or to disavow his own contribution. (p. 6)

Another strategy for speeding up analysis was advocated by French (1958) and Balint, Ornstein, and Balint (1972). These theorists recommended that analysts stop short of conducting a complete analysis and instead focus their work on one significant conflict or problem. This modification in the analytic process is sometimes referred to as **focal psychotherapy**.

THE PRACTICE OF PSYCHOANALYTIC THERAPY

The purpose of the following review of therapy techniques is not to prepare you to go out and conduct psychoanalytic therapy. Instead, this chapter can help you keep psychoanalytic or psychodynamic principles and techniques in mind as you provide therapy services.

Numerous specific methods for conducting therapy are derived from Freud's psychoanalytic theory and are outlined directly in his original works and the writing of others (Fenichel, 1945; Freud, 1966; Mosak & Kopp, 1973). As suggested in the preceding discussion of theoretical modifications of Freud's theories, there have been changes in the ways in which psychoanalysts use many of Freud's original ideas. The following section describes standard methods, techniques, and concepts that continue to be emphasized and employed to some extent by contemporary psychoanalytically oriented therapists (see Putting it in Practice 2.3).

Overall, the methods and techniques of psychoanalytic therapy have the following goals:

- To make the unconscious conscious or increase client awareness.

- To help clients develop greater self-control over maladaptive impulses.

- To help clients rid themselves of maladaptive or unhealthy internalized objects and replace them with more adaptive internalized objects.

- To repair self-defects through mirroring, presenting a potentially idealized object, and expressing empathy during optimal therapeutic failures.

Assessment Issues and Procedures

Traditionally, psychoanalytically oriented clinicians use two primary assessment procedures. First, they use clinical interviewing. Second, they use **projective testing** (aka generative assessment) with their clients. Projective tests used by analytic therapists include the Rorschach Inkblot Test, the Thematic Apperception Test, **free association** to specific words, and human figure drawings. Because they value direct interaction with clients and generative assessment procedures (in which the client generates information from his or her imagination), psychoanalytic therapists are often unimpressed by objective, psychometrically based questionnaires or assessment procedures.

For example, during a 2-hour weekly assessment seminar on my (John's) psychoanalytic internship, the supervisors spent 10 minutes reviewing results from the Wechsler Adult Intelligence Scales and the Minnesota Multiphasic Personality Inventory (MMPI) and 1 hour and 50 minutes talking about the Rorschach and human figure drawings. One supervisor in particular especially enjoyed turning the MMPI profile upside down and sideways to make fun of objective testing procedures. Although this behavior was a bit over the top, we interns had long stopped caring about his MMPI jokes. This was because he had already won our respect and admiration; in one of the first cases presented in the seminar, he accurately concluded that a woman he'd never met had been sexually abused solely on the basis of her first response to Card 1 on the Rorschach (this is a true story).

The empirical or scientific status of projective assessment is questionable (S. K. Erickson,

PUTTING IT IN PRACTICE 2.3

Informed Consent From the Psychodynamic Perspective

Contributed by Nicki Nance, PhD

A note from your psychotherapist:

As you complete your intake forms, you may be wondering, "What have I gotten myself into?" Beginning therapy is similar to taking a trip to an unknown destination with someone you don't know well yet. Knowing what to expect can be helpful, so before we begin I want to tell you more about how we'll work together.

The Map: I will get to know you by learning what brought you to therapy at this time. I will guide you in an exploration of your history to determine how you developed your current patterns of thinking, feeling, and acting. Together, we'll set goals to decrease your current discomfort and help you develop resources for moving forward. We will venture into the past and future to find help for what brought you here today.

The Vehicle: The relationship between a client and his or her therapist is the foundation of successful therapy. Gaining insight about what you experience in our relationship may help you become more insightful about other relationships. In the context of our relationship, you may also develop skills for identifying and expressing feelings, and taking emotional risks. I encourage you to be open and honest in our communications and I will support you in doing so by providing a safe space and a non-judgmental response. But I will also sometimes explore with you how your reactions to me may be similar to your reactions to other people in your life.

The Journey: People often struggle because they're bound to troublesome past experiences. Therefore, I'll be using techniques that help you put the past in a better perspective and live more fully in the present. During therapy, I may ask you to recall early experiences. Remembering can be uncomfortable, but what you discover from the past will help you to make changes for the future. I'm honored to be a part of this process, and I look forward to working with you.

Lilienfeld, & Vitacco, 2007; Wood, Nezworski, Lilienfeld, & Garb, 2008; Wood et al., 2010). Although psychodynamic-oriented therapists find projective assessment approaches useful, researchers, academics, and behaviorists have offered scathing critiques of their empirical status (Wood et al., 2008). Despite these critiques, including conclusions that the Rorschach does not accurately predict psychopathy, practitioners continue to use this traditional psychoanalytic assessment approach (Fabian, 2006). It may be true that some gifted Rorschach experts (like John's former supervisor) are exceptions to the empirical rule, but most reasonable scientists agree that projective assessments are not a valid means for establishing diagnoses, determining child custody, or for achieving typical psychological assessment goals. However, there are reasons beyond predictive validity why clinicians might find projective assessment procedures useful. These include: (a) rapport building through mutual exploration of deeper intrapsychic issues with clients; (b) determination of the presence or absence of more subtle thought disorders (e.g., psychotic symptoms); and (c) examination of ongoing therapy process and progress.

Critics of psychoanalytic approaches would likely contend that projective assessment procedures are invalid and therefore unethical (Lilienfeld et al., 2003). But as usual, in the big domain of psychotherapy practice, there's room for many perspectives. Consequently, if you're intrigued by projective assessment and want to learn specific projective assessment procedures, you'll be able to find the extensive training and supervision needed. Additionally, as we've noted, analytic therapists also use clinical interviewing assessment techniques. One example of a valuable and practical psychoanalytic interviewing assessment procedure is the screening interview used to determine whether an individual client is appropriate for psychoanalytically oriented treatment.

The Basic Rule

Traditional psychoanalysts begin each session the same way. They encourage clients to "Say whatever comes to mind." This is **the basic rule** in psychoanalysis; a variation of this approach is used in most psychoanalytically oriented therapies. The basic rule is designed to facilitate emergence of unconscious impulses and conflicts. To use the basic rule, analysts adhere to the following guidelines.

First, to let unconscious impulses and conflicts rise to consciousness, distractions or external stimuli must be minimized. This is one reason why Freud used a couch. If the client lies on a couch and the analyst sits behind it, the analyst cannot be seen; the analyst's distracting facial expressions are eliminated. Greater emphasis can be placed on what facial expressions (or thoughts and feelings) the client imagines the analyst is experiencing.

Second, the client's internal stimuli are minimized. When free associating, it's best not to be too hungry or thirsty or physically uncomfortable. If clients come to analysis hungry, thoughts about food will flood into their free associations. Similarly, if the client is physically uncomfortable, it will distract from the free association process. Even potential leaks in confidentiality associated with reporting information to insurance companies can inhibit the **free association** process (Salomon, 2003).

Third, cognitive selection or conscious planning is reduced. Free association is designed, in part, to counter intentional or planned thought processes. For example, if a client comes to therapy with a list of things to talk about, psychoanalytic practitioners might interpret this as resistance. You may wonder, "Why would the client's planning for the session be considered resistance?" The answer is that conscious planning is a defense for keeping control over sexual, aggressive, and other impulses. Traditional psychoanalytic theory presumes that these impulses are adversely affecting the client and need to be brought to consciousness. For contemporary theorists, client list making might be an interpersonal control strategy deserving collaborative exploration; awareness might be enhanced rather than the unconscious motives uncovered.

Interpretation

Traditional analysis views the unconscious as so charged with conflicted material that even free association doesn't allow direct access. Instead, ego defenses, designed to protect clients from their unconscious knowledge, distort information rising up from the unconscious, resulting in what's called unconscious derivatives. Depending upon the analyst's particular perspective, the derivatives may reflect primarily instinctual conflicts or primarily relationship or attachment conflicts.

The Freudian analyst's job is to listen for and interpret unconscious derivatives. This process is anything but simple. The analyst cannot just sit back and make interpretation after interpretation of unconscious derivatives. Fenichel (1945) stated the reason for this:

> The unprepared patient can in no way connect the words he hears from the analyst with his emotional experiences. Such an "interpretation" does not interpret at all. (p. 25)

Fenichel is saying that analysts must prepare clients before using interpretation. Proper client preparation involves steps described in the following sections.

Developing a Therapeutic Alliance

Mentioned in Chapter 1 as a common factor contributing to positive therapy outcome, the concept behind the term **therapeutic alliance** was first discussed by Freud (1958; originally published in 1911). He emphasized that a reality-based attachment between analyst and client was crucial and needed to coexist with the simultaneously occurring positive or negative transference distortions. Later, Zetzel (1956) was the first to actually use the term therapeutic alliance. Consistent with Freud, she believed that if clients had early parent-child interactions characterized by trust and affection, their ability to develop a positive therapeutic alliance was enhanced. Overall, it's easier to defensively disregard input from someone—even potentially helpful feedback—when you don't like the source.

Role Induction

When clients aren't given information about how psychoanalytic therapy proceeds, they often feel confused or annoyed. This is especially the case if you use interpretation as a therapy technique. To use interpretation more collaboratively, you might say something like this:

> As I do therapy with you, I may notice some patterns. These patterns might be related to your early childhood relationships, your relationship with me, or your descriptions of your relationships outside therapy. Is it okay with you if I

occasionally mention these patterns so we can explore them together and then hopefully come to a better understanding about how they might be affecting your life?

The term **role induction** refers to a process wherein therapists educate clients about their role in the therapy process (J. Sommers-Flanagan & R. Sommers-Flanagan, 2009).

Timing

Once a therapeutic relationship is established and role induction information provided, interpretation becomes a potential therapy tool. However, even then, psychoanalysts should proceed carefully. Fenichel (1945) articulated this point:

> Since interpretation means helping something unconscious to become conscious by naming it at the moment it is striving to break through, effective interpretations can be given only at one specific point, namely, where the patient's immediate interest is momentarily centered. (p. 25)

In this excerpt Fenichel is emphasizing that **timing** is essential. Here are several tips for timing interpretations:

- Watch for when the client is just a step away from becoming aware of something new.

- Wait for the client to show positive regard for you.

- Wait until you can say the interpretation clearly and articulately; if the interpretation is muddled in your mind, it probably won't be helpful.

- Wait until you have enough data to support your interpretation; in other words, you should be able to explain, based on your observations of the client and what he or she has said, why you're pointing out particular patterns and connections.

To make matters even more complex, good timing isn't everything. If you're conducting psychoanalytic therapy, you also need to know what to interpret . . . which you'll need to explore in a more advanced psychoanalytic text!

Transference

One of the unique and most lasting contributions of Freud's work was his discussion and analysis of transference (Luborsky, 1985). In the past half century, more than 3,000 books and professional journal articles have been published on **transference** phenomena (Kivlighan, 2002). As Kivlighan stated, "From a strictly classical stance, transference is a client distortion that involves re-experiencing Oedipal issues in the therapeutic relationship" (p. 167). Gelso and Hayes (1998) provide a more modern definition of transference that goes beyond Oedipal issues:

> The client's experience of the therapist that is shaped by the client's own psychological structures and past and involves displacement, onto the therapist, of feelings, attitudes and behaviors belonging rightfully in *earlier significant relationships*. (p. 51, italics in original)

More than anything else, transference is characterized by inappropriateness. As Freud stated, transference "exceeds anything that could be justified on sensible or rational grounds" (Freud, 1958). This is because transference involves using an old map to try to get around on new terrain, and, simply put, it just doesn't work very efficiently (J. Sommers-Flanagan & R. Sommers-Flanagan, 2009). Consequently, one way to detect transference is to closely monitor for client perceptions and treatment of you that don't fit correctly. Of course, to effectively monitor for inaccuracies in your client's perceptions, you must know yourself well enough to identify when your client is treating you like someone you aren't.

In one clinical case, I (John) had a client accuse me of being the most insensitive man she had ever had the displeasure of meeting. Eventually, after becoming fed up with her perception of my non-responsiveness, she shouted, "You're like a robot! I bet if I cut open your arms, I'd find wires, not veins."

Fortunately, as it turns out, this woman was having a transference reaction toward me. In her past, the consistent pattern was for men (including her father) to be relatively unresponsive until finally erupting into a rage toward her. And this was precisely what she was waiting for and finding so frustrating. From the corrective emotional experience and object relations perspective, my nonaggressive response to her may have been considered healing.

Countertransference

Countertransference was originally defined as the therapist's tendency to see the client in terms of his or her own previous relationships. In that sense, it's the same as transference, but it occurs when the transference is directed from the therapist toward the client. Freud conceptualized countertransference as a negative factor in therapy: "Recognize this counter-transference . . . and overcome it," he counseled, because "no psychoanalyst goes further than his own complexes and internal resistances permit" (Freud, 1957, p. 145).

As stated elsewhere, "Countertransference . . . consists of emotional, attitudinal, and behavioral responses that are inappropriate in terms of . . . intensity, frequency, and duration" (J. Sommers-Flanagan & R. Sommers-Flanagan, 2009). When working with clients, it's helpful to pay attention to your own emotions, thoughts, impulses, and behaviors. For example, during a session you may notice that you feel irritated or annoyed with a client. If you're the sort of person who occasionally feels annoyed with others, your feelings may not require much scrutiny—other than simply noting they've come up. However, when your annoyance is strong (intensity), comes up often (frequency), and sticks with you for a considerable length of time (duration), then you may be suffering from countertransference.

As you may have guessed, in the case where I (John) was accused of being like a robot, there was also evidence of countertransference. Specifically, as my client progressively increased the volume of her complaints about me, I found myself in a quick emotional retreat. The fact is that I've never been comfortable with highly intense emotional demands aimed toward me, and my typical response is emotional distancing and escape. Her transference had pushed my buttons. In a way, she was absolutely right: Although I didn't have wires for veins, I was progressively becoming more emotionally unresponsive toward her. I was experiencing a countertransference reaction that could have been explored through a relational or two-person process.

Moving beyond Freud, contemporary psychoanalytically oriented clinicians broadened the definition of countertransference to include all therapist emotional-cognitive-physical reactions to the client. This means that the therapist's reaction need not be viewed as a sign of personal unresolved conflicts activated by the client's transference responses. Using this conceptualization, many writers emphasize at least two potential beneficial aspects of countertransference (Beitman, 1987; Pipes & Davenport, 1999).

First, countertransference awareness can help therapists obtain a deeper understanding of their own issues. When therapists struggle with deeper awareness, it can give them greater compassion for clients. Second, if the therapist's reaction is unusual, it may have more to do with the client than the therapist. For example, if you're feeling afraid of a client, he or she may be subtly saying or doing something threatening; consequently, your reaction to the client helps you glimpse how the client usually affects other people. This glimpse can provide a foundation from which to make a transference interpretation.

From the two-person psychology frame within psychoanalytic theory, even if your reaction to a client is not unusual, it still may represent countertransference. The key question to keep in mind is "Who am I being asked to be in this situation?"

Triangles of Insight

Earlier we discussed the issue of what the psychoanalytic therapist should interpret. Now we focus on a common approach to interpretation. Later we look more closely at this process through case examples.

Beyond resistance, psychoanalytic therapists often focus their interpretations on **triangles of insight**. These insight triangles focus on either conflict or transference.

A **conflict-based triangle of insight** includes (1) the client's wish, aim, or drive; (2) the threat or imagined threat that makes the direct gratification of the wish impossible; and (3) the defensive compromise. Although in traditional Freudian analysis the client's wish has sexual or aggressive roots, in an object relations model the client's wish might have an interpersonal focus. For example, a young man might wish for greater emotional and physical distance from his mother. However, because when he was growing up his efforts toward individuation were met with abandonment from his mother, he feels too anxious and too guilty to assert his independence needs directly. Then, although he feels confused when his mother places demands on him, he denies and minimizes the issue by stating, "Oh it's just my mom being my mom; I don't really like it, but there's nothing else I can do." Using the triangle of insight model, an interpretation might focus on one or more of these three issues:

1. You wish you could have a little more independence or be a little more assertive with your mother.

2. But you don't say or do anything because you're afraid you'll hurt her or she'll just turn away from you in anger.

3. You've been trying to shrink the problem by saying it's no big deal, but you still end up feeling anxious, guilty, and confused more often than you'd like.

In contrast to a conflict-based approach, the **transference-based triangle of insight** includes:

- Observations based on the transference relationship.

- The client's reports of his early childhood relationship dynamics.

- The client's reports of his contemporary, outside-of-therapy relationships.

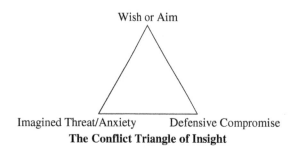

The Conflict Triangle of Insight

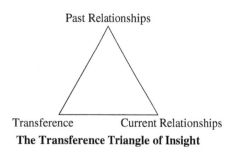

The Transference Triangle of Insight

FIGURE 2.1 Two Psychoanalytic Triangles of Insight

In the preceding case, to facilitate insight, the therapist (who happens to be a woman who is about 20 years older than the client) might say:

- Sometimes in here I feel you pulling away in a sort of charming way; you laugh and joke, but you seem to want to keep me away from knowing more personal or intimate things about you.

- You've told me before about how your mom would cling to you until finally you'd break free and then she'd punish you by being unavailable, and this seems connected to . . .

- how hard it is now for you to really open up to a woman, because you fear she'll clamp onto you and never let you out of her sight.

The transference triangle of insight may emerge and repeat itself in the client's dreams and waking narratives.

Dream Interpretation

Freud considered dreams "the royal road to the unconscious." He believed that client dreams constituted the best access he could get to repressed, unconscious, instinctual drives. Unfortunately, as it turns out, Freud's royal road is fraught with potholes and speed bumps.

Although dreams provide access to the unconscious, similar to client free association material, they consist of unconscious derivatives and require interpretation to produce insight. Viewing dreams as unconscious derivatives consequently places psychoanalysts in an authority position—the classical analyst interprets the dreams' meanings. This can be problematic because client dreams are a temptation for the psychoanalyst to project his or her own issues and conflicts onto ambiguous dream symbols and material. Certainly, one might conclude that Freud, because of his own interest (and perhaps preoccupation) with sexual issues, might have overinterpreted or misinterpreted client dream images as representing sexual instinctual drives. Additionally, based on his own theory, his own phallic (achievement) issues might have led him to insist to clients that his interpretations (rather than the clients') were sacred and correct.

This may be why psychoanalytically oriented therapists often have a reputation for giving out authoritarian, symbol-based interpretations of dream content. For example, in textbook descriptions of psychoanalytic dream analysis, if a male client dreams of struggling while climbing a tree, the tree trunk is interpreted as a penis and his struggle represents his problems associated with feeling sexually adequate. Similarly, a woman client with the same dream might be told she's experiencing penis envy and her efforts to climb the tree are symbolic of her wish to become a man.

In reality, contemporary psychoanalytic dream work doesn't rely on authoritarian, symbol-based, analyst-centered interpretations. Instead, it's a deeply personal and interactive process. Levy (1984) briefly described psychoanalytic dream analysis:

> Using dreams to their fullest advantage requires that the patient be encouraged to free associate to dream elements. The patient must be an active collaborator in dream interpretation in order to avoid a sense of speculation. . . . Whenever possible, the patient's own ideas should be sought so that he becomes familiar with unconscious

mechanisms that are sometimes most clearly seen in dream material. (p. 48)

This description is a reminder that psychoanalytic dream analysis, as currently practiced, is interactive. It emphasizes client reactions to and impressions of the dream's meaning. Although the analyst's perspective and interpretations are important, the method involves asking clients to free associate to their dreams, and then a collaborative exploration of responses ensues.

Psychodynamic Psychotherapy in Action: Brief Vignettes

In traditional psychoanalysis, psychological defenses are interpreted before conflict. The reason for this rule is simple. If you interpret underlying conflict first, then the client will simply use preexisting mechanisms to deny, minimize, repress or otherwise defend themselves from your insightful interpretation. For example, if you tell your client that the reason for her silence is fear of rejection, then she's likely to withdraw from you by using more silence. Instead, if you interpret the defense first, by opening up a discussion of how she uses silence to protect herself, then she may be able to begin using less distorting defenses, giving you both a clearer glimpse of the underlying conflicts and a better chance of understanding and accepting your eventual deeper conflict interpretations.

Vignette I: A Poor Application of Interpretation

Contrary to expectations, defenses don't promptly disappear upon interpretation. In fact, especially when used in an authoritarian or confrontational manner, interpretations can cause clients to react defensively (W. R. Miller & Rollnick, 2002). Consider this example:

Client: There's absolutely nothing about my past that causes me any trouble. I hated my older brother, but he's dead now. There's no point in talking about that. The past is over. It doesn't do any good to talk about it.

Therapist: I've heard you say this before. You close down an entire subject for discussion when, very possibly, there could be something uncomfortable worth talking about. It's like you put up a wall and say, "There's nothing there, end of subject." [Therapist makes confrontational interpretation of denial.]

Client: There really *is* nothing in my past to talk about! [Client persists in using denial to defend against exploring a potentially painful past.]

Therapist: There's that wall again.

This poor example of interpretation illustrates several problems. First, interpretations work best when nested in an empathic therapy alliance. In this case the therapist doesn't start with empathy, but instead rushes right to confrontation/interpretation. Second, timing is critical for interpretive success. This therapist appears to want to share what she or he knows and isn't following Fenichel's rule of waiting until the interpretive material is very close to the surface. Third, the therapist doesn't back off and focus on what might be so hard about talking about the brother. Instead, the interpretation is repeated, again, with no empathy or process focus on what's happening in the room.

Vignette II: Analysis of Resistance Leading to Transference Material

This example emphasizes the importance of gently exploring resistance as something valuable—something to be explored together by therapist and client to pursue the possible meaning of the resistance. In this case, the client falls silent. During the past several sessions the therapist had observed his client was having difficulties speaking freely and usually followed these struggles with apologies and scathing self-critique. The bracketed information that follows is in the original text.

Patient: I'm sorry. I feel like I don't have anything to say. [Silence, lasting a minute or two.]

Therapist: Let's try to understand the silence together and see what it tells us about you.

Patient: I just seem to run out of things to say. [Silence.]

Therapist: When you run out of things to say, how do you begin to feel?

Patient: I feel stupid. In fact, often, in the car on the way over here I worry about whether I'll have enough things to talk about to fill the time.

Therapist: You feel stupid.

Patient: After I've told you the news since my last appointment, I can't think of anything important to tell you. My mind wanders to dumb things, what to cook for dinner, my hair, stupid things like that.

Therapist: You label your more personal thoughts dumb or stupid. What does that bring to mind?

Patient: My parents. They were always telling me I was stupid, that my opinions were stupid if they were different from theirs.

Therapist: So when you are silent, you keep more personal things to yourself. I think you may do this to ward off the possibility that I, too, may find your more personal thoughts stupid, even if that doesn't consciously occur to you.

Patient: You know, I do worry that you'll think I'm stupid, although I never put that together with being silent. Stupid was a word my mother used constantly. She still does, whenever I don't do things her way. (Levy, 1984, p. 82)

This case shows how exploring resistance (silence) can produce transference material and insight. The transference issue revealed won't magically disappear, but its emergence provides the client and therapist with new and useful information leading to further work on the client's internalized harsh and critical self. It's also important to notice how the therapist uses empathy and is gently exploring the resistance together—with the client.

CASE ANALYSIS AND TREATMENT PLANNING

Althea Horner, a contemporary object-relations practitioner and theorist, warned about the educational use of case examples. She stated: "Because no two people are alike (being as idiosyncratic as their fingerprints or their DNA), as much as specific cases elucidate they can also mislead when applied to other situations" (Horner, 1998, p. xv). With Horner's warning in mind, we now proceed to an extended case analysis and treatment plan designed to help you see how psychoanalytic therapies might be applied in practice.

In a recent article, Wachtel (2010) described his psychoanalytic work with a male client (Andrew) struggling with feelings of disconnection in his marriage. As you read the following case, focus on how Andrew's childhood experiences created an internalized interpersonal model for relationships. Also, notice how Wachtel uses attachment theory to guide his interactions and interventions with the client. This case is integrated with an abbreviated treatment plan based on a four-point outline:

- The Problem List (or Goal List)
- Problem Formulation (What seems to create and/or sustain the client's problem or reason for treatment)
- Interventions
- Outcomes Assessment

Wachtel (2010) describes Andrew's problems and provides case formulation information.

> It had become apparent fairly early in the work that a central factor in Andrew's conflictual experience of the marriage was an enormous sensitivity to feeling coerced and crowded. He experienced his wife as "controlling" him, though a broader look at the pattern between them made it clear that her "control"—as is often the case—was in good measure a function of his own acquiescence. Put differently, part of what happened was that Andrew—both because of his concerns about his daughter and because of his own guilt over his wish to pull back from his wife—often went out of his way to be compliant with Jane's wishes, and then felt intruded on and "controlled." (pp. 562–563)

The Problem List

Andrew reports feeling controlled. Wachtel notes he also acquiesces or backs down from speaking about his personal needs for space or freedom.

Additionally, Andrew experiences depressive and anxious symptoms associated with his perception of being trapped in an unhappy marriage. The problem list for Andrew's treatment plan might look like this:

- Difficulty speaking up (aka subassertiveness).
- Anxiety (associated with speaking up and associated with feeling trapped).
- Depression (and related feelings of hopelessness linked to his perception of being trapped in an unhappy relationship).

Next, Wachtel discusses his integration of attachment theory into the psychoanalytic case formulation:

> [H]aving been stimulated by a recent immersion in the attachment literature and the related literature on mother–infant interaction, I articulated my understanding of Andrew's experience just a little differently than I had ... [in previous sessions].... Instead of saying that Jane's comment had felt intrusive (though it did, and though that would certainly have also been an empathically responsive comment), I said that it felt like Jane had been "overtracking" his experience. His [Andrew's] eyes lit up, and he said, excitedly: "Yes, that's exactly it. I love that word, overtracking, that's it!"
>
> I used that particular word because... Andrew's description of his experience brought to mind what I had been reading about the way that infants seem to do best with a moderate degree of tracking of their experience; that is, of the mother's interacting in a way that was responsive to the baby's cues. Too little responsiveness, of course, is hardly a good experience for the infant. He or she will feel, in some preverbal fashion, misunderstood, misread, unhelped. But, it turns out, too much tracking, too high a correlation between the cues coming from the infant and the behaviour coming from the mother seems not to feel so good either.
>
> The babies of mothers who undertrack tend to be insecure in the fashion that is called ambivalent or resistant in the attachment literature. They keep flailing about trying to get their mothers to be more responsive. But the babies of mothers who overtrack, who are too in sync, seem to have difficulties too; they tend to be insecure in the

fashion that is described as avoidant. They withdraw from contact in order to have any room for autonomy at all. (pp. 563–564)

Problem Formulation

In a general sense, psychoanalytic case formulations always have interpersonal foundations (Binder, 2004). These foundations are built from repeated child-caretaker interactions, subsequently internalized, and later manifest themselves in clients' daily lives. Consequently, Andrew's depressive and anxiety symptoms are traced to early childhood interpersonal experiences (or perceptions), observed within the therapy relationship (transference), and triggered in his contemporary interpersonal relationships (i.e., using the transference-based triangle of insight).

From an attachment-informed psychoanalytic perspective, Andrew's difficulty speaking up and associated anxiety and depression are maintained by an unconscious internalized working model triggered by specific relational interactions with his wife, who appears, at least from his vantage point, as overly close and controlling. If Andrew becomes aware of his part in this interpersonal dynamic or dance, then he can proactively and intentionally deal with his underlying fears (of being emotionally suffocated) and develop new behaviors that allow him to initiate more desirable interpersonal patterns in his marriage. This will help him address his needs for autonomy in a way that doesn't trigger anxiety over rejection or abandonment (being alone).

Wachtel discusses the therapeutic process he uses with Andrew—a process based on the problem formulation. Take special note of how Wachtel gathers detailed observations of Andrew before offering specific interventions:

> As Andrew and I continued to talk about the experience I had labeled as overtracking, Andrew conveyed both his great pleasure at the way I had labeled the experience and his experience of almost horror at what it felt like to be overtracked. In the midst of this, he suddenly did something I found very striking, but which I might well not have noticed (or might not have noticed with as much clarity or interest) had we not been talking

about this particular experience in this particular way (that is, had I not had the concept and the experience of overtracking reverberating in my consciousness). What happened was that Andrew continued to talk to me about the experience, but, while he was doing so, he turned his head so that he was not only facing away from me but was basically looking at right angles to me while he spoke. This continued for a few seconds, and then he turned back to look at me. He did not seem to notice at all that he had done this, and he continued to speak continuously and coherently through both the turning away and the turning back to face me.

What Andrew did, in a fashion that seemed completely outside his awareness, seemed to me to be both a confirmation and a poignant playing out of the very concern about overtracking we had just been discussing. Andrew had clearly felt keenly understood by me in my labeling of his "overtracking" experience. In many respects this was a gratifying and positive experience for him. But the very fact that I had understood him so well, I believe, also raised the anxiety that I too would understand him too well, that I too would overtrack, not leave him room for his needed zone of privacy. From that vantage point, turning away from me was a way of seeing whether he could still control our interaction, whether he could be understood and in contact when he felt like it rather than as an inexorable consequence of my "looming empathy."

In this sense, what happened between us in this interaction could be seen as . . . the patient unconsciously posing a "test" for the therapist. In this instance, I think that the unconscious test that Andrew was posing was whether he could control the degree of contact between us and whether we could remain in contact on his terms – that is, with his regulation of the intensity and nature of the contact. (p. 565)

Intervention

As he works with Andrew, Wachtel is formulating hypotheses based on his experience and observations of Andrew in-the-moment, Andrew as a child, attachment theory, and what he knows about Andrew's current relationships. At the same time, Wachtel is listening closely to Andrew and

moderating his therapeutic behaviors. An analysis of Wachtel's considerable multitasking helps illustrate why psychoanalytic or psychodynamic psychotherapies require rigorous training and supervision.

Working from a psychoanalytic model, Wachtel is developing a relationship with Andrew that respects Andrew's anxiety around closeness. As Wachtel demonstrates his respect for providing Andrew emotional space and builds trust around this relationship dynamic, Andrew's insight into and responsibility for his relationship behaviors can develop slowly and ways he might modify his behaviors can be facilitated through in-session experience and Wachtel's interpretations. In fact, as Wachtel acknowledges, because of Andrew's sensitivity to too much closeness, he (Wachtel) will need to avoid too much early interpretation as it might be viewed as "overtracking." This experiential component of therapy can be viewed as an example of what Alexander and French (1946) referred to as the *corrective emotional experience* and in this article, Wachtel notes that in this therapeutic situation, traditional interpretations should be employed secondarily—after indirectly communicating sensitivity to the therapeutic relationship dynamic. Toward the end of his case description, Wachtel describes how he carefully offered an indirect suggestion for Andrew to consider. He does this in a way designed to avoid activating Andrew's interpersonal anxiety; if he were to activate Andrew's anxiety, he might also activate Andrew's resistance.

> Later in the session I suggested that what he wished was possible between him and Jane was to be able to talk to her and not have to be gazing into her eyes at every moment, to be able to know that she is there and listening, but that he can glance over at the mail or do something else while talking to her. I offered this essentially in a metaphorical sense, as an image that captured the kind of experience with her that he desired rather than as a literal description of a specific mode of interaction. I also offered it without reference to what had transpired between us earlier in the session, but clearly with that experience in mind. Andrew was enthusiastically receptive to this comment, saying that yes, it captured very well what he longed for, and it seemed to create at least

a small opening for him to imagine a way of approaching Jane rather than having to retreat from her in order to prevent himself from feeling invaded.

Although psychoanalytic therapists are traditionally criticized for holding an assumption that all clients need is insight to initiate behavior change, in fact, effective psychoanalytic therapists are strongly oriented toward talking specifically about behavior change. Binder (2004) describes the typical change process in psychodynamic psychotherapy as including four parts:

1. Cognitive insight (usually of a repeating maladaptive interpersonal pattern).

2. Practice in detecting maladaptive mental and interpersonal patterns.

3. Creating new and more satisfying interpersonal experiences.

4. Internalization of new and more satisfying interpersonal experiences and the consequent modification of interpersonal schemas and corresponding internal working models of interpersonal relations. (pp. 132–133)

Outcomes Measurement

Psychoanalytic psychotherapists may avoid or dismiss outcomes assessment. Nevertheless, if psychoanalytic treatment providers wish to continue practicing their trade within a medical system, research support and valid outcomes assessment is needed. It's no longer enough for psychoanalytic approaches to base their proof—as they have historically—on case studies and anecdotal reports.

Although psychoanalytic therapists might be inclined to use traditional projective measures (e.g., the Rorschach Inkblots or Thematic Apperception Test) to evaluate client progress, projective assessment approaches have been strongly criticized and consequently, in and of themselves, should not be relied upon as valid evidence for positive outcomes (Wood et al., 2010). Instead, contemporary psychodynamic outcomes researchers are generally

using a combination of symptom-oriented measures (e.g., the Beck Depression Inventory; BDI) and interpersonal process measures. For example, Crits-Christoph and colleagues have used the 24-item California Psychotherapy Alliance Scale (Gaston, 1991) as a process measure that predicts positive treatment outcomes (Barber et al., 2008, Barber, Connolly, Crits-Christoph, Gladis, & Siqueland, 2009).

In his work with Andrew, Wachtel could use the CALPAS and/or the BDI to track process and symptom change every session or less-often, depending upon what they collaboratively agree on as a means of monitoring process and progress. Psychodynamic therapists are likely to view the collaborative agreement on process and outcomes measures as essential to treatment outcome as such collaboration is an active ingredient in building a therapeutic alliance.

Cultural and Gender Considerations

From the beginning, significant conflicts have characterized the relationship between gender/culture and psychoanalysis. Somewhat in keeping with this tradition, Wachtel never mentions Andrew's ethnic background. He also never mentions the societal-level learning that could also be influencing Andrew's interest or need for more independence or freedom in his relationship with his wife, Jane. It would be difficult for Andrew to be a married man in the 21st century without having been bombarded by social media messages about what it means to be a man . . . and that real men are not "controlled" by their wives or at least not comfortable sharing power or close communication in intimate relationships. Clearly, the nature of Andrew's beliefs about what marriage relationships should be like is influenced by factors other than his early relationship with his mother and may, in fact, be much more closely linked to his ethnic or cultural orientation and gender-based expectations.

Although Wachtel's use of attachment theory to inform his verbal interactions with Andrew are both intellectually interesting and have intuitive appeal, there are very strong questions as to whether the "Middle Class American" style of attachment theory can be applied directly to individuals outside Middle Class American culture. If Andrew were raised within an Israeli Kibbutz or African community, his "attachment" style might not neatly fit into an American model. On the other hand, in support of the multicultural sensitivity of psychoanalytic approaches, it should also be noted that Wachtel is carefully formulating a very personalized treatment plan for Andrew. And this plan is based on Andrew's unique (a) articulation of his concerns, (b) self-reported history, and (c) interactions within the therapy hour. Given this perspective, an attachment-informed psychoanalytic therapist might claim he or she is exceptionally multiculturally sensitive—and although there are still questions about the culturally appropriateness of treating an individual who has collectivist cultural values with individually-oriented psychoanalytic techniques, the depth and exploration associated with psychoanalytic approaches lends support to the potential for multiculturally sensitive adaptation.

As implied previously, the feminist critique of this case is perhaps somewhat less generous. Specifically, when discussing attachment theory, Wachtel always uses "mother" instead of "father, parent, or caretaker." This linguistic style tends to place mothers in positions of great child-rearing responsibility and consequently, can lead to mother-bashing or mother-blaming. In keeping with this frame, all of Andrew's needs for freedom and sensitivity to being controlled are traced to having a mother whom he experienced as smothering or as overtracking his every move throughout childhood. Although his relationship with his mother is likely important and relevant to therapy, the fluidity of attachments and attachment dynamics suggests that Andrew's repeating relationship problems (aka Core Conflictual Relationship Theme) shouldn't necessarily be viewed as an internalized working model that Andrew rigidly carries around in his head (Luborsky, 1984). To his credit, Wachtel acknowledges this potential oversimplification and generalization problem.

> Appropriately understood, attachment status is not a quality residing inside a single individual. . . . We describe people as securely or insecurely attached, as avoidantly or ambivalently attached, and so forth, as if they were that way with everyone and at all times—as if, that is, this was just "the way they are." This linguistic form, seeming to suggest that attachment status is a property the individual simply carries around with him in his head, reflects what Mitchell (1995, p. 65) called "a view of mind as monadic, a separable, individual entity," in contrast to "a view of mind as dyadic, emerging from and inevitably embedded within a relational field". . . . I utilized such monadic language myself earlier in this paper, referring to how particular patterns of tracking by the mother led to "securely," or "ambivalently," or "avoidantly" attached individuals. (pp. 567–568)

At their best, psychoanalytic approaches focus sensitively on subtle and personal client characteristics and utilize this focus to facilitate client development, maturity, and intentional and more satisfying individual decision-making. At their worst, these same approaches can over-emphasize mother-child interactions and then build meaning based far too much on the internal inferences made by individual (and sometimes neurotic) therapists, while ignoring real-world social forces that, unarguably, strongly influence human behavior.

EVIDENCE-BASED STATUS

Having just glimpsed an articulate and artistic application of psychoanalytic therapy by renowned writer and therapist, Paul Wachtel, we now turn to the question you've all been waiting for: What does the scientific research say about the efficacy of psychoanalytic or psychodynamic psychotherapy?

Conducting rigorous research on longer-term treatments, such as psychoanalytic therapy, is difficult in terms of practicalities and cost. Perhaps this is one reason why cognitive-behavioral outcomes studies are more often supported with grant funding. Further, psychoanalytic approaches are less symptom or diagnosis-focused, seeking instead to facilitate client insight and improve interpersonal relationships. As contemporary evidence-based criteria focus more on whether a specific psychological procedure reduces symptoms associated with a medical diagnosis, the challenges of "proving" the efficacy of more complex therapy approaches becomes increasingly difficult—especially when compared to the lesser challenges inherent in evaluating symptom-focused treatments. Historically, because of these challenges, psychoanalytically oriented psychotherapies have been view as less efficacious than cognitive and behavioral therapies.

The good news for psychoanalytic therapy fans is that evidence is accumulating to support treatment efficacy. The less good news is that some of the research support remains methodologically weak and the wide variety of psychoanalytic approaches makes it difficult to come to strong and clear conclusions. Nevertheless, Shedler (2010) in a recent *American Psychologist* article reviewed outcomes for psychodynamic therapies and concluded:

> The available evidence indicates that effect sizes for psychodynamic therapies are as large as those reported for other treatments that have been actively promoted as "empirically supported" and "evidence based." . . . Finally, the evidence indicates that the benefits of psychodynamic treatment are lasting and not just transitory and appear to extend well beyond symptom remission. (Shedler, p. 107)

Table 2.3 provides a sampling of meta-analytic evidence supporting psychodynamic therapies. For comparison purposes, we've included the original meta-analyses conducted by Smith and colleagues in Table 2.3 (M. L. Smith & Glass, 1977; M. L. Smith et al., 1980). In their initial meta-analyses 29 psychodynamic and 28 psychodynamic-eclectic treatment studies were evaluated. Overall, both treatment approaches showed medium to large effect sizes (psychodynamic = 0.69; psychodynamic-eclectic = 0.89). These early results suggested that psychodynamic approaches were significantly more efficacious than no treatment and approximately equivalent to other therapy approaches.

The data in Table 2.3 generally includes meta-analyses with effect sizes (ES) equal to or greater than those reported by Smith and colleagues. Additionally, for comparison purposes, the average ES for antidepressant medications is included (ES = 0.31 for serotonin-specific reuptake inhibitors or SSRIs). These data would suggest that psychodynamic psychotherapy is substantially more effective than general SSRI treatment. Perhaps of even greater significance is the fact that the benefits of psychoanalytic therapy tend to increase over time (Shedler, 2010). This implies that clients experiencing this therapeutic model develop insights and acquire skills that continue to improve their functioning over the long run—which is clearly not the case for antidepressant medication treatment (Whitaker, 2010).

Overall, as usual, we recommend you take the preceding research findings (and Table 2.3) with a

Table 2.3   A Sampling of Psychodynamic Psychotherapy Meta-Analyses

Authors	Outcome focus	# Studies	ES
Abbass et al., 2009	General psychiatric symptoms	8	0.6
Anderson & Lambert. 1995	Various	9	0.85
de Maat et al. 2009	Long-term treatment	10	0.78
Comparison Research			
Turner et al., 2008	Meds for Major depression	74	0.31
Smith et al., 1977	Different therapies Many problems	375	0.68
Smith et al., 1980	Different therapies Many problems	475	0.75

Note: This is only a sampling of meta-analytic psychoanalytic psychotherapy reviews. We've omitted several reviews with very high effect sizes (see Shedler, 2010 for a more complete review) partly because of criticisms related to their statistical methodology. The studies included are a reasonable representation of psychoanalytic psychotherapy meta-analyses.

grain of salt. This is because of challenges inherent in conducting systematic research on something as precarious and subjective as human mental and emotional problems. One such challenge, referred to by Luborsky and colleagues (1999) as the **allegiance effect,** suggests that the researcher's therapy preference or allegiance is a strong predictor of outcome study results. Specifically, Luborsky and colleagues analyzed results from 29 different adult psychotherapy studies and reported that about two thirds of the variation in outcome was accounted for by the researcher's theoretical orientation.

The implications of the allegiance effect are obvious. It likely explains why, shortly after Shedler's (2010) publication extolling the virtues of psychodynamic psychotherapy, several critiques and rebuttals were published (Anestis, Anestis, & Lilienfeld, 2011; McKay, 2011; Thombs, Jewett, & Bassel, 2011). These critiques generally claimed that Shedler's review was biased and overlooked a legion of weaknesses within the meta-analyses he reviewed (e.g., poor outcome measures, pooling the effects of small samples with little power and poor designs, lack of treatment integrity effects). Although we generally agree with the issues raised by Shedler's critics, it would be difficult to argue that these critics were completely objective and without bias of their own. The problem is that virtually all researchers (and writers) have an allegiance of one sort of another.

One of our favorite ways of understanding the allegiance effect is articulated in an old story about a man named Lawrence P. Berra, better known to most of us as the great New York Yankee baseball player, Yogi Berra. One day, when a player on Yogi's team was called out on a close play at second base in a crucial game, Yogi went charging onto the field to protest the call. The umpire explained that he, unlike Yogi, was an objective observer and that he, unlike Yogi, had been only about 5 feet from the play, while Yogi had been over 100 feet away, seated in the dugout. When Yogi heard the umpire's logic, he became even more angry than before and snapped back, "Listen ump, I wouldn't

have seen it, if I hadn't believed it" (adapted from Leber, 1991).

The "I saw it because I believed it" phenomenon is simply a reality to understand and appreciate when working with humans. We all have our biases. Consequently, psychoanalytically oriented individuals see support for their perspective and behavior therapists see support for theirs. However, despite all these caveats, based on accumulating research, psychodynamic approaches have a reasonably good record of efficacy (see Putting it in Practice 2.4).

CONCLUDING COMMENTS

Anyone whose collected works fill 24 volumes is likely to have—as we psychoanalytically informed mental health professionals like to say—achievement issues. Dr. Freud might even accept this interpretation. He himself stated that "A man who has been the indisputable favorite of his mother keeps for life the feeling of a conqueror, that confidence of success that often induces real success" (E. E. Jones, 1953, p. 5).

Judging him based on his own theoretical perspective, Freud clearly suffered from some Oedipal conflicts, and these were, in part, manifest in his intense striving for recognition. Eventually, for one reason or another, it may have been his penchant for stature that caused him to invent and then recant his seduction theory.

In 1937, 2 years before Janet's death, Edouard Pichon, Pierre Janet's son-in-law, wrote to Freud, asking him to visit with Janet. Freud responded:

> No, I will not see Janet. I could not refrain from reproaching him with having behaved unfairly to psychoanalysis and also to me personally and never having corrected it. He was stupid enough to say that the idea of sexual aetiology for the neuroses could only arise in the atmosphere of a town like Vienna. Then when the libel was spread by French writers that I had listened to his lectures and stolen his ideas he could with a word have put an end to such talk, since actually I never saw him or heard his name in the Charcot time: he has never spoken this word. You can get an idea of his scientific level from his utterance that the unconscious is une

PUTTING IT IN PRACTICE 2.4

In Retrospect

By Nicki Nance, PhD, LMHC

Prologue: I didn't set out to be a therapist. More than 40 years ago, I went to an employment agency after earning my BA in psychology and announced that I didn't want to work with old people or little children. The agent said, "How about heroin addicts?" Somehow, that seemed manageable to me at age 22, even though I'd never, to my knowledge, met an addict. From that point forward, my clinical career unfolded without much intervention from me. The State that hired me to work with addicts provided extensive training in Gestalt Therapy, Transactional Analysis, Reality Therapy, and Rational Emotive Therapy. Drug addicts acculturated me to a fast-paced, smooth and abrasive, candid and cryptic way of communicating that still defines me, both as a clinician and as a professor.

A Tale of Two Theories: I've always conceptualized cases in psychoanalytic terms. It's my first language, though it is generally only spoken in my head. Believe it or not, people make sense to me in the structural language of id, ego, and superego. Ego defense mechanisms adequately describe most behaviors that beg clinical attention. The emergence of the present condition from the past experience has face validity to me, and Erik Erikson's work provides a template that has mostly stood the test of increased life expectancy and multiculturalism. So for me there are two theories—psychoanalytic and "other."

Only When My Lips Are Moving: I believe that if one's counseling orientation is a good fit with their temperament, they evolve naturally. I internalized the language of the streets because it resonated with me. I like word play. Gestalt Therapy, Reality Therapy, and Rational Emotive Therapy afforded me the opportunity to speak in many ways . . . and therefore to think in many ways. As theories have emerged in the literature, I've attempted to learn their respective languages. By doing so, I've added to my fund of knowledge about people and how to serve them. Today, I teach theories to counselors-in-training. More is stuffed into the class every term. I lament that when humans realized that the earth was round, flat earth theories were (mostly) discarded. In psychology, though, new theories don't seem to replace old ones. They are simply tossed onto the theory pile. Still, for me, no theory has differentiated itself sufficiently to ascend from the "other" category.

The Bridge of Eclecticism: In the 1970s, Transactional Analysis (TA) made sense to me. The language, to me, was a conscious translation of Freud's structural theory, palatable to clients, practical to me, with behavioral prescriptions and contracts for change. Within the TA paradigm was a perspective of Lifescripts that simply proposed that people make decisions early in life in response to permissions and injunctions from significant others, and sometimes they need to make better decisions later. Much of my clinical work has been guided by this simple principle, with its psychoanalytic underpinnings and cognitive sensibilities. Once I was on the bridge of eclecticism, it was fairly easy to see what was on the other side—every "other" theory, entirely workable without betraying my psychoanalytic roots.

Epilogue: Since 1970, I've worked with both old people and little children, in addictions, corrections, psychiatric settings, and privately. I have sufficient evidence to back my practices. I learn new theories and techniques and teach them to my students. We make endless concept maps to illustrate the interrelatedness of theories. In the counselor chair, my intuition, informed by four decades of clients, is running the show. I trust myself and I trust human nature. Freud has become like a long-time partner whose idiosyncrasies are tolerable because he hasn't yet betrayed my trust.

facon de parler. No I will not see him. I thought at first of sparing him the impoliteness by the excuse that I am not well or that I can no longer talk French and he certainly can't understand a word of German. But I have decided against that. There is no reason for making any sacrifice for him. Honesty the only possible thing; rudeness quite in order. (Jones, 1961, pp. 633–634)

There was no special reconciliation for Freud. Toward the end of his life he suffered from many medical and psychological problems. His addiction to tobacco led to cancer and jaw surgery and considerable physical pain. In September 1939, he asked a fellow physician and friend, Max Schur, to assist in his suicide. Freud asked, "Schur, you remember our 'contract' not to leave me in the lurch when the time had come. Now it is nothing but torture and makes no sense" (Gay, 1988). After Schur responded, Freud replied, "I thank you" and followed this with, "Talk it over with Anna, and if she thinks it's right, then make an end of it" (Gay). Although Anna was initially against the plan, Schur argued otherwise and on 2 consecutive September days, he administered enough morphine to finally result in Freud's death (September 23, 1939).

Freud's legacy is often linked to negativity or pessimism. There are good reasons for this link,

as Freud focused on issues like the death instinct and primitive instinctual impulses that we have little awareness of or control over. But there's also hope associated with his work. One of his more hopeful statements is carved in a memorial to him in Vienna which reads,

The voice of reason is small, but very persistent.

CHAPTER SUMMARY

In the late 1800s and early 1900s, Sigmund Freud began practicing and writing about psychoanalysis. He subsequently gathered an impressive following and generated 24 volumes of work. He initially reported believing his clients had experienced sexual abuse, but later, for mysterious reasons, recanted his seduction hypothesis. He lived in a time when and a place where sex and sexuality were not generally spoken of openly.

Freud developed one of the giant theories of human development. In this chapter, four main parts (or approaches) to his theory were described. These included the: (1) dynamic approach; (2) topographic approach; (3) developmental stage approach; and (4) structural approach. Freud believed that everyone has the potential to develop psychopathology if exposed to the right type and amount of stress.

After Freud, psychoanalytic thought continued to develop in many different directions. Adler and Jung both left Freud's inner circle to develop their own theory and approach. Pine (1990) categorized the evolution of psychoanalytic thought as encompassing four stages: (1) drive; (2) ego psychology; (3) object relations; and (4) self-psychology. However, there are many other contemporary psychoanalytic or psychodynamic movements. These include time-limited psychodynamic psychotherapy, attachment psychotherapy, and relational psychoanalysis.

Psychoanalytic practitioners generally use free association (aka: the basic rule) to help clients articulate underlying unconscious processes. Then, as clients experience transference and resistance, the psychotherapist carefully uses interpretation to clarify and bring unconscious patterns into awareness. Consistent with a contemporary focus on human relationships as a primary motivator and developmental force, psychotherapists often focus their interpretations on problematic repeating interpersonal themes or patterns in the client's life. These patterns can often be seen in triangles of insight that include (a) current client relationships; (b) the client-therapist relationship (transference); and (c) past client relationships.

Psychoanalytic approaches have historically not been well-suited or friendly toward females and individuals from divergent cultures. Although this is changing, there is still a predominant orientation toward white and male ways of thinking.

Although somewhat controversial, over the years psychoanalytic approaches have garnered a considerable amount of research support. This research support indicates that for particular individuals and problems, psychoanalytic or psychodynamic approaches can be quite effective.

PSYCHOANALYTIC KEY TERMS

The Aetiology of Hysteria

Allegiance effect

Anal

Anxious-avoidant insecure attachment

Anxious-resistant insecure attachment

Attachment-informed psychotherapy

The basic rule

Conflict-based triangle of insight

Conscience

The conscious

Corrective emotional experience

Countertransference

Defense mechanisms

Denial

Developmental stage approach

Disorganized/disoriented attachment

Displacement

Dream interpretation

Dynamic approach

Ego

Ego-ideal

Ego psychology

Eight stage epigenetic psychosocial theory of development (Erikson)

Eros

Focal psychotherapy

Free association

Genital

Id

Internal working model

Interpretation

Latency

Libido

Normal-abnormal continuum

Object relations theory

Oedipal conflict

Oral

Phallic

Preconscious

Projection

Projective testing

Psychic determinism

Rationalization

Reaction formation

Regression

Relational psychoanalysis

Repetition compulsion

Repression

Role induction

Secure attachment

The seduction hypothesis

Self-psychology

Strange situation

Structural approach

Sublimation

Superego

Thanatos

Therapeutic alliance

Timing

Topographic approach

Transference

Transference-based triangle of insight

Triangles of insight

Two-person psychology or intersubjectivity

Unconscious

RECOMMENDED READINGS AND RESOURCES

The following readings and resources may deepen your understanding of psychoanalytic or psychodynamic therapy approaches.

PSYCHOANALYTIC JOURNALS

Reviewing the following journals will keep you up-to-date with the latest academic discourse in psychoanalytic theory and practice.

Contemporary Psychoanalysis

International Journal of Psychoanalysis

Journal of the American Psychoanalytic Association

Journal of Psychoanalytic Psychology

Psychoanalytic Dialogues

READINGS ON PSYCHOANALYTIC/PSYCHODYNAMIC THEORY AND THERAPY

Perusing the literature on psychodynamic psychotherapy can be overwhelming and mind-boggling. There is so much out there (including Freud's 24 volumes). However, if you want a little psychoanalytic snack or bedtime reading, here are a few classic and contemporary books and articles that may pique your interest.

Ainsworth, M. D., & Bell, S. M. (1970). Attachment, exploration, and separation: Illustrated by the behavior of one-year-olds in a strange situation. *Child Development, 41*, 49–67.

Erikson, E. H. (1963). *Childhood & society* (2nd ed.). New York, NY: Norton.

Fairbairn, W. R. (1952). *Psychoanalytic studies of the personality*. Oxford, England: Routledge & Kegan Paul.

Freud, S. (1949). *An outline of psychoanalysis*. New York, NY: Norton.

Freud, S. (1964). *New introductory lectures on psychoanalysis* (J. Strachey, Trans., Vol. 22). London, England: Hogarth Press.

Gay, P. (1988). *Freud: A life for our time*. New York, NY: Anchor Books.

Horner, A. J. (1998). *Working with the core relationship problem in psychotherapy: A handbook for clinicians*. San Francisco, CA: Jossey-Bass.

Levy, S. T. (1984). *Principles of interpretation*. New York, NY: Aronson.

Luborsky, L. (1984). *Principles of psychoanalytic psychotherapy: A manual for supportive-expressive treatment*. New York, NY: Basic Books.

Mahler, M. B., & Pine, F. (1975). *The psychological birth of the human infant: Symbiosis and individuation*. New York, NY: Basic Books.

St. Clair, M., & Wigren, J. (2004). *Object relations and self psychology: An introduction* (4th ed.). Belmont, CA: Brooks/Cole.

Shedler, J. (2010). The efficacy of psychodynamic psychotherapy. *American Psychologist, 65*(2), 98–109.

Strupp, H. H., & Binder, J. L. (1984). *Psychotherapy in a new key*. New York, NY: Basic Books.

Wachtel, P. L. (2010). One-person and two-person conceptions of attachment and their implications for psychoanalytic thought. *International Journal of Psychoanalysis, 91* (3), 561–581.

Weiner, I. B., & Bornstein, R. F. (2009). *Principles of psychotherapy: Promoting evidence-based psychodynamic practice* (3rd ed.). Hoboken, NJ: John Wiley & Sons.

TRAINING ORGANIZATIONS AND WEBSITES

The following websites include podcast links, newsletters, information on psychoanalytic/psychodynamic training, conferences, and other events.

American Psychoanalytic Association (APsaA; www.apsa.org)

American Psychological Association, Division of Psychoanalysis (Division 39; www.division39.org)

The C. G Jung Page (www.cgjungpage.org)

Freud Museum, Vienna (www.freud-museum.at/cms/index.php/en_home.html)

The International Psychoanalytic Association (IPA; www.ipa.org.uk)

National Psychological Association for Psychoanalysis (NPAP; www.npap.org)

VIDEOS/DVDs

The following video list includes professional demonstrations of psychoanalytic or psychodynamic psychotherapy/counseling. You can find how to order or view these or many other videos using an Internet search.

Your college or university library may have psychoanalytic/psychodynamic videos or DVDs available for checkout.

Carlson, J., & Kjos, D. (2000). *Object relations therapy with Dr. Jill Savege Scharff* [Video]. Boston, MA: Allyn & Bacon.

Davidson, F. (1995). *Old age I: A conversation with Joan Erikson* [Video]. San Luis Obispo, CA: Davidson Films.

Harris, J. (2006). *Psychodynamic counseling and psychotherapy* [DVD]. North Amherst, MA: Microtraining Associates.

Levenson, H. (2009). *Brief dynamic therapy over time* [DVD]. Washington, DC: American Psychological Association.

Wachtel, P. L. (2007). *Integrative relational psychotherapy* [DVD]. Washington, DC: American Psychological Association.

GOING FARTHER AND DEEPER

Additional psychoanalytic and psychodynamic counseling and psychotherapy resources are available at johnsommersflanagan.com.

Individual Psychology and Adlerian Therapy

THIS CHAPTER

- Reviews key figures and contextual factors contributing to the development and evolution of Adlerian theory and therapy (aka Individual Psychology)
- Outlines and describes core theoretical principles underlying Adlerian therapy practice
- Describes and discusses principles and techniques associated with the four stages of Adlerian therapy
- Offers brief vignettes and verbatim therapy examples to demonstrate Adlerian therapy principles and techniques in action
- Illustrates how treatment planning, outcomes assessment, and gender and cultural issues can be integrated into an Adlerian therapy approach
- Reviews the empirical status of Adlerian therapy approaches
- Offers resources for further study

We've often wondered about Alfred Adler. Officially, he's the founder of individual psychology. But where did he come up with his radical ideas? As this chapter unfolds, you'll find his beliefs were so out of step in the early twentieth century that he seems an anomaly: He's like a man from the future who somehow landed in the middle of Freud's inner circle in Vienna.

Some writers inappropriately label Adler as a neo-Freudian. Others wonder if Adler's Individual Psychology (IP) is relevant today. In fact, Adler's IP "is a psychoeducational, present/future-oriented, and brief approach" (R. E. Watts & Pietrzak, 2000, p. 22). Make no mistake about it, Adler was a contemporary—not a disciple—of Freud and his approach to the practice of counseling and psychotherapy remains impressively relevant.

Adler's psychology was far ahead of its time. He wove cognition into psychotherapy long before

Albert Ellis and Aaron Beck officially launched the cognitive therapy movement in the 1950s and 1960s. For example, in the following quotation Adler (1964; originally published in 1933) easily could be speaking about a cognitive rationale for a computerized virtual reality approach to treating fears and phobias (now growing in popularity in the 21st century):

> In a word, I am convinced that a person's behavior springs from his [or her] idea.... As a matter of fact, it has the same effect on one whether a poisonous snake is actually approaching my foot or whether I merely believe it is a poisonous snake. (pp. 19–20)

In his historical overview of the talking cure, Bankart (1997) claims "Adler's influence on the developing fields of psychology and social work was incalculable" (p. 146). This chapter is an exploration of Alfred Adler's individual psychology and his incalculable influence on modern counseling and psychotherapy.

BIOGRAPHICAL INFORMATION: ALFRED ADLER

Alfred Adler

Adler was the second eldest of six children born to a Jewish family on the outskirts of Vienna. His older brother was brilliant, outgoing, and handsome, and also happened to be named Sigmund. In contrast, Alfred was a sickly child. He suffered from rickets, was twice run over in the street, and experienced a spasm of the glottis. When he was 3 years old, his younger brother died in bed next to him (Mosak, 1972). At age 4, he came down with pneumonia. Later Adler recalled his physician telling his father, "Your boy is lost" (Orgler, 1963, p. 16). Another of Adler's earliest memories has a similar sickly, dependent theme:

> One of my earliest recollections is of sitting on a bench bandaged up on account of rickets, with my healthy, elder brother sitting opposite me. He could run, jump, and move about quite effortlessly, while for me movement of any sort was a strain and an effort. Everyone went to great pains to help me, and my mother and father did all that was in their power to do. At the time of this recollection, I must have been about two years old. (Bottome, 1939, p. 30, quoted in Bankart, 1997, p. 131)

In contrast to Freud's childhood experience of being his mother's favorite, Adler was more encouraged by his father. Despite his son's clumsy, uncoordinated, and sickly condition, Adler's father

Leopold, a Hungarian Jew, deeply believed in his son's innate worth. When young Alfred was required to repeat a grade at the same middle school Freud had attended 14 years earlier, Leopold was his strongest supporter. Mosak and Maniacci (1999) capture the nature of Adler's response to his father's support:

> His mathematics teacher recommended to his father that Adler leave school and apprentice himself as a shoe-maker. Adler's father objected, and Adler embarked upon bettering his academic skills. Within a relatively short time, he became the best math student in the class. (p. 2)

Adler's love and aptitude for learning continued to grow and he studied medicine at the University of Vienna. After obtaining his medical degree in ophthalmology in 1895, he met and fell in love with Raissa Timofeyewna Epstein, and he married her in 1897. She had the unusual distinction of being an early socialist and feminist who maintained her political interests and activities throughout their marriage (Hoffman, 1994).

HISTORICAL CONTEXT

Freud and Adler met in 1902. According to Mosak and Maniacci (1999), "Legend has it" that Adler published a strong defense of Freud's *Interpretation of Dreams*, and consequently Freud invited Adler over "on a Wednesday evening" for a discussion of psychological issues. Thereafter, "The Wednesday Night Meetings, as they became known, led to the development of the Psychoanalytic Society" (p. 3).

Adler was his own man with his own ideas before he met Freud. In fact, prior to their meeting he had already published his first book, titled *Healthbook for the Tailor's Trade* (Adler, 1898). In contrast to Freud, much of Adler's medical practice was with the working poor. Early in his career he worked extensively with tailors and circus performers.

In February 1911, Adler did the unthinkable. As president of Vienna's Psychoanalytic Society, he read a highly controversial paper at the group's monthly meeting. The essence of this paper, *"The Masculine Protest,"* was deeply at odds with Freudian theory. Instead of focusing on biological and psychological factors and their influence on excessively masculine behaviors in males and females, Adler emphasized the power of culture and socialization. He claimed that women were socially coerced into an underprivileged social and political position. Further, he noted that some women who reacted to this cultural situation by choosing to dress and act like men were suffering not from **penis envy**, but from a social-psychological condition he referred to as *the* **masculine protest**. Finally, he also claimed that overvaluing masculinity was driving men and boys either to give up and become passive or to engage in excessive aggressive behavior. In extreme cases, males who suffered from the masculine protest began dressing and acting like girls or women.

The response of the Vienna Psychoanalytic Society members was perhaps even more extreme than the response of Freud's colleagues upon his reading "The Aetiology of Hysteria" to the Vienna Psychiatric Society in 1896. Bankart (1997) describes the scene:

> After Adler's address, the members of the society were in an uproar. There were pointed heckling and shouted abuse. Some were even threatening to come to blows. And then, almost majestically, Freud rose from his seat. He surveyed the room with his penetrating eyes. He told them there was no reason to brawl in the streets like uncivilized hooligans. The choice was simple. Either he or Dr. Adler would remain to guide the future of psychoanalysis. The choice was the member's to make. He trusted them to do the right thing. (p. 130)

Freud likely anticipated the outcome. The group voted for Freud to lead them. Adler left the building quietly, joined by the Society's vice president, William Stekel, and five other members. They moved their portion of the meeting to a local café and established the Society for Free Psychoanalytic Research. The Society moved even farther from its psychoanalytic roots by quickly changing its name to the Society for Individual Psychology. The focus of this new group included the groundbreaking acknowledgment that human functioning was not only biologically based, but also powerfully influenced by social, familial, and cultural factors. Bankart (1997) summarizes the perspective of the Society for Individual Psychology: "Their response to human problems was characteristically ethical and practical—an orientation that stood in dramatic contrast to the biological and theoretical focus of psychoanalysis" (p. 130).

Adler's break with Freud gives us an initial glimpse of the shape of his theoretical approach. Adler identified with the common people. He was, surprising as it seems for his time, also a feminist. These leanings likely reflect the influences of his upbringing and his marriage. They reveal his compassion for the sick, the oppressed, and the downtrodden. For Adler, the key to psychotherapy, psychological health, and well-being is summed up in a single word: **encouragement** (Dinkmeyer & Dreikurs, 1963; Watts & Pietrzak, 2000). In contrast, the road to psychological ill health is paved with **discouragement**.

> When a doctor once said to Adler: "I do not believe you can make this backward child normal," Dr. Adler replied: "Why do you say that? One could make any normal child backward; one should only have to discourage it enough!" (Bottome, 1936, p. 37)

Before examining Adlerian theoretical principles, let's look at what he had to say about gender politics 85 years ago:

> All our institutions, our traditional attitudes, our laws, our morals, our customs, give evidence of the fact that they are determined and maintained by privileged males for the glory of male domination. (Adler, 1927, p. 123)

It's hard not to wonder if perhaps Raissa Epstein may have had a few pointed discussions with Alfred Adler—and more than just a little influence on his thinking.

> ### QUESTIONS FOR REFLECTION
>
> What are your thoughts on Adler's allegiance to feminism? Do you suppose he became more of a feminist because he married one? Or did he marry a feminist because he already had strong leanings that direction?

THEORETICAL PRINCIPLES

Adler and his followers have written about the theoretical principles of individual psychology extensively. Much of the material that follows is derived from Adler (1958), Ansbacher and Ansbacher (1956), Mosak and Maniacci (1999), and Carlson, Watts, and Maniacci (2006).

The Whole Person

Adler didn't believe in dichotomies or in breaking the individual into different functional parts. Instead, he emphasized unity of thinking, feeling, acting, attitudes, values, the conscious mind, the unconscious mind, and more. Watts and Eckstein (2009) described Adler's rationale for choosing the name Individual Psychology for his entire theoretical system: "Adler chose the name individual psychology (from the Latin, *individuum*, meaning indivisible) for his theoretical approach because he eschewed reductionism" (p. 281).

Adlerian **holism** is in direct contrast to Freud's reductionistic psychological models. Adler didn't believe in Freud's tripartite id-ego-superego psychology. He believed the whole person made decisions for which he or she was completely responsible. The idea of an id entity or instinct separately pushing for gratification from inside a person was incompatible with Adler's basic beliefs about holism.

Striving With Purpose

A central proposition of individual psychology is that humans actively shape themselves and their environments. We aren't passive recipients of our biological traits or simple reactors to our external environment. There is a third element—beyond biology and the environment—that influences and directs human behavior; Adler (1935) referred to this third force as "attitude toward life" (p. 5). Attitude toward life is composed of a delightful combination of individual human choice and purpose.

In a practical sense, everyday behavior can be analyzed as to its purpose. When an Adlerian therapist notices a maladaptive quality to her client's behavior patterns, she considers the behavioral goals. She doesn't interrogate her client with aggressive questions like "Why did you do that?"—but is curious about the purpose of her client's behavior. Mosak and Maniacci (1999) articulated how Adler's holism combines with purposeful behavior:

> For Adler, the question was neither "How does mind affect body?" nor "How does body affect mind?" but rather "How does the individual use body and mind in the pursuit of goals?" (pp. 73–74).

This concept of striving with purpose has been especially helpful in child psychology and parenting (see Putting it in Practice 3.1). Rudolph Dreikurs applied the concept of purposeful striving to children when he identified "the **four goals of misbehavior**" (Dreikurs, 1948). In keeping with Adler's and Dreikurs perspective on the need to understand children's motives, a popular Boston-based parent education organization has coined the phrase, "Get curious, not furious" as a mantra for parents when faced with their children's misbehavior (L. Braun, personal communication, January, 2003).

PUTTING IT IN PRACTICE 3.1

Why Children Misbehave

In keeping with Adler's philosophy of a practical psychology for the common person, his followers frequently applied his principles to everyday situations. Rudolph Dreikurs identified the four goals of children's misbehavior, a practical concept that has, for many years, has aided parents in their understanding of children's misbehavior.

Children, like all humans, have a motivation toward growth and personal development. Unfortunately, if they don't have a sense of growth—usually through feeling *useful* and feeling they *belong*—they're motivated by less positive goals. In his book *The Challenge of Parenthood*, Dreikurs (1948) identified the four main goals of children's misbehavior:

1. To get attention.
2. To get power or control.
3. To get revenge.
4. To display inadequacy.

The key point is that children don't behave randomly. Children want what they want. When we discuss this concept in parenting classes, parents respond with nods of insight. Suddenly they understand that their children, like them, have goals toward which they're striving. The boy who is "bouncing off the walls" is truly experiencing, from his perspective, an attention deficit. Perhaps by running around the house at full speed he'll get the attention he craves. At least, doing so has worked in the past. His parents undoubtedly feel annoyed and give him attention for misbehavior.

The girl who refuses to get out of bed for school in the morning may be trying for power. Maybe she feels bossed around or like she doesn't belong in the family, and so her best alternative is to grab power whenever she can. In response, her parents are likely to feel angry and activated—as if they're in a power struggle with someone who's not pulling any punches.

The boy who slaps his little sister may be seeking revenge. Everybody's always talking about how cute his sister is and he's sick and tired of being ignored, so he takes matters into his own hands. His parents likely feel scared and threatened; they don't know if their beautiful little daughter is safe from her vengeful brother.

There's also the child who has given up. Maybe she wanted attention before, or revenge, or power, but now she has given up and is primarily displaying her inadequacy. This isn't because she's inadequate, but because her striving for excellence, for completion, has—in

> her eyes—failed miserably. This child is acting out the concept of learned helplessness (Seligman, 1975). Her parents probably feel anxiety and despair as well. Or, unfortunately, as is often the case, they may finally begin giving her attention and inclusion and pampering, further reinforcing her behavior patterns and self-image of inadequacy.
>
> When teaching about the goals of children's misbehavior, we often include the following caveat: Children who misbehave may also be acting out due to basic biological needs. Therefore, the first thing for parents to check is whether their child is hungry, tired, sick, or in physical discomfort. After checking these essentials, parents should move on to evaluating the psychological purpose of their child's behavior.

Social Interest and Community Feeling

Humans are born into an interpersonal context. As a consequence, the development of individual personality is shaped by interpersonal factors. This is why IP places so much emphasis on understanding individuals within the context of their family constellations.

The interpersonal nature of humans leads to what Adler refers to as **community feeling**. When an individual experiences a deep sense of connection to others—an awareness of being a member of the human community—he or she is experiencing community feeling.

Social interest, or *Gemeinschaftsgefuhl*, is community feeling in action. Social interest is also a therapeutic goal. Watts (2000) stated: "The ultimate goal for psychotherapy is the development or enhancement of the client's social interest" (p. 323). As an individual's social interest develops, so does the capacity for empathy and altruism. Psychologically healthy individuals feel a sense of communion with others and strive to help other humans. As Mahatma Gandhi is quoted as saying,

> Consciously or unconsciously, every one of us does render some service or other. If we cultivate the habit of doing this service deliberately, our desire for service will steadily grow stronger and will make, not only for our own happiness, but that of the world at large. (Boldt, 1999, p. 59)

Social interest is unique to IP. It's unique for several reasons, not the least of which is that it acknowledges that the therapy approach is not value-free. Research has shown that social interest is positively related to spirituality, positive psychology, and human attachment (Leak, 2006; G. K. Leak & K. C. Leak, 2006; Weber, 2003). Some writers consider the positive aspects of religion to be a manifestation of social interest. This was Adler's position as well (Manaster & Corsini, 1982; Watts, 2000).

Striving for Superiority

Adler's most basic human motive, for children and adults, has been identified in the literature as **striving for superiority**. This doesn't mean that Adler believed humans inherently try to demonstrate interpersonal superiority by dominating one another—that would be contrary to *Gemeinschaftsgefuhl*. Instead, his emphasis was that individuals strive for a perceived plus in themselves and their lives. Mosak and Maniacci (1999) apply this concept to a clinical situation:

> How can self-mutilation move someone toward a plus situation? Once again, that may be a "real" minus, especially in the short-term situation. Long-term, however, that person may receive attention, others may "walk on eggshells" when near that person (so as to not "upset" him or her), and he or she may gain some sense of subjective relief from the act, including a sense of being able to tolerate pain. (p. 23)

As you can see from the preceding example, within the individual there's opportunity for both interpersonal gain and individual developmental gain. This is one of the inner pushes that fuels the

Adlerian psyche. But it should be emphasized that when it comes to basic human nature and potential, Adler is like Switzerland. He's neutral. He doesn't believe in the innate goodness or innate destructiveness of humans. Instead, he believes we are what we make ourselves; we have within us the potential for goodness and evil.

If you look at it in an interpersonal context, striving for individual superiority can take on a Western, individualistic quality. Fortunately (for humanity), this wasn't Adler's perspective. He viewed individualistic superiority striving as a sign of psychopathology. Striving for yourself or **self-interest** is considered unhealthy; Adler once claimed he could simplify his entire theory by noting that all neurosis was linked to vanity. Striving for self-interest translates into striving for superiority over others—which is striving without social interest or *Gemeinschaftsgefuhl* (Watts & Eckstein, 2009). A big question for Adlerians is whether you're striving primarily for self-interest or social interest.

Additionally, we should point out that the term *superiority* is an oversimplification of Adler's writings. Heinz Ansbacher articulated a more comprehensive and accurate view of Adler's concept of striving for superiority in a published interview:

The basic striving, according to Adler, is the striving for Vollkommenheit. The translation of Vollkommenheit is completeness, but it can also be translated as excellence. In English, only the second translation was considered; it was only the striving for excellence. The delimitation of the striving for excellence is the striving for superiority.

Basically, it all comes from the striving for completeness, and there he said that it is all a part of life in general, and that is very true. Even a flower or anything that grows, any form of life, strives to reach its completeness. And perfection is not right, because the being does not strive—one cannot say to be perfect—what is a perfect being? It is striving for completeness and that is very basic and very true. (Dubelle, 1997, p. 6)

Ansbacher's clarification helps us to see that there's much more to Adler than superiority striving. Adler also provided us with more information

about superiority striving when he stated, "The fundamental law of life is to overcome one's deficiencies" (Ansbacher & Ansbacher, 1956, p. 48). This motivation toward compensation is the flip side of superiority and another way to look at the concept of completeness. Optimally, individuals strive to (a) overcome their deficiencies, (b) with an attitude of social interest, and (c) to complete or perfect themselves. Of course, this striving is idealized and fictional . . . but serves as a great motivator toward improving oneself and working for the common social good.

Phenomenology

After reading the quote from Ansbacher about flowers and completeness and humans and individuality, we can't help but head down the road toward existentialism. You may be wondering, was Adler an existentialist? Did he, in some ways, predate modern existentialism in psychotherapy?

The answer is that Adler was indeed an early existentialist; the concept of **phenomenology** is a central assumption of individual psychology. In fact, Adler was writing about experiences of neuroses at around the same time and in about the same place as Edmund Husserl, the founder of the school of phenomenology (Mosak & Maniacci, 1999). As we see in Chapter 4, Adler had a profound influence on two key architects of modern existential theory, Viktor Frankl and Rollo May.

An Idiographic Approach

For Adler, general statements about humans and human psychology are helpful, but of limited use. Ansbacher's statement about a flower growing to completeness is an excellent example. Although it's an accurate statement about flowers in general, it tells us nothing about the particular completeness associated with a daisy, a rose, or a sunflower. Similarly, if you read about sunflowers in a book, the statements contained therein may tell you a lot about sunflowers in general, but not much about the particular sunflower plant that you're trying to grow in your shady garden in upstate New York.

In Adler's words, "a human being cannot be typified or classified" (Adler, 1935, p. 6).

Individual psychology is all about the psychology of the single, unique, whole individual. Therefore, being given general or nomothetic information about schizophrenia is only minimally helpful in our study of an individual who happens to have the diagnosis of schizophrenia. In the practical, sensible manner common to Adlerian approaches, it's more important that we meet and spend time with clients than it is for us to provide a diagnostic label. For Adlerians, research is best if its idiographic, not nomothetic (Kelly & Main, 1978).

Soft Determinism

At this point, it should come as no surprise to hear that IP is not a deterministic approach. Adler did not emphasize causal determinants of human behavior. An old story of Mulla Nasrudin, a mischievous but wise and perhaps mythical figure from Turkey, articulates **soft determinism**. The story is titled *Moment in Time*.

> "What is fate?" Nasrudin was asked by a scholar.
> "An endless succession of intertwined events, each influencing the other."
> "That is hardly a satisfactory answer. I believe in cause and effect."
> "Very well," said the Mulla, "look at that." He pointed to a procession passing in the street.
> "That man is being taken to be hanged. Is that because someone gave him a silver piece and enabled him to buy the knife with which he committed the murder; or because someone saw him do it; or because nobody stopped him?"
> (Shah, 1966, p. 110)

Soft determinism is the midpoint between deterministic, cause-and-effect thinking and nondeterminism, which assumes no causal connections. In the Nasrudin story, we could consider many other influential factors that may or may not have contributed to the man's committing a murder and going to be hanged. Perhaps he experienced child abuse, or was deeply hurt by the person he murdered, or believed he had no other recourse, or....

From the IP perspective, human behavior is a function of a combination of influences. There is no single, direct *causal* factor producing a single behavior. Instead, there are many influences or *contributing* factors.

Adler believed every individual is responsible for his or her behavior. People have freedom to choose from a menu (sometimes a limited menu) of behavioral options. Although the Adlerian position holds individuals responsible for their behavior, it doesn't blame individuals for their misdeeds. Instead, Adler holds open the possibility that an individual may not completely understand or be conscious of the potential consequences of her actions. Mosak and Maniacci describe this position: "People are not to be blamed, but to be educated" (1999, p. 19).

As implied by the preceding quotation, Adlerian theory is hopeful and optimistic. If you think about Adler and his life, his hope and optimism seem well founded. To begin as a young boy who was pronounced lost, who flunked a year of middle school, and who was hit by various vehicles in the street, and to end up as one of the most influential psychological thinkers of all time—how could he not become an optimist?

Style of Life (aka Lifestyle): The Biopsychosocial Map

Although we know that Adler became an optimist, we don't know exactly when and how he became an optimist. It just so happens that the theory of individual psychology provides us with reasonable hypotheses about when and how Adler came to his positive perspective. The theory suggests that Adler developed a style of life or **lifestyle** characterized by optimism. He probably became an optimist, at the very latest, before age 8 or 9, and more likely by age 5 or 6—which is when Adlerians believe the *style of life* has been formed (Ansbacher & Ansbacher, 1956).

Adler was deeply influenced by Hans Vaihinger, a philosopher who wrote a book titled *The Psychology of "As If"* (Vaihinger, 1911; Watts, Peluso, & Lewis, 2005). According to Vaihinger, we each create our own world and then live by the rules we've created. This world is necessarily subjective and essentially fictional—in the sense that it's based on our implicit and explicit personal beliefs rather than objective fact. This is why, early in his career, Adler referred to a client's *fictional goals* or **fictional finalism** as a future-oriented concept that influences an individual's present behavior. Toward the end of his career, Adler stopped using the term *fictional*, instead using **guiding self-ideal** and other phrases to articulate this concept (Watts & Holden, 1994).

Vaihinger's (1911) philosophy strongly contributed to the cognitive flavor of Adler's individual psychology and his formulation of the style of life concept, as we can see from the following anecdote from Adler (1931):

> Perhaps I can illustrate this [style of life concept] by an anecdote of three children taken to the zoo for the first time. As they stood before the lion's cage, one of them shrank behind the mother's skirts and said, "I want to go home." The second child stood where he was, very pale and trembling and said, "I'm not a bit frightened." The third glared at the lion and fiercely asked his mother, "Shall I spit at it?" The three children really felt inferior, but each expressed his feelings in his own way, consistent with his style of life. (p. 50)

An individual's style of life is subjective, created, and both conscious and unconscious. In contemporary terms, it is a cognitive schema or biopsychosocial map of how the world works (see Chapter 8). If as a child you learned from your father's example that men are harsh, critical, and to be feared, you will likely carry that schema with you for many years afterward. At times, you may be conscious of this belief, but you also may avoid being around men or respond to men in ways outside of your awareness.

The style of life also has similarities to what psychodynamic theorists call repetition compulsion or attachment theorists call the internal working model (Bowlby, 1988; Peluso, Peluso, Buckner, Kern, & Curlette, 2009). The style of life includes your beliefs or internalized model of yourself, of how the world works, and your personal ethical convictions—as well as your understanding of interpersonal dynamics. Your entire being is guided by your style of life. Lydia Sicher (1935), an early

Adlerian, claimed that even the apparently nonsensical behavior of psychotic patients can be understood through an understanding of their lifestyle:

> To the person not acquainted with the life history and life-style of this woman, her utterances would probably seem completely confused and incoherent, just as dreams seem when one tries to interpret them according to their content rather than in the light of their psychological purposes. To one fully acquainted with her life history and life-style, everything she said can be construed in connection with actual experience and real people. (Sicher, 1935, p. 55)

For an Adlerian, the future is now. This is because your conception of the future (your goals) strongly influence your everyday behavior (Carlson, Watts, & Maniacci, 2006). In addition, the future is then. This means that your future was established, to some degree, by your early childhood experiences. The overall theoretical construct operating here is continuity. Humans are characterized by continuity; the past, present, and future are all closely intertwined.

To this point, we've emphasized the Adlerian style of life's cognitive (psychological) and social dimensions, but it should be noted that there are also biological factors that contribute to style of life development. This is one place where Adlerian theory becomes rather complex. To explore this complexity further, see Carlson, Watts, and Maniacci (2006) or Sweeney (2009).

An individual's personal continuity or style of life may be more or less adaptive. Some people hold onto beliefs about the self, world, and others that cause them emotional pain and distress. Adler has referred to these beliefs as **basic mistakes**, and these cognitive mistakes are an obvious target of therapy. As you might expect, Adler is hopeful and optimistic about the possibility for helping individuals change their cognitive maps through therapy or through therapeutic life experiences. Despite the fact that humans are characterized by continuity, change is also possible. We examine Adlerian approaches to style of life assessment and analysis later in this chapter.

A summary of theoretical principles associated with individual psychology is in Table 3.1.

Table 3.1 Theoretical Principles of Individual Psychology

Theoretical Assumption	Description
Holism	Humans are a single complete unit; a whole that cannot and should not be divided into separate parts.
Superiority striving	Humans strive; we are active, creative, and persistent in our drive to move toward completion and excellence. We can become discouraged and resigned due to unfortunate life circumstances, but our natural state is forward moving.
Purpose	Human behavior is purposeful. We move toward specific goals in life. In this sense, humans are pulled by hopes for the future, rather than instinctual forces from the past. Adler originally referred to the endpoint of our future purposeful striving as fictional finalism because the endpoint is each individual's subjective fiction.
Social interest	In addition to striving for completion and excellence (also called superiority), humans also strive to connect socially, both with individuals and with the community in general. This motivating factor is referred to as social interest or community feeling (or, most accurately, both). If humans strive for superiority without a community-feeling motive, they are likely to become driven, selfish, and arrogant in pursuit of their goals.
Idiography	Although general information about humans can be helpful, every individual is unique. Therefore, to really understand an individual, a couple, or a family, you must work with that individual, couple, or family. Group or nomothetic research is of little value.
Phenomenology	Individual experience is subjective and based on each individual's perception. The individual actively creates and adapts his or her own personal reality.
Soft determinism	Adlerians believe in the power of biology and the environment to influence human behavior. However, biology, environment, and other significant factors do not directly cause specific behaviors to occur; instead, behavior is determined by a myriad of influencing factors.
Freedom to choose	Humans are free to choose their behavior from a limited set of options. Humans are also fully responsible for their choices, although they may make uneducated choices due to bad information or a lack of information. Therefore, education can help facilitate healthy, free choice and personal responsibility.
Style of life	The individual cognitive map or schema each of us uses to navigate through life is established in childhood. This map, referred to as lifestyle or style of life, is our personality: It gives us our continuity and tells us about ourselves, others, and how the world works. The map can include basic mistakes, but it can be modified through therapeutic, educational experiences, including counseling or psychotherapy.
Optimism	Adler was an optimist. Although he believed basic human nature was neutral, he was hopeful that the pull toward social interest and community feeling and the drive toward completeness would help individuals live together peacefully and happily.

QUESTIONS FOR REFLECTION

What continuities do you notice in your view of yourself and your life? This next question is harder: What basic mistakes do you make over and over again? Please don't worry about your answer because Adler believed we all repeatedly make *basic mistakes*—it's only a matter of whether the mistakes are large or small.

Tasks of Life

Adlerian theory is not just a psychological theory of the individual; it also includes assumptions about the demands the world places on individuals. Adler believed all individuals face three interrelated life tasks or challenges:

1. Work or occupation

2. Social relationships

3. Love and marriage

Later, Dreikurs and Mosak (1966, 1967; Mosak & Dreikurs, 1967), both of whom worked directly with Adler, identified two additional life tasks within the individual psychology framework:

4. Self

5. Spirituality

Finally, other Adlerian practitioners, Dinkmeyer and Sperry (1987) identified a sixth task:

6. Parenting and family

These six tasks constitute the challenges of life.

When clients come to therapy, they nearly always come because of difficulty with one or more basic life tasks. The difficulties arise from inaccuracies, mistakes, and maladaptive perceptions associated with their style of life. Therefore, the overarching goal of therapy is to help clients adjust or modify their style of life in ways that help them more effectively complete their life tasks.

Work or Occupation

Adler believed the best way to solve the life task of work or occupation was by solving the second life task, social relationships, through "friendship, social feeling, and cooperation" (Adler, 1958, p. 239). If a person is unable to work cooperatively, divide labor responsibilities, and maintain friendly relations, he or she is likely to struggle in the work area. Here's an example of how Adler described one particular work or occupational problem and its origin:

> There are some people who could choose any occupation and never be satisfied. What they wish is not an occupation but an easy guarantee of superiority. They do not wish to meet the problems of life, since they feel that it is unfair of life to offer them problems at all. These, again, are the pampered children who wish to be supported by others. (Ansbacher & Ansbacher, 1956, p. 429)

In this excerpt, Adler is linking the past to the present. He believes that the client who was pampered as a child will have occupational difficulties.

However, if the client can have experiences, inside or outside of therapy, that help change the assumption that life should offer no problems at all, then the occupational problem will not necessarily extend into the future.

Social Relationships

Adler was a strong proponent of positive social relationships. He felt that establishing healthy social relationships was an ultimate therapy goal and a key to solving the work or occupational problem. In essence, humans are interdependent. Lydia Sicher (1991) emphasized the centrality of this concept in the title of her classic paper "A Declaration of Interdependence." When we accept this interdependence and develop empathy and concern for others social relationships can prosper.

As a life task, the need for positive social relationships can also referred to as the *need to belong* (Baumeister & Leary, 1995; Dreikurs, 1950; Gere & MacDonald, 2010). Not meeting this life demand, or not perceiving one has met this demand, can result in both personal distress and misbehavior. For example, Dreikurs (1950) articulated that children who don't feel they belong are more likely to misbehave. More recently, substantial empirical research points to the importance of belonging and to the negative consequences of "not belonging." Some of the negative consequences include: (a) decreased or impaired cognitive functioning (Chen, Williams, Fitness, & Newton, 2008), (b) increased cortisol and/or stress levels (Blackhart, Eckel, & Tice, 2007; Zwolinski, 2008), and (c) increased preoccupation with social stimuli (Gardner, Pickett, Jefferis, & Knowles, 2005; Pickett, Gardner, & Knowles, 2004). It appears that everyone needs to belong to some social group. Meeting this need is a major life task.

Love and Marriage

Some theorists refer to this life task as *love* while others refer to it as *sex* (Mosak & Maniacci, 1999). For the purposes of our discussion here, we're using Adler's original terms, *love* and *marriage* (Ansbacher & Ansbacher, 1956).

Adler's writing and speaking about love and marriage were reportedly quite popular during his lifetime. Should you explore his original work in this area, you will find his writing very accessible, possibly even romantic. A brief excerpt of his original work follows, with the male-oriented language of his time included:

[E]ach partner must be more interested in the other than in himself. This is the only basis on which love and marriage can be successful.

If each partner is to be more interested in the other partner than in himself, there must be equality. If there is to be so intimate a devotion, neither partner can feel subdued nor overshadowed. Equality is only possible if both partners have this attitude. It should be the effort of each to ease and enrich the life of the other. In this way each will be safe; each will feel that he is worthwhile and that he is needed. The fundamental guarantee of marriage, the meaning of marital happiness, is the feeling that you are worthwhile, that you cannot be replaced, that your partner needs you, that you are acting well, and that you are a fellow man and a true friend. (Ansbacher & Ansbacher, 1956, p. 432)

Many clients come to therapy with intimacy problems, both sexual and nonsexual. For Adlerians, the road to recovery for these clients is the same as suggested previously: Modify the style of life, develop empathy (community feeling), and take decisive action by thinking and acting differently in everyday life.

Self
Dreikurs and Mosak (1967) and Schulman (1965) have written about the life task of self. They note that this task was implied, but not fully developed, in Adler's original work. Essentially, this task emphasizes that everyone has a relationship with himself or herself. Not surprisingly, the nature of your relationship with yourself is established during childhood.

Mosak and Maniacci (1999) describe four dimensions of the self-life task:

1. **Survival of self:** Am I taking good care of my physical self? Am I taking good care of my psychological self? Am I taking good care of my social self?

2. **Body image:** Is my perception of my body reasonable and congruent with my actual body?

3. **Opinion:** What is my opinion of me? To evaluate this in an interview, Adlerians often ask clients to complete the incomplete sentence, "I _____ me" (Mosak & Maniacci, 1999, p. 107).

4. **Evaluation:** Some clients have various extreme perspectives of the self. From the object relations perspective, the question would be "Am I good or am I bad?"

The optimal resolution of the self-task is characterized by good self-care, an accurate perception and expectations of one's body, a reasonably accurate and positive opinion of oneself, and a balanced view of oneself as not overly good or overly bad.

Spirituality
Much of Adler's writing focused on the need for community feeling, social interest, and cooperation. This is even the case with regard to some of his writing about religion. He stated: "The most important task imposed by religion has always been, 'Love thy neighbor'" (Adler, 1958, p. 253).

Mosak and Maniacci (1999) described five specific issues related to the spirituality task. As individuals grow up and face life, they must approach and deal with each of these issues:

- *Relationship to God:* Does the individual believe in God? If so, what kind of God does he or she perceive? If not, then what does he or she believe in?

- *Religion:* Addressing the issue of organized religion is different from addressing the issue of God. Does the individual embrace religious belief or avoid it? How are guilt and repentence dealt with (Mosak, 1987)?

- *Relationship to the universe:* Mosak and Maniacci state that "Some individuals see humans as simply another animal. Others see humans as the pinnacle of God's creation" (p. 108). This concept is interwoven with religious beliefs, but it can also be somewhat separate. The question is: What is the nature of the relationship of humans to the rest of the world and the universe?

- *Metaphysical issues:* Most individuals have beliefs about heaven, hell, reincarnation, karma, salvation, and so on. How individuals view these issues is a function of lifestyle, and an individual's lifestyle must conform to beliefs in this area.

- *Meaning of life:* A special emphasis is placed on the importance of finding meaning in life. Adlerians believe that healthy individuals lead meaningful lives in cooperative relationship to other members of the human community.

Parenting and Family

Giving birth to and raising children, and functioning as a family, are extensions of the love and marriage task discussed previously. However, these things also constitute a task in and of themselves. Some individuals function as single parents and raise children outside marriage. Individual parents also develop strong feelings and beliefs about how children *should* be raised. How individuals face the parenting and family task is both a function of and a challenge to their style of life.

Given that Adler believed an individual's personality is fully formed by about age 5, he obviously viewed parents or caregivers as having a tremendous influence on children's personality development and well-being (Adler, 1927). Rudolph Dreikurs worked with Adler and following Adler's death extended his work in the area of parenting. Dreikurs work has been exceptionally influential. In stark contrast to many popular parenting approaches at the time, the Adlerian-Dreikurian parenting approach has the following core characteristics (Gfroerer, Kern, & Curlette, 2004):

- The relationship between parent and child should be democratic-authoritative and not too autocratic/authoritarian or permissive.

- Parents should be responsive to their children's needs and yet firm in setting limits and boundaries.

- Discipline is designed to help teach children problem solving and therefore should be respectful with an emphasis on natural and logical consequences.

- Instead of overusing praise, parents should focus on encouraging their children.

- As noted previously, parents should "get curious, not furious" and work to understand the purpose of their children's misbehavior.

- Punishment is not an effective means of teaching children and generally is associated with long-term negative outcomes.

A substantial number of contemporary parenting authorities attribute many of their ideas to Adler and Dreikurs (J. Sommers-Flanagan & R. Sommers-Flanagan, 2011).

Although Adler didn't explicitly include parenting and family as a formal life task, his emphasis on the importance of family life supports its inclusion as a sixth life task.

Theory of Psychopathology

Adlerians generally define psychopathology as "discouragement," but there's much more to it than that.

The discouraged individual is unable or unwilling to approach and deal with essential life tasks; he or she lacks the courage to do so. With regard to psychopathology and life tasks, Adler stated:

> The three problems of life which I have already described must be solved somehow or other by every human being for the individual's relationship with the world is a three-fold relation. . . . [W]hoever can make friends with society, can pursue a useful occupation with faith and courage, and can adjust his sexual life in accordance with good social feeling, is immune from neurotic infection. But when an individual fails to square himself with one or more of these three inexorable demands of life, beware of feelings of abasement, beware of the consequent neurosis. Schizophrenia is the result of a failure in all three directions at once. (Adler, 1964, p. 20)

In the case of a mental disorder, one or more of the life tasks have become overwhelming. This is where discouragement fits in. The person struggling to adequately face a life task becomes discouraged.

He or she feels inferior or unable to successfully manage the life task demands and therefore symptoms arise.

Symptomatic patients are suffering from an interaction between their mistaken or maladaptive style of life and the demands of a life task. Symptoms become an answer to the question "What shall I do if I cannot successfully manage this life task?" From an Adlerian perspective, symptoms *have a purpose*—they are an attempted, albeit unhelpful effort to address the life tasks—and may help individuals avoid facing life tasks for which they feel ill-prepared or inadequate. Here are some examples:

- If I steal, then I won't have to communicate, cooperate, divide labor, or perform other basic social functions needed in the workplace.

- If I become depressed, I can communicate my anger and dissatisfaction indirectly. I will be taken care of and in control of the household.

- If I become anxious, I won't have to approach one or more of the basic life tasks. Perhaps I can avoid marriage or work. If I collapse from anxiety, surely someone will rescue me from the demands of life.

Adler articulated his formulation of many different mental disorders. Here is an example of his blunt description of the etiology of anxiety problems: "Anxiety neurosis is always symptomatic of a timid attitude towards the three problems of life, and those who suffer from it are invariably 'spoiled' children" (Adler, 1964).

Mosak (1989) also makes a clear statement about psychopathology from the Adlerian perspective when he says, "poor interpersonal relationships are products of misperceptions, inaccurate conclusions, and unwarranted anticipations incorporated in the life-style" (p. 86). This statement brings us back to discouragement. The maladaptive lifestyle and its associated interpersonal dysfunctions cause the client to experience disappointments, feelings of inferiority, and eventually discouragement.

In particular, IP emphasizes the significance of inferiority. Feelings of inferiority are natural because as small children we always grow up in the presence of caretakers that are bigger, stronger, and smarter than we are. However, inferiority can take on psychopathological dimensions. Carlson and colleagues (2006) described three inferiority dimensions:

1. **Objective inferiority:** From this perspective inferiority is measurable and contextual. Some people are taller, stronger, faster, more musically talented, or more intelligent than others. Objectively, most of us are vocally inferior to Sarah Brightman and Ramon Vargas, athletically inferior to Dwyayne Wade and Mia Hamm, and intellectually inferior to Stephen Hawking and Marilyn vos Savant.

2. **Inferiority feelings:** These are "global, subjective and evaluative" generalizations that are believed despite contrary evidence. "For example, [a] 5-foot, 10-inch man...may feel short no matter who is in the room with him" (Carlson et al., 2006, p. 58). This would be true if there was objective evidence of his shortness (e.g., being in a room with a 6'5" person) or no objective evidence (e.g., being in a room alone or only with shorter people). Individuals may have inferiority feelings, but these feelings are contained and not acted on.

3. **Inferiority complexes:** These are behavioral manifestations of inferiority feelings. Inferiority complexes can be normal or pathological. Similar to the *DSM*, the main criterion for judging normality is whether the inferiority complex causes significant impairment. For example, a woman might feel test anxiety because she feels intellectually inferior. This anxiety may cause her distress, but if she is able to cope with it adequately and it doesn't interfere with her life goals (she attends college, graduates, and moves successfully into the employment world), then she has a normal inferiority complex. In contrast, if her intellectual inferiority complex results in debilitating test anxiety and she fails tests and doesn't graduate from college and is unable to pursue her intellectual interests, then she has an inferiority complex that is psychopathological.

THE PRACTICE OF ADLERIAN THERAPY

Adler's Individual Psychology (IP) has been criticized as based on common sense. Although we agree that IP can seem like common sense, we find Adlerian therapy to be a sensitive and complex process, requiring rigorous training to do it well.

Consistent with its idiographic foundation, Adlerian therapy integrates assessment into the therapy process or phases. Consequently, we'll wait to discuss assessment issues until the appropriate therapy phase.

As you may recall from Chapter 1, there are many different perspectives on the differences or distinctions between counseling and psychotherapy. For Adlerians, counselors and psychotherapists use the same processes or procedures, but they have different therapy goals: Counseling focuses on making behavior changes within the lifestyle while psychotherapy involves changing the client's lifestyle itself—changing the deeper attitudes, beliefs, and life-goals (Sweeney, 2009).

Both counseling and psychotherapy involve a friendly and collaborative process consisting of **four stages** (Carlson et al., 2006; Dreikurs, 1969).

1. **Forming the therapeutic relationship.**
2. **Lifestyle assessment and analysis.**
3. **Interpretation and insight.**
4. **Reorientation.**

Forming the Therapeutic Relationship

The relationship between Adlerian therapists and their clients is egalitarian and characterized by effective listening and caring. Therapist and client sit on chairs of equal status and look more or less directly at one another. Of all therapist types, Adlerians may seem most like a friendly teacher or business consultant whose business it is to help the individual negotiate life more successfully (see Putting it in Practice 3.2: Informed consent From the Adlerian Perspective).

Therapists intentionally foster collaboration and communicate interest in the client as a person.

Bitter and colleagues (Bitter, Christensen, Hawes, & Nicoll, 1998) described how an Adlerian counselor might open a first session:

> We often start an interview with "What do you want me to know about you?" rather than, "What brought you in?" or "What did you want to talk about today?" Meeting and valuing the person is essential to positive change; the relationship may not be everything that matters, but [it] is *almost* everything that matters. (Bitter et al., 1998, p. 98)

Clients are encouraged to be active participants in therapy. Although the therapist is an expert and teaches, the client is an active—as opposed to passive—learner.

Goal Alignment

One way therapists communicate respect is by working hard to understand the client as a person and the client's goals for therapy. In particular, for therapy to proceed successfully, therapist and client must align their goals.

Although client and therapist goals for therapy should be aligned, the Adlerian therapist has preset ideas about appropriate therapy goals. Mosak (1995) includes the following goals as appropriate for Adlerian therapy:

- Fostering client social interest or community feeling.
- Helping clients overcome feelings of inferiority and discouragement.
- Helping clients change the basic mistakes imbedded in their lifestyle.
- Shifting client motivation from self-focused superiority to a community focus.
- Helping clients believe and feel as equals in their relationships.
- Helping clients become contributing members to society.

Mosak's goal list further articulates how clients and their problems—consistent with Adlerian theory—are viewed as inseparable units. Consequently,

PUTTING IT IN PRACTICE 3.2

Informed Consent From the Adlerian Perspective

Hello. I'd like to welcome you to my office and provide you with information about how I typically work with clients.

Usually people come to counseling due to problems or concerns with relationships, work, or family issues. My first goal is to make a connection with you so we can work together collaboratively. At the same time, I will be gathering information from you to better understand what's going on in your life now . . . but this information gathering will also involve many questions about your past, your family of origin, and your future goals.

The counseling approach I use is called *Adlerian*. Let me explain a little bit about what that means.

Our counseling together may be brief or longer as the length of counseling will depend on the concerns you have and how efficiently we can work together. The Adlerian approach emphasizes that we all develop ideas about ourselves, the world, and the future based on our early childhood experiences. Unfortunately, sometimes the ideas we learned from the past don't work perfectly well in the present. As a consequence, we'll take a good hard look at your beliefs or automatic assumptions about yourself, the world, other people, and the future. Then we'll work together to change or tweak those assumptions so they fit even better with the sorts of challenges you're facing in your life. Sometimes I'll give you assignments to try out new behavior or new attitudes and then we'll talk about how well those new behaviors or attitudes functioned for you in your life. Other times I'll offer you my opinion or recommendations about what I think is going on with you and what you could try to do to improve yourself and your life. Usually these recommendations will have to do with making sure the purpose of your specific behaviors and attitudes are a good fit for what you want to accomplish in life. We'll also probably focus on how you can improve your personal relationships—because from an Adlerian perspective, having healthy and balanced social relationships is very important.

Overall, counseling is about new learning and developing a new and different orientation toward life. This usually just involves small changes in how you think about yourself, others, the world, and the future. You might think of therapy as a tune-up for your basic assumptions about life.

I very much look forward to working with you.

in contrast to contemporary cognitive-behavior therapy, the therapist is unlikely to formulate a "problem list" with the client. The problem and the person are one entity and need not be separated, except for specific therapeutic purposes.

Focusing on Positives and Not Pathologizing

Adlerians focus on client strengths as well as problems. For example, it's common to ask about positive personal qualities (e.g., "What were some of your best traits as a child?" and "Tell me a story about one of your childhood successes"). Unlike solution-oriented therapy approaches, therapists show interest in the whole person, both problems and strengths. The goal is to establish an environment characterized by encouragement.

The Adlerian approach doesn't focus on pathologizing clients. Watts and Eckstein (2009) integrated several Adlerian theoretical concepts into their description of the therapeutic process:

> Adlerian counseling embraces a nonpathological perspective. Clients are viewed as discouraged. All persons struggle with feelings of inferiority. When persons creatively respond with courage and community feeling/social interest to the challenges of life and the concomitant feelings of inferiority, they are considered to be functioning well. When they do not, or if they respond without community feeling/social interest, they are discouraged and may have what Adler called an inferiority complex. Persons with an inferiority complex are more concerned with how others perceive them than they are with finding solutions to problems. They tend to be passive and withdrawn. Persons compensating for inferiority feelings by a superiority complex tend to be arrogant and boastful. In both cases, they are discouraged but responding to overwhelming feelings of inferiority in different ways. (p. 282)

Initial Lifestyle Interpretations

One of our old supervisors with an Adlerian-humanistic bent used to tell us, "Near the end of your first session, you should be able to share with your clients a few important things you've learned about them" (H. A. Walters, personal communication, December 1983). Although we didn't know it at the time, our supervisor was talking about making an initial *style of life interpretation*. The purpose of this early or initial interpretation is to further the connection between therapist and client and begin the process of a deeper problem analysis. Because it occurs so early in counseling, this first interpretation is really more of a collaborative guess than an interpretation and should be phrased as such. It also prepares the client for the Adlerian approach and further interpretations and techniques offered later in therapy.

Lifestyle Assessment and Analysis

Several approaches to lifestyle assessment are available. Although some researchers and practitioners use self-report questionnaires (e.g., the Basic Adlerian Scales for Interpersonal Success-Adult Form [BASIS-A Inventory]; Wheeler, Kern, & Curlette, 1991), the three main assessment strategies are conducted using a clinical interview format:

1. The family constellation interview
2. The question
3. Earliest recollections

The Family Constellation Interview

The **family constellation interview** is a particular approach to obtaining pertinent information about the client's childhood experiences. Topics covered include descriptions of each family member, descriptions of how family members interacted with one another, how each family member was viewed by the client, who fought, who didn't fight, and much more. Adler also considered psychological **birth order** to be a strong contributor to style of life (see Putting it in Practice 3.3). In particular, he emphasized that every individual is born into a different family; this is because with the addition of each new family member, family dynamics change and a new family is born.

An example of a family constellation interview, leading to interpretation and client insight, is included later in this chapter.

PUTTING IT IN PRACTICE 3.3

Birth Order and Lifestyle

Popular psychology has often oversimplified the Adlerian concept of birth order. At the worst, birth order is used like astrology to describe an individual's personality and to predict human behavior. This occurs despite the fact that Adler cautioned against using a simplistic birth order approach to understanding lifestyle. He stated:

> There has been some misunderstanding of my custom of classification according to position in the family. It is not, of course, the child's number in the order of successive births which influences his character, but the situation into which he is born and the way in which he interprets it. (Adler, 1937, p. 211)

Birth order is psychological, not chronological. For example, if a first-born child has illnesses or disabilities that reduce his/her abilities, a second-born may adopt personality characteristics more commonly associated with first-borns. In that situation, the chronological second born becomes the psychological first born.

As noted previously, psychological birth order is one of three psychosocial dynamics contributing to style of life development. Keeping Adler's caution in mind, the following birth order tendencies are offered.

Child's Position	Lifestyle Characteristics
Oldest	This child may be initially spoiled and later dethroned. She or he may be bossy, strict, and authoritarian; it's as if she or he has a right to power. She or he also may feel exceptionally responsible for others. The oldest child may strongly identify with father because she or he turns to him for support after the second child's birth.
Second	She or he always has an older rival, and this may make him or her competitive. The challenge is to develop a unique identity, so she or he may end up being a rebel. There is often an unfulfilled wish to be bigger, stronger, smarter, and more capable.
Middle	She or he is likely to be even-tempered, developing a sort of "take it or leave it" attitude. She or he may become overly sensitive to the overlooked or underprivileged. She or he can feel cheated out of her position of privilege and harbor resentments, sometimes quietly manipulating others to achieve her ends. She or he also may have trouble finding her niche in life.

Child's Position	Lifestyle Characteristics
Youngest	She or he is never dethroned and may feel she or he should be treated like royalty. She or he is likely to have unrealistic aspirations, dreaming of being bigger and more powerful than everyone else, but usually doesn't have the follow-through to achieve these dreams. This may make him or her chronically frustrated, and consequently he could choose to stay the baby, learning to manipulate others to get his/her way.
Only	This child has plenty of attention from both parents and therefore feels special, especially liking attention from adults. There may be problems with peer relationships due to lack of experience with give and take and tolerance. May believe s/he should be "taken care of."
Only boy among girls	He may need to prove he's a man, but is likely to be sensitive to feminine issues. He may be treated like a hero and therefore hold high self-expectations. He also may have strong expectations that others will quickly recognize his specialness and feel deep disappointment when he's treated just like everyone else.
Only girl among boys	She may become overly feminine or a tomboy, trying to compete with her brothers. She also may feel she has a special designation and, depending upon her relations with her brothers, may expect abuse from males or may expect them to be her protectors. She also may feel deep disappointment when her specialness goes unrecognized.

The Question

Recall that for Adlerians all behavior is purposeful. **The Question** is designed to uncover the purpose of the client's symptoms. The Question is "How would your life be different if you were well?" It can be phrased in many ways (e.g., "What would you be doing in your life if you no longer had your symptoms?"). The question is a straightforward method for determining if the client is obtaining special treatment or *secondary gain* for having problems.

After asking the question, the IP practitioner listens for activities or relationships clients might resume should their problems be resolved. In this way, the therapist is determining which life tasks the symptoms may be helping clients avoid. Carlson et al. (2006) described how the question assists with case formulation:

The answer to this question typically reveals what is being avoided by using the presenting problem. For example, one client may say, "If I didn't have

this anxiety, I'd be able to work better." He may be using anxiety as a safeguarding mechanism... as well as using it to buy double insurance. Another client may respond with "If I weren't so depressed, I'd be able to be nicer." She may be using depression to cover up some aggression and depreciation tendencies. (p. 110)

QUESTIONS FOR REFLECTION

How do you think "the Question" might help in formulating a treatment approach for an individual client? What if the question were posed to you? What would your answer be?

Earliest Recollections

Adler considered early memories as one of the most important discoveries of individual psychology. **Early recollections** are used as powerful tools for understanding the client's lifestyle and guiding self-ideal. Sweeney (2009) has succinctly articulated the Adlerian perspective on early recollections: "Early recollections are not a reflection of the past but a forecast of the future" (p. 105).

This perspective can be difficult to grasp. The point is that early memories are not so much memories as they are projections . . . a message from the past, still active in the client's present life (Clark, 2002; Taylor, 1975). As such, the accuracy of the memory is essentially irrelevant. The memory or projection is an active expression of the client's living lifestyle. It's no surprise that the memory is twisted into a shape that corresponds with the client's thoughts, feelings, and attitudes toward him- or herself and life. If the memory was not important *in the present*, there would be no purpose for the client to remember it (see Putting it in Practice 3.4 for a summary of how to use early recollections by Art Clark, author of *Early Recollections: Theory and Practice in Counseling and Psychotherapy* [2002]).

Although Adler's approach to exploring the meaning of early recollections was primarily intuitive and impressionistic, other authors have provided more detailed methods (see Clark, 2002). Additionally, in his Adlerian therapy text, Sweeney (2009) provided a list of questions that can be helpful in understanding the memory at a deeper level:

- Is the individual active or passive?

- Is he or she an observer or participant?

- Is he or she giving or taking?

- Does he or she go forth or withdraw?

- Is he or she alone or with others?

- Is his or her concern with people, things, or ideas [or animals]?

- What relationship does he or she place himself or herself in with others? Inferior? Superior?

- What emotion does he or she use?

- Are detail and color mentioned?

- Do stereotypes of authorities, subordinates, men, women, old, young, reveal themselves?

- Prepare a "headline" that captures the essence of the event.

- Look for themes and an overall pattern.

- Look for corroboration in the family constellation information (adapted from Sweeney, 2009, pp. 104–105).

Toward the conclusion of the assessment phase of therapy, an Adlerian becomes able to identify a client's "basic mistakes." Five examples of basic mistakes are identified by Mosak (1995):

1. **Overgeneralization:** There is no fairness in the world, or I'm always the one who has to take care of everything.

2. **False or impossible goals:** I have to be the boss to be acceptable, or others should always take care of my needs.

3. **Misperceptions of life and life's demands:** The world is against me, or the world is my oyster.

4. **Denial of one's basic worth:** I totally suck, or no one could ever love me.

5. **Faulty values:** A set of values at odds with social interest; I must win and be the best no matter how much it hurts others.

Interpretation and Insight

Insight is central to Adlerian therapy, but is conceptualized differently than psychoanalytic psychotherapy. For Adlerians, there's a strong link between insight, motivation, and action. Insight stimulates motivation, which stimulates action. Think about it: You discover a maladaptive lifestyle pattern or assumption in yourself (e.g., I think I must be perfect and in control at all times) and notice the cost to yourself of holding that maladaptive assumption (e.g., I'm always the one planning, organizing, and managing things and I never really let loose

PUTTING IT IN PRACTICE 3.4

Early Recollections

By Art Clark

Alfred Adler (1937) considered early recollections to be one of the most important discoveries of Individual Psychology. As a projective technique, early recollections involve eliciting and interpreting the meaning of memories from the first years of childhood. These remembrances frequently render an individual's ingrained convictions and perceptions of life. The directions for the assessment tool are fairly simple and brief: "Think back to a long time ago when you were little, and try to recall one of your first memories, one of the first things that you can remember. (Clark, 2002, p. 92)" Recollections must be visualized as a single event before a person is eight years of age. Utilizing an empathy-based model, it is possible to interpret various aspects of a person's narrations of early memories from three perspectives. Thematic topics clarify central or core ideas of a remembrance. Personality dimensions reflect qualitative levels of effective functioning in the memory. Perceptual modalities relate prominent sensory processes in the recollection of an individual.

The following framework outlines the three perspectives for interpreting early recollections:

1. Thematic Topics
2. Personality Dimensions

    Degree of Activity: Level of initiative, persistence, and engagement in events.

    Social Interest: Level of compassion, cooperation, and contribution with respect to others.

    Optimistic–Pessimistic: Level of contentment and experience of positive or negative events.

    Self-efficacy: Level of belief in ability to surmount challenges and anticipate success.

    Conscientiousness: Level of responsibility, reliability, and diligence.

3. Perceptual Modalities

    Senses: Vision, Hearing, Touch, Smell, and Taste.

    Color

    Place

    Objects

In applying the multiple perspective model, narrations of early memory renderings from two individuals in early adulthood will help clarify the interpretive process. In the first example, Sarah relates an early childhood memory: "I remember sliding down a hill near my house. I was sitting on a red sled in front of my mother, and was all bundled up in a cozy snow suit. We were laughing together as we went down the hill. The snow was nice and fluffy, and I turned the sled a little by pulling on the rope. I can still feel how pleasant the tingling snow felt on my cheeks."

Interpreting Sarah's memory from a thematic perspective, the centrality of affectionate relationships and stimulating experiences is apparent. In particular, Sarah has a close and supportive relationship with her mother. In relation to personality dimensions, Sarah's degree of activity is high in terms of engagement and initiative. An elevated level of social interest is notable as Sarah participates in a cooperative activity and contributes to its enjoyment. Sarah's sense of contentment is evident, and her positive experience indicates an optimistic orientation. Sarah demonstrates personal control and capability as functions of self-efficacy. Her diligent attention to the task of sledding and assumption of responsibility reflects qualities of conscientiousness. Relating to perceptual modalities, Sarah's visual and touch capacities are prominent and her observation of the red color of the sled suggests an aesthetic awareness or sensitivity. The outdoor location evokes a sense of place for Sarah within an interpersonal context. As an object, the sled provides a conduit or an outlet for satisfying physical and social activities. Formulations from the three perspectives of her early recollection contribute to an assessment of Sarah's higher level of wellness and positive outlook on life.

In contrast with Sarah's first memory, however, early recollections of clients in counseling comprise a range of narrations that may be less constructive or purposeful. In a second example, Keith is in counseling for an anxiety disorder and extensive stress in his life. He recounts an early recollection: "I was about six years old, sitting in a car with my father in a parking lot. When the car wouldn't start, he began yelling and hitting the steering wheel. My father kept turning the key and the engine made a grinding noise but wouldn't start. His eyes were bulging as he was yelling and swearing. It was kind of scary and I felt sad inside." Applying the multiple perspective early recollection interpretation model to Keith yields a less favorable outlook on life in comparison with Sarah. He endures a distressing and anxiety-laden experience from which he has no escape and instead he passively observes a futile event. An awareness of Keith's ingrained convictions and perceptions enables the counselor to enhance an empathic understanding of him and formulate a supportive treatment plan in counseling.

and have any fun). Don't you think that insight or self-discovery might motivate you to take action and make a few changes? This perspective leads Adlerians to believe that insight without action isn't true insight, but a sign that a client is playing at therapy, rather than taking it seriously.

Insight is often achieved through a collaborative interpretative process. Rather than employing authoritarian or authoritative interpretations, Adlerian therapists work collaboratively, often asking questions like, "Could this be true?" There are also many other techniques described in this chapter used to deepen insight. The purpose of interpretation is to articulate continuity of an inaccurate, maladaptive lifestyle; it's not important to show a causal connection between past and present. Once this continuity is revealed in a way clients can understand, the final phase of therapy, reorientation, has begun.

Reorientation (Specific Therapy Techniques)

The **reorientation** therapy phase involves the direct application of specific techniques to deepen insight and facilitate change. IP practitioners don't shy away from using specific techniques in the service of therapy process and outcome. In particular, because therapy is all about new learning—in the broadest sense of the term—using specific, action-oriented, techniques that facilitate client learning is not only an acceptable practice, but a desirable one as well. Mosak (1989) captures this Adlerian attitude toward the therapist's role and function: "There comes a time in psychotherapy when analysis must be abandoned and the patient must be encouraged to act in lieu of talking and listening. Insight has to give way to decisive action" (p. 91).

In honor of Adler, Mosak, and other individual psychology proponents, we now review several top Adlerian techniques.

The Future Autobiography

For the Adlerian, the future guides and shapes everyday behavior. Given this assumption, *the* **future autobiography** is an excellent technique to help clients become more intentional in shaping their futures. This technique is especially useful for clients who like to write. However, it can be adapted for clients who prefer drawing or storytelling.

You can use this technique in at least two ways. However, because Adlerians support counselor creativity, you may discover your own way to use a future autobiography.

First, this technique can be used for assessment. You might say:

> Everyone has a life story. So far, yours has a past and a present, and if I asked you to, you could write me a great story about everything you've experienced up to today. That would be tremendously interesting, but I'd like you to

do an even more interesting project. Between now and next week, write a story about the rest of your life. Make it as detailed or as sketchy as you want. Just look at who you are right now and project your life into the future—as you want it. In other words, finish your life story in the way you would like it to go. We can look at it together next week.

As an assessment procedure, the future autobiography can help identify clients' guiding self-ideal (or fictional life goals) and determine whether this ideal is facilitating or hampering their daily functioning. Additionally, a discussion of the client's future autobiography can help clients take greater conscious responsibility for directing and shaping their lives.

The future autobiography can also be used more therapeutically. If this is your preference, use it *after* gathering information about your client's past and lifestyle. Then, because you have an initial grasp or understanding of your client's basic beliefs about the world, self, and others, you can coach your client to write a realistic and adaptive future autobiography. For example, you might ask your client to address one of the basic mistakes within the context of this assignment:

> We've been talking about how you think you need to be perfect all the time. This belief causes you no end of anxiety. As an assignment for this week, write a "future autobiography." Write the rest of your life story, from here on out. And as you do that, keep this in mind: Write a story in which you're not perfect, one in which you make mistakes but, overall, live in an acceptable and loving way in the world. Okay?

The future biography assignment directly addresses the lifestyle and related future goals or ideals. It can be modified for clients who prefer not to write. Either an oral future biography or a pictorial future biography can be assigned.

Creating New Images

Clients naturally have images of themselves in the past, present, and future. As with most Adlerian techniques, this procedure can be used in many different ways. In some cases, the therapist may try to use a short phrase to visually and metaphorically capture a client's behavior, attitude, or value. I (John) have found this technique useful in my work with adolescents, perhaps because they love feedback, especially feedback that is unusual, compelling, sarcastic, and in the form of a sound bite.

A 15-year-old boy consistently criticized his mother's wealth. He didn't respect how she chose to spend her money. He liked to dress in ragged T-shirts and ripped-up baggy pants, and hung out with friends whose parents had little money. He claimed he was embarrassed to bring his friends over to his mother's nice home. However, this boy also regularly complained that his mother didn't provide *him* with enough money. This inconsistency raised the possibility that the boy was trying to control his mother and get everything he wanted for himself. To create a new image in therapy, John commented, "I just had an image of you come into my mind, can I share it?" (Client says, "Sure"). "I had an image of you as a closet spoiled rich kid. You want money and expect you should have money, but you're uncomfortable with your friends seeing you as rich. What do you think?" This image of "a closet spoiled rich kid" helped the young man more directly talk about his inner conflicts and expectations about money associated with his lifestyle.

Creating new images can also be used to encourage clients to actively develop new and more adaptive self-images. After analyzing your client's early recollections and basic mistakes, you can work to come up with a "new visual" (as our artistic friends like to say). This new visual is a self-generated image used to replace old more negative, disturbing, or maladaptive self-images.

Acting "As If"

Most people at least occasionally wish for traits they don't have. Some wish for self-confidence and others wish they were calm, instead of nervous and edgy. Still others wish they could focus, get organized, and follow through on a project.

The **acting as if** technique is used when clients are wishing for behavior change. When this wishing occurs, you can initiate the *as if* process by asking: "What if you were self-confident? How would

that look?" Then, if your client shares an image of self-confidence with you and it seems a positive step toward adjustment, you might suggest: "For the rest of our time today and throughout this week, how about you try acting *as if* you were filled with self-confidence." This can also be accompanied with a detailing of exactly what "self-confident" would look and sound like. Of course, there's always the possibility that your client will balk at this suggestion and claim that acting self-confident would be phony. Your job at that point is to encourage your client to try it anyway. Mosak (1989) gave an example of encouragement in this situation: "[E]xplain that all acting is not phony pretense, that one can try on a role as one might try on a suit" (p. 91).

This technique gives clients permission to try on new ways of being. Acting as if can bypass resistance because it frames a new behavioral experiment as "just acting." By engaging in these experiments and then talking about them in therapy, clients gain new perspectives and perhaps new motivation for behaving in different and more adaptive ways.

Reflecting As If

Watts (2003) created a modification of the classical Adlerian as if technique. This modification, **reflecting as if** (RAI), is based on an integration of Adlerian and social constructionist theoretical perspectives. Watts (2003) described this theoretical integration as it applies to couples counseling:

> The integrative reflecting as if procedure asks clients to take a "reflective" step back prior to stepping forward to act as if. This process encourages clients to reflect on how they would be different in their relationship if they were acting as if they were the couple they desire to be. By using reflective questions, counselors can help clients construct perceptual alternatives and consider alternative behaviors toward which they may begin moving. (p. 73)

There are three phases to the RAI procedure:

1. *Reflecting*: During the reflecting stage, therapists ask clients to reflect on how they wish they might act differently. For example: "If you were acting

as if you were the person you would like to be, how would you be acting differently? If I were watching a videotape of your life, what would be different?" (Watts & Peluso, 2005, p. 382). And, "What would be the first signs or signals that you're beginning to act in this way you'd like to act."

2. *Planning*: This phase involves building a hierarchy of specific behaviors linked to the self-ideal. First, therapist and client collaboratively brainstorm a list of specific behaviors likely to emerge in the acting as if scenario. Second, the therapist guides the client in ranking the relative difficulty of the various as if behaviors.

3. *Implementing*: As a homework assignment, the client identifies one or two as if behaviors that would be easiest to implement. Watts and colleagues (2005) describe the rationale for this in Adlerian language:

> Commencing with the least difficult behaviors increases the potential for client success, and success is typically encouraging for clients and often increases their perceived self-efficacy. Having had some success, clients' motivation to engage courageously the more difficult tasks on their list is usually stronger.

The RAI procedure is simple and straightforward. It's also a good example of not only the theoretical compatibility of Adlerian approaches, but also of their empirical base. Specifically, RAI employs several evidence-based techniques, including (a) collaborative goal setting; (b) collaborative brainstorming as a step in problem solving; (c) a focus on concrete and measurable behaviors; and (d) concrete behavioral planning. RAI can be used with individuals (Watts & Peluso, 2005; Watts, 2003), couples (Watts, 2003), and with children (Watts & Garza, 2008).

The Push-Button Technique

Adler believed that under every feeling there is a cognition. Based on this theoretical assumption, Mosak (1985) described a therapy technique he referred to as the **push-button technique**. The technique is designed to improve emotional control. Mosak outlines how to introduce this technique to clients:

> This is a three-part experiment. Please close your eyes and keep them closed until all three parts are over. First, I'd like you to dig into your memory and retrieve a very pleasant memory—a success, a beautiful sunset, a time when you were loved—and project that in front of your eyes as if you were watching it on a TV screen. Watch it from beginning to end and attach to it the feelings you had when the incident occurred. Go! Remember how wonderful it was! When you are through, hold up a finger to signal that you are through, and we'll go on to the next part....
>
> Now I'd like you to fish back in memory and retrieve a horrible incident. You failed. You were hurt or ill. Life screwed you. Someone died. You were humiliated. Watch that one from beginning to end as if it were on TV and attach to it the feelings you had at the time the incident occurred. Go! Remember how terrible it was! When you are through, hold up a finger to signal that you are through and we'll go on to the last part....
>
> Now I'd like to go into your memory and retrieve another pleasant memory. If you can't come up with another pleasant memory, go back to the first pleasant memory you had. Watch it on the TV screen from beginning to end and attach to it the feelings you had when the incident occurred. Go! Remember how wonderful it was! When you are through, please open your eyes. (1985, pp. 211–212)

The push-button technique is an ABA reversal experimental design that teaches clients the power of thoughts and images over feelings. After the client experiences affective changes with this procedure, you can make the point, "It's no wonder that depressed people feel depressed. It's because they're consistently thinking depressing thoughts." In the end, the therapist sends the client home with two make-believe push buttons (one happy and one sad) and the following persuasive statement:

> [I]f you come back next week and are *still* depressed, I'm going to ask you to explain why you *choose* to continue to feel depressed when you

have the happy button at your disposal. We'll find out what your investment in being depressed is. (Mosak, 1985, p. 212)

In this example, you've seen Mosak's approach to using the push-button technique in a session with a depressed adult. However, this technique can also be applied to children and adolescents in therapy and as a general emotional education technique in schools (J. Sommers-Flanagan & R. Sommers-Flanagan, 2001; J. Sommers-Flanagan & R. Sommers-Flanagan, 2007b).

Spitting in the Soup

Clients frequently avoid or evade demands and responsibilities associated with basic life tasks. **Spitting in the client's soup** is both a metaphor and technique for spoiling the client's use of a particular avoidance strategy. It speaks to how clients often obtain some "perverse" gratification from repeatedly avoiding responsibility and engaging in maladaptive behaviors. The purpose of spitting in the client's soup is to both enhance client awareness/insight and spoil the use of the maladaptive behavior pattern in the future. After all, who can enjoy eating his soup after someone has spat in it?

Spitting in the soup involves confrontation (J. Sommers-Flanagan & R. Sommers-Flanagan, 2009). Confrontation is an appropriate intervention when there is a strong client-therapist relationship and the therapist becomes aware of a discrepancy between what the client wants and what the client is doing. For example, spitting in the client's soup is appropriate for adolescent clients who repeatedly engage in destructive behaviors (e.g., theft and dishonesty) despite the fact that they profess to want greater personal freedom.

Carlson et al. (2006) provide a simple example of how spitting in the soup can spoil a client's underlying motive:

A male client who is too worried what other people must think of him whenever he goes in public is confronted with his vanity: Obviously, everybody must be noticing him. (p. 142)

This particular version of spitting in the soup has dimensions of paradox and reframing; it becomes

difficult for the man to worry about others without simultaneously becoming aware of the fact that it's also a signal of his vanity.

Spitting in the client's soup works best if therapists use the following guidelines:

- Develop a friendly and supportive relationship with the client characterized by good listening and encouragement.

- Identify a repeating and unhelpful behavior or thinking pattern (basic mistake) that the client uses repeatedly and plans to use in the future.

- Ask and get the client's permission to share an insight.

- Succinctly share the repeating and unhelpful pattern that the client is planning to continue using.

- Be open to discussing the client's reaction to having his or her soup spat in!

Another example of spitting in the soup is included in a counseling vignette later in this chapter.

Catching Oneself

Self-awareness and self-control are at the foundation of Adlerian theory. The technique of **catching oneself** is designed to help clients become aware of their maladaptive behavior patterns and goals. To use the technique, the therapist coaches the client on how to catch himself when he or she slips into old, unhelpful behaviors. For example, a college basketball player came to therapy because of problems with his explosive temper during practice. His coach had issued an ultimatum: "Deal with your anger more constructively or leave the team." The first step of his therapy involved having this young man catch himself when he began thinking or acting in ways that usually led to his angry outbursts. Because, for this client, the primary dynamics related to his anger were perfectionism and blame, he was given the following instructions:

During this session and throughout the week, we'll focus on your tendency to think you need to be perfect and then blame others when you aren't perfect. That's the beginning of your slippery slope toward anger. Your job is to simply notice when you're not performing perfectly and thinking critically about yourself. Just notice it, catch yourself, and think—ah, there it is again, that tendency to criticize myself. Also, notice when you shift from self-criticism to blaming others for your performance. Again, just notice it; there's no need to do anything about it for now.

The technique of catching oneself is a historical predecessor of behavioral and cognitive self-monitoring and thought stopping (see Chapters 7 and 8).

Task Setting and Indirect Suggestion

Adler employed an interesting, engaging, but not always direct therapy style. In the next section we talk about his most indirect strategy: namely, paradoxical instructions. However, as in the following excerpt, he sometimes used both a direct *task-setting strategy and an indirect or suggestive method* for implementing it. This style reminds us of the renowned hypnotherapist Milton Erickson, who mastered this approach and become famous for it several decades after Adler's death (see Chapter 11).

In this case, Adler is discussing a task-setting procedure he uses with depressed patients:

After establishing a sympathetic relation I give suggestions for a change of conduct in two stages. In the first stage my suggestion is "Only do what is agreeable to you." The patient usually answers, "Nothing is agreeable." "Then at least," I respond, "do not exert yourself to do what is disagreeable." The patient, who has usually been exhorted to do various uncongenial things to remedy this condition, finds a rather flattering novelty in my advice, and may improve in behavior. Later I insinuate the second rule of conduct, saying that "It is much more difficult and I do not know if you can follow it." After saying this I am silent, and look doubtfully at the patient. In this way I excite his curiosity and ensure his attention, and then proceed, "If you could follow this second rule you would be cured in fourteen days. It is—to consider from time to time how you can give another person pleasure. It would very soon enable you to sleep and would chase away all your sad thoughts. You would feel yourself to be useful and worthwhile."

I receive various replies to my suggestion, but every patient thinks it is too difficult to act upon. If the answer is, "How can I give pleasure to others when I have none myself?" I relieve the prospect by saying, "Then you will need four weeks." The more transparent response, "Who gives *me* pleasure?" I counter with what is probably the strongest move in the game, by saying, "Perhaps you had better train yourself a little thus: do not actually *do* anything to please anyone else, but just think about how you could do it!" (Adler, 1964a, pp. 25–26)

There are several rather marvelous components to Adler's description of this approach he uses with depressed clients. First, he is deeply engaged with his client. He has thought through the typical responses and is acting with the client—as in a "game." Second, it's clear that his task-setting for the client would be completely ineffectual without having a solid therapeutic relationship. Third, Adler is combining at least four approaches at once: (1) task-setting; (2) spitting in the client's soup; (3) paradox; and (4) indirect suggestion.

Although you might make the case that Adler is being ingenuine or manipulative during this exchange, you can also make the opposite argument. Perhaps Adler is being so much himself that he's able to let out his playful, artistic, and Socratic self—all in an effort to move the patient away from depression and toward social interest or community feeling.

Paradoxical Strategies

Many different authors have written about **paradoxical strategies**, but Adler was one of the first. Paradox in therapy generally involves prescribing the symptom. Specifically, if your client is overly self-critical, you might suggest that she negatively analyze and criticize herself at even a higher rate and intensity during the coming week.

Although some empirical evidence supports paradoxical approaches, they're generally considered high-risk (Hill, 1987). Consequently, when we use paradox, we generally use it in moderation. For example, with a 43-year-old woman who "worries constantly," we don't generally tell her to "worry more," but instead tell her to take 20 minutes twice daily to sit down or pace as she worries intensively. Often, the positive outcome of a paradoxical prescription is the interesting phenomenon of clients feeling more in control than they did previously. Paradoxical strategies are covered in more detail in Chapter 4.

Advice, Suggestion, and Direction

The Adlerian therapist offers advice freely. Of course, he or she does so only within the context of a friendly, collaborative, positive relationship.

Corsini (1998) offers a description of a directive, advice-giving technique he refers to as "*I'll Betcha.*" He claims that this technique is a form of turning the tables on the client, and in that sense it contains paradoxical qualities (but seems less risky than prescribing a symptom). He states:

> [This technique] is called "I'll Betcha." It goes as follows: Say that I suggest that a client do a particular thing to achieve a particular end and the client says it will not work. I will persist and finally will say, "I'll betcha it will." Then I outline the bet—always for exactly $2.00. If the client accepts my bet, the conditions are the following: He or she is to do exactly what I say. If it does not work, he or she wins the bet; if it does work, I win the bet. I have made about 50 such bets over the years and have not lost one. The interesting part is that my opponent decides whether it worked or not. (Corsini, 1998, p. 54)

Offering advice, suggestions, and direction occur deep within the reorientation stage of counseling. This is because, by this time, the client has already been provided with interpretations, and therefore insight and motivation are present. The motivation ignited through insight is the motivation for excellence and a drive toward improving one's lot in life. It's hard to think of a better time to offer a bit of helpful advice.

Adlerian Therapy in Action: Brief Vignettes

The following vignettes illustrate two common Adlerian interventions. As you read through these vignettes, try to imagine yourself as either the client or the therapist. How might it feel to have someone work with you in this way . . . and how might it feel to work this way with clients?

Vignette I: Using an Early Interpretation

This first vignette is an excerpt from a session John did with a 17-year-old male. It illustrates how a client's style of life can be surfaced very quickly in a session and then an early interpretation used to engage the client's interest and motivation.

The young many in this interview is a Job Corps student and has been asked to meet to talk about some anger problems he is experiencing. The young man is biracial; he is of both African and white descent (J. Sommers-Flanagan & R. Sommers-Flanagan, 2004).

John: So, I don't know you, you don't know me. Basically, we're kind of strangers. So, you know, I, I have different ways of trying to get to know people. One is just to ask you some things about what you like and what you don't like.

Sean: Alright.

John: So, I'll just do that if that's okay.

Sean: That'll work.

John: Okay. So now I'm gonna sometimes write things down, not always, but write a few things down. So, tell me, what's your favorite thing to do, your favorite recreational activity?

Sean: Um, there's a couple things. I like playing football. I like playing basketball. Um, I like to draw and write music.

John: Yeah? You write music or lyrics?

Sean: Um, lyrics.

John: Write lyrics, okay.

Sean: And that's about it.

John: Yeah. So those are the things you really like. Enjoy a lot.

Sean: Mmm hmm.

John: How about some things you hate? Sometimes you can tell a lot about somebody by finding out some things that they just hate.

Sean: The same things.

John: You hate football, you hate basketball, you hate drawing?

Sean: Those are my favorite things to do but they make me mad.

John: Yeah?

Sean: Cause I get frustrated when I like, when I play basketball if I don't play so well, it'll make me mad. Well, you know, I like to be QB when I play football. If I don't get a good pass or if somebody drops it I get mad. Um, when I draw if I can't think of nothin' to draw or mess up, I get mad. Or um, when I'm writing music if I can't think of anything I get writer's block, I get really mad. So, yeah, they're like my worst things to do, like what somebody wouldn't want me to do, but they're my favorite things to do, so I do them anyways.

John: That's interesting. So, I can tell you what the issue is already. [This offer to interpret the problem is, in some ways, very premature. Additionally, this would be more in keeping with an Adlerian approach if John asked permission to share his perspective. However, when working with adolescents who are intrigued with the counseling process, sometimes this quick problem formulation can provide a concrete issue to work on collaboratively.]

Sean: Alright.

John: You ready?

Sean: Yeah.

John: So, you know what the problem is about anger for you? You're a perfectionist.

Sean: I don't try to be. I don't really mean to be, though. [Despite the premature or early nature of the interpretation, the client accepts it and begins talking about how, for him, the perfectionism feels out of control.]

John: Yeah.

Sean: I don't like to be because if I don't play as good as I want to play in basketball, for example. If I miss a shot and I know I can make it, I know I should make it, it makes me mad. I mean really mad. I don't just be like "oh darn" you know,

I'm a little mad now. I'll flip out. [The client continues to share his style of life dynamic and the distress it causes him.]

John: You think you should do things right all the time. [This is a cognitive reflection.]

Sean: Yeah.

John: Yeah, that's tough. Man, you've got a huge burden. [This is more of an emotionally empathic statement.]

Sean: Yeah, well I don't mean to.

John: That's a lot of pressure.

Sean: Kind of. It's, it's a lot of stress because you know, it's just kind of the way that I was brought up. You know, I never wanted to lose at anything. I never wanted to be less than anybody. I've always wanted to be the best, but I've never gotten there yet. [The client rather naturally links his current lifestyle problem or basic mistake to his childhood experiences.]

For Adlerians the purpose of insight is to enhance motivation to change. You can see from this brief interaction that after the interpretation, the client becomes more verbal and begins disclosing information that may be useful for making personal changes.

Later in the therapy process this client discloses ways in which his biracial ethnic identity feeds into his needs to be perfect. This discussion is especially interesting because it is consistent with the literature on biracial identity development theory and validates the Adlerian emphasis on social and cultural factors shaping human behavior (R. E. Hall & Rowan, 2003; Hud-Aleem & Countryman, 2008; Poston, 1990).

Vignette II: Spitting in the Client's Soup

A 15-year-old boy was referred for therapy because he had taken explosives to school. He had been to see John previously and so they already had a reasonably positive therapy relationship. Partway through the session John had the impression that the boy was using criminal thinking errors to remain blame-free. John decided to use a variation of the spitting in the soup technique.

Client: Yeah. This whole thing is stupid. Everybody's just overreacting. It was just a big firecracker.

John: It seems to you like a big overreaction about a not-so-big deal.

Client: Right.

John: You know what, I'll bet I can guess exactly what you were thinking just before you decided to take those explosives to school.

Client: No you can't.

John: I'll bet I can.

Client: I'll bet you can't.

John: I bet you were thinking, "I won't get caught."

Client: That's crazy. How did you know?

John: (Smiling) It must be my psychic powers.

For this boy, the belief "I won't get caught" is one of several ideas related to his basic mistake of not having to take personal responsibility for his actions. His style of life went something like this: "I'm not responsible for the things I do. There's always a better explanation. Therefore, I can pretty much do what I please and get away with it because it's not my fault."

As Sweeney (2009) noted, after the spitting in the soup intervention, the client "may continue the behavior, but it won't taste as sweet any longer!" (p. 141). In this case, the boy illustrated how sometimes clients will cling tenaciously to the maladaptive beliefs associated with their style of life.

John: Well, I guess it turned out you were wrong.

Client: No I wasn't.

John: You're kidding right?

Client: No. I wasn't wrong.

John: Wait a minute, you just admitted that you were thinking to yourself, "I won't get caught" and then you took the explosives to school and then you got caught, so you were wrong.

Client: No I wasn't. I didn't get caught. Somebody must have narked on me.

At this point the client is now denying that John spit in his soup. It's like he's playing a game and he's saying, "Yeah I was thinking I won't get caught but because someone narked on me I can still say I didn't get caught now and in the future and it will be sweet because you're spitting in the wrong soup." This is one of several creative maneuvers clients can use as excuses for continuing with the same old maladaptive basic mistakes without changing their thinking or behavior. In this situation, continuing with a logical argument is likely to be ineffective and so John switches his approach to creating a new image.

John: Okay. No big deal. But it seems like the thought, "I won't get caught" could be some sort of signal for you. Like maybe it means trouble is coming. What if every time you had that thought, "I won't get caught" at the same time you saw a bunch of red or blue lights flashing. That way you might choose not to do whatever you're about to do and therefore avoid getting in any trouble.

Client: That's sort of dumb.

John: Let's try it anyway. I'll say the words and you think of flashing lights. Okay. "I won't get caught." Did you see the lights?

Client: I guess.

John: Cool. Good. Now let's try it again and try to see the blue and red lights as brightly in your mind's eye as possible. "I won't get caught."

Client: Okay.

John: Now let's try one more thing. What if you thought to yourself, right after you see those flashing lights, what if you thought, "I'm the kind of guy who makes good decisions!" Try that out. Go ahead and say it.

Client: I'm the kind of guy who makes good decisions.

John: All right. Now we'll be meeting again next week and I want to make a deal with you. I know you're into collecting baseball cards and so when you come in next week I'll ask you this question: "What kind of guy are you?" and if you can remember to say, "I'm the kind of guy who makes good decisions," then I'll give you this pack of baseball cards. Deal?

Client: Definitely. That's a deal.

In this case John tried spitting in the client's soup, but the client resisted the intervention and so John switched to creating a new image combined with a behavioral strategy for reinforcing the boy for adopting a new self-statement to replace the basic mistake of "I won't get caught." Although traditional Adlerians tend to avoid using positive reinforcement, the Adlerian approach is very flexible and mixes well with other approaches.

CASE ANALYSIS AND TREATMENT PLANNING

In this section we include excerpts of a family constellation interview H. Mosak conducted with a 17-year-old girl. This is a fabulous interview; if you get a chance, we recommend you read it in its entirety (Mosak, 1972).

In the first excerpt, Dr. Mosak asks the client, Ann, about her perceptions of her older sister, Debbie. As he gathers information, he occasionally shifts to connecting with the client through gentle interpretations:

Dr. M.: What kind of child was Debbie when you were growing up?

Ann: She was *very* studious all the time.... Well, from my point of view she was a goody-goody.... It's hard to talk about your own sister.

Dr. M.: Especially if you have to say such nice things about her.

Ann: No, she was *very* reliable and *very* responsible ... and *very* talkative.

Dr. M.: Did she get into trouble at school for that?

Ann: Occasionally.

Dr. M.: So, while she was a goody-goody, she still got into trouble occasionally. She wasn't quite perfect. What else was she like?

Ann: Well, she always tried to please my parents. And she was *very* sensitive. You know like she cried easily ... that's about all.

Dr. M.: I'm going to invite you, Ann, to look at all of this on the blackboard. If you had one word to describe your sister, what word would you use? Let me give you an incomplete sentence. She was ...

Ann: Responsible, I guess.

Dr. M.: That's a good word.

Ann: I can't do it all in one word.

Dr. M.: I can. Would you like to hear my one word?

Ann: Yes.

Dr. M.: She was *very* ... (Audience laughter) How does that sound?

Ann: Very good. (Ann and audience laughter)

As Mosak collects information, he consistently validates the client's perspective. His approach is vintage Adlerian: He's friendly, supportive, and perceptive. For example, he noticed that Ann used the word "very" four times in a short period and used it to resonate with Ann.

The Problem List

At this point it's really too soon to develop a problem list, but what's interesting is that Mosak has proceeded by asking Ann about her sister, which is an indirect way to evaluate her style of life. Asking about the sister works as an assessment tool because Ann, at least in part, has defined herself in comparison to her sister and this is a part of her style of life.

Children often compete with each other to find their own successful niches within the family value system. Each child needs to belong and be valued for his or her unique attributes. Even very young children can sense if they have a chance at being the "successful" one in the family on a particular dimension. This is why a second child who follows an academically successful sibling usually chooses to develop her own, different successful attributes (e.g., she may become the class clown). Without special encouragement, it can be too threatening to compete with an older, smarter child in the area of academic success (or athletic or musical prowess, etc.). Without parental support, the younger child has inferiority issues stimulated whenever she tries hard in the area in which the older child excels, and discouragement ensues.

A tentative initial problem list includes:

• Inferiority feelings or low self-esteem.

• A range of different maladaptive behaviors and cognitions. These can be detailed later, but they're maladaptive because they're based on Ann's conception of herself relative to her sister (who is described as "very") and not on Ann's deeper interests (this is a basic mistake). This problem might also be characterized as a weak sense of identity...from which problem behaviors flow.

Next, Dr. Mosak continues to identify Ann's unique status in the family and how it relates to her conception of herself.

Dr. M.: Who's the most industrious, and who the least?

Ann: Debbie, the most; me, the least.

Dr. M.: Who's the "goodest," and who rebelled openly?

Ann: Debbie was the "goodest," and I was the rebel.

Dr. M.: Proudly?

Ann: Yep!

Dr. M.: Who was the covert rebel, never fought openly, just did what he wanted?

Ann: Sam.

Dr. M.: Who demanded his own way, and who got it?

Ann: I demanded it, and Debbie got it.

Dr. M.: And Sam?

Ann: Sam got his way also.

Problem Formulation

Eventually, Dr. Mosak paints the picture of Ann as what he refers to as a "reverse puppet." This means that a primary basic mistake of Ann's is to inaccurately define defiance toward her parents as freedom. Due to inferiority issues, for her to exist in her family she had to be the opposite of (or different

from) her sister Debbie. Consequently, she turned into a tomboy who did poorly academically—the opposite of what her parents wanted. Of course, a reverse puppet is still a puppet, because it isn't free to do what it wants, but only the defiant thing. Ann wants her parents' acceptance and approval—she just wants it in an area where she has some measure of hope for success.

There is much more to this interview than can be included here. Dr. Mosak connects Ann's feelings of weakness and inferiority to her mother's weakness and her father's dominance. He also engages the audience to support and encourage Ann's potential new perception of her qualities of creativity and sensitivity as positive traits, rather than signs of weakness. In the end, he offers her an initial lifestyle interpretation (which, for our purposes, also works as a problem formulation).

Dr. M.: We can see, Ann, why you would not believe in yourself, growing up the way you did. I guess if I grew up in that spot, I would feel pretty much the way you feel. The question is, is it necessary now? Or do you want to stop being a "reverse puppet" and decide what *you* want to do in life? Not, "what *they* want me to do which I will not do." That's the issue you and your counselor will have to work out together. Is there anything else you would like to add, ask, or comment on?

Ann: I think you are just remarkable. I mean the way you can . . . (Audience laughter and applause)

Dr. M.: Thank you, you are very kind. Other than that . . .

Ann: I guess I didn't realize that I was the victim of, what I was suffering from, I think I can accept myself a lot easier now.

Dr. M.: You are suffering from the ignorance that you are a good, competent person. You *are* competent, you are good, but you are too busy looking at Debbie and your mother, and judging yourself negatively, instead of deciding what you want to do. (These excerpts from Mosak's interview are quoted in Sweeney, 1989, pp. 268–286.)

Interventions

In his interpretation, Mosak is compassionate, supportive, encouraging, hopeful, and direct. He is so much of these qualities that the client can easily digest the less positive interpretive feedback—that she is a reverse puppet who doesn't believe in herself—without becoming defensive.

Mosak's interpretation explicitly articulates what many psychodynamic interpretations imply: He asks the client if she wants to change her old, outdated, way of thinking about and being in the world. Mosak asks Ann, "The question is, is it necessary now? Or do you want to stop being a 'reverse puppet' and decide what *you* want to do in life?" If the timing is right, based on Adlerian theory, the client's basic motivation to strive toward excellence and completion will cause her to answer this important therapy question with, "Absolutely, yes! I want to change!" This answer—this articulation of the client's motivation—leads directly to the reorientation phase of Adlerian therapy.

Mosak's work with Ann was limited to a single consultation session. If we had access to additional therapy interactions with Ann and her IP practitioner, they would focus primarily on action, encouragement, and support. The following techniques could be applied to Ann and her situation, based on her family constellation interview.

- *Acting as if.* "During this next week, Ann, I'd like you to act 'as if' you're completely competent and good. As you practice this new way of thinking about yourself, notice the ways you feel, think, and act differently. Also, notice what activities spark your interest."

- *Spitting in the client's soup.* When the therapist notices Ann talking about her sister or mother, he or she might comment, "It seems like one of your favorite ways to avoid deciding what you want to do is to keep the spotlight on your mom and sis. When you do that you probably can't find your own direction."

- *Creating new images.* "Until now, you've had an image of your sister on a pedestal. It's like you're down below, looking up at her. Let's make a new and more useful image for you. What if you saw both you and your sister on the same level? Try to imagine it. How does it feel?"

Overall, Adlerian therapy helps clients develop more adaptive lifestyles and a variety of active techniques are used to facilitate positive change or reorientation. Adler sums up the modest nature of therapy goals for Ann or other Adlerian therapy recipients: "Our method enables us to replace the great mistakes by small ones.... Big mistakes can produce neuroses but little mistakes a nearly normal person" (Adler, 1964a, p. 62).

Outcomes Measurement

For Adlerians, assessment is integrated into the treatment process and assessment via lifestyle analysis occurs throughout therapy. As noted in Mosak's work with Ann, it's possible to obtain information regarding Ann's lifestyle while discussing her sister's childhood behaviors during a family constellation interview. However, gathering lifestyle information based on a family constellation interview is not likely to focus enough on diagnostic symptoms to an extent that meets contemporary scientific standards for outcomes research.

A primary goal of Adlerian therapy is to develop client social interest. Secondarily, Adlerians focus on the ability of clients to face and accomplish the tasks of life. Based on previous research, it appears that these counseling goals are measurable and relevant to treatment outcomes. For example, research shows that higher self-interest scores are associated with fewer psychiatric symptoms and lower diagnostic rates (Fish & Mozdzierz, 1991; Mozdzierz, Greenblatt, & Murphy, 1986; Mozdzierz, Greenblatt, & Murphy, 2007; Mozdzierz & Semyck, 1980). In addition to the Belonging scale of the BASIS-A Inventory (cited previously), the most commonly used social interest measures are listed below:

- Sulliman Social Interest Scale (Mozdzierz, Greenblatt, & Murphy, 1988; Sulliman, 1973)

- Social Interest Index (Greever, Tseng, & Friedland, 1973; K. B. Greever, Tseng, & Friedland, 1974)

- Social Interest Scale (Crandall, 1975; Crandall, 1977)

Although some life tasks are integrated into the preceding social interest scales, the ability to face and accomplish the tasks of life might be more directly measured through a broad array of scales focusing on an individual functionality. This measurement could be obtained through more general measures such as the Global Assessment of Functioning (GAF) from the *DSM* system or through any one of a wide variety of self-efficacy scales (DiIorio et al., 2001; Forcehimes & Tonigan, 2008). Due to its emphasis on the individual's belief in his or her ability to accomplish a specific task, Bandura's self-efficacy concept holds great promise for Adlerian therapists interested in monitoring their treatment outcomes (see Chapter 8 for more information on self-efficacy).

CULTURAL AND GENDER CONSIDERATIONS

Adler's IP is not value free. In particular, one value woven deep into his theory is social equality. You may have noticed as Mosak was working with Ann he was friendly and supportive of her—he sees her as a social equal. Currently, counselors and psychotherapists are more likely to use the term *social justice* when talking about this value, but the message is consistent: There should be a "fundamental valuing of each person as a social equal" (Sweeney, 2009, p. 28).

In his time, Adler was a radical feminist. Some of what he wrote continues to stand out as radical feminism. For example, he spoke directly about ways in which women's psychopathology is shaped by a prejudiced society:

It is a frequently overlooked fact that a girl comes into the world with a prejudice sounding in her ears which is designed only to rob her of her belief in her own value, to shatter her self-confidence and destroy her hope of ever doing anything worthwhile. If this prejudice is constantly strengthened, if a girl sees again and again how women are given servile roles to play, it is not hard to understand how she loses courage, fails to face her obligations, and sinks back from the solution of her life's problems. (quoted in J. B. Miller, 1973, p. 41)

He also believed strongly in the equal capabilities of women (Adler, 1958):

Boys actually do show greater talent for studies which are capable of preparing them for their masculine occupations but this is only a seemingly greater talent. If we investigate more closely we learn that the story of the lesser capability of women is a palpable fable (p. 109).

Adler's writings on social equality or egalitarianism place him as one of the first modern feminists and help make his approach very palatable to contemporary feminist thinkers and practitioners.

Adler's focus on the individual may appear to make his approach less sensitive to ethnic and cultural groups with collectivist values. However, IP focuses on the individual within a social context; it was the first traditional psychological theory to emphasize social and familial dynamics in shaping individuals. Also, Adler's clinical practice focused primarily on lower socioeconomic clients (circus performers and tailors), which likely made him sensitive to issues and struggles among the less wealthy (see Putting it in Practice 3.5 for a practitioner commentary focusing on Adlerian theory).

EVIDENCE-BASED STATUS

Adlerian concepts have been written about for nearly a century and the underlying theory has certainly lived up to Adler's hopes of creating a useful psychology: Professionals, teachers, and parents around the globe have applied IP principles within educational settings, for parent education, and for group, family, couple, and individual therapy. Even further, numerous contemporary approaches

PUTTING IT IN PRACTICE 3.5

Adlerian Theory Development

This essay was contributed by Veronica I. Johnson of Winona State University.

In graduate school, I felt immediately drawn to Adlerian theory. This attraction only solidified as I developed as a professional counselor and has continued now as a counselor educator. Adlerian theory fits with my belief system as to what causes human suffering and what promotes change. I feel these two factors are the most important components in choosing a theoretical orientation. From Carl Rogers we learn how important the counselor-client relationship is in promoting change and growth. Although Rogerian relationship principles are key, Adler goes further when he describes the concept of encouragement and how pathology develops as a result of discouragement.

My professional counseling identity is further matched with Adler's view that all humans strive for superiority or purpose in life and what we need to thrive is encourage-ment. This isn't an illness-oriented theory, but a wellness perspective—consistent with our counseling roots. Adler went beyond the relationship, emphasizing technique and purpose in his theory.

As I've learned more about Adler over the years, I'm affirmed in my belief that, as Adler would suggest, we choose counseling for a reason, often based on our own personal experiences, and those experiences shape how we see the world . . . and the theory that we choose to practice from and live our lives by. Our families are our first communities and we strive to belong to something. From our families we learn about ourselves and the world and we transfer that knowledge to our adult relationships and to our communities.

My passion is in working with couples and fostering healthy relationship skills and attitudes in young adults. I use Adlerian theory to describe how we develop our worldview and how this contributes to our behavior in romantic relationships. I love to see that "Aha!" look in client's faces when they develop insight as to how they came to think a certain way about their significant other, or why they behave the way they do in their relationships. Adler provides us with an explanation of human nature—thoughts, feelings, and actions—that just makes good sense.

Adler also helps me to be optimistic in my view of humanity. I'm optimistic to begin with, but working in the mental health field, it's easy to become less hopeful about clients' prognoses. I've worked with sexual abuse survivors, adolescents diagnosed with severe emotional disturbance, and adults with severe and persistent mental illness. Adlerian theory has given me a strong foundation from which to understand the human experience, communicate and connect with clients, and work effectively towards change. As long as I believe in the creativity of the human spirit, the ability to overcome obstacles with encouragement, and the power of striving with purpose, I remain hopeful that any client can change and grow. I acknowledge the uniqueness of all clients and identify what strengths they already possess that can aid in their current functioning. Adler also introduced humor to the counselor-client relationship, which I believe is very important. Adler was human with his clients, not simply a mirror or an objective bystander.

I love Adler's forward thinking. I wish that current and future theories gave more credit to how much Adler contributed to the human services field. There are glimpses of Adler in Cognitive-Behavioral theory, Choice theory, Existentialism, Constructive theories, and Feminist theory, just to name a few. As psychotherapy continues to move towards an integrative model of helping, Adlerian theory represents the epitome of integration. It's one of the most comprehensive, holistic, wellness-oriented theories I've encountered. This theory works with various populations. I've yet to find its flaws in working with couples, families, individuals, and diverse cultural groups. Because of its emphasis on uniqueness, it is flexible and malleable to most client situations. I use Adlerian theory to make sense out of situations that I confront in my own life; I use it to relate to and understand students; I use it in supervision; I use it with clients. I continue to be fascinated by and in admiration of Alfred Adler—his strength, courage, and foresight. I will continue to credit him in the courses I teach as one of the great contributors to what we know about human nature.

to therapy borrow extensively from IP, including cognitive-behavioral, solution-focused, existential therapy, and reality therapy.

Despite the prominent use of Adler's concepts, direct empirical research attesting to the efficacy of Adlerian therapy is sparse. Perhaps the greatest reason for this is the fact that Adler found nomothetic research that compares group outcomes to be relatively useless. Consequently, the Adlerian focus has been and primarily continues to be idiographic case studies.

Early research reviews, based on only four empirical studies of Adlerian psychotherapy, indicate that the procedures are slightly more effective than placebo treatment and have efficacy similar to psychoanalytic and person-centered therapy (Smith et al., 1980).

A number of studies have been conducted on Adlerian concepts (e.g., birth order) and the efficacy of techniques or approaches related to Adlerian theory and therapy.

Of Adler's theoretical concepts, birth order and social interest have obtained the greatest research attention. Based on a wide range of studies, the relationship of birth order to specific personality traits has been mixed and complex (Pollet, Dijkstra, Barelds, & Buunk, 2010; Sulloway & Zweigenhaft, 2010).

Social interest has been linked to a number of other psychological concepts and perspectives. For example, G. K. Leak and K. C. Leak (2006) reported a positive correlation between positive psychology and social interest and G. K. Leak (2006) found a similar positive relationship between social interest and spirituality. As Adlerians would hypothesize, higher social interest is associated with fewer psychiatric symptoms and an increased sense of well-being (Fish & Mozdzierz, 1991; Mozdzierz & Semyck, 1980; Mozdzierz et al., 2007).

Not surprisingly, the concepts of social interest and encouragement have found their way into a wide range of school-based curricula. Specifically,

Ready to Learn, a prekindergarten through first grade program based shows promising empirical support (Villares, Brigman, & Peluso, 2008) as well as a research-based school counselor intervention program titled *Student Success Skills* (Webb, Lemberger, & Brigman, 2008). Additionally, there are a few research studies attesting to the effectiveness of parenting programs based on Adlerian principles (e.g., Systematic Training for Effective Parenting [STEP]; Gfroerer et al., 2004; Spence, 2009).

Overall, although many therapy practitioners use Adlerian approaches, there remains little research to support Adlerian therapy efficacy. Despite the Adlerian theoretical aversion to group efficacy studies, if this approach is to remain a viable and popular option among practitioners, additional empirical research support is recommended.

CONCLUDING COMMENTS

In the end, there's little debate about the significance of Adler's contribution as a person, theorist, and practitioner to the fields of counseling and psychotherapy. Even Albert Ellis, not typically one to lavish praise on anyone, wrote a tribute to Alfred Adler, in which he referred to him as the "true father of modern psychotherapy" (Ellis, 1970, p. 11). Similarly, Ellenberger (1970) wrote, "It would not be easy to find another author from which so much has been borrowed from all sides without acknowledgement, than Adler" (p. 645).

Indeed, you will find that Adlerian psychology is everywhere. Sometimes he is cited; other times he is not. One possible explanation for Adler's omnipresence in modern counseling and psychotherapy is that he employed a psychology of common sense. And so it has been only a matter of time until the rest of the field began catching up with him.

Adler's writings are a treasure of quotations. We leave you with two of our favorites:

"An incalculable amount of tension and useless effort would be spared in this world if we realized that cooperation and love can never be won by force." (Adler, 1931, p. 132).

"Everything is a matter of opinion" (Adler, 1983, p. 1).

CHAPTER SUMMARY

Alfred Adler, the developer of individual psychology (IP) was a man ahead of his time. Having established himself and published a book before joining Freud's inner circle, he was an independent thinker who broke from Freud and eventually developed a comprehensive and practical psychology that remains highly influential today.

IP includes many theoretical concepts. It views individuals as whole persons who strive for purpose and superiority. It also emphasizes social interest over self-interest as a healthy counseling goal. Individuals are viewed as unique, behavior is determined by multiple factors, and people develop an internal cognitive map or "style of life" for how to accomplish tasks of life. These tasks include: (a) work or occupation; (b) social relationships; (c) love and marriage; (d) self; (e) spirituality; and (f) parenting and family.

Adlerian theory and therapy de-emphasizes psychopathology. Individuals who seek (or need) counseling are viewed as discouraged or as lacking the courage to directly face the challenges of the tasks of life.

Adlerian therapy is practiced in four overlapping stages. These include: (1) forming a friendly and egalitarian therapy relationship; (2) obtaining information leading to a comprehensive lifestyle (or style of life) assessment and analysis; (3) using collaborative interpretation to help clients achieve insight into their style of life; and (4) reorientation or a changing of one's style of life to better meet the tasks of life.

Adler was especially far ahead of his time in terms of his views on women and on egalitarian relationships. He viewed women as capable, but as oppressed by a male-dominated society. He also viewed individuals within a relational and social context. This makes his approach to therapy sensitive to culture and gender issues.

Although principles of IP are used in schools, parenting, and individual, couple, group, and family counseling, there's little systematic empirical research supporting its efficacy. There are several studies supporting its application in these various domains, but additional research is needed to demonstrate its efficacy.

In the end, Adler's IP theory remains immensely practical. His principles and techniques for working with people have been integrated into many different contemporary therapy approaches.

INDIVIDUAL PSYCHOLOGY KEY TERMS

Acting as if

Adlerian therapy

Basic mistakes

Birth order

Catching oneself

Community feeling

Creating new images

Discouragement

Early recollections

Encouragement

Family constellation interview

Fictional finalism

Forming the therapeutic relationship

Four goals of misbehavior

Four stages [of Adlerian therapy]

Future autobiography

Gemeinschaftsgefuhl

Goal alignment

Guiding self-ideal

Holism

I'll Betcha

Idiographic approach

Individual psychology

Individuum

Inferiority complexes

Inferiority feelings

Interpretation and insight

Lifestyle (aka style of life)

Lifestyle assessment

Objective inferiority

Offering advice, suggestions, and direction

Paradoxical strategies

Penis envy

Phenomenology

Push-button technique

Reflecting as if

Reorientation

Self-interest

Social interest

Soft determinism

Spitting in the client's soup

Striving for superiority

Task setting and indirect suggestion

Tasks of life

The masculine protest

The question

RECOMMENDED READINGS AND RESOURCES

The following resources provide additional information on Adler and Adlerian therapy.

ADLERIAN (INDIVIDUAL PSYCHOLOGY) JOURNALS

Journal of Individual Psychology
The Quarterly: Publication of the Adlerian Psychology Association of British Columbia

Individual Psychology: Journal of Adlerian Theory, Research & Practice
International Journal of Individual Psychology

READINGS ON ADLERIAN THEORY AND THERAPY

Adler, A. (1927). *Understanding human nature*. Garden City, NY: Garden City.

Adler, A. (1958). *What life should mean to you*. New York, NY: Capricorn.

Ansbacher, H. L., & Ansbacher, R. (Eds.). (1956). *The individual psychology of Alfred Adler*. New York, NY: Basic Books.

Bottome, P. (1939). *Alfred Adler, apostle of freedom*. London, England: Faber and Faber.

Carlson, J., Watts, R. E., & Maniacci, M. (2006). *Adlerian therapy: Theory and practice*. Washington, DC: American Psychological Association.

Clark, A. J. (2002). *Early recollections: Theory and practice in counseling and psychotherapy*. New York, NY: Brunner-Routledge.

Dreikurs, R. (1948). *The challenge of parenthood*. Oxford, England: Duell, Sloan & Pearce.

Mosak, H. H. (1985). Interrupting a depression: The pushbutton technique. *Individual Psychology*, *41*, 210–214.

Mosak, H. H., & Maniacci, M. P. (1999). *A primer of Adlerian psychology: The analytic-behavioral-cognitive psychology of Alfred Adler*. Philadelphia, PA: Taylor & Francis.

Sommers-Flanagan, J., & Sommers-Flanagan, R. (2001). The three-step emotional change trick. In H. G. Kaduson & C. E. Schaefer (Eds.), *101 more favorite play therapy techniques* (pp. 439–444). New York, NY: Jason Aronson.

Sweeney, T. J. (2009). *Adlerian counseling and psychotherapy: A practitioner's approach* (5th ed.). New York, NY: Routledge/Taylor & Francis.

Vaihinger, H. (1911). *The psychology of "as if."* New York, NY: Harcourt, Brace and World.

Watts, R. E. (Ed.). (2003). *Adlerian, cognitive, and constructivist therapies: An integrative perspective*. New York, NY: Springer.

TRAINING ORGANIZATIONS AND WEBSITES

Extensive information about Alfred Adler and the practice of individual psychology can be obtained from the following websites and training institutes.

Adler School of Professional Psychology (ASPP; www.adler.edu)

Alfred Adler Institute of New York (http://www.aai-ny.org/home.aspx)

Alfred Adler Institute of San Francisco and Northwest Washington (pws.cablespeed.com/~htstein/)

Center for Adlerian Studies (www.centroadleriano.org/links.html)

North American Society of Adlerian Psychology (NASAP; www.alfredadler.org)

The International Committee for Adlerian Summer Schools and Institutes (ICASSI; www.icassi.net/)

VIDEOS/DVDs

Carlson, J. (2005). *Adlerian therapy with Jon Carlson* [Video]. Washington, DC: American Psychological Association.

Carlson, J. (2006). *Adlerian therapy over time* [Video]. Washington, DC: American Psychological Association.

Carlson, J., & Kjos, D. (2000). *Adlerian therapy with Dr. Jon Carlson* [Video]. Boston, MA: Allyn & Bacon.

Sweeney, T. J. (2000). *Adlerian early recollections: Live demonstration including DCT assessment.* North Amherst, MA: Microtraining Associates.

GOING FARTHER AND DEEPER

Additional Adlerian counseling and psychotherapy resources are available at johnsommersflanagan.com.

CHAPTER 4

Existential Theory and Therapy

THIS CHAPTER

- Reviews the key figures and contextual historical factors associated with the development and evolution of existential theory and therapy
- Outlines and describes core theoretical principles of existential counseling and psychotherapy
- Describes and discusses principles and techniques associated with existential therapy practice including,
  - Formation of an I-Thou therapeutic relationship
  - Existential therapy strategies and techniques
  - Existential integration
- Offers two unique existential therapy vignettes that demonstrate existential strategies in action
- Illustrates how treatment planning, outcomes assessment, and gender and cultural issues can be integrated into an existential therapy approach
- Reviews the empirical status of existential therapy approaches
- Offers resources for further study

Get ready to get philosophical. This chapter is about life's big issues and concerns. Together, we explore meaning, death, responsibility, and more. Although some therapy approaches are more in line with the great American quick fix, existentialists are uninterested in and unimpressed by gimmicks and techniques (Schneider, Galvin, & Serlin, 2009). For existentialists, a narrowly defined psychotherapy administered as a technical procedure to be prescribed and applied to clients is viewed as an unhealthy manifestation of a deteriorating society. To capture the creative, non-linear, and meaning-focused nature of existential therapy, we begin with a quotation from Viktor Frankl (1969):

> [A]ctually, I have been told in Australia, a boo-merang only comes back to the hunter when it has missed its target, the prey. Well, man also only

returns to himself, to being concerned with his self, after he has missed his mission, has failed to find meaning in life. (p. 9)

Some forms of counseling and psychotherapy, such as Freud's psychoanalysis, evolved primarily from medical practice with disturbed patients. Others, such as behavior therapy, arose from experimental psychological research. Still others, such as person-centered therapy (Chapter 5) and individual psychology (Chapter 3), have roots in clinical practice, humanistic-existential philosophy, and, to some degree, psychotherapy research. In contrast, existential approaches to counseling and psychotherapy are directly and deeply linked to **existential philosophy**. This philosophical perspective focuses primarily on the inevitable conditions humans face during life, such as death, responsibility, freedom, and purpose. Existentialists typically eschew scientific research because of its inauthentic artificiality. Additionally, although they practice therapy with individuals, couples, families, and groups, their approach is systematically guided by philosophical perspectives, rather than knowledge obtained from therapeutic practice. As Irvin Yalom, a renowned existential therapist, has stated, "I have always felt that the term 'existential therapy' reflects not a discrete, comprehensive body of techniques, but, instead, a posture, a sensibility in the therapist" (Serlin, 1999, p. 143).

KEY FIGURES AND HISTORICAL CONTEXT

The roots of existential philosophical thought are diverse. There's no single philosopher from whom all existential thinking flows. Most texts point to nineteenth-century philosophers Soren Kierkegaard and Friedrich Nietzsche as major players in the formulation of existentialism, and, in fact, Kierkegaard and Nietzsche do capture and embody certain dimensions of the diversity of thinking inherent in existentialism.

Soren Kierkegaard

The Danish philosopher Soren Kierkegaard (1813–1855) lived nearly his entire life in Copenhagen. Kierkegaard was devoutly religious. He was powerfully shaken when he discovered, at age 22, that his father had not only cursed God, but also seduced his mother prior to marriage. Subsequently, Kierkegaard's writings focused primarily on religious faith and the meaning of Christianity. Eventually he concluded that religious faith was irrational and attainable only via a subjective experiential "leap of faith." For Kierkegaard, virtuous traits such as responsibility, honesty, and commitment are subjective choices—often in response to a subjective religious conversion. Kierkegaard did not describe himself as an existentialist, but his work is seen as precursor to the existential philosophical movement, which formally began some 70 years following his death.

Friedrich Nietzsche

In contrast to Kierkegaard who began from a position of firm religious faith, the German philosopher Friedrich Nietzsche (1844–1900) had strongly negative feelings toward Christianity. It was he who, in his book *Thus Spake Zarathustra*, stated "God is dead." Although he may have been referring to a societal emptiness, he also claimed that religion used fear and resentment to pressure individuals into moral behavior. Instead of following a religion, he believed, individuals should channel their passions into creative, joyful activities. Irvin Yalom offers a fascinating view of Nietzsche's psychological suffering in a historical fiction piece titled *When Nietzsche Wept*. In this novel, Yalom (1992) weaves existential principles into a fictional therapeutic encounter between Breuer, Freud, and Nietzsche.

Kierkegaard and Nietzsche represent an interesting paradox or **dialectic** in existential thinking. A dialectic involves a process where learning is stimulated from the integration of opposites. On the one hand, some existentialists profess extreme and devout religious faith, whereas others are staunchly atheistic. Still others claim a more agnostic middle ground. These differences in fundamental human beliefs are representative of the wide sweep of human intellectual diversity and provide fodder for some serious and fascinating philosophical explorations.

A Little Etymology

The etymological origin of **philosophy** is from the Greek "Philos" (meaning loving) and "Sophos" (meaning wisdom) and so the literal translation is "loving wisdom." In contrast, psychology comes from the Greek *psukh*, which started out meaning *breath* and eventually developed semantically into "soul, spirit" and "mind." Modern psychology is typically defined as the science of the mind or mental states and processes, although modern behavioral scientists would likely insist on the introductory textbook definition of "the science of behavior."

We provide this detour into etymology to activate your intellectual enthusiasm. Try thinking of existential psychology as a crossroads between loving wisdom and the science of behavior. Put another way, as you read this chapter let the data feed your soul.

Learning From Dialectics

It may be that polarized positions (or dialectics) regarding religion and other issues within existential philosophy and psychology are predestined. After all, as Fritz Perls emphasized in his existentially based Gestalt approach to treatment, humans seem hard-wired to take on polarizing positions. He stated: "every psychological phenomenon . . . [is] experienced as a polarity" (F. Perls, 1969a, p. 3).

Hegel believed human reasoning and ideas evolve through a **dialectical process**. Essentially, what happens is (a) a concept or idea is developed, which then, (b) fuels the generation of the opposite idea, which produces conflict between the ideas. It is through this conflict of polarized ideas that a new, synthesized, and higher level of truth can be developed.

Hegel's dialectic is relevant to counseling and psychotherapy. In fact, one of the most popular new approaches to therapy, dialectical behavior therapy (M. Linehan, 1993), involves, in part, a direct application of Hegel's dialectic. Specifically, DBT practitioners adopt the following dialectical position of radical acceptance when working with clients: "I accept you as you are and I am helping you to change" (J. Sommers-Flanagan & R. Sommers-Flanagan, 2007a).

The ongoing struggle between polarized factions within the individual can be seen as a primary pathway toward deeper understanding of the true nature of the self. This seems an appropriate outcome of the existential struggle because, for most existential practitioners, regardless of religious orientation, the overarching goal of therapy is to help the client discover and explore the authentic self.

Then again, as we consider the big questions, even the existence of the self is in doubt. For example, some multicultural and post-modern worldviews not only question the utility of thinking about an authentic self—they question its existence.

Hoffman and colleagues (Hoffman, Stewart, Warren, & Meek, 2009) describe this "crisis of the self":

> The influence of Eastern thought, particularly Buddhist philosophy, introduced recognition of no-self as an ideal (Mosig, 2006). Cultural analyses provided examples of cultures which did not have a traditional conception of self, but rather understood what is referred to as the self in Western thought in terms of roles which are much more fluid over time. . . . In the end, the necessity of a self conception, so basic to Western psychology, is now in question. (p. 136)

And so if we keep in mind the following:

- Humans naturally create polarities.
- These polarities generate conflict.
- Through this conflict there is a potential (it's not automatic) for synthesis and intellectual development.
- Some traditional theorists emphasize the centrality of the self, while postmodern and culturally diverse perspectives deemphasize the self.
- We learn from both perspectives—self as central and no-self as ideal—and develop a more wise and balanced view of self.
- This process links directly—albeit with complexity—to existential practice.

Of course, philosophy doesn't stop with Kierkegaard, Nietzsche, and Hegel; philosophy never stops. In particular, Pascal, Husserl, Vaihinger, Sartre, Heidegger, Jaspers, and Marcel were instrumental in popularizing and developing existential perspectives.

One final historical footnote before moving forward: Some writers speculate that the Zeitgeist or context of the 1940s was ripe for existentialism, especially European existentialism. This is because the devastation of World War I, followed by further global conflict in World War II, including ethnic cleansing of Jewish people in and around Germany, stimulated an introspective process focusing on death, personal responsibility, freedom, love, and other related existential topics.

Jean-Paul Sartre: The Existentialist Prototype

Existentialism is perhaps most aptly and succinctly articulated by French philosopher Jean-Paul Sartre, who claimed, with bold certainty, "Freedom is existence, and in its existence precedes essence" and "Man's essence is his existence" (Sartre, 1953, p. 5).

If you're not sure what Sartre's assertions mean, you're likely not alone. Existential philosophy is sometimes so utterly abstract that it's difficult to distill practical implications from philosophical statements. Grasping meaning from existential philosophy is especially challenging for practicing therapists and students of counseling and psychotherapy who are usually looking for concrete advice about exactly how to behave during a therapy session. We have only this minor reassurance for you as you embark on this chapter: In many ways, the entire purpose of existential philosophy is to struggle with individual, personal meaning. Therefore, as you grope and flail for meaning within the philosophy that embodies this chapter, you will also be experiencing existential psychology.

Rollo May (1962) explains Sartre's statement *Freedom is existence, and in its existence precedes essence*: "That is to say, there would be no *essences*—no truth, no structure in reality, no logical forms, no *logos*, no God nor any morality—except as man in affirming his freedom makes these truths" (pp. 5–6).

Sartre's philosophical proposition is that there are no absolute or essential truths (essences), but that we as individual human beings create our own truth and reality. His statement articulates the pure existential position. Once again, you may recognize that Adler's (Chapter 3) and Vaihinger's (1911) concepts of lifestyle and technique of acting as if, as well as his earlier ideas about fictional finalism are consistent with this proposition; each individual constructs his or her reality.

Paul Tillich discusses Sartre's second statement, "Man's essence is his existence."

> There are, however, only rare moments . . .
> in which an almost pure existentialism has
> been reached. An example is Sartre's doctrine
> of man. I refer to a sentence in which the whole

problem of essentialism and existentialism comes into the open, his famous statement that man's essence is his existence. The meaning of this sentence is that man is a being of whom no essence can be affirmed, for such an essence would introduce a permanent element, contradictory to man's power of transforming himself indefinitely. According to Sartre, man is what he acts to be. (Tillich, 1961, p. 9)

This description speaks to a key proposition of pure existential theory. That is, humans contain no permanent elements. This concept is further articulated in a popular phrase in the contemporary media, "to reinvent oneself." If you "reinvent yourself" (or even talk or think about anyone reinventing himself or herself), you're using the existentially based concepts of impermanence and emergence. For existentialists, transformation is within reach.

Following these lines of thought, existentialism strongly emphasizes personal choice, personal consciousness, and personal responsibility. If humans construct their own reality and are continuously capable of self-reinvention, then all behavior is owned by the individual. Sartre lays claim to the reality of human responsibility succinctly when he states: "I am my choices" (Sartre, 1953, p. 5).

Existentialism is, at its core, antideterministic. If you suggest to existentialists that human behavior is determined by particular factors, events, or mental processes, they're likely to roll their eyes. This is because existentialists reject the proposition that humans are enslaved by Freudian unconscious, instinctual drives, and they reject environmental stimulus-response determinants as well. In place of instinctual and environmental causes of behavior, existentialists posit individual choice and human freedom. The past does not and cannot determine the future. Our particular choices in this moment determine the now, and our choices in the next moment determine that moment.

But what, from a purely existential perspective, determines our daily, moment-to-moment choices? For Sartre, the answer is this: Human reality "identifies and defines itself by the ends which it pursues" (Sartre, 1953, p. 19). Of course, this theme should sound familiar because, once again, it resonates with Adler's ideas about purposeful, goal-oriented behavior and the style of life. The following quotation from Yalom's discussion of Frankl's existential perspective further clarifies this common theme:

> The difference is between drive and strive. In our most essential being, in those characteristics that make us human rather than animal, we are not driven but instead actively strive for some goal.... "Striving" conveys a future orientation: we are pulled by what is to be, rather than pushed by relentless forces of past and present. (Yalom, 1980, p. 445)

Although existentialists believe in the unconscious, their particular unconscious is not in the Freudian tradition. As Yalom talks about being *pulled by what is to be*, we cannot help but move forward toward an understanding of how existential philosophy was transformed into existential therapy.

Viktor Frankl and the Statue of Responsibility

Viktor Frankl

Viktor Frankl was the leading existentialist in Europe during his time. He was born to a Jewish family in Vienna and studied medicine at the University of Vienna before marrying Tilly Grosser in 1941. He, Tilly, and his parents were deported to a concentration camp less than a year later. Initially, Frankl worked as a physician and then as a psychiatrist in the concentration camp, with a focus on suicide prevention, sometimes delivering lectures to imaginary audiences. On October 19, 1944, his plight became even more bleak as he was transported to Auschwitz and then to a Nazi concentration camp affiliated with Dachau. While in these camps his father died and his wife and mother were murdered. In April 1945 Frankl was liberated from Dachau. He later married Eleonore Katharina Schwindt, a practicing Catholic and they continued honoring each other's religious beliefs by attending both the Catholic church and the Jewish synagogue while celebrating both Hanukah and Christmas (Redsand, 2007).

Frankl is author of the most widely read existential work of all time, *Man's Search for Meaning* (V. Frankl, 1963). This book, originally published as *trotzdem Ja zum Leben Sagen: Ein Psychologe erlebt das Konzentrationslager* (*Saying Yes to Life in Spite of Everything: A Psychologist Experiences the Concentration Camp*; 1946) and later as *From Death-Camp to Existentialism* (V. E. Frankl, 1959), describes Frankl's concentration camp experiences and outlines his particular therapeutic approach, **logotherapy**.

Frankl's logotherapy is centered around helping clients find meaning. He frequently quoted Nietzsche, stating: "He who has a why to live can bear with almost any how" (Frankl, 1963, p. 121). This perspective is distinctly different than Freud and Adler. Frankl (1963) wrote:

> The striving to find a meaning in one's life is the primary motivational force in man. That is why I speak of a will to meaning in contrast to the pleasure principle (or, as we could also term it, the will to pleasure) on which Freudian psychoanalysis is centered, as well as in contrast to the will to power stressed by Adlerian psychology. (1963, p. 121)

Although he was a strong proponent of freedom, Frankl believed freedom could and would degenerate without an equal valuing of personal responsibility. He recommended that a statue of responsibility be erected on the West Coast of the United States to balance the Statue of Liberty on the East Coast (Frankl, 1963). In fact, a prototype for the statue of responsibility has been developed and the non-profit Statue of Responsibility Foundation is soliciting funds for the project.

Rollo May: From Existential Theory to Existential Practice

Rollo May

Most historians credit Rollo May with formally introducing and integrating existential thought into American counseling and psychotherapy (R. May, Angel, & Ellenberger, 1958). After obtaining his bachelor's degree in English from Oberlin College in Ohio, May was a missionary teacher in Greece for 3 years in the early 1930s. During that time he traveled to Vienna in the summer, where he happened to take some seminars from Alfred Adler. In a 1987 interview, May described his experiences of taking a psychology course in college and then learning from Adler:

> Well, in college, I took one course in psychology and [although] I didn't learn much about human beings . . . I did learn a lot about pigeons and dogs. So I dropped the whole thing and majored in English literature.
>
> So the next summer, I went up to Alfred Adler's seminar in Vienna and there I learned what psychotherapy can really be. It changed me very deeply. It opened up a great deal of new possibilities in my life. (p. 425)

Following his time in Greece and Europe, May returned to the United States, where he obtained a bachelor's degree in divinity, working with and befriending the existential theologian Paul Tillich at Union Theological Seminary in New York.

May gave up the life of a pastor at a New Jersey church to study clinical psychology at Columbia University. Shortly thereafter he fell ill with tuberculosis and was on the brink of death, which forced him into 18 months of treatment in a sanitarium. Eventually May returned to Columbia, where he was granted a doctoral degree in clinical psychology in 1949 (DeCarvalho, 1996). His dissertation, *The Meaning of Anxiety* (1977), argued that anxiety

was an essential component of the human condition. Some of May's major works include *Man's Search for Himself* (1953), *Love and Will* (1969), *The Courage to Create* (1975), and *Freedom and Destiny* (1981). His edited volume, *Existence: A New Dimension in Psychiatry and Psychology* (May, Angel, & Ellenberger, 1958) was most instrumental in bringing existential thinking into the mainstream in the United States.

Although May was integral to bringing existential philosophy into psychological practice in the United States, he had predecessors in Europe. For example, nearly a decade before he began studying with Adler in the early 1930s, another early existential practitioner, young Viktor Frankl, had joined Adler's inner circle (in 1926). Gould writes,

> Frankl agreed with Adler's viewpoint. Adler saw a person's freedom of choice as central . . . and . . . freedom of choice became the starting point for the development of Frankl's own theories. (Gould, 1993, p. 4)

Overall, the presence of existential thought within modern therapeutic practice can be traced back at least to Alfred Adler, who had significant influence on both May and Frankl, both of whom initially popularized existential psychotherapy. Other, more recent major figures in existential psychotherapy and some of their key publications include:

- James Bugental (1915–2008): *The Search for Authenticity* (1965); *The Art of Psychotherapy* (1987); *Psychotherapy Isn't What You Think: Bringing the Psychotherapeutic Engagement into the Living Moment* (1999).

- Irvin Yalom (1931–): *Existential Psychotherapy* (1980); *Love's Executioner* (1989); *Momma and the Meaning of Life* (1999); *The Gift of Therapy: An open Letter to a New Generation of Therapists and their Patients* (2002); *Theory and Practice of Group Psychotherapy* (Yalom & Leszcz, 2005).

- Emmy van Deurzen (1951–): *Everyday Mysteries: Existential dimensions of Psychotherapy* (1997); *Paradox and Passion in Psychotherapy* (1998); *Existential*

Counseling and Psychotherapy in Practice (1988); *Psychotherapy and the Quest for Happiness* (2009).

- Kirk Schneider (1953–): *The Psychology of Existence: An Integrative, Clinical Perspective* (Schneider & May, 1995); *Rediscovery of Awe: Splendor, Mystery, and the Fluid Center of Life* (Schneider, 2004); *Existential-Integrative Psychotherapy: Guideposts to the Core of Practice* (2008); *Existential–humanistic therapy* (Schneider & Krug, 2010).

THEORETICAL PRINCIPLES

As noted previously, there's no single theorist or theory of existential psychotherapy. Consequently, although we focus on key existential philosophical and phenomenological principles, other existential writers and theorists may emphasize principles slightly different from the following.

The I-Am Experience

The **I-am experience** is the experience of being, of existing (R. May et al., 1958). The experience of being is often referred to as **ontological experience** (*ontos* means "to be" and *logical* means "the science of"). Literally, then, a major focus of existential therapy consists of exploring immediate individual human experience. You might think of it as suddenly waking up and being completely tuned into what it's like to be alive, to exist, to be here right now in this particular moment in time.

Existentialists like to use hyphens to capture the interconnectedness of phenomenological experience. For example, in contrast to May's I-am experience, Boss (1963) and Binswanger (1933) used Dasein (which is translated to being-in-the-world) to describe the sense-of-existence. Also, the phrase, "Dasein choosing," which is translated to the-person-who-is-responsible-for-his-existence choosing is used. We should note that this practice is in no way related to our own hyphenated last names, although it has inspired John to consider adding a hyphenated middle name so he can refer to himself in the third person as, "John-who-is-

responsible-for-his-existence-Sommers-Flanagan," which he thinks sort of rolls right off the tongue.

It follows, as-if-anything-really-follows-from-the-preceding, that existential therapy is almost always in the service of self-awareness or self-discovery. However, unlike psychoanalysts, existentialists seek to expand client self-awareness rather than interpreting client unconscious processes. This is because existentialists believe the entirety of an individual's human experience is accessible to consciousness. It's not so much a matter of uncovering an elusive unconscious as it is a matter of elucidating the conscious and deepening the relational.

Four Existential Ways of Being

There are four primary existential ways of being-in-the-world. They include:

1. *Umwelt*: Being-with-nature or the physical world.
2. *Mitwelt*: Being-with-others or the social world.
3. *Eigenwelt*: Being-with-oneself or the world of the self.
4. *Uberwelt*: Being-with-the-spiritual or over world.

The first three of these existential ways of being were described by Boss (1963), Binswanger (1963), and May et al. (1958). The fourth way of being was added by van Deurzen (1988).

These four dimensions of existence are ubiquitous and simultaneous. Some people focus more on one dimension than others or shift from one to another depending on particular intentions or situations. For example, while on a mountain hike up the Stillwater gorge in Montana, it's difficult not to become profoundly into being-with-nature as water powerfully cascades around you, making all conversation (being with others) impossible. However, depending on other factors, this experience can take people inward toward eigenwelt, toward an uberwelt spiritual experience, or stimulate a deep mitwelt (albeit a nonverbal one). In most cases the direction your being moves in a given situation is likely a combination of several factors, including anxiety, previous experiences, intention, and many other factors we discuss next.

The Daimonic

According to Rollo May, "The daimonic is any natural function which has the power to take over the whole person" (1969, p. 123, italics in original). *Daimon possession* has historically been used to explain psychotic episodes and is popularly referred to as *demonic possession*. However, May repeatedly emphasizes that daimonic and demonic are not the same concept, as in this response to criticism from Carl Rogers: "I never use the word demonic, except to say that this is not what I mean" (May, 1982, p. 11).

The **daimonic** includes both positive and negative potential. Similar to Jung's more general conception of libido, it's a form of psychic energy or an *urge* that's the source of both constructive and destructive impulses. May describes the daimonic in greater detail: "The daimonic is the urge in every being to affirm itself, assert itself, perpetuate and increase itself.... [The reverse side] of the same affirmation is what empowers our creativity" (May, 1969, p. 123).

Again, just as Jung emphasized the integration of the shadow archetype, May considers the harnessing and integration of the daimonic to be a central task in psychotherapy. He views psychotherapy as an activity that plumbs the depths of an individual's most basic impulses in an effort to acknowledge, embrace, and integrate every bit of being and energy into the whole person. May commented specifically about the need to integrate the daimonic and the danger of leaving it unintegrated:

> If the daimonic urge is integrated into the personality (which is, to my mind, the purpose of psychotherapy) it results in creativity, that is, it is constructive. If the daimonic is not integrated, it can take over the total personality, as it does in violent rage or collective paranoia in time of war or compulsive sex or oppressive behavior. Destructive activity is then the result. (May, 1982, p. 11)

The goal then is to integrate the biological and natural daimonic urges in ways that maximize constructive and creative behavior. May (Schneider et al., 2009) discussed this in the context of what's important in therapy:

> A therapy that is important, as I see it, is a therapy that enlarges a person, makes the unconscious conscious. Enlarges our view, enlarges our experience, makes us more sensitive, enlarges our intellectual capacities as well as other capacities. (p. 420)

The Nature of Anxiety

Existential philosophy generally views anxiety as leading to authenticity and freedom (Wulfing, 2008). Following this tradition, R. May (1953) was perhaps the first modern mental health professional in the United States to conceptualize anxiety as a good thing. He emphasized that it was a normal and essential by-product of human existence. His formulation of anxiety encourages us to embrace it as a part of our experience. We should explore it, experience it, engage it, and redirect it into constructive activities—and we should definitely not seek to avoid it.

The existential perspective identifies two types of anxiety: **normal anxiety** and **neurotic anxiety**. Normal anxiety is directly proportional to the situation. It is a meaningful message within our awareness (not requiring repression or other defensive processes) and can be used creatively. In contrast, neurotic anxiety is disproportionate to the situation; it is usually repressed, denied, or otherwise avoided, and is not used for creative or constructive purposes. Instead, it is destructive.

For example, as you read this chapter, you may simultaneously be aware of mounting anxiety over time pressures in your life. Perhaps you need to finish reading this chapter and study for an exam in your theories class. You also need to finish writing a proposal for a research class. At the same time, you're thinking about how you should get the oil changed in your car before your weekend road trip. In addition, you haven't found anyone to take care of your dog while you're away for the weekend. The pressure is rising.

If, in response to your pressure-packed situation, you respond by functioning creatively and efficiently, you're experiencing normal anxiety. Perhaps you decide to write your research proposal on an existential topic and hire your nephew to stay at your apartment and take care of your dog. You study as efficiently as you possibly can, and then get your oil changed on the way out of town. In the end, you heave a sigh of relief. You've faced your anxiety and dealt with the situation effectively.

In contrast, if you experience neurotic anxiety, you avoid facing your anxiety-provoking situation by going out and partying with your friends, blowing off your theories exam, writing up a minimal research proposal, and taking your misbehaving dog with you on the road in your car without rechecking the oil. The three key differences are (1) you deny the importance of your life demands, (2) you respond or react to the situation out of desperation, rather than responding proactively and with creativity, and (3) you end up increasing your chances of having difficulties down the road (literally) because you haven't responsibly maintained yourself (or your vehicle).

As the preceding example implies, existential treatment is not about doing away with normal anxiety; instead, the goal is to reduce neurotic anxiety. This is accomplished by helping clients live with and cope effectively and creatively with the normal anxiety that accompanies existence.

Normal and Neurotic Guilt

Guilt, like anxiety, has both positive and negative qualities. It may seem a bit odd, but guilt is good—**normal guilt**, that is. Guilt inspires people to act in thoughtful and conscientious ways. Normal guilt is like a sensor: When functioning well, it alerts us to what's ethically correct and guides us toward morally acceptable behavior.

Psychopathology arises, not from the human experience of normal guilt, but from **neurotic guilt**. Neurotic guilt usually consists of a twisted, exaggerated, or minimized version of normal guilt. For example, when a victim of domestic abuse feels guilty for provoking her abuser, it's a twisted guilt

and doesn't serve a productive purpose. Similarly, the abuser who feels only transient or minimal guilt after physically battering his romantic partner is neurotically denying or minimizing his personal responsibility. He may experience complete relief from guilt after delivering a quick apology and a dozen roses. Worse, he may relieve his guilt by blaming his partner and demanding an apology from her.

In contrast, some individuals feel massive guilt and responsibility for even the most minor, normal, human ethical transgressions. Excess guilt may make such people think they should be punished or make restitution for their unacceptable behaviors. For example, after making a mistake that cost her employer several hundred dollars, a guilt-ridden employee may commit unending hours of service to her employer, church, and community in an effort to relieve herself of her guilty feelings—and even then, the guilt feelings may continue.

Existential Psychodynamics

Similar to psychoanalytic theorists, existentialists believe humans are in conflict with powerful internal forces. However, instead of helping clients cope with instinctual drives or rework internalized object relations, existential therapists help clients face and embrace **existential psychodynamics** or **"ultimate concerns"** of existence (Yalom, 1980; Yalom, 1995). These ultimate concerns produce anxiety that must be dealt with either directly or indirectly via defense mechanisms (although for existentialists, defense mechanisms are not an elusive, automatic unconscious process, but a style or pattern of avoiding anxiety that can and should be brought to awareness).

In *Existential Psychotherapy*, Irving Yalom (1980) describes four ultimate concerns relevant to psychotherapy. These concerns are:

1. Death
2. Freedom
3. Isolation
4. Meaninglessness

These ultimate concerns capture the nature of reality for existentialists. Everyone who lives is confronted with real demands and truths inherent in human existence. In turn, we're free to choose our response to those demands and anxiety-producing truths.

Death

Yalom (1980) outlines two therapy-relevant propositions about death. First, he emphasizes that death and life exist simultaneously:

> [D]eath whirs continuously beneath the membrane of life and exerts a vast influence upon experience and conduct. (p. 29)

As a consequence, the possibility of death cannot be ignored. Any of us might suddenly face death in the next moment, next day, or next week—or we may live decades longer. Death is knowable and unknowable. We will die; it's only a question of when, where, and how. Death is one of life's realities.

Second, Yalom claims death is a "primordial source of anxiety" and therefore a main source of psychopathology (1980, p. 29). For anyone who has directly faced death, the potential influence of death anxiety is obvious. Years ago when I (John) was prematurely and inaccurately diagnosed as having cancer spreading throughout my body, I experienced several days of anxiety that I would prefer not to repeat. The continuous whirring of death to which Yalom refers became substantially louder. It was only after looking into the abyss of my own, possibly imminent death, that I could understand what it meant to directly encounter death anxiety—a phenomenon that I'd previously contemplated in only the most abstract and intellectual manner. The fortunate revision of my cancer diagnosis allowed the immediate anxiety to recede, but the experience left me with a greater appreciation of both life and death.

Despite the imposing and potentially debilitating fact that death is constantly rumbling beneath life's surface, confronting and dealing with death is also a potentially therapeutic mechanism of personal change. Yalom (1980) summarizes his existential perspective on this issue:

The matter can be summed up simply: "Existence cannot be postponed." Many patients with cancer report that they live more fully in the present. They no longer postpone living until some time in the future. They realize that one can really live *only* in the present; in fact, one cannot outlive the present—it always keeps up with you. Even in the moment of looking back over one's life—even in the last moment—one is still there, experiencing, living. The present, not the future, is the eternal tense. (p. 161)

The purpose of facing death for existentialists is to experience life more deeply and fully. To face death is to motivate oneself to drink with greater enthusiasm from the cup of life. This is *not* a call for morbid preoccupation about life's end, but instead a call to shed external trappings and roles and to live in the now as an individual self with freedom of choice. Research supports this idea that individuals can and do openly approach death by embracing the present and without increased emotional distress or mental disorders (Lichtenthal et al., 2009).

QUESTIONS FOR REFLECTION

A hospice chaplain told us that often, people with terminal diseases make peace with their impending death and their lives become more rich and full. In contrast, a famous Dylan Thomas poem urges, "Do not go gently into that good night. Rage, rage against the dying of the light." Peace or resistance? Rage or acceptance? Where do you find yourself?

Freedom

Freedom is generally considered a positive condition of life, eagerly sought by many individuals. But this isn't the existentialist's view. Sartre believed humans are *condemned to freedom*, and existential therapists have followed suit by articulating the many ways in which freedom is an anxiety-laden burden (Sartre, 1971).

Personal responsibility is the first and primary burden of freedom. If you are free, you are simultaneously responsible. Every action becomes a choice. There is no one to blame for your mistakes. Perhaps you were misled and made a poor choice, but the fact is that *you* were a participant in the misleading. You cannot even defend yourself by employing the pesky Freudian unconscious. As Yalom (1980) states, "To a patient, who insists that her behavior is controlled by her unconscious, a therapist says, 'Whose unconscious is it?'" (p. 216).

Complete and total responsibility is inescapable. In the end, the more freedom you experience, the more choices you have; and the more choices you have, the more responsibility you have; and having a large load of responsibility translates into a large load of anxiety.

To make matters even more daunting, you're responsible not only for your choices, but also for your *nonchoices*. This is because every choice you make represents, at the same time, the death of hundreds of other possibilities. Yalom (1980) provides a personal example based on Sartre's existentialism:

> There is, as I write, mass starvation in another part of the world. Sartre would state that I bear responsibility for this starvation. I, of course, protest: I know little of what happens there, and I feel I can do little to alter the tragic state of affairs. But Sartre would point out that I choose to keep myself uninformed, and that I decide at this very instant to write these words instead of engaging myself in the tragic situation. I could, after all, organize a rally to raise funds or publicize the situation through my contacts in publishing, but I choose to ignore it. I bear responsibility for what I do and for what I choose to ignore. Sartre's point in this regard is not moral: he does not say that I *should* be doing something different, but he says that what I *do* do is my responsibility. (p. 221)

Personal responsibility is a heavy burden to carry. It's so heavy that many individuals can't bear the weight. When the weight of personal responsibility is too heavy, individuals defend themselves with denial, displacement, and blaming. For example, when an employee underperforms, rather than claiming responsibility, he blames the situation ("I didn't have time to do a good job on the project") or a coworker ("Bob is impossible to work with. How can I be expected to produce a quality product?") or his employer ("I'm not paid enough or given enough respect to work any harder than I'm working").

QUESTIONS FOR REFLECTION

Governments vary dramatically in the amount of individual freedoms available to citizens. States vary, cities vary, even families and couples vary in this domain. What makes freedom safe or dangerous within human groups? Should human freedom sometimes be limited?

Nearly everyone considers acceptance of personal responsibility to be a virtue. Sartre's "I am my choices" is roughly the equivalent of former U.S. President Harry Truman's "The buck stops here." Not surprisingly, if you meditate on this concept for a while, you're likely to end up feeling empowered, which is why existentialists doggedly come back to ultimate personal freedom. For them, the best and most direct route to personal empowerment is awareness of personal responsibility, including fully experiencing the angst that comes along with it.

Overall, the essential point of freedom and responsibility for the existentialist is this: You, and you alone, are the author of your experiences. Don't bother pointing the finger of blame toward anyone but yourself.

Isolation

The existential assumption is that every individual is fundamentally alone in this world. In Yalom's words, there is "an unbridgeable gulf between oneself and any other being" (1980, p. 355). This is a terrible truth; we enter life as an individual being and we leave the same way. This is the nature of existential isolation.

There are also other, less deep and less permeating, forms of isolation. For example, many individuals who come for therapy come because of social problems that include feelings of disconnection and loneliness. In addition, some clients experience intrapersonal isolation, in that they feel cut off from or out of touch with their sense of self. Although both of these forms of isolation are important in therapy, they're examples of surface symptoms rather than directly representative of existential psychodynamics.

The ideal or goal of existential therapy with respect to isolation is to help clients connect as deeply as possible with others while at the same time acknowledging their incontrovertible separateness. Yalom refers to this as a "need-free" relationship. Need-free relationships are unselfish relationships in which one person knows another person intimately, gives love without a personal agenda, and acknowledges the other's separateness and independence of thought. When a need-free relationship exists, both parties usually feel more alive and engaged in life (Yalom, 1980).

Martin Buber, a Jewish philosopher and theologian, has written extensively on the **I-Thou relationship** (Buber, 1970). An I-Thou relationship involves the deepest of all possible connections between two individuals. It's a completely mutual and celebratory relationship, in which both self and other are experienced fully. Unfortunately, according to Buber, legitimate I-Thou moments are rare and relatively brief. This is the relation toward which we should strive, but it's impossible to live consistently in an I-Thou connection.

The practical interpersonal problem faced by most of us is the problem of isolation versus fusion. Like a newborn baby, sometimes we luxuriate in the illusion that someone will anticipate and meet our every need. Or in the blush of powerful infatuation, we're intoxicated by the possibility of complete fusion with another individual. Sometimes, even a brief glimpse of the reality of our existential aloneness can cause us to cling to whatever potential love object may be in our vicinity, often with less than desirable outcomes.

Yalom claims that denial is the most common way that humans deal with the conflict between being an individual and experiencing frightening existential isolation. One of the most common forms of denying isolation is through love or fusion with another individual. In his book *Love's Executioner*, Yalom (1989) complains of working with clients who are in love:

> I do not like to work with patients who are in love. Perhaps it is because of envy—I, too, crave enchantment. Perhaps it is because love and psychotherapy are fundamentally incompatible. The good therapist fights darkness and seeks illumination, while romantic love is sustained by mystery and crumbles upon inspection. I hate to be love's executioner. (p. 15)

No doubt you've sometimes been around friends, relatives, acquaintances, or clients who desperately seek social or intimate contact. These individuals loathe being alone, and if they're in an intimate relationship that ends, they move quickly to replace their former partner. They haven't developed the inner strength, identity, and sense of completeness necessary to face the piercing anxiety associated with existential isolation. Instead, they frantically seek connection with others because doing so gives them at least a brief experience of completeness.

Earlier in this chapter we noted that the overarching goal of existential therapy is to help clients discover and explore their authentic self. We should extend that definition to include the discovery and exploration of the authentic and complete, individual self—separate from others.

When done correctly, heightening a client's awareness of existential isolation should improve his or her ability to form healthy interpersonal relationships. Similar to death anxiety and angst over the burden of personal freedom, getting in touch with and embracing existential isolation has a positive consequence. To admit and face aloneness gives us the strength to face the world and the motivation to relationally connect in deep and meaningful ways with other individuals.

Many individuals find the existential musings (especially Yalom's) about love and eternal aloneness to be rather depressing. Consequently, for a more uplifting existential perspective on love we offer one of Viktor Frankl's (1963) reflections while being prodded by the butts of Nazi rifles in Dachau:

> A thought transfixed me: for the first time in my life I saw the truth as it is set into song by so many

poets, proclaimed as the final wisdom by so many thinkers. The truth—that love is the ultimate and the highest goal to which man can aspire. Then I grasped the meaning of the greatest secret that human poetry and human thought and belief have to impart: The salvation of man is through love and in love. I understood how a man who has nothing left in this world still may know bliss, be it only for a brief moment, in the contemplation of his beloved. (p. 37)

QUESTIONS FOR REFLECTION

Eastern philosophies often stress that our separations are illusions. We are all part of the great web of life. Does this argue against accepting and embracing our isolation? Is one view or the other true, or do they somehow both speak to ultimate reality?

Meaninglessness

The classic existential crisis or neurosis occurs when an individual faces the question "What is the meaning of my life?" Seeking life's meaning can be agonizing. This is probably why it's so easy for many of us to just stay busy on Facebook or with other distractions instead of grappling with life's biggest question. Leo Tolstoy captures the pain and torment associated with thinking too much about the meaning of one's life:

The question, which in my fiftieth year had brought me to the notion of suicide, was the simplest of all questions, lying in the soul of every man from the undeveloped child to wisest sage: "What will come from what I am doing now, and may do tomorrow? What will come from my whole life?" otherwise expressed—"Why should I live? Why should I wish for anything? Why should I do anything?" Again, in other words: "Is there any meaning in my life which will not be destroyed by the inevitable death awaiting me?" (Tolstoy, 1929, p. 20)

Many existentialists would respond to Tolstoy with something along the lines of "Life has no

inherent meaning. It's up to you to invent, create, or discover meaning in your life. Your challenge is to find meaning in an apparently meaningless world."

To begin our discussion of meaninglessness, we should emphasize that, similar to the other ultimate concerns, meaninglessness should be confronted, embraced, and dealt with directly. Viktor Frankl has written of his own personal struggle with meaninglessness:

I gladly and readily confess that as a young man I had to go through the hell of despair over the apparent meaninglessness of life, through total and ultimate nihilism. But I wrestled with it like Jacob with the angel did until I could say "yes to life in spite of everything," until I could develop *immunity* against nihilism. (Gould, 1993, p. 9)

Of all existential theorists, perhaps Frankl focused the most on living a meaningful life. He believed the "will to meaning" is a primary motive, surpassing the importance of Freud's pleasure principle and Adlerian superiority striving. He also emphasized that, similar to Adler's formulations of human motivation, meaning isn't a drive or push; instead it is characterized by striving or willing.

Many clients come to therapy because they're suffering from the absence of meaning in their lives. C. G. Jung also wrote about the preponderance of meaninglessness among clients with whom he worked:

Absence of meaning in life plays a crucial role in the etiology of neurosis. A neurosis must be understood, ultimately, as a suffering of a soul which has not discovered its meaning.... About a third of my cases are not suffering from any clinical definable neurosis but from the senselessness and aimlessness of their lives. (Jung, 1953, p. 83)

There is some research supporting Jung's observation. In the face of personal loss, a sense of meaningfulness, religiosity, and spirituality are all predictive of positive mental health (Fry, 2000; Fry, 2001).

Is Life Meaningful?

Frankl claims humans have a primary motivational pull toward meaning. And yet the question remains: Is there inherent meaning in life toward which all humans can or should strive? On the one hand, the ever-optimistic (just kidding here) Sartre says no:

> All existing things are born for no reason, continue for no reason, continue through weakness and die by accident.... It is meaningless that we are born; it is meaningless that we die. (Cited in Hepburn, 1965)

Fortunately, Sartre's position is that of a philosopher—not a therapist. In contrast, Frankl is more optimistic: "We do not just attach and attribute meaning to things, but rather find them; we do not invent them, we detect them" (V. Frankl, 1967, p. 16).

Frankl is claiming two things: First, humans have a will to meaning. Second, meaning *does* exist in the world, and it's up to us to find it. Further, Frankl emphasizes that the individual does not find meaning through preoccupation with the self. Instead, we must look outside ourselves to find meaning.

Frankl's approach to helping clients find meaning in life is **logotherapy** (*logos* = meaning; *therapeia* = healing). As noted previously, he developed this approach after being imprisoned in Nazi concentration camps in Germany. During this time, his previous beliefs in the importance of meaning to human survival were affirmed.

The key to logotherapy is to confront clients directly with the need for meaning, but not to tell them what they *should* consider personally meaningful. Logotherapy celebrates individual responsibility: Clients are completely responsible for their lives and choices regarding the pursuit of meaning. Although Frankl comes across as somewhat religious or spiritual in his writings, he emphasizes that logotherapy is a secular theory and practice.

In the end, there are a number of paths toward meaning that humans can discover and through which they can resolve their existential neuroses. The following possibilities are derived from Yalom (1980) and Frankl (1967):

- *Altruism:* Clients can choose to serve others through kindness and unselfishness.

- *Dedication to a cause:* Clients can dedicate themselves to political, religious, medical, familial, scientific, or other causes. The key is for the cause to take the person beyond selfishness.

- *Creativity:* Clients can choose to create something beautiful, powerful, and meaningful.

- *Self-transcendence:* Guilt, depression, personal salvation, and other self-oriented goals can be put aside to pursue selflessness.

- *Suffering:* Clients can face suffering with optimism, dignity, and integrity.

- *God/religion:* Clients can focus on serving God or their religion instead of serving self or pursuing material goals.

- *Hedonism:* Clients can choose to live life to the fullest each moment, to drink up the excitement, joys, and sorrows of daily life.

- *Self-actualization:* Clients can dedicate themselves to self-improvement, to meeting their potential.

These final two potentially meaningful pursuits (hedonism and self-actualization) are discussed by Yalom, but would not be considered suitably meaningful from Frankl's perspective because they focus exclusively on the self, rather than on something outside the self.

In summary, humans have an internal striving for meaning, meaningful pursuits exist in the world, and it is the counselor's task to help clients pursue and embrace meaning.

QUESTIONS FOR REFLECTION

What if you inferred the meaning of life from dominant media messages? Watch TV or read a few magazines and think about what messages about the meaning of life are being conveyed.

Existentialism and Pessimism

When we lecture on existential psychodynamics, many students justifiably complain about the inherent pessimism associated with existentialist thought. They have a legitimate foundation for their complaints. After all, when existentialists look at life, they see the rumblings of impending death. When they contemplate freedom, they become preoccupied with the burdens of responsibility. When they consider love, they lament that individual isolation is a permanent life condition. And when they talk about life's meaning, they throw themselves into the nihilistic pit of meaninglessness and can only dig themselves out by creating or discovering their own meaning.

There's no doubt that existential philosophy has its share of depressing thoughts. On the other hand, we believe that the whole point of existential thought is not to depress, but to provide hope. Life is a struggle. Life is filled with suffering. But most of all, life is to be lived. And that makes all the difference as we face the ultimate concerns—the realities of death, freedom, isolation, and meaninglessness.

Self-Awareness

Self-awareness is central to existential therapy. Earlier, we said the goal of therapy was to help clients get in touch with their authentic selves. Consistent with the spirit of existentialist thought, we're now revising the goal of existential therapy again (recall that because existence precedes essence, we are continually reinventing, revising, and updating ourselves). As Bugental (2000) stated:

> There is no final or definitive statement to be made. About psychotherapy, about human psychology, about life. We are always in the process of sketching possibilities, of discovering, of becoming. (p. 251)

And so for this moment, the goal of existential therapy is to facilitate self-awareness—including the awareness of death, freedom, isolation, and life's meaning. But stay alert (and aware) because before this chapter ends we'll shift the focus of self-awareness once again—next time we'll be talking about existential integration (Schneider, 2008; 2010).

Theory of Psychopathology

For existentialists, psychopathology results primarily from diminished self-awareness or self-understanding. Signs of diminished self-awareness might include some or all of the following interrelated characteristics:

- Emotional numbness or automaton living.
- Avoidance of one's anxiety, guilt, or other meaningful emotions.
- Avoidance of inner daimonic impulses.
- Failure to acknowledge and reconcile life's ultimate concerns.

Bugental (2000) described one version of existential psychopathology:

> Most of us spend the greater portion of our lives on tape. Without awareness we carry out preprogrammed actions, feel preset emotions, and act on predetermined judgments. This taped living comes not because we are helplessly the creatures of our habit systems, our environments, our glands, or our ancestry, but because we have lost our centers.

As we will see later, for many existentialists successful therapy is about finding one's center and living as fully in the moment as possible (Schneider, 2008; 2010).

Typically, neurotic or maladaptive behavior is linked to avoidance. As clients disavow natural urges and avoid ultimate concerns, they progressively or suddenly become decentered and develop psychological, emotional, or behavioral symptoms. The cure generally involves facing oneself, facing life, and embracing the realities of death, freedom, isolation, and meaninglessness. This does not mean life becomes easy. However, clients who face ultimate concerns with an integrated sense of self will experience normal anxiety and guilt, rather than neurotic anxiety and guilt.

Another way to look at psychopathology in the multidimensional world of existential therapy is to focus on how well individuals are able to lead a meaningful life wherein they experience authentic purpose (Keshen, 2006). Keshen described the following psychopathology sequence:

I. There is a will to meaning (or purpose) in life.

II. The individual is unable to "find or fulfill" authentic meaning or purpose.

III. The individual therefore experiences an "existential vacuum."

IV. Symptoms associated with this vacuum may include: Anhedonia, worthlessness, boredom, anxiety, apathy, emptiness, low self-esteem, or low mood.

V. The individual engages in an unfulfilling "purpose substitute" instead of directly addressing the need for purpose or meaning in life. This purpose substitute might involve addictions, excessive television viewing, overzealous emphasis on acquisition, and so on. (See Keshen, 2006, p. 288)

Consistent with the existential perspective, there are many ways to describe psychopathology, but none of them translate particularly well to the contemporary diagnostic system within the medical model.

THE PRACTICE OF EXISTENTIAL THERAPY

The ethical principle of informed consent mandates that therapists tell clients what to expect in therapy. There is perhaps no other form of therapy in which providing complete informed consent is more essential than the existential approach. This is because existential approaches, more than any other, include an immediate confrontational component. See Putting it in Practice 4.1 for a sample informed consent form from an existential perspective.

In addition to providing presession informed consent, initial here-and-now interactions with clients should proceed gently and educationally.

This is true whether the interaction is simply feedback about personal responsibility or involvement in an existentially oriented Gestalt experiments (see Chapter 6). Later in this chapter we illustrate gentle, educational therapist-client interactions within the context of specific techniques and case examples.

A Word (or Two) on Specific Therapy Techniques

Existential practitioners are generally reluctant to discuss therapy techniques because technical interventions are viewed as artificial or phony, detracting from the authentic I-Thou interpersonal existential encounter. Brief and superficial therapy designed to quickly help people feel better is anathema to existential therapists. This is because it's not only okay to feel negative emotions, it's good and healthy to feel them and in doing so, clients become, somewhat paradoxically, more open to positive emotions. In his 1987 interview, Rollo May lamented the psychotherapeutic quick fix:

> Therapy is becoming a bunch of places where you get fast food. And I think that's quite interesting, that the hamburger you can consume in 15 minutes is parallel to what you get in many of these clinics.
>
> Now I think existential therapy is something radically different. Its aims are different. As we were saying earlier, the aims are not to patch the person up. The aims are to open the person up. The aims are to help this person become more sensitive to life, to beauty. Now that sounds a bit sentimental, I know, but it's a very serious thing to me. And to love.
>
> As Freud said, to love and work, these are the two things that he hopes to influence in people. And that is a very different thing from giving them some gimmick by which they can make the boyfriend be faithful or some other tricks. (Schneider et al., 2009, p. 425)

Instead of techniques, the primary therapeutic force or factor employed by existentialists is the interpersonal therapeutic encounter. This interpersonal encounter is best articulated by Buber's

PUTTING IT IN PRACTICE 4.1

Informed Consent From the Existential Perspective

Welcome to therapy! As you may already know, therapy is an intense, engaging, exciting collaborative process. When you arrive at your therapy sessions, be prepared for a full-on interpersonal encounter. We will talk about anything and everything and I will give you feedback about every aspect of yourself that I can.

The purpose of therapy is for you to more deeply discover who you are, what you want, and how to get it. The philosophy underlying my work is that life should be lived to the fullest. This means that during our sessions we won't focus on how you can control your emotions more completely; instead, we will focus on how you can feel your feelings and experiences—both joy and sorrow—with more depth and authenticity both in therapy and in the world.

During therapy, I will do my best to honor you and your personal experience and perspective. However, I will also consistently provide you with feedback about your thinking patterns, feelings, gestures, and other behaviors that may be outside your awareness. In some ways, you should think of me as a mirror, designed to help you get to know yourself better. This means that I won't be playing any social games with you or dancing around the truth of what I see. Often, I will simply tell you what I see, what I think, and the emotional reactions I have to you and your behavior.

Finally, when you come to therapy, be prepared to have emotions stirred up. Therapy is not a calm place where you come to relax and detach from the world and your personal experiences. Our purpose together is to help you face and embrace all of life, rather than running from it. Therefore, much of what we do together will be a real, authentic, mini–life experience wherein you confront the challenges of life and existence within the relatively safe confines of the therapy office. We will use therapy for practicing life, rather than for avoiding life. . . .

I-Thou relationship (Buber, 1970). The therapist is the leader in this encounter. By being present with the client in the immediate moment, existential therapists partner with clients toward self-discovery and growth. As the interpersonal therapy encounter develops, therapists may utilize specific techniques designed to facilitate awareness, creativity, and self-development (Nanda, 2010).

Forming an I-Thou Relationship and Using It for Positive Change

The existential practitioner is first and foremost responsible for developing an approximation of an I-Thou relationship with clients (van Deurzen, 2010). This relationship is characterized by depth, mutuality, connection, and immediacy.

More than any other theoretical perspective, existentialists also emphasize therapist transparency and authenticity. The therapeutic endeavor flows from an interpersonal encounter where the therapist is spontaneous and open to his or her sensations, emotions, and intuition.

The existential perspective on therapist authenticity and spontaneity brings certain liabilities. For example, given that self-deception is a common characteristic among clients and therapists alike, it's quite possible for therapists to have intuitive impulses that are much more attuned to and therefore designed to address their own issues and agendas than that of their clients (Schneider, 2010). Of course, therapist self-deception is a concern for all therapy approaches, but it's a particular ethical concern for existential therapists because of their strong endorsement of therapist intuition and spontaneity.

Personal Responsibility

The theme of personal responsibility has direct implications for existential therapists (Sapienza & Bugental, 2000). As the therapist, you're completely responsible for your behavior within the therapy session. In Sartre's frame, you are your therapeutic choices. Also, although you aren't responsible for your client's welfare, you are responsible for the therapy process to which your client is exposed. It's the existential therapist's job to create conditions designed to facilitate an interpersonal therapeutic encounter and to avoid behaviors (e.g., too much self-disclosure) that might inhibit therapy progress (Geller, 2003).

Presence

Presence is a term often used to describe the therapist's initial approach to the therapy relationship. Therapists are alert, interested, and as fully in-the-room as possible during every minute of every session. If you feel bored or distracted (signs of what psychoanalysts refer to as countertransference), it's your responsibility to get reconnected and fully engaged in the process. Sapienza and Bugental (2000) recommended that when therapists feel boredom or disconnection, it's crucial to look within and then engage in activities designed to recapture one's aliveness.

Kirk Schneider (2010), a leading contemporary existential psychotherapist described presence as a critical component in the experiential liberation portion of his existential integrative approach:

> Presence serves three basic therapeutic functions: it holds or contains the therapeutic interaction; it illuminates or apprehends the salient features of that interaction; and it inspires presence in those who receive or are touched by it. (p. 7)

For some clients focused existential presence and an I-Thou relationship might be too intense. This could serve as one indicator of whether or not an existential approach is a good fit for a given client. Additionally, existential therapists should shift their intensity level depending on the particular client and, in most cases, begin with less intensity and move toward deeper intimacy as the relationship warms up.

Empathic Mirroring and Focusing

While present in the room with the client, existentialist therapists tune in as much as possible to all that is happening within the client. Although this tuning in always falls short of complete accuracy, mirroring back to clients all of what they're manifesting in the room is a powerful part of existential therapy. In Schneider's **existential integrative therapy** model (Schneider, 2008; 2010) he refers to empathic mirroring and focusing as a component of both presence and **invoking the actual**. It involves a "calling of attention [to] help clients to experience the expansive rage, for example, beneath their oppressive sadness, or the contractive melancholy beneath their expansive bravado" (p. 8). This description helps articulate how empathic mirroring or invoking the actual conceptually and technically overlap with therapist presence—yet another example of the indivisible nature of existential ways of thinking feeling, and behaving.

Schneider (2010) also identified three specific verbal invitations (i.e., techniques) to aid in the invoking the actual process. These include:

- *Topical focus*: "Take a moment to see what's present for you." "What really matters right now?" and "Can you give me an example?" (p. 9).

- *Topical expansion*: "Tell me more," "Stay with that (feeling) a few moments," or "You look like you have more to say." (p. 9).

- *Content-process discrepancies*: "You say you are fine, but your face is downcast;" or "Your body hunches over as you talk about your girlfriend, I wonder what that's about;" or "When you talk about that job, your eyes seem to moisten" (p. 9).

We should note that although we refer to Schneider's verbal invitations as techniques, they're not prescriptive techniques; therapists don't plan ahead to use these particular scripts in a therapy session. Instead, topical focus, topical expansion, and content-process discrepancies are ways therapists can be responsive or facilitative in the moment within therapy sessions.

Feedback and Confrontation

Whenever therapists are present and mirroring back to clients what they see, hear, and experience, feedback and confrontation are happening. In fact, feedback and confrontation flow from presence and empathic mirroring and focusing, partly because presence and empathic mirroring are explicitly designed to create an interpersonal feedback experience.

Depending on your personality style and the particular existential approach you're using, the feedback you give clients may be more or less directly confrontational. As a therapist, Fritz Perls tended to be more in-your-face confrontational (see Chapter 6), whereas Rollo May was more patient and reflective. Our advice is for gentle and progressive feedback and confrontation because without a strong therapeutic connection or alliance, feedback and confrontation can be too painful to integrate. For example, when discussing client resistances,

Yalom and Leszcz (2005) and Schneider (2010) emphasize the longstanding protective function of defense mechanisms and the need to treat defensiveness with respect and care. Further, Schneider notes that although there are no perfect guidelines for when to confront, generally confrontation is reasonable when there is a strong therapeutic alliance and a chronic pattern or entrenchment. Confrontation examples include:

- "You say you can't confront your wife, but you mean you won't!"

- "How many times are you going to keep debasing yourself [in ways you hate]?"

- "You'd rather argue with me than get on with your life!" (From Schneider, 2010, p. 12).

Mindfulness

Mindfulness is a traditional Buddhist approach to daily living (Nanda, 2009). Mindfulness emphasizes acceptance of one's thoughts and of challenging life situations. Although it's not generally associated with existential therapy, we include it here because of its consistency and compatibility with the existential approach. In addition, the case example detailed later features an integration of mindfulness and existential therapy (Nanda, 2010).

Mindfulness meditation is currently very popular as a psychotherapeutic approach. It was a formative factor in the development of dialectical behavior therapy (M. Linehan, 1993), acceptance and commitment therapy (Hayes et al., 1999), and Mindfulness Based Cognitive Therapy (Segal, Williams, & Teasdale, 2002). In contrast to traditional cognitive therapy approaches, mindfulness emphasizes the acceptance, instead of rational disputation, of internal cognitive thought processes. Nanda (2010) described commonalities of mindfulness and existential therapy principles:

Some common attitudes that are valued in Mindfulness . . . and Existential therapy . . . are the stance of a beginner's mind, openness to discover, allowing experience to be disclosed, suspending judgment, non-striving, letting go of any agenda of curing, fixing. All these approaches encourage "being with" experience, and an acceptance of what is present. (p. 332)

To the extent that mindfulness approaches can be integrated into existential therapy in a way that honors authenticity and the I-Thou relationship, it's a reasonable "technique" to employ.

Existential Therapy Techniques

Although most existential therapists reject techniques, both Frankl and Fritz Perls wrote extensively about technical interventions. Perls referred to his techniques as "experiments," a term that captures the immediate experiential nature necessary in an existential encounter (see Chapter 6, Gestalt Theory and Therapy). The following techniques are primarily derived from Frankl.

Paradoxical Intention

Paradoxical intention or anti-suggestion was originally employed by Alfred Adler. Frankl also wrote about and used this approach. In a case example, Frankl discusses a bookkeeper who was suffering from a chronic writer's cramp. The man had seen many physicians without improvement and was in danger of losing his job. Frankl's approach, implemented by one of his associates, was to instruct the man to:

Do just the opposite from what he usually had done; namely, instead of trying to write as neatly and legibly as possible, to write with the worst possible scrawl. He was advised to say to himself, "now I will show people what a good scribbler I am!" And at that moment in which he deliberately tried to scribble, he was unable to do so. "I tried to scrawl but simply could not do it," he said the next day. Within forty-eight hours the patient was in this way freed from his writer's cramp, and remained free for the observation period after he had been treated. He is a happy man again and fully able to work. (Frankl, 1967, p. 4)

Surprisingly, Frankl attributes the success of this approach, in part, to humor. He claims that humor is therapeutic in that it allows individuals to place distance between themselves and their situation. As a result of new perspectives facilitated by humor, the client can then let go of symptoms. Frankl emphasized that paradoxical intention is not superficial. He considered the attitude change achieved by paradoxical intention to be of considerable depth.

Given Frankl's emphasis on humor as an underlying therapeutic force in paradoxical intention, it's not surprising to find that he explains the mechanism underlying paradoxical intention with a joke:

The basic mechanism underlying the technique . . . perhaps can best be illustrated by a joke which was told to me some years ago: A boy who came to school late excused himself to the teacher on the grounds that the icy streets were so slippery that whenever he moved one step forward he slipped two steps back again. Thereupon the teacher retorted, "Now I have caught you in a lie—if this were true, how did you ever get to school?" Whereupon the boy calmly replied, "I finally turned around and went home!" (Frankl, 1967, pp. 4–5)

Frankl claims that paradoxical intention is especially effective for anxiety, compulsions, and physical symptoms. He reports on numerous cases, similar to the man with the writer's cramp, in which a nearly instantaneous cure results from the intervention. In addition to ascribing the cure to humor and distancing from the symptom, Frankl emphasizes that through this technique, clients are taught to intentionally exaggerate, rather than avoid, their existential realities.

> **QUESTIONS FOR REFLECTION**
>
> Think about a time when you experienced an annoying physical symptom that seemed beyond your control (e.g., an eye twitch, excessive sweating). Do you think intentionally "trying" to produce the symptoms might actually give you more control over them?

Cognitive (Meaning) Reframing

As a modern therapy technique, **cognitive reframing** probably has its origins in Adler's individual psychology. However, Frankl also employed this technique, and later cognitive therapists such as Albert Ellis and Aaron Beck more forcefully emphasized its power as a primary therapeutic technique.

Frankl (1967) describes using a reframing technique (although he doesn't refer to it as reframing) in the following case example:

> An old doctor consulted me in Vienna because he could not get rid of a severe depression caused by the death of his wife. I asked him, "What would have happened, Doctor, if you had died first, and your wife would have had to survive you?" Whereupon he said: "For her this would have been terrible; how she would have suffered!" I then added, "You see, Doctor, such a suffering has been spared her, and it is you who have spared her this suffering; but now you have to pay for it by surviving and mourning her." The old man suddenly saw his plight in a new light, and reevaluated his suffering in the meaningful terms of a sacrifice for the sake of his wife. (pp. 15–16)

This example illustrates Frankl's emphasis on helping clients find meaning. It flows from the classic Nietzsche quote offered earlier in this chapter—"He who has a why to live." In this case, suffering without meaning produces clinical depression. But when Frankl gives the man contextual meaning for his suffering, the depression is lifted.

Awareness and Existential Integration

For Schneider (2008, 2010), there are moment-to-moment dimensions to self-awareness that can and should be developed and harnessed to help people achieve at least a provisional or intermittent existential integration. Three phenomenological or experiential characteristics guide Schneider's (2010) work. As you study existential therapy, it will be informative to consider these phenomenological characteristics as areas toward which client self-awareness can be guided.

Constriction, Expansion, and Centering
Constriction and expansion are natural human rhythms that occur within individuals. Mahoney (1991) wrote that all individuals experience

intermittent periods of expansion and constriction. In other words, we're all intermittently experiencing constriction (drawing in) and expansion (venturing out). Mahoney described expansive periods as characterized by growth, risk, and moving forth assertively into the world. In contrast, constrictive periods are characterized by inhibition, a drawing back or retreat from contact with others and with the outside world.

As individuals deal with threatening life circumstances or exceptional opportunities, shifting from expansion to constriction to expansion is healthy. There are obvious times when we should shrink and other times to enlarge ourselves. Different situations produce a natural rhythm or flow between expansion and constriction.

In the existential tradition, Schneider (2008, 2010) helps clients focus not only on awareness of their personal constriction and expansion experiences, but also on understanding the meaning of these natural patterns. As clients work on developing awareness and understanding their personal meanings, existential integrative therapy moves clients toward a centering experience or "the capacity to be aware of and direct one's constrictive and expansive potentialities" (Schneider, 2010, p. 2). The goal is to be in the center while both observing and guiding oneself in constriction and expansion behaviors.

Existential Therapy in Action: Brief Vignettes

In traditional existential therapy, therapists are intermittently nondirective and directive, sometimes tracking their clients' emotions, anxiety, and avoidance and other times directing or leading them into deeper emotional waters. Existential therapy emphasizes the therapist as an instrument of change—therapists develop an I-Thou relationship and then push their clients to address difficult issues. Being the instrument of change places a great burden on the therapist and consequently, doing existential therapy requires substantial training and personal psychotherapy.

Vignette I: Using Paradox

Reginald was a 29-year-old African American professor of history. He came to therapy for a variety of reasons and worked extensively on these issues over the course of about nine months. About halfway through his therapy, Reginald brought up a relatively minor issue that caused him considerable distress. The issue was excessive sweating. He reported feeling "out-of-control" and that these feelings were typically initiated when he felt anxiety and then began sweating profusely. He had tried a number of strategies to enhance his control over sweating, but had been unsuccessful. He told a recent story of when he was challenged on a lecture issue by a student in class. During the ensuing exchange, he started sweating so badly that his glasses fogged over and he had to remove them.

The therapist guided Reginald to explore his feelings of being out of control. Reginald shrunk away from that part of his experience. He was intelligent, athletic, and in-control of his life. He told his therapist.

> I really like feeling in control. It's who I am. It's what I'm comfortable with.

The therapeutic discussion ranged back and forth from Reginald's intellectual talk of being comfortable to his gut-level distress over sweating. There weren't many therapeutic openings and so the existentially oriented therapist gave Reginald the following assignment.

> Reginald, it clearly hasn't worked when you try to control your sweating and so I have a new idea for you to experiment with. The next time you're in a situation and you begin sweating, just notice it and say to yourself—in your head, not aloud—"Go ahead and sweat away. Sweat as much as you want. Sweat as much as you need." The point is, I want you to try to make yourself sweat more.

Reginald reluctantly agreed to the homework assignment. The next week he came to therapy elated:

> I tried to make myself sweat more and I think the reverse happened. I actually stopped sweating sooner!

In their discussion that day, Reginald's therapist guided him toward a number of resolutions. These were cognitive and behavioral resolutions rooted in existential philosophy. Reginald resolved to:

- Embrace his sweating.
- Tell people he sweats a lot sometimes, rather than trying to hide or deny it.
- Tell people—including himself—that he's glad he sweats easily because it's a great way for the body to cool and cleanse itself.
- Tell himself that he loves himself—even when feeling out of control and even when sweating profusely.

Not surprisingly (at least from the existential perspective), at the end of therapy Reginald's decreased need for control had a positive effect on several different areas of his life.

Vignette II: Using Confrontation and Visualization to Increase Personal Responsibility and Explore Deeper Feelings

In this case, a Native American counselor-in-training is working with an 18-year-old Latina female. The client has agreed to attend counseling to work on her anger and disruptive behaviors within a residential vocational training setting. Her behaviors are progressively costing her freedom at the residential setting and contributing to the possibility of her being sent home. The client says she would like to stay in the program and complete her training, but her behaviors seem to say otherwise.

Client: Yeah, I got in trouble again yesterday. I was just walking on the grass and some "ho" told me to get on the sidewalk so I flipped her off and staff saw. So I got a ticket. That's so bogus.

Counselor: You sound like you're not happy about getting in trouble, but you also think the ticket was stupid.

Client: It was stupid. I was just being who I am. All the women in my family are like this. We just don't take shit.

Counselor: We've talked about this before. You just don't take shit.

Client: Right.

Counselor: Can I be straight with you right now? Can I give you a little shit?

Client: Yeah, I guess. In here it's different.

Counselor: On the one hand you tell me and everybody that you want to stay here and graduate. On the other hand, you're not even willing to follow the rules and walk on the sidewalk instead of the grass. What do you make of that?

Client: Like I've been saying, I do my own thing and don't follow anyone's orders.

Counselor: But you want to finish your vocational training. What is it for you to walk on the sidewalk? That's not taking any shit. All you're doing is giving yourself trouble.

Client: I know I get myself trouble. That's why I need help. I do want to stay here.

Counselor: What would it be like for you then . . . to just walk on the sidewalk and follow the rules?

Client: That's weak brown-nosing bullshit.

Counselor: Then will you explore that with me? Are you strong enough to look very hard right now with me at what this being weak shit is all about?

Client: Yeah. I'm strong enough. What do you want me to do?

Counselor: Okay then. Let's really get serious about this. Relax in your chair and imagine yourself walking on the grass and someone asks you to get on the sidewalk and then you just see yourself smiling and saying, "Oh yeah, sure." And then you see yourself apologize. You say, "Sorry about that. My bad. You're right. Thanks." What does that bring up for you.

Client: Goddamn it! It just makes me feel like shit. Like I'm f-ing weak. I hate that.

In this counseling scenario the client is using expansive and angry behaviors to compensate for inner feelings of weakness and vulnerability. The counselor uses the client's language to gently confront the discrepancy between what the client wants and her behaviors. As you can see from the preceding dialogue, this confrontation (and the counselor's use of an interpersonal challenge) gets the client to take a serious look at what her discrepant behavior is all about. This cooperation wouldn't be possible without the earlier development of a therapy alliance . . . an alliance that seemed deepened by the fact that the client saw the counselor as another *Brown Woman*. After the confrontation and cooperation, the counselor shifted into a visualization activity designed to focus and vivify the client's feelings. This process enabled the young Latina woman to begin understanding in greater depth why cooperating with rules triggered intense feelings of weakness. In addition, the client was able to begin articulating the meaning of feeling "weak" and how that meaning permeated and impacted her life.

CASE ANALYSIS AND TREATMENT PLANNING

Existential therapy focuses on moment-to-moment experiences inside and outside the therapy office. As such, this approach is not well-suited to the medical model and generally existential therapists are not keen on treatment planning. If therapy involves a spontaneous and authentic interpersonal encounter designed to open the individual to his or her deepest sensations and emotions, how can we design a concrete treatment plan with objective and measurable goals?

Consequently, when discussing existential treatment planning, it's best to begin with apologies and caveats. Undoubtedly, our efforts to capture existential depth psychotherapy will fall short. Similarly, our treatment plan will be either too narrow or too broad. Nevertheless, in this section we try squeezing an existential model into a medical model treatment plan.

The case we've chosen was originally reported by Jyoti Nanda (2010). Nanda described using the popular mindfulness-based cognitive therapy (MBCT;

Segel, Williams, & Teasdale, 2002) approach within existential psychotherapy to facilitate awareness of existential-phenomenological client themes. Nanda refers to this integration of mindfulness and existential psychotherapy as **Mindfulness-Based Existential Therapy** (MBET).

Nanda was working with a man (John) who came to therapy with a range of depressive symptoms. John was on antidepressant medications. The primary event that triggered his depressive symptoms was the stillborn death of his second child. He came to see Nanda about five months after the stillborn delivery. Nanda reflected on their first session:

> John spoke of his immense sorrow and loss at the death of their child. As I listened attentively sharing the space, the silences, and offering my understanding of his pain, what felt palpable for me was the human to human connection we had. While I have never experienced loss of this nature, I am no stranger to the human condition of pain and suffering. Perhaps John sensed that I felt his pain with him. (pp. 338–339)

During the second session John asked Nanda for direct advice.

Client (John): You must have had other people come to you with similar issues. In your experience, what do you think we should do, should we try for another baby?

Therapist (Jyoti): You are asking me to choose for you whether you and your wife should try for another baby?

John: What do you think?

Jyoti: I can see it is a difficult situation, and choosing one way or another is really hard. It is a real dilemma. I really don't know what the right choice is for you John. What do you and your wife want?

John looked crestfallen.

John: That's not very helpful. If I knew I wouldn't ask you.

Jyoti: You're looking for an answer from me, and I am not telling you what to do! (Pause) I can understand you are perhaps disappointed and perhaps annoyed with me. But you are assuming that I should know what the right choice is for you.

John looked perplexed and thoughtful.

Jyoti: (Silence) Perhaps the answer will emerge, as we find greater clarity about what is really important for you. (p. 339)

This exchange illustrates several features of existential therapy. First, the therapist is not comfortable offering directive advice. This is because it's inconsistent with existential philosophical values to impose her frame for living onto her client. This doesn't mean she never provides information to her client; it just means that when it comes to big life decisions, an existential therapist doesn't presume to know what's best for another person (Sapienza & Bugental, 2000).

Second, Nanda is transparent and open about discomfort she has in response to her client's direct question. There's no muted, emotionally neutral response followed by unguided exploration. Nanda simply states: "I really don't know what the right choice is for you, John."

Third, in some ways Nanda is modeling an existential way of being for her client. In reflecting on this interaction, she noted:

> Over the course of therapy, my feeling comfortable with the not knowing, and moving away from being the expert who knows the "right" answers from the "wrong" ones and someone who provides explanations of what is "wrong" and knows how to fix it, perhaps facilitated for John a greater comfort in staying with his own not knowing, and uncertainty. (p. 339)

Accepting one's inability to control or "know" everything is a tenet of existential therapy. To some extent, Nanda is *teaching* or demonstrating this value to her client by refusing the role of an all-knowing expert and modeling an ability to acknowledge not knowing.

The Problem List

Although it's not fair or right to shrink the client's existential being-in-the-world into a problem list, an initial and tentative list for John might look like this:

1. The client has grief and sadness related to profound disappointment and loss associated with the stillborn death of his second child.

2. The client is partially alienated from or avoiding his own experiences (taking antidepressants and wishing for a quick fix or answer to a question that is so deep it deserves greater reflection).

3. The client is immersed in contemporary world values that suggest he should somehow "know" the right thing to do and/or control uncontrollable life events.

As they continued working together, John reported that strong negative feelings about not having a second child were often triggered by seeing other couples with two children. These feelings also were linked to a sense of personal failure. Like a good existential therapist, Nanda took the opportunity to empathize with John's feelings, while at the same time, gently confronting his failure feelings. After John disclosed what seeing "two-child" families brought up for him, Nanda stated:

Jyoti: It feels like a reminder yet again, and of course it is painful. But I am not sure I understand why you see this as personal failure.

John: I didn't do enough to save our baby.

Jyoti: (after a silence, then saying softly) Didn't do enough to save your baby?

John: I should have saved our baby, somehow.

Jyoti: Of course, you wish you could save your baby. So do I. But I am still not sure I understand why you see this as personal failure.

John: It is pathetic, I feel helpless that as a father I couldn't somehow save our baby.

Jyoti: (after a silence saying softly) Of course, it feels helpless. Both of us wish it had been different. But can either of us control outcomes in matters like birth and death, which are beyond our control? Can either you or I know when and how we or our loved ones are going to die?

At this point Nanda is gently helping her client face an ultimate concern of death. She explains her reasoning (Nanda, 2010):

> The existential theme that we have choice only within the givens of our human limitations . . . informed my intervention. I acknowledged our shared desire for life, and our shared helplessness of what is beyond our control—birth and death. This intervention was possible within the strength and quality of our relationship. Without the relationship itself, it could sound quite clinical. Our being together with the pain and suffering of the human condition, sharing the space and the silences allowed John to reflect and re-consider what was beyond our control, that possibilities arise within limitations. (p. 340)

In addition to the confrontation, Nanda is existentially sharing a space with John. This involves helping him "be" rather than moving into an urgent sense of "doing" (as if there is really anything to be done in this situation).

Problem Formulation

Generally, the client's problems are related to diminished awareness, avoidance of death anxiety, and avoidance of acknowledging the limits of his personal control. As we look back at John's problem list and construct a problem formulation, it's important to note that John's three "identified" problems are overlapping and interrelated . . . which is natural because existentialists see human existence as indivisible.

John's chronic grief and sadness are directly related to the other two identified problems. Specifically, as he contemplates trying to conceive another child so soon after his loss, he's avoiding the full experiencing of his grief. In this way if he and his wife can deny their anxiety and sadness by focusing on hope for another child, they can postpone facing their human limitations. Additionally, he is allowing his personal illusions of control over the uncontrollable to protect him from fully facing death and other parts of life over which he has no control.

The problem formulation involves John's impulses to "do" something to eradicate his and his wife's suffering. His efforts to do things and not feel things or be with the situation are essentially avoidance. Actively avoiding his experience isn't working for John. He needs an intervention that helps him to be more fully with his grief and loss.

Interventions

The therapy process that helps John overcome his problems is not brief or surface-focused. The interventions, if we can call them that, include many of the therapy techniques discussed previously in this chapter. These include, but are not limited to: (a) establishing a therapeutic presence (i.e., I-Thou relationship), (b) empathic mirroring, (c) feedback and confrontation, (d) cognitive reframing, and (e) monitoring of John's constrictions and expansions with the goal of him becoming a more centered, self-aware, and intentional being.

Earlier in the therapy Nanda challenged John's beliefs about himself being a failure. She described this confrontation:

> Acceptance of his personhood did not prevent me from challenging his "sedimented" beliefs. Our relationship could be seen close to Buber's I-Thou relationship. It offered inclusion of John's way of being by me, while also confronting him with my own being. (p. 340)

As individuals work in existential therapy they have intermittent insights into why they are the way they are. Although behavioral and cognitive therapists dismiss the importance of insight, as Adlerians would counter, insight provides fuel for change in the form of enhanced motivation.

Nanda and John worked together just over two years. During their time together John was able to face the domineering nature of his father, his suppressed interest in art (he was in the finance industry due to his father's "choosing"), and the connection between his moods and fluctuations in the stock market. He also faced many other issues.

When John experienced a regression to deep sadness and grief during the one year anniversary of his child's death, he asked Nanda for more specific techniques to deal with his emotions. As a mindfulness-based practitioner herself, Nanda felt the tug to teach John mindfulness strategies. She also experienced the prohibition against techniques commonly associated with existential therapy. She articulated her dilemma:

> I was aware that the Existential approach is technique averse. I needn't have offered mindfulness. I could have stayed with John's distress in the manner that I had, and clearly that was helpful to John. Yet there was this whole body of research that I was aware of. Should I deny John a practice that I believed would be helpful? (p. 341)

After an internal debate about the appropriateness of integrating mindfulness into existential therapy, Nanda decided to go ahead, primarily because of the compatibility between mindfulness and existential acceptance of one's being. Interestingly, this decision was accompanied by an open discussion with John that she had never provided mindfulness training to a client previously. Consequently, for a period of time, Nanda provided 30 minutes of mindfulness training for John, without charge, prior to beginning their usual therapy sessions.

As John became more skilled with mindfulness and continued with existential therapy, he decided to explore discontinuing his antidepressant medication. Not surprisingly, another open discussion occurred and John then worked with his medical provider to titrate down and then discontinue the antidepressants. Nanda described John's experience:

> As the effect of the medication started waning, John reported experiencing his feelings with greater intensity, with greater nuances to them. The irritations and frustrations had greater intensity, but so did the pleasures and the joys. Colours seemed more vivid, and sharper. What he was noticing had a wider range to them. (p. 345)

In the end, John found he was able to function well without medication. He was reportedly more confident, less self-critical, not depressed, more calm, more able to be assertive with his father, and better able to talk about his needs with his wife. He also wrote Nanda a long description of the benefits he attributed to learning the mindfulness techniques.

Outcomes Measurement

Determining how to best measure treatment outcomes from an existential perspective is a perplexing conundrum. Therefore, before describing how to measure existential treatment outcomes, let's focus first on the existentialist arguments for why treatment outcomes aren't measured.

Traditional existential therapists don't believe in using assessment instruments. You can probably guess why that's the case, but here's a short story describing their rationale.

I (John) recall talking with colleagues over lunch at the University of Portland about their possible Myers-Briggs Type Indicator scores. The resident existentialist was clearly offended. She countered with, "You wouldn't ever use a questionnaire like that with a client, would you?" When I said I might, because I thought questionnaires and personality assessment could sometimes be therapeutic, she launched into a diatribe about how using such an instrument was unethical and inauthentic. Of course, she had an important point: All assessment measures fall short of measuring anything close to a real, complete person. The goal of existential therapy isn't to narrow an individual's conception of self, but to expand it. As a consequence, for existentialists, psychometric assessment procedures not only are useless, they also can be anti-therapeutic and/or unethical because they detract from the human encounter.

Despite existentialists' philosophical opposition, it's important for all practitioners to demonstrate accountability by monitoring their outcomes. Perhaps the best solution to this predicament is to use a few standardized outcomes measures focusing on depression, personal misery, meaninglessness,

and/or positive dimensions of life (e.g., happiness), while acknowledging that these are wholly insufficient for measuring existential therapy outcomes.

Another approach is to narrow the focus for existential therapy and then seek to measure specific behaviors or behavior patterns linked to this narrower focus. In this regard, Keshen (2006) recommended developing a "a more succinct, well-defined, and research-friendly model of existential psychotherapy" (p. 285). In his model, the focus is on purposelessness (or meaninglessness). He explained his rationale:

> I have decided to focus on purposelessness because, in my opinion, this concept is more tangible and amenable to quantitative evaluation than other existential foci (e.g. scales are available to evaluate purpose in life).

If you're operating from an existential perspective (or if Nanda wanted to employ specific outcomes measures in her work with John), tools for monitoring client outcomes might include some of the following:

- Life Regard Index (Battista & Almond, 1973)
- Purpose in Life Test (Crumbaugh, 1968; Crumbaugh & Henrion, 1988)
- Seeking of Noetic Goals Test (Crumbaugh, 1977)
- Spiritual Meaning Scale (Mascaro, Rosen, & Morey, 2004)
- Toronto Mindfulness Scale (Lau et al., 2006)

For a discussion on psychometric evaluations of meaning measures, see Mascaro and Rosen (2008).

CULTURAL AND GENDER CONSIDERATIONS

Existential therapy continues its paradoxical preoccupation with polarities with respect to its sensitivity to diversity. On the one hand, because of its emphasis on the sanctity of individual experience and discovery of the unique self, it can be viewed as very ethnoculturally sensitive. On the other hand, feminists and multiculturalists frequently complain that existentialism is a theory promoted by wealthy, dead, white, European men. As Prochaska and Norcross stated, "Only in existentialism and the movies do people possess unlimited freedom, construct their own meanings, and execute boundless choices. Save it for the wealthy, worried well" (Prochaska & Norcross, 2003, p. 133).

Despite the scathing critique from Prochaska and Norcross, there is evidence indicating that existential approaches *can be* diversity sensitive. As is often the case, it seems diversity insensitivity lies less with specific theories and more with individual practitioners and how theories are applied. For example:

- All three of the cases discussed in this chapter involved diversity.
- Vontress, Johnson, and Epp (1999) have written about cross-cultural counseling cases and issues from an existential perspective.
- The research of Paul Wong (2008a, 2008b) has shown the importance of meaningfulness for acculturation.
- Schneider (2010) noted in his existential integrative approach that when therapists confront client resistances, they should be careful not to do so out of cultural misunderstanding.

Writing from an existential perspective, counselor educator Kurt Kraus articulates very nicely the need for cultural sensitivity:

I remember a time in my career when with great anticipation I moved far away to be able to work with more clients of color, specifically Native American and African American peoples. When I found myself, White, for the first time in the minority, still experiencing life as a majority person, it dawned on me: Being well-trained and embracing a multicultural experience did not make me ready; privilege is a skin that is hard to shed.

When a supervisee errantly says, "I know how you feel" in response to a client's disclosure, I twitch and contort. I believe that one of the great gifts of multicultural awareness . . . for me [is] accepting the limitations to the felt-experience of empathy. I can only imagine how another feels, and sometimes the reach of my experience is so

short as to only approximate what another feels. This is a good thing to learn. I'll upright myself in my chair and say, "I used to think that I knew how others felt too. May I teach you a lesson that has served me well?" (Personal communication, August, 2002)

Kraus's multicultural lesson reminds us of Yalom's (1980, 1989, 1999, 2003) discussions of existential isolation. As individual entities traveling through human existence, we're destined to be separate from everyone else. To say "I know how you feel" is a violation of existential reality. In some ways, it's an easily detectable lie. Perhaps the best we can do is to communicate to clients, regardless of their cultural background, "I'm trying my best to understand how you feel," keeping in mind that we'll never fully succeed.

EVIDENCE-BASED STATUS

Schneider (2010) described several concrete changes clients can experience if and when they achieve existential integration:

It is not that all symptoms or problems are eradicated through such a process, it is simply that the major barriers to choice in a given area are removed. The result for such clients is that they experience more centeredness, less panic, and a greater capacity to respond to rather than react against their fears. For some clients, moreover, and for many at varying degrees of intensity, there is a whole new orientation toward life following [existential integrative] therapy; I call this orientation awe-inspiring: a renewed sense of the humility and wonder, indeed, amazement before, the whole of life. (p. 12)

Thinking about Schneider's description of existential integrative therapy outcomes is an excellent way to begin a discussion about existential treatment efficacy. As you may recall, in Chapter 1 there was a discussion about efficacy research and how outcomes associated with some therapies are less easy to measure using standardized objective assessments than others. How easy do you think it would be to measure "a renewed sense of the humility and wonder, indeed, amazement before, the whole of life?" Like many existentialists, Schneider isn't using language consistent with a modernist scientific paradigm.

For many students imbedded in a society where individuals who are experiencing emotional distress or behavioral disorders go see a medically oriented provider, receive a treatment, and then experience symptom reduction, it can be difficult to think about therapy like an existentialist. As a consequence, we offer May's (1983) discussion of the limitations of contemporary scientific methods.

[T]he existential movement in psychiatry and psychology arose precisely out of a passion to be not *less* but *more* empirical. Binswanger and the others were convinced that the traditional scientific methods not only did not do justice to the data but actually tended to hide rather than reveal what was going on in the patient. The existential analysis movement is a protest against the tendency to see the patient in forms tailored to our own preconceptions or to make him over into the image of our own predilections.

It is also important here to remind ourselves that every scientific method rests upon philosophical presuppositions. These presuppositions determine not only how much reality the observer with this particular method can see—they are indeed the spectacles through which he perceives....

The result in our day is that science gets identified with methods of *isolating* factors and observing them from an allegedly *detached base*—a particular method which arose out of the split between object and subject made in the seventeenth century in Western culture and then developed into its special compartmentalized form in the late nineteenth and twentieth centuries.

[As] Helen Sargent has sagely and pithily remarked, "Science offers more leeway than graduate students are permitted to realize." (pp. 45–46)

May is saying that scientific outcome studies only represent a single perspective on the nature and effectiveness of therapy. Of course, you (and psychotherapy efficacy researchers) may see this position as a cop-out—especially because based

on contemporary scientific standards, there are no RCTs attesting to existential therapy efficacy. There are case studies and anecdotal reports, but even those generally don't meet scientific standards for single-case controlled research with psychometrically acceptable measures.

There is a relatively small amount of research supporting existential group therapy outcomes. For example, one research team found significant changes in endocrine and immune functioning in breast cancer patients who participated in existential group therapy (van der Pompe, Duivenvoorden, Antoni, & Visser, 1997). This and other studies suggest that existential group therapy is both meaningful and helpful to individuals facing life threatening illnesses (Kissane et al., 2003; Page, Weiss, & Lietaer, 2002).

There is some published research on the effectiveness of paradoxical intention. For example, in a meta-analysis, paradoxical intention was shown to have a .99 effect size (K. A. Hill, 1987). This suggests that the average client treated with paradoxical approaches is better off than about 84% of clients not receiving treatment. Overall, this is a fairly strong outcome and slightly better than the .80 effect size typically attributed to psychotherapy in general (M. L. Smith et al., 1980). An alternative meta-analysis of paradoxical techniques was similarly positive (Shoham-Salomon & Rosenthal, 1987).

Although this should be common sense from the existential perspective, there's also research attesting to the importance of meaning in psychological well-being. Fry (2001) reported that personal meaning, religiosity, and spirituality predicted psychological well-being more significantly than other factors, such as physical health and social support. It seems clear that as individuals age and/or face death Yalom's (1980) observations that "Existence cannot be postponed" and that people experience a deepening of living in the present (Lichtenthal et al., 2009). There is also substantial evidence attesting to the contribution of meaningfulness as an aid in acculturation (Pan, Wong, Chan, & Joubert, 2008; Pan, Wong, Joubert, & Chan, 2008), buffering of stress (Mascaro & Rosen, 2006), and in reducing depressive symptoms (Mascaro & Rosen, 2005).

We should be clear that based on contemporary scientific standards, none of the preceding research clearly establishes existential therapy efficacy. However, in a review of Schneider's *Existential Integrative Psychotherapy* book, renowned psychotherapy researcher Bruce Wampold (2008) stated: "I have no doubt that [existential integrative] approaches would satisfy any criteria used to label other psychological treatments as scientific. Our current consensus on what is scientific is excruciatingly narrow."

The point is that contemporary quantitative counseling and psychotherapy research emphasizes symptom reduction and although symptom reduction can be a very good thing, it's not everything. Existentialists might ask: "Would you rather experience symptom reduction as your therapy outcome or a renewed sense of amazement before the whole of life!" Now that's a therapy outcome worth striving for (see Putting it in Practice 4.2 for musings from an existentially oriented practitioner).

CONCLUDING COMMENTS

Existential therapy is about finding meaning. It's about facing the fact that we die and that often we feel very much alone. Existential therapy is also about taking personal responsibility for the glorious choices we have before us each day . . . each hour . . . each minute . . . each second. To quote Mary Oliver (1992), "What is it you plan to do with your one wild and precious life?"

CHAPTER SUMMARY

Existential counseling and psychotherapy is an approach based on existential philosophy. Existential philosophy focuses on invariable conditions of human existence, including personal responsibility, isolation, death, and meaning.

Existential philosophers (and therapists) tend to view life in dialectical extremes and then gather knowledge and meaning from an integration of those two extremes. For example, Viktor Frankl

suggested that we need a statue of responsibility on the West Coast to balance the Statue of Liberty on the East Coast. By experiencing and embracing personal freedom, combined with complete responsibility for one's actions, individuals can be stimulated to learn and grow.

Many different principles are associated with existential theory. These include: (a) the I-Am experience; (b) the four existential ways of being (i.e., umwelt, mitwelt, eigenwelt, uberwelt); (c) the daimonic; (d) the nature of anxiety and guilt; (e) existential psychodynamics or ultimate concerns (i.e., freedom, death, isolation, meaninglessness); and (f) self-awareness.

Existential therapists don't believe in contemporary models of psychopathology. Instead, they work with individuals and groups to achieve greater awareness and to embrace all of what life has to offer—including the eventuality of death. By embracing all of existence, life can be lived to the fullest.

Existential therapists don't use prescribed techniques or procedures. Instead, they seek to form an "I-Thou" relationship with clients and use it for therapeutic change. Existential therapy process typically involves an intense interpersonal encounter that includes deep emotional sharing, feedback, confrontation, and encouragement. The goal is to achieve greater and greater awareness or existential integration.

As a therapy approach, existentialism isn't known for its sensitivity to gender or culture. Historically, this approach has been developed by white males and most often implemented with individuals who have the resources, time, and inclination to examine their lives in greater depth. However, there are many examples of existential therapy being used in culturally and gender-sensitive ways.

Basically, existentialists don't value modern empirical science. Existentialists even define the word empirically differently than contemporary scientists. For existentialists, the whole of human experience is what's important. This is an approach that focuses on helping people live their lives more fully and consequently, there is very little empirical research supporting its efficacy in alleviating symptoms.

PUTTING IT IN PRACTICE 4.2

Existential Musings

Kurt Kraus of Shippensburg State University wrote the following commentary:

As an existentially oriented phenomenologist I am often caught, conflicted by my theoretical belief and my clients' desire for someone in my chair whose beliefs are not mine. For me, the honoring of suffering, the anxiety of limited time, and the continuous presence of opportunities for personal meaning are often the very things that clients initially wish to be rescued from. It is a conflict that I very much appreciate, one that makes for the most interesting therapeutic alliances.

I often ask myself, "How can theory help me better understand some aspect of the client with whom I am working?" And then, when I have located one or two meaningful theoretical explanations, I store them in some recess of my mind—sort of as a backdrop or a map. I then proceed with my client to construct a personal meaning for his or her experience. One thing I try to remember is that no map gets you where you want to be: Movement does. It is, at least in therapy, the actual journey that gets the client where he or she chooses to go. Learning theories is a valuable means to an end, but the path is not paved in theory; it is paved with experience.

Sometimes theory texts afford great fantasy. If I adhere to one theory I will be clear in my professional identity, "I am a reality therapist, or I am Rogerian, or I do rational emotive behavior therapy." At times through these fantasies I can be Melanie Klein, or Alexander Wolfe, or Judith Jordan. I've never held on long enough to emerge as anyone other than myself—full of doubts about the veracity of any one theory over all others. Instead I study those that fit me, content in the notion that the theories of counseling and psychotherapy are quite occasionally transmogrified through my interpretation and through my unique relationship with each and every client with whom I sit.

EXISTENTIAL KEY TERMS

Cognitive reframing

Daimonic

Dialectic

Dialectical process

Eigenwelt

Existential integrative therapy

Existential philosophy

Existential psychodynamics

I-Am experience

Invoking the actual

I-Thou relationship

Logotherapy

Mindfulness

Mindfulness-based existential therapy

Mitwelt

Neurotic anxiety

Neurotic guilt

Normal anxiety

Normal guilt

Ontological experience

Paradoxical intention

Philosophy

Presence

Uberwelt

Ultimate concerns

Umwelt

RECOMMENDED READINGS AND RESOURCES

The following resources provide additional information on existential theory and therapy.

EXISTENTIAL JOURNALS

Existential Analysis
International Forum for Logotherapy
International Journal of Existential Psychology and
    Psychotherapy

Review of Existential Psychology and Psychiatry

READINGS ON EXISTENTIAL THEORY AND THERAPY

Buber, M. (1970). *I and thou*. New York, NY: Scribner.

Bugental, J.F.T. (1987). *The art of the psychotherapist*. New York, NY: Norton.

Frankl, V. (1963). *Man's search for meaning*. Boston. MA: Beacon.

Frankl, V. (1978). *The unheard cry for meaning*. New York, NY: Simon & Schuster.

Mascaro, N., & Rosen, D. H. (2008). Assessment of existential meaning and its longitudinal relations with depressive symptoms. *Journal of Social and Clinical Psychology, 27*(6), 576–599.

May, R. (1977). *The meaning of anxiety* (Rev. ed.). New York, NY: Norton.

May, R., Angel, E., & Ellenberger, H. F. (Eds.). (1958). *Existence: A new dimension in psychiatry and psychology*. New York, NY: Basic Books.

Nanda, J. (2010). Embodied integration: Reflections on mindfulness based cognitive therapy (MBCT) and a case for mindfulness based existential therapy (MBET). A single case illustration. *Existential Analysis, 21*(2), 331–350.

Sartre, J.-P. (1953). *Existential psychoanalysis* (H. E. Barnes, Trans.). Chicago, IL: Regnery.

Schneider, K. J. (Ed.). (2008). *Existential-integrative psychotherapy: Guideposts to the core of practice*. New York, NY: Routledge/Taylor & Francis.

Schneider, K. J., Galvin, J., & Serlin, I. (2009). Rollo May on existential psychotherapy. *Journal of Humanistic Psychology, 49*(4), 419–434.

Schneider, K. J., & Krug, O. T. (2010). *Existential–humanistic therapy*. Washington, DC: American Psychological Association.

van Deurzen, E. (2010). *Everyday mysteries: A handbook of existential psychotherapy* (2nd ed.). New York, NY: Routledge/Taylor & Francis.

Vontress, C. E., Johnson, J. A., & Epp, L. R. (1999). *Cross-cultural counseling: A casebook*. Alexandria, VA: American Counseling Association.

Yalom, I. D. (1980). *Existential psychotherapy*. New York, NY: Basic Books.

Yalom, I. D. (1989). *Love's executioner*. New York, NY: Basic Books.

Yalom, I. D. (2002). *The gift of therapy*. New York, NY: HarperCollins.

TRAINING ORGANIZATIONS AND WEBSITES

International Society for Existential Psychology & Psychotherapy (ISEPP; www.existentialpsychology .org)

Viktor Frankl Institute (logotherapy.univie.ac.at/)

Saybrook Institute, The Rollo May Center for Humanistic Studies (www.saybrook.edu)

Society for Existential Analysis (www.existentialanalysis .co.uk)

VIDEOS/DVDS

Carlson, J., & Kjos, D. (2000). *Existential-humanistic therapy with Dr. James Bugental* [Video]. Boston, MA: Allyn & Bacon.

Schneider, K. J. (2006). *Existential therapy* [DVD]. Washington, DC: American Psychological Association.

Schneider, K. J. (2009). *Existential-humanistic therapy over time* [DVD]. Washington, DC: American Psychological Association.

Yalom, I. (2002). *The gift of therapy: An interview with Irvin Yalom* [Video]. Pacific Grove, CA: Brooks/Cole.

GOING FARTHER AND DEEPER

Additional existential counseling and psychotherapy resources are available at johnsommersflanagan.com.

CHAPTER 5

Person-Centered Theory and Therapy

THIS CHAPTER

- Reviews the key figures and historical factors contributing to the development and evolution of person-centered theory and therapy
- Outlines and describes classical person-centered theoretical principles
- Describes and discusses principles and strategies associated with classical and contemporary person-centered therapy practice, including
  - Assessment issues
  - Therapist experiencing of congruence, unconditional positive regard, and empathic understanding
  - Specific strategies linked to motivational interviewing
- Provides short vignettes to demonstrate person-centered therapy principles in action
- Illustrates how treatment planning, outcomes assessment, and gender and cultural issues can be integrated into a person-centered approach
- Reviews the empirical status of classical and contemporary person-centered approaches
- Offers resources for further study

If Freud was a pessimist and Adler and Jung were optimists, then Carl Rogers—the primary theoretical figure of this chapter—was a super-optimist. His approach is founded on an abiding belief in the capacity for persons, when unfettered by social and familial obstacles, to develop into positive, creative, flexible, and altruistic beings. Rogers referred to this capacity as an **actualizing or formative tendency**. As you read about him, you'll see his trust in the positive nature of persons is unshakable. Emphasizing this perspective, in 1961, he wrote:

> [I]t is the client who knows what hurts, what directions to go in, what problems are crucial. (Rogers, 1961, pp. 11–12)

Rogers developed a distinctive approach to therapy: He listened. He listened to clients with immense respect. Additionally, in all aspects of his life, he strove to be a genuine and open person; he strove to be himself. As he interacted authentically with clients, he put himself so deeply into their worlds that he could sometimes feel their feelings right along with them.

At times, other theorists have viewed Rogers's optimism as frustrating and naive. For example, Rollo May, a person who regarded Rogers quite highly, once wrote to Rogers concerning his (Rogers's) extraordinarily positive view of the world's future:

> You paint a seductive and enticing picture, and anyone would like to believe it. But I recall the words of Warren Bemis in the film of you and him, when he characterized your viewpoint as "devilishly innocent." (Kirschenbaum & Henderson, 1989, p. 242)

We hope, despite his innocence, that you will embrace Carl Rogers and his person-centered theory and therapy with every part of your being. As one of the best listeners to walk the planet, Rogers deserves to have us stop whatever else we might be doing and, for the moment, listen to him.

BIOGRAPHICAL INFORMATION: CARL ROGERS

Carl Rogers

Carl Ransom Rogers was born in 1902. He was the fourth of six children raised on a farm in Illinois. His parents were rigid fundamentalist Christians, whom Rogers later described as "absolute masters of repressive control" (quoted in Bankart, 1997, p. 292). He described how his parents taught him to keep his distance when socializing with outsiders:

> Other persons behave in dubious ways which we do not approve in our family. Many of them play cards, go to the movies, smoke, dance, drink, and engage in other activities, some unmentionable. So the best thing to do is to be tolerant of them, since they may not know better, and to keep away from any close communication with them and live your life within the family. (Rogers, 1980, p. 28)

Rogers's family dynamics appear to have laid the groundwork for the social and personal transformation he later experienced. In many ways, Rogers as a therapist sought to create a completely accepting, permissive, and nonjudgmental environment. He tried to help his clients obtain an experience in stark contrast to what he experienced in relationship to his parents.

Despite his parents' distrust of intellectualism, Rogers went to college, initially following the family policy of majoring in agriculture. He also was involved in the campus Young Men's Christian Association group and was one of 12 students chosen to attend the World Student Christian Federation Conference in Peking, China (Rogers, 1961).

It was on this trip that, according to Bankart, "Rogers appears to have become Rogers" (Bankart, 1997, p. 292). He was away 6 months. Somehow this experience produced at least the following three changes in Rogers: (1) he rejected his parents' conservative religious ideology; (2) he decided to marry his childhood sweetheart; and (3) he decided to pursue graduate studies at the liberal Union Theological Seminary in New York City.

HISTORICAL CONTEXT

Not long after enrolling at Union Theological Seminary, Rogers transferred (across the street) to Columbia University Teachers College to study clinical psychology. His training was squarely within the domain of American academic psychology. At the time, Columbia University was inculcated with John Watson's behaviorism (see Chapter 7). Consequently, Rogers was oriented more toward the contemporary scientist-practitioner model in psychology than any theorist we've discussed to this point. His strong interest in research—he was the first person to tape-record actual therapy sessions—led some to refer to him as "the founder of psychotherapy research" (Bohart, 1995, p. 87; Rogers, 1942).

Professional and Personal Influences

Rogers's first clinical position was at the Adlerian-oriented Rochester Child Guidance Center. During this time, academic psychologists were staunchly behavioral, while clinicians were trained in either psychoanalytic or neo-analytic theory. Since Rogers wanted to help people (rather than work in a laboratory), he was trained in a diagnostic-prescriptive analytic approach:

> Rogers originally went to . . . Rochester . . . believing in this diagnostic, prescriptive, professionally impersonal approach, and it was only after actual experience that he concluded that

it was not effective. As an alternative, he tried listening and following the client's lead rather than assuming the role of the expert. This worked better, and he discovered some theoretical and applied support for this alternative approach in the work of Otto Rank and his followers. (Raskin & Rogers, 1989, pp. 160–161)

Rogers attended a 2-day seminar with Otto Rank and learned a great deal from a Rank-trained social worker, Elizabeth Davis, whom he hired to work for him in Rochester. Ms. Davis was able to tune into and articulate clients' feelings in a way that fascinated Rogers; he credits her as the inspiration for his best-known therapeutic approach. "What later came to be called the reflection of feeling sprang from my contact with her," he noted (Rogers & Haigh, 1983, p. 7).

During his 12 years in Rochester, Rogers wove many elements of Rankian practice into his approach, including the following ideas:

- Clients have creative powers.

- Therapy should help clients accept their personal uniqueness and self-reliance.

- The client is the central figure in the therapy process; the therapist only helps clients access their powers of self-creation.

- Therapists shouldn't seek to educate clients.

- Therapists shouldn't foster dependency with clients by becoming love objects.

- Therapy works when clients are able to experience the present within the therapy setting (adapted from Raskin & Rogers, 1989).

As a young American living in the 1930s, Rogers also was influenced by the social policies and person of President Franklin D. Roosevelt. Roosevelt was optimistic, empowered individuals by involving them in social and political activities, and supported the creativity of his subordinates (Bohart, 1995). At the same time, Rogers was influenced by the philosophy of John Dewey, whose statements about human development goals are similar to Rogers's goals for and attitudes toward psychotherapy: "Not perfection as a final goal, but the ever-enduring process of perfecting, maturing, refining, is the aim in living" (Dewey, 1920, pp. 176–177).

Rogers's relationship with his wife also powerfully affected him. Because of his sheltered childhood and poor social skills, she was the first person with whom he ever had a caring and sharing relationship. In 1980, at the age of 75, he wrote,

> During the first two years of marriage we learned a vitally important lesson. We learned, through some chance help, that the elements in the relationship that seemed impossible to share—the secretly disturbing, dissatisfying elements—are the most rewarding to share. This was a hard, risky, frightening thing to learn, and we have relearned it many, many times since. It was a rich and developing experience for each of us. (Rogers, 1980, p. 32)

Honoring the Client

Consistent with his theory, Rogers gave the most credit for the development of his theory to his clients; he learned about what helped and what didn't directly from them. In a published interview, his daughter, Natalie, acknowledged that she learned to learn from her clients from her father, "And so like Carl, I stayed open to learning from my clients. They are always our best teachers." (J. Sommers-Flanagan, 2007, p. 122).

Rogers's first book, *The Clinical Treatment of the Problem Child* (1939), helped him obtain a professorship in psychology at Ohio State University. He subsequently published *Counseling and Psychotherapy* in 1942, which pioneered the use of audiotape recordings to study therapy (another example of his emphasis on learning from his clients) and featured his nondirective psychotherapeutic approach.

Struggles With Psychiatry and Psychology

Rogers developed his client-centered approach to psychotherapy in a climate openly hostile to his ideas. He was an extremist, a dangerous sort of radical, who rapidly built a devoted following both within academia and out in the real world. He fought the behaviorism of academic psychology as well as the psychoanalysis that ruled the clinical world. However, one of his biggest battles was with psychiatry, a battle that he described as "an all-out war" (Rogers, 1980, p. 55).

During the 1930s and 1940s, psychiatry was adamantly opposed to letting nonphysicians practice psychotherapy. They also fought desperately to keep psychologists from assuming leadership roles within mental health agencies. At Rochester, Rogers battled with psychiatry to maintain his leadership position at the guidance clinic. Later, at the University of Chicago counseling center, he was accused of practicing medicine without a license and launched a "blistering counterattack" to earn psychologists the right to practice psychotherapy (Rogers, 1980, p. 54).

Rogers also had his battles with mainstream academic psychology. His ongoing debates with the noted behaviorist B. F. Skinner are the stuff of legend (see Chapter 7).

Overall, professional counselors, social workers, and educators have been more receptive to Rogers and his work than psychologists. He summarized his feelings about his impact on psychology:

> I believe an accurate statement would be that we have had very little influence on academic psychology, in the lecture hall, the textbook, or the laboratory. There is some passing mention of my thinking, my theories, or my approach to therapy, but, by and large, I think I have been a painfully embarrassing phenomenon to the academic psychologist. I *do not fit*. Increasingly I have come to agree with that assessment. (Rogers, 1980, p. 51)

Rogers was indeed an unusual academic psychologist. He fraternized with social workers, counselors, and teachers, even publishing in their journals. He rebelled against assigning course grades, allowing students to be their own teachers and evaluators. He participated in encounter groups and expressed disdain for the time-honored traditional class lecture. Nevertheless, Rogers still

earned significant respect from academic psychology. He was elected president of the American Psychological Association in 1946 and received a prestigious award for scientific contribution in psychology in 1956. These honors led Rogers to refer to himself as a "respected gadfly" within psychology (Rogers, 1980, p. 53).

Evolution of Person–Centered Therapy

Overall, Rogers's practice of person-centered theory and principles can be divided into four developmental periods.

- *Nondirective counseling*. This period began in the 1940s and was characterized by Rogers's growing aversion to directive, traditional therapy methods. His publication of *Counseling and Psychotherapy* marks this period (Rogers, 1942).

- **Client-centered therapy**. In the 1950s Rogers changed the name of his approach from *nondirective counseling* to *client-centered therapy*. During this period Rogers published *Client-Centered Therapy* (1951) and changed his focus from a nondirective process to an honoring of the client's ability to lead the therapy.

- *Becoming a person*. During the 1960s, Rogers focused on self-development. His work was strongly associated with the human potential movement. He published *On Becoming a Person* (1961) and moved from academia at the University of Wisconsin to California in 1964. Other major publications during this period reflected his application of person-centered theory to new situations and included *Freedom to Learn: A View of What Education Might Become* (1969) and *Carl Rogers On Encounter Groups, (1970)*. He changed the name of his approach to **person-centered therapy** (PCT).

- *Worldwide issues*. In the 1970s and 1980s, Rogers became more concerned with worldwide issues. He founded the Center for the Study of the Person in La Jolla, California, in 1968, and began dedicating much of his work to improving interracial relations and efforts toward world peace. He met with Irish Catholics and Protestants, visited South Africa and the Soviet Union, and conducted cross-cultural workshops in Brazil, Dublin, and Hungary. During this period he published *Carl Rogers On Personal Power* (1977) and *A Way of Being* (1980).

As with most popular theories, person-centered principles have moved beyond a focus on the life and achievements of the original founder (Cain, 2010). Contemporary variations on PCT are discussed later in this chapter.

THEORETICAL PRINCIPLES

The person-centered approach includes a theory of personality and a theory of psychotherapy. The theory of personality has 19 propositions (Rogers, 1959). It's surprisingly complex and difficult to articulate, which may be why it gets little attention. Even Rogers noted that his personality theory "is the most thoroughly ignored of anything I have written" (Rogers, 1980, p. 60).

Theory of Personality

Rogers's 19 theoretical propositions are collapsed into four core features of his personality theory.

Self-Theory

In the tradition of William James, Mary Calkins, and Gordon Allport, the person-centered theory of personality is essentially a **self-theory** (Bankart,

1997). Rogers postulated that every person exists within an ever-changing world in which he or she is the center. In addition, he believed that the *self* is not a fixed structure, but a structure in process, capable of both stability and change.

Rogers used the term **organism** to refer to the locus of all psychological experience. The organism is the entire realm of an individual's experience, while the self is the "me" portion of the organism. Rogers's self has both conscious and unconscious components.

The distinction between organism and self makes it possible for an individual's self to be inconsistent with its overall psychological experience. This discrepancy is referred to as **incongruence**. In contrast, when the self's experiences and perceptions are consistent with the organism's total experience, there is **congruence**. Congruence between self and organism is highly desirable; it leads to adjustment, maturity, and a fully functioning individual. The developmental goal is for the "me" or self to grow so that it takes up the entire organism (and in the process, the self becomes more fully aware—meaning that self-awareness is a key part of human or self-development).

Phenomenology and the Valuing of Experience

Rogers summarized his personality theory by stating, "This theory is basically phenomenological in character and relies heavily upon the concept of self as an explanatory concept" (Rogers, 1951, p. 532). Person-centered theory places a premium on direct personal experience. Although both intellectual/rational thinking and feelings/emotions are valued and crucial informational sources, experiencing is considered a more direct way of accurately knowing oneself and the world. Bohart states that "experiencing is the direct, nonverbal sensing of patterns and relationships in the world, between self and world, and within the self. It includes what is often called 'intuitive knowing'" (Bohart, 1995, p. 91).

In part, person-centered therapy (PCT) is designed to help clients be more open to their vast array of personal or organismic experiences. True learning is best achieved through lived experience wherein the "self" determines whether a particular action or feeling is enhancing or not.

Learning and Growth Potential

Rogers believed strongly in the inherent actualizing or formative tendency in humans. Some of this viewpoint was derived from his childhood farming and outdoor experiences, as he came to see the potential for many things in nature to grow and evolve toward completeness. Additionally, he attributes this viewpoint to several writers and philosophers, including Kurt Goldstein, Harry Stack Sullivan, Abraham Maslow, and Karen Horney. Rogers believed people have the capacity to learn on a moment-to-moment basis and have a formative tendency to "move toward greater order, complexity and interrelatedness" (Bohart, 1995, p. 89):

> There is one central source of energy in the human organism. This source is a ... function of the whole system [and] ... is most simply conceptualized as a tendency toward fulfillment, toward actualization, involving not only the maintenance but also the enhancement of the organism. (Rogers, 1980, p. 123)

As you may recognize, this actualizing tendency is also similar to Adler's striving for superiority and Freud's small, but persistent voice of reason. Generally, the idea that there's an actualizing tendency or developmental force underlying the behavior of individual humans is an oft-repeated philosophical or theoretical concept (J. Sommers-Flanagan & Sommers-Flanagan, 2011).

Conditions of Worth

In addition to the organism's need to maintain and enhance itself, there are additional, learned needs. The main two learned needs are the **need for positive regard** and the **need for self-regard**.

As babies and toddlers grow in relationship with caretakers, two things begin happening. First, the baby begins developing a greater and greater self-consciousness. Most parents see this behavior clearly in their children at about age two, when the child's favorite words become "mine!" and "no." Second, the growing child develops a strong need

for positive regard or approval. This need for positive regard—to be prized and loved—becomes so powerful that children automatically and consistently look to caretakers and significant others for acceptance and approval.

Rogers describes the ideal situation:

> If an individual should *experience* only *unconditional positive regard*, then no *conditions of worth* would develop, *self-regard* would be unconditional, the needs for *positive regard* and *self-regard* would never be at variance with *organismic evaluation*, and the individual would continue to be *psychologically adjusted*, and would be fully functioning. (Rogers, 1959, p. 224, italics in original)

Unfortunately, no child's home life is ideal, so although children consistently watch and listen for approval, it's not always forthcoming. Consequently, children begin distinguishing between approved and disapproved feelings and actions. They sense and understand the **conditions of worth** present in their lives (Kohn, 2005).

Eventually, children internalize their caretakers' appraisals, despite the fact that these appraisals are not completely consistent with their overall organismic experiences, because the alternative is to suffer the pain of negative regard. For example, if a young girl who loves to play roughly and aggressively with other boys and girls consistently experiences disapproval from her parents when she does so, then she is forced to one of the following three conclusions:

1. When I play rough I am bad (**negative self-regard**).

2. My parents don't like me because I play rough (negative regard from others).

3. I don't like to play rough (denial of a desirable organismic experience).

As you can see, none of these preceding conclusions value the child's total organismic love of rough-and-tumble play. Consequently, she experiences incongruence in one way or another.

Over time, if children continually experience conditions of worth incongruous with their organismic values, a conflict or discrepancy may develop between their conscious, introjected values and their unconscious genuine values. Hall and Lindzey (1970) describe this seed of psychopathology:

> If more and more true values of a person are replaced by values taken over or borrowed from others, yet which are perceived as being his [sic] own, the self will become a house divided against itself. Such a person will feel tense, uncomfortable, and out of sorts. He will feel as if he does not really know what he is and what he wants. (p. 532)

When individuals get out of touch with their true selves and desires, psychopathology develops. This can be thought of as a discrepancy between the **real self** and **ideal self**. The real self is the total organismic self—the self linked to actualization. In contrast, the ideal self is filled with unattainable shoulds derived from dysfunctional societal and familial conditions of worth. A discrepancy between the real and ideal self is known as incongruence. It can be associated with a growing but vague awareness of discomfort, of something being terribly wrong. This discomfort is especially likely to arise when clients are exposed to organismically desirable feelings, actions, or opportunities.

For example, when the little girl who was negatively judged for having aggressive impulses grows up and has an opportunity for aggressive expression, all sorts of twisted internal events may take place. She may project her desires for anger expression onto others, she may become aggressive and then condemn herself, or she may let loose with her aggression but then deny that she experienced any anger or gratification. Unless her self becomes more congruent with reality, she will continually reinterpret reality to fit whatever self-picture she needs to maintain, no matter how much this violates her true experience and external reality.

Rogers also believed individuals are capable of perception without awareness. Similar to other writers in the 1940s, he referred to this process as **subception** (McCleary & Lazarus, 1949). Subception occurs when a person unconsciously perceives a threatening object or situation (see *The Gift of Fear*, de Becker, 1997, for a related example). The object or situation is generally threatening because it represents an inner conflict between real desires and introjected desires. Further, subception is likely to result in visceral reactions (e.g., increased heart rate, high blood pressure, rapid respiration, and other anxiety sensations).

To summarize, Rogers's personality theory emphasizes several concepts. It is a theory of self, of experience, of striving for maintenance and enhancement of the self, and of learned needs for positive regard. It is also a theory of discrepancy, because it's the discrepancy between self and organismic experience, between what the caretakers value and what the organism values, that creates or determines psychopathology.

Theory of Psychopathology

In summarizing Rogers's ideas on psychopathology, Bohart (1995) states:

> Psychological problems are neither faulty beliefs or perceptions nor inadequate or inappropriate behavior per se. As humans confront challenges in life they will periodically misperceive, operate on mistaken beliefs, and behave inadequately. Dysfunctionality occurs if we *fail to learn* from feedback and therefore remain stuck in our misperceptions or inadequate behavior. Dysfunctionality is really a failure to learn and change. (p. 94)

The *failure to learn from experience* best characterizes person-centered psychopathology. This is why person-centered therapists work so hard to help clients become open to learning from new experiences. This is also why rigidity is considered the antithesis of psychological health. Rigidity impairs learning.

Psychopathology occurs when clients hang onto introjected parental conditions of worth instead of modifying their self-concept based on moment-by-moment, day-by-day personal experience. Since every moment is an opportunity for new learning, closing down and avoiding or ignoring these moments is pathological. Similarly, in their person-centered approach, *emotion-focused therapy*, Greenberg and colleagues focus especially on the importance of openness to emotional processing in normal human functioning (Elliott, Watson, Goldman, & Greenberg, 2004; Elliott & Zucconi, 2006; Greenberg, 2011; Paivio & Greenberg, 1995). When clients are unaware of or unable to access important emotional information, dysfunctional behavior or interpersonal interactions result.

Theory of Psychotherapy

Rogers's theory of psychotherapy is directly related to his theory of personality. If psychopathology originally stems from the individual's experience of judgment or invalidation of the self by significant others, it logically follows that a nonjudgmental atmosphere will facilitate psychological health. This premise is the foundation of Rogers's theory of psychotherapy.

Rogers believed that if therapists can trust clients and provide a therapeutic relationship, then clients will be able to begin trusting themselves; they will experience a steady and powerful movement toward greater personal development and psychological health. He described his general theory of psychotherapy in one sentence:

> If I can provide a certain type of relationship, the other person will discover within himself the capacity to use that relationship for growth, and change and personal development will occur. (Rogers, 1961, p. 33)

Rogers (1957) outlined his relationship-based theory of psychotherapy in a landmark article, *"The Necessary and Sufficient Conditions of Therapeutic Personality Change."* He used his academic-scientific orientation to describe the six conditions of effective psychotherapy:

> For constructive personality change to occur, it is necessary that these conditions exist and continue over a period of time:

1. Two persons are in psychological contact.

2. The first, whom we shall term the client, is in a state of incongruence, being vulnerable or anxious.

3. The second person, who we shall term the therapist, is congruent or integrated in the relationship.

4. The therapist experiences unconditional positive regard for the client.

5. The therapist experiences an empathic understanding of the client's internal frame of reference and endeavors to communicate this experience to the client.

6. The communication to the client of the therapist's empathic understanding and unconditional positive regard is to a minimal degree achieved. (Rogers, 1957, p. 95)

Because of their central importance in most forms of therapy relationships today, the core conditions of PCT—congruence, unconditional positive regard, and accurate empathy—are defined and described next. Later, when we focus on how to practice PCT, practical applications of these core conditions are discussed.

Congruence

Congruence is defined as authenticity and sometimes referred to as transparency. The congruent therapist is real, open, and honest. Rogers claimed, "The more that I can be genuine in the relationship, the more helpful it will be" (Rogers, 1961, p. 33). Rogers was very specific about why therapist congruence is essential. He stated, "It is only by providing the genuine reality which is in me, that the other person can successfully seek . . . the reality in him" (1961, p. 33). Counselor congruence provides a sort of grounding or reality so that clients' real selves have something to interact with.

Congruence implies that therapists should acknowledge and express both positive and negative feelings within the context of the therapy relationship. Rogers emphasized the importance of expressing less positive feelings when he wrote, "I have found this to be true even when the attitudes I feel are not attitudes with which I am pleased, or attitudes which seem conducive to a good relationship. It seems extremely important to be real" (1961, p. 33).

Unconditional Positive Regard

Unconditional positive regard is also referred to as acceptance, respect, or prizing. It involves an emphasis on valuing the client as a separate person whose thoughts, feelings, beliefs, and entire being are openly accepted, without conditions. Person-centered theory holds that if the therapist can accept clients completely, then clients can explore who they really are and what they really want. By accepting clients, therapists lead clients to begin accepting themselves.

Rogers described his discovery of unconditional positive regard as a therapeutic element:

> I find that the more acceptance and liking I feel toward this individual, the more I will be creating a relationship which he can use. By acceptance I mean a warm regard for him as a person of unconditional self-worth—of value no matter what his condition, his behavior, or his feelings. It means a respect and liking for him as a separate person, a willingness for him to possess his own feelings in his own way. (Rogers, 1961, p. 34)

Rogers went on to say that this acceptance should extend to the moment-to-moment changes and inconsistencies manifested by clients during sessions. He takes a stand against more directive interventions, such as confrontation and interpretation. It matters not whether clients claim to have a change of heart halfway through a session. At one moment they may identify only feelings of love and kindness toward someone, and at the next they may rage about the same person. To the person-centered therapist, both love and rage are important, valid, and equally worthy of attention. By simply listening and reflecting back the depth of both feelings, the therapist allows clients to accept or modify what's been expressed. Even further, Rogers believed that complete acceptance combined with accurate empathy could lead clients to an expanding awareness into previously unknown parts of the self. Hall and Lindzey (1970) noted that,

> [E]xplicitly recognized in Rogers' theory is the concept of an organism that has many experiences of which the person is not aware. Some of these unsymbolized experiences are denied entrance to consciousness because they are inconsistent with the self-image. If this is not repression, in the psychoanalytic sense, then the distinction between it and repression is so slight as to be negligible. The principal difference between Rogers and psychoanalysis lies in Rogers' conviction that repression can be prevented in the first place by the parents giving unconditional positive regard to the child. Or if the damage has been done, it can be corrected later by therapeutic intervention in which the therapist prizes the client. When he is given unconditional positive regard, the client eventually discovers his real self. (pp. 545–546)

Unconditional positive regard is challenging but essential in helping clients begin to accept their complete and uncensored selves. It can lead to a willingness to explore very personal feelings and to greater self-awareness.

Accurate Empathy or Empathic Understanding

Accurate empathy is the therapeutic condition professionals most directly linked to Carl Rogers and PCT. Based on what he initially learned from Elizabeth Davis, Rogers became more and more capable of noticing and reflecting his clients' feelings. At times, when listening to audiotapes of his work, he seems to slip completely into the client's world, seeing and experiencing exactly what the client sees and experiences. At such times, he sometimes shifts from using a second-person pronoun ("When he left, you felt betrayed and alone") to using a first-person pronoun ("If I'm getting this right, it's almost like, here I was, wanting to be close, and then he just up and left, and I felt betrayed and alone"). This pronoun shift is referred to as **walking within** and is discussed in greater depth later in this chapter.

Of the three core conditions, empathy has been most widely discussed and researched (Clark, 2010a; Elliott, Bohart, Watson, & Greenberg, 2011). Many theorists from many different theoretical orientations acknowledge the importance of empathy to psychotherapy. For example, it has been referred to as a prerequisite for therapy (Freud, 1923), a necessary condition (Bohart & Greenberg, 1997), and an enabling factor (Hamilton, 1995). It is also considered to have a variety of functions. Some say it's the basis for forming a patient-therapist bond (Kohut, 1959), others claim it dissolves client fear and denial (Barrett-Lennard, 1981), and still others promote it as a factor that provides clients with safety (Jenkins, 1997).

Empathy is a multidimensional concept (Clark, 2007; Clark, 2010a; Clark, 2010b; Elliott et al., 2011). In 1964, Rogers identified three ways of empathic knowing. Clark (2010a) described these:

> **Subjective empathy** enables a counselor to momentarily identify with a client through intuitive reactions and fleetingly imagine and experience what it is like to be a client. Using **interpersonal empathy**, the counselor attempts to grasp [and feedback] the phenomenological experiencing of a client from an immediate or extended perspective. **Objective empathy** features a counselor's use of theoretically informed observational data and reputable sources in the service of understanding a client. (p. 349, bold added)

Though empathy is a powerful factor in psychotherapy, from a person-centered perspective, empathic understanding is not a single variable leading to a particular outcome. Instead, it's used in conjunction with the other two therapeutic conditions, congruence and unconditional positive regard. In the following excerpt, Rogers (1961) discusses the importance of experiencing and conveying *both* empathy *and* unconditional positive regard when relating to clients:

> Acceptance does not mean much until it involves understanding. It is only as I understand the feelings and thoughts which seem so horrible to you, or so weak, or so sentimental, or so bizarre— it is only as I see them as you see them, and accept them and you, that you feel really free to explore all the hidden nooks and frightening crannies of your inner and often buried experience. (p. 34)

Despite all the research confirming that empathy is crucial to therapy, Natalie Rogers has commented that she believes it is still perhaps the most underestimated condition leading to positive change in therapy (Sommers-Flanagan, 2007). For some reason, people seem to take empathy for granted and don't believe that it's the powerful cure that Carl Rogers believed it to be.

The Magic of Person–Centered Listening

Person-centered listening isn't in vogue in the United States. It might be that most of us are too busy tweeting and expressing ourselves to dedicate time and space to person-centered listening. The unpopularity of person-centered approaches also might be related to the prominent "quick fix" attitude toward mental health problems. And so, call us old-fashioned, but we think that if you haven't learned to do person-centered listening, you're missing something big.

Years ago, when John was deep into the "Carl Rogers" stage of his development, he decided to create a person-centered video recording to demonstrate the approach. He recruited a volunteer from an introductory psychology course, obtained informed consent, set up a time and a place, welcomed a young woman into the room, and started listening.

Lucky for John, the woman was a talker. It's much harder to get the magic to happen with nonverbal introductory psychology students.

It wasn't long into the session when John attempted a short summary of what the woman had said. He felt self-conscious and inarticulate, but was genuinely trying to do the person-centered listening thing: He was paraphrasing, reflecting feelings, summarizing, walking within, and doing all he could to be present in the room and make contact or connect with the "client." After his rambling summary, there was an awkward silence. John remained silent, trusting that the client knew where to go next. And she did. She cut through the awkwardness with a disclosure of having been sexually molested as a child. John continued listening nondirectively as the woman told her story, shed a few tears, and spoke powerfully about her journey toward building inner strength.

The demonstration recording was a huge success . . . except for the fact that the audio was terrible. To hear the powerful disclosure and share in the magic of person-centered process, John had to force his class of 15 graduate students to gather within three feet of the television in perfect silence . . . which was rather awkward.

The lesson of person-centered listening is that sometimes when you put it all together the client can take you places you never knew existed. There are many things about our clients we'll never know unless and until we listen empathically, communicate genuinely, and experience respect for the other person with our heart and soul. As Rogers (1961) said, "the client knows what hurts" and so it's up to us—as therapists—to provide an environment where clients can articulate their pain and reactivate their actualizing tendency (see Putting it in Practice 5.1: An Interview With Natalie Rogers).

QUESTIONS FOR REFLECTION

Can you think of any problems with having too much empathy? Do you think therapists can get overinvolved and lose objectivity? What do you think about working with someone who is very similar to you? Would that make it harder to sit back and let the client tell you about his or her feelings and experiences?

THE PRACTICE OF PCT: A WAY OF BEING WITH CLIENTS

Generally speaking, there are two types of person-centered therapists: **classical** and **contemporary**. Cain (2010) describes the former:

> The classical group of practitioners continues to uphold the position that the six core conditions articulated by Rogers in 1957 are both necessary and sufficient, that Rogers's 1959 theory of personality and psychotherapy remains definitive, and that nondirective attitude and behavior on the part of the therapist is essential to practice. (p. 44)

In contrast, *contemporary* person-centered therapists believe in person-centered principles, but feel free to be more active, directive, and to blend PCT with other approaches. For example, focusing therapy (Gendlin, 1981; 1996), emotion-focused therapy (Greenberg, 2011), Natalie Rogers's (1996) integration of art and dance into therapy, and motivational interviewing (Miller & Rollnick, 2002) are all foundationally person-centered, but use alternative methods and modalities to help clients focus on self-exploration and self-development.

Natalie Rogers

Decades of psychotherapy research confirm that the relationship between therapist and client is a fundamental, active therapeutic factor (Lambert, 1992). One of our biases is that we firmly believe beginning mental health professionals should learn how to be purely person-centered before adding more directive approaches (J. Sommers-Flanagan & R. Sommers-Flanagan, 2009). Because Rogerian principles, like Adlerian principles, are integrated into virtually every other contemporary therapeutic approach, learning PCT is excellent foundational training for becoming any sort of therapist you want to become.

PUTTING IT IN PRACTICE 5.1

Why Is the Person–Centered Approach Undervalued in the United States?

An Interview With Natalie Rogers

In the following excerpt from two telephone interviews, Natalie Rogers discusses why person-centered approaches tend to be undervalued or overlooked in the United States.

John Sommers-Flanagan (JSF): Other than the managed-care focus and an emphasis on quick fixes, can you think of any reasons why more American therapists aren't practicing PCT?

Natalie Rogers (NR): That's a good question. Most psychology students I know only get a chapter or two in the academic world, and they don't really understand in any depth what the person-centered approach is about. And, most importantly, I think they haven't experienced it. They've read [about] it and they've talked about it and they've analyzed it, but my own belief is that it really takes in-depth experiencing of the client-centered approach to know the healing power of empathy and congruence and unconditional positive regard.

JSF: So it's almost like students get more of an intellectual understanding, but you're just not seeing them get the experiential part.

NR: Even the intellectual understanding is very superficial, because they read maybe a chapter and watch the old Gloria film (Rogers, 1965). The fact that there have been 16 books written on client-centered therapy and a lot of other books now that Carl's passed away and the research that he did is so profound . . . the in-depth research on what actually helps clients go deeper into their feelings and thoughts.

JSF: Right.

NR: You know, [how therapists can help clients go deeper into their feelings and thoughts] is hardly ever mentioned in academia as far as I know.

JSF: And what I remember from our last conversation was that you said you thought it didn't happen in the U.S. at all and maybe a little bit in Europe?

NR: I think it does happen a lot more in Europe, and most particularly in the United Kingdom, Scotland and England. They have really excellent training programs in the client-centered approach, and the books that are coming out are coming out from there. You know in Germany they have a several-year, very extensive training program that's also linked in, I believe, to becoming accredited or licensed as a therapist. Things are going that particular route in Europe, but none of that is here in the States.

JSF: That seems to reflect our own emphasis on the surface or the quick fix as well in that people just really haven't gone deeper and experienced the power of PCT.

NR: Right. And then again I think the other point is that the ego needs of the therapists [appear] to be strong here. Therapists in this country seem to need to have the attitude that "I have the answers" or at least that "I know more," and it's ... the old medical model that we still hold onto in this country a lot. The doctor knows what he needs to diagnose and treat, knows what's wrong and that there are ten steps to fix it.

JSF: Right, which seems to be the opposite of the person-centered therapy of "trust the individual, trust the person."

NR: Not just seems to be, it is the opposite. So, to actually believe, to have faith in the individual, to have faith that each person has the answers within himself or herself if given the proper conditions, and that's a big if. That philosophy takes a great deal of humility on the part of the therapist.

JSF: For us to realize that we don't have all the answers for another person.

NR: Right. I kind of like the gardener metaphor. That I'm the gardener and I help till the soil and I help water the plants and fertilize the plants, and care for them. And I need to understand what the plant needs, what conditions that plant needs for it to actually grow and become its full potential. That's very different. That's what I see as one metaphor for being a therapist. I don't know all the answers, but I'm a person who creates the conditions for the person to grow.

JSF: Kind of the fertile field metaphor. So ... what would you tell beginning therapists that would help them see the tremendous value of following person-centered principles?

NR: Well, I always ask my students to examine their own beliefs about psychotherapy and about what it is that creates psychological feelings and growth. I think it's a philosophical, spiritual belief system that we're looking at. People are using the words "methods" and "techniques," which always puts me off, because although there certainly are methods that we use, it's much bigger than that. It's a belief system about the connection between mind, body, and emotional spirit. And so I ask them what do they believe creates personal growth, and what have they experienced themselves that creates growth, and we get them to think and talk about their religious experiences, their psychotherapy experiences, their experiences in nature, and their experiences in relationships. I think they're all profound. And then when we focus in on relationships, which is what psychotherapy is about, then I want them to experience ... from me or my colleagues in hour-long demonstrations what it means to be client-centered. So then they experience it as witnesses and they can experience it as a client.

JSF: So more students need to directly experience, or at least witness, client-centered therapy.

NR: Let me give an example. I was talking to a colleague once who had some of my training and who said that he was now using brief therapy, brief psychotherapy, and I admitted I didn't really know what that was. We decided that he'd have to give me some ideas on what that's like. So I listened to him describe the theory and practice

> for quite a while and questioned him about it. And as he was describing it, I was wondering, how would I feel if I were in the client's chair and this was what was being done to me. And so then I felt pretty uncomfortable, and thought, "I guess I wouldn't like it." So I asked him, "Have you ever been a client in this kind of brief therapy yourself?" And he said "No," and I thought that was inexcusable. To practice something on somebody else that you haven't experienced in-depth yourself. I think it is inexcusable. So that illustrates in a kind of negative way the point that I wanted to make. You really need to have in-depth experience of that which you are going to have other people do.

Assessment Issues and Procedures

Classical person-centered therapists don't employ standardized assessment or diagnostic procedures. Rogers wrote that "psychological diagnosis as usually understood is unnecessary for psychotherapy and may be actually be detrimental to the therapeutic process" (Rogers, 1951, p. 220).

Assessment and diagnosis can contribute to client psychopathology. By judging or placing labels (aka conditions of worth) onto clients, self-appraisal moves further from clients. Also, when therapists diagnose or classify clients as having mental disorders, it becomes harder to view clients as unique individuals. Typical behavioral and cognitive therapy texts that focus on treatments for specific disorders such as major depressive disorder, generalized anxiety disorder, obsessive-compulsive disorder, or post-traumatic stress disorder miss the whole point of therapy—which is to treat the individual, not the disorder.

Despite drawbacks of diagnosis, person-centered therapists may use diagnostic procedures for insurance billing. Also, when communicating with other professionals, therapists may employ diagnostic terminology, but they take care to treat the client as a unique individual who deserves respect.

Contemporary person-centered approaches sometimes employ assessment procedures. For example, in emotion-focused therapy (EFT) the therapist assesses very specific areas of client functioning (Goldman & Greenberg, 1997; Greenberg, 2011). Goldman and Greenberg explain that assessment procedures are used in the service of idiographic case formulation, that assessments are never performed a priori, and that assessment data emerge best within the safety of a PCT environment. As an integrative approach, EFT is discussed in Chapter 14.

The Therapist's Opening Statement

From the person-centered perspective, clients take the lead in the therapeutic process. Essentially, the message given to clients is "You talk and I'll listen and try my best to understand what you're experiencing in your life and in yourself." An excellent model for how to start a therapy session comes from Carl Rogers:

> Anything you'd like to tell me about yourself that will help me to know you better, I'd be very glad to hear. (Rogers, 1963)

You may notice the preceding opening is very similar to initiating the basic rule or free association from a psychoanalytic perspective. This is because person-centered and psychoanalytic approaches have one big commonality: Both approaches use a process where clients talk, while therapists listen intently. Despite this commonality in process, psychoanalytic therapists are listening for material to judge and interpret, while person-centered therapists are listening to go as deeply as possible into the client's inner world—without judging. (See Putting it in Practice 5.2: Informed Consent From the Person-Centered Perspective.)

PUTTING IT IN PRACTICE 5.2

Informed Consent From the Person-Centered Perspective

I'm looking forward to working with you in counseling. The purpose of this form is to inform you about your rights as a client and to tell you what to expect during typical counseling sessions.

The first thing is there's no such thing as a typical counseling session. You're unique, and the problems and challenges in your life are unique. As a counselor, it's my job to help you express what you're thinking, feeling, and experiencing. You should think of me as a sort of companion. I will accompany you as you explore yourself, your problems, your life situation, and your personal experiences. Generally, I won't tell you what to do in your life. Instead, because the form of counseling I provide is "person-centered counseling" I'll help you focus on your own thoughts and feelings. There are two reasons why I don't tend to "advise" clients: First, you're a different person than I am and therefore I can't and shouldn't tell you how to live your life. Your personal decisions are completely up to you, and I respect and trust your ability to make informed decisions about your life. Second, I also don't give out expert advice because I've discovered that clients rarely benefit from such advice. You'll benefit more from struggling with your own personal decisions and discovering what's right for you.

Even though I won't be offering advice, that doesn't mean I won't sometimes express my opinions or feelings during counseling. At times, when I have a strong feeling or reaction, I'll tell you what I'm thinking or feeling as honestly as I can.

Being in counseling isn't always easy and it's never an emotionally neutral experience. Sometimes you may feel good because you're getting to express everything you're feeling and thinking while I'm trying my best to listen and understand. At other times you may find yourself talking about and feeling things that are hard and painful. Counseling is not a neutral experience because it requires you to face yourself more completely than you do in your ordinary life. It's like scrutinizing yourself in a mirror. Even though the mirror doesn't judge you, you may feel judgmental about things you see. As you explore yourself on the inside and on the outside, you may feel both pain and joy.

If you have questions or concerns about counseling, ask them any time. I'll do my best to respond to your questions. Overall, my view is that counseling is an excellent opportunity for you to explore, in greater depth, who you are, what you want, and how you want to live. I'm delighted to accompany you on your journey of self-discovery.

Experiencing and Expressing Congruence

Therapist congruence has particular implications for therapy and for the therapist (J. Sommers-Flanagan & R. Sommers-Flanagan, 2009). Both beginning and experienced therapists can struggle to communicate congruence to clients (Cain, 2010). Perhaps the most basic question is this: "Does being congruent mean I need to tell the client about my every thought and feeling?"

The answer to this question is a clear no. That's not to say therapists should be overly cautious about self-disclosing to clients. The point is that random or unhelpful therapist thoughts, no matter how spontaneous, need not be shared. Despite the openness and transparency of person-centered therapists, the main aim of openness is to communicate potentially helpful information to clients. Rogers (1958) discusses this issue directly:

> Certainly the aim is not for the therapist to express or talk about his own feelings, but primarily that he should not be deceiving the client as to himself. At times he may need to talk about some of his own feelings (either to the client, or to a colleague or superior) if they are standing in the way. (pp. 133–134)

The main message is that therapist verbal censoring is needed (Cain, 2010). An excellent way to see how much self-disclosure is appropriate from a person-centered perspective is to listen to Rogers doing therapy. In his audio and video therapy recordings, Rogers rarely self-disclosed, and when he did it was in the service of furthering the client's therapy work and not in the service of his own ego needs. If you're honest with yourself (i.e., congruent), most of the time you'll be unlikely to disclose because your disclosure is not relevant or helpful to the client.

Rogers viewed therapist techniques in a manner similar to self-disclosure. That is, when asked if it's ever appropriate for therapists to use techniques, Rogers said yes, but only when techniques come up spontaneously, from a genuine or congruent place, and not when they're preplanned.

Experiencing and Expressing Unconditional Positive Regard

Is it possible for anyone to ever experience unconditional positive regard for another person? After all, everyone is human, and it seems only human to judge others. Nevertheless, completely suspending judgment, accepting clients as they are, is one of Rogers's core therapeutic conditions, so we must face this challenge.

For now, let's assume it's possible, at least intermittently, for therapists to experience unconditional positive regard toward clients. There remains the problem of how to best express positive regard. Should you do it directly? Would it be appropriate to say, "I accept you completely and totally as the person you are" or "I prize and value your total being?"

The answer to that question is an "Absolutely not!" Other than the fact that talking like this is totally corny, most therapists eventually get themselves in trouble if they directly express unconditional positive regard to clients, for two reasons. First, expressing too much positive regard can be overwhelming to clients. Clients may react by wanting to break down therapy boundaries. Upon hearing positive, loving statements they naturally seek more closeness, perhaps a friendship or romantic relationship. Alternatively, some clients may react to direct expressions of affection with fear. These clients may firm up the boundary between themselves and the therapist, moving away from the intimacy the therapist is overtly offering.

Second, saying "I care about you" or "I won't judge you" can be viewed as phony or unrealistic, especially if the therapist hasn't spent much time with the client and therefore doesn't really know him or her well. These phony or unrealistic statements often backfire because eventually the client begins noticing ways in which the therapist does not care or is judgmental.

If it's inappropriate to directly express unconditional positive regard to clients, then how can therapists communicate this important message? In our *Clinical Interviewing* text, we've detailed several ways that therapists can indirectly communicate unconditional positive regard:

> How do you express positive regard, acceptance, and respect to clients indirectly? Here are some ideas: First, by keeping appointments, by asking how your clients like to be addressed and then remembering to address them that way, and by listening sensitively and compassionately, you establish a relationship characterized by affection and respect. Second, by allowing clients freedom to discuss themselves in their natural manner, you communicate respect and acceptance. Third, by demonstrating that you hear and remember specific parts of a client's story, you communicate respect. This usually involves using paraphrases, summaries, and sometimes interpretations. Fourth, by responding with compassion or empathy to clients' emotional pain and intellectual conflicts, you express concern and acceptance.... Fifth, clinical experience and research both indicate that clients are sensitive to an interviewer's intentions. Thus, by clearly making an effort to accept and respect your clients, you are communicating a message that may be more powerful than any therapy technique. (J. Sommers-Flanagan & R. Sommers-Flanagan, 2009, p. 118)

To return to our initial question, is it possible for therapists to feel unconditional positive regard toward some or all of their clients? The realistic answer is, probably not. However, this is likely the wrong question anyway. Rogers was an optimist and an idealist, but he wasn't a fool. The more important question is this: Is it possible for therapists *to try* to feel unconditional positive regard toward their clients? We think the answer to this revised question is an enthusiastic "Yes!" (See Putting it in Practice 5.3.)

Most person-centered writers acknowledge a difference between completely accepting all client thoughts, feelings, and behaviors and practical applications of unconditional positive regard. In most cases, a line is drawn between accepting clients thoughts and feelings vs. accepting or endorsing all client behaviors (Cain, 2010). In a telephone interview, Natalie Rogers described this in terms of her experience growing up with Carl Rogers as her father and in terms of misunderstandings regarding his educational theories:

> And in terms of Carl's theories about education, I remember hearing him talk and audiences asking about permissiveness and freedom, but I think the permissiveness often has been misunderstood. He said that any thoughts and feelings are OK, but not all behavior is acceptable. Unless that is really made clear, both in the theory and in the practice, it can be disastrous. (Sommers-Flanagan, 2007, p. 122)

Experiencing and Expressing Empathic Understanding

Consistent with the existential-humanistic tradition, person-centered therapists don't believe it's possible for one individual to directly know and experience another individual's feelings (Rogers, 1959). As with unconditional positive regard, what appears important regarding empathy is not that therapists perfectly experience and express empathy, but they *try their best* to do so. Rogers described the empathic way of being in 1975:

> The way of being with another person which is termed empathic has several facets. It means entering the private perceptual world of the other and becoming thoroughly at home in it. It involves being sensitive, moment to moment, to the changing felt meanings which flow in this other person, to the fear of rage or tenderness or confusion or whatever, that he/she is experiencing. It means temporarily living in his/her life, moving about in it delicately without making judgments, sensing meanings of which he/she is scarcely aware, but not trying to uncover feelings of which the person is totally unaware, since this would be too threatening. (Rogers, 1975, p. 4)

The following sections are organized around Rogers's (1975) description of what it means to be empathic.

Entering and Becoming at Home in the Client's Private Perceptual World

Entering the client's private world requires preparation and intentionality. You need to begin your encounter with your client deeply valuing an

PUTTING IT IN PRACTICE 5.3

Stretching Your Ability to Experience Unconditional Positive Regard

Trying to experience and express unconditional positive regard for clients is very hard. In the following situations, see if you can imagine yourself experiencing unconditional positive regard as a therapist.

- You're working with a sex offender who's talking about the gratification he gets from sexual encounters with young children.
- You're working with a battered victim of domestic violence who insists her husband loves her and that she must go back and live with him again—for the fifth time.
- You're working with a pyromaniac. He tells you about how he masturbated after setting a local historical building ablaze.
- You're working with a teen girl. She tells you about her promiscuous sexual exploits and regular use of strangulation or the drug ecstasy to increase her sexual gratification.

From the person-centered perspective, it's essential to experience unconditional positive regard for the client. Do you think you could experience unconditional positive regard in the preceding situations? What might prevent you from feeling unconditional positive regard? Which situations would be easier for you? Which ones would be harder?

One way to experience positive regard in these difficult situations is to find within yourself positive regard simply for the suffering human being in the room with you—not positive regard for the behaviors, but for the yearnings, longings, losses, and fears the behaviors represent. Rogers firmly believed every person was born with the potential to develop in positive, loving ways, given the right environment, but some folks don't get much of a chance. When doing person-centered therapy, you become their next chance, maybe their last chance, to be welcomed, understood, and accepted. Your acceptance may create the conditions needed for change.

understanding of the client's perspective. You need to be open to feeling what the client feels and willing to ask the subjective empathy question "How would I feel if I were _____ and saying these things?" (Carkuff, 1987, p. 100). Technically, the procedures employed to enter the client's world include reflection of feelings, empathic exploration, and clarification.

As a former full-time mental health practitioner, John recalls when he initially became aware of the psychological and emotional shift involved with the person-centered listening experience.

I remember going to the office to meet with my first client of the day. Sometimes, just before beginning the counseling process I was very much in my own head. My thoughts were bouncing around like a room full of ping-pong balls being batted around by a rambunctious bunch of fifth graders. I was thinking about my own life, my family, my business, financial issues, personal conflicts, my professional and personal future, community issues, and gritty details associated with these topics.

I know in an ideal world, I would have been able to settle and center myself before inviting my first client into the counseling room, but I couldn't manage to do that. Instead, it would become time for the session to start and so I would start, despite my brain being a busy construction zone that should have had an accompanying sign reading: "Danger. Man at work. Do not disturb."

But when I sat down with my first client, a funny thing happened. My personal thoughts drifted away. Just like that. As I began listening to another living, breathing person, I could almost see my self-centered thoughts drift away and fall off the edge of my consciousness. For the hour, the gentle (and sometimes less gentle) pull of my clients private perceptual world landed me in their world, not mine. It wasn't so much that I entered; I just slipped in through some random window or door or crack or crevice and began making myself at home. And I didn't move in. I just entered for a mystical 50 minute visit. In retrospect, I think of the emotional and psychological shift from my world to my clients' worlds as a form of meditation. Nearly always, spending an hour making myself at home in my clients' inner worlds, left me calmer and helped shrink my own emotional over-reactions to life.

We have a social work friend who likes to say that the door to children's emotions locks from the inside (J. Sommers-Flanagan & R. Sommers-Flanagan, 2011). This implies that children have to unlock the door to their emotions for us to gain entry. We can't barge in, without doing damage. The same process seems true for adults. As Rogers theorized, we must establish an environment of safety and trust so clients will be motivated to unlock their emotional doors and let us into their private and personal worlds.

Being Sensitive From Moment to Moment With the Client's Changing Meanings and Emotions

Moment-to-moment sensitivity requires focused attention to your client's constantly changing way of being. In emotion focused therapy Greenberg recommends focusing on meaning and poignancy associated with client verbalizations (Greenberg, 2011). For example, Goldman and Greenberg (1997) recommended that as the client offers a narrative, the therapist keep his or her attention focused by continually asking internal questions such as "What is the core meaning or message that she or he is communicating?" or "What is most alive?" or "What is being felt?" (p. 408). These questions help articulate the importance of not getting stuck on what the client said previously, because your focus is on the new information or the new emotion that is occurring in the now.

This is a crucial concept for mental health professionals to understand and practice. Being all too human, clients can be unintentionally inconsistent. They will say one thing one moment ("I miss my mom") and another thing the next ("I'm glad I live 1,000 miles from my mother"). As a careful and rational listener, you may be inclined to jump in and confront client inconsistencies ("Wait a minute, you just said you miss your mother and now you're saying you're glad you live far away from her. Which is really true?"). As you'll see later when we discuss motivational interviewing, it's not the therapist's job to confront every client discrepancy . . . partly because it's perfectly natural for clients to feel deep ambivalence. Instead, as Rogers taught, it's the therapist's job to keep listening to these moment to moment changes. In these situations, confrontation is undesirable because it can reduce trust and increase resistant behaviors (Miller & Rollnick, 2002).

Temporarily Living, and Moving About Delicately, in the Client's Life

To reside in another person's life is serious business. It's important to notice that Rogers suggested we do this *temporarily—not permanently*. This is a warning of the dangers of diving too deeply into another's world. In 1967, Rogers wrote of an experience in which he became too involved with a client and lost his way:

> I stubbornly felt that I should be able to help her and permitted the contacts to continue long after they had ceased to be therapeutic, and involved only suffering for me. I recognized that many of her insights were sounder than mine, and this destroyed my confidence in myself, and I somehow gave up my self in the relationship. (Rogers, 1967a, p. 367)

Ideally, your goal is to have one foot in the client's world and one foot firmly planted in your own world, letting yourself flow into the client's being for periods of time without losing a more objective perspective on what's happening in the therapy session. As noted in Chapter 4, Martin Buber, the Jewish theologian, referred to this sort of experience as an I-Thou relationship and emphasized that it's impossible to constantly maintain such a relationship. For a transcript of a 1957 dialogue between Rogers and Buber, see Kirschenbaum and Henderson (1989).

Sensing Deep Meanings, But Not Uncovering Feelings That Are Too Far Out of Awareness

Rogers sometimes talked about working on the edge of his clients' consciousness. In this regard his approach is consistent with psychoanalytic practice. You may recall from Chapter 2 that psychoanalytic principles suggest that therapists should interpret unconscious material *just as* insights are about to break through. Similarly, Rogers respects the client's pace and comfort. As a person-centered therapist moving about gently within your client's world, if you have an impulse to tell a client about something completely outside of his or her awareness, it's probably best to hold your tongue. Even though there is room for intuitive input, your main job is to follow the client's lead, not to forge your own path.

Motivational Interviewing: A Contemporary PCT Approach

PCT principles have been integrated into most other therapies. However, there are three specific approaches that are explicitly new generation person-centered therapies. These include:

1. **Motivational interviewing**

2. **Emotion-focused therapy**

3. **Nondirective play therapy**

Next, we discuss motivational interviewing. Due to its strong integrational characteristics, emotion-focused therapy is covered in Chapter 14. Additional resources are available on nondirective play therapy (Landreth, 2002).

Moving Away From Confrontation and Education

In his research with problem drinkers, William R. Miller was studying the efficacy of behavioral self-control techniques. To his surprise, he found that structured behavioral treatments were no more effective than an encouragement-based control group. When he explored the data for an explanation, he found that regardless of treatment protocol, therapist empathy ratings were the strongest predictors of positive outcomes at 6 months ($r = .82$), 12 months ($r = .71$), and 2 years ($r = .51$; W. R. Miller, 1978; W. R. Miller & Taylor, 1980). Consequently, he concluded that positive treatment outcomes with problem drinkers were less related to behavioral treatment and more related to reflective listening and empathy. He also found that active confrontation and education generally led to client resistance. These discoveries led him to develop motivational interviewing (MI).

MI builds on person-centered principles by adding more focused therapeutic targets and specific client goals. Rollnick and Miller (1995) define MI as "a directive, client-centered counseling style for eliciting behavior change by helping clients to explore and resolve ambivalence" (p. 326).

Focusing on Client Ambivalence

Client ambivalence is the primary target of MI. When it comes to substance abuse and other health related behaviors, Miller and Rollnick (2002) view ambivalence as natural. Most all problem drinkers recognize or wish they could quit, but continue drinking for various reasons. Miller and Rollnick described what happens when therapists try to push healthy behaviors on clients:

> [The therapist] then proceeds to advise, teach, persuade, counsel or argue for this particular resolution to [the client's] ambivalence. One does not need a doctorate in psychology to anticipate what [the client's] response is likely to be in this situation. By virtue of ambivalence, [the client] is apt to argue the opposite, or at least point out problems and shortcomings of the proposed solution. It is natural for [the client] to do so, because [he or she] feels at least two ways about this or almost any prescribed solution. It is the very nature of ambivalence. (pp. 20–21)

In many situations, humans are naturally inclined to resist authority. Therefore, when resistance rises up in clients, MI advocates person-centered attitudes and interventions. This leads to Miller and Rollnick's (2002) foundational person-centered principle of treatment:

> It is the client who should be voicing the arguments for change (p. 22).

Although Miller and Rollnick describe Rogers as collaborative, caring, and supportive—they emphasize that he was not nondirective (W. R. Miller & Rollnick, 1998). Instead, they note that Rogers gently guided clients to places where they were most confused, in pain, or agitated and then helped them stay in that place and work through it. The four central principles of MI flow from their conceptualization of Rogers's approach (W. R. Miller & Rollnick, 2002). According to these principles, it's the therapist's job to:

- Use reflective listening skills to *express empathy* for the client's message and genuine caring for the client.

- Notice and develop the theme of discrepancy between the client's deep values and current behavior.

- Meet client resistance with reflection rather than confrontation (Miller and Rollnick refer to this as "rolling with resistance").

- Enhance client self-efficacy by focusing on optimism, confidence that change is possible, and small interventions that are likely to be successful.

MI is both a set of techniques and a person-centered philosophy or style. The philosophical MI perspective emphasizes that motivation for change is not something therapists can effectively impose on clients. Change must be drawn out from clients, gently and with careful timing. Motivational interviewers do not use direct persuasion.

A Sampling of MI Techniques

Miller and Rollnick (2002) provide many excellent examples of how reflection responses reduce resistance. The following interactions capture how reflection of client efforts lessens the need for resistance:

Client: I'm trying! If my probation officer would just get off my back, I could focus on getting my life in order.

Interviewer: You're working hard on the changes you need to make.

or

Interviewer: It's frustrating to have a probation officer looking over your shoulder.

Client: Who are you to be giving me advice? What do you know about drugs? You've probably never even smoked a joint!

Interviewer: It's hard to imagine how I could possibly understand.

Client: I couldn't keep the weight off even if I lost it.

Interviewer: You can't see any way that would work for you.

or

Interviewer: You're rather discouraged about trying again. (pp. 100–101)

In the following excerpt from *Clinical Interviewing* (2009), we describe the MI technique of **amplified reflection**:

> Recently, in hundreds of brief interviews conducted by graduate students in psychology and counseling with client—volunteers from introductory psychology courses, consistent with Miller and Rollnick's (2002) motivational interviewing work, we found that clients have a strong need for their interviewers to accurately hear what they're saying. When their interviewer made an inaccurate reflection, clients felt compelled to clarify their feelings and beliefs—often in ways that rebalanced their ambivalence.
>
> For example, when an interviewer "went too far" with a reflection, the following exchange was typical:

Client: I am so pissed at my roommate. She won't pick up her clothes or do the dishes or anything.

Interviewer: You'd sort of like to fire her as a roommate.

Client: No. Not exactly. There are lots of things I like about her, but her messiness really annoys me.

> This phenomenon suggests that it might be possible for interviewers to intentionally overstate a client's position in an effort to get clients to come back around to clarify or articulate the more positive side of an issue. In fact, this is a particular motivational interviewing technique referred to as amplified reflection.
>
> When used intentionally, amplified reflection can seem manipulative, which is why amplified reflection is used along with genuine empathy. Instead of being a manipulative response it can also be viewed as an effort on the interviewer's part to more deeply empathize with the client's frustration, anger, discouragement, and so on. Examples of this technique include:

Client: My child has a serious disability and so I have to be home for him.

Interviewer: You really need to be home 24/7 and really need to turn off any needs you have to get out and take a break.

Client: Actually, that's not totally true. Sometimes, I think I need to take some breaks so I can do a better job when I am home.

Client: When my grandmother died last semester I had to miss classes and it was a total hassle.

Interviewer: You don't have much of an emotional response to your grandmother's death—other than it really inconveniencing you.

Client: Well, it's not like I don't miss her, too.

> Again, we should emphasize that amplified reflection is an empathic effort to get completely in touch with or resonate with one side of the client's ambivalence (from J. Sommers-Flanagan & Sommers-Flanagan, 2009, pp. 316–317).

PCT in Action: Brief Vignettes

In classical PCT, therapists are nondirective and follow their clients' lead. Meier and Davis (2008) refer to this as **pacing** and write eloquently about the difference between pacing and leading. Our main hope is that you'll develop enough self-awareness to recognize when you're pacing and when you're leading. Another way to think of this is to know the difference between following your client's agenda versus following your own agenda. In the first brief vignette, we provide an example of a cognitive-behavioral therapist conducting an intake interview.

Vignette I: Person-Centered Therapy (Not!)
In contrast to PCT, cognitive-behavioral therapy (CBT) involves setting an explicit agenda and then working from that agenda (see Chapter 8). The following excerpt from Ledley, Marx, and Heimberg (2010) illustrates how in the CBT approach, therapists may push their agenda. In this excerpt, all [bracketed comments] are added by us and not in the original:

Clinician: So, you consider the panic attacks your biggest problem right now?

Client: Yeah. For sure.

Clinician: Hmmmm. That surprises me a bit. During our assessment, you told me that you have panic attacks pretty infrequently. [Hmmmm. In this situation the therapist is using the word "surprise" to move toward a confrontation—where the discrepancy between what the client rates as most troubling is contrasted with what the therapist views as most troubling.]

Client: Yeah, I do. But they're pretty awful when they come on.

Clinician: So, when they do happen, they get you pretty stressed out and kind of foul up your day? [This is a motivational interviewing technique, called **coming alongside** (Rosengren, 2009). The therapist slightly overstates the client's position hoping the client will correct him/her with a more moderate statement. Note the therapist both reflects the client's experience ("get you pretty stressed out") and then overstates

Client: Yeah. They definitely stress me out. I don't know about fouling up a whole day, though. They don't last that long, you know. [As predicted from the motivational interviewing perspective, the client pulls back from the more extreme statement.]

Clinician: How about the problems with your eating? Can they foul up a whole day? [Now the cognitive-behavioral therapist is confronting, albeit somewhat indirectly, the client's choice to work on her panic attacks instead of her eating behaviors.]

Client: They foul up every day. I already told you—I'm bingeing like three times a day. And then I throw up. And I feel so gross that I have to have a shower to get cleaned up and calm down. It's awful. I've missed five classes in the past week. [The client concedes that the eating problem is more disruptive to her daily life.]

Clinician: So, it sounds like the bulimia might be interfering more than the panic attacks. [This is a person-centered reflection of content or paraphrase that appears to be intentionally

selected to highlight what the therapist wants the client to admit.]

Client: I guess. [The client concedes, but seems less than enthused.]

Clinician: It sounds like you might be feeling like working on the eating is a bit more stressful right now than working on the panic. [Another paraphrase.]

Client: Well, obviously.

Clinician: It can be very hard, I agree. Is it worth giving it a try for a few weeks and seeing how it goes? [The therapist acknowledges the client's perception that working on the eating "can be very hard," but follows that with, "How about we do this my way first and then evaluate?" In contrast, person-centered therapists would not put their goals and strategies as a higher priority than the client's.]

Client: I guess [again, the client concedes, but without much motivation] (pp. 78–79).

Vignette II: Person-Centered Goal-Setting

Next, we've reworked the preceding vignette to be consistent with PCT. In contrast to the CBT example, the person-centered therapist respects both sides of the client's ambivalence and works to help the client decide, for herself, how to move forward. The vignette begins with the same two opening responses.

Clinician: So, you consider the panic attacks your biggest problem right now. [From the PCT perspective, this is framed (and phrased) as a statement, not as a question.]

Client: Yeah. For sure.

Clinician: When you were talking earlier you said you're really struggling with your eating. And now I hear you saying your feelings of panic are also a major priority for therapy. [In the PCT approach, the therapist, having listened closely, simply brings the two conflicting statements together in space and time and then lets the client clarify the discrepancy. There's no judgment or "surprise," just a gentle noticing.]

Client: They're both priorities. They both make me feel miserable.

Clinician: It's like you're saying, "they both make me feel so miserable that I'm not even sure which one to talk about first." [This is an example of the PCT method of "walking within." The therapist is metaphorically stepping into the client's psychological world and speaking from that perspective using first-person pronouns. When done well, clients typically don't notice this wording shift. When done poorly, it can sound terribly phony—which is why Rogers would likely recommend using this method only when it bubbles up naturally.]

Client: I wish I could deal with the eating, but it's overwhelming. It takes over my whole life and so I'm afraid if we try to work on this first, we'll fail and then I'll know I'll never be able to change. [This process allows the client to begin articulating deeper fears.]

Clinician: It feels like, "If I were to try to change my eating behaviors and fail, then things will be hopeless." Do I have that right? [Another walking within, centered on fear of failure and hopelessness.]

Client: Exactly. It just feels too risky. What do you think I should do? [It's not unusual, when repeatedly prompted to self-reflect, for clients to then turn to the therapist for direct guidance.]

Clinician: I hear you wishing you could deal with your eating struggles, but it's so scary that you also wish for expert guidance. You're the one experiencing this and you're the only one who knows what sort of risk and fear you feel inside. Do you mind if I just tell you what I think? [The therapist summarizes some of the internal dynamic the client is struggling with and then asks the client's permission to be open.]

Client: That's exactly what I'd like you to do. [Of course, the client affirms this, because she's already asked for it.]

Clinician: Like you, I wish I could look into the future and say with absolute certainty exactly what you should do. And I may come to the point where I feel clear enough that I can share that with you. But for now I hear you saying you're deeply afraid of the risk of working directly on your eating behavior . . . and so before we decide together what you should work on first, it seems important for us to continue exploring your fears and hopes. It also seems important, as much as possible, for you to be your own guide in this process . . . with me along for clarification and support. [This is very PCT. The rule is to respond to every client question, but not to answer every question. This is also an example of informed consent or role induction where the therapist leads the client back toward self-exploration, rather than to a reliance on external validation. From the PCT perspective, many client problems exist or are exacerbated because of nonreliance on the self. For example, an eating disorder can be conceptualized as a repeated pattern where the client is feeling out of control and not in charge of her own behavior. Additionally, she may have body image issues related to self-rejection instead of self-acceptance. Consequently, self-rejection and denial of her personal power likely contributes to her eating disorder and so, even in cases of modified PCT where therapists eventually integrate a more directive approach (e.g., CBT), initially a deeper exploration of the self and issues around self-acceptance are emphasized.]

Client: It's so hard being me right now. I just want to have someone else take over and rescue me from myself. [The client acknowledges her feelings of self-alienation and wish to have someone else take over and rescue her.]

Looking at this case through the PCT lens allows for consideration of the pros and cons of working from the PCT perspective. Specifically, you can see the client is now asking for guidance and yet the therapist is reluctant to provide guidance, instead wanting the client to continue painful self-exploration.

CASE ANALYSIS AND TREATMENT PLANNING

In the following case example, Carl Rogers is conducting a single-session demonstration with a hospitalized woman, known here as Ms. PS (Rogers, 1963). This is an abridged version of the session, with ellipsis following responses where portions were deleted. Again, this case is integrated with an abbreviated treatment plan and our comments are in [brackets].

Carl Rogers (CR): What'd I like is for you to tell me anything you're willing to tell me about yourself and your situation and how you feel about yourself and your situation. Or I guess another way of putting it is, anything you're willing to tell me that would help me to know you better, I'd be very glad to hear. [This is a vintage Rogers opening. His goal is clear: He wants to hear whatever she's willing to say and to get to know *her* better.]

PS: Where do you want me to start?

CR: Where ever you would like to. [This is a standard PCT response to the client's hesitation over where to begin. Rogers gives the client full permission to begin wherever she likes.]

PS: Well, I'll start with my childhood. When I was, uh, when I was a little girl, I had this cross eye since I was about 7 years old. And, I mean kids poked fun of me and as the years got longer and I start going into the higher grades. I mean I never had no boyfriends or anything I mean I had girlfriends but after the girls started going

around with the boys I mean and the boys would tell them, don't go around with me or something like that. And actually I ended up without any girlfriends at all. And around my neighborhood there was no girls my age so I was counting on the school and they sort of let me down. And I felt just like I, I wasn't wanted.

CR: So you sort of wound up with no friends at all and am I getting it right, that you feel that was due, basically, due to your eye condition, or.... [As described by Wickman and Campbell (2003), Rogers commonly provided clients with "invitations for repair" (p. 179). These invitations allow clients to correct Rogers, in case his perceptions of the client's inner experience is inaccurate.]

PS: [There's a 2-minute gap and then the interview continues.] That's what I always say (5 seconds of silence). And then my home situation now, is um, well that's part of it, my husband won't let me go anyplace. But then there's my mother too. My husband's brother's staying downstairs with my mother and I just don't, I don't like the idea of it. I mean, my mother isn't married to him, and yet he acts like he's a father to my two brothers and we're living upstairs in my mother's place and even though I'm married, he tries to boss me around.

CR: So that's another thing you don't like, you don't quite like the situation your mother is in and you don't like him, because he acts like he's married to her.... [Rogers initiates a pattern where, when the client goes silent, he waits expectantly for her to continue speaking. Also, the client is focusing repeatedly on what she *doesn't* like, and Rogers is staying right with her.]

PS: No, she's only living on 20 dollars a month for food already and with having to have him stay there and eat and, my God, they practically eat beans all the time, it wouldn't be that bad if he wasn't there. Gotta be buying cigarettes and all that stuff. They could be saving that money for food. Actually with the little money she gets he's actually living off her.

CR: Sounds like you feel pretty resentful of that. [This is Rogers's first response that can be categorized as a "reflection of feeling."]

PS: Yes, well, I mean I don't care for it. I mean everybody's up against it, like my mother's mother. [The feeling reflection with the word *resentful* may have disorganized the client a bit, as she appears to struggle expressing herself.]

CR: I'm sorry. I didn't get that.

PS: My mother's mother don't like it either.

CR: I see, um hmm.

PS: She don't like to have her daughter talked about by my mother's brothers and sisters.

CR: Uh huh. Uh huh. So I guess you're saying, "I'm not the only one that feels that way about her and her situation." [Notice that Rogers uses a first-person quotation—for the first time in this session—to deepen his empathic connection with this client. This is another example of "walking within." He also steers clear of his client's muddled verbal output, commenting only on the main message in the communication, which appears to be an effort to justify her feelings.]

PS: Yes. I mean, I'm not the only one, but if anybody tells her anything, she's so bull-headed and knot-headed that she, she just, if somebody tells her to do something or get away from him or something, she just stay with him. I mean she just wants to do things her own self. But, even though I'm married, she wants to try to run my life. I mean. I hate the idea of everybody telling me what to do. Even my husband, he'll tell me what to do. Even though I'm young and I'm married, I mean I'm a human being and I like to run my life myself. I mean I don't want to feel like I'm still in a baby buggy or something like that.

CR: You feel that your mother and your husband and everybody tries to run your life. [Another paraphrase.]

PS: Yes. That's why I feel, I was old enough to bear a baby and that's surely a lot of pain. But yet they won't let me make up my mind for myself.

CR: Here I was old enough to have a child and yet nobody thinks I can make my decisions or run my own life. Is that what you're saying? [Here he's both walking within and using an invitation for repair.]

The Problem List

Most of the time person-centered therapists aren't really thinking about problem lists. However, somewhat surprisingly, although Rogers has yet to ask a traditional problem-oriented question, based on these first few minutes of this first session, a tentative problem list can be generated. The initial and tentative problem list for Ms. PS might look like this:

- Unspecified social problems (an apparent sense of disconnection or alienation).

- Problems with assertiveness and self-esteem (Ms. PS appears to have difficulties speaking up for herself and reports feeling controlled by others; it's likely this is related to self-esteem issues).

- Unresolved anger/resentment (Ms. PS is angry toward several people and may need assistance exploring this and dealing with it more effectively).

- Thinking difficulties that may be exacerbated by either anger or anxiety (Ms. PS seems to have difficulties expressing herself clearly, which could be related to mental disorganization).

The interview continues...

PS: Yes. I mean like, this is when my husband and I went to California, with our little boy.... But, being back in the whole situation it's just not good. His mother is the kind of person who would talk behind her own brother's back. Uh, I mean her own son's. My husband has six brothers and one sister. And I mean she'll talk to one of her sons about one of her other sons. I mean, she's that kind of person. And although she don't come right out and tell me to my face that she don't like me, I know by the way she's talking about the other people behind their backs, that she's talking about me, too.

CR: You feel she's just a gossip and you feel she doesn't like you. [Another paraphrase.]

PS: Oh, I know she don't like me (laughs).

CR: No doubt about that. [Rogers goes with the client's correction of his paraphrase.]

PS: Oh, no doubt (11 seconds of silence). Uh, mostly that's, uh, that's the point. And my little girl she passed away a couple of months ago. And my mother did another thing. See, when my little girl was born, I asked my mother, I said, um, "How come her leg, her one leg, is turned a little bit?" and she said, "All babies are like that when they're small." She said, "You can't expect them to get up and walk right away," and I said, "I know that." And she said, "Don't worry about it" and so I didn't worry about it and then after my little girl passed away, my mother told me that my daughter was cripple. She kept it from me again. She keeps things from me like that. And, and in a way I felt responsible for my little girl's death. You know, she would be sitting down and um, well, I'd sit her up in the davenport, in the corner and I'd put her little legs in, but if I would have known she was cripple, I surely wouldn't do that. [This is a key interaction. Following Rogers's validation of her correction of his paraphrase, the client becomes silent. Rogers allows the silence to be. Then Ms. PS moves into an emotionally significant issue. In essence, his responses to her have allowed her to go deeper.]

CR: That really concerns you that that was kept from you and it concerns you that maybe you didn't deal with her right, not, not knowing that she was crippled.... [Paraphrase.]

PS: She let me down. I mean, my mother she, I always took the blame home. My mother always, always liked my oldest brother. I always took the blame home, whether I did something wrong or not. I got along a lot better with my father. Then my father passed away and then, and well actually, I mean I took most, I took all the blame I

wanna say, than my brother and now my youngest brother that's home, he's going through the same darn thing I am. He's taking all the blame home.

CR: You feel when you were home, whatever went wrong, you took the blame for it, within yourself. [Even though he uses the word "feel" this is just a paraphrase.]

PS: No, uh, my brother would say that I did this and that.

CR: I see. That's what I wasn't quite clear about, you were blamed for everything. [This is an example of a correction or repair.]

PS: Yeah.

CR: Whether you had done it or not. Is that...?

PS: Yes I was.

CR: It isn't so much you felt you were to blame, but, but, others blamed you. [Repair continues.]

PS: I mean my brother actually got away with everything.

CR: I guess you feel that was sort of true with everybody except your father. Is that.... That things went somewhat better between you and your father. [At this point Rogers leads the client toward talking about her father.]

PS: Yes. Yes they did. I mean, I could go and he'd take me, well, my mother and my father we used to go out a lot of times, but they went sort of late you know and by that time I'd be asleep and I used to fool 'em all the times because I knew they were gonna stop at the hamburger shop. And I'd make believe I was asleep and when they'd stop and I'd say, "Oh, I'm awake, I'm awake, you gotta get me one too." And I mean, I used to have a lotta fun when I used to go out with my mother and father and mostly when I went away with my father I used to help him pile wood and I mean we had a lotta fun the neighborhood kids would come over, boys and girls and they'd help my father pile up the wood and help him cut it with a saw and after that, we'd all pile in the car and went down got an ice cream cone.

CR: Those are really kind of pleasant memories. [A simple reflection of feeling.]

PS: Uh hmm.

CR: (10 seconds of silence) I don't know, but it looks as though, thinking about those things, make you feel a little bit weepy, or am I wrong? [Once again, Rogers lets the silence do its work and then tentatively comments on the client's affect.]

PS: A little bit.

CR: A little bit.

Problem Formulation

Ms. PS has experienced conditions of worth. It also seems she has not relied on her own judgments, perhaps because of not trusting herself. Instead, she has allowed others to control her or tell her how to lead her life. This pattern of submitting to others may have led to her feeling deep anger and resentment and yet there's also the question of whether she's developed herself enough to make mature and healthy decisions on her own. This problem formulation implies that part of the therapy work will involve this client developing a clearer and more direct way to both rely on herself and her own judgment, while at the same time considering input from others.

It's also likely that her low self-worth adversely affects her ability to express anger directly. Although a behavioral approach might emphasize skill development through practice and role playing, PCT works on improving her self-worth and her situational appraisal skills so she can become confident enough to speak up appropriately.

Finally, it may be that she has unresolved feelings of loss and guilt around the death of her daughter. The guilt seems associated with her self-evaluation that she should have relied on her own feelings or beliefs when her mother was misleading her about her daughter's health condition.

The session continues...

PS: I can remember, I don't exactly know how it went, but I know I was pretty young, but um, we went over by, my father, yes his brother, we went over by, it was I and David, my oldest brother.

Anyway, the two guys, they decided to go out and then my mother and my aunt and my brother were there and two children, gee, I don't know if I'm getting this quite clearly. [Again, Rogers has created an atmosphere that allows the client to continue going deeper into an early childhood memory.]

CR: It's hard to remember. [A process-focused paraphrase.]

Toward the end of the session the client commented on her counseling experience with Rogers:

PS: Gee, that's funny, I never said these things before to the other doctors (16 seconds of silence). [The patient's comment at this juncture reflects the fact that Rogers is, indeed, different than the other doctors. As Natalie Rogers has put it, her father's approach uses a different language and is revolutionary (N. Rogers, May, 2003, personal communication). Thus far, he has shown deep interest in the client as a person, while showing no interest in the client's symptoms. One can see why this client said things to Rogers that she'd never said to any other doctors.]

As the session continued, the client spoke about many deeply personal and powerful issues. Finally, toward the end she admits to having previously wanted pity from others, but states she wants to start making her own decisions and no longer wants pity. In one of her final apt references to her self-development, she states: "It's just like everyone's got a part of me...like one's got one leg the one's got one arm (laughs), just like they all got part of me and I ain't got none of myself."

Interventions

The PCT intervention is always the same and yet always unique. Ms. PS needs to be exposed to Rogers's "certain kind of environment" characterized by congruence, unconditional positive regard, and empathic understanding. As this environment (intervention) is provided, she will begin to develop greater insight into what she really wants. She also will begin to trust her own judgment and her actualization tendency will be activated.

For the most part, Rogers will track or pace what Ms. PS says in therapy. He will feed back to her his understanding. Through this treatment process, he will help her become more aware and sensitive to her own emotions and judgments. At times, as he did in this interview when he guided Ms.PS toward talking about her father, Rogers will gently lead her to explore new psychological and emotional territory. The purpose of this is to help her to freely "explore all the hidden nooks and frightening crannies of" her "inner and often buried experience" (p. 34).

For those of us oriented toward the quick fix world of psychotherapy and medicine, this approach raises questions. What good does this "free" exploration do? How can we understand what Rogers is offering via PCT?

It may be helpful to think about PCT using behavioral terminology (see Chapter 7). PCT's freedom to explore the self can be reformulated as exposure treatment, using a classical conditioning model. In some ways, Rogers is doing systematic desensitization. As Ms. PS talks about her fears and emotional pain within an accepting environment, she is being exposed to her fears and is systematically extinguishing them. In the end, she can leave therapy without fear of herself or her judgment. She may develop the skill of balanced judgment—to be able to explore her feelings and opinions, while considering others' input. In this way therapy has facilitated her "development" or maturation into a more fully functioning person.

Outcomes Measurement

Similar to psychoanalytic and existential therapists, person-centered therapists don't have much use for objective, pencil-paper outcomes measures. Because treatment focuses on self-development and not solely on symptom reduction, symptom checklists, or other behaviorally oriented measures may not be optimal for measuring outcomes. However, as pressure to demonstrate positive outcomes has increased, researchers with humanistic perspectives have begun using more symptom-based measures in combination with measures sensitive to changes that humanistic therapies are likely to produce. For example, in an "allegiance-balanced randomized clinical trial" comparing the efficacy of cognitive-behavioral therapy (CBT) and process-experiential therapy (PE; aka emotion-focused therapy) for treating clinical depression, two self-report measures sensitive to person-centered outcomes were used (Watson, Gordon, Stermac, Kalogerakos, & Steckley, 2003):

1. A 10-item version of the Rosenberg Self-Esteem Inventory (Bachman & O'Malley, 1977).

2. The 127 item Inventory of Interpersonal Problems (Horowitz, Rosenberg, Baer, Ureño, & Villaseñor, 1988).

These measures were used in addition to more traditional, symptom-based inventories like the Beck Depression Inventory (BDI; Beck, Ward, Mendelson, Mock, & Erbaugh, 1961).

In considering outcomes assessment with Ms. PS or in other person-centered clinical settings, brief instruments evaluating her self-esteem, assertiveness, and depression/anxiety might all be appropriate and not interfere with the person-centered treatment process. Additionally, Hubble, Duncan, and Miller (1999) developed a four-item Outcomes Rating Scale, a humanistically oriented process-outcome measure designed to be used every session as a means for both tracking progress and empowering clients to provide their therapists with ongoing feedback about how the therapy process is going (Duncan et al., 2010).

CULTURAL AND GENDER CONSIDERATIONS

Rogers was empowering of all persons, including women. This makes his approach much more acceptable to feminist therapists (Brown, 2010). In his work with Ms. PS, he is following her lead, listening to her, and empowering her (albeit indirectly) to articulate her wants and needs. The main feminist critique of PCT is that it's not directly activist—PCT doesn't advocate for clients, but waits for clients to become ready to advocate for themselves.

At first glance, PCT appears very culturally sensitive. After all, it's an approach characterized by deep trust in and respect for individuals. Rogers developed PCT "in the 1940s because he believed the therapies available at that time tended to be too 'therapist-centered.'" (Cain, 2010, p. 144). This is an approach especially designed to address the needs and interests of unique clients, while activating their inner potential for positive change and growth. What could be more culturally sensitive?

As is turns out, there are a number of ways in which PCT isn't culturally sensitive or appropriate. First, PCT focuses very much on individuals—which may not work well with culturally diverse clients with collectivist worldviews. PCT's emphasis on self-actualization is a poor fit for clients who are more oriented to family life, collectivist goals, and social or community interest.

Second, PCT's focus on emotions and emotional expression is also a poor fit for individuals from cultures that avoid individual emotional expression. For example, within the Latino or Asian cultures male emotionality can be viewed as a weakness. Somewhat similarly, many First Nations or Native American people, as well as Asians, simply don't talk about their personal issues outside the family (D.W. Sue & D. Sue, 2008). In fact, research has shown that many culturally diverse clients expect expert advice and consequently prefer directive therapies (Atkinson, Lowe, & Mathews, 1995; Atkinson, Maruyama, & Matsui, 1978). This makes classical PCT a poor treatment choice for some culturally diverse clients.

Person-centered approaches may be too indirect for some cultures, but in some cases they may actually be too direct. For example, if counselors are too congruent they may openly express thoughts and feelings more overtly and directly than is acceptable within some cultures. If so, instead of serving as a facilitative condition, the counselor's congruence might increase client anxiety and thereby impair the therapy process.

To this point, we've primarily described the limitations of PCT as an approach to counseling clients from diverse cultures. Of course, as always, there's an alternative view. Rogers noted that many of his philosophical ideas have an Eastern flavor. He discussed the Taoist principle of wu-wei, sometimes referred to as the principle of nonaction, and he shared several of his favorite sayings, most of which were Eastern in origin. In particular, he cited the following quotation from Lao-tse as possibly his very favorite:

> If I keep from meddling with people, they take care of themselves,
>   If I keep from commanding people, they behave themselves,
>   If I keep from preaching at people, they improve themselves,
>   If I keep from imposing on people, they become themselves. (Rogers, 1980, p. 42)

Over the years PCT has remained internationally popular. Although classical PCT is likely on the decline in the United States, person-centered approaches remain popular in Japan, South Africa, South America, and in a number of European countries and the United Kingdom (Cain, 2010).

Although PCT may not be a perfect fit for clients from diverse or collectivist backgrounds, due to the general sensitivity behind this approach, it would never be forced onto a client who doesn't desire to work in this way (see Putting it in Practice 5.4). Based on the work of Rogers, it's hard to imagine him ever advocating that PCT be generally applied to anyone who isn't comfortable or interested in PCT.

EVIDENCE-BASED STATUS

Rogers was the first modern scientist-practitioner. He took the unusual and risky step of recording and empirically evaluating his therapeutic approach. He also applied PCT to extremely challenging

PUTTING IT IN PRACTICE 5.4

Four Cornerstones of Being a Therapist

You may already be aware of the work of Sherry Cormier. Dr. Cormier is co-author of *Interviewing Strategies for Helpers*, a very well-respected book on interviewing within the mental health field. Her text, subtitled *Fundamental Skills and Cognitive Behavioral Interventions*, is frequently adopted in departments of psychology, counseling, and social work. So why would we include a comment by someone known for her cognitive-behavioral text within this person-centered chapter? Dr. Cormier's description of her theoretical orientation is an excellent integration of the evolutionary stages of person-centered theory and therapy. As you can see below, her description of herself is clearly within the spirit of contemporary person-centered therapy:

I don't use a single or a particular counseling technique or theoretical approach with all clients, and I consider this an ethical issue. To me the one-size-fits-all approach places loyalty to a technique or an orientation above the welfare of the client. There are, however, four things that are very important to me in working with people.

The cornerstone of all of my interactions with people is respect. To me this is a fundamental quality necessary for any effective human interaction, and I try to be as respectful as possible whether I am counseling, teaching, parenting, partnering, or shopping. In this sense I am a Rogerian, in that back in 1957 Carl Rogers defined positive regard and respect as one of the three core facilitative conditions for counseling and psychotherapy.

I think respect has been an internal quality I have had with myself for a very long time. More recently, I have come to believe that breathing is another very important part of human interactions. What I mean by this is that it is important for me to pay attention to my own breathing when I am with a person. When I am tense or uncomfortable I notice my breath gets faster and more shallow. As I deepen my breath and slow it down, I feel more centered, and when I am more centered I am more fully present and more alive in the interaction. In some instances I also pay attention to the breath patterns of the other person as well. This seems to reflect both Rogerian and Gestalt influences.

The third quality that is important to me in working with people in all kinds of interactions is intuition. This is also a much more recent development in the evolution of how I am with people.

As I have gotten older, I have recognized my capacity to be intuitive, and, perhaps more importantly, have learned to trust it. Over the years there have been instances when I have turned away from my intuition and have come to regret this. So now when I get a hunch or a feeling in my gut about a client or a person I pay attention to that for a period of time. Sometimes my intuition shows up in my dreams. If I am unclear about what the intuitive images mean, I seek consultation about them, or sometimes I draw about them in order to create meaning. This, I think, reflects both Jungian and narrative approaches.

> At the same time, I am also influenced by techniques, interventions, and approaches that are evidence-based; that is, they have some sort of literature base or empirical support for their use with certain clients and certain issues. This reflects my cognitive-behavioral roots. In recent years, one such approach that I rely on greatly in all person-to-person interactions is the Prochaska, DiClemente, and Norcross stages of change model. I find myself conceptualizing clients, students, my family, my friends, and so on in terms of this model, and this conceptualization seems to help me understand and be more empathic and more patient with their process.
>
> I have enjoyed sharing this with you. I wish each of you the very best in developing your own orientation and approaches to working with people.

clinical populations and openly reported his less-than-stellar findings.

One of Rogers's early and most ambitious studies was with hospitalized schizophrenics in Wisconsin. This study examined client-centered relationship variables in the treatment of 16 hospitalized schizophrenics. Rogers reported:

It is a sobering finding that our therapists—competent and conscientious as they were—had over-optimistic and, in some cases, seriously invalid perceptions of the relationships in which they were involved. The patient, for all his psychosis, or the bright young college student with no knowledge of therapy, turned out to have more useful (and probably more accurate) perceptions of the relationship. (Rogers, 1967b, p. 92)

The patients made little progress in this treatment study. However, consistent with later research pointing to the crucial nature of empathy in positive treatment outcomes, patients who rated themselves as experiencing a higher degree of empathy, warmth, and genuineness had shorter hospital stays than patients who rated their therapists as less empathic, warm, and genuine.

More recent research on PCT effectiveness has yielded small, but positive results. First, PCT is consistently more effective than no treatment. Second, it is marginally more effective than placebo treatment. Third, it is often somewhat less effective than more structured cognitive and behavioral treatments for specific problems. For example, in their large meta-analysis, Smith and Glass reported

an effect size of .63 for client-centered therapy, a moderate-size effect (Smith & Glass, 1977; Smith et al., 1980). In contrast, behavioral and cognitive therapies obtained effect sizes ranging from .73 to 1.13 (Smith & Glass, 1977; Smith et al., 1980).

More recent research results tend to vary based on researcher allegiance. For example, in a review of 18 client-centered treatment versus no treatment studies, emotional-focused therapy researchers Greenberg, Elliot, and Lietaer (1994) reported a large effect size (ES = .95) for client-centered therapy. In contrast, family therapy and behavioral research teams reported PCT as less efficacious than family and behavioral therapies (Szapocznik et al., 2004; Weisz, Weiss, Alicke, & Klotz, 1987; Weisz, Weiss, Han, Granger, & Morton,1995). Two more recent studies showed no significant differences between cognitive-behavioral therapy, psychodynamic therapy, and PCT (Stiles, Barkham, Mellor-Clark, & Connell, 2008) or between cognitive therapy and PCT (Marriott & Kellett, 2009).

Given the empirical facts, most professionals, academics, and students conclude that cognitive and behavioral treatments are more scientifically valid than PCT. Although this may well be the case, there's another perspective. It may be that, when measured using scientifically validated clinical outcome instruments, PCT appears less effective than therapies targeting specific behaviors, symptoms, and cognitions. In fact, it would be surprising to discover the opposite—that a more general phenomenological treatment outperforms structured educational treatments on symptom-focused measures. As existentialists would inevitably argue, it's impossible for empirical research to quantify and measure people's capacity to love, accept, and prize themselves—an outcome toward which PCT strives.

In contrast to classical PCT, research on motivational interviewing has flourished. MI is viewed not only as an empirically supported treatment, but as the preferred treatment for substance-related problems. Research shows it's both brief and highly efficacious. In a large-scale study of an early four-session form of MI, MI was equivalent to 12 session 12-step and cognitive-behavioral therapy at immediate outcome and more effective than CBT with less motivated clients. Additionally, a meta-analysis of 72 studies showed MI was equivalent to other more long term and directive treatments (Hettema, Steele, & Miller, 2005).

Before leaving this section, we should comment on the empirical status of Rogers's bold claim, made in 1957, that a special relationship between therapist and client is *necessary* and *sufficient* for positive therapy outcome. Most researchers have disproven this claim, at least to their satisfaction. For example, Parloff, Waskow, and Wolfe (1978) stated:

> the evidence for the therapeutic conditions hypothesis [as necessary and sufficient] is not persuasive. The associations found are modest and suggest that a more complex association exists between outcome and therapist skills than originally hypothesized.

In the phrasing of their statement, these writers show a typical lack of understanding of PCT. They make the common mistake of evaluating Rogers's therapeutic conditions as "therapist skills" rather than therapist attitudes. This oversimplified and inadequate articulation of PCT could be associated with poorer outcomes and may be linked to the allegiance effect. Natalie Rogers would contend that most U.S. researchers "don't get" PCT and therefore are unlikely to represent it accurately or adequately (Sommers-Flanagan, 2007). Similarly, Rogers himself came to despair the "parrot-like" translations of PCT.

Despite all the preceding research disadvantages, Rogers's core conditions remain empirically robust, though perhaps not as robust as he originally claimed. Even person-centered therapists acknowledge that Rogers's conditions are best described as facilitative, instead of necessary and sufficient (Raskin, 1992). However, and these are two critical final points, (1) as Michael Lambert, an esteemed outcomes researcher noted, "The efficacy of client-centered psychotherapy for the client rests on 50 years of outcome and process research" and "Few therapies have such a long, storied, and successful research base" (Lambert & Erekson, 2008, p. 225), and (2) of all the factors that therapists bring to the therapeutic endeavor, client ratings of their therapist's empathy is the strongest predictor of positive treatment outcomes (Bohart, Elliott, Greenberg, & Watson, 2002). These two points give PCT a very distinguished status in the evidence-based world.

CONCLUDING COMMENTS

Rogers, more than anyone before or after him, understood the central role of relationship in therapy. The person of the therapist and the attitudes the therapist holds are more important than problems or techniques. We can't generate a more apt or succinct concluding comment than that of Rogers himself:

> [T]he relationship which I have found helpful is characterized by a sort of transparency on my part, in which my real feelings are evident; by an acceptance of this other person as a separate person with value in his own right; and by a deep empathic understanding which enables me to see his private world through his eyes. (Rogers, 1961, p. 34)

CHAPTER SUMMARY

Carl Rogers was a super-optimistic and positive man who developed person-centered therapy. He was raised in a strict and judgmental home, but ended up developing one of the most nonjudgmental and respectful therapies ever conceived.

In 1942 Rogers claimed that all that was necessary and sufficient for positive personality change was to provide clients with a special type of relationship characterized by congruence, unconditional positive regard, and empathic understanding. Due to his radical views, he engaged in many professional struggles with psychiatry and psychology.

The development of Rogers's therapy approach was characterized by four phases: (1) nondirective counseling; (2) client-centered therapy; (3) becoming a person; and (4) worldwide issues.

Rogers developed a complex theory of human personality focusing on self-development. This theory emphasized the full development of a self that is consistent with an individual's total organismic experience. Unfortunately, most children are exposed to conditions of worth that cause them to have conflicts between their real (what they want) and ideal (what they should want) selves. This contributes to a negative self-regard and to individuals not trusting themselves. Psychopathology is defined as a failure (for the self) to learn from experience.

Person-centered therapy is designed to address these developmental issues by providing clients (persons) with an environment characterized by three therapist attitudes: (1) congruence; (2) unconditional positive regard; and (3) empathic understanding.

In practice, PCT is a way of being with clients. This way of being is not skill-based, but instead based on therapist attitudes. As a consequence, it's the therapist's role to experience and express congruence, unconditional positive regard, and empathic understanding. These attitudes or conditions are generally expressed indirectly, as this is not a skill-based or technique-based approach.

Motivational interviewing (MI) is a contemporary form of PCT. Initially developed for working with alcohol-abusing clients, this approach uses reflective, empathic techniques to focus on client ambivalence and help clients develop their own motivation for change. This approach to therapy has become popular in the past two decades.

As a person-centered and empathic approach, PCT is generally viewed in a positive manner by feminists and feminist therapists. Although it doesn't go far enough in advocating for women, it's generally seen as a supportive form of therapy. In contrast, for several reasons, PCT may not be a good fit for some ethnic minority clients. The strong focus on the individual (in contrast to collectivism) and emphasis on authenticity and emotional expression, may conflict with some cultural values.

There is strong evidence to support some of PCT's key concepts. In particular, empathy is generally considered one of the most robust therapist attitudes and behaviors related to positive treatment outcome. Most empirical research indicates that classical PCT is better than no treatment, but less efficacious than more structured and explicitly educational therapies. However, this may be related to researcher bias.

PERSON-CENTERED KEY TERMS

Accurate empathy

Actualizing or formative tendency

Amplified reflection

Becoming a person

Classical PCT

Client-centered therapy

Coming alongside

Conditions of worth

Congruence

Contemporary PCT

Emotion-focused therapy (aka: process-experiential psychotherapy)

Ideal self

Incongruence

Interpersonal empathy	Pacing
Motivational interviewing	Person-centered therapy
Necessary and sufficient conditions	Phenomenology
Need for regard	Real self
Need for self-regard	Self-theory
Negative self-regard	Subception
Nondirective counseling	Subjective empathy
Nondirective play therapy	Unconditional positive regard
Objective empathy	Walking within
Organism	Worldwide issues

RECOMMENDED READINGS AND RESOURCES

The following resources provide additional information on person-centered approaches.

PERSON-CENTERED JOURNALS

Journal of Humanistic Counseling, Education and Development
Journal of Humanistic Education

Journal of Humanistic Psychology
Person-Centered Journal
Person-Centered Review

READINGS ON PERSON-CENTERED APPROACHES

Axline, V. M. (1964). *Dibs in search of self*. New York, NY: Ballantine Books.

Cain, D. J. (2010). *Person-centered psychotherapies*. Washington, DC: American Psychological Association.

Clark, A. J. (2007). *Empathy in counseling and psychotherapy: Perspectives and practices*. Mahwah, NJ: Erlbaum.

Elliott, R., Bohart, A. C., Watson, J. C., & Greenberg, L. S. (2011). Empathy. *Psychotherapy, 48*(1), 43–49.

Gendlin, E. T. (1996). *Focusing-oriented psychotherapy: A manual of the experiential method*. New York, NY: Guilford Press.

Kirschenbaum, H. (2007). *The life and work of Carl Rogers*. United Kingdom: PCCS Books.

Miller, W. R., & Rollnick, S. (2002). *Motivational interviewing: Preparing people for change* (2nd ed.). New York, NY: Guilford Press.

Rogers, C. R. (1961). *On becoming a person*. Boston, MA: Houghton Mifflin.

Rogers, C. R. (1977). *Carl Rogers on personal power*. New York, NY: Delacorte Press.

Rogers, C. R. (1980). *A way of being*. Boston, MA: Houghton Mifflin.

Rogers, N. (1996). *The creative connection*. New York, NY: Science and Behavior Books.

Sommers-Flanagan, J. (2007). The development and evolution of person-centered expressive art therapy: A conversation with Natalie Rogers. *Journal of Counseling & Development, 85*(1), 120–125.

TRAINING ORGANIZATIONS AND WEBSITES

Association for the Development of the Person-Centered Approach (www.adpca.org/)

Center for Studies of the Person (CSP; www.centerfortheperson.org)

The Focusing Institute (www.focusing.org)

Motivational Interviewing Network of Trainers (MINT; http://www.motivationalinterviewing.org/)

Person-Centered International (PCI; http://personcentered.com/pcalinks.html)

Person-Centered Expressive Therapy Institute (PCET; www.nrogers.com)

World Association for Person-Centered and Experiential Psychotherapy and Counseling (WAPCEPC; www.pce-world.org)

VIDEOS/DVDs

Cain, D. J. (2010). *Person-centered therapy over time*. Washington, DC: American Psychological Association.

Carlson, J., & Kjos, D. (2000). *Person centered therapy with Dr. Natalie Rogers* [Video]. Boston: Allyn & Bacon.

Miller, W. R., & Rollnick, S. (1998). *Motivational interviewing* (Vols. 1–7) [Video]. Albuquerque, NM: Horizon West Productions.

Raskin, N. J. (2007). *Client-centered therapy* [DVD]. Washington, DC: American Psychological Association.

GOING FARTHER AND DEEPER

Additional person-centered counseling and psychotherapy resources are available at johnsommersflanagan.com.

CHAPTER 6

Gestalt Theory and Therapy

THIS CHAPTER

- Reviews key figures and historical factors associated with the development and evolution of Gestalt theory and therapy
- Outlines and describes theoretical principles underlying Gestalt theory and therapy
- Describes and discusses specific Gestalt therapy strategies and techniques, including
  - Assessment procedures
  - Training guidelines
  - Gestalt therapy experiments
- Provides short vignettes that demonstrate Gestalt therapy principles in action
- Illustrates how treatment planning, outcomes assessment, and gender and cultural issues can be integrated into a Gestalt therapy approach
- Reviews the empirical status of Gestalt therapy approaches
- Offers resources for further study

Fritz Perls, the primary force behind Gestalt theory and therapy, was a charismatic and controversial figure. He was very talented at articulating and demonstrating key therapeutic concepts. For example, one of his most famous and apt descriptions of Gestalt therapy was: "Lose your mind and come to your senses" (1969, p. 69). This statement captures the physical and experiential nature of Gestalt therapy.

In addition, Perls was much more likely to demonstrate Gestalt therapy than talk about it. During an interview with a professional journalist (Bry, 1973), Fritz was asked, "What is Gestalt therapy?"

He responded:

"Discussing, talking, explaining is unreal to me. I hate intellectualizing, don't you?"

He then refused the interview, instead, convincing the journalist to experience Gestalt therapy in the *here and now*. He urged her to *be the patient* so he could teach her Gestalt therapy (and not teach her *about* Gestalt therapy).

We include this anecdote because it captures an essential Gestalt therapy perspective: Gestalt therapy is not a time to *talk about* one's experiences; instead, every moment of therapy is an experience to embrace and confront. The goal is self-awareness.

Similar to how he handled professional interviews, when asked to lecture, Perls typically lamented that learning was unlikely to occur. He viewed lectures as too intellectual and too sterile for real, useful learning to occur.

Perls's emphasis that Gestalt therapy is a first-person, here-and-now experience, leaves us with a conundrum. How can we use a textbook (a format steeped in intellectual tradition) to teach Gestalt therapy? Although the challenge is significant, we'll do our best impersonation of Fritz as we engage you in a Gestalt experience.

Because there's no substitute for a Gestalt experience, this chapter is sprinkled with experiential activities. Feel free to skip them if you like. Then again, you might as well choose to snooze because you'll just be avoiding an opportunity to "Wake up, lose your mind, and come to your senses."

BIOGRAPHICAL INFORMATION: FRITZ PERLS AND LAURA POSNER PERLS

As you prepare to engage in the Gestalt theory and therapy experience of this chapter, take a moment to get in touch with your current sensory experience. Look at the words on this page as if you were seeing letters and words for the very first time. Notice your face. How does *your face* feel? Do you notice any facial tension? Now . . . pay attention to your whole body. Where's the tension? Where's the calmness? Intentionally breathe in. Now let your breath out. Now, notice your posture. Are you in the posture you aspire toward? Take an intentional moment to assume a learning posture. Assume *your* learning posture.

A defining feature of Gestalt therapy involves cultivating self-awareness by paying attention to your body. As we travel through this chapter together . . . remember to pay attention to your body. Do that now. Now.

And then, think about that word.

Now.

We'll come back to talking about now later.

Now shift your attention again, this time to your imagination. As you read life history anecdotes about Fritz and Laura, go into your imagination. Visualize and feel what you're reading. Make it personal.

Friederich Salomon Perls was born and raised in Berlin. He and his family were Jewish. His older sister was killed by the Nazis.

Both Friederich and his younger sister recall that he was a difficult boy—a boy who challenged his lower middle-class parents. At one point he flunked the 7th grade. Then he flunked it again. He was enrolled in the conservative Mommsen Gymnasium that had a reputation for rigidity and anti-Semitism. They asked him to leave school.

For a short time Friederich worked for a merchant, but he was dismissed for being a prankster. He returned to school at the more liberal Askanishe Gymnasium at age 14. Somehow, he turned his life around and did very well, persevering to the point where he decided to study medicine. At age 23, he volunteered and served as a medical corpsman in World War I. He subsequently earned his medical degree with a specialization in psychiatry from Friedrich-Wilhelm University.

In the early to mid-1920s Fritz moved to Vienna for training in psychoanalysis. He spent 7 years in psychoanalysis with three of the leading analysts at the time, Otto Fenichel, Wilhelm Reich, and Karen Horney. He described his experience:

> In 1925, I started seven years of useless couch life. I felt stupid. Finally, Wilhelm Reich, then still sane, began to make some sense. Also, there was Karen Horney, whom I loved. . . . From Fenichel I got confidence; from Reich, brazenness; from Horney, human involvement. (1969, p. 38)

During this time Perls began working for Kurt Goldstein at the *Goldstein Institute for Brain-Damaged Soldiers* in Frankfurt. Goldstein, now best known for first coining the term self-actualization, was using a Gestalt psychology approach to help soldiers focus on their perceptions. His emphasis on placing "the total organism of the individual in the foreground" (Goldstein, 1939, p. 17) was an intellectual and practical predecessor of Gestalt therapy.

Lore Posner was born in Pforzheim, Germany, to a wealthy family right about when Fritz was flunking 7th grade. She was fabulously bright and ambitious. She was involved in modern dance, a concert-caliber pianist, attended law school, obtained a doctorate in Gestalt psychology, and studied existential psychology with Paul Tillich and Martin Buber. Prior to her collaborations with Fritz, Lore was a dynamic force of her own.

While working on her PhD in Gestalt psychology, Lore studied with Kurt Goldstein and met Frederick Perls in 1926. She was 21 and he was 33. Frederick and Lore were married in 1929. Together they transformed into Fritz and Laura, forming a union that would produce one of the most provocative personal change strategies ever developed.

Not long after their marriage they fled Germany and the Nazis with the clothes on their backs and about $25, moving briefly to Amsterdam, then to South Africa.

HISTORICAL CONTEXT

In Germany in the 1930s, several different ideas about psychotherapy were bubbling about. The biggest bubble was psychoanalysis and so it's not surprising that Fritz was an early fan of Freud. As noted previously, one of his training analysts was Wilhelm Reich.

A Muscular Digression

As we follow our moment-to-moment awareness, we should briefly digress and note that Wilhelm Reich is both famous and infamous (Reich, 1975; Reich, Higgins, Raphael, Schmitz, & Tompkins, 1988). He developed a psychotherapy that focused on observing clients' facial expressions and body positions. He believed libido was a positive life force or energy characterized by excitement. This excitement could be viewed in the human body, but it was directly suppressed by society. He came up with the term **character armor** to describe muscular resistance through which clients defended against their libido.

Even more interesting, Reich moved to the United States and turned away from his psychoanalytic work, developing a telephone booth–size device called the **Orgone Accumulator**. This device (purportedly used by J. D. Salinger and written about by Jack Kerouac and Orson Bean) was designed to charge the body with **orgone** collected from the atmosphere. Unfortunately (or perhaps fortunately, depending on your perspective) the U.S. Food and Drug Administration obtained a federal injunction banning interstate distribution of orgone materials. Reich violated the injunction, was arrested, and sent to prison where he died (Mann, 1973; Sharaf, 1994).

Now we return to our main story.

Fritz and Laura in South Africa

In 1934 Fritz and Laura settled in South Africa for about 12 years. They quickly established the *South African Institute for Psychoanalysis*. Then, in 1936, Fritz had a profound experience that further shaped his life . . . he met Sigmund Freud at a conference in Europe. Fritz described this meeting in his free-flowing autobiography, *In and Out the Garbage Pail:*

> I made an appointment, was received by an elderly woman (I believe his sister) and waited. Then a door opened about 2 1/2 feet wide and there he was, before my eyes. It seemed strange that he would not leave the door frame, but at that time I knew nothing about his phobias.
> "I came from South Africa to give a paper and to see you."
> "Well, and when are you going back?" he said. I don't remember the rest of the (perhaps four-minute long) conversation. I was shocked and disappointed. (F. Perls, 1969b, p. 56)

For Perls, this meeting was ultimately invigorating and motivating. It freed him from the dogma of psychoanalytic thinking and propelled him to embrace existentialism and his own approach to psychotherapy.

In South Africa, Fritz and Laura collaborated on their first major written work, *Ego, hunger and aggression* (F. S. Perls, 1945). Although Laura wrote several chapters she received only an acknowledgment and even that was deleted from future editions.

Laura reported that their initial discoveries began when she was mothering their two children in South Africa (Rosenfeld, 1978). She observed their children's eating and chewing behaviors, which led to linking the real chewing of food with the metaphorical process of assimilating ideas.

Chewing, eating, and digesting became consistent themes in Gestalt theory and therapy. When people eat, they bite off what they can chew. When they're exposed to ideas, they take in what they can and mentally chew it to digest the ideas. They used the term **mental metabolism** to describe this process.

QUESTIONS FOR REFLECTION

Let's explore mental metabolism. What foods "go down easy?" What ideas do you find yourself easily digesting? What foods give you a stomach ache? What ideas give you a headache? Now, one step further: What foods make you want to vomit? And . . . what ideas do you find repulsive?

The Gestalt Therapy Bible

In a published interview, Laura described how Gestalt therapy was named:

Actually when we first started we wanted to call it "Existential therapy", but then existentialism was so much identified with Sartre, with the nihilistic approach, that we looked for another name. I thought that with Gestalt therapy, with the word "Gestalt", we could get into difficulties. But that criticism was rejected by Fritz and Paul [Goodman]. (Rosenfeld, 1978, p. 11)

The second major work of Fritz and Laura's, *Gestalt therapy: Excitement and growth of the human personality*, was published in 1951 (F. Perls, Hefferline, & Goodman, 1951). Once again, Laura received no credit. The book was reportedly primarily written by Goodman. The first half of the book includes Gestalt activities Hefferline used with his students at Columbia University. The second half of *Gestalt therapy* was a dense immersion into Gestalt theoretical principles. Although not initially well received or accessible (Goodman was apparently a rather plodding writer), this book remains a cornerstone of contemporary Gestalt therapy. For example, Margherita Spagnuolo Lobb, founder and director of the Istituto di Gestalt in Italy, wrote:

Our founding book, Gestalt Therapy, is strange and difficult to understand because it does not lend itself to rational categorizations, but it is provocative and intellectually challenging. It stimulates readers to reflect and generate new ideas. This effect is not dependent on culture or time or place; it happens any time one reads it—50 years ago or today. For this reason, it is often referred to as the "bible" of Gestalt therapists. (Lobb & Lichtenberg, 2005, pp. 22–23)

Although Lobb is referring to the theoretical section of the book, written by Goodman, this is still a good time for you to drop everything and fully participate in the Gestalt therapy activity, **Feeling the Actual** (see Putting it in Practice 6.1).

Fascism and World War II

Gestalt therapy was developed in the wake of World War II. Bowman and Nevis (2005) describe the conditions:

The rise of fascism, the Holocaust, and World War II were arguably the most influential factors in the development of Gestalt therapy since Freud and Breuer's development of the "talking cure." The list of indispensable contributors to Gestalt therapy who were forced to flee their homelands in search of safety and freedom from fascism is extensive—The Perlses, Buber, Lewin, Goldstein, Wertheimer, Koffka, Kohler, and Reich, to name but a few. Many lost entire families, and all lost loved ones and their worldly belongings. (p. 12)

Given this context, it's not surprising that Gestalt therapy has anarchistic roots. There's skepticism toward bureaucracy that can lead to friction between Gestalt practitioners and bureaucratic systems in psychology and medicine (Bowman & Nevis, 2005).

This anti-establishment or anti-authoritarian stance seems natural within a fascist context. Consistent with this sensitivity to authoritarian control and oppression, after 12 years in South Africa, in 1946, Fritz and Laura moved away from the growing Apartheid regime and toward the freedom of New York City.

From 1948 to 1951, Fritz, Laura, and Paul Goodman conducted Gestalt therapy workshops.

PUTTING IT IN PRACTICE 6.1

The Gestalt "Feeling the Actual" Experiment

This is experiment 1 from *Gestalt Therapy* (1951). It illustrates a concrete therapy technique *and* captures the basic philosophy of Gestalt therapy. After you've experienced it, you may want to try it with someone else, possibly a fellow student, or a willing practicum client (with your supervisor's permission).

This experiment tunes you into what is actual and now. Too often, our attention is divided and we're numb to life or we experience anxiety or apprehension that focuses our attention, but true contact with the environment and with your self is different from an anxiety state.

To participate in this experiment, follow these instructions: "Try for a few minutes to make up sentences stating what you are at this moment aware of. Begin each sentence with the words 'now' or 'at this moment' or 'here and now'" (F. Perls et al., 1951, p. 37).

For example, "Now, as I type, I'm aware of soreness in my lower back. Now I'm thinking about what I've done to myself and why I've chosen to sit for so long. Now I think I should move. Now I'm aware of thinking I should stop thinking. At this moment I wonder what my body wants. Here and now it wants to lie down and rest. But at this moment I remain sitting, resisting what I know is good for me. Now I'm fighting with myself about whether to type another word or to stretch my back and stare at the ceiling."

Okay. Now it's your turn. Start "Feeling the actual" now.

Debriefing section [Don't read any further until you've spent five minutes Feeling the actual.]

How did it feel to participate in this experiment? For some, it feels silly or awkward. For others, it seems phony and contrived. Still others feel resistance or opposition. In **Gestalt experiments**, your individual here-and-now reaction to the experiment is just as important as any "content" you generate. You're a total being, capable of both experiencing an experience and, at the same time, reacting to the experience.

If you felt this experiment to be phony, don't be surprised. Sometimes, after living in disconnected ways, it's possible to feel like you're acting when you're beginning to really experience life.

In contrast, if you felt opposed and resistant to this experiment, perhaps you're using *deflection*: You're avoiding contact with the environment by pulling back and being uninvolved.

Gestalt therapy can be repetitive. But the purpose of repetition isn't in the service of numbness. Instead, it's to awaken you. To "wake up" is to value your physical-sensory experience. Repeatedly experiencing the mundane (even this book!) as well as the extraordinary as fully and completely as possible means your awareness is elevated and consciousness expanded.

In New York, Cleveland, and then California, Fritz's already big personality appears to have grown even bigger. He relocated to Big Sur, California, as a member of the Esalen staff and prominent figure in the human potential movement. By this time Fritz had stopped doing individual psychotherapy work in favor of large group demonstrations, sometimes referred to as "circuses" (Bowman & Nevis, 2005).

> For Gestalt therapy specifically, the most unfortunate effect of . . . Perls's circuses was a perception of Gestalt therapy as, ironically, significantly less than the sum of its parts. Gestalt therapy became known as a therapy of techniques, quick cures, or even gimmicks. (p. 15)

Toward the end of his life Fritz fled from what he perceived as increasing fascist trends in the United States under the Nixon administration. He settled in Cowichan, B.C., establishing a communal utopian anarchy. Fritz died in 1970.

Although the contributions of Laura Posner Perls to Gestalt therapy practice were immense, she never received much credit, partly due to the flamboyant extraversion of Fritz and partly due to the fact that her name, somewhat mysteriously (at least to us) didn't appear on many publications. She did, however, comment freely—and perhaps somewhat bitterly—on Fritz's productivity at the twenty-fifth anniversary of the New York Institute for Gestalt Therapy (an organization that she co-founded with Fritz).

> Without the constant support from his friends, and from me, without the constant encouragement and collaboration, Fritz would never have written a line, nor founded anything. (L. Perls, 1990, p. 18)

Gestalt Therapy's Roots and Branches

Gestalt therapy is an integration of several different divergent intellectual and historical forces. These included:

- Psychoanalysis.
- Developmental psychology.
- Gestalt psychology.

- Field theory.
- Existential philosophy.
- World War II, fascism, and anarchist rebellion.
- Reich's focus on body awareness.
- Experiential learning during workshops and demonstrations.

Gestalt theory and therapy is an amalgam, an integration, a flourish of immediacy, a powerfully human encounter, and more. It's an open system where everything is interrelated, and consistent with anarchistic roots, friction, rebellion, and reconfiguration prevail.

Like all systems and cultures, Gestalt theory and practice continues to evolve. The two biggest developments, woven into this chapter, are *relational Gestalt therapy* (Yontef, 2010) and *emotion-focused therapy* (J. C. Watson, Goldman, & Greenberg, 2011).

THEORETICAL PRINCIPLES

Gestalt theoretical principles are both praised and castigated. On the one hand, Fritz and Laura were onto something profound. On the other hand, as Laura Perls noted, Fritz was not very adept at writing in English (Rosenfeld, 1978). This may have been partly why he preferred demonstrations over more traditional academic publications.

To provide an initial caveat to our theoretical discussion, we quote Wagner-Moore's (2004) helpful summary of the status of Gestalt theory:

> The "Perlsian" form of Gestalt therapy primarily embodies the history and personality of Perls himself, rather than a scientific, structured, empirically derived or theoretically consistent model of psychotherapy. Gestalt theory is an intellectually fascinating, philosophically complex set of diverse but poorly articulated and poorly substantiated beliefs.

As Wagner-Moore implies, examining Gestalt theoretical principles is challenging. There is classical Gestalt theory derived from the previously mentioned *Gestalt Bible* (Perls et al., 1951). There is the less formal and more accessible *Gestalt therapy verbatim* (F. S. Perls, 1969) a compilation of verbatim transcripts of Perls's in weekend dream retreats and a 4-week intensive workshop, which many contemporary Gestalt figures consider the best representation of his work (Prochaska & Norcross, 2010). And there are theoretical modifications and extensions of his work (E. Polster & M. Polster, 1973; Woldt & Toman, 2005; Yontef, 1988).

Our look at Gestalt theory is an effort to simultaneously honor Fritz's original thinking while incorporating ideas, revisions, and new emphases provided by recent and contemporary Gestalt theorists and practitioners.

Existential and Gestalt Psychology Foundations

Gestalt theory and therapy is an approach with existential-humanistic and Gestalt psychology roots. Similar to other existential-humanistic therapies (e.g., person-centered theory), there's an underlying belief in individuals as having self-actualizing potential. This actualizing potential can be activated and clients can move toward their potentials given proper therapeutic experiences.

Self-Actualization and Self-Regulation

Instead of self-actualization as articulated by the existential-humanists, Gestalt theory focuses on individuals' **self-regulation**. If you notice that the term self-regulation has a physical feel, you're sensing an important component of Gestalt theory. Gestalt has a greater emphasis on physical awareness and the body or musculature than most other therapy approaches.

Self-regulation depends on awareness. We can't self-regulate until self-awareness brings the need for self-regulation into focus. The process includes:

- An initial state of equilibrium—All is well in the organism.
- Disruption of equilibrium through emergence of a need, sensation, or desire from the background—Dis-equilibrium begins to occur,

but may still not have completely emerged from the background.

- Development of awareness of the need, sensation, or desire—Individuals may need help from a therapist to facilitate this awareness (aka: the emergence of the need from the background to the figure).
- Taking actions or making contacts to deal with dis-equilibrium—The aware individual is able to take intentional action to address the situation and finish whatever "business" needs to be finished.
- Return to equilibrium—All is well until the next moment when another dis-equilibrating experience occurs.

Based on this natural self-regulation model, it's clear that the therapist's primary role is to help clients become aware of their needs, sensations, and desires so they can be dealt with more directly and authentically.

The Gestalt (Holism)

Gestalt is a German word referring to the unified whole or complete form. A primary idea associated with Gestalt is that "the whole is different or greater than the sum of its parts." This idea can be traced back at least to Aristotle's *Metaphysica* in about 350 b.c. (Warrington, 1956). During Perls's time, the term **holism** was coined by South African Prime Minister Jan Smuts, author of *Holism and evolution* (Smuts, 1927).

The fact that wholes are greater than the sums of their parts is a phrase that's easier to state than understand. The following comment about holism helps articulate how individual components can combine to form new, unique, and unpredictable qualities.

> For example, carbon atoms have particular, knowable physical and chemical properties. But the atoms can be combined in different ways to make, say, graphite or diamond. The properties of those substances—properties such as darkness and softness and clearness and hardness—are not properties of the carbon atoms, but rather properties of the collection of carbon atoms. Moreover, which

particular properties the collection of atoms has depends entirely on how they are assembled—into sheets or pyramids. The properties arise because of the connections between the parts. I think grasping this insight is crucial for a proper scientific perspective on the world. You could know everything about isolated neurons and not be able to say how memory works, or where desire originates. (Christakis, 2011; retrieved, July 2, 2011 from http://www.edge.org/q2011/q11_6.html)

QUESTIONS FOR REFLECTION

Can you transfer Christakis's commentary on chemistry and physics to humans? Speculate on how, you personally, are greater or more unique than the sum of your parts . . . and then extend that speculation to the next person with whom you make contact.

Gestalt theory views mind-body as an inseparable whole; it's a physical-mental-emotional theory. Gestalt therapists actively comment on their client's physical positions, postures, gestures, and so on, as these motor movements represent emotional and cognitive events within the person. Much of this emphasis comes from Reich's influence on Perls. As Wallen (1970) stated, "Gestalt therapists consider repression as essentially a muscular phenomenon" (p. 7). We'll return to focusing on the body when we discuss Gestalt therapy techniques.

Phenomenology

Like Adlerian and Rogerian theories, Gestalt theory is phenomenological. Gestalt therapists are primarily interested in direct experiencing in therapy. Koffka (1935) described this: "as naive and full a description of direct experience as possible" (p. 73). This means clients (and therapists) are encouraged to drop their baggage and biases and report their direct experience. Direct experiencing and authenticity in therapy and life facilitates growth.

Field Theory

Kurt Lewin (1951) originally described and discussed **field theory**. **Field theory** emphasizes that individuals and the environment are together within a field of constant interaction. Field theory is a holistic concept. As Yontef (2002a) articulates (much better than we ever could), everything is relational within field theory:

> Field theory looks at all events as a function of the relationship of multiple interacting forces. Interacting forces form a field in which every part of the field [affects] the whole and the whole [affects] all parts of the field. No event occurs in isolation. The whole field determines all events in the field, with some forces being in figural awareness and some operating in the background. (p. 19)

There are several ways in which a belief in field theory fundamentally guides therapist behavior and practice (see Parlett, 2005, pp. 47–51).

1. The therapist is not detached or separated from the field. This concept is consistent with modern subatomic physics. As Yontef (2002) said, people are not so much in a field, but "of a field." We prefer the more holistic perspective on this: People are both in the field and of the field.

2. The field is organized and so the therapist and client explore the field together. All fields have patterns and inter-relationships that repeat and that are interdependent. In essence, the Gestalt therapist is saying, let's wade right into the field and try to both see it as a functioning whole and, at the same time, become more intimately familiar with the workings of its parts.

3. Gestalt therapists work in the immediate, present, and here-and-now field. Time is relativistic and captured in memories and so everything of importance is in the here-and-now field.

Gestalt therapists attend to what's happening within the whole field; the point of contact or boundary between the person and environment is of special interest. As these boundary contacts are explored, awareness is stimulated in clients and therapists. Awareness, in turn, stimulates self-regulation.

The Figure-Formation Process

Humans constantly shift their cognitive or perceptual focus. This may be especially true in our contemporary, media-based society where distractibility is normative. In Gestalt psychology, this is referred to as the **figure-formation process**.

Let's enter this domain through a brief activity:

An amazing human quality is the ability to intentionally shift the focus of consciousness. If you're reading these words your focus (figure) is the words on this page (or screen) and their meaning. This process puts you in your head—literally. You're all eyes and intellectual processing.

This visual and intellectual experience is a function of your focus, but you might just as well focus on something else. If, as you read these words you intentionally shift focus to your ears, what happens? Or, if you are listening to this book instead of reading, shift to the smells in the room. Can you simultaneously focus completely on every sound wave or every odor bouncing around you without losing your intellectual focus? You may still be seeing or hearing the words, but now they've drifted into the background. If you consciously focus on auditory perception, then sound will take over the foreground or figure. And if we take this further we could have you alternate between different sounds and smells in your environment (maybe there's music or a dull hum of lights, or your breathing, or someone's perfume or your gym clothes in the corner, or . . .). In each case, your attention is shifting, more or less, and placing different perceptual experiences at the forefront. You're engaging in a figure-formation process.

Perhaps an everyday example will help even more. Let's say you're driving the Interstate in Montana. The speed limit is 75 mph (yes, thanks to the federal Department of Transportation, we do have a speed limit). There aren't many cars on the road because you're in Montana. A signal from your cell phone pops into your awareness, triggering a social need, which then produces disequilibrium, and so you decide to take action and check your new text message. You steer with one hand, hold your phone with the other, and shift your eyes back and forth from the road to the phone. Three seconds

on the road, 3 seconds reading text on the phone. At first the road and steering wheel is figure and the phone in your hand is background. Then the phone and text message is figure and the road and steering wheel is background.

Suddenly, you have a background thought about what you're doing. Having passed your driver's test you possess internal knowledge about how far you travel in three seconds at 75 mph. You're covering 333 feet—over the length of a soccer or football field—every 3 seconds. This internal memory emerges from background to figure along with a realization that you could have run over 111 deer on the highway standing side-by-side while checking three seconds of your text message. Another linked thought crystalizes into figure and you can almost hear your parents in your head telling you they love you so much that they'd like you not to text and drive.

The figure-formation voice in your head brings with it a surge of anxiety and you tap your brake and slow down to an unheard of 55 mph so that you're only covering 243 feet every 3 seconds. Somehow you rationalize and justify that you're safe enough to text and equilibrium is restored.

The point is not so much that you're endangering your life and the lives of hundreds of innocent deer, but that you're always missing something when figure recedes into background and gaining something when figure-formation occurs. This losing or gaining is, to some extent, under voluntary control. You may choose to miss out on the text message or you may choose to miss out on the 333 feet of road—but you can't have it both ways because something has to be figure and something has to be ground.

From the Gestalt perspective, you're always just a little bit aware of the ground (or background) and part of the purpose of therapy is to turn up background noise volume by shifting your focus or awareness so you can evaluate whether whatever's bubbling around in the background might be meaningful or useful. During Gestalt therapy not everything you focus on will be meaningful or useful. However, many parts of your human experience (including unfinished business from the past that's affecting you in the present) might prove useful and meaningful.

This is the essence of Gestalt therapy: Shift your focus and then shift it again to embrace here and now awareness and the personal development it might stimulate. At the same time, you recognize that not every 333-foot stretch of Montana highway will be immediately and profoundly important, but you stay with that focus because to do otherwise threatens your existence.

The figure-formation perceptual process, as applied to therapy, suggests that the primary or dominant needs of an individual can emerge from background (ground) into focus (figure) at any given moment. This is why Gestalt therapists believe that a client's unfinished business from the past will inevitably be brought into focus as therapists keep clients in the here and now.

I and Thou, Here and Now, What and How

Yontef (2010, p. 31) used the preceding nine words to succinctly describe Gestalt therapy. These words speak to three core theoretical factors or processes in Gestalt therapy:

1. *I and Thou*: An authentic therapist-client relationship.

2. *Here and Now*: Immediacy or being present in the here and now.

3. *What and How*: An emphasis on process over content; moment-to-moment examination of what's happening and how it's happening.

I and Thou

Fritz Perls was dynamic and confrontational. Much of his work occurred in group contexts. He often intentionally frustrated clients to produce reactions and worked in ways considered adversarial. Consequently, his approach is often not directly generalizable to individual or group psychotherapy. Fortunately, many historical and contemporary Gestalt therapists have moved away from trying to *be like Fritz* and instead expanded on the original

Gestalt theoretical model, de-emphasizing the therapist as authoritative and confrontational (Clarkson, 1997; R. Hycner & Jacobs, 2009; Yontef, 2005).

The Gestalt therapy relationship is viewed as an authentic contact between two collaborative experts working to develop and refine client self-awareness. The therapist is an expert on the Gestalt change process; the client is an expert on his or her own experience. These two individuals are interdependent and both responsible for therapy process and success (Yontef, 2002b). Although in keeping with an existential framework therapists hold clients responsible for their experiences, they don't blame them for their problems or for impasses in the therapy process. E. Polster (1966) provides a description of this kinder and gentler Gestalt therapy relationship:

> They may engage simply, saying and doing those things which are pertinent to their needs, the therapist offering a new range of possibility to the patient through his willingness to know the truth and to be an authentic person. Ideally this would be enough. It is curative for both to speak freshly, arouse warmth, and encounter wisdom. (pp. 5–6)

In keeping with Buber's I-Thou relationship, Gestalt therapists strive to connect deeply with their clients. They work to have compassion. Although they acknowledge moving in and out of an I-Thou connection, they do so to guide clients toward greater self-awareness and personal discovery.

Here and Now

> I maintain that all therapy that has to be done can only be done in the now. (Perls, 1970, p. 16)

We have a friend who has an interesting wristwatch. It's an old-fashioned watch with an hour-hand, a minute-hand, and a second-hand. However, in place of numbers around the watch dial there a word—the same word sits in each number's usual position. That word is NOW.

Although other existential therapists also focused on the constantly unfolding present, no one did it with the passion and tenacity of Fritz. For Perls, the individual always brings everything into the room—past, present, and future—and it's all accessible in the Now.

The opposite of Here and Now is Then and There. The operation of Then and There is to distance ourselves from ourselves. We can tell stories about our experiences rather than accessing our experiences directly. Although this may feel safer, it also is more dead and less alive. For Gestalt therapists the lively now is all there is that's worthy of focus.

You may wonder how the past can be accessed by focusing on the Now, but Gestalt therapists emphasize that the past can only be accessed in the Now. This is because the past is unchangeable—it is over. The only way the past is accessible is to bring it into the Now. Perls made his position clear in a lecture he delivered in Atlanta in 1966:

> This is why I am absolutely dogmatic in regard to the fact that nothing exists except in the now, and that in the now you are behaving in a certain way that will or will not facilitate your development, your acquisition of a better ability to cope with life, to make available what was unavailable before, to begin to fill in the voids in your existence. (F. S. Perls, 1970, p. 18)

Perls took this idea even further by outlining ways in which a psychoanalytic focus on the past causes clients to remain infantile or childish. He believed that when clients talk about themselves they (a) give over authority to therapists who then profess to understand or interpret client behavior, and (b) remain in a dependent and child-like position. Instead, in Gestalt therapy the past comes into the Now so clients can choose to take personal responsibility. He stated, "We are infantile because we are afraid to take responsibility in the now" (Perls, 1970, p. 17).

Perls talked about anxiety or fear, including the fear of taking responsibility for oneself in the Now, as a form of "stage fright" (Perls, 1970, p. 15). He based his reasoning in part on a quotation from Freud: "Denken ist probearbeit" ("Thinking is trial work"). Perls noted that thinking about ourselves and the future is all simply rehearsal for the main event of living. For better or worse, really living and being in the moment requires the discontinuation of thinking as rehearsal and actually stepping up and out onto the stage. Instead of allowing a client who is racked with anxiety to continuously focus on the future and wonder in session, "How will I talk with my parents about wanting to study dance instead of computer science?" a Gestalt therapist might encourage the client to bring the future into the present by acting out the conversation using an empty chair technique. This technique would bring the stage fright anxiety more into the client's control and then moment-to-moment sensory awareness could be explored—giving the client both practice at talking about her desire to dance professionally and increased awareness of both unfinished business from the past and anxieties imported from the future.

What and How

It may already be obvious, but we should emphasize that Gestalt is a therapy approach that focuses on process over content. To support this process orientation, Gestalt therapists generally avoid using the question "Why" because it's viewed as promoting intellectualization. Instead, therapists use questions that start with What ("What would your feet tell you right now if they could speak?") or How ("How would you describe the sound of your voice as you say that?").

Contact and Resistance to Contact

> The Gestalt concept of contact can be defined as the exchange of information between I-ness and otherness. (Tønnesvang, Sommer, Hammink, & Sonne, 2010, p. 588)

Based on field theory, individuals are organisms in and of the world (field) that come in contact with other objects and organisms. **Contact** is perceptual. We recognize that we've made contact through our senses. If you can, imagine yourself on a nature walk where you're smelling flowers, seeing green leaves and grass, hearing the river rush by, touching rough bark on a tree, feeling a sense of movement. In this scene you're making contact with a variety of objects in nature. Now imagine that you meet a person on the trail. You smell the person's scent in the gentle breeze. Is it perfume or cologne or body odor?

The possibility of contact implies boundaries. When the scent of another person reaches your nose and into your brain, two human boundaries have made contact and depending on the particular odor and your mental representations of that odor in your past, you may approach or withdraw; you may seek to prolong or shorten your boundary contact. The function of boundaries are to connect and to separate.

Erving and Miriam Polster (1973) consider contact as the "lifeblood of growth" (p. 101). All learning possibilities involve contact. For example, as you read these words you're making contact with Gestalt theory and therapy. What happens with this learning may or may not be characterized by intentionality. You may make contact with Gestalt theory and therapy and then experience one of five different **boundary disturbances**, which we discuss in the next section.

Theory of Psychopathology

When thinking about psychopathology it's helpful to define healthy functioning. Healthy functioning in the Gestalt world is characterized by contact, full awareness, full sensory functioning, and spontaneity. In this state the individual experiences excitement and a sort of graceful flow. There's little need for overthinking or planning as being oneself in the spontaneous moment is possible.

Psychopathology as Contact Disturbance

Psychopathology occurs when natural processes of contact, excitement, self-regulation, and new learning are disturbed. Consequently, Gestalt therapists view psychopathology through the lens of contact and *resistance to contact*.

Every contact evokes excitement and presents the possibility of new learning. However, some contacts are especially challenging and can potentially damage individuals. These challenging contacts must be faced and assimilated or integrated into one's being. The individual or organism needs to face the

contact, bring it into figure (awareness), bite into it (the experience of contact), and then using maximal self-awareness, digest what is organically vital and discard the rest.

Given this model, psychopathology is defined as an individual's or organism's (client's) "creative adjustment" in a difficult situation (Lobb & Lichtenberg, 2005, p. 33). Lobb provides an example:

> [i]f a young girl spontaneously feels the desire to hug her father and she encounters his coldness, she stops her spontaneous movement toward him, but she doesn't stop her intentionality to contact him. The excitation of "I want to hug him" is blocked in an inhaling movement (where she holds her breath), and she becomes anxious. To avoid this anxiety, she learns to do other things and eventually may even forget the anxiety. What she does is establish contact via styles of interrupting or resisting spontaneity. (p. 33)

Individuals may have characteristic styles of interrupting or resisting contact. Because learning is an essential byproduct of contact, repeatedly interrupting or resisting contact constitutes psychopathology. Five different boundary disturbances (aka: ways of having **resistance to contact**) and examples are described in Table 6.1.

THE PRACTICE OF GESTALT THERAPY

> Gestalt therapy was conceived as a comprehensive, organismic approach. But later on, particularly in the West, but in the East, too, it became identified mostly with what Fritz did at the time. It became very well-known in the last five years of his life when he was predominantly using his hot-seat method. That method is fine for demonstration workshops, but you can't carry on a whole therapy that way; yet people do. I think they are limiting themselves and doing a lot of harm. (Rosenfeld, 1978, p. 17)

Doing Gestalt therapy is tricky business. As modeled by Fritz, it's potentially a very powerful approach. But because of his tendency to be a showman and to use frustration and confrontation

Table 6.1   The Five Boundary Disturbances

1. *Introjection*: This boundary disturbance involves uncritical acceptance of other's beliefs and standards. In other words, a contact occurs and whatever values and standards are associated with the contact are swallowed whole. There's not much thinking or chewing involved.

    Miguel meets Marlon on the nature walk. Miguel tells Marlon he has found a special plant off the trail that produces a "natural high" when eaten. Marlon joins Miguel in eating some of the plant. [Reflect for a moment on what consequences you think might be associated with Marlon's uncritical acceptance and swallowing of Miguel's ideas and values (as well as the plant!).]

2. *Projection*: This boundary disturbance occurs when one person places (or projects) his or her emotions or traits onto others. Often the emotions or traits are those that we would like to disown or those that make us uncomfortable, but that we can identify with.

    Susan meets Latisha on the nature walk. Susan was just in a fight with her romantic partner and has some residual anger. After stopping and having a short conversation with Latisha, Susan walks on, thinking to herself: "Wow, that was one angry woman. I'm glad I'm not like that."

3. *Retroflection*: This disturbance has two variations. First, it occurs when someone turns back on him/herself something s/he would like to do to another person. For example, when working with suicidal clients, one of our former supervisors used to always ask: "Who is the client wanting to commit suicide at?" Second, it involves the doing to ourselves what we would like someone in the environment to do to or for us.

    Marco meets Polo on the nature walk. Marco falls immediately in love with Polo, but Polo doesn't return his affection. After they separate, Marco comes upon a lake. He looks into the clear water, sees his reflection, and falls in love with himself.

4. *Deflection*: This boundary disturbance involves a distraction designed to diffuse or reduce contact or avoidance of contact. This can include avoiding physical contact, using humor excessively, and talking about others instead of the self. This is also similar to what Perls refers to as "Aboutism," which involves talking about things or about the self instead of directly experiencing contact.

    LeBron meets Veronica on the nature walk. They walk together for over two hours. During this time LeBron tells Veronica all about his athletic accomplishments from 20 years ago. As a consequence, LeBron and Veronica never really feel anything close to an intimate connection.

5. *Confluence*: This occurs when there's a merging of boundaries. There can be a feeling of not really knowing where one person stops and the other begins. This style can be associated with excessively over-accommodating behavior among people who desperately want to be liked and approved by others.

    Romeo meets Juliet on the trail. In just a few minutes they begin holding hands. They feel as though they're experiencing something mystical and as if they've known each other forever. It doesn't take long for them to begin completing each other's sentences. They're surprised and pleased to discover they agree on everything.

to facilitate dramatic change, it's all the more important for beginning and advanced practitioners to understand the process, be sensitive to client responses, and use caution when implementing Gestalt techniques. In fact, research shows that when using Gestalt and experiential treatments there's an increased risk for negative therapy outcomes (Lilienfeld, 2007).

Polster (1966) identified three specific therapeutic devices or phases within the Gestalt approach. These included:

1. Encounter

2. Awareness

3. Experiment

Below we use Polster's three general therapeutic categories to organize our discussion on Gestalt therapy practice. But first we begin with a crucial focus on assessment and training practices.

Assessment Procedures and Training Guidelines

Gestalt therapy approaches have historically underused formal assessment and diagnostic processes. There are several reasons for this. First, as we've seen in previous chapters, existential-humanistic therapists typically avoid assessment and diagnosis. Second, Gestalt therapy was modeled by Fritz during workshops and retreats; there was little focus on screening participants or formal problem assessment. Third, Gestalt techniques were formulated as growth stimulators, meaning there was more focus on pushing people forward toward growth than there was on a systematic problem assessment. Finally, in some ways, the entire Gestalt therapy approach involves facilitation of self-assessment. It is through self-awareness that humans change. Without self-awareness, there can be no self-regulation. Assessment occurs continuously as Gestalt therapists help clients focus on moment-to-moment self-awareness (Clarkson, 2003; Melnick & Nevis, 1998). Of course, this assessment approach translates poorly to the modernist scientific paradigm.

In recent years Greenberg and colleagues have conducted extensive research on **emotion-focused therapy** (formerly called **process-experiential therapy**; Elliott & Greenberg, 2007):

> Drawing together person-centered, Gestalt and existential therapy traditions, [emotion-focused therapy] provides a distinctive perspective on emotion as a source of meaning, direction and growth. (p. 241)

Because Gestalt therapists typically don't use formal assessment procedures, minimizing client risk includes a focus on two main factors: (1) emphasizing collaboration; and (2) clinical training guidelines related to goodness of fit.

Emphasizing Collaboration

For the past two decades there has been a revisiting and reemphasis on developing positive and collaborative client-therapist relationships. Earlier applications of Gestalt therapy focused quickly on therapy tasks and experiments designed to facilitate self-awareness. Less time and attention was spent on cultivating the therapy bond or relationship (L. S. Greenberg & Watson, 1998).

Working toward a positive therapy relationship is consistent with classical Gestalt therapy, but needed renewed emphasis. A number of contemporary Gestalt theorists and therapists have been advocating for this rededication to a therapy relationship as a manifestation of Buber's I-Thou relationship and characterized by presence, inclusion, nonexploitativeness, and authenticity (R. Hycner & Jacobs, 2009; R. A. Hycner, 1990; R. H. Hycner, 1985; Lobb, 2009).

Adopting a phenomenological stance implies that therapists should work collaboratively with clients to determine whether a Gestalt approach is appropriate. This collaborative work begins with a suitable informed consent—where clients can read about what a Gestalt approach entails and begin appraising whether the approach sounds appealing (see Putting it in Practice 6.2). However, clients can't be considered wholly responsible for understanding all of what Gestalt therapy is based on reading a short descriptive informed consent. It's

PUTTING IT IN PRACTICE 6.2

Informed Consent From the Gestalt Perspective

By Nicki Nance, PhD, L.M.H.C.

A note from your counselor:

Often a new client will say, "If I knew what therapy was, I'd have been here a lot sooner." In fact, it's common to put off a first appointment for fear of the unknown. Now that you've taken that important first step, I want to tell you more about how we will work together.

Ownership: You are the owner of yourself, your struggles, and your solutions, and as such, your experiences are the map for our sessions. What we address in any session will be determined by your ongoing experiences in the session. I will actively guide that process to help you become more deeply aware of how you think, act, and feel, but I'll try my best to avoid telling you what to believe, how you should feel, or what you should do.

Genuineness: You may have heard that I'm a "straight shooter." I do, in fact, constantly search for the most excellent truth and the clearest way to state it. Sometimes the sudden revelation of a truth is like a bright light being turned on in a dark room—uncomfortable at first, but ultimately helpful for finding your way. I encourage you to be genuine as well. It may be uncomfortable to confront reality, disclose personal experiences, or speak your mind, so our sessions are intended to provide a safe place where you can be your most authentic self.

Presence: Although a review of the past may provide a context for understanding your current experience, the past doesn't get any better. Our primary focus will be less about *why* you are the way you and more about *how* to connect with yourself and engage in your current life. For that reason, I'll be vigilant in keeping our work in the "here-and-now."

Enactment: At times, I will challenge you to try some alternative statements or behaviors during our sessions. Talking about your issues is valuable, but allowing yourself to participate in actual experiences is often more effective in deepening your knowledge of yourself. The action-based techniques will also help me to know you better, and therefore provide you with more precise feedback.

Connection: Our ability to work together is based on mutual respect, commitment to a common goal, and the knowledge that our work is time-limited. The relationship itself can be richly rewarding and serve as a foundation for your future interpersonal successes. I hold the opportunity to be a part of your process in high regard, and I look forward to working with you.

also the therapist's job, as a therapeutic partner, to explain and discuss his or her approach. There also may be opportunities for therapists to introduce small and relatively nonthreatening **Gestalt experiments** to obtain both direct and observational feedback on the client's experience.

In contrast to many of Fritz's demonstrations, contemporary and ethical Gestalt therapists don't jump right into here-and-now Gestalt experiments. Instead, there's a warming up period, collaborative exploration of client problems, and communication of empathy, compassion, and respect. Without this collaborative foundation, Gestalt experiments carry heightened client risk.

Clinical Training Guidelines Based on Goodness of Fit

As briefly discussed in Chapter 1, Beutler (2009) emphasized that goodness of fit between client and therapy is a strong predictor of positive (and negative) treatment outcomes. Emphasizing a collaborative I-Thou relationship with clients can help make a *goodness of fit* determination. However, Beutler's research and other reviews have identified three specific client types for whom Gestalt and experiential therapies are likely a poor fit. These include:

1. Clients with depressive symptoms who are also highly reactive or sensitive to feedback.

2. Clients with depressive symptoms who also have tendencies to externalize their problems (e.g., these clients more naturally blame others or their environment for their depressive symptoms).

3. Clients who exhibit observable deterioration when engaging in an expressive-experiential, emotionally activating treatment.

Based on these research findings, Gestalt and experiential therapists should develop methods for identifying clients who exhibit these patterns. When these patterns are identified, different approaches that are less intense and less emotionally activating should be employed (Castonguay et al., 2010).

There are additional guidelines in the literature for when and how to use experiential techniques. These include:

- When clients have a borderline personality disorder diagnosis or show similar emotional instability, therapists should take more time to establish a therapeutic alliance before implementing therapeutic tasks; this means using Gestalt experiments such as the empty chair technique less often early in therapy and more sparingly throughout. Therapists using experiential tasks or Gestalt experiments should be patient and not rush into tasks or experiments prematurely.

- Therapists should avoid using interpretations when implementing Gestalt experiments. Using interpretations can leave clients feeling disempowered and pushed around by an expert therapist. Although Fritz was often highly confrontational and sometimes interpretive, Gestalt theory and therapy (as articulated by Fritz himself) strongly emphasized that therapists don't engage in interpretation; interpretation is left to the client. For example, with regard to dreamwork, Fritz stated: "In working with a dream, I avoid any interpretation. I leave this to the patient since I believe he knows more about himself than I can possibly know" (1970, p. 32).

These cautions about how to approach and apply Gestalt therapy are an example of why counseling and psychotherapy is taught, tutored, and supervised within rigorous professional training programs. Experiential approaches are emotionally activating. Other therapies are more ego-supportive and/or intellectually educational. Professional training and supervision will help you develop skills for determining when and how to apply these powerful techniques collaboratively, ethically, and respectfully (Staemmler, 2004; G. Wheeler, 2006).

Encounter: The Dialogic Relationship in Gestalt Therapy

Polster identified the therapeutic encounter as the initial phase of the Gestalt therapy process:

> First is encounter, the interaction between patient and therapist, each of whom is in the present moment a culmination of a life's experiences. They

may engage simply, saying and doing those things which are pertinent to their needs, the therapist offering a new range of possibility to the patient through his willingness to know the truth and to be an authentic person. (Polster, 1966, pp. 5–6)

Within the present moment Gestalt therapists and their clients are in dialogue. Each party strives to communicate authentically. Therapists express warmth and empathy and work toward development of an I-Thou relationship. In recent years Gestalt writers have begun integrating concepts from relational psychoanalytic psychotherapy (Jacobs, 2001). As you may recall, in Chapter 2 relational psychoanalysis was briefly described. Essentially, relational psychoanalysis and **relational Gestalt therapy** hold a common view; both the therapist and client bring subjectivity into therapy and neither subjective view is considered inherently authoritative (R. Hycner & Jacobs, 2009; Jacobs, 1992; Jacobs, 2001; Jacobs, 2009; Yontef, 2005). This view is in contrast with former one-person psychology models where therapists were experts whose perceptions and ideas dominated the therapeutic exchange.

Gestalt therapists encourage clients to attend to their moment-to-moment experiences in session. The therapist tries to create a safe therapeutic environment where clients can explore their experiences, enhance their awareness, and engage in Gestalt experiments. To help make the therapy environment safe, Gestalt therapists try to act as a nonjudgmental partner in the client's self-awareness journey. Yontef (2002) has emphasized that this dialogic relationship requires therapist humility, respect for client-therapist differences, personal therapy, and the ability to bracket or suspend one's own thoughts, emotions, and judgments.

Awareness

Polster's (1966) second phase of Gestalt therapy is awareness. This *awareness* runs the gamut from body sensations to emotions and values. He noted:

Awareness is necessary for recovering liveliness, inventiveness, congruence, and courage to do that which needs doing.... In Gestalt Therapy

self-awareness is fostered through techniques requiring phenomenological articulations of self-experience. An inward look is required, one which goes beyond taking life for granted. This look encompasses the breathing process, tightness of sphincters, awareness of movement and an infinite number of similar details ranging from small and physical aspects to larger awarenesses like expectancy, dread, excitement, relief, etc. (p. 6)

Consistent with a Reichian model, Gestalt therapists emphasize body awareness. Both Reich and Perls believed client **resistance to contact** was manifest physically or muscularly. As a consequence, Gestalt therapists attend closely to client physical movements, gestures, flushing, and other physical manifestations of emotional and psychological processes.

Body Feedback

As therapy proceeds, Gestalt therapists will consistently point out or notice client nonverbal behavior. This process can be very intense. As you may recall from personal experience, having someone comment on your posture or facial expression can feel either intimate or intrusive.

QUESTIONS FOR REFLECTION

Think of a time when someone commented on your physical self. Maybe they mentioned that you looked sad or angry. Perhaps they noticed your leg bouncing or some flushing on your neck. Can you remember how that felt? Was it pleasant to have someone noticing your physical behaviors or did you feel scrutinized?

In a series of studies focusing on emotional expression, Pennebaker and colleagues (Pennebaker, Zech, & Rimé, 2001), tested the idea that physical-emotional inhibition adversely affects health. For example, in one study, two groups of college students engaged in a personal journaling assignment. In one randomly assigned group, members were instructed to keep a journal of trivial daily events. In the second group, members kept journals that included an exploration and articulation of their deeper thoughts and feelings. Pennebaker's hypotheses were supported; inhibiting expression of deeper thoughts and emotions appeared to exert a physical toll.

Overall, Pennebaker et al. (2001) reported that students who expressed their deeper thoughts and feelings were healthier as measured by visits to the university health service and blood tests of immune functioning. Although this study was unrelated to Gestalt therapy per se, it can be viewed as supportive of Reich and Perls's ideas that resistance to contact (or in this case, authentic disclosure) may have a muscular dimension.

Gestalt therapists also contend that emotional inhibition exacts an emotional price. Therefore, they might be inclined to comment, relatively freely, on any of the following physical observations.

- Tightness in a client's jaw.

- Repeated opening and closing his fists.

- The movement of one hand to the neck several times when talking about father.

- Grimacing or puckering of the lips.

- Redness or flushing of the neck begins to emerge.

In the following example, Naranjo (1970) illustrates the Gestalt therapist's focus on the physical (in the dialogue T is the therapist and P is the patient):

P: I don't know what to say now . . .

T: I notice that you are looking away from me.

P: (Giggle.)

T: And now you cover up your face.

P: You make me feel so awful!

T: And now you cover up your face with both hands.

P: Stop! This is unbearable!

T: What do you feel now?

P: I feel so embarrassed! Don't look at me!

T: Please stay with that embarrassment.

P: I have been living with it all my life! I am ashamed of everything I do! It is as if I don't even feel that I have the right to exist! (p. 78)

In this next example, Engle and Holiman (2002) use physical observations and feedback as a foundation for initiating a Gestalt empty-chair experiment:

Therapist: I'm struck by how much your face changes as you move from talking about your son to talking about work. It's an important conflict for you, and you seem to rush past your tenderness about your son and move quickly back to your struggles with work. Let me offer you a way to address this struggle and to acknowledge both parts of yourself. Let me set up two chairs facing one another, and, if you are willing, you can dialogue between those two parts of yourself . . . the part that loves the role of mother, and the part that can't resist the high-profile career. (p. 156)

Engle and Holiman's (2002) therapy example provides an opportunity to discuss the therapist as an interpretive authority. As you look back at the therapist's statement, notice the words, "It's an important conflict for you." Unless the client has previously acknowledged the importance of this conflict, the therapist is using an interpretation. Additionally, when the therapist says, "Let me offer you a way . . . " the therapist is acting as an authority. Although there will be individual variability of how much interpretation and authority is included within Gestalt therapy process, generally speaking, less interpretation and less authority is preferable and more consistent with Gestalt theory and practice.

Language and Voice Quality
Gestalt therapists also attend closely to client language and voice quality. Some of the most common

examples of language and voice use that can be used to enhance awareness include:

- *Moving clients from using "it" or "you" to "I"*: "When you're talking about yourself it can be helpful to use the word 'I.' Are you willing to try that on?"

- *Moving clients from talking in past tense to talking in present tense*: "I just noticed that you're talking about your relationship with your daughter and telling me a story about what happened yesterday. If you're okay with it, I want you to try speaking to me as if the incident is happening right now. Instead of telling me a story about what happened, describe it as if it's happening right here and right now."

- *Having clients transform their questions into statements*: Perls (1970) was very clear on this. He stated:

  > You may have wondered about the fact that I almost never answer questions during therapy. Instead I usually ask the patient to change the question in to a statement.... You will find that nothing develops your intelligence better than to take any question and turn it into a genuine statement. (pp. 30–31)

- *Noticing when clients use passive language*: Clients will frequently use language that represents their sense of passivity or disempowerment. They will speak with qualifiers like "maybe," "sort of," "kind of," and "I don't know." Gestalt therapists may ask clients to use more direct language and drop the qualifiers. And then as clients speak more directly the therapist checks in on how that change feels.

- *Notice client voice tone and quality*: Client voice tone and quality may change significantly when they speak about different issues or people. These changes may reflect unfinished business or any of a range of emotions ranging from guilt (resentment) to fear. Gestalt therapists often encourage clients to speak differently and then examine

how it feels. For example, clients who speak very softly might be asked to raise their voice and then talk about what sensations, thoughts, and emotions this change stimulates.

Because clients are whole beings, they can't help but express part of who they are and what they've experienced in the past through language and voice tone. Gestalt therapists take advantage of this to turn the client's inner world inside out—what the client is experiencing internally is open to examination.

Unfinished Business

In many ways Gestalt therapy is a here-and-now therapy that's all about there and then. The whole point is to get clients to bring their baggage or **unfinished business** out of their crusty old closet and into the present moment. When that happens, change is possible.

Bankart (1997) described this Gestalt process:

> How does Gestalt psychotherapy help the individual become self-regulating again? Here, I think, Perls showed us the true genius of the talking cure. Perls believed that the conflicts manifest in the unconscious must be brought out of the past—out of the demilitarized zone of fantasy, dream, and memory—and into the here and now. The therapeutic session must become a living theater of the mind where dreams and impulses are lived out, usually symbolically but always immediately and fully. As awareness bursts into consciousness, the person must become the reality of what she or he is experiencing. The empty chair next to the client becomes the mother who withheld love; the foam bat placed in the client's hands becomes the sword with which she or he can "stab" the betraying father in the heart; the dream symbol is unlocked and its power unleashed to reveal the unfinished situations that prevent us from experiencing life here and now. (p. 321)

As Bankart emphasizes, the Gestalt approach pulls the long-dead but still influential past into the living present. Because everything is happening *now*, we watch the client's personal issues and neuroses unfold in the therapy session.

Another example from Naranjo (1970) illustrates how the past can be pulled into the present.

P: I would like to face this fear and bring out whatever it is that I am avoiding.

T: Okay. That is what you want now. Please go on with your experiences in the moment.

P: I would like to make a parenthesis to tell you that I have felt much better this week.

T: Could you tell me anything of your experience while making this parenthesis?

P: I feel grateful to you and I want you to know it.

T: I get the message. Now please compare these two statements: "I feel grateful," and the account of your well-being this week. Can you tell me what it is you felt that makes you prefer the story to the direct statement of your feeling?

P: If I were to say, "I feel grateful to you," I would feel that I still have to explain.... Oh! Now I know. Speaking of my gratefulness strikes me as too direct. I feel more comfortable in letting you guess, or just making you feel good without letting you know my feeling.

T: Now see what it feels like to tell me of your gratefulness as directly as possible.

P: I want to thank you very much for what you have done for me. I feel that I would like to recompense you for your attention in some way.... Wow! I feel so uncomfortable saying this. I feel that you may think that I am being a hypocrite and a boot-licker. I guess that I feel that this was a hypocritical statement. I don't feel that grateful. I want you to believe that I feel grateful.

T: Stay with that. How do you feel when you want me to believe that?

P: I feel small, unprotected. I am afraid that you may attack me, so I want to have you on my side.

This example is pure Gestalt. The client is in the moment and has two incidents where he spontaneously has an insight (self-awareness shifts) and he changes course. Additionally, although the final statement may be associated with unfinished

business, the therapist makes no interpretation or connection. If the client makes a connection to the past, the therapist will track and reflect... but the therapist doesn't initiate interpretive activity.

Specific Gestalt Experiments

Polster's (1966) third phase of Gestalt therapy process involves implementation of **Gestalt therapy experiments**:

> The third therapeutic force is the experiment, a device which creates new opportunities for acting in a safely structured situation. Included are suggestions for trying one's self out in a manner not readily feasible in everyday life. (p. 6)

The Gestalt experiment is a powerful treatment method. Unfortunately, powerful psychological methods can be abused. This abuse can take place unintentionally. A well-intended therapist may feel frustrated with a client's plodding therapy pace and implement a Gestalt experiment based on his or her own schedule and not on a schedule in sync with the client's readiness.

Perhaps due to his eccentric, flamboyant, and extraverted personality, Fritz modeled an excessive use of Gestalt experiments. After all, they made for much more exciting theater than using Rogerian reflections. However, in defense of Perls, he was aware of the dangers of abusing techniques:

> A technique is a gimmick. A gimmick should be used only in the extreme case. We've got enough people running around collecting gimmicks, more gimmicks and abusing them. These techniques, these tools, are quite useful in some seminar on sensory awareness or joy, just to give you some idea that you are still alive, that the myth that the American is a corpse is not true, that he *can* be alive. But the sad fact is that this jazzing-up more often becomes a dangerous substitute activity, another phony therapy that *prevents* growth. (F. Perls, 1969a, p. 1)

In this statement, Perls makes several issues clear. First, Gestalt therapy is not technique-driven. Second, the goal of therapy is to facilitate self-awareness and personal growth in the long run (not the short term). Third, Gestalt techniques, inappropriately used, can be phony and antitherapeutic. To these cautions we would add, consistent with Gestalt theory and the renewed emphasis on therapy relationships described previously, Gestalt techniques must be employed within the context of an authentic, I-Thou, dialogue relationship.

Although the following techniques are designed for use with adult clients, Gestalt therapy also has been used with child and adolescent populations (Blom, 2006; Oaklander, 1978; Oaklander, 1997; Oaklander, 2001; Oaklander, 2006).

Staying With the Feeling

Gestalt therapy places an emphasis on immediate feelings. Feelings are to be faced and confronted, not avoided. **Staying with the feeling** is less a specific technique than a general therapy strategy or philosophy.

Gestalt therapists use a variety of techniques to encourage clients to stay with feelings they're avoiding. These include:

- Therapists persistently and repeatedly ask questions like: "What are you aware of now?" or "What are you noticing inside yourself right now?"

- Clients are instructed to give "voice" to their feelings and sensations (e.g., "Let your anxiety have a voice and let it speak for a while").

- Clients are encouraged to act on or act out their feelings in the here and now. Perls often had clients pull on and "stretch" him when they felt inner tension and conflict. He believed that by acting on feelings outside of themselves, clients would identify and reintegrate their disowned feelings.

- As in the preceding Naranjo (1970) case example, sometimes therapists simply say, "Stay with that."

Therapists encourage clients to stay with their feelings because doing so enhances full contact, improves awareness (sometimes including an "Ah ha!" or "Wow!" exclamation of insight), and stimulates self-regulation and personal development.

I Take Responsibility For . . .

This experiment is used to fulfill one of the basic underlying principles of Gestalt and existential therapy. As Baumgardner states, "Gestalt therapy is an existential therapy, concerned with the problems evoked by our dread of accepting responsibility for what we are and what we do" (Baumgardner & Perls, 1975, p. 9).

To use this experiment, clients use **I take responsibility for** as a prefix to what they're saying in therapy. For example, if clients are feeling bored, they might be instructed to say, "I'm bored and I take responsibility for my boredom." The technique is especially useful when clients are externalizing symptoms.

QUESTIONS FOR REFLECTION

Think about how you might use "I take responsibility for" with clients suffering from anxiety and depressive disorders. How does it feel to imagine having clients say, "I'm depressed and I take full responsibility for my depression?" How about "I take responsibility for my anxiety?"

Playing the Projection

Much of Gestalt therapy as practiced by Perls was conducted in group settings. He routinely put group participants on the hot seat and exhorted them to become involved in Gestalt experiments and then give them feedback. An old supervisor of ours who was in a group facilitated by Perls noted—with enthusiasm—that being in the hot seat was one of the most frightening and exhilarating experiences in his life.

Playing the projection is especially applicable to group therapy. Similar to psychoanalytic object relations theorists, Perls believed that much of what happens in interpersonal relationships to be projective. In therapy groups, when Perls observed a group member making a statement about someone else that seemed to have much more to do with herself, Perls would ask the participant to play the projection. For example, if the participant commented that she thought Robert (another group member) was too critical of other group members, Perls might say, "Try that on. Stand up and let yourself be critical of everyone here. Go around the room and criticize everyone."

Another way to apply this technique is to direct your client, "Tell me something especially annoying you've noticed about someone else." When the client responds with something like "I hate it when Juan is so selfish and insensitive," ask the client to act selfish and insensitive. You can also have the client amplify these selfish and insensitive feelings using an empty-chair dialogue, with one part being selfish and insensitive and the other part being unselfish and sensitive. As the dialogue ensues, be sure to encourage the client to focus on what thoughts and feelings come up as he plays the two parts or roles. We discuss the empty-chair technique in more detail in an upcoming section.

The Reversal Technique

This technique is designed to get clients in touch with parts of themselves they ordinarily minimize, deny, or ignore. You may recall that one dimension of psychopathology from the Gestalt perspective is the disowning of one's feelings or emotions. To help clients reclaim their complete selves, the reversal experiment is used.

You might have passive individuals behave aggressively, exhibitionists inhibit themselves, and a person who talks least talk the most. As with the playing-the-projection experiment, **the reversal technique** is often employed in group therapy. However, it can be modified for individual clients. The main emphasis is for clients to notice physical sensations, feelings, and thoughts that emerge as they engage in these less prominent behaviors.

The Exaggeration Experiment

In **the exaggeration experiment** clients are instructed to exaggerate their subtle nonverbal behaviors. These nonverbals may or may not be consistent with the client's overall behavior pattern or verbal statements. Exaggerating subtle nonverbal behaviors helps clients reclaim their entire self—including their bodies—and can amplify the meaning of behaviors that may have been outside awareness.

This experiment is used with additional awareness instructions. For example, a client who brushes her hand past her neck might be asked to exaggerate the motion and then to focus on what she feels. The therapist might say, "Make that motion again, only make it bigger. What are you aware of now?"

The Empty-Chair Technique or Dialogue Experiment

This technique (also known as the two-chair technique) is the best known and best researched of all the Gestalt experiments (Greenberg & Foerster, 1996; Greenberg & Malcolm, 2002; Paivio & Greenberg, 1995a). There are two ways to use the **empty-chair dialogue** in therapy.

Working out an internal conflict. In the first version of empty-chair, clients are instructed to switch seats when playing two different parts of the self. Typically, this approach to the empty-chair results in the client taking on the "**top dog**" and "**underdog**" polarities. For example, if a client is experiencing a neurotic conflict about getting her college assignments and projects completed in a timely manner, the following therapy interaction might ensue:

Therapist: If you're up for it, I'd like you to try an experiment. It involves putting your two most extreme attitudes about doing your class assignments and projects into each of these chairs. In this chair you put all your feelings and beliefs about getting your assignments done on time; in this other chair put all your procrastination feelings and beliefs. Then you move back and forth between the chairs and have a dialogue. Okay?

Client: Okay. I'll try it.

Therapist: Which chair would you like to start in?

Client: I'll be in this one (moves into chair). It's the procrastination side. It doesn't want to do any homework at all.

Therapist: Okay. Good. But now that you're sitting in that seat, use the word "I" instead of "it" and keep everything in the present tense and try it again.

Client: I don't want to do any homework at all!

Therapist: Nice. Now stay with that and keep looking at the empty chair and saying how you feel.

Client: Homework sucks. What's the big deal? I don't know why I have to do it. I think mostly all the professors just give it because they think they have to. It's just busy work. I really, totally, don't care at all about homework. (Pause.)

Therapist: Sit in the other chair and see what comes up.

Client: What should I do?

Therapist: Look over at the chair you were just in and respond to what you heard.

Client: You're so irresponsible. If you don't do your projects, you'll get bad grades. Then you might flunk. Then you'll lose your scholarship. And then you might as well plan on flipping burgers at a fast food restaurant all your life. Is that what you want?

Therapist: How do you feel as you say that?

Client: This is totally my mom. I think she took over my body and spoke for me. That's weird.

Therapist: What else?

Client: It's like I want to do homework, but when I hear that voice I want to punch myself.

Therapist: What's that about?

Client: I don't want to do the homework because of being afraid to get bad grades. I don't want to do anything out of fear. I want to do homework because I want to do homework, not because someone's scaring me or forcing me or for any other reason.

Therapist: Okay. So stay in that chair that wants to do homework and say what you're feeling.

Client: I want to do homework because I want to be smart. (Client takes a deep breath)

Therapist: What's that like.

Client: That feels right. It feels nice.

Therapist: Okay. See what's left in the other chair.

Client: (Switches.) I'm not afraid of flipping burgers. You'll never scare me into doing anything. But I can totally honor what you're saying about wanting to be smart.

Therapist: What do you want when you sit in that chair?

Client: I don't want to flip burgers, but I'm not afraid to. I do want to have some fun. I won't let you study all the time and forget about having fun. If you try to do that I'll screw everything up.

Therapist: What sort of fun do you want?

Client: Just to be with friends. To hang out. To talk and laugh. I just want two things. I want to have fun with my friends and I want you to stop with all the crazy threats about flipping burgers. That doesn't help. It just makes me want to sabotage everything.

Therapist: What does the other side think of that?

Client: (Switches.) I think we can make a deal. I will own my desire to be smart and do well in school. I think I can stop with the threats. And I'm totally okay with having some fun.

This sequence is simplified, but it illustrates the Gestalt top-dog/underdog phenomenon. Perls writes about this split:

[O]ne of the most frequent splits in the human personality . . . is the topdog-underdog split. The topdog is known in psychoanalysis as the superego or the conscience. Unfortunately, Freud left out the underdog, and he did not realize that usually the underdog wins in the conflict between topdog and underdog. I give you the frequent characteristics of both. The topdog is righteous, some of the time right, but always righteous. . . . The topdog always says you should and the topdog threatens . . . However, the topdog is pretty straightforward. Now the underdog looks for the different method. The underdog says, yeh, or I promise, or I agree . . . or . . . if only I could. So the underdog is a very good frustrator. And then the topdog, of course, doesn't let him get away with it and praises the use of the rod and the self-torture game or self-improvement game, whatever you want to call it, goes on year in and year out, year in and year out and nothing ever happens. Right? (Perls, 1973, p. 125)

One goal of the empty-chair technique is to help clients break out of being stuck in a self-torture game. In the preceding example, as the dialogue proceeds, polarization begins, but the client suddenly becomes aware of her own desire to do well in school. It appears she may have introjected (swallowed whole) threatening ideas about what might happen if she chooses to have fun instead of study. When she spits out the threatening piece of her self-torture game, she's able to make contact with her own motivation and begins depolarizing. She's able to quickly construct a creative adjustment to her competing internal demands.

In this case, the top-dog entity that wants class assignments completed is connected with an early parent figure, and the underdog is the child. The conflict represents unfinished business. By bringing the unfinished business into the here and now, the empty-chair experiment provides an opportunity to finish the unfinished business. When this exchange occurs, it's often desirable for emotions to run high, which seems to facilitate resolution (Malcom & Greenberg, 2000).

Working out interpersonal conflicts. In the second empty chair alternative, clients act out old or a contemporary life conflicts in the now. For example, if a female client is in the midst of a conflict with her husband, she would play both parts of a dialogue with her husband while simultaneously examining the feelings that emerge. Although this procedure begins differently from the first version of the empty chair dialogue, it often progresses into the top-dog versus underdog dialogue. In the first case, the dialogue emerges from an inner conflict. In the second case, the dialogue emerges from an external conflict. However, considering the dynamic of defensive projection, intense conflicts are usually strongly characterized by projected parts of the self onto others and the empty chair helps the disowned parts of the self become reintegrated. When working out an old or contemporary interpersonal conflict using an empty chair technique, sometimes the focus is entirely on monitoring, reflecting, and coming to terms with the client's emotional experiences. This approach, during which the client remains in one chair, is illustrated in the extended case example in this chapter.

The Gestalt Approach to Dream Work

Dream work was a central component to traditional Gestalt psychotherapy. Fritz often worked with dreams in workshop settings and viewed them as especially important.

> The dream is an existential message. It is more than an unfinished situation; it is more than an unfulfilled wish; it is more than a prophecy. It is a message of yourself to yourself, to whatever part of you is listening. The dream is possibly the most spontaneous expression of the human being, a piece of art that we chisel out of our lives. And every part, every situation in the dream is a creation of the dreamer. (Perls, 1970, pp. 31–32)

Dreams are the royal road to integration. They should be experienced, not interpreted. In keeping with existential philosophy, the dreamer is 100% responsible for all dream images. If your client dreams of a monster murdering an innocent victim, both monster and victim were "created by" the dreamer.

There are four main steps to Gestalt dream work.

1. The dreamer tells the dream story.

2. The dreamer "revives" the dream by changing the language: Instead of telling the dream in the past tense, it's reported it in the present tense.

3. The dreamer becomes a director and organizes the dream as a play, moving around, setting the stage, and describing where everyone is and where every object is.

4. The dreamer then acts out the dream, always using the personal pronoun "I" to enhance identification with each object and character in the dream.

Overall, the goal of dream work is for the dreamer to

> [b]egin on his own to re-identify with the scattered bits and pieces of his personality, which had only been held together superficially by the expression "I." Then when the click comes, the dynamic, the Elan vital, the life force that has been

disowned and projected into others will begin to follow into his own center and he will begin to be himself again. (Baumgardner, 1975, p. 119)

Gestalt Therapy in Action: Brief Vignettes

The following vignettes focus on how repetitive phrasing with dreamwork and how conversing with body parts can help clients increase personal awareness and achieve insights leading toward positive change.

Vignette I: And This Is My Existence

Perls had an uncanny ability to use repetitive phrases to produce client insight. He used the **"and this is my existence"** technique especially with dreams, fantasies, and other repeating images. The technique is straightforward and formulaic. You simply tell the client to describe a dream image with a brief phrase, then follow the phrase with the statement "and this is my existence." When introducing the technique you should emphasize that it will feel silly or phony, but just to focus on the experience. The following example illustrates the technique with a 26-year-old male who came for treatment because of anxiety connected with achievement in the academic arena.

Client: I dreamt I was racing my brother home. We were kids again. He got ahead of me and cut me off. I tackled him from behind. The next thing I knew we were all muddy and my mom was scolding us.

Therapist: Just go through the dream one thought at a time. Say it slowly and clearly. Then, after each thought, add the statement "and this is my existence." I know this sounds silly and phony, but just try it and see what it feels like.

Client: I'm racing my brother . . . and this is my existence.

We're heading home . . . and this is my existence.

Therapist: That's it. Keep your focus on your body and your feelings and see what happens.

Client: He's ahead . . . and this is my existence.

I can't catch up because he's blocking me . . . and this is my existence.

I'm tackling him from behind . . . and this is my existence.

I'm muddy and a big mess . . . and this is my existence.

My mom is standing over me . . . and this is my existence.

She's telling me I'm stupid . . . and this is my existence.

And that I should leave my brother alone . . . and this is my existence.

Therapist: What's happening?

Client: I can't believe it. This dream is my life!

Therapist: What is there you don't want to believe?

Client: That I'm still competing with my brother. I'm still losing. And I'm still worried about what my mother will think.

Therapist: How do you want to change the dream?

Client: What do you mean?

Therapist: I mean you can go ahead and change the dream. It's your dream. Tell it to me again, only this time change it into how you want it to be right now.

This example illustrates several Gestalt therapy principles.

- The dreamer owns the dream, whether he wants to or not. The simple "existence" technique only amplifies reality as it is.

- The therapist facilitates, but doesn't interpret. Interpretation is the job of the client, not the therapist.

- As the client sinks into the process, he begins sensing connections. These connections fit into his reality like pieces of a puzzle. It feels like an "aha" experience. The client's insight represents the unfinished business that's dominating his life. As awareness increases, the client can take control and guide his life in the present, rather than spending energy battling the unfinished business from the past.

- When the therapist asks the client to re-create his dream, the client is empowered to actively live his life, rather than being an automaton trudging forward without an independent spirit.

Vignette II: Hand-to-Hand Conversation

This vignette is from a therapy session John had with an 11-year-old African American client named DeWayne. The client was in therapy due to impulsive and sometimes aggressive behavior. During the following exchange, John was working with DeWayne on a repeating aggressive behavior pattern. DeWayne would sometimes hit his younger sister and other times hit inanimate objects (e.g., trees, walls).

John: Hey I noticed you've got a scab on your hand. What happened?

DeWayne: I got mad and punched a tree in my yard.

John: And you ended up with that scab.

DeWayne: Yeah. It doesn't hurt.

John: Yeah. I'm thinking you're pretty tough and strong and so I'm not surprised it doesn't hurt you any.

DeWayne: Yeah.

John: Do you mind if we do something weird in here. I mean you're tough and strong and all that and so I think you can do this, but it's pretty weird.

DeWayne: I can do it. What is it?

John: Well, it's sort of like acting. I want you to try to have a conversation with your hand.

DeWayne: That is weird.

John: Let me show you what I mean. [John looks at his hand and begins talking].

John: Hey, how's it going?

John's hand: Uh, pretty good.

John: Yeah, well, what'cha been doing?

John's hand: I'm just hanging here on the end of your arm.

John: Yeah. I know that. But what have you been doing lately?

John's hand: Not much. Staying out of trouble I guess. Sometimes I've been grabbing food and stuffing it into your mouth.

John: And you do a really good job of that . . . thanks for keeping me well fed!

John: Okay. Do you see what I mean?

DeWayne: Yeah. I get it.

John: Now which hand do you usually hit things with . . . is it the one with the scab?

DeWayne: Yeah. I pretty much always hit things with my right hand.

John: All right. Go for it. Just be yourself and then have a conversation with your hand like I did. Sometimes when you're talking I might ask you a question or I might ask your hand a question, and you just keep right on going. Okay?

DeWayne: Okay.

DeWayne: How you doing down there?

DeWayne's hand: I'm all right. I just hit a tree this week and got this scab.

DeWayne: [Looks at John] This is weird.

John: Yes it is, but you're doing great. Just go with it like you're acting in a play and just forget about everything else and let yourself have an interesting conversation with your hand.

DeWayne: Yeah. I can see your scab. It looks kind of cool.

DeWayne's hand: Yeah. I think it makes me look tough. But it hurt a little when it was bleeding.

DeWayne: Yeah. I remember that, too.

DeWayne's hand: Yeah. I don't always like scabs. And I don't like it when you pick at scabs.

DeWayne: But it's hard not to.

John: Can I ask your hand a question?

DeWayne: Sure.

John: (Looking at DeWayne's hand) Do you always like hitting things?

DeWayne: Not always.

John: So sometimes you'd like not to hit things?

DeWayne: Yeah, but it's hard when somebody makes me mad I just swing.

John: (Still looking at DeWayne's hand) What do you think you could do instead of swinging at things?

DeWayne: I could get put in a pocket.

John: Cool. I suppose you'd be safe in there.

DeWayne: Yep.

John: What else could you do?

DeWayne: I could hold my dad's hand. Then I wouldn't be able to hit my sister.

John: So sometimes it would be nicer to just get close to your dad and hold his hand. Sometimes you'd rather do that instead of hitting your sister?

DeWayne: Yeah.

John: (Looking up at DeWayne) What do you think it would be like to tell your dad this?

DeWayne: I could do that.

John: Let's practice that. Let's pretend your dad is in that empty chair. Tell him what your hand would rather do than hit your sister. Start off with, "Hey Dad . . ."

DeWayne: Hey Dad. Sometimes if I feel like hitting Josie would you mind if I held your hand instead?

John: What did that feel like?

DeWayne: It felt good. I think my dad would like that because he doesn't like me to hit Josie. I think it would be good.

In this situation it becomes clear that DeWayne would prefer contact with his father over expressing his anger aggressively. Although we can't know for sure, it's possible that some of DeWayne's anger was related to jealousy. This possibility made DeWayne's solution generated through a conversation with his hand a reasonable behavioral alternative . . . because he can get the closeness he wants with his father more directly and not experience the negative consequences associated with his aggressive behavior.

At the end of the session DeWayne's father was invited in and DeWayne was able to offer his suggestion. The father was receptive and later reports indicated DeWayne was engaging in substantially reduced physical aggression.

CASE ANALYSIS AND TREATMENT PLANNING

This case was reported by Watson, Goldman, and Greenberg (2007) in their book titled, *Case Studies in Emotion-Focused Treatment of Depression: A Comparison of Good and Poor Outcome*. The book is an important contribution to the literature for several reasons: (a) the authors report detailed descriptions of six prototypical therapy cases; (b) three cases have positive outcomes and three cases have neutral or negative outcomes; (c) the sequence of therapeutic tasks is explained well; and (d) the authors employ a variety of standardized psychological measurements to track treatment process and outcomes.

The following is a summary of a 20-session case with Gayle, a 37-year-old woman who was married and mother of two children. She was diagnosed with major depression, as well as other psychiatric disorders. This was one of the positive outcome cases reported by Watson et al. (2007).

Before beginning, we should note that emotion-focused authors and researchers consider EFT as primarily a person-centered approach that employs the Gestalt empty chair technique as a means of focusing on emotion. We include it here as an illustration of the empty chair technique and will discuss the EFT model in more detail in Chapter 14.

The Problem List

Watson et al. (2007) describe Gayle's problems in a narrative:

> [Gayle] was concerned about being viewed as a "bad mother," was dissatisfied with her parenting, and felt like giving up. She was afraid of perpetuating her family history with her children. She was also concerned with having been unfairly considered "the screwed up one" by her parents and her parents-in-law. She felt unsupported and judged by everybody. She also perceived her life as a "mess" and was afraid of being disdained for

being depressed. The stressors that were identified when she entered therapy were her inability to parent her children, conflict with her family of origin, and lack of support. (p. 53)

Gayle also reported feeling "screwed up," "not good enough," "stupid," and ashamed of her binge eating (p. 53). She very much wanted to fix her problems with her parents and gain their approval.

A pretherapy *DSM* multiaxial diagnosis was provided (Watson et al., 2007, p. 54):

Axis I: Major depressive disorder

Axis II: Borderline, dependent, and fearful/anxious personality features

Axis III: Back and weight problems

Axis IV: Problems with primary support system, discord with parents and brother, and discord between son and daughters

Axis V: GAS = 49

Gayle's pretherapy Beck Depression Inventory (BDI) score was 33 (in the severely depressed range).

Problem Formulation

Watson et al. (2007) described the case formulation:

Gayle's core maladaptive emotion scheme was of sadness and a sense of abandonment. These feelings became the central focus of therapy early in the treatment within the context of working on her unresolved feelings toward her mother. The goals of therapy were to resolve her unfinished business with her mother and to have Gayle become less self-critical and more self-validating. Her therapist thought that she needed to separate her feelings of anger and sadness, which were fused into complaint and helplessness, to acknowledge the hurt and grieve the loss of not having a supportive family and to stop condemning herself for being sexually abused by a neighbor. Gayle appeared to be aware of her feelings; however, she silenced them to avoid conflict with others. One of the primary tasks was to help her change her behavior so that she could become more expressive of her feelings and needs and differentiate herself from significant others. (p. 55)

There are several specific stages within this therapy model. These include: (a) bonding and awareness; (b) evoking and exploring feelings; and (c) transformation. From the beginning Gayle was extremely emotional in her therapy sessions. The authors reported "510 coded emotion episodes" during Gayle's 20-session treatment. This is about double the average with this therapy model. They also reported that by the third session, a bond and collaborative focus had been established so they could begin working on: "[Gayle's] unfinished business with her mother and her need for support" (p. 56).

Interventions

In Session 3 the therapist introduced the empty chair technique.

Gayle: When I had the big argument with my mom it was like "You always fight with your brother, you know you need to grow up," and it's like all me, me, me, me, I'm the one.

Therapist: Ah, so she was saying it was your fault.

Gayle: Yeah. I'm the one that used to try and make his bed and show him my love and buy all these stupid things, where I was used like a dog and I said, "Don't tell me that I didn't try."

Therapist: You're really just brimming.

Gayle: Yeah. I'm, like I said to Barry the whole week, I said, "I'm like a volcano; I'm gonna explode, and I don't want to." But, you know, my mom keeps phoning me; I haven't phoned her.

Therapist: I'd like us to try something. I think it might be helpful.

Gayle: [blowing nose] OK.

Therapist: What I'd like to try is for you to imagine your mom here.

Gayle: OK.

Therapist: In this chair. Can you imagine her here and have a dialogue with her? How does that sound?

Gayle: [laughs] I don't know. I do it in my head all the time [laughs].

Therapist: Yeah. OK. Why don't we see where it goes, and I'll be right there next to you. We'll just see what happens, OK? Can you imagine your mom there?

Gayle: Sort of.

Therapist: What do you see?

Gayle: Well, she wants to be accepted, and she doesn't think she's doing anything wrong.

After intermittent discussion of the technique, the empty chair dialogue begins in earnest. This is the intervention. The therapist functions as a facilitator and supporter while expressing empathy as the empty chair dialogue proceeds.

Gayle: Yeah. You hurt me so bad as a kid, Mom.

Therapist: That's so deep, yeah. What do you want from her?

Gayle: I want some space right now.

Therapist: Can you tell her that? "Mom, I just..."

Gayle: [sighs, blows nose] I'm sorry.

Therapist: That's OK.

Gayle: I'm a cry baby. It happens [laughs]...

Therapist: Good. That's why you're here. [laughs] This is the place to cry.

Gayle: Well, Mom, I'd really like some space. I know you don't understand, and it's not that I don't care, but I feel like you control me, and I can't be myself when you're around.

The therapy process is fairly repetitive. As Gayle exhibits escalating emotions (which is viewed through her physical body, voice tone, and speech content) the therapist initiates repeated empty chair dialogues. These dialogues enable Gayle to focus on her emotions and become clearer about where these feelings originate and how she can deal with them behaviorally. In this next excerpt, the focus is on a sexual abuse incident.

Gayle: I was really angry [crying] that nobody was there to help me. Why wasn't my mother there when I needed her?

Therapist: Yeah. Do you want to put your mother in the chair, Gayle, and tell her now?

Gayle: [crying] Why weren't you there when I needed you, Mom?

Therapist: Yeah.

Gayle: Why did you let me go to a stranger's house, and you didn't really know them?

Therapist: Yeah. Tell her what it was like for you.

Gayle: I felt very mad and wrong, and I felt very ashamed and scared, and I wanted to be protected. It's like I couldn't trust you again because you didn't protect me.

Therapist: Yeah. "So I didn't trust you after that."

Gayle: And I always felt that I had to meet your needs because you never met mine, I needed to be protected.

Therapist: "I was a little girl; I was only 5."

Gayle: I was so little.

Therapist: Yeah.

Gayle: I was so little, and you were just so concerned with [blows nose] I was out of your way and not bothering you.

Therapist: Yeah. Tell her why you were sad.

Gayle: [blows nose] I really resent the hurt I felt for years and blaming myself and for you not recognizing the signs of the depression.

Therapist: "So I resent you for not seeing my pain."

Gayle: Yeah.

Therapist: All those years?

Gayle: And I bottled it so much to the point where it was just exploding, and you didn't see any of it; you didn't recognize it.

Therapist: Yeah. "So you didn't protect me from the abuse, and then you didn't see pain."

Gayle: And you didn't help me.

Therapist: "As a result you didn't help me."

Gayle: It was very painful.

Therapist: What did you need from her then?

Gayle: I needed it not to happen.

Therapist: Yeah. "I needed you to be an adult."

Gayle: And then when it did happen [cries], I needed you to hug me and tell me it was OK and that she would get disciplined and that you would still love me, that it wasn't my fault.

Therapist: Yeah.

Gayle: I needed you to help me feel better about myself because I hated myself for it happening, and I was just so afraid of you [Blows nose]. I was afraid that if you ever found out you would hate me and throw me out of the house.

Therapist: Uh-huh. "So you needed to feel that I could tell you to feel safe."

Gayle: I feel like I've lost your love and approval, and you don't understand [cries] what I've been through.

Therapist: Yeah. "You don't know me; you don't understand my pain."

Gayle: Because you're not processing your own, so how can you process mine?

Therapist: Yeah. So kind of like "because you're so out of touch with your own pain, you can't share mine."

Gayle: No, even if I did, it was just bouts.

Therapist: What do you want from your mother now?

Gayle: I just want what I'm allowing myself. I want her to let me go as a kid. I'm not a kid anymore. Let me go; let me grow up.... I have to make my own standards. It doesn't mean that they have to be different. I can still want to be a good person and want to do good things.

Therapist: Uh-huh.

Gayle: But I don't have to run under the pressure of the guilt.

Therapist: That's all we have as children when terrible things happen to us and nobody protects us. Our own minds take over and try to protect, and by trying to convince you that you're responsible, in a way what the critic is saying is that because you're responsible, if you do everything right it will never happen again.

Gayle: That's why I'm so driven to perfection.

Therapist: Exactly! (pp. 76–77)

Outcomes Measurement

This case was a part of a research protocol and so several outcomes measures were employed. In a real-world setting fewer measures would be used to track progress. Most likely, the BDI would be used to track depressive symptoms.

Gayle outcomes were very positive. After 20 sessions she "was able to function normally" and "was no longer afraid of becoming depressed" (p. 81). Her BDI score went from 33 at pretherapy to zero. Her scores on other distress-related measures also dropped to zero. These positive outcomes were "maintained at 18-month follow-up" (p. 81).

CULTURAL AND GENDER CONSIDERATIONS

As Wheeler (Wheeler, 2005; 2006) noted, Gestalt approaches can be compatible with multicultural work. Gestalt experiments in general, and the empty chair technique in particular, can help bicultural and culturally diverse clients living in the dominant white culture deepen their self-awareness and live more authentically within challenging cultural situations. However, this cultural compatibility is more theoretical than real. In fact, many clients from diverse cultural backgrounds are reluctant to engage in emotionally focused, experiential therapies. The emotional focus can be inconsistent with collectivist cultural values and with cultural rules about emotional expression (Joyce & Sills, 2010).

Additionally, to date, an explicit valuing of multicultural contact and awareness has not been a major focus in Gestalt professional journals. Specifically, in a database search of all Gestalt professional journals, only 5 of 1,078 articles included the words diversity, multicultural, or cultural in the title. We should note that a simple title search doesn't speak to the implicit valuing of all forms of contact and learning inherent to Gestalt approaches. There are Gestalt training texts that discuss diversity issues directly (Joyce & Sills, 2010; Woldt & Toman, 2005). However, it appears that a greater emphasis on reaching out to and addressing diversity issues is both possible and needed.

The situation regarding Gestalt therapy's sensitivity to women and feminist issues is similarly mixed. Although women have been deeply involved in the development and evolution of Gestalt therapy this hasn't resulted in many publications focusing on how Gestalt approaches address women's issues. Similar to the Gestalt journal publications on diversity, only 6 of 1,078 articles dating back to 1978 included the words gender in the title—and five of these six articles were commentaries on a single featured piece (Amendt-Lyon, 2008). Perhaps of greater significance was the fact that there were no professional Gestalt journal articles with titles that included the word "feminist" or the word "women."

On the other hand, because it's an approach that emphasizes emotional focusing, Gestalt therapy may be easier for women than men. Due to gender-based expectations, female clients may be more interested in and comfortable with an intensive and active focus on emotions. Additionally, the work of Laura Posner Perls and Miriam Polster has been central to the training of Gestalt therapists worldwide (Polster, 1991).

Finally, Gestalt therapy could also do a better job of explicitly focusing on GLBT issues. There have been writings that focus on applications of Gestalt approaches to (a) the coming out process (Iaculo & Frew, 2004), (b) gay survivors of domestic abuse (Kondas, 2008), and (c) lesbian couple counseling (Brockmon, 2004), but these publications represent a small minority of articles in Gestalt journals (5 of 1,078). There isn't yet a systematic or rigorous effort within the Gestalt professional community to articulate and address GLBT therapy needs and concerns.

EVIDENCE-BASED STATUS

To the tough-minded, empirically oriented scientist an evaluation of Gestalt theory is very simple. Fritz and Laura Perls and their associates and followers came up with an interesting set of ideas about human functioning. Unfortunately, these ideas are nearly all untestable and unverifiable. To talk of confluence and of peeling the onion and of muscular manifestations of resistance is one thing... but to scientifically demonstrate that such things exist and operate in a measurable way in humans is another. Also, although Gestalt theorists sometimes talk about leaps of insight, they haven't taken even the smallest steps toward empirically validating their interesting ideas.

This may be strong criticism, but as you might expect, Fritz was occasionally critical of academia and science (this is understated sarcasm in case you weren't sure). And so let's look at the alternative polarity on scientific verification.

> The first approach is science, or as I call it, "aboutism," which lets us talk about things, gossip about ourselves or others, broadcast about what's going on in ourselves, talk about our cases. Talking about things, or ourselves and others as though we were things, keeps out any emotional responses or other genuine involvement. In therapy, aboutism is found in rationalization and intellectualization, and in the "interpretation game" where the therapist says, "This is what your difficulties are about." This approach is based on noninvolvement. (1970, p. 12)

Perls was generally against therapy outcome studies and nomothetic approaches to understanding the individual. He emphasizes that discovering what works should not and cannot be determined through research. Instead, to determine the effectiveness of an approach, the focus should be on the individual: "[W]e present nothing that you cannot verify for yourself in terms of your own behavior" (F. Perls et al., 1951, p. 7).

Perls's perspective notwithstanding, the standardized empirical research on Gestalt therapy is moderately positive. This empirical result was initially articulated by M. L. Smith et al. (1980) in their meta-analysis of 475 outcome studies (which also included a number of Gestalt therapy studies). Further research has consistently shown that Gestalt therapy is slightly better than placebo treatment and perhaps somewhat less effective than cognitive and behavioral treatments (Greenberg, Elliott, & Lietaer, 1994). It also has been shown to be most effective with reserved, internalizing clients who are open to participating in Gestalt experiments (Daldrup, Beutler, Engle, & Greenberg, 1988). However, before concluding that Gestalt therapy is a less effective therapy, we should note that some researchers have suggested that the slightly lower effectiveness of Gestalt therapy during clinical studies can be more than accounted for by the researcher allegiance effect. The bias of cognitive and behavioral researchers may produce the aforementioned results (Elliot, Greenberg, & Lietaer, 2002).

CONCLUDING COMMENTS

In this final excerpt from *The Gestalt Approach and Eyewitness to Therapy*, Fritz Perls has switched seats with his client, and so she is now playing the role of Fritz, while Perls takes the role of a very resistant client. Finally, after battling his resistance, she moves Perls toward a breakthrough. The following dialogue took place as a live demonstration in front of an audience.

Barbara: I notice that no matter what happens, the burden returns to me. No matter what I suggest, you say no, you do it for me, I don't know how.

Fritz: Of course. If I weren't so incapable, I wouldn't be here. This is my illness, don't you see?

Barbara: Talk to your illness.

Fritz: But my illness isn't here. How can I talk to my illness? And if I could talk to the illness, the illness wouldn't listen, because this is the illness.

Barbara: I'll listen. Did someone give you the illness?

Fritz: (Slowly.) Yes.

Barbara: Who?

Fritz: Sigmund Freud. (There is much laughing among the group at this point.)

Barbara: I realize that Sigmund isn't here, that he's . . .

Fritz: But for seven years I got infected.

Barbara: (Giggling.) Oh, I'm three years above you because I spent 10 years with an analyst. Don't tell me how bad it is! Could you talk to Sigmund?

Fritz: Oh no, I can't. He's dead.

Barbara: You've changed. That's the first time you've slipped. What are you aware of now?

Fritz: (Soberly.) A great sorrow that Freud is dead before I really could talk as man to man with him.

Barbara: (Gently.) I think you could still talk to him. Would you like to?

Fritz: Uh huh.

Barbara: Fine. (Pause.) I'd like to listen.

Fritz: Now I'm stuck. I would like to do it. I would like to be your patient in this situation, and uh . . . (speaking very slowly) Professor Freud . . . a great man . . . but very sick . . . you can't let anyone touch you. You've got to say what is and your word is holy gospel. I wish you would listen to me. In a certain way I know more than you do. You could have solved the neurosis question. And here I am . . . a simple citizen . . . by the grace of God having discovered the simple secret that what is, is. I haven't even discovered this. Gertrude Stein has discovered this. I just copy her. No, copy is not right. I got in the same way of living—thinking, with her. Not as an intellectual, but just as a human plant, animal—and this is where you were blind. You moralized and defended sex; taking this out of the total context of life. So you missed life. (There is quiet in the room for several moments. Then Fritz turns to Barbara.) So, your copy of Fritz wasn't so bad. (Gives Barbara a kiss) You did something for me.

Barbara: Thank you, Fritz. (F. Perls, 1973, pp. 207–208)

Gestalt therapy is about much more than just isolated sexual and aggressive impulses, or altering reward schedules or errant cognitions. Gestalt therapy is a about living life to the fullest in the present moment.

CHAPTER SUMMARY

Gestalt theory and therapy is a powerful experiential approach to counseling and psychotherapy that was developed by Fritz Perls and Laura Posner Perls.

They met at Kurt Goldstein's lab in Germany, but soon afterwards had to move to South Africa to flee the Nazis. In South Africa and later in New York, they collaborated with others to produce several publications leading to the theory and practice of Gestalt therapy.

Gestalt theory is a composite or integration of many different theoretical perspectives. There is a foundation of psychoanalysis combined with Gestalt psychology, field theory, existentialism, phenomenology, holism, and the personalities of Fritz and Laura. Gestalt therapists form an I-Thou relationship with clients, work in the here-and-now during sessions, and ask clients what-and-how questions about their moment-to-moment experiences.

Contact with other people and life experiences is considered the lifeblood of Gestalt therapy. Unfortunately, for one reason or another, people develop stylistic resistances to contact and therefore lead lives characterized by numbness. The ways in which people resist contact or can have boundary disturbances include: (a) introjection; (b) projection; (c) retroflection; (d) deflection; or (e) confluence.

Gestalt experiments are very emotionally activating for clients and therefore therapists should work collaboratively and follow counseling and psychotherapy training guidelines. Typically, clients enter therapy with unfinished business from the past that can be brought into the present and worked on actively. The therapist seeks to establish a genuine relationship, facilitate client awareness, and engage clients in Gestalt experiments.

Gestalt experiments can be uncomfortable for individuals or groups from diverse cultures who don't value direct emotional focusing and expression. Although this approach might be especially well-suited to women who, due to gender socialization, tend to be more comfortable with emotional expression, there aren't many Gestalt publications focusing on women. The same is true for cultural minorities and gay, lesbian, bisexual, and transgendered populations.

Although there is some evidence that Gestalt therapy is effective, the research is minimal. This may be because Fritz Perls had an existential orientation and was not interested in modernist scientific research. However, emotion-focused therapy, an approach that integrates person-centered therapy with empty chair dialogues, has shown empirical promise.

GESTALT THERAPY KEY TERMS

And this is my existence

Body feedback

Boundary disturbances

Character armor

Confluence

Contact

Deflection

Dreamwork

Emotion-focused therapy

Empty chair dialogues

Feeling the actual

Field theory

Figure-formation process

Gestalt therapy Bible

Gestalt experiments

Hand-to-hand conversation

Here-and-now

Holism

I and Thou

I take responsibility for

Introjection

Mental metabolism

Orgone

Orgone accumulator

Phenomenology

Playing the projection

Process-experiential therapy

Projection

Relational Gestalt therapy

Resistance to contact

Retroflection

Self-regulation

Staying with the feeling

The exaggeration experiment

The reversal technique

Top dog

Underdog

Unfinished business

What-and-how

RECOMMENDED READINGS AND RESOURCES

The following resources provide additional information on Gestalt therapy.

GESTALT JOURNALS

The Gestalt Review
Gestalt Theory

International Gestalt Journal

READINGS ON GESTALT APPROACHES

Hycner, R., & Jacobs, L. (Eds.). (2009). *Relational approaches in Gestalt therapy*. Cambridge, MA: Gestalt-Press Book.

Joyce, P., & Sills, C. (2010). *Skills in Gestalt counseling and psychotherapy* (2nd ed.). London: Sage.

Oaklander, V. (1978). *Windows to our children*. Moab, UT: Real People Press.

Oaklander, V. (1997). The therapeutic process with children and adolescents. *Gestalt Review, 1*(4), 292–317.

Perls, F. (1969a). *Gestalt therapy verbatim*. Moab, UT: Real People Press.

Perls, F. (1969b). *In and out the garbage pail*. Moab, UT: Real People Press.

Perls, F. (1970). Four lectures. In J. Fagan & I. L. Shepherd (Eds.), *What is Gestalt therapy?* (pp. 11–49). New York, NY: Science and Behavior Books.

Perls, F., Hefferline, R. F., & Goodman, P. (1951). *Gestalt Therapy*. New York, NY: Bantam Books.

Perls, L. (1990). A talk for the 25th anniversary. *Gestalt Journal, 13*(2), 15–22.

Polster, E., & Polster, M. (1973). *Gestalt therapy integrated: Contours of theory and practice*. New York, NY: Brunner/Mazel.

Rosenfeld, E. (1978). An oral history of Gestalt therapy: I. A conversation with Laura Perls. *Gestalt Journal, 1*, 8–31.

Woldt, A. L., & Toman, S. M. (2005). *Gestalt therapy: History, theory, and practice*. Thousand Oaks, CA: Sage.

TRAINING ORGANIZATIONS AND WEBSITES

Association for the Advancement of Gestalt Therapy (www.agt.org)

Center for Gestalt Development (www.gestalt.org)

Gestalt Center for Psychotherapy and Training (www.gestaltnyc.org)

New York Institute for Gestalt Therapy (www.newyorkgestalt.org)

VIDEOS/DVDs

Harris, J. (2006). *Experiential counseling and psychotherapy* [DVD]. North Amherst, MA: Microtraining Associates.

Oaklander, V. (2001). *Gestalt therapy with children* (DVD). Psychotherapy.net

Polster, E. (2001). *Psychotherapy with the unmotivated patient*. Psychotherapy.net

Wheeler, G. (2004). *Gestalt therapy* [DVD]. Washington, DC: American Psychological Association.

GOING FARTHER AND DEEPER

Additional Gestalt counseling and psychotherapy resources are available at johnsommersflanagan.com.

CHAPTER 7

Behavioral Theory and Therapy

THIS CHAPTER

- Reviews key figures and historical factors contributing to the development and evolution of behaviorism and behavior therapy
- Outlines and describes core behavioral theoretical principles
- Describes and discusses principles and strategies associated with behavior therapy practice, including
  - Assessment issues and procedures
  - Operant conditioning approaches
  - Systematic desensitization and other exposure techniques
  - Behavioral skills training
- Provides short vignettes to demonstrate behavior therapy principles in action
- Illustrates how treatment planning, outcomes assessment, and gender and cultural issues can be integrated into a behavior therapy approach
- Reviews the empirical status of behavior therapy
- Offers resources for further study

The story of behaviorism and its therapeutic application, behavior therapy, is deeply linked to the story of science within academic psychology. Behaviorism and behavior therapy sprang from scientific efforts to describe, explain, predict, and control observable animal and human behavior. Behaviorism and behavior therapy are often considered reactions to unscientific psychoanalytic approaches in psychology (Fishman & Franks, 1997).

In some ways, behaviorism is philosophically opposed to psychoanalysis, and in other ways the two approaches are quite similar. The biggest difference between behaviorism and psychoanalysis is that psychoanalysts subjectively focus on inner dynamics or mental concepts, whereas behaviorists strictly focus on observable phenomena or materialistic concepts (Lazarus, 1971). In addition, behaviorists use therapy techniques derived from scientific research, whereas psychoanalytic techniques are usually derived from clinical practice. However, both perspectives are similar in that they are highly mechanistic, positivistic, and deterministic approaches to understanding humans. These similarities led the late Michael Mahoney, an influential behavioral theorist who later adopted a constructive perspective (see Chapter 11), to refer to psychoanalysis and behaviorism as the yin and yang of determinism (Mahoney, 1984).

For behaviorists, all behavior is learned. Even the most complex human behaviors are explained, controlled, and modified using learning procedures. This chapter explores the application of behaviorism to the human therapeutic enterprise.

KEY FIGURES AND HISTORICAL CONTEXT

Three major historical stages characterize the evolution of behavioral approaches to human change:

1. Behaviorism as a scientific endeavor.

2. Behavior therapy.

3. Cognitive behavior therapy.

Behaviorism

John B. Watson

In the early 1900s, North American scientific psychology was on the move. Led by the ambitious John B. Watson, a new and different mechanistic view of humans was becoming more popular. This view, dubbed *behaviorism*, was in stark contrast to prevailing perspectives. For example, although most early twentieth-century academic psychologists were interested in human consciousness and free will and used a procedure called *introspection* to identify the inner workings of the human mind, behaviorists systematically excluded consciousness and introspection, and believed in determinism rather than free will.

Prior to Watson, William James, the innovative thinker credited with launching the field of psychology in the United States, was much more comfortable identifying himself as a philosopher than as a scientist. When, in 1889, James was told by the president of Harvard University that he would soon be appointed the first *Alford Professor of Psychology* at Harvard University, James allegedly retorted: "Do it, and I shall blow my brains out in front of everyone at the first mention of my name" (Bankart, 1997, p. 218). James had little regard for the scientific foundation of psychology; writing in 1892, he claimed it consisted of:

a string of raw facts; a little gossip and wrangle about opinions; a little classification and generalization on the mere descriptive level; a strong prejudice that we *have* states of mind, and that our brain conditions them: but not a single law in the sense in which physics shows us laws, not a single proposition from which any consequence can causally be deducted.... This is no science, it is only the hope of a science. (James, 1992, p. 433)

John Watson's perspective was much different. Watson believed in psychological science. He immersed himself in experimental psychology, the classical conditioning learning model as demonstrated by Pavlov's salivating dogs (Pavlov, 1906). He was aware of Thorndike's (1911) problem-solving cats and the law of effect (a precursor to operant conditioning). For Watson, behaviorism was far beyond "the hope of a science." His behaviorism was based on verifiable scientific data. In publishing his behaviorist manifesto in 1913, he essentially redefined psychology as pure science: "Psychology as a behaviorist views it is a purely objective branch of natural science" (Watson, 1913, p. 158). The young field of psychology was ready for Watson and enthusiastically embraced his ideas. He was elected to the presidency of the American Psychological Association in 1915, at the age of 35.

In opposition to James's free will and human autonomy, Watson's scientific psychology, his behaviorism, was designed to predict and control human behavior. Similar to Pavlov and Thorndike, much of his work focused on nonhuman animal behavior. Watson viewed humans and other animals as indistinguishable. His claims about the potential of behaviorism in predicting and controlling human behavior were as bold and startling then as they are now.

Give me a dozen healthy infants, well-formed, and my own specified world to bring them up in and I'll guarantee to take any one at random and train him to become any type of specialist I might select—doctor, lawyer, artist, merchant-chief and yes, even beggar-man and thief, regardless of his talents, penchants, tendencies, abilities, vocations, and race of his ancestors. (Watson, 1924, p. 104)

From the beginning, Watson was strongly interested in applying behavioral scientific principles to human suffering. This may have been because he experienced a nervous breakdown as a young man and had not found psychoanalysis helpful (Bankart, 1997).

Little Hans and Little Albert

Watson began testing his beliefs about the origins of human psychopathology partly as a reaction to what he viewed as ridiculous notions of psychoanalytic treatment. In 1909, Freud reported an analysis of a 5-year-old boy who experienced a profound and debilitating fear of horses. Freud explained that his patient, *Little Hans*, was afraid of being bitten by a horse because of unresolved Oedipal issues and castration anxiety (Freud, 1909).

In contrast, Watson sought to demonstrate that severe fears and phobias were caused not by obscure psychoanalytic constructs but by direct **classical conditioning** of a fear response. In his now famous experiments with 11-month-old Little Albert, Watson quickly made his point. After only five trials in which Watson and his research assistant Rosalie Raynor paired the presentation of a white rat to Albert with the striking of a metal bar, Albert developed a strong fear and aversion to white rats (Watson & Rayner, 1920). Classical conditioning was quick and efficient despite the fact that Albert had previously been a calm and happy baby who eagerly played with white rats. Even worse (for Little Albert), his conditioned fear response generalized to a variety of furry or fuzzy white objects, including a rabbit, a dog, cotton wool, and a Santa Claus mask. Although Watson had further conditioning and deconditioning plans in store for Little Albert, after the initial five trials the boy's mother apparently decided that enough was enough and removed Little Albert from Watson's experimental clutches (Beck, Levinson, & Irons, 2009).

Mary Cover Jones and Little Peter

In 1924, Watson's former student, Mary Cover Jones, conducted an investigation of the effectiveness of **counterconditioning** or deconditioning with a 3-year-old boy named *Little Peter*. It was Jones's study and not Watson's that dramatically illustrated the potential of classical conditioning techniques in the remediation of psychological fears and phobias.

Mary Cover Jones

Jones initially documented the presence of an intense fear reaction in Little Peter. Prior to his involvement in the behavioral experiments, Little Peter exhibited fear in response to several furry objects, including rabbits, fur coats, and cotton balls (Jones, 1924b). Jones proceeded to systematically decondition Little Peter's fear reaction by pairing the gradual approach of a caged rabbit with Peter's involvement in an enjoyable activity—eating his favorite foods. In the end, Peter was able to touch the rabbit without fear; his fear response was extinguished.

Jones's work was extensive and profound. Over time, she worked with 70 different children, all of whom had marked and specific fear responses. The children upon whom she conducted her experiments were institutionalized; her efforts were uniformly designed to eliminate their fears, not create them. Overall, her conclusions are clear and constitute the basic framework for contemporary (and scientifically verifiable) behavioral approaches to treating human fears and phobias (Jones, 1924a). She stated:

> In our study of methods for removing fear responses, we found unqualified success with only two. By the method of direct conditioning we associated the fear-object with a craving-object, and replaced the fear by a positive response. By the method of social imitation we allowed the subjects to share, under controlled conditions, the social activity of a group of children especially chosen with a view to prestige effect. [Other] methods proved sometimes effective but were not to be relied upon unless used in combination with other methods. (Jones, 1924, p. 390)

As illustrated by Watson's and Jones's experiments, the behavioral emphasis on observable behavior and rejection of mental concepts is well suited to laboratory research with animals and humans. Early behaviorists made many important contributions to psychological science. Highlights include:

- The discovery by Pavlov, Watson, and their colleagues that physical and emotional responses could be involuntarily conditioned in animals and humans via classical conditioning procedures.

- The discovery by Mary Cover Jones that fear responses could be deconditioned by either (a) replacing the fear response with a positive response or (b) social imitation.

- The discovery by Thorndike (of the law of effect) and its later elaboration by Skinner that animal and human behaviors are powerfully shaped by their consequences.

Behavior Therapy

In a testament to the behavioral zeitgeist of the 1950s, three different research groups in three different countries independently introduced the term *behavior therapy* to modern psychology.

B. F. Skinner in the United States

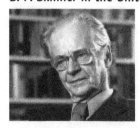

B. F. Skinner

Skinner's early work was an immense experimental project on operant conditioning with rats and pigeons in the 1930s (Skinner, 1938). At that time, his emphasis was on the extension of Thorndike's *law of effect*. He repeatedly demonstrated the power of positive reinforcement, negative reinforcement, punishment, and stimulus control in modifying animal behavior. Within the confines of his well-known Skinner box, he was able to teach pigeons to play ping-pong via operant conditioning procedures.

In the 1940s, Skinner began extending operant conditioning concepts to human social and clinical problems. His book *Walden Two* was a story of how operant conditioning procedures could be used to create a utopian society (Skinner, 1948). His next book, *Science and Human Behavior*, was a critique of psychoanalytic concepts and a reformulation of psychotherapy in behavioral terms (Skinner, 1953). Finally, in 1953, Skinner and his colleagues first used *behavior therapy* as a clinical term referring to the application of operant conditioning procedures to modify the behavior of psychotic patients (Skinner, Solomon, & Lindsley, 1953).

Joseph Wolpe, Arnold Lazarus, and Stanley Rachman in South Africa

Joseph Wolpe's interest in conditioning procedures as a means for resolving neurotic fear began with his doctoral thesis (Wolpe, 1948). Later, he conducted "experiments in neurosis production" with 12 domestic cats (Wolpe & Plaud, 1997, p. 968) and eventually established the first nonpsychoanalytic, empirically validated behavior therapy technique (Wolpe, 1954, 1958). His book *Psychotherapy by Reciprocal Inhibition* outlined the therapeutic procedure now called systematic desensitization (Wolpe, 1958). In the late 1990s, Wolpe reflected on his treatment technique:

> As the therapy procedure has evolved, the anxious patient is first trained in progressive muscle relaxation exercises and then gradually exposed imaginally or in vivo to feared stimuli while simultaneously relaxing. (Wolpe & Plaud, 1997, p. 969)

Wolpe's approach is similar to Jones's first counterconditioning principle wherein a conditioned negative emotional response *is replaced with* a conditioned positive emotional response (Jones, 1924b). Wolpe's revolutionary work attracted the attention of two South African psychologists, Arnold Lazarus and Stanley Rachman. Both contributed significantly to the behavior therapy movement. In fact, Lazarus claims credit for first using the term *behavior therapy* in a scientific journal. He states:

> The first time the terms behavior therapy and behavior therapist appeared in a scientific journal was when I endeavored to point out the need for adding objective, laboratory-derived therapeutic tools to more orthodox psychotherapeutic techniques. (Lazarus, 1971, p. 2)

Lazarus is perhaps the first mental health professional—and certainly the first behavior therapist—to openly embrace eclecticism. Early on, and throughout his career, he advocated the integration of laboratory-based scientific procedures into existing clinical and counseling practices (Lazarus, 1958; Lazarus, 1991). He is an adamant opponent of narrow therapy definitions or conceptualizations. Because of his broadly eclectic practices, we explore his multi-modal behavior therapy approach in Chapter 14.

Over the years, Rachman also influenced developing behavior therapy procedures. He was editor of the journal *Behaviour Research and Therapy* for decades. His initial unique contribution involved the application of aversive stimuli to treating what he described as neurotic behavior, including addictions (Rachman, 1965).

Hans Eysenck and the Maudsley Group in the United Kingdom

British psychiatrist Hans Eysenck independently used the term *behaviour therapy* to describe the application of modern learning theory to the understanding and treatment of behavioral and psychiatric problems (Eysenck, 1959). Eysenck's subsequent quick publication of two edited volumes (a behaviorally based textbook of abnormal psychology and a collection of case studies in behavior therapy) led to the widespread dissemination of behavior therapy as a procedure through which surface symptoms are directly treated as a means of alleviating neurotic functioning (Eysenck, 1960; Eysenck, 1964).

As a consequence of the work of all these pioneering researchers and practitioners, behavior (or behaviour) therapy was born.

Cognitive Behavior Modification

Most behavior therapists now acknowledge and work with cognition. For example, in the compilation *The Best of Behaviour Research and Therapy*, which included journal articles written over 35 years, many selected articles specifically focused on thoughts, expectations, and emotions (Rachman, 1997). Additionally, after considerable thought, the Association for the Advancement of Behavior Therapy (AABT) renamed itself the Association for Behavioral and Cognitive Therapies (ABCT).

Behavior therapy continues to evolve. This shouldn't be surprising because, as articulated by Cyril Franks, behavior therapy is designed to evolve: "Above all, in behavior therapy a theory is a servant that is useful *only until better theory and better therapy come along*" (Franks & Barbrack, 1983, pp. 509–510; italics added).

THEORETICAL PRINCIPLES

Over the years there have been many formulations and reformulations of behavioral theory and therapy (Farmer & Nelson-Gray, 2005). For the most part, two primary convictions characterize behaviorists and behavioral theory—both then and now:

1. Behavior therapists employ techniques based on modern learning theory.

2. Behavior therapists employ techniques derived from scientific research.

Some behaviorists have criticized even these most basic behavioral tenets. For example, in his book *Behavior Therapy and Beyond*, Lazarus states:

> Eysenck's ... insistence that behavior therapy denotes "methods of treatment which are derived from modern learning theory" amounts to little more than a beguiling slogan....
>
> The danger lies in a premature elevation of learning principles into unwarranted scientific truths and the ascription of the general term of "modern learning theory" to what in reality are best described as "modern learning theories." (Lazarus, 1971, pp. 4, 5)

Lazarus's point is that behavior therapy is based not on learning theory, but on learning theories (in the plural). He asserts that even psychoanalytic formulations of what occurs in therapy constitute learning hypotheses, many of which remain unsubstantiated.

Theoretical Models

Despite the fact that learning theory models are continually in flux and revision, we turn now to a brief description of the two main models of learning that form the theoretical foundation of behavior therapy (Farmer & Nelson-Gray, 2005; Fishman & Franks, 1997). In Chapter 8 we look at two more learning theory models that focus more directly on cognitive learning.

Operant Conditioning: Applied Behavior Analysis

Applied behavior analysis is a clinical term referring to a behavioral approach based on **operant conditioning** principles. The operant conditioning position is straightforward: *Behavior is a function of its consequences.*

Operant conditioning was developed by B. F. Skinner. Skinner expanded on Thorndike's (1932) original learning theory. Thorndike stated that behavior followed by a "satisfier" would strengthen responses and behavior followed by an "annoyer" would weaken responses. Skinner (1938) changed the terminology and conducted extensive research. The term operant refers to how behaviors operate on the environment, thereby producing specific consequences.

Operant conditioning is a **stimulus-response (SR) theory**; no cognitive or covert intervening variables mediate the organism's response to a particular stimulus. Similarly, applied behavior analysis focuses solely on observable behaviors. Therapy proceeds primarily through manipulating environmental variables to produce behavior change.

The main procedures used by applied behavior analysts are reinforcement, punishment, extinction, and stimulus control. These procedures are used to manipulate environmental contingencies (e.g., environmental rewards and punishments). The goal is to increase adaptive behavior through reinforcement and stimulus control and to reduce maladaptive behavior through punishment and extinction.

In theory, and sometimes in practice, **positive reinforcement** and **punishment** concepts are simple. For example, when your cat meows at the front door and gets a bowl of tasty cat food, the likelihood of your cat returning to your front door and meowing again is increased. In contrast, if you spray cold water on your cat when it meows (or administer an aversive electric shock), the meowing behavior is likely to diminish (or, as sometimes occurs with punishment, erratic or aggressive behaviors may develop).

Unfortunately, operant conditioning procedures are not always simple and straightforward in real life. Take, for example, the hypothetical parents of 5- and 15-year-old girls. The parents are trying to teach their 5-year-old to tie her shoes. Therefore, whenever she engages in shoe-tying behavior they coo and clap, and when she finally gets it right they give big bear hugs and high fives. In this situation the parents' cooing and clapping are likely to serve as positive reinforcements and the 5-year-old's shoe-tying behavior will increase.

At the same time, the parents are also trying to teach their 15-year-old daughter to speak to them more respectfully. Because positive reinforcement worked so well with their 5-year-old, they initially try cooing, clapping, and hugging in response to their daughter's respectful communication. Unfortunately, when they hug her, she recoils (especially in front of her teenage friends) and responds by saying, "Just get away from me!" After discovering that their positive reinforcement plan doesn't work with their older daughter, the parents decide to try using punishment. Together, they resolve to shout and scold her whenever she speaks disrespectfully. This time their efforts backfire even worse—she responds by shouting right back at them.

Finally, in desperation, the parents visit a counselor. When the counselor suggests using a behavioral plan, the parents roll their eyes and exclaim, "We've already tried that, it doesn't work!" In reality, the only thing the parents discovered is that operant conditioning is more complex than most people believe.

Classical Conditioning: The Neobehavioristic, Mediational Stimulus-Response Model

The **neobehavioristic mediational SR model** is based on classical conditioning principles. Its tenets were developed and articulated by Pavlov, Watson, Mowrer, and Wolpe.

Classical conditioning is sometimes referred to as associational learning because it involves an association or linking of one environmental stimulus with another. In Pavlovian terms, an **unconditioned stimulus** is one that naturally produces a specific physical-emotional response. The physical response elicited by an unconditioned stimulus is mediated through smooth muscle reflex arcs, so higher-order cognitive processes are not required for conditioning to occur. The following clinical example described by Wolpe illustrates how fear or anxiety responses are classically conditioned.

> A 34-year-old man's four-year fear of being in automobiles started when his car was struck from behind while he was waiting for a red light to change. At that moment he felt an overwhelming fear of impending death; subsequently he was afraid to sit inside even a stationary car. That the fear was purely a matter of classical autonomic conditioning (automatic response to the ambience of a car's interior) was evidenced by the fact that he had no expectation of danger when he sat in a car. (Wolpe, 1987, pp. 135–136)

In Wolpe's example, the experience of being struck from behind while waiting for a red light is the unconditioned stimulus (Wolpe, 1987). This stimulus automatically (or autonomically) produces a reflexive fear response (or **unconditioned response**). As a consequence, the 34-year-old man suffered from a debilitating fear of impending death (a **conditioned response**) when exposed to the interior of an automobile (a **conditioned stimulus**). As Wolpe emphasizes, this scenario represents classical autonomic conditioning or learning because the man has no cognitive expectations or cognitive triggers that lead to his experience of fear when

sitting inside an automobile. Because of the lack of cognitive processing involved in classical conditioning, when an individual experiences a purely classically conditioned fear response, often he or she might say something like, "I don't know why, but I'm just afraid of elevators."

Classical conditioning principles also include stimulus generalization, stimulus discrimination, extinction, counterconditioning, and spontaneous recovery.

Stimulus generalization is defined as the extension or generalization of a conditioned fear response to new settings, situations, or objects. For example, in the preceding example, if the man begins experiencing intense fear when sitting in an airplane, stimulus generalization has occurred. Similarly, in the case of Little Albert, stimulus generalization occurred when Albert experienced fear in response to objects (stimuli) similar in appearance to white rats (e.g., Santa Claus masks or cotton balls).

Stimulus discrimination occurs when a conditioned fear response is not elicited by a new or different stimulus. For example, if the 34-year-old man can sit in a movie theater without experiencing fear, stimulus discrimination has occurred. Apparently the movie theater setting (stimulus) is different enough from the car setting that it doesn't elicit the conditioned response. In the case of Little Albert, stimulus discrimination occurred when Little Albert did not have a fear response when exposed to a fluffy white washrag.

Extinction involves the gradual elimination of a conditioned response. It occurs when a conditioned stimulus is repeatedly presented without a previously associated unconditioned stimulus. For example, if Watson had kept working with Little Albert and repeatedly exposed him to a white rat without a frightening sound of metal clanging, eventually Little Albert might lose his conditioned response to rats. Extinction is not the same as forgetting; instead, it involves relearning that the conditioned stimulus is no longer a signal that precedes the unconditioned stimulus.

In contrast, Mary Cover Jones's work with Little Peter is an example of successful counterconditioning or deconditioning. **Counterconditioning** involves new associative learning. The subject learns that the conditioned stimulus brings with it a positive emotional experience. For example, when Jones repeatedly presented the white rat to Little Peter while he was eating some of his favorite foods, eventually the conditioned response (fear) was counter-conditioned. The same counterconditioning principle is in operation in Wolpe's systematic desensitization.

Spontaneous recovery within a classical conditioning paradigm was initially discussed by Pavlov (1927). Spontaneous recovery occurs when an old response suddenly returns (is recovered) after having been successfully extinguished or counter-conditioned. For example, if after successful counterconditioning through systematic desensitization, Wolpe's client suddenly begins having fear symptoms associated with the interior of automobiles, he is exhibiting spontaneous recovery.

Theory of Psychopathology

For behaviorists, maladaptive behavior is always learned and can be either unlearned or replaced by new learning. The idea that human learning is at the core of human behavior guides how behavior therapists approach client assessment and treatment. Truax (2002) articulates this link between psychopathology, assessment, and treatment:

> The basic assumption in behavioral theory is that both adaptive and maladaptive behaviors are acquired, maintained, and changed in the same way: through the internal and external events that proceed and follow them. This means that behavioral case conceptualization involves a careful assessment of the context within which a behavior occurs, along with developing testable hypotheses about the causes, maintaining factors, and treatment interventions. (p. 3)

Psychopathology may be a function of inadequate learning or skill deficits. For example, an underlying premise of assertiveness or social skills training is that individuals who exhibit too much passive or too much aggressive behavior simply have social skill deficits; they haven't learned how to appropriately use assertive behavior in social situations. Consequently, the purpose of assertiveness skills training (a behavioral treatment) is to teach clients assertiveness skills through modeling, coaching, behavior rehearsal, and reinforcement.

Interestingly, the successful outcomes associated with assertiveness training can be explained through either classical conditioning or operant models. For example, Wolpe considers assertive behavior to be incompatible with anxiety; therefore an anxiety response is counter-conditioned and replaced by an adaptive, incompatible response (Wolpe, 1973). In contrast, contemporary assertiveness trainers usually focus more on the contingencies—reinforcements and punishments—that establish and maintain passive, aggressive, and assertive social behavior (Alberti & Emmons, 2008).

As a means of better understanding client psychopathology, behaviorists apply scientific methods to clinical or counseling settings. Behaviorists systematically:

- Observe and assess client maladaptive or unskilled behaviors.

- Develop hypotheses about the cause, maintenance, and appropriate treatment for maladaptive or unskilled behaviors.

- Test behavioral hypotheses through the application of empirically justifiable interventions.

- Observe and evaluate the results of their intervention.

- Revise and continue testing new hypotheses about ways to modify the maladaptive or unskilled behavior(s) as needed.

Behaviorists are on the cutting edge when it comes to applying specific treatment procedures to specific clinical problems. More than any other practitioner group, behavior (and cognitive-behavioral) therapists insist on empirical support for their treatment methods. As a consequence, the majority of empirically supported treatments (ESTs) are behavioral or cognitive-behavioral (Chambless et al., 1998; Chambless et al., 2006; Chambless & Hollon, 1998).

THE PRACTICE OF BEHAVIOR THERAPY

When preparing to do behavior therapy, be sure to get out your clipboard, because behavior therapists take notes and think like scientists. You may even need graph paper or a white board for illustrating concepts to clients. As a behaviorist, you're a teacher and educator: Your job is to help clients unlearn old, maladaptive behaviors and learn new, adaptive behaviors.

A sample excerpt from a behaviorally oriented informed consent form is included in Putting it in Practice 7.1.

What Is Contemporary Behavior Therapy?

In this chapter we've included a description of therapeutic interventions that are primarily behavioral but that occasionally focus on cognitive variables. Not all the therapies in this chapter are purely behavioral. Similarly, although the next chapter includes interventions derived from the cognitive therapy movement and that are predominantly cognitive in nature—we recognize that nearly all cognitive therapies are used in conjunction with the primarily behavioral techniques described in this chapter.

This leaves us in a conundrum regarding the definition of cognitive-behavioral therapy (CBT). As you may already know, CBT is currently the most popular and scientifically evaluated approach to psychotherapy. This approach explicitly combines cognitive and behavioral techniques, viewing them as both compatible and as enhancing one another's impact.

To make matters more complex, there are now several *2nd generation* cognitive-behavioral therapies. These therapies include:

- Dialectical Behavior Therapy (DBT)
- Action and Commitment Therapy (ACT)
- Eye Movement Desensitization Reprocessing (EMDR)

Some theories texts include these new generation behavior therapies in the behavior therapy chapter. However, partly because we'd rather not risk the wrath of the late, great Joseph Wolpe, we view them as horses of a different therapeutic color. Consequently, we review DBT, ACT, and EMDR in Chapter 14. And although you may be chomping at the therapeutic bit (to continue our stretched horse metaphor), you'll have to delay your gratification and learn more about these three very important evidence-based therapy approaches later.

Assessment Issues and Procedures

In a perfect behavioral assessment world, behavior therapists would directly observe clients in their natural environment to obtain specific information about exactly what happens before, during, and after the occurrence of adaptive and maladaptive behaviors. The main goal of behavioral assessment is to determine the external (environmental or situational) stimuli and internal (physiological and sometimes cognitive) stimuli that directly precede and follow adaptive and maladaptive client behavioral responses.

Functional Behavior Analysis

Behaviorists typically refer to a formal assessment of behavior contingencies as a **functional behavioral analysis** (FBA) or assessment (Drossel, Rummel, & Fisher, 2009; Haun & Truax, 2007). An FBA can also be described as an assessment of the **behavioral ABCs** (Spiegler & Guevremont, 2010):

- A = The behavior's *antecedents* (everything that happens just before the maladaptive behavior is observed).
- B = The *behavior* (the client's problem specifically defined in concrete behavioral terms; e.g., rather than being called an "anger problem," it's referred to as "yelling or swearing six times a day and punching others twice daily").
- C = The behavior's *consequences* (everything that happens just after the maladaptive behavior occurs).

PUTTING IT IN PRACTICE 7.1

A Behavioral Informed Consent Form

The following is a sample excerpt from a behavior therapy informed consent. As you read it, pretend you're sitting in a therapist's waiting room, about to go in for your first behavior therapy session.

I specialize in behavior therapy, a research-based and highly effective form of therapy based on modern learning theories.

Humans are constantly learning. As you know from experience, humans learn everything from tying shoelaces and riding bicycles to complex emotional responses, like love, jealousy, and nervousness. Everyone has a tremendous capacity for learning.

Whether you've come to therapy because of a difficult situation, a problem relationship, or a troubling emotion, I'll help you unlearn old troubling habits and learn new, more positive habits. Research has proven that behavior therapy is very helpful for many problems.

Sometimes people think behavior therapy is boring and impersonal, but nothing could be further from the truth. In therapy, we'll work as a team, and we'll talk in detail about some of the hardest things you're facing in your life. Then we'll develop a plan for helping you overcome the problems and symptoms that cause you distress.

In most cases, our plan will include several different approaches to learning and to changing. Some new learning will happen right in our sessions, and some will happen outside our sessions. That means I'll give you assignments to complete between our meetings. If you complete your assignments, then the new learning we're working on will happen even faster.

Behavior therapy is a brief therapy. You won't come to therapy forever; depending on your problem and your situation, it may take only a few therapy sessions or it may take several months. We'll regularly evaluate our work together and talk openly and directly about your progress.

My job is to work in partnership with you to improve your life and relieve your uncomfortable symptoms. Therefore, I'll regularly explain exactly what we're doing and why we're doing it. And whenever you have questions, feel free to ask; I'll do my best to provide you with the answers you deserve.

A functional behavior analysis is designed to determine the function of a given behavior. The basic question we try to answer in an FBA is: What reinforcers are operating in the environment to maintain a specific problem behavior? A goal of the FBA is to develop a functional causal model (or hypothesis) to explain behavior (O'Brien & Carhart, 2011). For example, if a child client is disrupting class in school, *unobtrusively* observing the child at various times during the day could be scheduled. Through direct observation, the behavior therapist gathers data and watches for patterns. The child's class disruptions may be preceded by a particular stimulus. Perhaps this stimulus (e.g., in-class reading assignments) produces an aversive, uncomfortable state (i.e., anxiety) and so the child experiences negative reinforcement when the reading assignment is avoided. Or, perhaps the child is obtaining positive reinforcement (e.g., attention from the teacher and classmates) immediately after engaging in disruptive behavior.

Unfortunately, direct behavioral observation is inefficient. First, most therapists can't afford the time required to go out and observe clients. Second, many clients object to having their therapist come into their home or workplace to conduct a formal observation. Third, even if the client agreed to have the therapist come perform an observation, the therapist's presence is unavoidably obtrusive and therefore influences the client's behavior. The therapist observer is more than an observer, also becoming a participant within the client's environment—which means that an objective and natural observation cannot be obtained.

Because behavior therapists usually cannot use direct behavioral observation, they typically employ a variety of less direct methods to gather data and construct a functional causal hypothesis.

The Behavioral Interview

The clinical or behavioral interview is the most common assessment procedure (Craig, 2005; J. Sommers-Flanagan & R. Sommers-Flanagan, 2009). During interviews, behavior therapists directly observe client behavior, inquire about antecedents, problem behaviors, and consequences, and operationalize the primary therapy targets (Cormier, Nurius, & Osborn, 2009). For behaviorists, the operational definition or specific, measurable characteristics of client symptoms and goals are crucial behavioral assessment components.

Defining the client's problem(s) in precise behavioral terms is the first step in a behavioral assessment interview. Behavior therapists are not satisfied when clients describe themselves as "depressed"

or "anxious" or "hyper." Instead, behaviorists seek concrete, specific behavioral information. Typical queries during a behavior therapy intake interview might include:

- "Tell me about everything that happens during the course of a day when you're depressed. Let's start with when you wake up in the morning and cover everything that happens until you go to bed at night . . . and I even want to know what happens throughout the night until the next morning."

- "Describe the physical sensations you experience in your body when you're feeling anxious."

- "You said you were acting 'hyper.' Tell me what that looks like . . . describe it to me so I can see it, as if I were a mouse in the corner watching it happen."

Behaviorists value information about both the internal (mood or physiology) and the external (behavior), as long as the information is clear, specific, and measurable.

Despite many practical advantages of behavioral or clinical interviews, this assessment procedure also has several disadvantages:

- Low interrater reliability.

- Lack of interviewer objectivity.

- Inconsistency between behavior in a clinical interview and behavior outside therapy.

- False, inaccurate, and subjective reports from clients.

Behavior therapists compensate for the inconsistent and subjective nature of interviews through two strategies: First, they employ structured or diagnostic interviews such as the *Structured Clinical Interview for the Diagnostic and Statistical Manual of Mental Disorders*, fourth edition, which helps improve interview reliability (American Psychiatric Association, 2000; First, Spitzer, Gibbon, & Williams, 1997). Second, they use additional assessment methods beyond interviewing procedures, to obtain client information (J. Sommers-Flanagan & R. Sommers-Flanagan, 2009).

Self-Monitoring

Although it's often impractical for behavior therapists to directly observe client behavior outside therapy, they can train clients to observe and monitor their own behavior. For example, clients can monitor food intake or keep track of the number of cigarettes they smoke. In cognitive-behavior therapy, clients frequently keep thought or emotion logs that include at least three components: (1) disturbing emotional states, (2) the exact behavior engaged in at the time of the emotional state, and (3) thoughts that occurred when the emotions emerged.

Client **self-monitoring** has advantages and disadvantages. On the positive side, self-monitoring is inexpensive and practical. The other big benefit is that self-monitoring is not simply an assessment procedure, it also typically shows therapeutic benefits (Davies, Jones, & Rafoth, 2010; Young, Medic, & Starkes, 2009). The downside is the client can easily collect inadequate or inaccurate information, or resist collecting any information at all.

Standardized Questionnaires

Behaviorists famously prefer "objective" assessment measures over more "subjective" projective assessment procedures (Groth-Marnat, 2009). Objective psychological measures include standardized administration and scoring. Additionally, behaviorists prefer instruments with established reliability (i.e., internal consistency and consistency over time) and validity (i.e., the instrument measures what it purports to measure). Radical behaviorists also emphasize that objective measurement must focus solely on overt or observable behaviors rather than internal mental processes.

Overall, behaviorists employ questionnaires as one way of determining whether a specific treatment is working. Objective measurement isn't perfect, but repeated measurement of client symptoms and behavior help keep therapist and client on the right track. Case examples in this chapter illustrate behavior therapist's use of standardized questionnaires.

Operant Conditioning and Variants

In the tradition of Skinner and applied behavior analysis, perhaps the most straightforward application of behaviorism to therapy is direct operant conditioning. Skinner's emphasis is completely on environmental manipulation rather than processes of mind or cognition. In one of his more dramatic statements, he noted:

> I see no evidence of an inner world of mental life.... The appeal to cognitive states and processes is a diversion which could well be responsible for much of our failure to solve our problems. We need to change our behavior and we can do so only by changing our physical and social environments. (Skinner, 1977, p. 10)

Contingency Management and Token Economies

Using operant conditioning for human problems requires an analysis of the naturally occurring behavioral consequences in the client's physical and social environment. This process is sometimes referred to as **contingency management**. Contingency management is formally defined as:

> the systematic delivery of reinforcing or punishing consequences contingent on the occurrence of a target response, and the withholding of those consequences in the absence of the target response. (Schumacher et al., 2007, p. 823).

Contingency management is used most frequently in institutional, educational, family, and drug treatment settings.

To illustrate contingency management in action, let's return to the parents who wanted their 15-year-old to stop speaking disrespectfully. If you recall, the parents' efforts to modify their teen's behavior using positive reinforcement and punishment backfired. Essentially, the parents failed because they didn't use the procedure appropriately. Operant conditioning involves several systematic steps.

First, the parents need to operationalize the target behaviors and identify behavioral objectives. This requires precisely defining behaviors of interest. It also requires determining whether they want to increase or decrease the frequency of each target behavior. In conjunction with their applied behavior analyst, the parents agreed on the following goals:

- Decrease profanity (use of traditional "cuss words") in the home or toward the parents.

- Decrease disrespectful gestures or nonverbal behaviors (e.g., giving "the finger," rolling her eyes, giving long heaving sighs).

- Decrease derogatory comments about the parents or their ideas, such as "You're stupid," "That sucks," or "This family is so lame."

- Increase their 15-year-old's smiling behavior, compliments toward the parents and younger sibling, and compliance with parental suggestions and advice.

Second, the therapist helped the parents develop a system for measuring target behaviors. They were each given a pencil and notepad to track their 15-year-old's behaviors. Additionally, they used a digital audiotape recorder to keep an ongoing record of verbal interactions preceding and following their daughter's behaviors.

After analyzing the parents' notepads and audio-recorder data, the therapist helped the parents identify contingencies that were maintaining disrespectful speech and lack of respectful speech. During a 2-week baseline monitoring period, 16 incidents of undesirable behavior and 3 incidents of desirable behavior were recorded. Their home was an aversive environment for all four family members.

It was determined that the parents' reaction to the disrespectful speech—giving into demands, getting emotionally upset, or engaging in a protracted argument—were positively reinforcing problem behavior, whereas their relative lack of response to more pleasant behaviors was extinguishing the behaviors they wanted to increase. Further, a variety of potential positive reinforcements were identified, including (a) taking their daughter to dinner, (b) allowing her to rent DVDs online, (c) taking her for driving lessons, (d) allowing extra cell phone time in the evening, and (e) spending money on her. This analysis led to the third stage of treatment:

modification of existing environmental and social contingencies.

The parents were instructed in a very specific reinforcement and extinction procedure.

- The parents initiated a $10 weekly allowance program. This program provided their teen with money to spend as she wished. The only contingency for receiving the money was that whenever the 15-year-old used profanity, disrespectful gestures, or derogatory comments, she automatically lost $1 of the allowance, which she was scheduled to receive every Friday at 6 p.m.

- In response to the previously identified undesirable behaviors, the parents would calmly and immediately state, "Okay, that's one dollar you've lost."

- Using a variable-ratio reinforcement schedule, the parents provided one of the four reinforcers (a meal out, online DVD rental, extra phone time, or practice driving) immediately after their teen displayed one of the aforementioned desirable target behaviors. To implement the variable ratio schedule, the parents were given a six-sided die. They were instructed to roll the die and then, depending upon the number they rolled, provide a positive reinforcer after that number of positive behaviors. Then, immediately after providing a reward, they rolled the die again (privately, of course), and if the die came up "3," they planned to reward her again after three desirable behaviors. To reduce the number of positive reinforcements they provided, thereby fading her from the reinforcement program, the parents were given an additional die to use after every 2 weeks of increasing positive behaviors.

Third, the parents were instructed on how to continuously monitor and evaluate the effects of their new contingency schedule. This is a key factor in operant conditioning. The therapist explained this important principle to the parents:

> As behaviorists, we believe the only way we can
> tell if something is a positive reinforcer is to test it.
> What you discovered last time you tried positive

reinforcement with your 5- and 15-year-olds was that hugging and high fives functioned as positive reinforcements for your 5-year-old, but not for your 15-year-old. Perhaps the most important part of our intervention with your 15-year-old is for us to evaluate her response to the specific consequences you provide. This will help us understand how to increase and how to decrease her behaviors.

After using this operant conditioning program for eight weeks, the parents and therapist agreed that continued therapy was unnecessary. The parents said in their last session, "Thank you so much for your help. It's like we're getting acquainted with a new daughter."

Following Skinner's original work aimed at modifying the behavior of psychotic patients, operant conditioning or contingency management within institutions came to be known as token economies (Ghezzi, Wilson, Tarbox, & MacAleese, 2009; Skinner, 1954). Within **token economy** systems, patients or students are provided points or poker chips (symbolic rewards) for positive or desirable behaviors. These tokens are used like money, to obtain goods (e.g., food or toys) or privileges (e.g., computer or recreational time).

Token economies have been both lauded as highly effective and criticized as coercive and as not having lasting effects that generalize to the world outside the institution (Glynn, 1990; Matson & Boisjoli, 2009; Reitman, Murphy, Hupp, & O'Callaghan, 2004). In an ideal behavioral setting, reinforcements and punishments would be tightly controlled and then, after desirable behavior patterns are well established, behavioral contingencies would be slowly decreased (as in the case of the 15-year-old teen whose reinforcements were progressively decreased). This procedure is referred to as **fading** and is designed to generalize learning from one setting to another. The desired outcome occurs when a child, teen, or institutionalized adult internalizes the contingency system and continues positive behaviors independent of a token system.

Critics of behaviorism contend that people have a natural desire to behave in positive ways and that contingency management can interfere with that desire. For example, Kohn (2005) stated:

> I once heard someone . . . declaring that "human nature is to do as little as necessary." This prejudice is refuted not just by a few studies but by the entire branch of psychology dealing with motivation. Normally, it's hard to stop happy, satisfied people from trying to learn more about themselves and the world, or from trying to do a job of which they can feel proud. The desire to do as little as possible is an aberration, a sign that something is [terribly] wrong. It may suggest that someone feels threatened and therefore has fallen back on a strategy of damage control, or that rewards and punishments have caused that individual to lose interest in what he's doing, or that he perceives a specific task—perhaps incorrectly—as pointless and dull. (p. 90)

Kohn (2005) believes that applying tangible rewards to people who are already motivated undermines intrinsic motivation. In fact, many studies have shown that positive reinforcement adversely affects intrinsic motivation (Deci, 1971; Deci, Koestner, & Ryan, 2001; Ryan, Lynch, Vansteenkiste, & Deci, 2011). Of course, there's also a body of literature rebutting this hypothesis and claiming that positive reinforcement, when properly conceptualized and administered, can increase intrinsic motivation (Carton & Nowicki, 1998; Maag, 2001). In the end, if you want to employ operant techniques in a consistently helpful fashion, additional training is needed.

Although positive reinforcement has had its share of criticism, punishment or **aversive conditioning** as a therapeutic technique generates far more controversy. Historically, Thorndike (1932), Skinner (1953), and Estes (1944) all concluded that punishment led to behavior suppression but wasn't an effective method for controlling behavior. Punishment was viewed as insufficient to completely eliminate a learned response. Somewhat later, Solomon (1964) reopened the book on punishment by reporting that punishment alone could generate new, learned behavior. Currently, although punishment is a powerful behavior modifier, it's also viewed as having major drawbacks. In particular, within the attachment and trauma literature, excessive punishment by caregivers leads to what has been referred to as *trauma bonding*. A description of Harry Harlow's studies on attachment behaviors in monkeys (see Harlow, Harlow, Dodsworth, & Arling, 1966; Harlow, Harlow, & Suomi, 1971) provides a vivid example of the terrors of mixing love and punishment: "When Harlow presented baby macaques with mechanically devised spike-sprouting surrogates or mothers that suddenly puffed blasts of air, the infants gripped all the tighter to the only security they knew" (Hrdy, 1999, p. 398).

Despite problems with punishment as a learning tool, aversive conditioning (the term used to describe the use of punishment for behavior modification purposes) is sometimes used to reduce undesirable and maladaptive behavior. It has been applied with some success to smoking cessation, repetitive self-injurious behavior, alcohol abuse or dependency, and sexual deviation.

While discussing the use of corporal punishment with children, former American Psychological Association President and renowned behaviorist Alan Kazdin (2008) provides an excellent description of what the research says about using punishment (including spanking children):

> study after study has proven that punishment all by itself, as it is usually practiced in the home, is relatively ineffective in changing behavior....
>
> Each time, punishing your child stops the behavior for a moment. Maybe your child cries, too, and shows remorse. In our studies, parents often mistakenly interpret such crying and wails of I'm sorry! as signs that punishment has worked. It hasn't. Your child's resistance to punishment escalates as fast as the severity of the punishment does, or even faster. So you penalize more and more to get the same result: a brief stop, then the unwanted behavior returns, often worse than before....
>
> Bear in mind that about 35% of parents who start out with relatively mild punishments end up crossing the line drawn by the state to define child abuse: hitting with an object, harsh and cruel hitting, and so on. The surprisingly high

percentage of line-crossers, and their general failure to improve their children's behavior, points to a larger truth: punishment changes parents' behavior for the worse more effectively than it changes children's behavior for the better. And, as anyone knows who has physically punished a child more harshly than they meant to—and that would include most of us—it feels just terrible. (pp. 15, 16, 17)

Kazdin's point about how using punishment changes the parent's behavior for the worse is another example of operant conditioning. Specifically, when parents spank children, immediate compliance often occurs, which relieves parents of tension and discomfort. This cycle gives parents a powerful dose of negative reinforcement for using physical punishment.

In a meta-analysis of the effects of corporal punishment on children's behavior (Gershoff, 2002; Gershoff & Bitensky, 2007), punishment was associated with 1 desirable outcome (i.e., immediate behavioral compliance) and 10 undesirable outcomes, including less internalization of moral principles, potential abuse, delinquent behavior, and later abuse within adult relationships. Despite this fairly clear scientific indictment of corporal punishment, many adults remain in favor of its use as a disciplinary technique (Baumrind, Larzelere, & Cowan, 2002; Gershoff & Bitensky, 2007).

Behavioral Activation

Over half a century ago, Skinner suggested that depression was caused by an interruption of healthy behavioral activities that had previously been maintained through positive reinforcement. Later, this idea was expanded based on the initial work of Ferster (1973) and Lewinsohn (Lewinsohn, 1974; Lewinsohn & Libet, 1972) who focused on observations that:

> depressed individuals find fewer activities pleasant, engage in pleasant activities less frequently, and obtain therefore less positive reinforcement than other individuals. (Cuijpers, van Straten, & Warmerdam, 2007, p. 319)

From the behavioral perspective, the thinking goes like this:

- *Observation*: Individuals experiencing depression engage in fewer pleasant activities and obtain less daily positive reinforcement.

- *Hypothesis*: Individuals with depressive symptoms might improve or recover if they change their behavior (while not paying any attention to their thoughts or feelings associated with depression).

Like good scientists, behavior therapists have tested this hypothesis and found that behavior change—all by itself—can produce positive treatment outcomes among clients with depression. The main point is to get clients with depressive symptoms to change their behavior patterns so they engage in more pleasant activities and experience more positive reinforcement.

Originally, **behavioral activation** was referred to as activity scheduling and used as a component of various cognitive and behavioral treatments for depression (A. T. Beck, Rush, Shaw, & Emery, 1979; Lewinsohn, Steinmetz, Antonuccio, & Teri, 1984). During this time activity scheduling was viewed as one piece or part of an overall cognitive behavior treatment (CBT) for depression.

However, in 1996, Jacobson and colleagues conducted a dismantling study on CBT for depression. They compared the whole CBT package with activity scheduling (which they referred to as behavioral activation), with behavioral activation (BA) only, and with CBT for automatic thoughts only. Somewhat surprisingly, BA by itself was equivalent to the other treatment components—even at two-year follow-up (Gortner, Gollan, Dobson, & Jacobson, 1998; Jacobson et al., 1996).

As is often the case, this exciting research finding stimulated further exploration and research associated with behavioral activation. In particular, two separate research teams developed treatment manuals focusing on behavioral activation. Jacobson and colleagues (Jacobson, Martell, & Dimidjian, 2001) developed an expanded BA protocol and Lejuez, Hopko, Hopko, and McNeil (2001) developed a brief (12-session) behavioral activation

treatment for depression (BATD) manual and a more recent 10-session revised manual (Lejuez, Hopko, Acierno, Daughters, & Pagoto, 2011).

Implementation of the BATD protocol is described in a short vignette later in this chapter.

Relaxation Training

Edmund Jacobson was the first modern scientist to write about relaxation training as a treatment procedure (Jacobson, 1924). In *Progressive Relaxation*, he outlined principles and techniques of relaxation training that therapists still employ in the twenty-first century (Jacobson, 1938). **Progressive muscle relaxation** (PMR) was initially based on the assumption that muscular tension is an underlying cause of a variety of mental and emotional problems. Jacobson claimed that "nervous disturbance is at the same time mental disturbance. Neurosis and psychoneurosis are at the same time physiological disturbance; for they are forms of tension disorder" (Jacobson, 1978, p. viii). For Jacobson, individuals can cure neurosis through relaxation. Currently, PMR is viewed as either a counterconditioning or extinction procedure. By pairing the muscle-tension conditioned stimulus with pleasurable relaxation, muscle tension as a stimulus or trigger for anxiety is replaced or extinguished.

Progressive muscle relaxation remains a common relaxation training approach, although others—such as breathing retraining, meditation, autogenic training, imagery, and hypnosis—are also popular (Benson, 1976; Logsdon-Conradsen, 2002; Philippot & Segal, 2009). However, clinical training guidelines suggest that beginning therapists understand how, when, and for how long relaxation procedures should be implemented (Castonguay, Boswell, Constantino, Goldfried, & Hill, 2010; Lilienfeld, 2007). This is because of the well-documented research finding that ironically, relaxation can trigger anxiety (Braith, McCullough, & Bush, 1988; Heide & Borkovec, 1984; Ley, 1988).

Information on implementing relaxation procedures with clients is outlined in Putting it in Practice 7.2. Be sure to discuss appropriate implementation of these procedures in class and with your supervisor.

PUTTING IT IN PRACTICE 7.2

Prepping Clients (and Yourself) for Progressive Muscle Relaxation

Before using relaxation training with clients, you should experience the procedure yourself. You can accomplish this either by going to a behavior therapist and asking to learn the procedure, using a PMR CD or podcast, or asking your professor to demonstrate the procedure in class.

We recommend that you make your own PMR recording and use it for practicing. Getting comfortable with the right pace and voice tone for inducing a relaxed state is important. It's also helpful to try out your relaxation skills with your classmates and ask for feedback.

When working with clients, keep the following issues in mind:

- Have a quiet room and a comfortable chair available. Noise and discomfort are antithetical to relaxation. Reclining chairs are recommended. Lighting should be dim, but not dark.

- Give clients clear information as to why you're teaching PMR. If the rationale isn't clear, they may not participate fully.

- Explain the procedure. Say something like "I'll be instructing you to create tension and then let go of tension in specific muscle groups. Research shows that tensing your muscles first and then relaxing helps you achieve a deeper relaxation than if you just tried to relax them without tensing first." You might demonstrate this by flexing and then relaxing your arm or shoulder muscles.

- Seat yourself in a position that's not distracting. A face-to-face arrangement can make clients uncomfortable. Instead, place seats at a 90° to 120° angle.

- Emphasize that, like most skills, the ability to relax is best learned through repeated practice. Assure your client that it is possible to learn to be relaxed and peaceful.

- Tell your clients that they're in control of the relaxation process. To become relaxed, all they have to do is listen to you and follow along, but whether they listen and follow along is totally their choice.

- Warn clients that they may feel unusual body sensations: "Some people feel tingling, others feel light and maybe a little dizzy, and still others feel heavy, like they're sinking into the chair. I don't know exactly how you'll feel, but we'll take a few minutes afterward to talk about how it felt to you."

- Let clients know they can keep their eyes open or shut. Some clients are uncomfortable closing their eyes and their discomfort should be respected. Don't worry about whether your client's eyes are open or shut. Relaxation is possible either way and more likely if the client is doing whatever is comfortable.
- Let clients know they can move around if it helps them be more comfortable. If they wear glasses, they might want to remove them. The key is to facilitate physical comfort.
- Check for physical conditions (e.g., a knee or back problem) that might be aggravated by tensing muscles. Omit painful or injured body parts from the procedure.
- Let clients know their minds may wander while you're talking and they're relaxing. That's okay. If they notice their minds wandering, all they need to do is gently bring attention back to whatever you're saying.
- Help clients have realistic, but optimistic, expectations: Most people who do progressive relaxation find that it helps them relax a bit, but don't find it amazing or dramatic. Some people find it extremely relaxing and wonderful.
- Be sure to acknowledge that practicing relaxation actually causes some people to feel more anxious. This can be due to unusual sensations, a trauma history, feeling a loss of control, or fears that something bad may happen during the process (Castonguay et al., 2010; Goldfried & Davison, 1994; Lilienfeld, 2007).

Additional detailed information about using PMR is available from several sources (Bernstein & Borkovec, 1973; Field, 2009; Goldfried & Davison, 1994).

Systematic Desensitization and Other Exposure-Based Treatments

Joseph Wolpe (1958) formally introduced systematic desensitization as a treatment technique. In his original work, Wolpe reported a highly controversial treatment success rate of 80%, and therapists (especially psychoanalysts) criticized and challenged his procedures and results (Glover, 1959). However, Wolpe staunchly defended his claim of impressive success rates for systematic desensitization (Wolpe & Plaud, 1997).

Systematic desensitization is a combination of Jones's deconditioning approach and Jacobson's PMR procedure (M. C. Jones, 1924). Jacobson articulated the central place of relaxation in curing clients of anxious or disturbed conditions, stating that "to be relaxed is the direct physiological opposite of being excited or disturbed" (Jacobson, 1978, p. viii).

After clients are trained in PMR techniques, they build a fear hierarchy in collaboration with the therapist. Systematic desensitization usually proceeds in the following manner:

- The client identifies a range of various fear-inducing situations or objects.
- Typically, using a measuring system referred to as subjective units of distress (SUDs), the client, with the support of the therapist, rates each fear-inducing situation or object on a scale from 0 to 100 (0 = no distress; 100 = total distress).
- Early in the session the client engages in PMR (see Putting it in Practice 7.2).
- While deeply relaxed, the client is exposed, in vivo or through imagery, to the least feared item in the fear hierarchy.

- Subsequently, the client is exposed to each feared item, gradually progressing to the most feared item in the hierarchy.

- If the client experiences significant anxiety at any point during the **imaginal or in vivo exposure** process, the client reengages in PMR until relaxation overcomes anxiety.

- Treatment continues systematically until the client achieves relaxation competence while simultaneously being exposed to the entire range of his or her fear hierarchy.

In the traditional systematic desensitization protocol clients were taught PMR and exposed to a feared stimuli using visual imagery. More recent research suggests that PMR is not necessary and that in-vivo exposure is superior to imaginal exposure (D. Dobson & Dobson, 2009).

Imaginal or In Vivo Exposure and Desensitization
Systematic desensitization is a form of **exposure treatment**. Exposure treatments are based on the principle that clients are best treated by exposure to the very thing they want to avoid: the stimulus that evokes intense fear, anxiety, or other painful emotions. Mowrer (1947) used a two-factor theory of learning, based on animal studies, to explain how avoidance conditioning works. First, he explained that animals originally learn to fear a particular stimulus through classical conditioning. For example, a dog may learn to fear its owner's voice when the owner yells due to the discovery of an unwelcome pile on the living room carpet. Then, if the dog remains in the room with its owner, fear continues to escalate.

Second, Mowrer explained that avoidance behavior is reinforced via operant conditioning. Specifically, if the dog manages to hide under the bed or dash out the front door of the house, it is likely to experience decreased fear and anxiety. Consequently, the avoidance behavior—running away and hiding—is negatively reinforced because it relieves fear, anxiety, and discomfort. **Negative reinforcement** is defined as the strengthening of a behavioral response by reducing or eliminating an aversive stimulus (like fear and anxiety).

Note that exposure via systematic desensitization and the other procedures detailed hereafter are distinctively behavioral. However, the concept that psychological health is enhanced when clients face and embrace their fears is consistent with existential and Jungian theory (van Deurzen, 2010; see online Jungian chapter: www.wiley.com/go/counselingtheories).

There are three ways to expose clients to their fears during systematic desensitization. First, exposure to fears can be accomplished through mental imagery. This approach can be more convenient and allows clients to complete treatment without ever leaving their therapist's office. Second, in vivo (direct exposure to the feared stimulus) is also possible. This option can be more complex (e.g., going to a dental office to provide exposure for a client with a dental phobia), but appears to produce outcomes superior to imaginal exposure (Emmelkamp, 1994). Third, computer simulation (virtual reality) has been successfully used as a means of exposing clients to feared stimuli (Emmelkamp et al., 2001; Emmelkamp, Bruynzeel, Drost, & van der Mast, 2001).

Psychoeducation is critical to effective exposure treatment. D. Dobson and K. S. Dobson (2009) state:

> A crucial element of effective exposure is the provision of a solid rationale to encourage your client to take the risks involved in this strategy. A good therapeutic alliance is absolutely essential for exposure to occur. (p. 104)

Further, D. Dobson and K. S. Dobson (2009) provide a sample client handout that helps inform clients of the exposure rationale and procedure.

> Exposure treatment means gradually and systematically exposing yourself to situations that create some anxiety. You can then prove to yourself that you can handle these feared situations, as your body learns to become more comfortable. Exposure treatment is extremely important in your recovery and involves taking controlled risks. For exposure treatment to work, you should experience some anxiety—too little won't be enough to put you in your discomfort zone so you can prove your fears wrong. Too

much anxiety means that you may not pay attention to what is going on in the situation. If you are too uncomfortable, it may be hard to try the same thing again. Generally, effective exposure involves experiencing anxiety that is around 70 out of 100 on your Subjective Units of Distress Scale. Expect to feel some anxiety. As you become more comfortable with the situation, you can then move on to the next step. Exposure should be structured, planned, and predictable. It must be within your control, not anyone else's. (p. 104)

Massed (Intensive) or Spaced (Graduated) Exposure Sessions

Behavior therapists continue to optimize methods for extinguishing fear responses. One question being examined empirically is this: Is desensitization more effective when clients are directly exposed to feared stimuli during a single prolonged session (e.g., one 3-hour session; aka: *massed exposure*) or when they're slowly and incrementally exposed to feared stimuli during a series of shorter sessions (such as five 1-hour sessions; aka: *spaced exposure*)? Initially, it was thought that massed exposure might result in higher dropout rates, greater likelihood of fear relapse, and a higher client stress. However, research suggests that **massed and spaced exposure** desensitization strategies yield minimal differences in efficacy (Ost, Alm, Brandberg, & Breitholz, 2001).

Virtual Reality Exposure

Technological advancements have led to potential modifications in systematic desensitization procedures. Specifically, **virtual reality exposure**, a procedure wherein clients are immersed in a real-time computer-generated virtual environment, has been empirically evaluated as an alternative to imaginal or in-vivo exposure in cases of acrophobia (fear of heights), flight phobia, spider phobia, and other anxiety disorders (Krijn et al., 2007; Ruwaard, Broeksteeg, Schrieken, Emmelkamp, & Lange, 2010).

In a meta-analysis of 18 outcome studies, Powers and Emmelkamp (2008) reported a large effect size ($d = 1.11$) as compared to no treatment and a small effect size ($d = .35$) when compared to in

vivo control conditions. These results suggest that virtual reality exposure may be as efficacious or even more so than in vivo exposure.

Interoceptive Exposure

Typical panic-prone individuals are highly sensitive to internal physical cues (e.g., increased heart rate, increased respiration, and dizziness). They become especially reactive when those cues are associated with environmental situations viewed as potentially causing anxiety (Story & Craske, 2008). Physical cues or sensations are then interpreted as signs of physical illness, impending death, or imminent loss of consciousness (and associated humiliation). Although specific cognitive techniques have been developed to treat clients' tendencies to catastrophically overinterpret bodily sensations, a more behavioral technique, **interoceptive exposure**, has been developed to help clients learn, through exposure and practice, to deal more effectively with physical aspects of intense anxiety or panic (Lee et al., 2006; Stewart & Watt, 2008).

Interoceptive exposure is identical to other exposure techniques except that the target exposure stimuli are internal physical cues. There are at least six interoceptive exposure tasks that reliably trigger anxiety (Lee et al., 2006). They include:

- Hyperventilation
- Breath holding
- Breathing through a straw
- Spinning in circles
- Shaking head
- Chest breathing

Of course, before interoceptive exposure is initiated, clients receive education about body sensations, learn relaxation skills (e.g., breathing training), and learn cognitive restructuring skills. Through repeated successful exposure, clients become desensitized to previously feared physical cues (Forsyth, Fusé, & Acheson, 2009).

Response and Ritual Prevention

Mowrer's two-factor theory suggests that, when a client avoids or escapes a feared or distressing situation or stimulus, the maladaptive avoidance behavior is negatively reinforced (i.e., when the client feels relief from the negative anxiety, fear, or distress, the avoidance or escape behavior is reinforced or strengthened; Spiegler & Guevremont, 2010). Many examples of this negative reinforcement cycle are present across the spectrum of mental disorders. For example, clients with Bulimia Nervosa who purge after eating specific "forbidden" foods are relieving themselves from the anxiety and discomfort they experience upon ingesting the foods (Agras, Schneider, Arnow, Raeburn, & Telch, 1989). Therefore, purging behavior is negatively reinforced. Similarly, when a phobic client escapes from a phobic object or situation, or when a client with obsessive-compulsive symptoms engages in a repeated washing or checking behavior, negative reinforcement of maladaptive behavior occurs (Franklin & Foa, 1998; Franklin, Ledley, & Foa, 2009; March, Franklin, Nelson, & Foa, 2001).

It follows that, to be effective, exposure-based desensitization treatment must include **response prevention**. With the therapist's assistance, the client with bulimia is prevented from vomiting after ingesting a forbidden cookie, the agoraphobic client is prevented from fleeing a public place when anxiety begins to mount, and the client with obsessive-compulsive disorder is prevented from washing his or her hands following exposure to a "contaminated" object. Without response or ritual prevention, the treatment may exacerbate the condition it was designed to treat. Research indicates that exposure plus response prevention can produce significant brain changes in as few as three psychotherapy sessions (Schwartz, Gulliford, Stier, & Thienemann, 2005; Schwartz, Stoessel, Baxter, Martin, & Phelps, 1996).

Participant Modeling

In addition to operant principles, social learning principles have been empirically evaluated for anxiety treatment (Bandura, Blanchard, & Ritter, 1969). Recall that, in her work with Little Peter and other fearful children, Jones reported that social imitation (**participant modeling**) was one of two effective deconditioning strategies (Jones, 1924).

Like most behavioral techniques, to have a positive effect, participant modeling needs to be conducted in an appropriate and sensitive manner. For example, individuals with airplane or flight phobias generally don't find it helpful when they watch other passengers getting on a plane without experiencing distress. In fact, such observations can produce increased feelings of humiliation and hopelessness; seeing others easily confront fears they find paralyzing is discouraging to phobic clients. The problem is that there is too large of a gap in emotional state and skills between the model and the observer so maximal vicarious learning doesn't occur. Instead of providing clients with general models of fear-free behavior, behavior therapists provide models of successful coping that are more relevant or close to what clients are capable of accomplishing. This is why published treatment protocols for panic disorder often recommend using a group therapy format to take advantage of participant modeling effects (Craske, 1999; Freeman, Pretzer, Fleming, & Simon, 2004).

Skills Training

Skills training techniques are primarily based on skill deficit psychopathology models. Many clients suffering from behavioral disorders haven't acquired requisite skills for functioning across a broad range of domains. Consequently, behavior therapists evaluate their clients' functional skills during the assessment phase of therapy and then use specific skills training strategies to remediate client skill deficits. Traditional skills training targets include assertiveness and other social behavior as well as problem solving.

Assertiveness and Other Social Behavior

In the behavioral tradition, Wolpe, Lazarus, and others defined *assertiveness* as a learned behavior (Alberti & Emmons, 1970; Lazarus, 1973). Generally, individuals are evaluated as having one of three possible social behavior styles: passive, aggressive, or assertive. *Passive* individuals behave in submissive ways; they say yes when they want to say no, avoid speaking up and asking for instructions or directions, and let others take advantage of them. *Aggressive* individuals dominate others, trying to get their way through coercive means. In contrast, ideal or *assertive* individuals speak up, express feelings, and actively seek to meet needs without dominating others.

Assertiveness training became popular as an individual, group, or self-help treatment for social difficulties in the 1970s. A number of self-help books on this treatment were published, including the highly acclaimed *Your Perfect Right: Assertiveness and Equality in Your Life and Relationships*, now in its ninth edition (Alberti & Emmons, 2008). The most common social behaviors targeted in assertiveness training are (a) introducing oneself to strangers, (b) giving and receiving compliments, (c) saying no to requests from others, (d) making requests of others, (e) speaking up or voicing an opinion, and (f) maintaining social conversations. Within a counseling context, assertive behavior is taught through the following strategies:

- *Instruction*: Clients are instructed in assertive eye contact, body posture, voice tone, and verbal delivery.
- *Feedback*: The therapist or group members give clients feedback regarding how their efforts at assertive behavior come across to others.
- *Behavior rehearsal or role playing*: Clients are given opportunities to practice specific assertive behaviors, such as asking for help or expressing disagreement without becoming angry or aggressive.
- *Coaching*: Therapists often whisper feedback and instructions in the client's ear as a role-play or practice scenario progresses.
- *Modeling*: The therapist or group members demonstrate appropriate assertive behavior for specific situations.
- *Social reinforcement*: The therapist or group members offer positive feedback and support for appropriate assertive behavior.

- *Relaxation training*: For some clients, relaxation training is needed to reduce anxiety in social situations.

Assertiveness training remains a viable treatment option for many clients. However, most practitioners will be more likely to use the terms **skills training** or social skills training instead of assertiveness. Components of assertiveness training for individuals with specific social anxiety and social skills deficits are still of great interest. For example, Social Phobia—a condition characterized by an excessive, irrational fear of being scrutinized and evaluated by others—is frequently treated with a combination of relaxation and social skills training that includes almost all the components of traditional assertion training (e.g., instruction, feedback, behavior rehearsal, social reinforcement) and graduated or massed exposure to challenging social situations and interactions (McNeil, Sorrell, Vowles, & Billmeyer, 2002). Additionally, DBT includes a social skills or assertiveness training component (see Chapter 14).

Problem-Solving Therapy

D'Zurilla and Goldfried (1971) originally described a therapeutic approach that eventually became known as **problem-solving therapy** (PST). PST is a behavioral treatment with cognitive dimensions. PST is based on the rationale that effective problem solving is a mediator or buffer that helps clients manage stressful life events more effectively and therefore achieve improved personal well-being (Chang, D'Zurilla, & Sanna, 2004; D'Zurilla & Nezu, 2010).

There are two main components to problem-solving therapy:

1. Problem orientation.
2. Problem-solving style.

Problem orientation involves teaching clients to have a positive attitude toward problem solving. This attitude includes: (a) seeing problems as a challenge or opportunity; (b) seeing problems as solvable; (c) believing in one's own ability to solve problems; and (d) recognizing that effective problem-solving requires time and effort (A. C. Bell & D'Zurilla, 2009).

Problem-solving style refers to how individuals approach social problems. In PST, clients are taught a *rational problem-solving* style that includes four steps (A. M. Nezu & C. M. Nezu, in press):

1. *Problem definition*: Clarifying a problem, identifying goals, and identifying obstacles.

2. *Generating of alternatives*: Brainstorming a range of potential solutions designed to overcome obstacles and solve the problem.

3. *Decision making*: Predicting likely outcomes, conducting a cost-benefit analysis, and developing a solution plan (this is sometimes referred to as *means-ends thinking* or *consequential thinking*).

4. *Solution implementation and verification*: Trying out the solution plan, monitoring outcomes, and determining success.

PST has been employed as an intervention for coping with and resolving a wide range of problems, including depression, suicide ideation, non-cardiac chest pain, and many other stressful life circumstances (Malouff, Thorsteinsson, & Schutte, 2007; Nezu et al., 2007; A. M. Nezu & C. M. Nezu, 2010). PST has also been used as a treatment for working with children and adolescents with conduct disorder (Kazdin, 2010; Kazdin, Siegel, & Bass, 1992). In addition to teaching some variant on the four-step approach previously listed, child and adolescent behavior therapists often focus specifically on a number of cognitive and behavioral concepts, such as means-ends thinking, generating behavioral alternatives, consequential thinking, and perspective taking (Shure, 1992; J. Sommers-Flanagan & R. Sommers-Flanagan, 2007b; Spivack, Platt, & Shure, 1976). Step 2 of the problem-solving approach (generating behavioral alternatives) is illustrated in one of the chapter vignettes.

Behavior Therapy in Action: Brief Vignettes

As you may recall from Chapter 1, traditional approaches to counseling and psychotherapy tended to emphasize clients achieving insight through talking (i.e., the talking cure). In contrast, many contemporary therapies focus more on therapists providing clients with an educational experience. Behavior therapy is a good example of an approach that actively teaches new life skills. Although behavior therapy also involves client-learning activities, therapists place a strong emphasis on psychoeducation. The following case vignettes capture this style.

Vignette I: Behavioral Activation Treatment for Depression (BATD)

This vignette briefly illustrates an approach called the revised behavioral activation treatment for depression (BATD-R). The full BATD-R manual is published in *Behavior Modification* and forms for this therapy are free online (Lejuez et al., 2011). Although BATD-R is a 10-session manualized protocol, research supports its flexible application.

The authors (Ruggiero, Morris, Hopko, & Lejuez, 2007) describe the case:

> Adrienne was a 17-year-old European American high school student referred for treatment to address symptoms of depression as well as difficulties in her relationship with her foster mother. She was socially pleasant and was of average intelligence. She lived with her foster mother and several younger children, all of whom were unrelated to Adrienne (two were foster children, two were the foster mother's biological children). (p. 67)

Adrienne attended an initial assessment session. During this session, Adrienne was accompanied by her caseworker (the foster mother could not attend) and the behavior therapist conducted a semi-structured clinical interview to determine her presenting symptoms and possible comorbid complaints. In the behavioral tradition, behavioral antecedents and consequences were also explored and analyzed. Ruggiero and colleagues reported that Adrienne had:

> [S]everal symptoms of depression and expressed concern about verbal conflicts with her foster mother that had been escalating in frequency. When asked for details about her daily routine, Adrienne described that she typically had minimal

time to herself, rarely spent time with friends after school, and had numerous household and babysitting responsibilities.

BA is based on the fundamental premise that clients with depressive symptoms are experiencing too few positive reinforcements and too many aversive stimuli. As a consequence, a thorough behavioral assessment process was initiated with Adrienne. This process involved guiding her in how to complete two assessment instruments: (1) the Beck Depression Inventory (BDI); and (2) the Daily Activity Log (Hopko, Armento, Cantu, Chambers, & Lejuez, 2003).

Adrienne obtained a score of 13 (mildly depressed) on the BDI. Her responses to the DAL, a 24-hour daily monitoring form were very revealing and help capture the rigor of behavioral assessment:

> The completed DAL covered 152 hours (6.3 days) during which her activities were allocated roughly as follows: 50 hours of sleep (about 8 hours per day), 35 hours in school, 24 hours of chores and responsibilities unrelated to school (e.g., cleaning the house, chores for her foster mother), 22 hours of school-related and miscellaneous activities (e.g., homework, preparation for school and church, meals), and 21 hours of discretionary time. Perhaps most striking, of her 21 hours of discretionary time, none were used to communicate and/or visit with similar-age peers and nearly all were spent watching television and using the Internet. One hour was used to interact with adult neighbors, and 2 to 3 hours were used to entertain young children.

Based on this assessment information combined with information from the initial clinical interview, two primary goals were established.

- Goal 1: Reduce frequency of verbal conflict between Adrienne and her foster mother.
- Goal 2: Reduce depressive symptoms.

To guide BA treatment, the therapist gathered additional information pertaining to the antecedents and consequences associated with Adrienne-foster mother verbal conflicts. Although nailing down the specific patterns was challenging, the therapist found:

- Parent-child conflict was "temporally connected" to the foster mother's increased after school volunteer commitments and activities.
- Adrienne was expected to babysit the four younger children for several hours after school.
- Because the foster mother was more fatigued, she was asking Adrienne to complete additional household tasks.
- Conflicts were also "linked to unpredictable, uncontrollable, and/or short-notice requests to baby-sit or perform household tasks" (p. 70).
- Partly due to her increased workload at home and partly due to her own poor choices regarding healthy social and physical behavior, Adrienne had discontinued her previously enjoyable activities (e.g., going to the mall with friends, photographing birds and animals).

Although the treatment process and progress was more complex than described below, in conjunction with the foster mother's acknowledgment that Adrienne needed more discretionary time, the following behavioral interventions were implemented. This description provides you with a sense of the detail involved in a BATD intervention:

> [T]hree feasible and pleasurable activities were prescribed for the following week and monitored with the Weekly Behavior Checkout (form 8). The three activities were (a) to make at least one phone call to at least one friend on each of 5 days, (b) to exercise for at least 30 minutes on each of 3 different days, and (c) to take one or more pictures of animals or natural settings on at least 1 day. These activities were selected because they were identified by Adrienne as pleasurable, were related to multiple life-goal domains, and were all clearly within household rules. Also, they had all been activities in which she had engaged at least once during the prior month, suggesting that likelihood for success was satisfactory. (p. 71)

The authors reported a positive outcome in this case. At her final BATD session, Adrienne obtained a score of 2 on the BDI. She also recognized how her daily routine and depressive symptoms were related. She reported engaging in a much wider range of healthy social and recreational activities and had expanded her social contacts. Interestingly, the authors noted that because Adrienne possessed positive social skills, she didn't need to have social skills training be a focus of her treatment.

BA treatment as reported in this case and as described in treatment manuals doesn't address client cognitive processes. This is an advantage for some clients—especially clients who are either less cognitively inclined or perhaps too capable of over-analyzing or overthinking life situations. Hopko and colleagues (2003) provide a nice description of this important distinction between behavioral activation and cognitive approaches to treating depression and a fitting conclusion to this case vignette:

> Based on this paradigm, activation partially involves teaching patients to formulate and accomplish behavioral goals irrespective of certain aversive thoughts and mood states they may experience. This clear focus on action makes it unnecessary to attempt to control and change such thoughts and mood states directly. (Hopko et al., 2003, p. 703)

BA is a promising approach for both clients and therapists who prefer to focus on behaviors rather than cognitions.

Vignette II: Generating Behavioral Alternatives With an Aggressive Adolescent

As noted previously, problem-solving therapy (PST) focuses on teaching clients steps for rational problem solving. In this case vignette, the thera-pist (John) is trying to engage a 15-year-old white male client in stage 2 (generating solutions) of the problem-solving model. At the beginning of the session, the client had reported that the night before, a male schoolmate had tried to rape his girlfriend. The client was angry and planning to "beat the s*** out" of his fellow student. During the session, John worked on helping the boy identify behavioral alternatives to retributive violence.

The transcript below begins 10 minutes into the session.

Boy: He's gotta learn sometime.

JSF: I mean. I don't know for sure what the absolute best thing to do to this guy is...but I think before you act, it's important to think of all the different options you have.

Boy: I've been thinking a lot.

JSF: Well, tell me the other ones you've thought of and let's write them down so we can look at the options together.

Boy: Kick the shit out of him.

JSF: Okay, I know 2 things, actually maybe 3, that you said. One is kick the [crap] out of him, the other one is to do nothing...

Boy: The other is to shove something up his a**.

JSF: And, okay—shove—which is kinda like kicking the s*** out of him. I mean to be violent toward him. [Notice John is using the client's language.]

Boy: Yeah, Yeah.

JSF: So, what else?

Boy: I could nark on him.

JSF: Oh.

Boy: Tell the cops or something.

JSF: And I'm not saying that's the right thing to do either. [Although John thinks this is a better option, he's trying to remain neutral, which is important to the brainstorming process; if the client thinks John is trying to "reinforce" him for nonviolent or prosocial behaviors, he may resist brainstorming.]

Boy: That's just stupid. [This response shows why it's important to stay neutral.]

JSF: I'm not saying that's the right thing to do...all I'm saying is that we should figure out, cause I know I think I have the same kind of impulse in your situation. Either, I wanna beat him up or kinda do the high and righteous thing, which is to ignore him. And I'm not sure. Maybe one of those is the right thing, but I don't know. Now, we got three things—so you could nark on him.

[John tries to show empathy and then encourages continuation of brainstorming.]

Boy: It's not gonna happen though.

JSF: Yeah, but I don't care if that's gonna happen. So there's nark, there's ignore, there's beat the s***. What else?

Boy: Um. Just talk to him, would be okay. Just go up to him and yeah... I think we need to have a little chit-chat. [The client is able to generate another potentially prosocial idea.]

JSF: Okay. Talk to him.

Boy: But that's not gonna happen either. I don't think I could talk to him without, like, him pissing me off and me kicking the s***... [Again, the client is making it clear that he's not interested in nonviolent options.]

JSF: So, it might be so tempting when you talk to him that you just end up beating the s*** out of him. [John goes back to reflective listening.]

Boy: Yeah. Yeah.

JSF: But all we're doing is making a list. Okay. And you're doing great. [This is positive reinforcement for the brainstorming process—not outcome.]

Boy: I could get someone to beat the s*** out of him.

JSF: Get somebody to beat him up. So, kind of indirect violence—you get him back physically—through physical pain. That's kind of the approach.

Boy: [This section is censored.]

JSF: So you could [do another thing]. Okay.

Boy: Someone like...

JSF: Okay. We're up to six options. [John is showing neutrality or using an **extinction** process by not showing any affective response to the client's provocative maladaptive alternative that was censored for this book.]

Boy: That's about it....

JSF: So. So we got nark, we got ignore, we got beat the s*** out of him, we got talk to him, we got get somebody else to beat the s*** out of him,

and get some.... [Reading back the alternatives allows the client to hear what he has said.]

Boy: Um... couple of those are pretty unrealistic, but. [The client acknowledges he's being unrealistic, but we don't know which items he views as unrealistic and why. Exploring his evaluation of the options might be useful, but John is still working on brainstorming and relationship-building.]

JSF: We don't have to be realistic. I've got another unrealistic one. I got another one... Kinda to start some shameful rumor about him, you know. [This is a verbally aggressive option which can be risky, but illustrates a new domain of behavioral alternatives.]

Boy: That's a good idea.

JSF: I mean, it's a nonviolent way to get some revenge.

Boy: Like he has a little dick or something.

JSF: Yeah, good, exactly. [John inadvertently provides positive reinforcement for an insulting idea rather than remaining neutral.]

Boy: Maybe I'll do all these things.

JSF: Combination.

Boy: Yeah.

JSF: So we've got the shameful rumor option to add to our list.

Boy: That's a good one. (Excerpted and adapted from J. Sommers-Flanagan & R. Sommers-Flanagan, 1999)

This case illustrates what can occur when therapists conduct PST and generate behavioral solutions with angry adolescents. Initially, the client appears to be blowing off steam and generating a spate of aggressive alternatives. This process, although not producing constructive alternatives, is important because the boy may be testing the therapist to see if he will react with judgment (during this brainstorming process it's very important for therapists to remain positive and welcoming of all options, no matter how violent or absurd; using judgment can be perceived and experienced as a punishment, which can adversely affect the therapy relationship).

As the boy produced various aggressive ideas, he appeared to calm down somewhat. Also, the behavioral alternatives are repeatedly read back to the client. This allows the boy to hear his ideas from a different perspective. Finally, toward the end, the therapist joins the boy in brainstorming and adds a marginally delinquent response. The therapist is modeling a less violent approach to revenge and hoping to get the boy to consider nonphysical alternatives. This approach is sometimes referred to as *harm reduction* because it helps clients consider less risky behaviors (Marlatt & Witkiewitz, 2010). Next steps in this problem-solving process include:

- Decision making
- Solution implementation and verification

As the counseling session proceeded, John employs a range of different techniques, including "reverse advocacy role playing" where John plays the client and the client plays the counselor and provided "reasons or arguments for [particular attitudes] being incorrect, maladaptive, or dysfunctional" (A. M. Nezu & C. M. Nezu, in press).

CASE ANALYSIS AND TREATMENT PLANNING

Discerning differences between cognitive and behavioral therapies is difficult. Most behavior therapists use cognitive treatments and most cognitive therapists use behavioral treatments. This is why the most popular current terminology for these approaches is cognitive-behavioral therapy.

Although the following case illustrates a cognitive-behavioral approach, in this chapter we focus on the behavior therapy techniques for panic disorder, while in the next chapter (Chapter 8) we continue this case, adding cognitive components from a comprehensive cognitive-behavioral approach for panic disorder and agoraphobia (Craske, 1999a).

Richard, a 56-year-old white male, referred himself for therapy due to anxiety, phobic, and depressive symptoms. Richard was afraid to leave his home because of fears of having a panic attack. He reported experiencing more than 10 attacks in the past month. These attacks were increasing in intensity. During his intake session he indicated that panic attacks trigger fears that he's having a heart attack. Richard's father died of a massive heart attack at age 59.

Richard's health was excellent. He had been rushed to the emergency room during two recent panic episodes. In both cases Richard's cardiac functioning was evaluated and found to be within normal limits. Nonetheless, his fear of panic attacks and heart attacks was escalating, and his increasing seclusion was adversely affecting his employment as a professor at a local vocational college. His wife, Linda, accompanied him to his intake session. At the time of the referral, Richard had stopped driving and was having his wife transport him.

Richard was administered the *Anxiety Disorders Interview Schedule for DSM-IV* (Grisham, Brown, & Campbell, 2004). This semistructured interview indicated that Richard's symptoms were consistent with panic disorder with agoraphobia.

During the intake interview, Richard was instructed in self-monitoring procedures and given a packet of rating scales to further assess the quality and quantity of his panic and agoraphobic symptoms. He was asked to use the self-monitoring scales to rate the duration, intensity, situational context, and symptom profile of each panic attack that occurred during the 10 days between his intake interview and his first treatment session. Richard also kept a food and beverage log during this 10-day period to determine if there were any links between food and beverage consumption and his anxiety symptoms.

In Richard's case there were two primary reasons to seek a medical consultation. First, panic and agoraphobic symptoms can be caused or exacerbated by various medical conditions. These conditions include heart disease, diabetes, hypoglycemia, hyperthyroidism, mitral valve prolapse, stroke, and more. Second, clients who obtain behavioral treatment for panic and agoraphobia often receive pharmacological treatment. However, adding medications appears to help some clients while adversely affecting others due to physical side-effect sensitivity and motivation reduction. Empirically oriented behavior therapists often consult with medical professionals to determine whether pharmacological treatment should be offered in each individual case.

Based on Richard's medical information, it was determined that he was suffering from primary rather than secondary panic symptoms (i.e., he did not have any medical conditions that were either causing or maintaining his anxiety symptoms). Additionally, after a conference with Richard and his physician regarding his physical sensitivity to medications, it was determined that behavioral treatment should initially proceed without adjunctive pharmacological treatment.

The Problem List

One characteristic of behavior therapy is the generation of a clear and concrete problem list. These problems are defined in behavioral terms and measurable.

Richard's problem list included:

1. *Specific fears of having a panic attack*: Fear of a heart attack, fear of death, and fear of public humiliation.

2. *Repeated un-cued panic attacks*: Physical symptoms included heart palpitations, sweating, dizziness, shortness of breath. Richard's symptoms triggered catastrophic thoughts of death and dying (a cognitive symptom also associated with Problems 1, 3, and 4).

3. *Social isolation/withdrawal*: Richard reported diminished social contact.

4. *Loss of independence*: Richard had begun relying on his wife and others to transport him to various destinations.

5. *Depressive symptoms*: Richard also had several depressive symptoms including low mood most days, anhedonia, and self-deprecatory thoughts; however, these symptoms were viewed as secondary to his anxiety and therefore not a primary target of treatment.

Each behavior therapy session included four parts: (1) check-in and homework review, (2) educational information about panic and behavior therapy, (3) in-session behavioral or cognitive tasks, and (4) new homework assignments.

Sessions 1 and 2. Richard's homework was reviewed. During the 10 days since his intake interview, he left home eight times and had four panic attacks. Although specific environmental cues were not identified for every panic attack, his panic symptoms were associated with caffeine consumption: Three of four panic episodes were preceded by consumption of caffeinated sodas, coffee, or both.

The first two sessions primarily focused on psychoeducation.

Therapist: Richard, excellent job on your homework. Looking this over gives us both a much better idea of how to get you back on track in your life.

Richard: Well, thanks.

Therapist: One of our main goals for today is to talk about what your panic symptoms mean. Let's start there.

Richard: Okay. That sounds good.

Therapist: First, even though the intense panic feelings you've been getting seem strange, they're completely natural. Humans are designed to experience panic just like you've been experiencing it. Why do you suppose that is?

Richard: Um. I've always figured that when my heart starts pounding and I get dizzy and all that, it must mean that something is terribly wrong.

Therapist: Exactly! The human internal panic response is an alarm system. Some people call it the fight-or-flight response. When it's working properly, the panic alarm is a great survival device. It increases blood pressure, tenses up muscles, and gets you ready to run or fight. It's supposed to go off exclusively during moments of extreme danger—like when you're crossing a street and a car is barreling straight at you, or when you're attacked by a mugger. Your main problem is that your alarm is misfiring. It's going off when you don't need it. You've been having a series of false alarms. Think about that. When you've had your panic attacks, have there been any extreme dangers you're facing?

Richard: Not exactly. But when I start to feel panicked, I'm sure I must be having a heart attack, just like my dad did when he was about my age.

Therapist: What have the doctors said about that?

Richard: Well, they've told me my heart is fine. That it's in good shape.

Therapist: So the false alarm you're feeling has two parts. There are physical symptoms of heart pounding, dizziness, and shortness of breath—that's one part. And then there's the thought of "I'm going to die from a heart attack just like my dad" that grabs you. Both these signals, the physical sensations and the thought you're going to die, are false. There is no immediate big danger, and your heart is fine. Right?

Richard: That's what they say.

Therapist: I know it feels incredibly scary and it's a horrible feeling. I don't expect you to instantly believe what I'm saying or what your doctor is saying, because the feelings are real and you've been having them repeatedly. But let's take it a step further. What would happen if you were in a movie theater and a false alarm went off? What would happen if you just sat there, because you *knew* it was only a false alarm?

Richard: I—um, I think, uh, I'd get pretty freaked out sitting there if everybody else was rushing out.

Therapist: Perfect. So you'd feel fear, but let's say you just sat there anyway and felt your fear, but you *realize* it's a false alarm and so you *know* that jumping up and running out isn't necessary. What would eventually happen?

Richard: I guess your point is that the fear would eventually go away. Is that it?

Therapist: That's right. Just like we talked about during your intake interview, eventually your heart stops pounding and returns to normal, your breathing slows down, and your body's alarm shuts off and it returns to normal.

Problem Formulation

During the preceding exchange the therapist is using psychoeducation to inform Richard regarding the natural role of panic and anxiety in humans. This education is both an initial component of a behavioral intervention as well as an example of collaborative problem formulation.

During these sessions the following points are highlighted:

• Anxiety is composed of three parts: thoughts, feelings, or sensations, and actions.

• With practice, Richard can become better at objectively observing his anxiety-related thoughts, feelings, and actions.

• His panic symptoms, although very disturbing and uncomfortable, are harmless.

• His panic symptoms are not caused by a "chemical imbalance." Anxiety and panic are natural human responses to danger.

• When Richard feels intense physical sensations associated with panic, but there is no clear external danger, his mind tries to find an explanation for his panic.

• Even though his father died from a heart attack when he was Richard's age, there's no medical evidence that the same thing will happen to Richard. (We explore this cognitive dimension to his panic in Chapter 8.)

• Because Richard leaves or avoids situations where he expects he might have a panic attack and then his symptoms decrease or abate, he's experiencing negative reinforcement (reduction of aversive feelings when leaving or avoiding stressful situations). This is a big part of the learning that contributes to Richard's panic. He's not giving himself a chance to learn that his symptoms will subside even when he stays in the situation.

As a consequence of this behavioral problem formulation, it becomes logical to conclude that solutions to Richard's panic include the following: (a) learn new skills for coping with the symptoms,

(b) use these skills to face the panic symptoms, (c) relearn through deconditioning that there's nothing to fear from his physical panic symptoms.

Interventions

To address these specific problems, Richard's behavior therapist used a five-component panic disorder protocol developed by Barlow and Craske (Barlow & Craske, 2000; Craske, 1999b). The five components included:

1. Education about the nature of anxiety (which has already begun).

2. Breathing retraining.

3. Cognitive restructuring.

4. Interoceptive exposure.

5. Imaginal or in vivo exposure.

In the preceding therapy excerpt it was obvious that Richard didn't completely buy the new explanation for his panic. Nevertheless, the next steps are distinctly behavioral: Richard needs to (a) cut down on his caffeine intake (because it contributes to symptom emergence), (b) develop behavioral coping skills, and (c) directly experience panic, face it, and deal with it effectively.

Therapist: Okay, Richard, we're about done for today, but of course I've got some homework for you again. You did such a great job with the first set, I'm guessing that doing homework comes naturally. This week I'd like you to slowly cut back on the caffeine intake. How do you think you might accomplish that?

Richard: I suppose I can get some of that caffeine-free soda. Well, actually my wife already picked some up.

Therapist: Excellent. So you've got an option waiting at home for you, and your wife is very supportive. And make that same switch to decaf coffee.

Richard: Okay.

Therapist: And keep up your self-monitoring panic log. The more we know about the patterns and symptoms, the better our work together will go.

Session 3. The main purpose of this session is to introduce breathing retraining as a method of relaxation and symptom control. It begins with a hyperventilation **overbreathing** demonstration. After a discussion of Richard's homework (he managed to make it one week without caffeine, had only one panic attack, and completed his panic log very thoroughly) the therapist moves into a learning activity.

Therapist: Richard do you remember last week we talked about your panic symptoms being a natural, but false, alarm?

Richard: Yeah, I remember.

Therapist: I got the impression that you weren't totally convinced of that idea, so if you want, we can discuss it a bit further, do a brief demonstration, and then focus on a new breathing technique that will help you calm yourself.

Richard: Yeah, I'm a skeptic about everything. But I have to admit I'm feeling a little better, and I think the no caffeine rule is helping.

Therapist: I'm sure it is, because like we've talked about, caffeine produces some of the physical sensations that trigger a panic attack. When the caffeine hits your system and your heart rate and breathing increase just a little bit, your body notices it, and the false alarm can start that much easier.

Richard: Yeah. That seems right to me.

Therapist: What we want is for you to be able to turn off the false alarm. One of the best ways to do that is to practice a little controlled breathing. Watch me. [Therapist demonstrates diaphragmatic breathing, inhaling for about 3 seconds and exhaling for about 3 to 4 seconds.] Okay, now you try it. The point is to breathe in slowly for about 3 seconds and then breathe out slowly for 3 or 4 seconds. If you keep this up for a minute, you end up taking about 10 breaths in a minute. [Richard places one hand on his abdomen and begins the breathing process.]

Therapist: Okay, that's great. Now let's have you try it for 1 minute.

Richard: Okay. [Richard breathes slowly for 1 minute.]

Therapist: Nice job, Richard. You had a slow and steady pace. How did it feel?

Richard: It was fine. I felt a little uptight to start, but it got easier, smoother as I went along.

Therapist: Excellent. Now I'm going to show you something that's called overbreathing or hyperventilation. Watch. [Therapist stands up and breathes deeply and rapidly, as if trying to quickly blow up a balloon. After about 1 minute, he sits down and slows down his breathing again.] So, Richard, what did you see happening to me as I did the overbreathing?

Richard: I don't know what you felt like on the inside, but your face got red and when you sat down you looked a little unsteady.

Therapist: Right. I intentionally hyperventilated and felt some of what you feel during a panic attack. I got dizzy, light-headed, and my hands felt tingly. When I sat down and did the diaphragmatic breathing I could feel my heartbeat slowing back down.

Richard: That's pretty intense.

Therapist: You can probably guess what's next. I want you to try the same thing, and as soon as you start to feel any dizziness or heart pounding or any of the symptoms that bother you, I want you to sit down and do your diaphragmatic breathing until the feelings subside. Got it?

Richard: I'm not so sure. How do you know I won't have a full-blown attack?

Therapist: Actually, that's a big part of this activity. If you have a full-blown attack, I'll be here and guide you through the breathing and the symptoms will pass. Of course, our goal is for you to just feel a tiny bit of the symptoms and then sit down and relax and breathe. But even if it gets more extreme for you, we have plenty of

time, so I'll be here and you'll get control back over your body. Ready?

Richard: Okay. [Richard rises from his chair, overbreathes for about 30 seconds, then sits down and, guided by his therapist, breathes steadily and slowly for about 90 seconds.]

Therapist: Now, Richard, tell me what you felt when overbreathing and what you're feeling now.

Richard: I'm okay now, but I did get dizzy. And my hands got tingly. It was amazingly similar to my attacks. But I'm okay now, maybe a little shaky, but okay.

Therapist: So you feel okay now. Actually, you look good too. And you gave your body an excellent lesson. Your body is starting to know that the panic alarm can get turned on intentionally and that you can turn it back off yourself.

Richard and his therapist continue debriefing his overbreathing experience. The therapist explains the exact physiological mechanisms associated with hyperventilation. At the end Richard was asked to practice diaphragmatic breathing for 10 minutes, twice daily, until his next weekly session. He also was asked to continue abstaining from caffeine and keeping his panic logs.

At the beginning of Session 4, Richard and his therapist begin working on cognitive restructuring. The next phases of Richard's cognitive-behavioral therapy for panic disorder are in Chapter 8.

Outcomes Measurement

Behavior therapists routinely use a variety of outcomes measures. These measures are geared to the client's specific symptoms.

Richard was given several standardized objective assessment instruments to provide treatment planning, monitoring, and outcomes information. These included the:

- Body Sensations Questionnaire (Chambless, Caputo, Bright, & Gallagher, 1984)

- Mobility Inventory Questionnaire (Chambless, Caputo, Gracely, Jasin, & Williams, 1985)

- Agoraphobia Cognitions Questionnaire (Chambless et al., 1984)

Depending on client problems and symptoms, behaviorists use many other behaviorally oriented questionnaires to monitor progress and outcomes.

CULTURAL AND GENDER CONSIDERATIONS

Consistent with the medical model, behavior therapy focuses directly on specific client problems and symptoms. As illustrated in the preceding case, client cultural background is less important than symptom presentation. When a client like Richard comes to counseling with anxiety symptoms, an evidence-based intervention will be offered—regardless of cultural or ethnic background.

As scientists, behavioral and cognitive-behavioral therapists are drawn toward using evidence-based treatments. When presenting behavioral and cognitive-behavioral therapies to consumers, behavior therapists tend toward explaining their practice by telling clients they're "scientifically inclined" and use "techniques that have been shown to be effective in carefully performed research studies" (Ledley, Marx, & Heimberg, 2010, p. 86).

When we review the evidence (in the next section) we'll see behavior therapists are speaking truthfully when they say they use treatments that are scientifically supported. However, this statement doesn't address an important question. That is: Is behavior therapy efficacious with culturally diverse clients?

Michelle Craske (2010), a prominent cognitive-behavioral therapist comments on this issue:

> The empirical support for CBT [cognitive-behavioral therapy] derives almost entirely from studies with white middle class Europeans or Westerners. In general, CBT is aligned with European and North American values of change, self-disclosure, independence and autonomy, and rational thinking, all of which are at odds with values of harmony, family and collectivism, and spirituality that define many other cultures. (p. 123)

Although some research indicates behavioral treatments are effective with minority clients (Penedo et al., 2007; Pina, Silverman, Fuentes, Kurtines, & Weems, 2003; Weber, Colon, & Nelson, 2008), Craske (2010) admits that generally cognitive and behavioral therapies are not yet proven efficacious in the multicultural domain. This means behavior therapists need to make multicultural adjustments. Therapy should proceed cautiously, with openness to the client's reaction to specific treatment approaches. For example, if Richard (from the case example discussed earlier) happened to be a Native American client, the therapist might say:

> You have symptoms that fit with a panic disorder diagnosis. Fortunately we have a scientifically supported treatment for panic disorder available. However, I should also tell you that most of the research has been with white clients, although there have been a few Native Americans and clients from other cultures involved in the research studies. It's likely this approach will be helpful to you, but as we proceed, let's talk about how it's working for you. If there's anything about this treatment that doesn't feel right, please let me know and we'll make adjustments. Is that okay with you?

There are several ways in which scientifically supported behavior therapies might not fit for culturally diverse clients. For example, a behavioral activation protocol like the one implemented with Adrienne might not work if Adrienne and her family had strong collectivist values. It could be offensive to conceptualize solutions to Adrienne's problem as requiring time away from the family … and Adrienne might resist behavioral activation homework if she doesn't view her personal and independent pleasure as important.

This discussion may lead you to worry that offering diverse clients treatments that are scientifically supported by research predominantly with white clients is culturally insensitive. However, it turns out that regardless of empirical support for treatment outcomes, many ethnic minority clients prefer an active, directive, problem-focused form of therapy over less-directive insight oriented therapies (Atkinson, Lowe, & Mathews, 1995). D. W. Sue and D. Sue (2008) discuss why diverse clients might prefer directive therapies:

> the culturally diverse client is likely to approach the counselor with trepidation: "What makes you any different from all the Whites out there who have oppressed me?" "What makes you immune from inheriting the racial biases of your forebears?" "Before I open up to you [self-disclose], I want to know where you are coming from." . . . [W]e contend that the use of more directive, active, and influencing skills is more likely to provide personal information about where the therapist is coming from (self-disclosure). Giving advice or suggestions, interpreting, and telling the client how you, the counselor or therapist, feel are really acts of counselor self-disclosure . . . [and] . . . a culturally diverse client may not open up (self-disclose) until you, the helping professional self-disclose first. (p. 147)

Overall, like most contemporary counseling and psychotherapy approaches, behavior therapists have more work to do to determine the cultural acceptability and efficacy of specific behavioral interventions (Craske, 2010).

QUESTIONS FOR REFLECTION

With more diverse students enrolling in counseling and psychology programs, minority therapists will increasingly be working with white clients. How do you think the trust issues articulated by Sue and Sue might affect a white client working with an African American, Latino, Asian, or Native American therapist?

Behavior therapy doesn't specifically address or ignore women's issues. Most likely, the extent to which behavior therapy is viewed in a positive light by feminists depends on individual practitioners. As in the vignette with Adrienne, behavior therapy can be very empowering for women . . . even though it doesn't necessarily endorse a political agenda explicitly focused on empowering women (Hunter & Kelso, 1985; Wolfson, 1999). Overall, as long as behavior therapy is implemented in a way that

supports women and helps them feel empowered to address their symptoms, it can be seen as supporting a feminist perspective. However, if individual practitioners blame women for their symptoms and ignore systemic problems that create and exacerbate women's problems and symptoms, then feminist therapists would be highly critical.

An electronic search for professional books and articles specifically focusing on gender, gay, lesbian, bisexual, and transgender issues revealed very little empirical work in this area (Martell, 2008). Again, this finding is likely due to the apolitical scientific stance of most behavior therapists. However, to the extent behavior therapists are interested in working with and advocating for GLBT populations, additional intentional focus on these areas is needed.

EVIDENCE–BASED STATUS

Behavioral and cognitive therapies are far and away the largest producers and consumers of therapy outcomes research. Behaviorists (including cognitive therapists) produce more empirical research in 1 year than all other theoretical orientations combined produce in a decade. Because research on behavioral approaches is so voluminous, space does not allow us to provide a systematic review here. Instead, we offer a quick overview of research related to intervention approaches discussed in this chapter.

To begin, we should note that the most recent APA Division 12 list of ESTs includes 60 different treatment protocols, most of which are behavioral or cognitive-behavioral. Consistent with this empirical orientation, all the behavior therapy approaches featured in this chapter have a substantial empirical base. We offer a brief sampling of this support:

- Token economies and contingency management systems are effective treatments within institutional programs. A meta-analysis of contingency management outcomes with individuals who were both homeless and abusing cocaine showed that day treatment and contingency management and contingency management alone were more effective in producing drug abstinence than day treatment alone (Schumacher et al., 2007).

- Extensive research indicates that behavioral activation is effective in treating depression in a wide range of different clinical populations (e.g., college students, hospitalized patients, clients with suicide ideation; Cuijpers, van Straten, & Warmerdam, 2007; Sturmey, 2009).

- Progressive muscle relaxation and other forms of relaxation are often used as a treatment component in behavioral and cognitive behavioral therapies. However, for treating insomnia and panic disorder, relaxation training alone shows efficacy (Morin et al., 2006; Ost et al., 1995; Spiegler & Guevremont, 2010).

- Exposure plus response or ritual prevention is one of the most well researched procedures, consistently producing robust outcomes. It has demonstrated its efficacy as a treatment for many different anxiety disorders as well as bulimia nervosa (Forsyth et al., 2009; McIntosh, Carter, Bulik, Frampton, & Joyce, 2011; Powers & Emmelkamp, 2008).

- Problem-solving therapy has substantial research support for treating depression and for contributing to effective treatment with children and adolescents with behavioral disorders (Bell & D'Zurilla, 2009; Cuijpers et al. 2007; Kazdin, 2010; A. M. Nezu & C. M. Nezu, 2010).

CONCLUDING COMMENTS

During their careers, B. F. Skinner, a strong proponent of behavioral determinism, and Carl Rogers, long an advocate of free will and human dignity, had numerous professional interactions. In the following excerpt, Rogers comments on an exchange they had while presenting their work together on a conference panel.

Along with the development of technology has gone an underlying philosophy of rigid determinism in the psychological sciences which can perhaps best be illustrated by a brief exchange which I had with Prof. B. F. Skinner of Harvard at a recent conference. A paper given by Dr. Skinner led me to direct these remarks to him. "From what I understood Dr. Skinner to say, it is his understanding that though he might have thought he chose to come to this meeting, might have thought he had a purpose in giving his speech, such thoughts are really illusory. He actually made certain marks on paper and emitted certain sounds here simply because his genetic make-up and his past environment had operantly conditioned his behavior in such a way that it was rewarding to make these sounds, and that he as a person doesn't enter into this. In fact if I get his thinking correctly, from his strictly scientific point of view, he, as a person, doesn't exist." In his reply Dr. Skinner said that he would not go into the question of whether he had any choice in the matter (presumably because the whole issue is illusory) but stated, "I do accept your characterization of my own presence here." I do not need to labor the point that for Dr. Skinner the concept of "learning to be free" would be quite meaningless. (Rogers, 1960, pp. 15–16)

Although Rogers offers an amusing critique of Skinner, contemporary behavior therapy has moved beyond rigid determinism. In fact, behavior therapy represents not only a flexible approach to therapy, but is also open to incorporating new techniques. The only rigidity inherent in the behavioral approach is its strict adherence to scientific validation of therapeutic techniques. Most of the behavior therapy perspective can be summed up in one sentence: If it can't be empirically validated, then it's not behavior therapy.

Overall, behavior therapists deserve credit for demonstrating that their particular approaches are effective—based on a quantitative scientific-medical model. Even more impressive is the fact that behavior therapy research has begun identifying which specific approaches are more likely to be effective with which specific problems. However, the question remains open regarding whether behavior therapy techniques are generally more effective than other techniques or whether behavior therapy researchers are simply better at demonstrating effi-cacy. Either way, we close with Skinner's remarks as an apt summary of the behavioral scientist's credo:

> Regard no practice as immutable. Change and be ready to change again. Accept no eternal verity. Experiment. (Skinner, 1970, p. viii)

CHAPTER SUMMARY

The behaviorism movement strongly shaped American psychology beginning in the early 1900s. Perhaps most significantly, Mary Cover Jones conducted research on young children with fears and phobias in the 1920s that identified treatment principles that continue to guide contemporary behavior therapy for anxiety problems. Led by B. F. Skinner, Joseph Wolpe, Arnold Lazarus, and other leading researchers and practitioners, behavior therapy was officially born in the 1950s.

Behaviorists are first and foremost scientists. Over the years they've primarily focused only on procedures and processes that are observable and supported by scientific research.

There are three main behavioral theoretical models. These models include: (1) operant conditioning (aka: applied behavior analysis); (2) classical conditioning (aka: the neobehavioristic, mediational stimulus-response model); (3) social learning theory (which is discussed in Chapter 8). For all behavior therapists, psychopathology is caused by maladaptive learning and is treated by providing clients new learning experiences.

Contemporary behavior therapy consists of a variety of empirically based assessment and intervention procedures. Assessment procedures include (a) functional behavioral assessment (including self-monitoring); (b) behavioral interviewing; and (c) standardized questionnaires.

Although there are many evidence-based behavior therapy procedures, in this chapter we focused primarily on five. These included (1) token economies and contingency management; (2) behavioral activation; (3) relaxation training; (4) systematic desensitization and exposure treatments; and (5) skills training.

Behavior therapy tends to focus exclusively on symptoms, sometimes ignoring social and political factors contributing to client problems. Although this focus is helpful for symptom reduction, feminists and multiculturalists tend to complain that behavior therapy can blame clients for their problems. There is also little research that specifically addresses whether behavior therapy is efficacious or effective for minority populations.

The good news is that behavior therapy is proven efficacious and effective for a wide range of problems for members of the dominant culture. This is partly because behaviorists are inclined to conduct research, embrace the modern scientific paradigm, and are comfortable with the medical model. Most of the therapies listed as highly efficacious or likely to be efficacious by Division 12 of the American Psychological Association are either behavior therapies or cognitive-behavioral therapies.

BEHAVIOR THERAPY KEY TERMS

Applied behavior analysis

Assertiveness training

Aversive conditioning

Behavioral ABCs

Behavioral activation

Classical conditioning

Contingency management

Conditioned response

Conditioned stimulus

Counterconditioning

Exposure treatment

Extinction

Fading	Punishment
Functional behavioral analysis	Response prevention
Imaginal and in vivo exposure	Self-monitoring
Interoceptive exposure	Skills training
Massed versus spaced exposure	Spontaneous recovery
Negative reinforcement	Stimulus discrimination
Neobehavioristic mediational SR model	Stimulus generalization
Operant conditioning	Stimulus-response (SR) theory
Overbreathing	Systematic desensitization
Participant modeling	Token economy
Positive reinforcement	Unconditioned response
Problem-solving therapy	Unconditioned stimulus
Progressive muscle relaxation	Virtual reality exposure

RECOMMENDED READINGS AND RESOURCES

The following resources provide additional information on behavior theory and therapy.

BEHAVIOR THERAPY JOURNALS

Although there are dozens more behavior therapy journals available, we only list some of the main professional resources here.

Behavior Modification
Behaviour Research and Therapy

Behavior Therapy
Child and Family Behavior Therapy
Journal of Applied Behavior Analysis
Journal of Behavior Therapy and Experimental Psychiatry

READINGS ON BEHAVIORAL APPROACHES

Bernstein, D. A., & Borkovec, T. D. (1973). *Progressive relaxation training: A manual for the helping professions*. Champaign, IL: Research Press.

Farmer, R. F., & Nelson-Gray, R. O. (2005). *The history of behavior therapy*. Washington, DC: American Psychological Association.

Gershoff, E. T. (2002). Corporal punishment by parents and associated child behaviors and experiences: A meta-analytic and theoretical review. *Psychological Bulletin, 128*(4), 539–579.

Goldfried, M. R., & Davison, G. C. (1994). *Clinical behavior therapy* (Exp. ed.). Oxford, England: John Wiley & Sons.

Jones, M. C. (1924). The elimination of children's fear. *Journal of Experimental Psychology, 8*, 382–390.

Mahoney, M. (1979). *Self-change: Strategies for solving personal problems*. New York, NY: Norton.

Pavlov, I. P. (1972). *Conditioned reflexes* (G. V. Anrep, Trans.). London, England: Oxford University Press.

Skinner, B. F. (1953). *Science and human behavior*. New York, NY: Macmillan.

Skinner, B. F. (1971). *Beyond freedom and dignity*. New York, NY: Knopf.

Skinner, B. F. (1977). Why I am not a cognitive psychologist. *Behaviorism, 5*, 1–10.

Spiegler, M. D., & Guevremont, D. C. (2010). *Contemporary behavior therapy* (5th ed.). Belmont, CA: Wadsworth/Cengage Learning.

Watson, J. B. (1924). *Behaviorism*. Chicago, IL: University of Chicago Press.

Wolpe, J. (1958). *Psychotherapy by reciprocal inhibition*. Stanford, CA: Stanford University Press.

Wolpe, J., & Plaud, J. J. (1997). Pavlov's contributions to behavior therapy: The obvious and the not so obvious. *American Psychologist, 52* (9), 966–972.

TRAINING ORGANIZATIONS AND WEBSITES

Association for Behavioral and Cognitive Therapies (ABCT; www.abct.org)

Association for Applied Behavior Analysis International (ABAI; www.abainternational.org)

VIDEOS/DVDs

Goldfried, M. R. (1994). *Cognitive-affective behavior therapy* [DVD]. Washington, DC: American Psychological Association.

Harris, J. (2006). *Behavioral counseling and psychotherapy* [DVD]. North Amherst, MA: Microtraining Associates.

Hays, K. (2007). *Exercise* [DVD]. Washington, DC: American Psychological Association.

Persons, J. B., Davidson, J., & Tompkins, M. A. (2000). *Activity scheduling* [DVD]. Washington, DC: American Psychological Association.

Turner, S. M. (1998). *Behavior therapy for Obsessive-Compulsive Disorder* [DVD]. Washington, DC: American Psychological Association.

GOING FARTHER AND DEEPER

Additional behavioral counseling and psychotherapy resources are available at johnsommersflanagan.com.

CHAPTER 8

Cognitive–Behavioral Theory and Therapy

THIS CHAPTER

- Reviews key figures and factors in the history and development of cognitive theories of behavior change
- Outlines and describes key concepts of social learning theory and cognitive appraisal theories and their integration into cognitive-behavioral theory and therapy
- Describes how cognitive-behavioral theorists and therapists view psychopathology
- Describes and discusses principles and procedures associated with cognitive-behavioral counseling and psychotherapy practice, including
  - Assessment procedures
  - Psychoeducation
  - Methods for identifying and exploring automatic thoughts and core beliefs
  - Implementation of specific cognitive-behavioral techniques
- Offers case vignettes to demonstrate cognitive-behavioral techniques in action
- Illustrates how treatment planning, outcomes assessment, and gender and cultural issues can be integrated into a cognitive-behavioral approach
- Reviews empirical evidence supporting cognitive-behavioral therapy practice
- Offers ideas for further study

In the beginning, most behaviorists made it very clear that they didn't really want to think much about cognition. Nevertheless, a few behaviorists purposefully included cognition in their work. One such behaviorist, Joseph Wolpe, opened Skinner's black box just enough to let in a little mental imagery for doing systematic desensitization (Wolpe, 1958). In some ways, this implies that Wolpe was at least partially responsible for starting the cognitive movement in behavior therapy.

We suspect Wolpe wouldn't appreciate our observation. At the 1983 annual meeting of the Association for the Advancement of Behavior Therapy (AABT then, *Association for Behavioral and Cognitive Therapy* now; ABCT), we listened as Wolpe condemned Michael Mahoney's use of "mirror time" or "streaming" with a very disturbed young man. Streaming involved having the client free-associate while looking at himself in a mirror (Williams, Diehl, & Mahoney, 2002). Wolpe was adamant: There were events happening at the conference far outside the behavior therapy realm. Mahoney and other "cognitive types" had stepped over the line.

But this wasn't the first behavioral-cognitive spat. As Meichenbaum (2003) noted years later, a 1970s zeitgeist caused a split between behaviorists who embraced cognition and behaviorists who eschewed cognition. In an interview, he recalled:

- [A] letter by a very senior and prominent behavior therapist was circulated in AABT to have individuals who advocated for cognitive factors in therapy to be kicked out of the behavior therapy association.

- The number of presentations on cognitive factors at AABT conferences were limited, if not excluded.

- Certain behavioral journals would not permit the use of the word "cognition" in any articles.

- Researchers in...CBT were professionally threatened if they continued to challenge the behavioral approach.

- CBT researchers were challenged as being "oxymoronic" and were labeled as "malcontents." (Meichenbaum, 2003, p. 127)

Of course, pressure from behaviorists didn't dampen the "cognitivists'" resolve. They pushed back and in 1977 a new journal, *Cognitive Therapy and Research*, was founded, with Michael Mahoney as editor.

Although there were initial conflicts and a split between staunch behaviorists and cognitivists, in recent years there has been substantial rapprochment and integration. As a consequence, when one of our favorite reviewers suggested we rename this chapter from Cognitive Theory and Therapy to Cognitive-Behavioral Theory and Therapy, we happily complied because it's now nearly impossible to distinguish between cognitive therapy and cognitive-behavioral therapy. In keeping with this trend, Judith Beck (Kaplan, 2011) recently announced:

[W]e are changing our name from the Beck Institute for Cognitive Therapy to the Beck Institute for Cognitive Behavior therapy because people now seem more familiar with the term CBT. (p. 36)

Judith Beck

As J. Beck noted, CBT is the popular term when referring to cognitive-behavioral therapy. However, because we emphasized behavior therapy in the previous chapter, this chapter, as in the past, focuses primarily on the cognitive dimension of CBT. Our main emphasis is on exploring the origins, nature, and practice of integrating cognition into the behavior therapy process (see Putting it in Practice 8.1 for Judith Beck's explanation for why she's a cognitive behavior therapist).

HISTORICAL CONTEXT AND BIOGRAPHICAL INFORMATION

Wilhelm Wundt used introspection as a scientific technique when he established the first psychology laboratory in 1879. Introspection was viewed as a method of studying internal cognitive processes ...or cognition (Wozniak, 1993). Wundt studied sensation, perception, memory, reaction time, and other psychological processes. Although 1879 seems like long ago, introspection doesn't begin with Wundt. It dates at least back to Socrates, who often used an approach now referred to as **Socratic questioning** to uncover and discover an individual's method of reasoning.

In the first half of the 20th century, introspection as a means of studying consciousness was on the decline. John Watson and B. F. Skinner had banished it from academic psychology and might well have considered holding a memorial service to celebrate its death. But as far as we know, that particular cognition never crossed their minds.

It's just as well. Cognition is a slippery and persistent phenomenon that just keeps popping up. Have you ever tried to banish a particular set of cognitions (thoughts) from your mind? Typically, when humans try to stop thinking about something,

PUTTING IT IN PRACTICE 8.1

Why Do I Practice Cognitive Behavior Therapy?

The following commentary was written by Judith S. Beck, PhD, president of the Beck Institute for Cognitive Behavior Therapy at the University of Pennsylvania.

Why do I practice cognitive therapy? Aside from the familial connection (my father, Aaron T. Beck, MD, is the "father" of cognitive therapy), it is the most widely researched form of psychotherapy; it has been shown in several hundred research studies to be effective. If I had an ear infection, I would first seek the treatment that has been demonstrated most efficacious. Why should it be different for psychiatric disorders or psychological problems?

Other than research efficacy, it is the one form of psychotherapy that makes sense to me. Take a typical depressed patient. Nancy, a 32-year-old married sales clerk with a young child, has been clinically depressed for almost a year. She has quit her job, spends much of the day in bed, has given over most of her child-rearing responsibilities to her mother and husband, goes out only infrequently, and has withdrawn from family and friends. She is very sad, hopeless, weighted down, self-critical; she gets little if any pleasure from activities or interactions with others and little sense of achievement from anything she does.

It just makes sense to me to work directly on the problems Nancy has today, teaching her cognitive and behavioral skills to get her life in order and decrease her depression. Behaviorally, I help Nancy plan a schedule: getting out of bed at a reasonable time each morning, getting bathed and dressed immediately, and preparing breakfast for herself and her daughter. We include calling friends, doing small household tasks, taking walks, and doing one errand. Cognitively I help her identify and respond to her negative thinking. Some of her dysfunctional thoughts are related to the behavioral tasks I have suggested: "I'll be too tired to get out of bed. I won't know what to make for breakfast. [My friend] Jean won't want to hear from me. It won't help to take a walk." Other dysfunctional thoughts are about herself ("I'm worthless"), her world ("Life is too hard"), and the future ("I'll never get better").

We tackle Nancy's problems one by one. In the context of discussing and solving problems, I teach her the skills she needs. Cognitive skills include identifying her depressed thoughts, evaluating her thinking, and developing more realistic, adaptive views. I also help her respond to her deeper-level ideas, her beliefs or basic understandings that shape her perception of her experience, ideas that, left unmodified, might contribute to a relapse sometime in the future.

> While doing cognitive therapy, I need to use all my basic counseling skills to establish and maintain a strong therapeutic alliance. I am highly collaborative with the patient, working with her as a "team" to help her get better; I provide rationales for the strategies I use; I use active listening and empathy, and I provide support. And I ask for feedback at every session to make sure that I have understood the patient correctly and that the process of therapy is amenable to her. But perhaps most importantly, I am quite active in the session—providing direction, offering suggestions, teaching her skills. Doing all of these things helps the patient recover most quickly.
>
> Why do I specialize in cognitive therapy? Because it is humane, it is effective, and it is the quickest way to alleviate suffering.

the banished thoughts return…sooner or later. Humans are a very cognitive species and so despite Watson's and Skinner's best efforts, cognition (now sometimes disguised as "information processing") returned to academic psychology and has become central to contemporary counseling and psychotherapy.

Three primary historical figures and trends characterize the history and evolution of cognitive therapy. These include:

- Albert Ellis and Rational Emotive (Behavior) Therapy
- Aaron Beck and Cognitive Therapy
- Donald Meichenbaum and Self-Instructional Therapy

Albert Ellis and Rational Emotive Behavior Therapy

Albert Ellis

Albert Ellis is generally credited with the initial discovery and promotion of modern rational (cognitive) approaches to psychotherapy. Ellis was born in Pittsburgh, Pennsylvania, in 1913 to Jewish parents. Similar to Adler (see Chapter 3) he had a challenging childhood. Eldest of three children, he described his

father as a minimally successful businessman who was often away from home. He described his mother as self-absorbed and as having bipolar tendencies. Ellis became very sick with a kidney ailment at age 5 and was hospitalized eight times from age 5 to 7 years. He believed his health struggles taught him to confront feelings of inferiority. His parents divorced when he was 12 years old.

Initially, Ellis wanted to be a writer, but his first eight novels were rejected. Eventually he entered the Columbia University clinical psychology program in 1942. After graduating he pursued training in psychoanalysis and, like Fritz Perls (see Chapter 6), was analyzed by Karen Horney.

Ellis formulated his approach after progressively discovering he was ineffectual in his traditional psychoanalytic practice. But he didn't blame himself for his being ineffectual. Instead, he blamed the psychoanalytic method. In his own words, here's what he discovered about psychotherapy (Ellis & Grieger, 1977):

I realized more clearly that although people have remarkable differences and uniquenesses in their tastes, characteristics, goals, and enjoyments, they also have remarkable sameness in the ways in which they disturb themselves "emotionally." People have, of course, thousands of specific irrational ideas and philosophies (not to mention superstitions and religiosities) which they creatively invent, dogmatically carry on, and stupidly upset themselves about. But we can easily put almost all these thousands of ideas into a few general categories. Once we do so, and then actively *look for* these categories, we can fairly quickly find them, show them to disturbed individuals, and also teach them how to give them up. (pp. 4–5)

This statement is an efficient summary of five bedrock components of Ellis's approach:

1. People dogmatically adhere to irrational ideas and personal philosophies.
2. These irrational ideas cause people great distress and misery.
3. These ideas can be boiled down to a few basic categories.
4. Therapists can find these irrational categories rather easily in their clients' reasoning.
5. Therapists can teach clients how to give up their misery-causing irrational beliefs.

Ellis began using more directive therapy approaches in the late 1940s and early 1950s. He acknowledges that many of his contemporaries were already heading the same direction—away from traditional psychoanalysis and toward more active-directive, cognitive-oriented therapy. He wrote:

Actually, they attributed to me more originality than I merited. By the late 1940s quite a few other therapists, most of them trained as I was in the field of psychoanalysis, had begun to see the severe limitations and myths of the analytic approach and had, whether they consciously acknowledged it or not, moved much closer to Adler than to Freud. (Ellis & Grieger, 1977, p. 4)

Not only does Ellis credit Adler's pioneering acceptance of cognition, he also noted that his "rational psychotherapy" is based, in part, on the philosophical writings of ancient Greek and Roman stoics, particularly Epictetus. The late J. W. Bush (2002) described Epictetus's history.

The first cognitive behavior therapist, so to speak, in the Western world was the philosopher Epictetus (c. 50–138 a.d.). He was born a slave in the Greek-speaking Roman province of Phrygia, in what is now central Turkey.

One day when Epictetus was working in the fields chained to an iron stake, his master approached him with the idea of tightening his leg shackle. Epictetus suggested that making the shackle tighter was not needed to keep him from running away, but would merely break his leg. The master was not persuaded, and sure enough Epictetus's leg was broken. But he did not protest or give any sign of distress. His master asked him why, and was told that since the leg was already irreversibly broken, there was really no point in getting upset about it. His master was so impressed by this demonstration of unflappability that he eventually set Epictetus free, and sent him away with money so he could become an itinerant philosopher. Epictetus considered this preferable to being a philosopher chained to a stake, and eventually came to Rome, then the capital of the Western world. Among the prominent Romans he influenced was the emperor Marcus Aurelius. (Retrieved October 12, 2011: http://www.anxiety insights.info/read/page/jwb_epictetus_fundamentals .htm)

Ellis initially referred to his therapy approach as *rational psychotherapy*, later changing the name to *Rational-Emotive Therapy*. In 1993, he inserted the word *behavior*, thus creating **Rational Emotive Behavior Therapy (REBT)**, a phrase that better reflects the strong behavioral components of his therapy approach.

There's little argument that Ellis was one of the biggest characters in the history and practice of psychotherapy. His influence was profound, from the publication and dissemination of many rational humor songs (including the infamous Albert Ellis Christmas Carols), to the direct training of thousands of REBT practitioners. When we heard him speak, there were two consistent occurrences. First, he found a reason to break into song (despite his very poor voice and tune carrying abilities). Second, he always managed to slip the "F" word into his presentations.

Given Ellis's eccentric, direct, and sometimes abrasive characteristics, it's tempting to minimize his accomplishments. But he produced more than 700 scholarly journal articles and 60 professional books. Additionally, he probably provided therapy to more individuals than any other practitioner in the history of psychotherapy. In 1987 alone, he reported he was working with 300 individual clients and five groups, while demonstrating his procedures at weekly "Five-Dollar Friday Night Workshops" in New York City (Ellis, 1987). Moreover, he continued this incredible pace into the twenty-first century—amassing more than 50 years of applied clinical experience. For detailed information on Ellis's personal history, see Dryden (1989).

Not long after Ellis began formulating his rational approach to psychotherapy another formal cognitive approach entered the scene.

Aaron Beck and Cognitive Therapy

Aaron Beck

Aaron Beck was born in 1921 in Providence, Rhode Island. His parents were Russian Jewish immigrants. He was the youngest of five children. By the time he was born an older brother and older sister had died of influenza, causing his mother to become very depressed. Beck reportedly saw himself as a replacement for his deceased older siblings (Weishaar, 1993).

Similar to Adler and Ellis, Beck also had a physical problem during childhood. He broke his arm and missed a substantial amount of school due to a long recovery period in the hospital. During this time he was held back a year in school and began believing he was not very smart. He overcame this difficult situation and his negative thoughts, eventually obtaining a medical degree from Yale in 1953.

Like Adler, Rogers, Perls, and Ellis, Beck was psychoanalytically trained. Early on, he became interested in validating Freud's anger-turned-inward-upon-the-self theory of depression. Instead he ended up rejecting Freud's theory and articulating his own (A. T. Beck, 1961; A. T. Beck, 1963; A. T. Beck, 1970).

Many psychoanalytic colleagues ostracized Beck for questioning Freud (Weishaar, 1993). However, over time, Beck's work on depression was recognized as empirically valid. His theory of depression and specific approaches to its treatment represents one of the best-known and most scientifically supported discoveries in the field of counseling and psychotherapy.

Beck described how he discovered the centrality of cognition to human functioning while conducting psychoanalysis:

> [T]he patient volunteered the information that while he had been expressing anger-laden criticisms of me, he had also had continual thoughts of a self-critical nature. He described two streams of thought occurring at about the same time; one stream having to do with his hostility and criticisms, which he had expressed in free association, and another that he had not expressed. He then reported the other stream of thoughts: "I said the wrong thing . . . I shouldn't have said that . . . I'm wrong to criticize him . . . I'm bad . . . He won't like me . . . I'm bad . . . I have no excuse for being so mean." (Beck, 1976, pp. 30–31)

This finding led Beck to conclude that focusing on this *other stream of consciousness* was more valuable than the free association material targeted by traditional Freudian analysts.

Beck's approach to therapy has come to be known simply as *cognitive therapy*. He reasoned that:

> [P]sychological problems can be mastered by sharpening discriminations, correcting misconceptions and learning more adaptive attitudes. Since introspection, insight, reality testing, and learning are basically cognitive processes, this approach to the neuroses has been labeled cognitive therapy. (Beck, 1976, p. 20)

Similar to Ellis's REBT, which often is delivered more forcefully, cognitive therapy has taken on many of Beck's personal qualities. As a therapist, Beck has always been recognized as someone who provided therapy in a collaborative and practical manner. His approach was always as gentle as Ellis's approach is forceful. Beck isn't interested in rational argument with clients. Instead, cognitive therapists using Beck's style engage in what Beck called **collaborative empiricism**. The therapist works together with clients to help them discover for themselves the maladaptive nature of their automatic thoughts and core beliefs. A key distinction between these two cognitively oriented therapists is that whereas Ellis emphasizes the forceful eradication of irrational thoughts, Beck emphasizes the collaborative modification of maladaptive thoughts (A. T. Beck, Rush, Shaw, & Emery, 1979; D. A. Clark, Beck, & Alford, 1999).

Donald Meichenbaum and Self-Instructional Strategies

Unlike Adler, Ellis, and Beck, Donald Meichenbaum followed the path of behavior therapy into the field of cognitive therapy and beyond. He described himself as learning to be a people-watcher as he grew up in New York City. He noticed that people on the streets in New York would sometimes talk to themselves.

In his early research Meichenbaum focused on impulsive schoolchildren and hospitalized adults diagnosed with schizophrenia. To his surprise, he discovered that both schizophrenics and children, similar to people on the New York streets, could improve their functioning after being taught to talk to themselves or to think aloud (Meichenbaum, 1969; Meichenbaum & Goodman, 1971).

A consummate observer and researcher, Meichenbaum's perspective has evolved over time. Initially, he integrated the work of Soviet psychologists Vygotsky (1962) and Luria (1961) with Bandura's (1965) vicarious learning model and the operant conditioning principle of fading to develop a systematic method for teaching children to use self-instructions to slow down and guide themselves through challenging problem-solving situations. His work with self-instruction led him to conclude that

> [E]vidence has convincingly indicated that the therapist can and does significantly influence what the client says to [the therapist]. Now it is time for

the therapist to directly influence what the client says to himself. (Meichenbaum & Cameron, 1974, p. 117)

During his early career, Meichenbaum's focus was on **self-instructional training** (SIT), which, consistent with his behavioral roots, he referred to as cognitive behavior modification (Meichenbaum, 1977). He emphasized that "behavior change occurs through a sequence of mediating processes involving the interaction of inner speech, cognitive structures, and behaviors and their resultant outcomes" (Meichenbaum, 1977, p. 218).

He later developed **stress inoculation training** (also SIT), a specific approach for helping clients manage difficult stressors (Meichenbaum, 1985). Throughout this early and middle phase of his career, Meichenbaum focused on empirical research and validation of highly practical approaches to helping clients. His style was similar to Beck's; he was collaborative and worked to help clients change their inner speech. Meichenbaum's model emphasized self-instructional coping skills more than Ellis or Beck. His style is also more openly empathic and emotionally oriented than many cognitive therapists.

More recently, along with other behavioral and cognitive therapists, Meichenbaum shifted toward an empirically oriented constructive model (Hoyt, 2000; Meichenbaum, 1992). As his thinking evolves, he's redefining cognitive therapy as an integrational approach. For example, at the Second Evolution of Psychotherapy Conference, he stated:

> [Cognitive behavior therapy,] which is phenomenologically oriented, attempts to explore by means of nondirective reflective procedures the client's world view. There is an intent to see the world through the client's eyes, rather than to challenge, confront, or interpret the client's thoughts. A major mode of achieving this objective is for the [cognitive behavior] therapist to "pluck" (pick out) key words and phrases that clients offer, and then to reflect them in an interrogative tone, but with the same affect (mirroring) in which they were expressed. The [cognitive behavior] therapist also may use the client's developmental accounts, as well as in-session client behavior, to help the

client get in touch with his or her feelings. (Meichenbaum, 1992, pp. 117–118)

Meichenbaum's progression—from behavior therapy, to cognitive behavior modification, to cognitive-behavioral therapy, to constructive cognitive-behavioral therapy—reflects a trend toward integration that we'll explore more later (see Chapter 14).

THEORETICAL PRINCIPLES

CBT was never intended to become a school, nor a fad. It does not advocate a specific treatment approach, nor orientation. CBT is a critically-minded, empirically based treatment approach. (Meichenbaum, 2003, p. 128)

Like behavior therapy, CBT is based on learning theory. This means that whenever we examine cognitive-behavioral theory, we're also looking directly at the two learning theories discussed in the previous chapter:

1. Classical conditioning
2. Operant conditioning

Cognitive-behavioral therapy also functions on the basis of two additional learning theories: (1) social learning theory; and (2) cognitive appraisal theory. These theories emphasize cognition in initiating and sustaining specific behaviors.

Social Learning Theory

Social learning theory was developed by Albert Bandura (Bandura & Walters, 1963). As a theoretical model, it's viewed as an extension of operant and classical conditioning. Social learning theory includes stimulus-influence components (classical conditioning) and consequence-influence components (operant conditioning), but it also adds a cognitive mediational component.

Social learning theory emphasizes two main cognitive processes: *observational learning* and *person-stimulus reciprocity*.

A significant portion of human learning is observational in nature (Bandura, 1971). For example, in Bandura's famous Bobo doll experiment, he showed **observational or vicarious learning** was a powerful behavior changing force (Bandura, Ross, & Ross, 1963). This process is also referred to as **modeling**. Observational learning includes covert or private mental processes that cannot be directly observed by experimenters (or therapists).

Social learning theory also emphasizes **reciprocal interactions** that occur between the individual's behavior and the environment (Bandura, 1978). Bandura postulated that individuals can have thoughts about the future, behavioral consequences, and goals. These thoughts form a sort of feedback loop and influence current behavior. In combination with observational learning, it becomes possible for clients to learn how to approach or avoid specific situations never having directly experienced positive or negative reinforcement—based completely on watching what happened to someone else. These reciprocal interactions make individuals capable of self-directed behavior change. In contrast to Skinner and Watson, Bandura sees free will and self-determination as possible.

One of Bandura's most important cognitive concepts is self-efficacy (Bandura & Adams, 1977; Bandura, 1977). **Self-efficacy** is defined as:

The conviction that one can successfully execute the behavior required to produce an outcome. (Bandura, 1977, p. 193)

Self-efficacy is different from self-esteem or self-confidence. Its specificity has made it more helpful to researchers and clinicians. There are many different self-efficacy measures in the scientific literature.

Self-efficacy can have an interactive or reciprocal influence on client behavior. As a positive expectation or belief about the future, higher self-efficacy is associated with more persistence, greater effort, and willingness to face obstacles. For example, if you really believe in your skills to study and successfully pass an upcoming midterm in this class, you have high self-efficacy and will behave in ways that make your success more likely to become reality. However, lower self-efficacy is associated with negative self-talk or preoccupation, giving up easily, and reduced concentration. As you can see, low self-efficacy won't help with your exam-taking success.

Several factors can increase or improve client self-efficacy:

- Incentives.
- Knowledge and skills.
- Positive feedback.
- Successful performance accomplishment.

Based on Bandura's reciprocal interactions model, a primary therapy goal would be to help clients develop and strengthen their self-efficacy. For example, a client who comes to therapy to quit smoking cigarettes may initially have little confidence in her ability to quit. If therapy is to be successful, it will be necessary to enhance the client's smoking cessation self-efficacy. This may come about when the therapist teaches the client self-monitoring procedures, progressive muscle relaxation, and strategies for coping with uncomfortable feelings associated with nicotine withdrawal. As the client's skills develop, so might her belief in her ability to successfully quit smoking. Therapists also may model a strong and positive belief in their client's success. In this way behavioral techniques can produce change indirectly; they provide clients with tools that positively impact their beliefs in their ability for success at a variety of challenging tasks.

Cognitive Appraisal Theories

The essence of cognitive theory can be summarized in one sentence that Ellis attributes to Epictetus (Ellis & Dryden, 1997):

> People are disturbed not by things, but by the view which they take of them.

Cognitive theory and, in particular, cognitive behavioral theory are expansions of behavior therapy. Consider Watson's position that "Introspection forms no essential part of [behavior therapy]

methods" (Watson, 1924, p. 158). Watson's objection was scientific; introspection was subjective and not amenable to measurement and so it was outside the purview of behaviorism. In contrast, for cognitive theorists, discovering the client's subjective interpretation of reality is *the whole point*. For example, many clients have classically conditioned fear responses, but these responses are cognitively mediated. Research supports this cognitive mediation theory. Individuals with anxiety disorders tend to:

- Pay too much attention to negative incidents or cues.
- Overestimate the likelihood of a negative event occurring.
- Exaggerate the significance or meaning of potential or real negative events. (Davey, 2006)

Similarly, if we look at Skinner's theoretical position, "Behavior is a function of its consequences," then cognitive theory transforms "consequences" from an objective to a subjective phenomenon. Now, behavior is a function of *what the organism thinks about its consequences*.

The cognitive revision of behavioral stimulus-response (S-R) theory is **stimulus-organism-response (S-O-R) theory**. Beck (1976) stated it this way:

> [T]here is a conscious thought between an external event and a particular emotional response. (p. 27)

Cognitive theory emphasizes the individual organism's processing of environmental stimuli as the force determining his or her specific response

The ABCDEF Cognitive Model
In Ellis's REBT model humans are viewed as having the potential for thinking rationally. However, humans also have a strong tendency to think in exaggerated, tangled, contradictory, mistaken, and irrational ways—and this is the primary source of human misery.

Ellis used an *A-B-C model* to describe and discuss S-O-R theory. In REBT, "A" represents the **activating event** or stimulus that has occurred in an individual's life; "B" refers to the **belief** about the activating event; and "C" refers to **consequent emotion** and behavior linked to the belief.

The **REBT ABCs** are best illustrated through an example:

Jem comes to therapy feeling angry, depressed, hurt, and resentful. Last night his romantic partner, Pat, wasn't home at 6 p.m. for dinner as they had arranged. This event troubled him greatly. In REBT terms, the fact that Pat wasn't home on time is the *activating event (A)*. When Pat was late, Jem began thinking, "Pat doesn't care enough about me to be home for dinner on time." He also started imagining Pat was romantically involved with someone else. Jem found himself thinking over and over: "Pat doesn't really love me and prefers to spend time with someone else."

Pat finally arrived home at 7:45 p.m. The explanation, "I was stuck in a meeting at work and couldn't call because my cell phone battery was dead" didn't convince Jem; his feelings continued to escalate. He yelled at Pat for being so insensitive and then said, "I know what's going on. You can't fool me. I've seen the way you look at that younger man from your office."

When Jem shows up for his appointment with Dr. Ellis, the doctor says: "What the Hell. You can blame Pat for your problems if you want, but you're the one making yourself miserable." He spells out the ABCs:

A. Jem's Activating Event: Pat is late for dinner.

B. Jem's Belief: Pat doesn't love or respect him anymore. Pat's probably having an affair.

C. Jem's Consequent Anger: sadness, hurt, resentment, and jealousy.

D. Feelings and Behavior: yelling and accusing Pat of having an affair.

The main thrust of REBT is to demonstrate to Jem that his current belief about Pat's lateness is irrational. Ellis referred to this as an **irrational belief** (iB). The purpose of REBT is to substitute a **rational belief** (rB) for an irrational belief (iB), which will result in more positive and more comfortable **new feeling** (F).

Ellis was well known for his direct and confrontational therapy style. Although it's easy to directly associate Ellis's style with REBT, not all Rational Emotive Behavior therapists are as direct and confrontational as Ellis.

Ellis's main intervention is to dispute (D) the irrational belief. He might directly dispute Jem's belief by asking,

- Is it true that Pat must always be home right on time to prove you're loved?

- Isn't it true that sometimes Pat can be late and that it's really not all that awful—it doesn't mean you're not lovable, but instead it's an inconvenient behavior that sometimes happens to the best of couples?

If all goes according to theory, Ellis's **disputation** (D) of Jem's irrational belief (and Jem's own subsequent and ongoing disputations of his irrational belief) will have an **emotional effect** (E) on Jem. Hopefully, this effect will be the development of a set of alternative, rational beliefs. Finally, if therapy is successful, Jem will experience a *new feeling* (F).

QUESTIONS FOR REFLECTION

In this example, Jem concluded that because Pat was late that Pat's having an affair. As he waits home alone at the dinner table, what other interpretations or beliefs could Jem use to explain Pat's lateness? Have you ever had a similar experience?

Beck's Cognitive Theory

The theoretical principles of Beck's cognitive therapy are similar to Ellis's REBT. Similarities include:

- Cognition is at the core of human suffering.

- The therapist's job is to help clients modify distress-producing thoughts.

There are several distinctions between cognitive therapy and REBT. Beck criticizes Ellis's use of "*irrational*" to describe the rules by which people regulate their lives. For example, he stated:

> Ellis (1962) refers to such rules as "irrational ideas." His term, while powerful, is not accurate. The ideas are generally not irrational but are too absolute, broad, and extreme; too highly personalized; and are used too arbitrarily to help the patient to handle the exigencies of his life. To be of greater use, the rules need to be remolded so that they are more precise and accurate, less egocentric, and more elastic. (Beck, 1976, p. 33)

Beck's cognitive theory includes the following five components:

1. Due to genetic predisposition, modeling by early caregivers, and/or adverse life events, individuals develop negative and/or inaccurate beliefs about themselves.

2. These deep beliefs about the self—also referred to as *self-schema*—lie dormant in the individual until they're activated by stressful life events or negative mood states, especially events and mood states that match or are consistent with the underlying belief or schema.

3. When these beliefs are activated, individuals respond with automatic thoughts that are inaccurate or systematically distorted in line with the underlying beliefs.

4. Repeated activation of underlying negative beliefs results in biased information processing and cognitive content consistent with specific mental disorders.

5. These automatic thoughts, core beliefs, and their associated emotional disturbances, can be modified via cognitive therapy—a procedure that doesn't require exploration of the past. (Adapted from J. S. Beck, 2005, p. 953)

A. Beck provides an example of how his theory plays out:

> [C]ognitions (verbal and pictorial "events" in [the] stream of consciousness) are based on attitudes or assumptions (schemas), developed from previous experiences. For example, if a person interprets all his experiences in terms of whether he is competent and adequate, his thinking may be dominated by the schema, "Unless I do everything perfectly, I'm a failure." Consequently, he reacts to situations in terms of adequacy even when they are unrelated to whether or not he is personally competent. (Beck et al., 1979, p. 3)

You may notice that Beck's core beliefs sound like Adler's style of life. Automatic thoughts are also very similar to basic mistakes (Schulman, 1985).

Beck's cognitive theory also promotes a different procedure (than Ellis's system) for modifying client thinking. Although both theorists emphasized teaching and learning, cognitive therapists use a more temperate approach, collaborative empiricism, to help clients discover inaccurate or maladaptive thoughts. Collaborative empiricism includes three main components:

1. Client and therapist work together collaboratively.

2. The therapist employs Socratic questioning to uncover the client's idiosyncratic and maladaptive cognitive rules or thinking patterns.

3. The therapist uses Socratic questioning and a variety of different techniques to help clients evaluate or test the validity or usefulness of their automatic thoughts and core beliefs.

This approach requires therapists to try to see the world through the client's eyes (Shaw & Beck, 1977). It emphasizes that clients aren't irrational or defective but may need to adjust the lens through which they're viewing the world (A. T. Beck, Emery, & Greenberg, 1985; Craske, 2010).

Meichenbaum's Self-Instructional Theory

Meichenbaum's cognitive self-instructional model emphasizes internal speech or verbal mediation. He stated that,

> [B]ehavior change occurs through a sequence of mediating processes involving the interaction of inner speech, cognitive structures, and behaviors and their resultant outcomes. (Meichenbaum, 1977, p. 218)

His model is a reciprocal one; it emphasizes an interactive relationship between the individual and the environment.

Meichenbaum's self-instructional model is one small step removed from behavior therapy. He takes inner speech or self-talk out of the client's head and brings it into the therapy office. Then he works with clients to develop more adaptive speech. Finally, he works with clients to internalize a newly learned and more adaptive way of talking to themselves.

Similar to REBT and cognitive therapy, **self-instructional training** focuses on patterns of responding to stressful life events (e.g., activating events or emotional triggers). How clients handle stressful events is addressed temporally.

- Preparation: Inner speech that occurs before the stressful situation.
- Coping: Inner speech that occurs during the stressful situation.
- Aftermath: Inner speech that occurs after the stressful situation.

When clients learn to give themselves helpful instructions before, during, and after stressful events, the events are handled more smoothly and competently.

QUESTIONS FOR REFLECTION

Meichenbaum's model emphasizes inner speech. Is his model compatible with Ellis's and/or Beck's? Where would you place Meichenbaum's ongoing, coping-oriented inner speech in Ellis's ABC model and Beck's model?

Theory of Psychopathology

In REBT, psychopathology is a direct function of irrational beliefs. Ellis's theory of psychopathology is largely consistent with Horney's (1950) "tyranny of the shoulds." Ellis described his views with his usual flair:

[E]very single time my clients talk about their depression, obsession, or compulsion, I can quickly, when using RET, within a few minutes, zero in on one, or two, or three of their major musts: "I *must* do well; you *must* treat me beautifully; the world *must* be easy." I then show these clients that they have these *musts* and teach them to surrender them. Now, they have many subheadings and variations on their musts but they all seem to be variations on a major theme, which I call "musterbation, absolutistic thinking or dogma," which, I hypothesize, is at the core of human disturbance. (Ellis, 1987, p. 127)

Like Ellis, the REBT theory of psychopathology is direct, straightforward, and sometimes offensive. To further capture his perspective, another quotation is pertinent: "I said many years ago, that masturbation is good and delicious, but musterbation is evil and pernicious" (Ellis, 1987, p. 127).

Initially, Ellis compiled a list of 12 basic irrational beliefs that caused emotional suffering. He later added a 13th; other REBT writers have added even more irrational beliefs. Ellis eventually decided that all irrational beliefs could be boiled down to the three basic beliefs, all of which connect to musterbation:

1. I *must* do well and be approved by *significant* others, and if I don't do as well as I *should* or *must*, there's something really rotten about me. It's terrible that I am this way and I am a pretty worthless, rotten person. That irrational belief leads to feelings of depression, anxiety, despair and self-doubting. It's an ego *must*. I have to do well or *I'm* no good.

2. "You other humans with whom I relate, my original family, my later family that I may have, my friends, my relatives, and people with whom I work, must, ought, and should treat me considerately and fairly and even specially, considering what a doll I am! Isn't it horrible that they don't and they had better roast in hell for eternity!" That's anger, that's rage, that's homicide, that's genocide.

3. "Conditions under which I live—my environment, social conditions, economic conditions, political conditions—must be arranged so that I

easily and immediately, with no real effort, have a free lunch, get what I command. Isn't it horrible when those conditions are harsh and when they frustrate me? I can't stand it! I can't be happy at all under those awful conditions and I can only be miserable or kill myself!" That's low frustration tolerance. (Ellis, 1987, p. 126)

Beck's theory of psychopathology is similar to Ellis's. However, in contrast to focusing on three basic irrational beliefs, Beck emphasizes *cognitive distortions* or faulty assumptions and misconceptions. As described previously, these distortions, triggered by external or internal events (e.g., a romantic break-up or drug/endocrine reaction) produce **automatic thoughts**, which are linked to **core beliefs or schemas**. Beck has defined seven different types of cognitive distortions, some of which overlap somewhat with one another and are similar to Ellis's irrational beliefs (Beck, 1976; Beck et al., 1979, 1985). Other authors have identified up to 17 different distorted thinking styles (D. Burns, 1989; Leahy, 2003). A list and description of some of the most common and practical cognitive distortions are in Table 8.2.

Beck also theorized that specific automatic thoughts and core beliefs were indicative of particular mental disorders (Beck, 1976). As a consequence of his extensive research on depression, he identified a cognitive triad associated with depressive conditions. Beck's **negative cognitive triad** consists of:

- Negative evaluation of self: "I am unworthy."
- Negative evaluation of the world or specific events: "Everything is just more evidence that the world is falling apart."
- Negative evaluation of the future: "Nothing will ever get better."

To help make Beck's cognitive triad clearer, we like to present it as the adolescents with whom we work express it:

- I suck.
- The world sucks.
- Everything will always suck.

Beck's theoretical work on depression has had an immense impact on the formulation and treatment of depressive disorders.

From the perspective of self-instructional theory, psychopathology is a function of dysfunctional inner speech. For example, individuals with anxiety tend to engage in disturbing inner speech long before facing stressful situations. To prepare for difficult situations they're likely saying very unhelpful things to themselves (e.g., "Lions, tigers, and bears, oh my!"). Instead of engaging in coping self-talk during an incident, they're likely in the midst of a self-critique that takes away from their ability to focus on and deal with the situation. Finally, after the incident ends, they're probably talking to themselves about how they're an abject failure who will never be able to handle difficult tasks.

THE PRACTICE OF COGNITIVE-BEHAVIORAL THERAPY

Sometimes cognitive-behavioral therapy seems very simple. It's as easy as 1, 2, 3:

1. Access clients' irrational or maladaptive thoughts or dysfunctional inner speech.

2. Instruct clients in more adaptive or more rational thinking and/or teach internal verbal instructional coping strategies.

3. Support clients as they apply these new and developing skills in their lives.

Unfortunately, cognitive therapy isn't as easy as it appears. Whatever model you follow, you'll need extensive training and supervision to achieve competence. For example, in the now classic text *Cognitive Therapy of Depression*, Beck and his colleagues included an 85-point checklist to measure therapist competency (Beck et al., 1979).

CBT begins with the initial contact between therapist and client. During this initial contact cognitive-behavioral therapists focus on developing a positive therapy relationship and on educating clients about CBT (a sample excerpt from a cognitive-behavioral informed consent is included in Putting it in Practice 8.2).

Assessment Issues and Procedures

According to Ledley, Marx, and Heimberg (2010) two primary goals are associated with CBT assessment.

1. Arriving at a diagnosis that best describes client symptoms.

2. Developing a tentative cognitive-behavioral treatment formulation that can be used for treatment planning. (p. 40)

To accomplish these goals, cognitive-behavioral therapists employ various assessment strategies. These strategies include collaborative interviewing, setting an agenda, developing an initial problem list, self-rating scales, cognitive-behavioral self-monitoring, and case formulation.

Collaborative Interviewing

In contrast to other theoretical orientations, some CBT practitioners consider the therapy relationship secondary. This is partly because CBT is focused on remediation of client problems and partly because existing research on whether the therapeutic alliance contributes to positive outcomes is mixed (Kazdin, 2007). Overall, some cognitive-behavioral therapists are more focused on developing a positive therapy relationship (Hardy, Cahill, & Barkham, 2007) and others consider the therapy relationship as less important (Craske, 2010).

Cognitive-behavioral therapists universally emphasize collaboration. The therapist is not the expert on whom all therapy success depends. Instead, expertise is achieved when the client and therapist join together, using collaborative empiricism to guide assessment and treatment.

Setting an Agenda

CBT is agenda-driven. The norm is to set an agenda in the first few minutes. During an initial session the therapist might begin with an organizing statement:

Welcome to therapy. We have a number of items to take care of today, but there's also flexibility. The first two items on my list are to go over the consent form and then discuss confidentiality. After that I'd like to do an interview with you, focusing on the problems and symptoms that bring you to therapy. Finally, toward the end we can talk about an initial plan for how we can best address the problems we discuss today. How does that sound to you?

Depending on the cognitive-behavioral therapist's style and preference a more formal structured clinical interview might be used (e.g., the Structured Clinical Interview for *DSM-IV*; SCID-IV; First, Spitzer, Gibbon, & Williams, 1997) or a less formal interview loosely focused on generating a problem list could be initiated.

The Problem List

A central assessment task is to establish a clear and comprehensive problem list. Items on **the problem list** should be described in simple, descriptive, concrete terms. Persons and Tompkins (1997) recommend including about five to eight items on a problem list. For example, Susanna, a 25-year-old female, generated the following problem list during a collaborative interview:

1. *Depressive thoughts.* Susanna reports depressive thoughts. She believes she is a worthless loser (negative evaluation of self), that the world is a rotten place (negative evaluation of the world), and that her life will continue to be miserable (negative evaluation of the future).

2. *Social isolation.* She is greatly dissatisfied with her social life. She has social contact outside of her workplace only once weekly or less.

3. *Procrastination and lack of self-discipline.* She struggles with timely payment of bills, keeping her house clean, personal hygiene, and organization.

4. *Internet preoccupation.* She spends many hours a day on the Internet. She reports enjoying this, but that her Internet activity increases markedly when she needs to pay bills, has a social opportunity, or is facing deadlines.

PUTTING IT IN PRACTICE 8.2

A Cognitive-Behavioral Informed Consent

I specialize in cognitive-behavioral therapy. Cognitive-behavioral therapy (or CBT for short) has more scientific research supporting its effectiveness than any other therapy approach.

CBT is an active, problem-focused approach to helping you improve your life. There are several important and unique parts of CBT.

CBT is collaborative: When many people think of therapy they sometimes think they'll be coming to see an all-knowing therapist who will make pronouncements about the causes of their problems. That's not the way CBT works. Instead, because you're the best expert on what's going on in your life, we'll work together to develop ideas and plans for how to reduce whatever symptoms or troubles you're having.

CBT is educational: As we work together, I'll share with you essential information about how thinking and behavior patterns effect emotions. This doesn't mean I'll be lecturing you; instead, I'll offer demonstrations about the ways in which situations, thoughts, behaviors, and emotions affect each other.

CBT is time-limited and active: Research shows that CBT is most effective when we work together actively to address the problems in your life. This means there will be homework and I'll act as both coach and cheerleader in helping you face your problems and complete your homework.

CBT focuses on current thoughts and behaviors: Most people develop problems due to events that happened during childhood or due to traumatic experiences. Even though the cause of your problems is important, we'll spend most our time talking about what's happening right now in your life.

CBT is not for everyone: Although CBT has more scientific evidence behind it than any other treatment approach, it's not a perfect therapy for everyone. You may have uncomfortable reactions to some parts of CBT. When this happens I want you to tell me and hopefully we can work it through. Therapy isn't always comfortable and I'll be encouraging you to face and deal with the problems that are blocking you from what you want in life. However, if you have strong cultural or personal values that don't fit well with CBT we should talk and I can try to connect you with a professional who will offer you the treatment you want.

I look forward to working with you to solve your problems. Please feel free to ask me questions at any time. My goal is for us to work together to achieve your treatment goals.

5. *Lack of academic progress.* She would like to finish her bachelor's degree, but after enrolling quits attending class.

6. *Disrupted sleep patterns.* She reports difficulty sleeping, which she sees as related to problems with procrastination.

Generating a problem list is helpful in several ways. First, it gives therapists a chance to show interest in and compassion for client problems. Second, as clients describe their problems, cognitive and behavioral antecedents and consequences are identified and initial hypotheses about client core beliefs can be generated. Third, as therapists utilize Socratic questioning to explore problems, clients become oriented to the CBT process.

Greenberger and Padesky (1995) provided specific examples of questions to use when exploring client problems. These questions help elucidate the client's cognitive world:

- What was going through your mind just before you started to feel this way?

- What does this say about you?

- What does this mean about you . . . your life . . . your future?

- What are you afraid might happen?

- What is the worst thing that could happen if this were true?

- What does this mean about the other person(s) or people in general?

- Do you have images or memories in this situation? If so, what are they? (Greenberger & Padesky, 1995, p. 36)

In Susanna's case, she reported feeling like "a loser" who had "no willpower" and who had always "been a miserable failure at initiating social relationships." She also thought others were critiquing her inadequacies. These core beliefs became the main target for change in her therapy.

Self-Rating Scales

At the beginning and throughout therapy, cognitive-behavioral therapists make liberal use of **self-rating scales**. For example, Beck developed the widely used *Beck Depression Inventory* (BDI) to evaluate and monitor depression during treatment (A. T. Beck, Ward, Mendelson, Mock, & Erbaugh, 1961). Empirically minded therapists often have their clients complete the BDI at the beginning of each session. Similar rating scales that cognitive therapists frequently use include the *Beck Anxiety Inventory* (A. T. Beck, Epstein, Brown, & Steer, 1988), the *Penn State Worry Questionnaire* (Meyer, Miller, Metzger, & Borkovec, 1990), and the *Children's Depression Inventory* (Kovacs, 1992).

Cognitive-Behavioral Self-Monitoring

Cognitive-behavioral self-monitoring is effective for helping clients develop awareness of automatic thoughts and associated emotions and behaviors. Cognitive-behavioral self-monitoring and the exploration of maladaptive or irrational thoughts begin within therapy sessions, but self-monitoring homework is also very important (D. D. Burns & Spangler, 2000).

Several cognitive-behavioral self-monitoring procedures are available. Persons (1989) recommended using a generic "thought record." To use a **thought record**, clients are instructed to jot down the following basic information immediately after experiencing a strong emotional response:

- Date and time of the emotional response.

- Situation that elicited the emotional response.

- Behaviors the client engaged in.

- Emotions that were elicited.

- Associated thoughts that occurred during the situation.

- Any other related responses.

The client's thought record provides a foundation for cognitive interventions. Beck and colleagues

Table 8.1   Thought Record Sample

Situation	Emotion	Automatic thoughts	Cognitive distortion	Rational response	Outcome/new feeling
Briefly describe the situation linked to the unpleasant feelings	Specify and rate the emotion (Sad, Anxious, Angry) on a 0–100 scale	State the automatic thought that accompanied the emotion	Classify the cognitive distortion present within the automatic thought	Replace the automatic thought with a more rational (or adaptive) response	Rate the feelings again to see if the rational response modified them
Home alone on Saturday night	Sad: 85	"I'm always alone. No one will ever love me. No one will ever want to be with me."	Dichotomous thinking and catastrophizing	Being home on Saturday night is better than being with someone I don't like. Just because I'm not in a relationship now doesn't mean I'll never be in one.	Sad: 45

(Beck et al., 1979), and other cognitive authors (Burns, 1989), recommend transforming generic thought records into more specific theory-based tools by having clients use the language of automatic thoughts, cognitive distortions, and rational responses. Table 8.1 provides a sample of an expanded thought record. Therapists operating from an REBT perspective would use the A-B-C-D-E-F model articulated by Ellis (1999a).

QUESTIONS FOR REFLECTION

If you were a client, can you imagine using a three-column cognitive self-monitoring log or Thought Record on a regular basis? What might stop you from using this sort of assessment procedure on yourself? What would motivate you to use a Thought Record?

Case Formulation

In CBT, **case formulation** (aka case conceptualization) is an essential bridge from assessment to treatment. Although manualized treatments are available, rarely do clients in the real world present with an uncomplicated single disorder (Persons, 2008). A case formulation helps practitioners develop a treatment plan that comprehensively addresses individual client issues.

Persons (2008) described four key elements for cognitive-behavioral case formulation:

1. Creating a problem list.

2. Identifying mechanisms underlying or causing disorders and problems.

3. Identifying precipitants activating current client problems.

4. Consideration of the origins of the client's current problems.

You may be surprised to see a CBT problem formulation that includes "consideration of the origins of the client's current problems." Consistent with Beck's original work, cognitive therapists are open to talking about the past—even though the past is not a primary focus. The purpose of considering the past is twofold: First, clients often believe that talking about the past is important, so allowing some past discussion can facilitate rapport. Second, glimpsing the origins of a problem can give therapists greater insight into the thoughts and behaviors that are maintaining the problem in the present.

Psychoeducation

Psychoeducation is an essential CBT component (J. S. Beck, 2005; Leahy, 2004). Most clients don't enter treatment with much knowledge about the nature of their problems. Just as physicians educate patients about medical rationale, problems, and procedures, cognitive-behavioral therapists educate their clients about the psychological (CBT) rationale, problems, and procedures.

Psychoeducation for CBT Rationale
It's generally recommended that cognitive-behavioral therapists educate clients, but lecturing is not desirable (Ledley et al., 2010). Instead, many therapists use stories, demonstrations, and life examples to illustrate CBT rationale (Freeman, Pretzer, Fleming, & Simon, 2004). We sometimes use a "bump in the night" scenario to initiate a discussion of how cognition can influence emotion.

Therapist: I know it's hard to believe that what you think has such a big influence on your emotions, but it's true. Let me give you an example.

Client: Okay.

Therapist: Let's say you're lying in bed at night, trying to go to sleep, and suddenly, out of nowhere, you hear a thud somewhere in your house. What would you feel?

Client: I'd probably be scared.

Therapist: Okay, so the first thing that comes to mind is that you'd feel scared. How about if you were taking care of a very pesky dog for a friend of yours, how would you feel then?

Client: Well, if I knew it was the dog being pesky, then I'd feel annoyed. I'd feel irritated that the dog was making noise while I'm trying to sleep.

Therapist: Perfect. So you've demonstrated that it's not the thud that produces your emotional reaction, but what you think about the thud. Tell me, when you first said you'd probably be scared in reaction to the thud, what thoughts went through your mind that would lead to that feeling?

Client: I thought you were suggesting that the thud meant that a burglar had broken into my house, and then of course I'd be scared.

Therapist: Exactly. In the absence of information about what caused the thud, you inserted the possibility of a burglar, and that would, of course, produce fear. But if you think it's a pesky dog, then you feel annoyed. And how about if your grandmother was staying at your house and you heard an unusual thud, what might come to mind then?

Client: I'd feel scared that she might have hurt herself. I'd get right up and go check on her.

Therapist: So now you're telling me that what you think not only directly affects your emotions, but also your behavior, because if you thought it was a burglar then you probably wouldn't jump up and check, you'd do something different, right?

Client: I'd hide under the covers in my bed!

Therapist: And I suppose that might work, but my point is that it's not the thud or what happens to you that produces your emotions and behavior, it's what you're thinking about a situation. It's your assumption or belief about the situation that causes you to feel and act in particular ways.

Client: I see what you mean.

In this example the therapist used Socratic questioning and dialogue to educate the client about the cognitive theory of emotional disturbance.

Psychoeducation About Client Problems
J. Beck (2005) provides an example of using psychoeducation to discuss the problem of depression.

Therapist: You know, these are all important questions you have, essential questions. And I think therapy can help you figure out some of the answers, though many of us struggle with them to some degree throughout our lives. (Pause) What we've found, though, is that people find these questions almost impossible to answer when they're depressed. (Pause) Once they get treated for the depression and the depression lifts, then they have more success.

Arthur: Hmmm.

Therapist: What do you think about that? (p. 148)

This example is a good template for how psychoeducation occurs during CBT. In the midst of the assessment or therapy process that the therapist senses a need to provide information and does so slowly and clearly. Then the therapist checks to determine the client's reaction. This process is crucial because it's important to know how clients are reacting to the information.

Psychoeducation for CBT Rationale, Client Problems, and CBT Procedures

The following case excerpt illustrates how a skilled cognitive-behavioral therapist can interactively and simultaneously provide psychoeducation about CBT rationale, client problems (i.e., anxiety and avoidance), and CBT procedure (i.e., exposure):

Clinician: Among people with anxiety disorders, we see a lot of avoidance behaviors. Why do you think this is the case? [Although most therapy approaches discourage "why" questions, in CBT clients are asked "why" in an effort to deepen their understanding of different phenomena.]

Michael: Because it helps?

Clinician: What do you mean, "it helps"? [The therapist wants the client to dig deeper into a potential rationale for avoidance.]

Michael: Well, it keeps the anxiety in check. If coffee and snacks are served after a meeting at the seminary, I am much more comfortable if I talk to the few guys that I am comfortable with than if I go right up to the father superior and talk to him.

Clinician: So, in the short term, avoidance is a pretty good strategy? [The therapist is noting the limited usefulness of avoidance behavior.]

Michael: I think so. Do you?

Clinician: I do, actually. But there is another side to consider. What about in the long run? [This is Socratic questioning.]

Michael: Not such a good strategy.

Clinician: Why? Sounds like you could just feel calm forever by avoiding the situations that make you anxious. [Similar to motivational interviewing techniques, Socratic questioning is used so the client makes the case for the rationale.]

Michael: Well, it doesn't seem do work that way, does it?

Clinician: What do you mean?

Michael: It's landed me in therapy.

Clinician: That's true. So, what do you think is so detrimental about avoidance? [Again, the therapist wants a deeper description of what's detrimental about avoidance.]

Michael: You never get over the things that make you nervous.

Clinician: What would you need to do in order to get over it?

Michael: I guess just do it and see that it isn't that bad.

Clinician: That's right. That's where exposures come in—doing the frightening things and seeing that they aren't that bad. [Now the therapist has a chance to make a pitch for exposure treatment.]

Michael: Right, I can see the point now.

Clinician: That's good. It's an important point to think about. We're going to be talking some more about the approach to treatment next time, but before we do, I want to spend some time considering how these three components of anxiety fit together. (From Ledley et al., 2010, pp. 119–120, bracketed material added)

Following this exchange, intermittent psychoeducation continues with the therapist interactively discussing how cognitive, physiological, and behavioral anxiety components are interrelated.

Methods for Exploring and Identifying Automatic Thoughts and Core Beliefs

Early CBT work often focuses on helping clients develop an awareness of their automatic thoughts and core beliefs. Sometimes clients develop this awareness very quickly; some clients seem to have a natural talent for accessing their thinking processes. For other clients, developing cognitive awareness is more challenging. Fortunately, many techniques exist for helping clients become more tuned in to their cognitions (Leahy, 2003).

Guessing the Thought

For many different reasons clients can have difficulty identifying specific thoughts associated with emotions and behaviors. When this occurs, J. Beck (1995) recommends that therapists take a guess at the underlying thought. We've found this strategy useful in our work with adolescents who have anger and aggression issues.

John: You said that lots of times you end up in fights and you didn't even plan to get in a fight. What sorts of thoughts are usually going through your head when that happens?

Pedro: I don't know. I just black out.

John: What kind of thing does the other person say that gets you so mad you black out? [John hits a dead end regarding exploration of thoughts and so he shifts to exploring a concrete anger trigger; information about specific anger triggers can help with later efforts to guess underlying thoughts.]

Pedro: If somebody disses my family. Then I'm all over them.

John: So you know what kinds of things people say to piss you off... but I'm still wondering what does that make you think? Like, let's say someone says something nasty about your mom. What does through your mind then? [John goes for underlying thoughts again.]

Pedro: I don't know. I just go crazy on them.

John: Let me take a guess about what you might be thinking. Is that okay with you? [Because the client seems unable to identify thoughts, John asks permission to take a guess.]

Pedro: Fine with me. Go on.

John: I'm wondering if maybe you start thinking, "That F—ing son of a B— has got no business saying that sh—. I'm gonna teach that A— a lesson for saying that." [John uses profanity to show empathy for the thoughts or inner speech the client is likely experiencing.]

Pedro: Yeah. That's amazing. That's exactly what I'm thinking.

In this case it was easy for John to take an educated guess about what the young man was thinking. We've also found that when doing this technique with youth who get very angry it helps to throw in profanity because that's the type of self-talk that gets activated in provocative situations (J. Sommers-Flanagan, Richardson, & Sommers-Flanagan, 2011).

Vertical Descent (aka: the Downward Arrow)

The purpose of **vertical descent** or downward arrow is to uncover underlying core beliefs (D. D. Burns, 1989; Leahy, 2003; Leahy, 2004). Leahy (2003) describes why he uses this technique and provides a good illustration:

> I use this technique frequently, because I have found that I can never really tell what the patient's underlying beliefs and fears might be. (p. 20)

Therapist: You said that you sometimes fear you might have cancer. Even though the doctor has reassured you that you are Okay, what would it mean to you if you did have cancer?

Patient: I'd be afraid that I might die.

Therapist: Almost everyone has a fear of that, of course, but let me ask you about your own fears of dying. Complete this sentence: "I'd be afraid of dying because..."

Patient: I'd be afraid that I wasn't really dead—that I was only in a coma—and that I would wake from the coma in my grave, buried alive. (p. 20)

This is a great illustration of how sometimes client underlying fears or beliefs can be different from what we expect.

Chasing Cognitive Distortions

In the early 1960s, Beck began identifying common **cognitive distortions** associated with mental and emotional problems. He originally identified seven cognitive distortions (A. T. Beck, 1976). Following Beck, other authors have written about these distortions using language that's more user-friendly (see Burns, 1989; Leahy, 2003). Five common cognitive distortions are in Table 8.2.

You might notice that some clients seem to use the same distortions all the time. These distortions have been internalized and tend to color many of the client's perceptions.

Cognitive distortions are typically used in the service of core beliefs or self-schema. All of the techniques discussed in this chapter can help reveal cognitive distortions. Once distortions are clarified and clients become aware of them, therapists can use many different techniques to question the validity or utility of these distortions. For example, Leahy (2003) recommended:

1. *Conducting a cost-benefit analysis* (to mind reading): Do you think that mind reading (or another distorted thinking style) gives you valuable information? How would your thoughts, feelings, and behavior change if you did less mind reading?

2. *Applying the double standard technique* (to dichotomous thinking). Would everyone see it this way? Why not? How might someone else describe this situation?

There are many other techniques for exploring the validity and usefulness of specific cognitive distortions (see Beck, 1995; Freeman, Pretzer, Fleming, & Simon, 2004; Leahy, 2003, 2004).

Specific Therapy Techniques

There are numerous, highly accessible, and highly practical cognitive therapy techniques practitioners can employ. The following techniques come from Ellis and Meichenbaum, but many other excellent resources for specific CBT techniques are available (D. Burns, 1989; Ellis, 1999b; Leahy, 2003; McMillin, 1986).

Vigorous and Forceful Disputing: A Favorite Technique From Albert Ellis

In the book *Favorite Counseling and Therapy Techniques* (Rosenthal, 1999), Albert Ellis shared his approach for *vigorously disputing irrational beliefs*. This technique stems from Ellis's view that an individual can begin to lightly adopt a rational belief (e.g., "I want people to like me, but I can live happily if they don't") while at the same time strongly holding onto an opposing irrational belief with more intensity (e.g., "But I really absolutely need their approval and have nothing to live for if I don't get it!").

To help clients who have this problem, Ellis suggests explaining that "vigorous, forceful, and persistent" disputing of irrational beliefs is often needed to "actually replace them with rational beliefs" (Ellis, 1999, p. 76). Next, clients are provided with the following written instructions, encouraging them to partake in this homework assignment to vigorously dispute their irrational beliefs.

> One way to do highly powerful, vigorous disputing is to use a tape recorder and to record one of your strong Irrational Beliefs into it, such as, "If I fail this job interview I am about to have, that will prove that I'll never get a good job and that I might as well apply only for low-level positions!" Figure out several Disputes to the Irrational Belief and strongly present them on this same tape. For example: "Even if I do poorly on this interview, that only will show that I failed this time, but never will show that I'll always fail and can never do well in other interviews. Maybe they'll still hire me for the job. But if they don't, I can learn by my mistakes, can do better in other interviews, and likely can get the kind of job I want."
>
> Listen to your Disputing. Let other people, including your therapist or members of your therapy group, listen to it. Do it over in a more forceful and vigorous manner and let them listen

Table 8.2   Five Common Cognitive Distortions in CBT

The following cognitive distortions are adapted from Leahy (2003) and Beck (1976). Leahy's book, *Cognitive therapy techniques: A practitioner's guide* includes more than 100 techniques and many useful forms for assigning client CBT homework. Leahy (2003) lists 17 possible cognitive distortions, but only five are listed here.

Dichotomous or polarized thinking: Although nearly everyone sometimes engages in "Black-White" thinking, this distortion is often dominant among clients with borderline or narcissistic personality traits. People and situations are usually evaluated as black or white, good or bad. When these clients come to counseling, they often either love or hate their therapist, with automatic thoughts like "This is the best therapist I've ever known. He's incredible. He's so insightful." The underlying schema may be "I must stay very close to good people and get away from the danger of bad people."

Labeling and mislabeling: All humans use labels to describe themselves and others. Unfortunately, sometimes people hang onto inaccurate or maladaptive labels, despite their emotional cost. For example, when a client consistently labels himself a "loser" or a "wimp," the labels can have a powerful and negative effect on client behavior and may be linked to a depressive condition. Similarly, even an overly positive but inaccurate label can have maladaptive features (e.g., if a woman with narcissistic qualities labels herself "The Queen").

Magnification and minimization: This distortion is also referred to as *overestimation and underestimation* and is illustrated in the case of Richard later in this chapter. It occurs when clients make a mountain out of a molehill (and vice versa). For example, when clients exaggerate the likelihood that they will flunk a test, magnification has occurred. When clients minimize the extent of their hard work and its likelihood of paying off in the future, minimization has occurred. Magnification is especially common among anxiety disorders and this style is also known as *Catastrophizing*.

Mind reading: This distortion involves the assumption that the client knows what other people think, even in the absence of direct evidence. For example, clients might conclude: "He thinks I'm a loser" or "I can tell she doesn't like me." Although these thoughts may or may not be accurate, clients who use this distortion are fairly certain their mind reading assumptions are correct. This style can be associated with a variety of different mental disorders because the content of what messages clients "read" will vary based on core beliefs or self-schema.

Personalization: Clients using this distortion tend to take everything personally. If someone doesn't say hello, they conclude that it's their fault. If the cashier gives them back incorrect change, they think the person is purposely taking advantage of them for some specific reason. This distortion style is often associated with paranoia. Automatic thoughts might include, "I know she's out to get me; she's been out to get me ever since I came in this store." This distortion may be connected to an underlying schema of "People are always untrustworthy. If I don't watch everybody all the time, I'll get taken advantage of."

to it again, to see if you do it better and more forcefully, until they agree that you are getting more powerful at doing it. Keep listening to it until you see that you are able to convince yourself and others that your Disputing is becoming more and more powerful and more convincing. (Ellis, 1999, pp. 76–77)

Ellis's prescribed homework involves repeated practice at forceful cognitive disputations. This assignment flows from his therapy style: If clients can mount a forceful and rational counterattack against their irrational beliefs, they can minimize and hopefully eliminate their irrational thinking.

Stress Inoculation Training

Stress inoculation training (SIT) has been used for a variety of clinical problems (Meichenbaum, 1985; Meichenbaum, 1996; Novaco, 1979). SIT includes three interrelated treatment phases.

1. *Conceptualization.* This phase includes (a) developing a collaborative relationship, (b) using Socratic questioning to educate clients about stress and how to conceptualize stressful situations as "problems-to-be-solved" (Meichenbaum, 1996, p. 4). When stress is viewed as a challenge, the therapist begins assisting clients in formulating individualized methods for preparing for, confronting, and reflecting on stressful experiences.

2. *Skills acquisition and rehearsal.* Specific coping skills are taught and practiced in the office and eventually in vivo. Skills taught are related to the individual's problems. Examples include relaxation training, self-instructional training, emotional self-regulation, and communication skills training.

3. *Application and follow-through.* Clients apply their new coping skills to increasingly challenging stressors. Personal experiments are used to help inoculate clients from later stressful situations. Relapse prevention strategies, attribution procedures (in which clients take credit for their accomplishments), and booster sessions are built into this final phase of the SIT model.

The unique component of Meichenbaum's theory is his emphasis on three types of self-statements. For example, Novaco coaches clients with anger problems to use **preparation self-statements**:

- This could be a rough situation, but I know how to deal with it.
- I can work out a plan to handle this. Easy does it.
- Remember, stick to the issues and don't take it personally. (Novaco, 1979, p. 269)

Later, when potentially angry or aggressive individuals are in the midst of a confrontation, clients practice **coping self-statements**:

- My muscles are getting tight. Relax and slow things down.
- Time to take a deep breath. Let's take the issue point by point.
- He probably wants me to get angry, but I'm going to deal with it constructively. (Novaco, 1979, p. 269)

Finally, at the end of the process, clients with anger issues are taught to make self-reinforcing or constructive self-statements:

- I did all right. I stayed calm.
- I think I can do even better next time if I focus more on my breathing.

Stress inoculation training is an empirically supported treatment for helping adults cope effectively with stress (Saunders, Driskell, Hall, & Salas, 1996). The application of self-instructional procedures in the treatment of children with impulsive behavioral problems continues to influence current treatment and research, but outcomes in that area have been more mixed (Kendall, 2000).

Other Cognitive Techniques

There are many more cognitive techniques available to cognitive therapists. Most of these techniques focus on using mental strategies—usually verbal, linguistic, or based on visual imagery—to manage or eliminate problematic symptoms.

Cognitive-Behavioral Therapy in Action: Brief Vignettes

One fascinating thing about doing counseling or psychotherapy from different theoretical perspectives is that you can get really good at focusing on different dimensions of human functioning. In the following vignettes three techniques for focusing on cognitions are illustrated. Although these techniques focus on cognitions, cognitions are always linked with situations, behaviors, and emotions. Cognitive-behavioral therapists can use cognitions narrowly or to initiate a focus on multiple dimensions of human functioning.

Vignette I: Generating Alternative Interpretations

In Chapter 7 we gave an example of the technique of generating behavioral alternatives. **Generating alternative interpretations** is based on the same model, with the specific focus being on thoughts or interpretations rather than behaviors.

Generating alternative interpretations is a useful technique with clients who hold onto maladaptive or irrational automatic thoughts despite the fact that other, more reasonable, interpretations or explanations exist. As McMillin (1986) noted, the first interpretation of a scene is often the worst, the most negative, or the most catastrophic. Unfortunately, first interpretations can be difficult to counter. This technique teaches clients to immediately counter first interpretations with at least four other reasonable alternatives, using the following guidelines:

1. Clients keep a written log of the worst emotions experienced during a 1-week period. This log includes a brief description of the activating event (A) and a brief description of the first interpretation (iB).

2. At the next session homework is reviewed and clients are given an additional assignment: "After logging your initial interpretation, add four different but equally plausible interpretations." The following example is adapted from McMillin (1986):

Situation: Sophia, a single 25-year-old female just broke up with her boyfriend.

First interpretation: There's something wrong with me. I'm inadequate, and I'll probably never have a long-term romantic relationship.

Alternative interpretations:

- I haven't met the right guy.
- I'm not interested in giving up my freedom right now.
- My boyfriend and I didn't have the right chemistry.
- My boyfriend was afraid of commitment. (McMillin, 1986, p. 12)

3. At the next session, the therapist (Karla) helps determine which interpretation has the most supporting evidence. She helps Sophia use an objective review of data rather than subjective impressions or hunches by asking questions like:

- What's the evidence supporting the possibility that there's something wrong with you and you'll never have a long-term relationship?
- How about the idea that you haven't met the right guy yet? What evidence do you have to support that?

4. Sophia is instructed to continue using this four alternative interpretation procedure when an emotionally distressing event occurs. Additionally, she is coached to write down alternative interpretations, but to wait and decide which interpretation is best only after time has passed to distance her from the event. Karla asks Sophia to practice this procedure with every upsetting event for the next month until it becomes an automatic response. (McMillin, 1986)

Like generating behavioral alternatives (see Chapter 7), this technique is especially useful with adolescents. In a series of studies, Kenneth Dodge and his colleagues have demonstrated that youths who consistently display aggressive behavior often do so, in part, because they've quickly and incorrectly interpreted the behavior of other youths as hostile (Dodge, 1980; Dodge & Frame, 1982; Dodge & Somberg, 1987). This phenomenon is called **misattribution of hostility**. For example, if a youth who often behaves aggressively is walking through the hall at school and another student inadvertently bumps him, the youth is likely to attribute the bump to an intentional hostile act. This attribution increases the potential for retaliation.

In our work with aggressive youths, we've used this technique with two minor modifications. First, in-session we use a stopwatch to add real-world pressure to the process: "Okay, you've got 60 seconds to come up with as many alternative explanations as possible. Starting now!" Second, we sometimes add incentives (stickers, money, baseball cards) to enhance motivation: "I'll give you one baseball card for every 'good' alternative you come up with" (see Sommers-Flanagan & Sommers-Flanagan, 2007).

Vignette II: Thinking in Shades of Gray and Exploring the Consequences of Giving Up the "Should" Rule

Thinking in shades of gray is a technique from Burns (1989). It involves taking automatic thoughts, assumptions, or conclusions about a specific performance and placing them on a concrete, measurable scale.

In the following case, Jackson, a 35-year-old engineer, was referred to therapy because his perfectionistic standards were causing extremely slow work performance. He was also suffering from depressive symptoms associated with his perfectionism at work. After focusing on his automatic thoughts, he produced the following written description of himself and his core beliefs or self-schema:

> I'm basically defective. Therefore, to prove I'm not defective, I have to do a better, higher quality job on my work than anyone else. Every task I do must be performed flawlessly, or there is just more proof that I'm defective. Accomplishing one or two tasks perfectly isn't sufficient proof of my adequacy. I've got to keep being perfect... or I've

failed. My basic assumption is that to fail at one task is to fail altogether.

Jackson was suffering from a terrible case of the "tyranny of the shoulds" (Horney, 1950). Although several cognitive and behavioral procedures are employed in his overall treatment, as one strategy to begin questioning his rigid and negative self-schema, we used **thinking in shades of gray**.

Jackson's therapist worked with him to develop a 100-point performance rating scale. Initially, Jackson confided that a normal scale might include ratings from zero to 100, but for him the meaning of each rating from zero to 95 would be "failure." To illustrate, he drew the scale shown in Table 8.3.

In Jackson's cognitive world, the only way he could achieve complete success was to have a performance that he rated as 96 to 100.

Collaborating with his therapist, Jackson developed a new rating scale that he could experiment with when evaluating his work-related performance. His new scale is in Table 8.4.

Jackson's new scale represented a compromise between him and his therapist. To continue thinking in shades of gray, Jackson took his new scale for a "test drive" by using it for a week at work. His assignment was to rate himself using this new scale and to occasionally double-check his ratings with his supervisor's feedback. To Jackson's surprise, his supervisor always rated the quality of his

Table 8.3 Jackson's "Black-White" Rating Scale

96–100	Complete success
75–95	Complete failure
50–74	Complete failure
25–49	Complete failure
0–24	Complete failure

Table 8.4 Jackson's "Shades of Gray" Rating Scale

96–100	Complete success
85–95	Partial success
75–84	Marginally acceptable
0–74	Complete failure

performance in the top two categories, and Jackson himself discovered that all of his self-ratings were also in the top two categories. Even more important, Jackson's supervisor was very pleased that Jackson was completing his projects more quickly.

This technique is a variation of response prevention discussed by Beck and colleagues (Beck et al., 1979; Shaw & Beck, 1977). It was employed in Jackson's case because much more work was needed to help him change his self-schema. Specifically, Jackson was instructed to clearly verbalize his "should" rule, to predict what would happen if the should was not followed, to carry out an experiment to test the prediction, and to revise his should rule according to the outcome of the experiment (Beck et al., 1979, p. 255).

Jackson was given a series of activities designed to test his should statement: "Every task I do must (should) be performed flawlessly or there is just more proof that I'm defective." He predicted that he might receive a reprimand from his boss if he ignored this should and turned in poor-quality work. His homework was to perform several work tasks as quickly as he could, while keeping his overall work quality within the 75 to 84 "marginally acceptable" range. Jackson successfully completed this test of his should rule and discovered that instead of receiving a reprimand from his boss, he received a pat on the back for a job well done.

CASE ANALYSIS AND TREATMENT PLANNING

In Chapter 7, we described the first three sessions of the case of Richard, a 56-year-old professor at a vocational college who referred himself for CBT due to recurring panic attacks. This case continues next, with a primary focus on cognitive components of Richard's treatment.

The Problem List

Five items were included on Richard's initial problem list. The main cognitive item was Problem #1:

1. *Specific fears of having a panic attack*: Fear of a heart attack, fear of death, and fear of public humiliation.

Richard believes his physical symptoms are signaling an imminent heart attack. This can be viewed as either an irrational or maladaptive belief. The following sessions address many issues, including Richard's belief that he will have a heart attack and die.

Session 4. Richard's homework was reviewed. Between sessions he had one full-blown panic attack and two minor incidents that he coped with by using diaphragmatic breathing. He reported no use of caffeine or other stimulants. He also reported practicing diaphragmatic breathing 12 times over the course of 7 days. During his major panic episode, Richard was out with his wife shopping, became separated from her, and then began worrying about her because she never leaves him alone when they're out together. The entries in his panic log included several references to catastrophic thoughts and overestimations (see the Problem Formulation section for more on these distorted thinking processes).

The first item on the agenda for Session 4 was a review of Richard's homework. This review stimulated a psychoeducational discussion about maladaptive thoughts.

Therapist: I see here on your panic logs that when you got separated from your wife, Linda, your mind started running a hundred miles an hour. Tell me about what you were thinking and feeling when you couldn't find her.

Richard: She said she was just going to the restroom. So I was browsing around by the restrooms and I never saw her come out. I kept waiting and waiting; it felt like forever. I got all worked up. Ever since this panic stuff started, she's been like my shadow. When she didn't come out I kept thinking that she must be hurt or sick or, my God, that maybe she was passed out or even dead. I finally got a woman to go in and check on her, and she wasn't in there, and then my mind really started racing. I thought she'd left me. I was sure that she'd finally gotten sick and tired of dealing with me and had snuck away. [Richard does a nice job articulating his anxiety-producing thoughts.]

Therapist: Where was she?

Richard: Oh, I guess there was an elderly woman in the bathroom who had gotten confused, and Linda took her to the help desk and they asked a bunch of questions. She said she felt terrible about being gone so long, but she had to help this woman, and then the woman got frightened and didn't want her to leave. I guess I must have wandered away a little ways when Linda came out with the woman, since I never saw them at all.

Therapist: How did you and Linda get back together and then what happened?

Richard: Linda found me in a cold sweat by the restrooms. I was trying to figure out why she would leave me and was imagining life without her. She came dashing up and started to explain everything, but I was in such a panic state I just had to go home. I couldn't get myself to focus and breathe and calm down. I had to go home to settle myself down. I'm sorry.

Therapist: It sounds like that was terribly frightening. There's no need to apologize. Like we've talked about before, those false alarms you've been having aren't going away all at once. You've been making great progress. What's important is that we take a good hard look at what happened and learn from it so you can keep getting the upper hand on the panic.

Richard: Yeah, I know. But I can't help feeling I disappointed myself and you, too.

Therapist: Well, overall, it looks like you had an excellent week. You practiced the diaphragmatic breathing and used it to calm yourself. And we can use the incident that happened with Linda to understand even more about what's causing the panic. [The therapist provides an in-session counter to Richard's overestimation of the importance of his panic attack.]

Richard: You think so?

Therapist: Absolutely. The next item on today's agenda is for us to talk about this thing we call "automatic thoughts." As most people go through the day, things happen and then their minds quickly produce automatic thoughts about whatever just happened. When you were waiting for Linda and she didn't come out, you immediately started thinking something terrible was wrong. You said you thought she was hurt or sick or dead in the bathroom. Those are terribly stressful thoughts. And then, as soon as the woman went in there and told you the bathroom was empty, it sounds like your first thought was that Linda was so sick of you that she had up and left you. Is that right?

Richard: Yeah. That's right.

Therapist: Okay, now that you're calm, I want to ask you some questions about what you were thinking in the store. Ready?

Richard: Yeah.

Therapist: Has Linda ever gotten hurt or injured in a public restroom before? [Socratic questioning begins.]

Richard: No. I know. That's a crazy thing for me to think.

Therapist: Actually, it's not totally crazy, it's just a big overestimation. Based on the fact that she's in good health and the fact that this has never happened before makes the odds that she would get hurt in the bathroom very unlikely. Possible, but very unlikely.

Richard: Okay.

Therapist: Another question: Do you think you can tell the difference between a thought and a fact?

Richard: I'm not sure what you mean.

Therapist: This happens to lots of people. We have a thought—yours was that Linda got hurt and maybe even died in the bathroom. But that's not a fact. One thing that helps people sometimes is to get clear in your mind about the difference between a thought and a fact.

Richard: I think I follow.

Therapist: Let's test it: Sometimes when your heart starts beating faster you say to yourself "I'm having a heart attack." Is that a thought or a fact?

Richard: That's a thought. But it could happen.

Therapist: Yes. Good point. Many of our thoughts could happen…but when we think they will happen it's called fortune-telling. But now let me ask you, the fact that your heart is beating faster than usual, is that a thought or a fact?

Richard: That's a fact.

Therapist: Right. And so the trouble starts not with the facts, but with your thoughts about what the facts might mean. If it's okay with you, I'm going to put a little "Thoughts or facts" assignment in your homework package.

Richard: That's fine.

Therapist: And here are some more questions. Does Linda love you?

Richard: Yes. I'm sure of that.

Therapist: And has she ever said that she's tired of being with you?

Richard: Nope.

Therapist: And were the two of you in a fight or having a bad time at the store?

Richard: Oh no. We like to shop together. We always have fun going out shopping. We don't buy all that much, but we have a good time looking.

Therapist: Okay, so the thought that she'd up and left you is not really overestimating. It's what we call a catastrophic thought. You automatically thought of the worst possible relationship catastrophe—even though there was absolutely no evidence to support it. You and Linda have been together for thirty years. She says she loves you and is happy to be with you and you were having a good time, but somehow you assumed that she must be tired of you and therefore she had left you permanently.

Richard: Man. That does sound pretty crazy. You're right. When we talk about this it's like that thought came out of left field. Maybe I'm a little tired of myself, but Linda hasn't ever complained. But you know, at the time, for about five horrible minutes, I had myself convinced it was true.

Therapist: So you had a catastrophic thought that came out of the blue, but it might be kind of related to your own weariness with yourself. Your brain grabbed onto a convenient explanation. You've been tired of yourself, and so the best, ready-made explanation for Linda's absence was the same, that she was tired of you, too.

Problem Formulation

In Session 4 the therapist is working through the problem formulation at a deeper level than can be done in an initial session. Although Richard received previous psychoeducation about how thoughts affect emotions and behavior, now his thoughts are being categorized. This will help make it easier for him to engage in more precise cognitive self-monitoring.

Richard's problem formulation includes the following components:

- He has automatic thoughts that include overestimations (of bad outcomes), catastophizing, and fortune telling.

- He has a core belief that he's physically defective.

- He has a secondary core belief that gets activated when he's feeling defective. His secondary core belief is that because he's defective he's also undesirable and will end up alone in the world.

- When something happens that activates Richard's core beliefs, he has automatic thoughts that distort reality and produce debilitating anxiety.

Interventions

Cognitive interventions are designed to target Richard's core belief that he's defective, his associated core belief that he's undesirable, and his distorted and unhelpful automatic thoughts. Five main interventions are used, some of which have already been applied and others that will be implemented soon:

1. *Psychoeducation* focused on how it's natural, but not helpful, to have automatic thoughts that are inaccurate or distorted.

2. *Cognitive self-monitoring*, including a focus on tracking his distorted thinking.

3. *Socratic questioning* designed to help Richard immediately respond to his overestimation and catastrophizing with curiosity and rational or Socratic questioning of his own.

4. *Distinguishing thoughts from facts technique* (Leahy, 2003). As illustrated in the preceding section.

5. *Generating alternative interpretations technique* (McMillin, 1986). This is also called cognitive restructuring because it teaches Richard to gently dispute his automatic thoughts and replace them with alternative interpretations.

Sessions 5–8. The therapist continues implementing the preceding five interventions.

Psychoeducation: Richard and his therapist discuss and explore differences between maladaptive overestimation, catastrophizing, and fortune-telling. An overestimation is the inflation of the likelihood of a negative outcome. Since it was possible that Linda was sick or hurt in the bathroom, Richard's automatic thought is classified as an overestimation. However, his quick assumption that Linda has left him has no support whatsoever, so it's categorized as a catastrophic thought. The thought that he will die of a heart attack is fortune-telling.

Richard's homework includes a cognitive monitoring thought record. This record includes a column for the situation (e.g., standing in line at a movie theater), behaviors engaged in (e.g., fidgeting and shallow breathing), emotions or feelings (e.g., anxiety and worry), and automatic thoughts (e.g., oh no, we won't get into the movie and it's my fault, and if we don't get in Linda will be disappointed, and she'll get so sick of me that she'll want a divorce). Richard categorizes his automatic thoughts on the thought record.

Richard had one panic attack between Sessions 5 and 6. Upon arrival he expressed discouragement and disappointment. The therapist was empathic and then used Socratic questioning to help Richard question his distorted thinking. Together, Richard and his therapist reviewed the fact that he's in the process of teaching his body how to turn off a false alarm system that's been functioning for years. After using empathy, reassurance, and psychoeducation information, the therapist began several interoceptive exposure trials.

Therapist: Okay, Richard, today we have a 90-minute appointment so we can get you started on some antipanic practice. Is that still okay with you?

Richard: Well, uh, okay. If you think I'm ready.

Therapist: I'm sure you're ready. Our first activity is called the chair spin. It's designed to get you feeling dizzy, which is one of the symptoms you have when your panic alarm goes off. You spin yourself till you're slightly dizzy, and then you can use both of the coping skills we've been working on to calm your body back down. So, once you're dizzy, do the breathing and the rational thinking exercise.

Richard: Okay. What should I say to myself for the rational thinking?

Therapist: Remember what we talked about last week? You had some great rebuttals for your overestimations, catastrophizing, and fortune-telling. For today, the main thing is to identify whatever automatic thought comes into your mind and replace it with one of those four rebuttals.

Richard: I can't remember them very clearly.

Therapist: Okay. I'm glad you mentioned that. It's good to get prepared. I've got them here in my notes. [Therapist pages through file for about 15 seconds.] Okay. Here they are. When you feel your body's alarm going off, you can say, "This is my false alarm. I can get my body back to normal with some deep breathing." Or, "I have proof from my doctor that my heart is in great shape." You also wrote: "It's okay to ignore minor physical sensations" and "These sensations will go away on their own...they always do." Remember?

Richard: Yeah. I've got it.

Therapist: Let's write those thoughts out on a piece of paper and for today you can practice saying them out loud while you do your breathing, okay?

Richard: Yeah. Good idea. That way I don't have to suffer from brain lock like I do sometimes.

The therapist led Richard through three separate interoceptive exposure activities. These included chair spinning, breathing through a straw until some panic feelings emerged, and hyperventilation. Richard calmed himself down each time. During the third activity, he chose to think his automatic thought-counters internally instead of saying them out loud. Richard left the session more optimistic than when he arrived.

Richard didn't have any panic episodes during these weeks. His optimism continued to rise, and he and his therapist began talking about termination in session 8. During these sessions he continued interoceptive exposure practice and diaphragmatic breathing.

QUESTIONS FOR REFLECTION

As a therapist, what problems or worries do you imagine facing as you lead a client through interoceptive exposure activities? How could you prepare yourself to implement these empirically supported strategies?

Session 9. Richard had two panic attacks between Sessions 8 and 9 and came into therapy very discouraged. Much of this session focused on Richard's "explanation" for his relapse.

Richard: I went backwards this week. I'm just a basket case. I guess this stuff works for most people, but I guess I'm weaker than most people.

Therapist: Okay, Richard, you had a relapse. That's the reality. But I hear you coming up with a fictional explanation for your relapse. I know we've been working hard on the breathing and

dealing with your automatic overestimations, catastrophizing, and fortune-telling and so I'm pretty sure you can figure this out. What type of thought is this explanation that you're too weak to be successful?

Richard: Geez. You mean this is just another one of those crazy thoughts?

Therapist: Right. It's not a crazy thought, but it's still that old unhelpful overestimation thought combined with fortune-telling. So you had a relapse and then came up with an explanation. What would you say about the work we've done together . . . is that the work a weak person does?

Richard: No. You're right. I'm working hard and it's going pretty well, but not perfectly.

Therapist: I agree with that. You're not a weak person. You've been dealing with this stuff like a hero. You've kept going to work; you've shown me great self-discipline. Let's toss your weakness theory and come up with a better explanation.

Richard: I guess I'm stumped on that one.

Therapist: What did we talk about for about 15 minutes last week?

Richard: [20 seconds of silence.] Um. Yeah, I think we talked about me stopping therapy in a few weeks.

Therapist: Right. That's a much better explanation. So what you're telling me with these two panic attacks is that we need to deal with the end of your counseling slowly and carefully because your *thoughts* of ending counseling are a new *trigger* for your false alarm system. The other thing it reminds me of is your tendency to quickly think that Linda will abandon you forever for one reason or another. Let's take a look at another trigger for your panics that we haven't really focused on much yet. Those automatic thoughts you have about Linda and the ones you just had about being weak seem to be what we call weakness or "defect thoughts." Somewhere inside, you think you're weak and defective, and so when something goes wrong, you've got this instant explanation. Unfortunately, your explanation makes things worse.

Richard: Do you really think it's possible for me to overcome this?

Therapist: I'll answer that, but first, how about if you look at the evidence and tell me what you think? What do you think your chances of recovery are?

Richard's response to this question revealed significant optimism, and the therapist let him take the lead in a discussion of what he needed for counseling to end smoothly. Richard suggested they continue counseling for a total of 15 sessions. He said he wanted two more weekly sessions and then to cut back to every other week for two sessions and then possibly do monthly sessions. The therapist added that even after therapy was over, Richard could still do telephone check-ins or even schedule a booster session. These possibilities seemed to greatly relieve Richard, which helped initiate a further discussion about his abandonment anxiety. Of course, when discussing this issue the therapist stuck with the cognitive-behavioral model and recommended that Richard begin some imaginal exposure to losing Linda in their next session. After that, they progressed to in-vivo exposure where Richard spent time apart from Linda.

Sessions 10–15. During these sessions Richard began spending short periods of time away from Linda to practice dealing with abandonment anxiety. He continued practicing his breathing, and worked hard on cognitive restructuring by inserting new and better explanations for situations that previously caused him excessive anxiety and panic. In the end, Richard was seen for a total of 15 sessions and one additional follow-up at 6 months after treatment.

Outcomes Measurement

CBT is a problem (or symptom) focused treatment. Consequently, the best way to measure treatment success is to measure the extent of Richard's problems before, during, after, and at 6-month follow-up.

As noted in Chapter 7, Richard was administered the following questionnaires at intake and then intermittently.

- Body Sensations Questionnaire (Chambless et al., 1984)
- Mobility Inventory Questionnaire (Chambless et al., 1985)
- Agoraphobia Cognitions Questionnaire (Chambless et al., 1984)

Although he also was given the Anxiety Disorders Interview Schedule for *DSM-IV* at intake, this was not readministered. Richard's scores on these three measures were all consistent with the fact that he was not experiencing panic attacks or agoraphobia symptoms at termination and at 6-month follow-up.

CULTURAL AND GENDER CONSIDERATIONS

CBT focuses on symptoms as manifest within individuals. This position is often considered culture and gender blind. For most cognitive-behavioral therapists, culture and gender are not of primary significance.

This position is obviously a two-edged sword. In the featured case, Richard is a white male living a life squarely in the middle of the dominant culture. The therapist was committed to Richard's well-being. If the client had been an Asian Indian or a bisexual or a woman experiencing domestic abuse the cognitive-behavioral therapist would have been equally committed to the client's well-being. This is the positive side of CBT's culture and gender blindness.

The negative side is that CBT can be viewed and experienced as blaming the client for his/her symptoms, when, in fact, the symptoms may be a function of gender or culture bias. Addressing the potential for CBT to feel blaming, D. Dobson and K. S. Dobson (2009) stated,

> By virtue of looking for distorted thoughts, cognitive-behavioral therapists are more likely

than other therapists to find them. Furthermore, some clients do react to the terms distorted, irrational, or dysfunctional thinking. We have heard clients say something to the effect—"Not only do I feel bad, but now I've learned that my thoughts are all wrong." (p. 252)

Awareness of the possibility of unfairly blaming Richard for symptoms that may be a function of his culture is a good first step towards gender and cultural sensitivity. For example, if Richard were a black American male his therapist might notice that Richard's thought record included many examples of personalization. In this situation it would be important for his therapist to be aware of and explore the contribution of microaggressions in Richard's daily life.

The term microaggression was initially coined by Chester Pierce (1978). **Microaggressions** were originally defined as "the everyday subtle and often automatic 'put-downs' and insults directed toward Black Americans" but now this is expanded so they "can be expressed toward any marginalized group in our society" (Sue, 2010, p. 5).

Microaggressions are typically unconscious. For example, we had a female client come to us in great distress because her vocational instructor had told her "You're pretty strong for a girl." Although the vocational instructor defended his "compliment," the young woman clearly didn't experience the statement as a compliment. In this circumstance if a therapist is insensitive to culture and gender issues, the young woman might feel blamed for having irrational thoughts and overreactive behaviors. Sue (2010) recommends that mental health professionals exercise vigilance to address microaggression issues inside and outside of counseling.

Let's briefly pretend that Richard is a 6'7" Black American male. In his thought record he notes:

Situation: Walking into the local grocery store. Young female makes eye contact with me and then quickly turns around and goes back and locks her car.

Thoughts: She thinks I'm going to steal her car.

Emotions: Anger.

Behavior: I act rude toward her and toward other white people I see in the store.

If the black American version of Richard has a therapist who looks at this thought record and then talks with Richard about the distorted thinking style of mind-reading ("Richard, you didn't really know what she was thinking, did you?") this therapist is showing cultural insensitivity and will likely be fired by Richard. This is an example of one of the many growing edges CBT should address with respect to women and minority clients.

EVIDENCE-BASED STATUS

As is the case with behavior therapy, the efficacy of CBT is well documented. There isn't enough space available to provide a detailed review of the many scientific studies evaluating the efficacy and effectiveness of CBT packages and components. (For a more systematic review, see Epp & Dobson, 2010; they reviewed CBT efficacy as it pertains to 20 different mental disorders in adults).

There are two main lists published that categorize psychological treatments as either (a) well-established; (b) probably efficacious; and (c) possibly efficacious. One list focuses on treatments for adults; the other list focuses on treatments for children and adolescents.

Before providing information about which treatments are on these lists we should digress into a brief discussion about EST lists. Obviously these lists are controversial and criticized on many fronts. However, as competition for health care dollars intensifies, more pressure for generating lists develops.

In an effort to de-politicize EST lists, Rosen and Davison (2003) published an article advocating a shift away from treatment lists and toward treatment principles. They noted that many treatment packages have an entrepreneurial side and consequently there becomes more room for bias in research process, outcomes, and reporting. This sort of bias is clearer in medicine and with pharmaceuticals, but Rosen and Davison imply that the same sort of bias affecting psychotropic drug research might also influence psychotherapy outcomes research (and likely already has on a smaller scale).

On the APA Division 12 (Society of Clinical Psychology) website, 29 treatments are listed as having "well-established" efficacy for treating specific mental disorders and other problems. Of these, 26 are behavioral, cognitive, or cognitive-behavioral. The three non-CBT treatments are brief dynamic psychotherapy for heroin abuse and interpersonal psychotherapy (for depression and for binge eating).

APA Division 12 lists 33 treatments as probably efficacious. Of these treatments, 25 are essentially behavioral, cognitive, or cognitive-behavioral. The eight non-CBT treatments include eye movement desensitization reprocessing (EMDR) for noncombat Posttraumatic Stress Disorder, brief dynamic psychotherapy for depression, interpersonal psychotherapy, hypnosis plus CBT for obesity, and four different forms of couple or family treatment. Overall 51 of 62 of the well-established or probably efficacious treatments are ostensibly CBT.

The treatment list provided for child and adolescents is developed by Division 53 (the Society of Clinical Child and Adolescent Psychology) of the APA and cosponsored by the Association for Cognitive and Behavior Therapy (ABCT). This list includes 14 treatments that are well-established (10 CBT, 3 family therapies, and interpersonal psychotherapy for depression). There are 34 probably efficacious treatments (27 CBT, 6 family or parent-child therapies, and interpersonal psychotherapy for bulimia).

In conclusion, it's worth noting that 82.3% of adult-oriented treatments classified as ESTs are essentially CBT and 77.0% of child/adolescent-oriented treatments are CBT-related. These numbers are impressive. The scientific treatment of choice is nearly always CBT.

But there are other competing conclusions. Non-CBT practitioners claim that federal grants are biased toward CBT and that CBT researchers and organizations are heavily involved in identifying and selecting ESTs. Additionally, perhaps the clearest statement about CBT is that it's a treatment approach amenable to the dominant modernist scientific paradigm and that CBT researchers have pursued their research agendas with great vigor.

When it comes to evaluating CBT efficacy, Ellis brought an additional interesting issue to the forefront. Specifically, he claimed throughout his career that the therapeutic relationship is minimally important to therapy success. Of course, this flies in the face of common factors research, empirically supported therapy relationships (Norcross & Lambert, 2011), as well as the perspective of most researchers, clinicians, and writers. For example, in their *Evidence-Based Practice of Cognitive-Behavioral Therapy* book, D. Dobson and K. S. Dobson (2009) flatly stated: "To provide effective cognitive-behavioral therapy, it is necessary to have a good therapeutic relationship" (p. 66). Nevertheless, Ellis commented on this issue with his usual charm:

> [S]everal recent studies have shown that during the therapy sessions . . . clients tend to feel better when their therapists are warm and accepting.
>
> Of course! What client would not feel better when the therapist kisses his/her ass in the office? Damned few! Many such clients, however, actually become more needy of approval and hence become unhealthier, if the therapeutic alliance becomes too damned close. (Ellis, 1996, p. 151)

As usual, both perspectives are important. The therapeutic relationship or working alliance—including factors such as agreement to engage in therapeutic tasks designed to address collaboratively generated goals and formation of a working bond between client and therapist—appears to contribute to positive outcomes (Borden, 1979). However, Ellis's point is also useful. Sometimes therapists can be overly focused on

QUESTIONS FOR REFLECTION

What are your thoughts on Ellis's criticism of therapy relationships that are "too damned close"? Do you think there's an ideal degree of closeness that might be associated with optimal outcomes? Might that closeness vary with different clients and different forms of therapy?

relationship components, wanting to be liked or admired, and cater too much to the client's perspectives. This pattern might make it so that serious therapeutic work is avoided or, as Ellis contends, clients may become too dependent on their therapists for approval and support.

CONCLUDING COMMENTS

There's little doubt about the efficacy of CBT. Both philosophically and empirically it has demonstrated itself to be a logical and effective form of treatment for many disorders. CBT also provides us with an excellent general metaphor representing the many paradoxes of counseling and psychotherapy theory.

In a relatively short time period, cognitive therapies have garnered considerable scientific support. So have we arrived? Do cognitive-behavioral techniques provide the ultimate answer to human suffering? Is cognitive therapy the way forward for human growth and actualization? Wherever there is certainty, there is always room for doubt, and Mahoney provides us with some. He stated:

> I do not believe that the simple cueing, recitation, or reinforcement of positive self-statements or the rationalistic "reconstruction" of explicit beliefs are optimal or sufficient approaches for facilitating significant and enduring personal development. (Mahoney, 1985, p. 14)

Even further, in his magnum opus, *Human Change Processes* (Mahoney, 1991), he quoted Hayek (1979), suggesting there may even be a superstitious quality to scientific validation:

> An age of superstitions is a time when people imagine that they know more than they do. In this sense the twentieth century was certainly an outstanding age of superstition, and the cause of this is an overestimation of what science has achieved—not in the field of comparatively simple phenomena, where it has, of course, been extraordinarily successful, but in the field of complex phenomena, where the application of the techniques which prove so helpful with essentially simple phenomena has proved to be very misleading. (Hayek, 1979, p. 176)

Hayek's comments suggest that it might be possible to ask larger, more complex questions than "does this technique make this symptom go away?" Cognitive and cognitive-behavioral approaches are very effective and, in many ways, very satisfying. Failing to at least think about using cognitive and behavioral techniques in certain situations and with certain diagnoses might almost be considered malpractice. But the question remains: Shall we continue searching for even more optimal approaches for facilitating enduring personal development, or perhaps entertain the notion that there will always be a need for multiple approaches?

CHAPTER SUMMARY

Cognitive-behavioral therapy (CBT) represents a combination of behavioral and cognitive approaches to human change. Initially, including cognitive variables in behavior therapy was resisted, but now most practitioners and researchers consider the two approaches as an integrated form of counseling and psychotherapy.

In the 1940s and 1950s progressively more therapists began breaking out of the psychoanalytic mode and using more active and directive therapy approaches. Albert Ellis was a leader in this area and he developed an approach he named rational emotive therapy (which he later changed to rational emotive behavior therapy). Not long after Ellis, Aaron Beck developed an approach named cognitive therapy. While Ellis's approach was confrontational and focused on irrational thoughts, Beck's approach was more collaborative and focused on maladaptive thoughts. Later, Donald Meichenbaum developed a third slightly distinctive cognitive-behavioral approach named self-instructional training.

Cognitive-behavioral therapies have several underlying theoretical principles. These include the classical and operant conditioning theories discussed in Chapter 7 as well as social learning theory and cognitive appraisal theories. Social learning theory, developed by Albert Bandura focuses on observational or vicarious learning as well as reciprocal person-environment interactions. His concept of self-efficacy has been especially important to CBT. Cognitive appraisal theories focus on how individuals subjectively interpret their environments. Psychopathology is defined as the presence of persistently irrational, maladaptive, or dysfunctional patterns in thinking and internal speech.

CBT places less emphasis on establishing a therapy relationship than most therapy approaches. Therapists seek to develop a collaborative and educational relationship with clients. Assessment includes a collaborative interview during which the therapist sets an agenda, identifies a problem list, uses various self-rating scales and procedures, develops a case formulation, and provides psychoeducation.

There are many methods for exploring and identifying clients' automatic thoughts and core beliefs. Therapists may sometimes guess the underlying thoughts, use the vertical descent technique, and use monitoring procedures to chase down and identify distorted or irrational thinking patterns. Among the many CBT interventions available, using vigorous and forceful disputing, stress inoculation training, generating alternative interpretations, and cognitive restructuring were illustrated.

CBT has not focused extensively on providing services specifically designed for minority populations, including ethnic groups, women, and the GLBT populations. Although there is extensive research supporting CBT, research with these minority populations has lagged behind and will likely be a focus of future research.

COGNITIVE–BEHAVIORAL THERAPY KEY TERMS

Activating event

Association for Behavioral and Cognitive Therapy (ABCT)

Automatic thoughts

Belief

Case formulation

Chasing cognitive distortions

Cognitive distortions

Collaborative empiricism

Collaborative interviewing

Consequent emotion

Coping self-statements

Core beliefs or schemas

Disputation

Emotional effect

Generating alternative interpretations

Guessing the thought

Irrational belief

Microaggressions

Misattribution of hostility

Modeling

Negative cognitive triad

New feeling

Observational or vicarious learning

Preparation self-statements

Psychoeducation

Rational belief

Rational emotive behavior therapy (REBT)

REBT ABCs

Reciprocal interactions

Self-efficacy

Self-instructional training

Self-rating scales

Setting an agenda

Social learning theory

Socratic questioning

Stimulus-organism-response (S-O-R) theory

Stress inoculation training

The problem list

Thinking in shades of gray

Thought record

Vertical descent (aka downward arrow)

Vigorous and forceful disputation

RECOMMENDED READINGS AND RESOURCES

The following resources offer additional information on cognitive or cognitive-behavioral therapy.

COGNITIVE–BEHAVIORAL JOURNALS

Cognitive and Behavioral Practice
Cognitive Therapy and Research

Journal of Cognitive Psychotherapy
Journal of Rational-Emotive and Cognitive-Behavior Therapy

READINGS ON COGNITIVE–BEHAVIORAL APPROACHES

Beck, A. T. (1976). *Cognitive therapy and the emotional disorders*. New York, NY: New American Library.

Beck, A. T., Rush, A., Shaw, B., & Emery, G. (1979). *Cognitive therapy of depression*. New York, NY: Guilford Press.

Beck, J. S. (1995). *Cognitive therapy: Basics and beyond*. New York, NY: Guilford Press.

Beck, J. S. (2005). *Cognitive therapy for challenging problems: What to do when the basics don't work*. New York, NY: Guilford Press.

Burns, D. (1989). *The feeling good handbook*. New York, NY: Morrow.

Dobson, D., & Dobson, K. S. (2009). *Evidence-based practice of cognitive-behavioral therapy*. New York, NY: Guilford Press.

Dryden, W. (1989). Albert Ellis: An efficient and passionate life. *Journal of Counseling and Development, 67*, 539–546.

Ellis, A. (1999). *How to make yourself happy and remarkably less disturbable*. San Luis Obispo, CA: Impact.

Ellis, A., & Harper, R. (1997). *A guide to rational living*. North Hollywood, CA: Wilshire.

Epp, A. M., & Dobson, K. S. (2010). *The evidence base for cognitive-behavioral therapy*. New York, NY: Guilford Press.

Greenberger, D., & Padesky, C. A. (1995). *Mind over mood: Change how you feel by changing the way you think*. New York, NY: Guilford Press.

Ledley, D. R., Marx, B. P., & Heimberg, R. G. (2010). *Making cognitive-behavioral therapy work: Clinical process for new practitioners* (2nd ed.). New York, NY: Guilford Press.

Meichenbaum, D. (1977). *Cognitive behavior modification: An integrative approach*. New York, NY: Plenum.

Meichenbaum, D. (1985). *Stress inoculation training*. New York, NY: Pergamon Press.

Persons, J. B. (2008). *The case formulation approach to cognitive-behavior therapy*. New York, NY: Guilford Press.

TRAINING ORGANIZATIONS AND WEBSITES

Albert Ellis Institute (AEI; www.rebt.org)

American Institute for Cognitive Therapy (www
.cognitivetherapynyc.com/)

International Association for Cognitive Psychotherapy
(www.the-iacp.com/)

National Association for Cognitive Behavioral Therapy
(NACBT; www.nacbt.org)

The Beck Institute for Cognitive Behavior Therapy
(www.beckinstitute.org)

VIDEOS/DVDs

Harris, J. (2006). *Cognitive counseling and psychotherapy* [DVD]. North Amherst, MA: Microtraining
Associates.

Holden, J., & Gladding, S. (2002). *Cognitive counseling* [DVD]. North Amherst, MA: Microtraining
Associates.

Marlatt, G. A. (1998). *Cognitive-behavioral relapse prevention for addictions* [DVD]. Washington, DC: American
Psychological Association.

Olatunji, B. O. (2011). *Cognitive-behavioral therapy for
anxiety and panic* [DVD]. Washington, DC: American
Psychological Association.

Vernon, A. (2010). *Rational emotive therapy over time*
[DVD]. Washington, DC: American Psychological
Association.

Young, J. (2007). *Schema therapy* [DVD]. Washington,
DC: American Psychological Association.

GOING FARTHER AND DEEPER

Additional cognitive-behavioral counseling and psychotherapy resources are available at johnsommersflana
gan.com.

CHAPTER 9

Choice Theory and Reality Therapy

THIS CHAPTER

- Reviews the key figures and historical factors contributing to the development and evolution of choice theory and reality therapy
- Outlines and describes core choice theory principles
- Describes and discusses principles and strategies associated with choice theory and reality therapy practice, including
  - Assessment issues
  - Building a therapeutic relationship
  - Reality therapy and confrontation
  - Helping clients with planning
- Provides short vignettes to demonstrate choice theory and reality therapy principles in action
- Illustrates how treatment planning, outcomes assessment, and gender and cultural issues can be integrated into a reality therapy approach
- Reviews the empirical status of reality therapy
- Offers resources for further study

Reality therapy was officially birthed when *Reality Therapy: A New Approach to Psychiatry* (Glasser, 1965) was published. As is true of many therapeutic approaches, reality therapy was initially the product of one person, William Glasser. Glasser speaks of the inspiration he got from mentors and colleagues, and the guidance his students and patients offered. He also expresses gratitude for the support he receives from his wife, Carleen H. Glasser. Although William Glasser remains a revered figure in the dissemination and application of reality therapy, other certified reality therapists now provide training in reality therapy (Burdenski et al., 2009; Robey, 2011; Wubbolding, 2000; Wubbolding, 2009; Wubbolding, 2011).

BIOGRAPHICAL INFORMATION: WILLIAM GLASSER

William Glasser

William Glasser was born May 11, 1925, in Cleveland, Ohio. Perhaps because reality therapy explicitly focuses on the present (and not the past), there's not much written about Glasser's childhood.

However, in *Choice Theory*, Glasser (1998) briefly described his parents:

> If the Olympics had an event in controlling, my mother could have gone for the gold medal. My father was totally choice theory. Never in the more than sixty years that I knew him did I ever see him try to control another person except when he was being goaded by my mother. And even then, his heart was not in it. (p. 90)

Despite his parents' "incompatibility," Glasser indicated that they "were always loving" toward him (1998, p. 89).

As a young adult, Glasser initially became a chemical engineer, but he then changed his focus and began a PhD program in clinical psychology. He obtained his master's degree in clinical psychology in 1948, but his advisors apparently rejected his dissertation. Subsequently, he was admitted to medical school at Western Reserve University and obtained his MD at the very young age of 28 (in case you're keeping track, Glasser finished three challenging degrees—a B.S. in chemical engineering, an M.A. in clinical psychology, and an MD—by age 28). By 1957, Glasser had completed his psychiatric residency at the Veterans Administration and UCLA. He became board certified in psychiatry in 1961.

During his psychiatric residency at UCLA, Glasser began questioning "the basic tenets of conventional psychiatry" (Glasser, 1965, p. xxv). In *Reality Therapy* (1965), he writes about how he told his mentor, psychiatrist G. L. Harrington, MD, of his doubts about traditional psychiatry: "When I hesitatingly expressed my own concern, he reached across the desk, shook my hand and said 'join the club'" (p. xxv). Glasser goes on to convey a deep gratitude to Harrington, whom he referred to as "my mentor . . . [and] the most skillful psychiatrist I've ever known" (1998, p. 5). Even further, he wrote, "Nothing that I can say briefly or in many pages could express how grateful I am for the time he generously spent to make this [reality therapy] possible" (p. xxv).

HISTORICAL CONTEXT

Because of the overlap in concepts and ideas, it's sometimes difficult to determine the inspiration and roots of a particular individual's thinking. There are clear historical and theoretical predecessors to Glasser, but how these earlier thinkers influenced him is unknown.

At first glance, because reality therapy involves teaching clients how to think, plan, and behave more effectively, some modern textbooks classify it as a cognitive-behavioral approach. However, basing our conclusions on Glasser's work and conversations with Glasser and other reality therapists, we believe classifying reality therapy as a cognitive or behavioral therapy is inaccurate (Glasser, 1998). This is partly because Glasser is adamantly opposed to behaviorism (Onedera & Greenwalt, 2007).

Much of Glasser's approach is consistent with humanistic-existential theory (Prochaska & Norcross, 2010). For example, Corey stated, in his review of one of Glasser's books, "I particularly like the existential emphasis on the roles of choice and responsibility" (Glasser, 2000, p. i). Clearly, Glasser's emphasis on the personal choice of an individual—the individual's inherent freedom—has an existential feel. His orientation toward personal responsibility is in the tradition of great existentialists such as Viktor Frankl and Irvin Yalom (see Chapter 4). Additionally, Glasser focuses almost exclusively on the present and places immense value on the authentic encounter between therapist and client. He views the therapy relationship as a key factor in treatment success (Onedera & Greenwalt, 2007). For Glasser, the relationship between therapist and client is characterized by kindness, connection, and a genuine desire to help the client combined with teaching choice theory principles. The following statement illustrates his emphasis on authenticity and connection:

> [T]herapy is not perfect. Psychiatrists make mistakes like everyone else. I handled that mistake by admitting it and learning something from it. When I admit a mistake, it makes me more human

and increases the connection. If I don't admit it,
I risk harming our connection or looking stupid.
(Glasser, 2000, p. 91)

Besides the link between existential-humanistic philosophy and reality therapy, other writers have speculated on the roots of Glasser's thinking. Croll (1992) described how reality therapy's emphasis on personal responsibility can be traced to Ralph Waldo Emerson's concept of self-reliance. In contrast, Rozsnafsky (1974), Whitehouse (1984), Petersen (2005), and Carlson (Carlson & Glasser, 2004), link Glasser's theory to Alfred Adler's individual psychology. Additionally, Wubbolding (2011)—whose name, after Glasser's, is most strongly associated with reality therapy—considers reality therapy to have similarities with many different theoretical approaches, but emphasizes that reality therapy is a unique approach.

QUESTIONS FOR REFLECTION

What are your first impressions of where choice theory fits as a theoretical perspective? If you don't have any impressions yet, as you read this chapter be sure to speculate on the historical factors and bodies of knowledge that may have influenced Glasser's development of choice theory.

THEORETICAL PRINCIPLES

Choice theory holds that humans are internally motivated. If you compare this basic assumption of choice theory to the primary theoretical assumption of behaviorism, you can appreciate the fundamental contradiction between choice theory and behaviorism. As you may recall, B. F. Skinner believed behavior is a function of its consequences (see Chapter 7). Skinner's position implies that humans have little internal choice over their behavior, because behavior is controlled by environmental factors. In contrast, according to choice theory, environmental

factors only provide humans with information; after obtaining and processing external information, we then choose how we want to behave.

Glasser (1998) claims that behaviorism—which he unaffectionately refers to as **external control psychology**—currently dominates human thinking and reasoning. He stated:

> The simple operational premise of the external control psychology the world uses is: Punish the people who are doing wrong, so they will do what we say is right; then reward them, so they keep doing what we want them to do. This premise dominates the thinking of most people on Earth. (pp. 5–6)

Further, Glasser considers the domination of our thinking by external control psychology to be an unfortunate reality with many negative consequences. He blames much of our current social and psychological distress on external control psychology. In his words,

> [T]his psychology is a terrible plague that invades every part of our lives. It destroys our happiness, our health, our marriages, our families, our ability to get an education, and our willingness to do high-quality work. It is the cause of most of the violence, crime, drug abuse, and unloving sex that are pervasive in our society. (1998, p. 7)

Not surprisingly, Glasser would like the world to discard external control psychology and replace it with his approach to human psychology: choice theory. Glasser views choice theory as the road to human happiness. In contrast, Wubbolding notes that it is not choice theory, per se, that leads to human happiness, but learning and utilization of an internal control psychology system (R. E. Wubbolding, personal communication, September 17, 2011). The reason internal control psychology can make us happy is this: If we understand the principles of internal control, we will stop trying to control others and recognize we can only control our own behavior. This shift in thinking will help people meet their basic human needs in more direct, healthy, and adaptive ways.

From the behavioral perspective, if you're reading this book, you're doing so to avoid punishment, to obtain reinforcement, or both. You might be reading to avoid failing an upcoming test or to gain rewards associated with knowledge acquisition—perhaps your professor or a fellow student will smile at you or compliment you if you make an informed comment in class. In contrast, from the choice theory perspective, you're reading this book only because you're choosing to read this book. You might, at any time, regardless of potential environmental and external consequences, decide to put this book down and stop reading. For the choice theorist, decisions are based on internal factors.

If choice theory posits that humans make decisions based on internal factors, the next reasonable question is one that philosophers and psychologists have struggled with for centuries. What internal forces or factors guide human decision making? Or, as Glasser (1998) has put it, what is the "underlying motivation for all our behavior?" (p. 25)

The Five Basic Human Needs

According to choice theory, all humans are motivated to satisfy one or more of five basic, genetically encoded needs:

1. Survival (or self-preservation)
2. Love and belonging
3. Power (or achievement or inner control)
4. Freedom (or independence)
5. Fun (or enjoyment)

Choice theory may be simple, but it's not simplistic. As we explore the needs in greater detail, you'll discover that humans are not directly acted upon by each independent need. Instead, sometimes survival needs are linked with needs for love or power, and each individual experiences a unique blend of human need states. It's as if the human needs derived from choice theory are five separate primary colors on an artist's palette. Consider the unlimited number of colors you could generate by mixing these five primary colors. If you can imagine the skilled artist noticing the unique hue or texture

in an original painting, then you can probably also imagine the skilled reality therapist noticing the unique blend of human needs being articulated by the behavior, thoughts, feelings, and physical condition of an individual undergoing therapy.

In contrast to the other four needs, the first human need, survival, is a physical need. Glasser (1998) has written extensively about the **five basic human needs** in *Choice Theory*. In the following sections, we summarize each.

Survival

In most of our daily lives, the need to survive and the concept of struggling for basic **survival** is rather distant. Directly confronting life-threatening conditions on a regular basis is rare.

There's a big difference between survival as an intellectual concept and survival as a personal experience. Glasser (1998) provides an example of conceptual survival, the kind of survival we all can talk about from an intellectual distance:

> All living creatures are genetically programmed to struggle to survive. The Spanish word *ganas* describes the strong desire to engage in this struggle better than any word I know. It means the desire to work hard, carry on, do whatever it takes to ensure survival, and go beyond survival to security.... If you are looking for a mate you can count on to help build a family and a life with you, find one with *ganas* and treat him or her well. Try not to criticize this motivated mate; you don't want the *ganas* turned against you. (p. 31)

Conceptual survival is intellectually intriguing. Often, abstract theoretical discussions about survival take people to the related topic of species survival and evolutionary biology. Glasser addresses this issue in choice theory, noting that sexual pleasure, a genetically wired-in human response, is a very effective means of insuring species survival. For Glasser, individual survival needs are expressed through total behavior (including our thoughts, behaviors, feelings, and physiology).

Love and Belonging

Glasser believes the need to love and belong is the primary human need. This is because we need other people in our lives to meet the rest of our needs.

The influence and primacy of **love and belonging** are everywhere. If you doubt this statement, just turn on the television or the radio, or look at a few popular magazine covers. There are more songs, jokes, books, and other materials about love, sex, and friendship than any other topic, including survival. Shakespeare's play, *Romeo and Juliet*, articulates the power of love. When faced with a choice between love and survival, Romeo and Juliet poignantly express their preference. They choose to give up survival rather than giving up love.

From the perspective of choice theory, suicide is usually a choice that arises out of a conflict between survival and another basic need. Recall Patrick Henry, who spoke eloquently of his choice between survival and freedom when he said, "Give me liberty, or give me death." Similarly, young children, in their uniquely direct manner, articulate their preference for power and fun over survival when they threaten to hold their breath until they get what they want.

Glasser has made many interesting statements about the need for love and belonging to help individuals address their needs in this very important area. One bit of advice he provides for anyone looking for romantic love is this: "Especially ask yourself, 'If I were not hormonally attracted to this person, would he or she be someone I would enjoy as a friend?' If the answer is no, there is little chance for that love to succeed" (1998, p. 36).

The need for love and belonging in humans runs strong and deep. It includes acquaintanceship, sexual love, friendship love, and romantic love. Be sure to watch for it in yourself and your clients. Unfortunately, needs for love and belonging are often confounded by our human need for power. In this regard, Glasser (1998) states:

> To keep any love, sexual or not, going, we need to go back to . . . friendship. . . . Unlike lovers or even many family members, good friends can keep their friendship going for a lifetime because they do not indulge in the fantasies of ownership. (pp. 35–36)

In other words, according to choice theory, love relationships are often derailed by the human need for power.

QUESTIONS FOR REFLECTION

Think about love relationships you've seen in your friends and family. Based on these observations, do you think power needs interfere with love relationships? Can you think of when one or both persons' power needs damaged or destroyed a loving relationship?

Power

Wubbolding (2000) has noted that **power** needs are often viewed negatively. He prefers more positive descriptors of this basic human need, such as achievement, inner control, or accomplishment.

Most humans enjoy having at least a little power. This is true partly because being completely powerless is aversive and partly because having power and influence is intrinsically gratifying. Imagine that you're very hungry. You walk into a restaurant, but no one greets you or offers to serve you. Out of desperation, you call out for help, but still there's no response. Finally, in even greater desperation, you pull cash out of your purse or wallet and wave it around, but still no one offers to help you. Although this example may seem silly, if you think about conditions faced by African Americans in the southern United States in the early 1960s, you get a taste of what it may have been like to experience the powerlessness associated with racial discrimination.

In contrast to the preceding example, some individuals in the world, due to wealth or status, wield immense power. For example, the queen of England or the crown prince of Saudi Arabia will probably never experience the sort of powerlessness and helplessness frequently experienced by individuals living in poverty, or those who happened to be born female, or of a nondominant or persecuted race within certain geographic regions. From the perspective of choice theory, either extreme, excessive striving for power or experiencing oneself as powerless may result in unhappiness and a need for counseling. In contrast to some reality therapy practitioners (Wubbolding, personal communication, September 17, 2011), Glasser (1998) considers an excess need for power to be a deeply destructive force within our Western culture:

> Driven by power, we have created a pecking order in almost everything we do; social position, neighborhoods, dwellings, clothing, grades, winning, wealth, beauty, race, strength, physique, the size of our breasts or biceps, cars, food, furniture, television ratings, and almost anything else you can think of has been turned into a power struggle. (p. 38)

Freud might have considered our culture's problems with power as stemming from a fixation in the phallic stage of psychosexual development. Interestingly, like Freud, Glasser discusses early childhood as a time when our human needs for power, and the gratification associated with meeting those needs, become recognized. He stated:

> As infants, once we get a taste of power through seeing our parents or others jump to attention to give us what we want, our need for more power starts to take over. By the time we are teenagers, power pushes us far beyond what we would do if our only motivation was to survive and get loving attention. (p. 38)

Often, when we teach or counsel parents of young children, the parents bitterly complain about having a "manipulative" child. Based on choice theory, it's natural for children to try to manipulate or gain power in their family situation. However, as Glasser (2002) points out in his book, *Unhappy Teens*, children become too focused on power and freedom only when their needs for love and belonging are unmet (this is also a basic concept in individual psychology; see Chapter 3). Unfortunately, many parents have difficulty setting basic limits with their children and therefore base their relationship on the exchange of goods and services from the external control perspective. Consequently, the children's primary means of having needs fulfilled gets transferred into power and freedom. Glasser describes part of this process in the case of Jackie, a teenager featured in *Unhappy Teens*:

> If she is unable to satisfy her need for love and belonging, she turns to the two needs, power and freedom, that may seem easier to satisfy but which will further disconnect her if she succeeds in satisfying them. She uses all that violent language for gaining both power and freedom. If she can't find a way to get connected again, she'll stay the same or get worse. (2002, p. 85)

It's tempting to cast a negative light on the human need for power. After all, it's been said that "power corrupts, and absolute power corrupts absolutely." But from the choice theory perspective, power is just another human need: "By itself, power is neither good nor bad. It is how it is defined, acquired, and used that makes the difference" (Glasser, 1998, p. 38). As with other human needs, individuals can become preoccupied with needs for power, and they can go about obtaining their power needs in cruel, insensitive, or overly selfish ways.

People get preoccupied with power, freedom, or fun for two main reasons. First, their preoccupation is caused by their inability to be involved in a satisfying relationship. The need for love and belonging is primary, so when it's not fulfilled, efforts to meet other needs may get out of control. Second, some people incorrectly turn to external control theory as a means for getting their love and belonging needs met. This causes them to pursue power or fun needs because, somewhere inside, they think having more property, more power, more toys, and more fun will get them what they really want: a loving and fulfilling relationship.

People who use power as a substitute for intimacy often seem addicted to power. They want to get ahead, to dominate the competition, to greedily acquire money and property, to win at all costs, or to control the lives and livelihoods of others. Without the concept of power needs, it's hard to explain why very wealthy people continue to accumulate material possessions. Clearly, many wealthy people have already accumulated a number of possessions that extends far beyond addressing their basic needs for survival, love, freedom, and fun. Why do some people keep purchasing more and more material objects beyond their basic needs? Who really needs 20 cars, 10 boats, a 40,000-square-foot house, and a large staff of servants and maids?

Consistent with the writings of Carl Rogers (*On Personal Power*, 1977) and Alfred Adler's social interest, Glasser claims power can be used for positive purposes. He even admits to his own power needs: "[M]any people gain power working for the common good.... I have written this book to try to help people, and if I succeed, I will feel very good and very powerful" (1998, p. 38). In addition, Wubbolding (2000) emphasizes that having an internal sense of achievement or accomplishment is a strong, positive, and constructive basic need that individuals experience. He also pointed out, in his review of this chapter, that the preceding discussion about power needs was overly negative because the word power brings with it so much definitional baggage. For example, he stated:

> The need for power or inner control need not be competitive. Satisfying this need is not a zero sum game. For instance, when a physician states that you are in excellent health you feel happy and your need for power is satisfied. In this case, there is not a winner and a loser. (Wubbolding, personal communication, September 17, 2011)

QUESTIONS FOR REFLECTION

What do you think of Wubbolding's idea of using *achievement* as a synonym, perhaps even a preferred synonym, for *power*? Do you feel more positive about having achievement needs or power needs or needs for inner control?

Freedom

Many teenagers long for the day they receive their driver's license; they yearn for their very own car. When they get behind the wheel and independently drive away from their family home for the first time, they sometimes want to shout in joy at their new-found freedom. Not surprisingly, this need is sometimes referred to as independence (Wubbolding, personal communication, September 17, 2011).

As Glasser (1998) states, "freedom concerns us mainly when we perceive that it is threatened" (p. 39). Examples of how human concern for freedom is increased in the presence of threats abound. Think of the increasing concerns for civil liberties in the United States following the passing

of the Patriot Act, protests in Tunisia, Egypt, Libya, and other Middle Eastern countries. Oppressed people throughout the world sometimes turn to violence to obtain and maintain their liberty.

The fact that many teenagers respond to the clarion call for **freedom** suggests, from the perspective of choice theory, that teenagers see themselves as being denied freedom by their parents (J. Sommers-Flanagan & R. Sommers-Flanagan, 2011). In fact, many parents throughout the world use the psychology of external control with their children (Glasser, 2002; Kohn, 2005). Consequently, it should be no surprise to discover teenagers striving hard to meet their basic human needs for freedom. In the words of Glasser (1998), "I believe that the need for freedom is evolution's attempt to provide the correct balance between your need to try to force me to live my life the way you want and my need to be free of that force" (p. 40).

Choice theory postulates that creativity in humans is directly connected to freedom. For example, if you're unable to express yourself or if no one listens to you when you do express yourself, you may channel your creative impulses into a destructive behavior pattern or an illness. In a case of a college-age woman who was experiencing auditory hallucinations, Glasser (2000) wrote:

> Rebecca is fearful that the life she is choosing to lead ... will alienate her from her mother and family. This fear, coupled with all the pressure she is putting on herself to give up that satisfying life, is triggering her creativity to produce the voices [auditory hallucinations]. My task is to create a good-enough relationship with her so that I can encourage her to live the life she wants. (p. 123)

This case illustrates how a problem related to limited freedom—or the perception of limited freedom—can cause clients to produce creative symptoms. From the choice theory perspective, many women of Freud's era who were experiencing hysteria symptoms were probably creatively expressing their pain and frustration at the limits and abuses imposed upon them by society.

Glasser also notes that creativity, when unburdened from control or freedom limitations, is often much less focused on the self and can be used more naturally to benefit others.

Fun

When we teach graduate courses in psychology and counseling, many students are pleased that Glasser places fun on his short list of human needs. Of course, we remind them that Glasser was not the first psychological theorist to emphasize the importance of **fun or enjoyment** to psychological development. As far as we know, Leon Saul (1973), a respected psychoanalyst, originally proposed that play be added to Freud's very short psychoanalytic list of the basic human activities, love and work.

Glasser (1998) believes that "the need for fun became built into our genes" (p. 41). He directly links the need for fun to play, and, even further, he links playing to learning, asserting that "[t]he day we stop playing is the day we stop learning."

Glasser has also stated that fun "is the easiest need to satisfy" and "is best defined by laughter" (p. 41). Having your need for fun met is commonly linked to or blended with having other needs met. In particular, for many people, fun is deeply intertwined with the most primary human need, the need for love and belonging.

Your Quality World

According to choice theory, **your quality world** or your world of wants "may be best thought of as a mental 'picture album' that holds images of all that we value and/or possess, or wish to eventually value and/or possess" (Smith, Kenney, Sessoms, & Labrie, 2011, p. 54). These mental pictures or memories are typically associated with obtaining one or more of your basic needs. For example, if someone helped you survive, experience love, or have fun, you're likely to put that person into your quality world. Glasser posits that your quality world includes three categories:

1. **People**

2. **Things or experiences or activities**

3. **Ideas or systems of belief**

He states that

> the overwhelming reason we chose to put these particular pictures into our quality worlds is that when we were with these people; when we owned, used, or experienced these things; and when we put these beliefs into action, they felt much better than did other people, things, or beliefs. (1998, p. 45)

Everyone's quality world is different. For example, one person might have Barack Obama (person), baseball (activity), and Buddhism (belief system) in her quality world and be married to someone with Sarah Palin (person), butterfly collection (activity), and (Christianity) in his. At the same time, somehow the two of them got into each other's quality worlds!

People, things/activities, and ideas or systems of belief move in and out of our quality worlds. The quality world of most people is a relatively stable place; with the possible exception of romantic love interests, the pictures in our quality worlds tend to come and go rather slowly. In fact, it can be very difficult for some people to let someone get out of their quality world—which, as you can imagine, may result in some serious problems, including stalking or murder.

Therapists need to do two things with respect to a client's quality world. First, you need to do your best to understand what's in your client's quality world. Second, to have a chance at helping your client use choice theory to improve his or her life, you need to get into your client's quality world.

Glasser and other reality therapists use different strategies to get into a client's quality world. These strategies are founded on this underlying principle: Act with clients in a way that gives them both hope for, and an experience of, having their basic human needs met. In a 2007 interview, Glasser described the initial process of a reality therapy session:

> So when you started you would say, "Tell me the story." And you would listen to the story and they would say this, that, or something else, and the story would . . . usually . . . have . . . unhappiness. . . . And you would listen and say, "Well it seems to me like you're just not a very happy person." And they would say, "I'm not." And then you could say to them, "Well, what if we [do] . . . counseling

and ... I am able to help you to understand why you are unhappy and how you can change your behaviors so you are happy and improve your relationships?" And in a moment or two you would say, "Let's take a look at your important relationships and tell me about your important relationships." Well in no time at all you'll find out that they do not have the kind of relationships that they would like. (Onedera & Greenwalt, 2007, p. 82)

In this excerpt, you can see Glasser is offering to help the client feel more happy (personal power or freedom) and offering to work with the client (relationship, or love and belonging). By doing so, he begins establishing a working relationship and enters the client's quality world.

Total Behavior

According to choice theory, all we do from birth to death is behave. But for Glasser, behavior is very inclusive, as choice theory includes a concept referred to as **total behavior**. Total behavior includes four distinct, but inseparable, components that are always occurring simultaneously:

1. **Acting**

2. **Thinking**

3. **Feeling**

4. **Physiology**

Total behavior is often described using an automobile analogy. Imagine you're sitting in the driver's seat of a front-wheel-drive vehicle. You place the key in the ignition and turn on the engine. According to choice theory, the engine represents your basic needs, because it's your desire to have those needs fulfilled that powers your overall system. As you put the car into gear and step on the accelerator, you keep a firm grip on the steering wheel. Because you want your needs met as efficiently as possible, when you get up in the morning and hop in your choice theory car, you almost always steer toward the same exciting destination— you steer in the direction of your quality world

or your inner world of wants. That's because you learned early in your life that doing so gives you the best possible chance of getting your five basic needs met.

If you're interested in love and belonging, you may steer your car in that direction by making breakfast for your romantic partner. If you want power, you may down a triple latte from the drive-through espresso stand on your way to work. If your first thoughts focus on survival, you may move as quickly as possible to a place that affords you food, water, shelter, and clothing. If you have a strong need for freedom or fun, well, you can imagine where those needs might take you.

In the car analogy, the two front wheels represent acting and thinking. These parts of our total behavior are under our direct control. We act and think in ways to get what we want. Although sometimes it might feel like we have little control over our thoughts, Glasser believes that thoughts, like behaviors, are chosen. In contrast, the back wheels of the car represent feelings and physiology. According to the total behavior concept of choice theory, our feelings and physiology are a product of indirect choice. This is because the ways in which we choose to act and think directly affects our feelings and physiology.

Choice Theory and Psychopathology

Glasser has a particular view of client psychopathology that some reality therapists share, but that others strongly oppose. As you read about Glasser's three primary principles of psychopathology, keep in mind that it's entirely possible to practice reality therapy while completely disagreeing with Glasser's stance on psychopathology (Wubbolding, personal communication, September 17, 2011).

Glasser's perspective on psychopathology includes three primary principles.

There Is No Such Thing as Mental Illness

Briefly stated, *Glasser does not believe in the existence of mental illness.* He expressed this position in 1965, while working as a psychiatrist at a school for delinquent girls, and has not wavered. He wrote: "The philosophy which underlies all treatment at the Ventura School is that mental illness does not exist" (Glasser, 1965, p. 85). Glasser's position on psychopathology and mental illness is similar to that of Thomas Szasz (1970) and Peter Breggin (1991). Although he works directly with human problems and human suffering, he doesn't believe mental illness exists (except for extreme forms in which brain pathology is clearly present, such as Alzheimer's disease, brain trauma, or brain injury). Despite his medical background, he doesn't prescribe or recommend psychotropic medications for clients and believes such medications are harmful. In 2003, he published a book titled, *Warning: Psychiatry Can Be Hazardous to Your Health* and on many occasions he has made statements similar to the following:

> Other mental health professionals don't talk about mental health, don't think about mental health. They focus on what psychiatrists and other people now believe are mental illnesses and focus on telling you that there is something wrong with your brain, that you need some kind of psychiatric drug to correct what's wrong with your brain, which they claim is some sort of a chemical imbalance. And [they] tell you that you can do nothing to help yourself. You should never tell anyone that he or she can do nothing to help himself or herself. That's a terrible thing to say. And certainly if you diagnose people as mentally ill who are not, and treat them with drugs that could harm them, this is a disaster in the country where we are not only spending billions of dollars doing that, which is bad enough, but the billions of dollars . . . harm the mental health of the people we are spending it on. (Onedera & Greenwalt, 2007, p. 80)

Glasser's extreme position—that we choose our behavior and are completely responsible for all our emotional, behavioral, and some physical problems—often makes students, clients, and even practicing reality therapists uncomfortable. Specifically, when Glasser uses verbs like *headaching*, *depressing*, and *angering* to describe human problems, some people view him as blaming the deeply distressed or the "mentally ill" for their problems. It's very important to keep in mind that the principles of choice theory and reality therapy don't

require practitioners to adopt every single viewpoint of Willian Glasser. In fact, there are many reality therapists who are quite comfortable working within the traditional medical model and who refer clients for medication interventions.

In contrast, Glasser sees himself as holding individuals responsible for their symptoms. And if you watch him in action, he doesn't act, write, or talk about clients in ways that reflect insensitivity. Instead, he encourages people to think and act in ways that give them more power over their symptoms and life situation.

As you might imagine, many individuals and many clients who come for counseling are not the least bit interested—at least initially—in using a choice theory model to explain their problems. That's because it's often more appealing to use an external control theory model and abdicate personal responsibility. Unfortunately, from the choice theory perspective, hanging onto external explanations for problems may initially feel better, but, in the end, believing you don't have choices that can help address your symptoms will increase your suffering and decrease your chances of recovery.

Unhappy Relationships

Glasser contends that most clients come to therapy because of unhappiness in an important relationship. He believes the unhappiness usually is caused by one person trying to control another person. He views the effort to control others (external control psychology) as a primary cause of unhappiness. The two antidotes to this particular problem are (1) to learn the first axiom of choice theory "The only person whose behavior we can control is our own" and (2) the positive relationship inherent in reality therapy.

For Glasser, symptoms—even symptoms of psychosis—are generally efforts to control others, or to feel in control, or obtain the basic need for freedom in one's life. He explains how his approach to counseling psychotic clients is consistent with how he counsels all other clients:

> Contrary to much current thinking, there is no problem doing psychotherapy with a person who hears voices or suffers from delusions. Although

I accept that the symptoms are there, I rarely refer to them in therapy. Most psychotic people can be reached if you concentrate on what they do that is sane.... I focus on these sane behaviors and work hard to try to create what I know every client I have ever seen, psychotic or not, wants: *good relationships that start with me.* (2000, p. 122)

For Glasser and reality therapy, then, your ability to relieve clients of problems and suffering hinges on two main factors: how well you can establish a positive therapy relationship (and thereby enter into your client's quality world) and how effectively you can teach your client to use choice theory in his or her life. Teaching clients to use choice theory involves the distinct process of teaching clients to use Wubbolding's Wanting Doing Evaluating and Planning (or **WDEP**) model (see Putting it in Practice 9.2).

Three Explanations

If there's no such thing as mental illness, then how does choice theory explain why otherwise perfectly intelligent people would act and think in ways that cause them physical and emotional misery? What causes pathological or maladaptive behavior?

Glasser (1998) described three logical reasons why so many people choose to think and act in ways he calls depressing, anxietying, phobicking, paining, and so on. As before, we should emphasize that many reality therapists don't agree with Glasser's more extreme positions on psychopathology. We include the following information to illustrate Glasser's more provocative and controversial perspectives.

The three logical explanations for pathological behavior might be better described as **purposes**. In other words, the purpose of pathological behavior is to accomplish the following three goals: (1) **restraining anger**, (2) **getting help**, and (3) **avoiding things** we don't want to face.

Restraining Anger

Depressing is the most common solution to the problem of anger. Similar to—but not the same as—the psychoanalytic conceptualization of depression as anger turned inward, depressing is viewed by reality therapists as a means by which anger

is restrained or managed. Using the language of choice theory, here's how the process works.

Something in your life doesn't go just the way you want it to go. For example, you wanted your boyfriend to meet you at the movies, and he doesn't show up. When this happens, you probably feel upset, frustrated, and out of control. Then, just like most people, on the heels of your frustration, you're likely to have an immediate impulse to anger.

Anger is a normal survival-related response built into our genes. As Glasser said, "Angering is the first total behavior most of us think of when someone in our quality worlds does something that is very much out of sync with what we want the person to do" (1998, p. 80). Although Wubbolding also presents anger as a natural reaction, he emphasizes that "[h]urt and fear are the primary feelings—then comes anger" (personal communication, September 17, 2011).

To return to Glasser's perspective, you probably learned that angering is not a very effective or acceptable choice for getting your love and acceptance needs met, so you may choose instead to depress. Depressing is, for the most part, much safer than angering, but it also has many drawbacks, not the least of which is that it feels absolutely miserable. While discussing the case of "Todd," Glasser described the immediate benefits of depressing over angering:

> Depressing prevented Todd from going after his wife, harming her, and even killing her, a common behavior in this country where weapons are so available. It also might have prevented him from killing himself. Suicide is another total behavior that people choose when they have given up on the idea that they will ever be able to get their lives back into effective control. (1998, p. 81)

If, like Todd, you're restraining your anger by depressing, reality therapy can relieve the problem by helping you find a better way (a better choice) to regain more direct control over fulfilling your need for love and acceptance. Part of this better way will undoubtedly include understanding one of the basic axioms of choice theory: You can only control yourself! Of course, everyone knows it's possible to control others—but what we believe Glasser means is that ultimately, we're healthier when we focus on ourselves rather than on controlling others.

Getting Help

Depressing and other forms of misery are often ways for us to get the love, power, or freedom we crave. Unfortunately for everyone involved, depressing can be a very effective method of controlling important people in your life in unhealthy ways. It can also be an effective method for gaining sympathy, support, and medications. This is one reason why Glasser firmly believes mental health professionals should be compassionate, and yet not pay too much attention to their clients' symptoms. He stated, "If it is coupled with compassion, not allowing anyone to control us with depressing helps them to see that there are much better choices than to depress" (1998, p. 82).

In a practical sense, reality therapists must sometimes pay attention to their clients' symptoms, because to ignore them is incompatible with being compassionate. The challenge is to gently and empathically help clients critically evaluate whether their symptoms are helping them fulfill their basic needs (Wubbolding, Brickell, Loi, & Al-Rashidi, 2001).

Avoiding Things

Everyone engages in avoidance sometimes. It may have to do with fear, aversion to doing something, or lack of motivation. For example, you may need to talk to your advisor or department chair about a thesis or dissertation topic, but you're nervous about what he or she might think about your idea. In that case, it would be easy to find other things to do and avoid scheduling an advising session. Or maybe you've had conflicts with your parents (probably because they're trying to control or advise you in one way or another), and so you're reluctant to call or visit them on your semester break. As it turns out, depressing, panicking, obsessing, and many other behaviors commonly considered to be mental illness are excellent ways to avoid dealing with life situations that need to be addressed. In these situations Glasser would say you have two choices: "Change what you want or change your behavior" (1998, p. 83). In other words, if you want more happiness in your life, take more responsibility for attaining it—there's almost always more we can do to fulfill our needs than what we're currently doing.

Choice Theory in a Nutshell

As a review of the theoretical material covered so far and a preview of upcoming sections focusing on reality therapy, Glasser's (1998) *Ten Axioms of Choice Theory* are listed below.

1. The only person whose behavior we can control is our own.

2. All we can give another person is information.

3. All long-lasting psychological problems are relationship problems.

4. The problem relationship is always part of our present life.

5. What happened in the past has everything to do with what we are today, but we can only satisfy our basic needs right now and plan to continue satisfying them in the future.

6. We can only satisfy our needs by satisfying the pictures or specific wants in our quality world.

7. All we do is behave.

8. All behavior is total behavior and is made up of four components: acting, thinking, feeling, and physiology.

9. All total behavior is chosen, but we only have direct control over the acting and thinking components. We can only control our feeling and physiology indirectly through how we choose to act and think.

10. All total behavior is designated by verbs and named by the part that is the most recognizable.

THE PRACTICE OF REALITY THERAPY

To do reality therapy you must learn and apply choice theory. Even better, you can obtain a reality therapy certification through the Willam Glasser Institute (http://www.wglasser.com/) or the Center for Reality Therapy (http://www .realitytherapywub.com/). Additionally, be sure to read Putting it in Practice 9.2 by Robert Wubbolding to better understand the interface between choice theory and reality therapy (and see Putting it in Practice 9.1 for a sample reality therapy informed consent).

PUTTING IT IN PRACTICE 9.1

Informed Consent From the Choice Theory/Reality Therapy Perspective

Welcome to therapy! I'm very glad you've chosen to meet with me to work on improving yourself and your life situation.

My approach to working with clients is called reality therapy. Reality therapy is refreshingly straightforward. We will spend almost all our time focusing on the present—what's going on in your life right now—and your future. This approach to therapy doesn't require digging around in your past. In fact, the only reason I might ask you about your past would be to find out about some of your past successes. Overall, as I work with you in reality therapy, I like to focus on three primary goals.

First, we'll need to spend time getting to know each other and getting comfortable. My main interest is to help you accomplish your goals and so I'll be asking you questions that help me understand what you value and what you want in your life.

Second, reality therapists emphasize something called choice theory. Choice theory emphasizes that we only have control over ourselves and although it's tempting to try to control others, things usually don't work out very well when we focus too much on changing other people. We'll focus on what you want, what you're doing, and whether what you're doing is getting you what you want. Choice theory is about helping you make the choices that get you what you want.

Third, an important part of choice theory involves active and detailed planning to help you achieve what you want in life. That means we'll focus a lot on your personal planning, making sure you have the best plan in place for accomplishing your goals.

Overall, I'm delighted to be working with you. What I want is to help you identify what's meaningful in your life and then to help you successfully accomplish your personal goals.

PUTTING IT IN PRACTICE 9.2

The Interface Between Choice Theory and Reality Therapy

Robert E. Wubbolding

Robert E. Wubbolding, EdD, director of the Center for Reality Therapy, provided the following commentary.

Reality therapy, based on choice theory, has long been criticized as a short-term, symptom-oriented problem-solving method. Now that brief, outcome-based counseling has become fashionable, reality therapy is gaining prominence and acceptance. To gain its rightful place in academia, however, will require more extensive research-based studies. Nevertheless, contrary to common belief, there are studies validating its effectiveness.

I have found that when students learn the theory accurately they see it as a comprehensive explanation of human behavior. To enhance its practicality, I have summarized the delivery system WDEP. *W* means exploring clients' wants and perceptions (i.e., what they want from the world around them and how hard they are willing to work to satisfy their wants). They also examine how they perceive themselves in the world as well as what they can control and not control. In the *D* component, the counselor helps clients describe their choices, their self-talk (e.g., "even though my choices are ineffective, I'll continue to do the same thing"), and their feelings—such as hurt, fear, anger, depression, and many others. The cornerstone in the practice of reality therapy is *E*, self-evaluation. No one changes a behavior without first determining that current choices are ineffective. In *Reality Therapy for the 21st Century,* I describe 22 types of reality therapy self-evaluation based on choice theory. A few of the self-evaluation questions follow:

- "Is what you're doing helping or hurting?"
- "Is what you want realistically attainable?"
- "Does your self-talk help or impede need satisfying choices?"

I have found this component to be increasingly necessary with clients, many of whom come from substance abusing, attention-deficit/hyperactivity disordered or simply tumultuous families in which expectations are, to say the least, inconsistent. In such an environment children grow up lacking the ability to self-evaluate; hence the need for a mentor to teach this skill.

In counseling any client my goal is to become part of his or her inner discourse. I cannot do this by communicating a lack of interest in the presenting issue—depression, blaming others, external perceived locus of control. I *always* deal directly with these issues and *then* proceed to discuss his or her relationships and choices by listening carefully for wants. For me, anything less demeans clients, worsens their frustration, and communicates that my agenda is more important than their pain.

The **WDEP** system is clearly based on an environment that avoids the toxic ABCs: arguing, blaming, criticizing, demanding, and getting lost in excuses. The helpful components of the environment include being determined, courteous, and enthusiastic; using paradoxical techniques; using informed consent; respecting boundaries; creating a sense of anticipation; discussing problems not as problems but as client solutions that have not helped; suspending judgment; using reflective listening; and many others.

One of my missions as a counselor, psychologist, and university professor is to make reality therapy academically both respected and respectable. A second goal is to promote it as a usable system, not as a cult. So I urge you, as students hoping to be respected therapists and helpers, to realize that reality therapy is a system practical *for you.* You need not imitate the style of anyone else. Adapt it to your own personality: assertive, laid-back, action-centered, or more cognitive. Select one, two, or three ideas from this excellent chapter that you will use!

Assessment Issues and Procedures

Glasser doesn't use standardized assessment procedures. He relies exclusively on choice theory to guide his treatment approach. Other reality therapy practitioners may or may not use traditional assessment procedures. This distinction is a good example of why it's important to separate the theorist from the therapeutic practice. Glasser is generally against testing, medications, and diagnostic procedures, but many reality therapists find choice theory and reality therapy completely compatible with these standard mental health practices.

Choice theory assessment initially focuses on an assumption regarding the primary reason why humans become unhappy and seek therapy. Glasser articulates the root problem as always involving an unsatisfying relationship:

> From the perspective of forty years of psychiatric practice, it has become apparent to me that all unhappy people have the same problem: They are unable to get along well with the people they want to get along well with. (Glasser, 1998, p. 5)

This theoretical stance—that the presenting problem is always a relationship problem—makes the therapist's assessment task straightforward.

As they interview clients, reality therapists reflect on the following assessment issues or questions directly related to choice theory. These are not necessarily questions that the reality therapist asks the client directly; these are questions the reality therapist is evaluating and addressing when providing counseling (for many additional questions, see Wubbolding, 2000).

- What is the nature of the client's unsatisfying relationship or relationship-related conflict?

- Will the client be able to understand and use choice theory to improve his or her ability to meet the basic needs? If so, the therapist can move quickly into explaining choice theory. If not, the therapist will need to use various strategies, such as in-session demonstration, rational persuasion, reframing, and so on, to help the client understand how choice theory works.

- Who and what is within the client's quality world?

- How is the client going about meeting his or her needs for survival, love and belonging, power, freedom, and fun?

- Is the client overemphasizing any of the basic human needs?

- What's going wrong as the client tries to meet his or her basic human needs?

- Have there been past successes that can show the client that he or she can use choice theory to meet these needs now and in the future?

- What are the perceptions of other people and how do they act in relation to you? What is the impact of their behaviors on you?

Somewhat recently, reality therapy practitioners have developed at least three different assessment instruments designed to measure the basic human needs. These include: (1) the Basic Needs Self-Assessment (Mickel & Sanders, 2003); (2) the Contextual Needs Assessment (T. Brown & Swenson, 2005), and (3) the Student Need Survey (M. K. Burns, Vance, Szadokierski, & Stockwell, 2006).

Building the Relationship

In recent years, Glasser has written in greater detail about relationship-building and relationship-destroying behaviors or habits. He considers these habits to be consistently positive or negative for all relationships, both within and outside of therapy. That being the case, his **seven caring habits** and **seven deadly habits** provide excellent guidelines for how reality therapists should and shouldn't behave toward clients. Glasser's seven caring habits are listed here along with brief descriptions and examples.

1. *Supporting*. Reality therapists help clients focus on what they want from life. By doing so, and by helping them obtain it in a direct and constructive way, reality therapists communicate support. Another way reality therapists communicate support to clients is by working with them on specific tasks. For example, to a client who wanted to write a letter to an important person, Glasser suggests, "Write the letter and bring it in to me. We'll look it over together before you send it. Is that okay?" (1998, p. 68).

2. *Encouraging*. Reality therapists are positive and encouraging with clients. Technically, this emerges in several forms: When focusing on the person or, in rare cases, on the person's past, the reality therapist emphasizes successes and positive identity; also, there is an emphasis on connection between therapist and client. For example, with a client who was struggling with a reluctance to talk, Glasser used an encouraging statement in a direct manner that has come to be associated with reality therapy: "Well, say it anyway. This is the place to say hard-to-say things" (1998, p. 65).

3. *Listening*. Many non-reality therapists view reality therapy as directive and confrontational. In truth, reality therapists emphasize listening. Their listening is less in the mold of nondirective Carl Rogers listening and more in the mold of a friend's listening to another friend. Additionally, reality therapists actively listen and respond when clients talk about their successes, plans, and efforts to connect with others, and listen less actively when clients' talk about symptoms or negative past experiences. Consistent with the WDEP model, reality therapists listen for what clients want (W); what clients are doing (D); self-evaluations (E); and plans (P).

4. *Accepting*. Reality therapists accept the fact that all clients want to fulfill their five basic human needs. This provides an excellent foundation for empathy and connecting within the therapy session. However, reality therapists never accept client statements that externalize responsibility. This is probably why many students and professionals inaccurately view reality therapy as being harshly confrontational. Reality therapists use teaching techniques—not harsh confrontation—when clients externalize responsibility.

5. *Trusting*. Reality therapists communicate trust in many ways. For example, in the Case Analysis later in this chapter, when Glasser tells Teresa to call and that he'll call her back, he's building a trust relationship.

6. *Respecting*. Reality therapists respect what people want. The following excerpt from a case in which Glasser is working with a married man

who wants to become a woman illustrates his emphasis on both connecting with clients and respecting them:

> I could turn him over to someone else, but we've made a good connection. He may think I am afraid to deal with his problem, and we'll lose the connection. It's that connection that's all important. Even his wife will look for that connection—that I really want to help him; that I respect him even though he wants to be a woman. (2000, pp. 90–91)

7. *Negotiating differences.* Reality therapy is all about negotiating differences. A basic assumption of choice theory is that although all individuals have the same five basic needs, there are unique ways in which they want those needs fulfilled. Reality therapists help clients negotiate differences between what they want from life and what they're getting. In couples therapy, Glasser emphasizes a concept called "the solving circle" to help clients constructively negotiate their differences. With regard to the solving circle, he tells couples: "Unless both of you are in the circle, you cannot negotiate; all you can do is argue" (1998, p. 95).

Reality Therapy and Confrontation

Because reality therapy has been misconstrued as harshly confrontational, once again we want to emphasize that reality therapy is gently confrontational. It helps clients learn and deeply understand the power, control, and choice they have in their lives (Wubbolding & Brickell, 2000). To articulate reality therapy's stance against harsh confrontation, we list the seven deadly habits of choice theory:

1. Criticizing
2. Blaming
3. Complaining
4. Nagging
5. Threatening
6. Punishing
7. Bribing or rewarding to control

In his usual style, Glasser is direct and clear about the negative consequences of using the seven deadly habits. He states: "There is nothing intangible about any of them; they are clear and explicit. Exhibiting them in any relationship will damage that relationship. If you keep doing so, the relationship will be destroyed" (2002, p. 13).

Helping Clients Develop Effective Plans

Wubbolding (1988, 1991, 2000, 2011) has written extensively about how reality therapists help clients develop plans for making positive life changes. Nearly always, therapists help clients make positive and constructive plans. Wubbolding (1988) uses the acronym *SAMIC³* to outline the essential ingredients of an effective plan:

S = Simple: Effective plans are simple. If a plan generated in reality therapy is too complex, the client may become confused or overwhelmed and therefore not follow through.

A = Attainable: Effective plans are attainable or realistic. If the plan is unattainable, the client will probably become discouraged. As Glasser does in the case of Teresa discussed later in this chapter, you should help your client adopt a small and realistic plan.

M = Measurable: Effective plans are measurable. Clients need to know if the plan is working and if they're making progress.

I = Immediate: Effective plans can be enacted immediately, or at least very soon. If clients have to wait too long to implement a plan, the immediate motivation and/or the memory of exactly what to do may be compromised.

C = Controlled: Effective plans are controlled exclusively by the planner. Be sure to avoid having clients develop plans that are contingent on someone else's behavior.

C = Committed: Clients need to commit to their plans. Obviously, if a client is only half-heartedly invested in the plan, then the plan is less likely to succeed.

C = Continuous: Effective plans are continuously implemented. This is where the practice of choice theory and reality therapy is similar to Eastern or mindfulness approaches to mental health. When functioning well, reality therapy clients have continuous awareness of what they want and of their plan for getting what they want. This high level of awareness reminds us of mindfulness or conscious-raising therapeutic techniques.

Wubbolding (1988) also recommends that individuals learning to conduct reality therapy develop a plan for themselves. In particular, he notes that to be effective reality therapists, it's very useful for practitioners to eventually obtain consultation and/or supervision from certified reality therapists (in addition, we recommend that you practice living your life using choice theory rules; see Putting it in Practice 9.3).

Reality Therapy in Action: Brief Vignettes

Similar to Adlerian therapy, reality therapy involves encouragement and intentional planning. The counselor establishes a positive working relationship and then persistently keeps the therapeutic focus on what's within the client's solving circle or circle of control. Maintaining a clear focus on positive actions and thoughts is what makes reality therapy an efficient and brief counseling approach.

Vignette I: Using Encouragement—Not Critical Confrontation

The following is an example of the type of confrontation often inaccurately associated with reality therapy. The counselor is confronting a teenage client on his efforts to find a job.

Counselor: Where else did you go?

Client: I tried a couple other [gas] stations, too. Nobody wants to look at me. They don't pay too good anyway. [Screw] them!

Counselor: So you haven't really done too much looking. Sounds like you want it served on a silver plate, Joe. Do you think looking at a couple of gas stations is really going to get you a job? (Ivey et al., 2002, p. 219)

Based on this very brief exchange it appears the counselor is trying to help the client be successful in obtaining employment. Consequently, we can assume that having gainful employment (or at least making money) is a "want" (the W in WDEP) and in the client's quality world. Although this counselor is supposedly doing reality therapy, his critical statements ("you haven't done too much looking" and "you want it served on a silver platter") are inconsistent with reality therapy principles. A reality therapist would use a more supportive and encouraging approach. For example:

Counselor: Where else did you go?

Client: I tried a couple other [gas] stations, too. Nobody wants to look at me. They don't pay too good anyway. [Screw] them!

Counselor (Reality therapy response): It sounds like you really want a job and you feel very frustrated. What else could you do to help you get what you want?

Notice that the reality therapist keeps the focus on what the client wants, empathizes with the frustration, and ignores the client's desire to quit trying. This approach is encouraging because the counselor is maintaining confidence in the client's ability to act and think in ways that will move him toward his quality world.

Generally, when counselors use confrontation, the goal is to help clients engage in self-examination. The process for nearly all therapy approaches is similar—counselors help clients increase their awareness or have insights, which then leads to motivation and eventual change. Consistent with this process, Wubbolding referred to client self-evaluation as a "prelude to change" (1999, p. 196).

In working with this young man on employment issues, the following exchange uses concepts and questions adapted from Wubbolding (1999).

Counselor: Hey Joe, do you think the overall direction of your life is more of a plus or more of a minus?

PUTTING IT IN PRACTICE 9.3

Living Choice Theory: The Four Big Questions

Four questions have been developed to help students and clients live the choice theory lifestyle (Wubbolding, 1988). These questions are derived from Wubbolding's *WDEP* formula. During one full week, do your best to keep these four reality therapy questions on your mind:

1. What do you want? (Wants)

2. What are you doing? (Doing)

3. Is it working? (Evaluation)

4. Should you make a new plan? (Planning)

In reality therapy, every day you're operating with a personal plan. The plan may or may not be any good and it may or may not be clear. The point is this: You're thinking and doing things aimed toward getting your basic needs met. Therefore, consistently ask yourself the four preceding questions. This will help make your plan and your choices more explicit.

Wubbolding's four questions are incredibly powerful and practical. Think about how you might apply them when doing therapy with a teenager. Now think about how you might apply them as a consultant for a local business. The fact is, whether you're consulting with a teenager or a business leader, there are hardly any other four questions that are more relevant and practical.

In the space that follows each question, answer the four questions for yourself today.

1. What do you want?

2. What are you doing?

3. Is it working?

4. Should you make a new plan?

After you've answered the questions, go back and think about what you've written as your answer for Question 1.

Client: I don't know. I suppose it's kind of a neutral. I don't have a job and I'm not really going any direction.

Counselor: That's interesting. No direction. I guess my question about that is whether going no direction is really the direction you want...or whether maybe you want something else?

Client: Yeah. I'd love to have some money. Right now the economy sucks, so I don't really see the point of looking for work.

Counselor: The odds of getting a job right now aren't great, that's for sure. Do you suppose the odds are better if you stay home or better if you get out and drop off a few applications?

Client: I see what you're saying. I guess my odds are a little better if I get out there. But I think my odds of making money are probably better if I just got out there and sold drugs, like some other guys I know are doing.

Counselor: I'm just trying to follow along and track what you want. It does sound like you want money. And you might be right about the drug selling scene, I don't know much about that. But let's be serious, do you think selling drugs would genuinely be good for you? I guess another way of asking that is, "Will selling drugs help or hurt you in getting what you want in the long run?" [This confrontation does what a reality therapy confrontation is supposed to do: It directly questions the usefulness of excuses.]

Client: I'm not saying I think selling drugs is a good thing to do. I'm just frustrated and sick of being broke and poor.

Counselor: Yeah. I hear you saying it's very hard. But I'm your counselor and it's my job to keep pushing you in positive directions. And so I'm asking you this because I think you can do better than how you're doing. Is the way you're thinking about this—that it's too hard, the economy sucks, and you're likely to fail—is that line of thinking helping you get a job or hurting your prospects?

Client: Yeah. I guess having a pity-party isn't helping much.

Counselor: And I'm sure having a pity party can feel good sometimes. But I'm with you on the fact that it's not helping much. So we've got to try out something different.

Because the preceding questions ask the client to look at himself and self-evaluate, they're inherently confrontational, but also supportive and encouraging. Many additional reality therapy questions that help clients self-reflect and plan are in *Reality Therapy for the 21st Century* (Wubbolding, 2000).

Vignette II: Collaborative Planning

This vignette extends the previous case into the reality therapy collaborative planning process.

Client: Well. What sort of different approach do you suggest?

Counselor: If it were up to me, I'd suggest we make a very clear plan for you to try out this week. The plan would focus on how you can get what you want: a job so you can start earning money. And we'd develop this plan together and we'd be honest with each other about whether our ideas would really give you the best chance possible to get a job.

Client: How about I go down to the Job Service and sign up there?

Counselor: That's one good idea. Of course it doesn't guarantee you a job, but nothing will because you don't have control over whether someone hires you, you only have control over your strategy or plan. Do you know what I mean?

Client: Not really.

Counselor: Thanks for being honest about that. Whenever you make a plan or set a goal, it's important for it to be completely within your control and not dependent on anyone else. That's because the only person whose behavior you can control is your own. For example, if your plan is to "get hired," you can be doomed to frustration and anger because you won't be making the hiring decision. Instead, a good plan involves developing a detailed, step-by-step process. For example, your plan could be to revise your resume and then submit it along with a well-crafted cover letter to 10 places where you think your skills are a good fit. You have complete control over all that.

Client: Okay. I get it. I could do that, but I'm not very good with writing and resumes and all that.

Counselor: How can you make sure those things are in good shape then?

Client: I could get my sister to look it over.

Counselor: When could you do that?

Client: Next week, I suppose.

Counselor: What would make it possible to do that sooner, like this week?

Client: You know, you're really kind of pushy.

Counselor: Do you think you'd do better with someone who lets you put things off until next week? Would that be more helpful in getting you a job sooner?

Client: Right. Right. Okay. I call my sister tonight and ask if she can help me as soon as she's available.

Counselor: That's sounds like a great start. What time will you call her tonight?

Client: Seven o'clock. I know. Why not six? Well I figure she'll be done with dinner by seven and so that's why.

Counselor: Good planning. I guess maybe I don't have to be so pushy after all.

The preceding dialogue illustrates how counselors can use gentle and persistent questioning to lead clients toward planning that's consistent with Wubbolding's principles (i.e., SAMIC³). It also illustrates how reality therapists function as a collaborator in helping clients or students plan for success. Burdenski (2010) commented on this collaborative or "coaching" model that distinguishes reality therapy from solution-focused postmodern approaches that generally inhibit counselors from providing input to help clients or students solve problems:

the [choice theory/reality therapy] practitioner is encouraged to use his or her knowledge and experience to help clients widen their perception of choices and new possibilities. I don't think of [choice theory/reality therapy] as an "expert" model, but rather as a "coaching model." (p. 14)

When it comes to planning for success, reality therapists are engaged and involved with students and clients in the here-and-now. In contrast to some postmodern approaches, reality therapists offer ideas and push an agenda. As with the case example in this section, reality therapists also work hard to make the planning process simple, straightforward, and concrete. This emphasis on concreteness is in contrast to postmodern approaches (e.g., the miracle question; see Chapter 11) that can be more challenging for children who haven't yet developed abstract thinking skills. Burdenski (2010) offers an example of how a school counselor might apply the practical and concrete aspects of this model with elementary students:

When working with an elementary-aged child struggling with paying attention in class, the counselor using reality therapy might ask: "How did your morning go in Ms. Smith's class?" "How did you spend your time?" "What did you try doing to help you pay attention better?" "What can you try later today?" "Are you willing to make a plan and tell me how it goes?" "Can you show me your commitment to the plan by giving me a nice firm handshake?" (p. 14)

Finally, we should note that Burdenski's inclusion of the "nice firm handshake" is another signature piece from reality therapy. Not only does the handshake symbolize the collaborative partnership, it also emphasizes the human connection between counselor and client. The human connection—love and belonging needs—is so central to choice theory and reality therapy that some Glasser Quality School consultants recommend that teachers begin their day standing at the classroom door and shaking hands or fist-bumping or somehow making a connection as each student enters the classroom.

CASE ANALYSIS AND TREATMENT PLANNING

The following case example is from *Counseling with Choice Theory* (2000). The client, Teresa, is a woman with depressive symptoms that appear primarily associated with her husband "leaving her."

Before meeting with Teresa, Glasser has access to her mental health history. He's aware of her marital break-up and depressive symptoms. Based on this information, he formulates his approach.

Prior to presenting the case, Glasser (2000) articulates the thinking that guides his initial behavior with Teresa:

> I was determined not to ask Teresa to tell me her story and, especially, not to ask her how she felt. I had to try to convince her that she was making ineffective choices in her life, knowing full well that my claim that she was making choices, especially choosing to depress, would be the furthest thing from her mind. If I couldn't begin to convince her on the first visit, there was little chance of any measurable progress. (p. 129)

Glasser is illustrating several reality therapy concepts. First, he prepares himself to focus on the positive. He plans to avoid asking Teresa about her symptoms. Second, his goal is to "try to convince her" that she's making poor choices. As you can see from his language, he understands that she won't be expecting to be held responsible for her depressive symptoms. Third, Glasser is set on working quickly. He wants to convince her of the merits of choice theory before she leaves his office.

Although reality therapy is predominantly an educational approach to client change, it also includes experiential components. Note Glasser's next move:

> I started by rising briskly, greeting her warmly, and offering my hand. Teresa was surprised by my energy and enthusiasm to see her. I was not the first therapist she had seen, and she was used to using her depressing to take over the interview. (p. 129)

Glasser anticipates that Teresa will use her depressing style to disempower the therapy and depress the therapist. This illustrates an early assessment and educational or role-induction rule for reality therapists: Do your best to determine how clients use people to confirm their external

control view of the world, and then behave in a way that doesn't validate their style. This can also be seen through a behavioral lens: Instead of reinforcing his client's depressing style, Glasser ignores depressive behaviors and models choice theory: He remains upbeat and positive, despite the client's interpersonal cues for depressing and hopelessness.

The Problem List

In the case of Teresa, Glasser doesn't use any formal assessment procedures. Instead, even before Teresa enters the office, he assumes she is *depressing*. This assumption is based on diagnostic referral information and generalization from his previous experiences as a therapist and with choice theory. He could be completely incorrect in his initial assumptions. If so, he would likely modify his behavior to fit with the client's unique needs . . . while maintaining his initial counseling objectives of teaching choice theory and connecting with the client.

At this point, the problem list is brief.

1. Clinical depression (Teresa is presumed to be engaging in a pattern of *depressing total behaviors*).

Most reality therapists would engage in a more systematic assessment or problem/goal identification process. As discussed previously, Wubbolding (2000) recommends a series of very specific questions aimed at stimulating self-evaluation. From Wubbolding's more systematic orientation, the initial focus would be on identifying Teresa's wants (W), what she's doing (D), evaluating/determining whether her total behavior is getting her what she wants (E), and components of a new plan (P). Then, the problem list might include the following four items:

1. Depressed mood (Teresa wants to be happier).

2. Social disconnection (Teresa complains of social isolation or inactivity).

3. Lack of energy (Teresa wants to feel more energetic).

4. Unhappiness with herself. (This might also be formulated as the depressive symptom of low

self-esteem or self-deprecation and from a choice theory perspective Teresa's self-critical thoughts are not helpful and therefore a problem that needs to be changed.)

Goal: Develop a (SAMIC^3) plan for increasing social connection.

As the case proceeds, Glasser uses an explanation or psychoeducation to inform Teresa about what to expect from him and from therapy. His explanation is also functioning as an intervention:

> Teresa, therapy is not easy. I have to ask you some hard questions that may even confuse you a little, but I'm doing it because I want very much to help you. But please, if I say anything that you don't think is right, ask me why, and I'll explain as well as I can. This isn't really a hard question, but I'd like you to try to do your best to answer it. What do you think a psychiatrist can do for you? (pp. 130–131)

When he says, "I want very much to help you" and "I'd like you to try to do your best" Glasser is directly expressing what he wants and then leaving the rest to Teresa, a strategy in line with choice theory Axiom 2: All we can give another person is information.

Teresa's response to Glasser's question about what a psychiatrist can do for her is: "Help me to feel better." He then uses a positive cognitive frame to direct Teresa toward the positive and toward experiencing hope. He responds, "Fine, that's the answer I was hoping for: You think you can use some help; you haven't given up" (p. 131). This is an example of Glasser beginning to impose choice theory onto Teresa's situation and symptoms.

Teresa has preconceived notions about therapy and mental illness stemming from previous therapy experiences. She has learned external control concepts that are incompatible with choice theory. In particular, Teresa expects to talk about her past and believes she's suffering from clinical depression, an illness that may require medication. The question is: How can Glasser introduce his beliefs about the nonexistence of mental illness without offending Teresa?

Glasser: Now I'm going to ask you a question that may not make much sense. Are you willing to try to answer it?

Teresa: You're the doctor, ask me, and I'll try to answer.

Glasser: Is it okay if we don't talk at all about how you feel or about your life? You said it was a disaster; I'd just as [soon] not talk about it. (p. 131)

Not only does Glasser ask Teresa a question, he also clearly states that his preference is to not talk about Teresa's feelings. He continues to apply his choice theory model.

It's likely that Teresa is taken aback by Glasser's question and perspective. She probably can't help but wonder what's up with this therapist who doesn't want to talk about her troubles. From her point of view, if he doesn't want to talk about her troubles and misery, then what on earth could he want to talk about?

Problem Formulation

It may even seem strange to you, the educated reader of this book, that Glasser doesn't want to listen to Teresa talk about her problems, but this position flows from his problem formulation, which is: Teresa is not suffering from a condition called clinical depression, *she is depressing*. That is, *the total behaviors that she's choosing are depressing her*.

Like solution-oriented therapists (see Chapter 11), Glasser has reasons for avoiding depressing talk. The main reason is that Teresa has been habitually meeting her love and belonging or power needs through depressing behaviors. It may be that people take care of her, listen to her, and think about her when she acts depressed. Or it may be that somewhere inside she feels better, because if she's depressed, then she has a good, legitimate reason for being lonely (and for not having her needs for love and belonging met).

A practical issue that reality therapists must address is the issue of timing and client readiness. Unlike Glasser in this case, it's often best for reality therapists to talk with clients about their symptoms and their misery. As Wubbolding states, "Avoiding a discussion of the presenting problem is a sure way to lose the client!" (personal communication, September 17, 2011). Glasser is obviously very direct—which may be more palatable to clients when the therapist is an elderly, caring man who happens to be the creator of his own therapy approach (see Putting it in Practice 9.4).

Although he's been operating on choice theory from the get-go, in this next exchange, Glasser begins to formally introduce choice theory. However, Teresa pushes back and expresses her interest in talking about her feelings.

Glasser: Please, Teresa, tell me. Has it done any good to talk about your misery to anyone? Like, do you choose to feel better after telling someone how miserable you are? [I'm tangentially introducing the idea that she can choose to feel better. I wonder if she'll pick up on it? She didn't.]

Teresa: Wait a second, you're getting me confused. I've got to tell you how I feel. How can you help me if you don't know how I feel?

A little later, Glasser is even more direct about choice theory. Again, Teresa resists his perspective.

Glasser: Everyone who comes in here is choosing to feel bad. No one who chooses to feel good ever comes in. At least they've never come to see me. I don't think it's [feeling bad] a very good choice. That's why I don't want to talk about it.

Teresa: I don't know what you're talking about. I don't choose to feel bad. (p. 132)

In the preceding exchange Teresa makes it clear that she's not giving up her external control theory without a fight. When practicing reality therapy, you must be prepared to use a variety of skills and strategies to teach clients choice theory. You often must be doggedly persistent, repetitive, and ready to provide evidence and demonstrations.

On the other hand, unlike Glasser, many reality therapists are much less blunt, more empathic, and more patient as they help clients understand the power of their choices. Glasser's version of reality

therapy is similar to Ellis's version of cognitive therapy. As is the case with cognitive therapy, there are kinder and gentler ways to use the approach.

Rarely do clients grasp choice theory immediately. This is partly because most individuals are steeped in external control psychology. They come to therapy believing they have a chemical imbalance, or believing they have a thing called schizophrenia or anxiety, and they've often been taught to think of themselves as having very little personal control over their symptoms.

Interventions

Based on the problem formulation, reality therapy interventions will naturally focus on helping Teresa change her actions and thoughts. Common reality therapy techniques include questioning (both for the purpose of confrontation and rational analysis or persuasion), reframing, staying focused on the positive, in-session demonstrations, and out-of-session experiments or homework.

In his session with Teresa, Glasser frequently uses questioning designed to persuade Teresa to adopt a choice theory mind-set.

Glasser: Well, if you don't choose to feel bad, then how come you feel bad?

Teresa: I feel bad because my life is a disaster. What else could I feel?

Glasser: But does choosing to feel bad help you in any way to feel better? I realize I'm confusing you, but I'm trying to help you. How you feel is a part of the way you choose to live your life. You chose what you did all day yesterday. Did you feel good or bad yesterday? (p. 132)

He then moves quickly to an in-session demonstration:

Glasser: Think about how you feel now and how you felt a few minutes ago when you walked in the door. Let's say hello again. Here, give my hand a good shake. [I reach out my hand, and she gives it a much more vigorous shake than she did when she came in.]

Teresa: Okay, you're right. I feel a little better. I do.

Glasser: Aren't you choosing to feel better? You could have chosen to continue to feel the way you did when you came in.

And then he moves back to questioning for the purposes of rational persuasion:

Glasser: If you were suffering from clinical depression, how could you feel better all of a sudden?

As you can see, Glasser is persistent in teaching Teresa that her "depression" is a function of her choice to depress, not of a chemical imbalance or a diagnostic label. Further, he eventually emphasizes to every client that their problems are a result of their unsuccessful efforts to deal with an unsatisfying relationship or the lack of any relationships at all. With Teresa, he used the following question to get her to focus on her relationship loss and loneliness:

Glasser: When you give up on your life, what is it that you really give up on? Think a minute. If you can answer that question, I think you can really get some help. (p. 134)

For Teresa, giving up on life coincided with her husband's walking out on her. Like many people who respond well to choice theory, she had previously felt better and functioned better because she was previously making more positive choices. Consequently, at least one avenue for helping Teresa make good choices was to have her reflect, even if briefly, on the fact that she made positive choices in the past. This is the exception to the general rule that reality therapy does not focus on the past; there is a focus on the past if the focus includes something positive or successful. Then, Glasser used more questioning:

Glasser: When you felt good, what did you choose to do that you've totally stopped doing now? (p. 134)

When Teresa answers, Glasser uses reframing to mold her response into something that better fits with choice theory.

Teresa: I did things, I saw people, I took care of my children, I wasn't broke all the time. I had a life.

Glasser: That's a perfect answer except for one little detail. You chose all those good things; you chose to have a life.

Teresa: Okay, okay, but that's all gone. In your words, tell me how I can choose to have a life now. (p. 134)

Teresa is signaling to Glasser that she's willing to give his theory a try. Once a client has accepted some basic parts of choice theory, it's time to move toward application. Subsequently, Glasser assigns homework that captures two themes. First, the assignments help Teresa experience the fact that front-wheel actions and/or thinking directly affects rear-wheel feelings and physiology. In our work using reality therapy with teens, we often sketch out the reality therapy car to illustrate total behavior concepts. Second, reality therapy homework includes active and effective planning. In the following excerpt, both forms of homework are illustrated.

Glasser: That's right, you can't separate choosing how you feel from choosing what you do. They go together. But you can go home and spend the rest of the day saying to yourself: *Teresa, face it. Good or bad, happy or sad, you're choosing everything you do all day long.* (p. 135; italics in original)

Then, a bit later, Glasser uses a homework assignment to help Teresa establish a short-term plan.

Glasser: All right, let's start.... What could you choose to do tomorrow that would be better than today?

Teresa: I could choose not to sit around all day.

Although Teresa generated a plan, she generated a negative and vague plan. As a result, Glasser uses confrontation and rational persuasion to help her establish a more positive plan.

Glasser: No, that won't work. It'd be like trying to choose not to eat so much. I'm not looking for you to choose not to do anything. I'm looking for you to start to choose to do something better than you're doing now. Something active, so that you have to get up and get going. [Then she said something that made us both smile. She was getting it.]

Teresa: I could choose to clean the house. It's a mess. (p. 135)

Rather quickly in this exchange Teresa is ready to go home and choose different, more positive, and more constructive behaviors. But the next thing Glasser does in this case is somewhat surprising. After a brief period of praising Teresa for "getting it," he makes a special, spontaneous-sounding contractual agreement with her. He asks her to call and leave him a message every time she chooses to do something all week. He also asks her to leave her number on his answering machine and tells her he'll find time to call her back.

At the end of Teresa's therapy, Glasser takes another step that's somewhat unusual. He asks Teresa if she's read *The Divine Secrets of the Ya-Ya Sisterhood*. And then he offers to help her start her very own "Ya Ya group" (p. 138). He concludes with this charge:

Glasser: For thousands of years, women have supported women. It may even be why the human species has survived. I say, take advantage of your genetic good fortune. Care for each other. (p. 138)

QUESTIONS FOR REFLECTION

After reading this case, what do you think you might be able to incorporate into your own counseling practice? Are there any behaviors that Glasser engages in that you think would be a poor fit for you? Is there anything he does that you really want to try out?

Outcomes Measurement

In schools, reality therapy is sometimes referred to as responsibility training. This is because choice theory and reality therapy hold people responsible for their thinking, actions, feelings, and physiology. It follows that the general goal of reality therapy is for clients to gain a sense of personal control over their choices. This intrinsic control should then help clients become more capable of meeting their basic human needs in ways that are responsible and satisfying.

Given these general goals, reality therapy treatment outcomes can focus on virtually any issue related to personal control. Not surprisingly, locus of control measures have often been used as outcomes measures in reality therapy research (Rose-Inza & Mi Gu, 2001). However, nearly any measure linked to client total behavior (thoughts, actions, feelings, physiology) would be acceptable. For example, if a client comes in with an anger/aggression problem (angering) then an anger or aggressive behavior measure would be appropriate for monitoring progress. Reality therapists also use measures of personal satisfaction, emotional control, or relationship satisfaction as a way of determining treatment efficacy. For Teresa, a specific depressive symptom scale would be most appropriate (e.g., the *Beck Depression Inventory*). Additionally, when working with student populations, Burdenski and Faulkner (2010) have developed several basic need measures that can be used by teachers or school counselors to measure baseline student need satisfaction and any gains made over time in the classroom or counseling setting.

CULTURAL AND GENDER CONSIDERATIONS

Choice theory and reality therapy has been practiced with an impressively wide range of ethnic groups and there are William Glasser Institutes in at least 16 different countries. The lead journal, the *International Journal of Choice Theory and Reality Therapy* (formerly the *International Journal of Reality Therapy*, 1997–2009; and formerly the *Journal of Reality Therapy*, 1980–1996) has a distinctly international flavor with many articles from international practitioners (Jusoh, Mahmud, & Ishak, 2008; J. Kim, 2007; Liu, Ting, & Cheng, 2010). In 1998, Wubbolding and associates published an article promoting

PUTTING IT IN PRACTICE 9.4

The Risks of Insensitivity

To begin with, consider this: Glasser's approach to psychiatry, psychology, and counseling is radical. His beliefs that mental illness doesn't exist and that anxiety, depression, and schizophrenia are the responsibility of the client run counter to most contemporary approaches to therapy and mental disorders. Consequently, if you choose to fully imitate Glasser rather than integrating reality therapy principles into your practice, you may end up offending clients or even other mental health professionals because of your unorthodox views and approach.

In addition, reality therapy is sometimes viewed as a directive and insensitive form of therapy that permits therapists to simply confront clients with the reality of the consequences of their choices. For example, in the case of Teresa, at one point Glasser tells her, "you don't have to tell me how you feel. I know how you feel" (p. 132). Obviously, this statement can be considered blatantly insensitive and in direct violation of existential-humanistic principles of empathy and an I-Thou relationship (see Chapters 4, 5, and 6).

From our perspective, Glasser's work with Teresa is neither unsympathetic nor unethical. However, taken out of context, Glasser's words are insensitive and blunt. And this is where the main ethical danger lies.

Sometimes reality therapy may appeal to students and professionals who are somewhat bossy and directive in their personality styles. Reality therapy becomes most offensive and potentially unethical when employed in a confrontational manner by naturally directive therapists who don't understand choice theory or how to use reality therapy appropriately.

We have especially seen this tendency in poorly trained professionals who work with juvenile delinquents. The end result is that the professional becomes demanding, bossy, confrontational, and insensitive—all in the name of "reality therapy." Of course, in our opinion, demanding, bossy, confrontive, and insensitive therapist behavior is not reality therapy; it's just bad behavior and may well be unethical. In fact, when practiced in this manner, reality therapy is transformed into just another effort to apply external control tactics to difficult youths (who are already reacting to adult efforts at external control).

In conclusion, this is our advice: It's quite possible for you to read this chapter or Glasser's or Wubbolding's work and be able to try out reality therapy ideas, strategies, and techniques immediately. There's nothing wrong with integrating reality therapy approaches into your counseling or psychotherapy practice. However, if you begin developing a strong interest in reality therapy, then we recommend that you take advantage of advanced reality therapy training and perhaps even become a certified

> reality therapist yourself (see Recommended Readings and Resources). On the other hand, if you choose to inappropriately twist reality therapy approaches into another form of external control psychology because you haven't obtained adequate training on how to really conduct reality therapy, then you run the risk of behaving unethically—or simply of doing poor therapy.

reality therapy as an approach that can be modified and adapted to many cultures (Wubbolding et al., 1998). This article was prepared by 11 signatories from 10 different countries.

Glasser, in an interview with Wubbolding, emphasized his perspective on the multicultural applicability of choice theory:

> [C]hoice theory is strongly based on the idea that built into our genetic structure are five basic human needs, and that all people on earth today, regardless of their size, shape, color, or anything else, have exactly the same genetic structure. We are all one race. (Wubbolding, 2000, p. 61)

From a multicultural perspective, Glasser's comment captures only one of two important realities. Although he emphasizes the culturally universal, he completely neglects the culturally specific (D. W. Sue & D. Sue, 2008). In his writings he doesn't address the potential genetic differences and non-shared environmental experiences common to ethnically diverse populations.

In contrast, Wubbolding and others (Wubbolding, Brickell, Imhof, Kim, Lojk, & Al-Rashidi, 2004) have written with more balance and sophistication about the application of choice theory and reality therapy to non-Western individuals and groups. His books devote sections or chapters to multicultural and international applications of choice theory. As an example of his pioneering efforts to apply reality therapy to Japanese individuals, he notes: "There is no exact Japanese translation for the word 'plan,' just as there is no exact word for 'accountability'" (2000, p. 181).

Wubbolding's message is that reality therapists must respect specific language and cultural differences when applying choice theory to individuals from different cultures. He emphasizes that asking questions like "What do you want?" or "Would that help?" may be too direct and possibly difficult for Asian clients to interpret. Instead, he suggests modifications such as "What are you looking for?" and "Would that be a minus or a plus?" Asian students with whom we have worked concur with Wubbolding's ideas for modifying choice theory for Asian clients.

From a feminist perspective choice theory and reality therapy have potential for empowerment, but also do not address important social power dynamics. Specifically, Ballou (1984) criticized the fact that reality therapists hold individual women completely responsible for their behaviors when there are external forces, both historical and contemporary, that limit women's rights and power. More than 20 years later, Linnenberg (2006) reviewed Ballou's concerns and found they had, for the most part, not been addressed. Perhaps in the next 20 years reality therapists will begin to more systematically and effectively incorporate social issues and feminist perspectives into their practice.

EVIDENCE-BASED STATUS

Overall, given the relatively high frequency with which choice theory and reality therapy is and has been practiced in schools and in counseling settings, very few well-controlled efficacy or effectiveness studies have been conducted. This may be due to four reasons:

1. Existential therapists have historically discounted the validity of the scientific research paradigm and traditional outcomes research.

2. Reality therapy has been extensively and pragmatically applied within school settings. This

particular setting is often burdened and under-funded which may have contributed to a mini-malist research agenda.

3. Certification in reality therapy does not include research training.
4. Large-scale grant funding typically goes toward cognitive-behavioral research and not reality therapy research.

The paucity of empirical research also may be related to Glasser's attitude toward outcomes. For example, when asked about evidence-based treatment, he stated:

> Well, I have a lot of evidence about what I do, it's in my books, it's in other books.... There's a group of references that will support what I am saying. And therefore when you use choice theory, you have tremendous evidence. But the biggest evidence of all is that it works. The people will say to you, "My goodness gracious, I'm much happier than I was, and I owe it to you because I've changed the way I'm living my life." (Onedera & Greenwalt, 2007, p. 83)

Consistent with the existential tradition, Glasser's response focuses on anecdotal and experiential evidence. Unfortunately, the evidence he's talking about is not viewed as "tremendous" within the dominant scientific efficacy or effectiveness paradigms.

In contrast to Glasser, other reality therapy proponents acknowledge the need for more scientific evidence to support reality therapy's efficacy (Wubbolding, 2011). Specifically, Wubbolding noted that although substantial anecdotal and less-controlled research evidence exists, future research should include studies that are (a) more tightly controlled, (b) longitudinal, and (c) conducted by objective evaluators. Similarly, Burdenski (2010) noted that reality therapy's less prominent position within academic counseling and psychology may be related to a lack of empirical research.

Highlights of the existing scientific research include:

- In a comparison study of a 12-week choice theory-based (CT) group intervention ($n = 93$) versus a 12-week motivational interviewing (MI) group intervention ($n = 98$) for college students with an alcohol-related violation, no differences were found between the CT and MI approaches on the Daily Drinking Questionnaire and self-reported negative alcohol-related incidents (B. Smith, Kenney, Sessoms, & Labrie, 2011). This was viewed as a positive outcome for the choice theory intervention because CT was shown to be as effective as MI, an empirically supported treatment (EST).

- A meta-analysis of 43 studies conducted in Korea showed that students within educational institutions receiving reality therapy interventions scored higher on self-esteem and locus of control outcome measures than students in control or comparison groups (Kim & Hwang, 2001).

- Reality therapy, cognitive coping training and their combination were more effective in helping empty nester Nigerian retirees with their adjustment than participants in a control group (Chima & Nnodum, 2008).

- A 15-week reality therapy based group guidance program for underachieving Taiwanese elementary students learning Mandarin produced improved learning attitudes, motivation, learning strategies, and grades (Liu et al., 2010).

- A dissertation report of a randomized controlled trial with domestic violence perpetrators showed that 15 reality group therapy participants had more significant positive changes on the Stets Control Scale than 15 cognitive-behavioral therapy (CBT) group participants after a 12-week intervention (Gilliam, 2004).

- Kim (2007) reported positive outcomes for reality therapy in treating Internet addiction.

- In a study of a reality therapy–based group therapy for chronic pain management, 22 veterans reported increased coping skills, greater need satisfaction, and overall satisfaction with the treatment (Sherman, 2000).

Going forward, the good news about reality therapy and research is that reality therapy is a short-term, directive form of therapy that would be relatively easy to evaluate. Additionally, the William Glasser Institute has made a renewed commitment to scientific research (Burdenski et al., 2009; Glasser, 2010).

CONCLUDING COMMENTS

The mission of the William Glasser Institute is to teach all people Choice Theory® and to use it as the basis for training in reality therapy, lead management, and Glasser Quality School education (http://www.wglasser.com/index.php?option=com _content&task=view&id=12&Itemid=64). The institute has existed for more than 44 years and there are now approximately 8,000 certified reality therapists worldwide and over 75,000 who have obtained substantial advanced reality therapy training.

William Glasser turned 86 while we were writing this chapter. For the most part he has passed on the choice theory and reality therapy torch. Wubbolding is the director of the Center for Reality Therapy. There are also many young professionals and academics who have embraced the mission of teaching choice theory to the world.

Although currently suffering from health problems, Glasser remains unabashedly enthusiastic about the value of his work. In support of his efforts, we end this chapter with a Glasser quotation that reflects both his idealism and his ambition:

> It is my vision to teach choice theory to the world.
> I invite you to join me in this effort.
>
> —William Glasser, *Unhappy Teenagers* (2002, p. 190)

CHAPTER SUMMARY

Choice theory and reality therapy is the brainchild of William Glasser (1965). Initially conceived in the 1960s it has attracted a significant following and is commonly employed as a model for individual counseling and for working for youth in the schools. As a model it has strong existential and Adlerian components, but due to its focus on actions (behavior) and thoughts (cognition), it's frequently mis-categorized as a cognitive-behavioral approach.

Choice theory posits that humans have five basic needs. These needs include (1) survival; (2) love and belonging; (3) power or recognition; (4) freedom; and (5) fun. All humans seek to have these needs met and if one or more are not met, then there may be efforts to meet them by overemphasizing one need over the others. All humans also have an internal quality world or inner world of wants. The quality world, developed and established during childhood, consists of pictures of people, things or activities, and ideas or systems of belief that we deeply value. Humans then use their total behaviors to meet their basic human needs and to pursue the pictures that exist in their quality worlds.

Glasser's position is that mental illness does not exist. This is a controversial position and not held by all reality therapy practitioners. He also believes that much of human psychopathology stems from unhappy relationships and most unhappy relationships develop because one or more people in the relationships are trying to control others. Glasser also believes that individuals display "psychopathology" in order to restrain their anger, get help, or avoid things.

Reality therapy does not rely on formal assessment procedures, but individual practitioners may integrate such procedures into their practice as they see fit. More often, individuals are evaluated through an interview process focusing on how well they're functioning in the world using choice theory. The therapy process is characterized by building the relationship, asking direct questions that focus on the four questions of choice theory, and planning for success. The four choice theory questions as developed by Robert Wubbolding include: (1) What do you want? (2) What are you doing? (3) Is it working? (4) Should you make a new plan? Once there is clarity around these four questions, then much of therapy involves planning for how clients can successfully meet their needs.

Glasser is a cultural universalist and not especially sensitive to gender and culture issues. In contrast, other choice theory and reality therapy advocates such as Wubbolding, have sought to modify reality therapy to make it more culturally sensitive.

Although some research supports choice theory concepts and reality therapy practice, there's very little systematic research on reality therapy efficacy. Future research needs to focus on more tightly controlled studies conducted by unbiased researchers and that focus specifically on treatment or educational outcomes.

CHOICE THEORY/REALITY THERAPY KEY TERMS

Acting

Avoiding things

External control psychology

Feeling

Five basic human needs

Freedom (or independence)

Fun (or enjoyment)

Getting help

Ideas and beliefs

Love and belonging

People

Physiology

Power or achievement

Restraining anger

SAMIC^3

Seven caring habits

Seven deadly habits

Survival

Ten axioms of choice theory

Things or experiences

Thinking

Total behavior

WDEP

Your quality world

RECOMMENDED READINGS AND RESOURCES

The following resources provide more information about choice theory and reality therapy.

CHOICE THEORY AND REALITY THERAPY JOURNAL

International Journal of Choice Theory and Reality Therapy

READINGS ON CHOICE THEORY AND REALITY THERAPY

Burdenski, T. K. (2010). What does the future hold for choice theory and reality therapy from a newcomer's perspective? *International Journal of Choice Theory and Reality Therapy, 29*(2), 13–16.

Glasser, W. (1965). *Reality therapy: A new approach to psychiatry*. New York, NY: Harper & Row.

Glasser, W. (1998). *Choice theory: A new psychology of personal freedom*. New York, NY: HarperCollins.

Glasser, W. (2000). *Reality therapy in action*. New York, NY: HarperCollins.

Glasser, W. (2002). *Unhappy teenagers: A way for parents and teachers to reach them*. New York, NY: HarperCollins.

Glasser, W. (2003). *Warning: Psychiatry can be hazardous to your health*. New York, NY: HarperCollins.

Robey, P. A. (2011). *Reality therapy and choice theory: An interview with Robert Wubbolding*. Family Journal, 19(2), 231–237.

Wubbolding, R. E. (2011). *Reality therapy*. Washington, DC: American Psychological Association.

Wubbolding, R. E., Brickell, J., Imhof, L., Kim, R. I., Lojk, L., & Al-Rashidi, B. (2004). Reality therapy: A global perspective. *International Journal for the Advancement of Counseling*, 26(3), 219–228.

TRAINING ORGANIZATIONS AND WEBSITES

The William Glasser Institute (www.wglasser.com)

Center for Reality Therapy (www.realitytherapywub.com)

VIDEOS/DVDs

Carlson, J., & Kjos, D. (2000). *Reality therapy with Dr. Robert Wubbolding* [Video]. Boston, MA: Allyn & Bacon.

Hamann, E. (2010). *Three Approaches to Counseling One Client: Solution Focused, Reality Therapy, and Cognitive-Behavioral*. North Amherst, MA: Microtraining Associates.

Wubbolding, R. (2007). *Reality therapy* [DVD]. Washington, DC: American Psychological Association.

GOING FARTHER AND DEEPER

Additional choice theory and reality therapy counseling and psychotherapy resources are available at johnsommersflanagan.com.

CHAPTER 10

Feminist Theory and Therapy

With MARYL J. BALDRIDGE

THIS CHAPTER

- Reviews the key figures and historical factors contributing to the development and evolution of feminist theory and therapy
- Outlines and describes feminist theoretical principles
- Describes and discusses principles and strategies associated with feminist therapy practice, including
  - Assessment issues and procedures
  - Therapy relationships
  - Therapist self-disclosure
  - Therapy focus and strategies
- Provides short vignettes to demonstrate feminist therapy principles in action
- Illustrates how treatment planning, outcomes assessment, and gender and cultural issues can be integrated into a feminist therapy approach
- Reviews the empirical status of feminist therapy
- Offers resources for further study

Feminist ideas are inherently radical and push boundaries and realities of what most of us are taught via the dominant social and cultural media. This is why consciousness raising—raising awareness of social and cultural influences on how we think of femaleness and maleness—is so central to the feminist perspective. With this in mind, read the following comment by Kaschak (1992) and see what feelings and insights it might create in you:

> For years, psychiatric journals have touted the salutary effects of antidepressants by printing "before" and "after" pictures showing a woman leaning on a mop looking despondently at her kitchen floor, and then happily mopping it after taking her medication. (p. 22)

As you process your reactions to the image of a medicated woman feeling happy mopping her floor, we offer another gender-expectation-busting story.

At a recent American School Counselor Association National Conference in Seattle (2011), Georgie Bright Kunkel, a 90-year-old woman, delivered a keynote address. She bounded onto the stage—not looking a day over 80. She introduced herself as the oldest stand-up comic in Washington state (Was there an older stand-up comic somewhere else on the planet?). She proceeded to crack jokes about everything from sex to . . . well . . . sex, and then sex again. In the middle of her routine, she slipped in a serious story that went something like this:

> I was working as a school counselor at an elementary school. To kick off our career day, I contacted a woman friend of mine who was an airplane pilot. She agreed to land her one-person

plane in the middle of our schoolyard. We were all very excited. We gathered the students outside and watched as she guided the plane down, smoothly landing on the playground. The students crowded around as she emerged from the tiny plane, helmet in hand. When it became apparent she was a woman, a male student turned to me and asked, "Where's the pilot?" It was clearly a one-person plane, but in this boy's mind, *men were pilots and women were stewardesses*. This was a sad truth for many of our students. But what interested me more was the impact of this event on our students' career ambitions. We had decided to take a student survey before and after career day. Before my friend landed on our playground, exactly 0% of our female elementary students listed "airplane pilot" as one of their potential career choices. After career day, about 40% of the girls listed airline pilot as a career to consider in the future.

This is an example of a feminist working therapeutically to raise awareness and bring about development, change, options, and liberation. Feminist therapy can be transformative. It was designed, in part, to break down unhelpful stereotypes and free all humans to fulfill their potentials.

> **QUESTIONS FOR REFLECTION**
>
> At this early point in the chapter you should try calling yourself a feminist therapist. Say aloud, "I'm a feminist therapist." Notice how that feels. What are your gut reactions? What are your intellectual musings? Can you embrace that label? Can you let it embrace you? If not, what gets in the way?

Similar to existential approaches, but in contrast to many others, feminist therapy is informed by a strong connection to a particular set of philosophies or beliefs. It wasn't developed by a single person, it doesn't have neat boundaries, it can't be easily described, and there are many ways to put it into practice. Feminist therapy, like feminist theory, reflects the work of women and men involved in grass-roots movements, and ideas and concerns formulated from the ground up. It's eclectic and inclusive. If you're interested in working with

people who struggle with real problems and you believe social forces, society, politics, hierarchies, and other paternalistic cultural factors contribute heavily to those problems, then you should consider pursuing training in feminist therapy.

The uniting perspective of everyone interested in feminist therapy (including male feminists) is an acknowledgment that sexism, racism, classism, and patriarchy are direct contributors to the problems and suffering in the world. Those engaged as feminist therapists take active steps toward addressing these influences. Without acknowledging and addressing sexism and patriarchy, therapists will contribute to their clients' oppression and be complicit in pathologizing natural reactions to abuse, denial of freedom, and denial of human rights. Remembering this common thread will be useful as you read this chapter.

Understanding feminist perspectives as a philosophy that explores attitudes about gender and oppression rather than thinking of it as exclusively applying to women will help you understand its relevance to all clients. There are a number of steps to take in the development of a feminist counseling and psychotherapy practice; it requires personal introspection and self-knowledge, as well as sociological awareness and education about the impact of sexism and patriarchy on society and individuals.

HISTORICAL CONTEXT

Feminist theory and therapy has been and continues to be influenced by social activists outside the counseling and psychotherapy disciplines. Consequently, we begin our journey by examining recent evolutionary movements in feminist thought within the United States.

Influences Outside Counseling and Psychotherapy: Three Feminist Waves

Themes of feminist thought have emerged, receded, reemerged and developed further throughout history. For example, Plato (c. 440 b.c.) included consideration of women for leadership positions within the ruling elite. John Stuart Mill, influenced in part by his friendship and marriage to feminist Harriett Taylor, wrote essays decrying the oppression of women, pointing out great costs to society that resulted from this oppression. Historically, women's rights and freedoms have ebbed and flowed in a manner suggesting that only great leaps in global social and gender consciousness could solidify current gains and make future progress possible.

To understand how feminism applies to modern counseling and psychotherapy, it's useful to have an awareness of feminist history in the United States. This is a topic worth volumes; we hope this limited synopsis will help you understand how feminism evolved over time and glimpse how it has influenced counseling and psychotherapy today.

Recent feminist history is typically organized into three movements. These movements are referred to as different "waves" of feminism, a descriptor that highlights the influence each time period had on the next, and the continuous nature of feminism's evolution.

First Wave Feminism

First wave feminism refers to the feminist and liberation-oriented activities occurring around and before the women's suffrage movement. Some of the roots extended into the anti-slavery movement, before the focus shifted to equal rights for women. During this time, feminists lobbied for all women's rights to vote, own property, and be acknowledged as citizens. Sometimes students ask us about the relevance and contribution of feminism in their lives. Usually we respond with something like, "If you're female and you can vote and own property or you're a male who thinks females should be able to vote and own property, then you owe at least a small debt to feminism."

Contemporary feminists honor the first wave feminism period and its leaders, while also acknowledging its inherent limits. For instance, stories of racial minorities who were also working hard for change are rarely acknowledged when discussing the suffrage movement. As feminist consciousness continues to expand, efforts are being made to develop more inclusive historical representations of early feminism (Collins, 2009).

Second Wave Feminism

Second wave feminism describes the feminist movement during the mid-1900s (Collins, 2009). This wave is characterized by the Women's Liberation movement, the formation of NOW (National Organization of Women), and shifting toward a focus on women's political and personal experiences. During this time, feminists worked toward changes in their relationships, health care, and career opportunities. Many people think of second wave activists when they hear the word, "feminism," as this was when feminist activists were highlighted (and often demonized) in the media (Collins, 2009). This movement significantly addressed policy and attitudes about women and gender in political, relational, and professional realms. This wave also initiated feminist explorations of masculinity and the oppression of men under patriarchy.

Although minority women's voices are included in some historical references to second wave feminism, and many women of color contributed significantly, the movement is retrospectively seen as predominantly white. For example, when "Women's Lib" advocated for a woman's right to work, the fact that many poor women and women of color had no choice and had to work low-wage jobs was largely ignored. At that time the women who were fighting for the right to work were generally wealthy enough to have the option of working or not working (although it was difficult for women to work in positions of power equal to men). Second wave feminism was also associated with a "women versus men" mentality. In retrospect, this mentality is viewed as part of a developmental process of differentiation and self-definition.

Third Wave Feminism

Contemporary or **third wave feminism** is an explicitly more expansive and inclusive feminism (Espín, 1993). In contrast to second wave feminism, contemporary feminism has expanded further into areas beyond women's issues. There's a broad focus on how sexism and patriarchy impact all members of society (Barrett et al., 2005; Espín, 1997; Kawahara & Espín, 2007; Yakushko & Espín, 2010). The concept of women versus men—the battle of the sexes—popular back in the 1970s and early 1980s is viewed as too simplistic. Third wave feminism brings women and men together to work against social injustice. Contemporary analyses of power and gender look well beyond sex-defined boundaries. Third wave feminism challenges underlying systems of oppression—the fight is against all systems that oppress and limit societal members regardless of where they fall along the gender continuum (Enns, 2004).

Although second and third wave feminists address many of the same issues, there are a number of contrasts in terms of how these issues are addressed. For example, second wave feminism challenged the meaning of and limits associated with being a woman (Collins, 2009). Women were encouraged to move beyond their traditional employment options and into traditionally male dominated vocations (e.g., firefighting, police work, medicine, welding). This chapter's opening story of the woman airplane pilot is a good example of second wave feminism.

Similar to the second wave, third wave feminism has an agenda that honors all occupations and roles as legitimate and valuable, and takes these concepts further. The mothers' movement is one of many examples of this shift (Bridson, 2010). Another distinction is that in the past, great emphasis was placed on minimizing differences between men and women (Collins, 2009). This was ostensibly because all qualities associated with being female were devalued and subject to discrimination. Now, feminism focuses on respecting and celebrating potential differences between men and women, while at the same time highlighting the fluidity of gender and the individual experiences of each person's gender definition. In this respect, wearing make-up or spike heels are considered women's (and men's) choices—as long as those choices are accompanied by awareness and empowerment of alternative choices. The film *Erin Brockovich* as a third wave manifesto, demonstrated how "showing cleavage" could be symbolized not only as a women's right, but also as a means of employing female attributes, including sexual attributes, as a source of power.

Feminism Continues to Evolve

As with all social justice movements and cultural revolutions, feminism has gained ground, lost ground, and regained it. Whether considered first, second, third, or even fourth wave, at the core feminism is about liberation. bell hooks (2000) articulates this in the following statement:

> All of us, female and male, have been socialized from birth on to accept sexist thought and action. As a consequence, females can be just as sexist as men. And while that does not excuse or justify male domination, it does mean that it would be naïve and wrongminded for feminist thinkers to see the movement as simplistically being for women against men. To end patriarchy (another way of naming the institutionalized sexism), we need to be clear that we are all participants in perpetuating sexism until we change our minds and hearts, until we let go of sexist thought and action and replace it with feminist thought and action. (pp. viii–xi)

Key Figures and Factors in the History of Feminist Theory and Therapy

Despite many obstacles women faced in the early 1900s, there were many original feminist thinkers within psychotherapy and counseling. Two of the most prominent were Raissa Epstein Adler (see Chapter 3) and Karen Horney (see Chapter 2).

Raissa Epstein Adler was a radical socialist and intellectual from a wealthy Jewish family in Russia. She moved from Russia to study zoology, biology, and microscopy in Zurich because, at the time, women weren't allowed to attend Russian universities. While in Vienna she met and married Alfred Adler in 1987. Although she was primarily involved in raising the couple's four children (two of whom, Alexandra and Kurt, became psychiatrists), Raissa was also deeply involved in the development of Alfred Adler's theory of Individual Psychology. Raissa took minutes at meetings of the Society for Free Psychoanalytic Research and undoubtedly influenced Alfred's views on women (R. Adler, 1982). Alfred Adler's public comments on sexual equality remain radical today.

Karen Horney

As we've seen from previous chapters, Karen Horney was a powerfully influential woman within psychology and psychoanalysis. She analyzed at least two very influential historical figures within psychotherapy (i.e., Fritz Perls, Chapter 6 and Albert Ellis, Chapter 8). Her work on tyranny of the shoulds is often viewed as an intellectual predecessor of REBT and cognitive therapy. She was persistent and sometimes provocative. She provided a strong "push back" to traditional Freudian psychoanalytic theory. Her views on womb envy and other feminist psychological phenomena are featured in Chapter 2.

From the early twentieth century forward, in psychiatry, as in many fields, women slowly, against great odds, began joining the ranks of educated male professionals. The inclusion of women in doctoral programs was initially and vehemently resisted. One can imagine that the "Old Boys in Academia Club" might have choked a bit when reading Horney's 1922 paper addressing the genesis of the castration complex in women. She wrote:

> In this formulation we have assumed as an axiomatic fact that females feel at a disadvantage because of their genital organs, without this being regarded as constituting a problem in itself—possibly because to masculine narcissism this has seemed too self-evident to need explanation. Nevertheless, the conclusion so far drawn from the investigations—amounting as it does to an assertion that one half of the human race is discontented with the sex assigned to it and can overcome this discontent only in favorable circumstance—is decidedly unsatisfying, not only to feminine narcissism but also to biological science. (Horney, 1967, p. 38)

Three Groundbreaking Feminist Publications

Many different publications contributed to dynamic feminist changes within psychology and counseling beginning in the 1970s. In this section we describe three particularly groundbreaking publications identified by Brown (2010).

Phyllis Chesler was a psychological researcher turned critic of the patriarchic mental health system. Following the 1969 meeting of the American Psychological Association where she was exposed to a feminist protest, she decided to use her skills to support the movement (Chesler, 1995). Her work articulated the following points:

- Psychotherapy for women replicated conditions associated with a society that was sexist and oppressive toward women.

- Women were labeled as disturbed simply because they did not want to engage in full-time parenting or wanted to venture into the working world.

- Many women were sexually violated during psychotherapy.

According to Brown (2010), **Women and Madness: Exposing Patriarchy in the Consulting Room** (Chesler, 1972) remains relevant today.

Naomi Weisstein was studying comparative and physiological psychology at Harvard University in the 1960s. As a woman, she had substantial obstacles; she wasn't allowed access to laboratory facilities or the library. In 1968, Weisstein published a highly controversial article, **Kinder, Kuche, Kirche as Scientific Law:** Misogyny in the Science of Psychology. The article was subsequently included in a feminist anthology, Sisterhood Is Powerful (Morgan, 1970). Weisstein's article was especially provocative and indicting because she used the German words Kinder (children), Kuche (kitchen), and Kirche (church), which harkened to the role of women as originally articulated by Kaiser Wilhelm II and later endorsed by the Nazi Third Reich. In her article, Weisstein described ways in which broad generalizations about women were articulated by experimental psychologists—even when women were rarely included in the research studies. Brown's (2010) description of Weisstein's argument (and reflection back to Karen Horney) illustrates this point:

> Weisstein—perhaps echoing Karen Horney's (1967) earlier observation that the concept of penis envy might simply reflect the egocentric musings

of a now-grown male child who was himself so attached to his penis that he could not imagine how those not possessing one would not envy him—critiqued then-pervasive psychoanalytic formulations of women as being less morally capable, more dependent, and less fully adult than men. She pointed out the complete absence of empirical, research-based support for these assertions upon which most of psychotherapy with women was founded. While today such assertions about women might seem outrageous, rereading Weisstein reminds us that in 1968 and for many years afterward, they were the conventional wisdom about women ascribed to by almost all practicing psychotherapists. (pp. 15–16)

This quotation deserves a brief commentary: When she refers to "almost all practicing psychotherapists" Brown isn't referring to Carl Rogers whose approach to psychotherapy focused on valuing all persons (yes, even women). Also, although "such assertions about women" might be seen as "outrageous" today, anyone capable of conducting a brief Internet search can uncover many examples of individuals and groups that continue to not only denigrate women, but to strongly express their view of women as clearly inferior to men.

A third groundbreaking publication hit the presses in 1970. Broverman, Clarkson, Rosencrantz, and Vogel (1970) published results from a study focusing on professional psychologists judgments of healthy males, females, and adults. Not surprisingly, it turned out that healthy males and healthy adults were essentially identical. What stood out was the finding that:

> The mentally healthy adult woman was not, in fact, an adult; in the eyes of the typical psychotherapist of the time, she was a lesser being whose attributes were less socially desirable. (Brown, 2010, p. 17)

In many ways the psychotherapists of the time were simply reflecting the social climate (Collins, 2009). Women were devalued. Women were considered inferior—even childlike in their ability to reason. But the psychotherapists should have known better, because after all, they were

scientists; they were objective. Well, as it turned out, they were scientists—but they weren't objective. And to steal (and paraphrase) a line from the film *Network* (1976), the women of psychology were mad as Hell and weren't going to take it anymore.

Consciousness–Raising Groups and Recent Developments

Women and madness (1972), Kinder Kuche, Kirche as scientific law (1968), and sex-role stereotypes and clinical judgment of mental health professionals (1970) came from and contributed to a bubbling grassroots feminist phenomenon in the United States in the late 1960s and early 1970s. The phenomenon was labeled as the feminist **consciousness-raising groups**. These were loosely structured and non-hierarchical meetings sweeping through the United States and catalyzing the women's movement within and outside psychology. Worell and Remer (2003) described how these groups promoted psychological awareness:

> In response to their growing awareness of personal dissatisfaction and unexplained malaise, groups of women began to congregate to discuss their life situations. In sharing experiences of restricted and stereotyped expectations for how they should conduct their lives, they discovered that their problems were voiced and mirrored by others. (p. 6)

These feminist consciousness-raising groups illustrated a two-sided principle associated with positive psychological development in general and women's positive psychological development in particular.

- Isolating women enables oppression, but . . .
- Connecting women with each other facilitates awareness, motivation, and change.

More recent contributors to feminist thinking have pursued this and other core principles. For example, Jean Baker Miller (1976), Judith Jordan (1997, 2010), and other therapists/scholars were instrumental in developing **relational-cultural therapy** (RCT). RCT is a contemporary feminist-informed therapy approach currently gaining in popularity. Jordan (2010) described the distinctly feminist conceptual principles of RCT:

> The practice of RCT is based on a new model of human development that places connection at the center of growth. The fundamental principles of RCT, as it emerged over the years, posit that we grow in relationship throughout our lives. RCT sees the ideal of psychological separation as illusory and defeating because the human condition is one of inevitable interdependence throughout the lifespan. (p. 3)

Interestingly, as observations of women's consciousness-raising groups illustrated years earlier, RCT contends that psychological connection for women (and men) has developmentally stimulating and growth producing effects (Gilligan, 2003; Jordan, 2010). Additionally, the migration in thinking from second wave to third wave feminism is visible. No longer are women required to compete with men to fit men's theories of healthy development. Instead, women's ways of being are valued in their own right and used to describe human health and well-being.

We should also note that Laura S. Brown is another historical and contemporary leader within the feminist therapy literature. We've used several of Brown's popular feminist works as a guide in writing this chapter. Some of her books include *Diversity and Complexity in Feminist Therapy* (Brown & Ballou, 1990), *Subversive Dialogues* (1994), *Rethinking Mental Health and Disorder* (Ballou & Brown, 2002), and *Feminist Therapy* (Brown, 2010).

Working Definitions

For the purposes of clarification, we offer several working definitions of concepts central to feminist theory. These definitions are evolving, even as feminism is evolving.

Feminism

The essence of feminist theory involves a belief in human equality and an understanding that an essential step in creating this equality is to shift existing paradigms about gender, sexuality, power,

and patriarchy. Funderburk and Fukuyama (2001) define **feminism** as:

> The belief that human beings are of equal worth and that the pervading patriarchal social structures which perpetuate a hierarchy of dominance, based upon gender, must be resisted and transformed toward a more equitable system. (p. 4)

Of course, feminism has never been easy to define. We should consider the famous quote by Rebecca West who lived from 1892 to 1983.

> I myself have never been able to find out precisely what feminism is: I only know that people call me a feminist whenever I express sentiments that differentiate me from a doormat.

Subversive

In *Subversive Dialogues* (1994), Brown framed feminist therapy as a subversive partnership. She succinctly describes and defines subversion in her most recent book:

> Subversion is a concept that broadly represents the psychotherapeutic strategies by which therapist and client, working together collaboratively, use the tools of psychotherapy to undermine the internalized and external patriarchal realities that serve as a source of distress and as a brake on growth and personal power for all humans. (Brown, 2010, p. 4)

It's important to note that Brown isn't really suggesting that psychotherapy *could* be **subversive**, she's contending that it *should* be subversive. If you think about it, subversive feminist psychotherapy constitutes a significantly transformative leap from oppressive psychotherapy as written about by Chesler in 1972.

Patriarchy

In the preceding (and following) pages we frequently use the word patriarchy. It can be easy to look at that word and assume it represents anger towards men or specific criticism of men's leadership styles. To clarify, criticizing patriarchy isn't necessarily male-focused. Many women participate heartily in the dominant hierarchical patriarchy, and have the ability (and sometimes desire) to oppress, discriminate, and hold others back. Third wave feminism emphasizes that this isn't about blaming men. Instead, it's about working through gender, racial, cultural, spiritual, and other partnerships to develop awareness and solutions.

With that in mind, here's Brown's (2010) definition of **patriarchy**:

> Patriarchies are the near-universal hierarchical social systems in which attributes associated with maleness are privileged and those attributed to women are denigrated . . . no matter the sex of the individual in whom these qualities are found. Patriarchical systems are identified by feminist therapy and theory as the primary sources of human distress, including those kinds of distress that are organized into diagnostic categories and labeled psychopathology by the mental health disciplines. The actual distress or dysfunction about which an individual initiates therapy is thus seen not as pathological per se, no matter how much it impairs a person's functioning, but most likely a response to being immersed in toxic patriarchal realities. Such toxic social hierarchies of value are construed inherently inimical to personal power and healthy function for all people, even those apparently privileged by patriarchal norms of dominance and hierarchy. (Brown, 2010, p. 5)

QUESTIONS FOR REFLECTION

What cultural forces and practices do you think are psychologically damaging to women? In contrast, what cultural forces and practices do you think are psychologically damaging to men? Is it fair to suggest that patriarchal systems are to blame for this damage to women and men?

Feminist theory and therapy inherently critique the damaging dominant patriarchy and the pathological use of power over others. Since the 1960s, feminist mental health theorists, researchers, and therapists have exercised increasing influence in counseling and psychotherapy (Enns, 2004).

Feminist theories in general and feminist theories of mental health in particular have sought to identify and address cultural forces and practices that are sexist and psychologically damaging.

THEORETICAL PRINCIPLES

Feminist theory is at once complex and simple, innocent and insidious, common sense and deeply profound. What can be more obvious (at least to the Western European mind) than the notion that every baby born deserves to pursue her or his calling to the fullest, with no obstacles arbitrarily put in place due to sex, race, or culture? Who disagrees with this ideal of universal fairness and equal opportunity?

On the other hand, fairness and equal opportunity is deeply disturbing to some individuals and groups. The problem is apparent on many levels. Universal fairness and equal opportunity immediately call into question the status quo. It disrupts the natural (or unnatural) order of things. If your sex should not in any way determine your role in culture or excuse you from culturally identified adult obligations, what are the implications?

- Equal responsibility for serving in the military.

- Equal responsibility for providing income to your family.

- Equal responsibility for nurturing your children.

- Equal opportunity for all employment options.

- Equal opportunity to attend the college of your choice.

- No more enhanced opportunities or limits based on skin color, shape of your body, native language, or ethnic origin.

About 20 years ago, in a psychology of women class at a small, private university, Rita asked the 14 female students, "Do you believe you should have the options of either being a stay-at-home mom with your children or joining the workforce and hiring nannies or using a day care to take care of your children?"

The response was unanimous. These young women were adamant: Yes! The choice to either stay home or enter the workplace should be theirs. Rita then posed a second question: "If you're in a heterosexual partnership or marriage, should your children's father have the same option? Is it totally okay for him to choose to be a stay-at-home dad?"

This time the response was muted and mixed. A few women dared to share that they wouldn't want to marry someone who chose to stay at home with the children and expected her to work. An excellent discussion followed. When we ask this question now, depending on the group, the age of the respondents, etc., the responses are different, but what's clear is that men's and women's rights and choices are inextricably bound together. Allowing men equal freedom to choose to stay home and take care of a baby affects his partner. One respondent recently pointed out, "The bottom line is this: We're in this together and so we'd better start talking and negotiating to develop more functional, mutual, and fair partnerships."

Sex and Gender Powerfully Affect Identity

The first principle of feminist psychological theory is that *both* biologically determined sexual characteristics *and* socially constructed gender-role expectations play a central role in understanding client experiences. As we explore this principle, keep in mind distinctions between the scientific meaning of the words *sex* and *gender*.

- **Sex** refers specifically and exclusively to the biological, physiological, and anatomical characteristics associated with being female or male. (Keeping in mind that intersex conditions or the presence of hermaphrodites within the general populations require that we realize there are more than two dichotomous "sexes.")

- **Gender** refers to the socialized or socially constructed roles, behaviors, activities, and attributes associated with identifying as female or male.

Put another way, female and male refer to sex differences and feminine and masculine refer to gender differences (see Putting it in Practice 10.1 for an activity focusing on sex and gender distinctions). Maleness and femaleness doesn't vary a great deal across cultures, but what is considered feminine or masculine can vary drastically.

Biological Sex

There are a few biological distinctions that classify humans as male or female. These include the sex chromosomes and sex-determining genes, the H-Y antigen, gonads, certain hormones, and internal reproductive organs (Zucker, 2001). The majority of those classified as female are born with clitorises, labia, vaginas, and uteruses and at puberty will develop breasts capable of milk production and begin a menstrual cycle that will last until midlife. The majority of those classified as male will have testicles and penises and at puberty will experience a hormonally driven change in their vocal cords that lowers their voices.

Although well over 90% of human biology is identical for both sexes, there are important physical and hormonal differences. These physical and hormonal differences vary greatly within any group of males or females and a significant number of babies (about 1.0% to 1.5%) are born with less pronounced physical sexual characteristics (Reis, 2009). Given culture's insistence on male and female as dichotomous categories, these individuals often struggle to find their sense of identity—or there is immediate surgery to modify the condition (Cull, 2002; Reis, 2007). Although **intersex conditions** were recently labeled as **disorders of sexual development** (DSD), some authors are advocating for a less pathologizing label, recommending instead that these conditions be referred to as **developmental sex divergences** (Reis, 2007). This language reduces stigma and endorses reality, especially when surgical intervention is inappropriate or unnecessary.

There's also a significant population of people who feel they were born into the wrong body in term of sexual designation. Transgendered populations continue to lack equal rights and acknowledgment in our society, and a large part of their struggle

PUTTING IT IN PRACTICE 10.1

Distinguishing Between Sex and Gender

To help make sex and gender distinctions even clearer try out the following activity.
   After reviewing our examples, make a list of different sexual characteristics associated with females and males:

- Women have uteruses and vaginas—men do not.
- Men have penises and testicles—women do not.

Now try generating some sex differences on your own:

- Women _____—men do not.
- Men _____—women do not.

In terms of gender, there are no hard and fast rules and so caveats are included to note the differences are not universal:

- In the United States, women wear skirts and dresses—men do not.
- In the United States, men can go topless in public—women do not.
- In the United States, men play American football—women do not.
- In some Arabic countries, men drive cars—women do not.
- In some African countries, women tend gardens—men do not.

As you read through the preceding list, you may have noticed yourself disagreeing with some of the statements. There are always exceptions, and gendered behaviors are always evolving. Try your hand at generating your own gender differences list:

- In _____, men _____—women do not.
- In _____, women _____—men do not.

Did you notice yourself focusing on any particular cultures or countries as you made your distinctions? What insights did you have about your own male/female biases . . . or perhaps you have no biases?

stems from two factors: (1) their presence in the population disturbs the neat and tidy normative sexual divisions between male and female and (2) they are pathologized by psychiatry, mental health, and the general public. Although homosexuality was removed from the *Diagnostic and Statistical Manual* (*DSM*, 2000), gender identity disorder continues as a psychiatric diagnosis. Feminists consider pressure to conform to a dichotomous sexual classification system as the primary causal factor in gender identity disorder. In other words, if the culture accepted this condition as a normal human variation, the pathology assigned to the condition would disappear.

Gender

Beyond the few biological differences that theorists identify as sexual differences, humans add many layers to maleness and femaleness. Much of the behavior we classify as male or female is culturally constructed, not biologically determined. As it turns out, at least based on science, women are not from Venus and men are not from Mars—we reside together on planet Earth in a complex set of culturally and biologically diverse bodies, working things out as best we can. And we may not be as different as we think. In a review of 46 meta-analyses, Hyde (2005) reported that females and males are strikingly similar across a wide range of psychological variables.

Gender is a social construction. As such, it's characterized by surprising fluidity and rigidity. In some cultures, it's feminine to be emotionally needy and unstable. In others, it's considered feminine to be stoic, centered, and a source of family stability. Some cultures prefer physically aggressive males. Others value intellectual skills as indicators of maleness. Sometimes gender-related behaviors will shift in a matter of minutes as when an executive transitions from the office, to the car, and to the nightclub. Determining just what's biological and what's socially constructed has been the goal of many research projects, the source of much controversy, and fuel for heated arguments at the dinner table (Unger, 2001). Regardless of exactly where divisions lie, feminist theory rejects the notion that biology is destiny and holds suspect most claims of innate male-female behavioral differences, noting that such differences are often used to exclude, exploit, or devalue individuals on the basis of sex or gender.

Human Development

Human development theorists believe our first self-defining insight is the realization, occurring during infancy, that mommy (or daddy or primary caregiver) is distinct from the self (Mahler, Pine, & Bergman, 1975). The second, identity-delineating insight is an awareness of our biological sex. Researchers believe that by as early as 18 months, many toddlers know their sexual identity and have begun selectively processing information accordingly. This is highly significant in the world of identity formation. Think about it. The first two human developmental insights are:

1. I am.

2. I am a girl (or boy).

This awareness—and associated drive to fit with one's sexually identified group—opens the door for culture to step in and offer developing boys and girls (and those with developmental sexual divergences) all sorts of potentially useful and harmful guidance. From religious instruction to Saturday morning cartoons, from the lyrics of popular music to parental role modeling, young people generally follow cultural rules for expressing their gender identity (Powlishta, Sen, Serbin, Poulin-Dubois, & Eichstedt, 2001).

No matter what you believe about the relative contributions of biology and environment on human behavior, sexual identity is a defining feature of human identity. Think about how often male and female differences get magnified and broadcast into your homes on television or through the Internet. For the most part, social forces in the United States seem to want the differences between females and males to be large and unequivocal... and sometimes, when comparing individuals to individuals, the differences seem substantial and obvious. However, there are many exceptions to these marked differences between the dichotomous sexes. This is in keeping with what Gilbert and Scher (1999) dubbed the **iron rule**, which states that "for any psychological or cognitive variable studied by psychologists, the differences within each sex are always greater than the differences between the two sexes" (p. 37). Hyde's (2005) meta-analytic review supports the iron rule.

QUESTIONS FOR REFLECTION

The iron rule means that the average differences between males and females on all cognitive measures, including the SAT, ACT, and GRE, are smaller than the average differences within groups of males and within groups of females. Why do you think some people still insist on emphasizing differences despite this scientific fact?

Deviance Comes From Dysfunctional Culture

Much of human suffering and distress comes from inequities suffered by women and others who were not born into the white, male, privileged class in North America and Western Europe. In the dominant cultural setting, patriarchy reigns and male is normative.

Male as Normative

Although male and female babies are born at roughly the same rate throughout the world, most cultures place greater value on male babies and regard maleness as normative (Enns, 2004; Nutt, 2005). But what does "male as normative" mean?

Male as normative means that maleness sets the standard for whatever is considered normal, average, or representative (Kaschak, 1992). Conversely, it means that anything deviating from male can be considered abnormal and inferior (Beauvoir, 1952).

Male as normative also includes an inherent assumption of male is valuable. If you're not male and you regularly experience maleness as more normal and more valuable than your femaleness

then you will likely also regularly experience distress. This distress may or may not be completely conscious . . . just as distress of undervalued minority populations may not always be consciously accessible. If you're male, take a moment to pretend you live in a world that devalues your existence and considers you as less than, as not completely normal, and as not inherently valued. Then, wish yourself a warm welcome to the world of women and minorities—where you can be labeled abnormal or inferior simply because of what you're not.

New Research: Similarities and Differences

Remnants (and more) remain of male as normative in psychology, although significant progress is being made. For example, while working with the renowned moral development theorist, Lawrence Kohlberg, Carol Gilligan began wondering if Kohlberg's stages of moral development were complete, since he had done most of his research using male subjects. Gilligan's (1982; Gilligan & Attanucci, 1988) research led her to hypothesize that an **ethic of caring** for others might constitute a different type of moral reasoning, one more readily displayed by females in our particular culture. For example, someone who makes a moral decision based on relieving someone else's emotional pain might constitute a higher moral reasoning (or at least as high) as people who base their decision on a rational analysis of fairness.

Gilligan's revised perspective on moral development has generated controversy for moral philosophers and feminists alike. What's important about Gilligan's contributions is that she provided an example of what's left out when we don't include multiple perspectives. Having a divergent moral model that includes women's voices creates a more complete model.

Stress researcher and social psychologist Shelly Taylor made a similar contribution when researching the well-known *fight or flight phenomenon* (Taylor et al., 2000). She and her colleagues wrote:

> A little-known fact about the fight-or-flight response is that the preponderance of research exploring its parameters has been conducted on males, especially on male rats. Until recently, the

gender distribution in the human literature was inequitable as well. Prior to 1995, women constituted about 17% of participants in laboratory studies of physiological and neuroendocrine responses to stress. (2000, p. 412)

Reanalysis of existing data and new research revealed significant differences in the ways in which females and males respond to stressful situations. Taylor and colleagues (2000) concluded:

> We propose a theory of female responses to stress characterized by a pattern termed "tend-and-befriend." Specifically, we propose that women's responses to stress are characterized by patterns that involve caring for offspring under stressful circumstances, joining social groups to reduce vulnerability, and contributing to the development of social groupings, especially those involving female networks, for the exchange of resources and responsibilities. We maintain that aspects of these responses, both maternal and affiliative, may have built on the biobehavioral attachment caregiving system that depends, in part, on oxytocin, estrogen, and endogenous opioid mechanisms, among other neuroendocrine underpinnings. (p. 422)

The preponderance of the research suggests that in fact, that male ways of being aren't always normative for females, or even for all males. There are physical and psychological similarities between females and males, but there are also differences. In this case, it would be inappropriate to make the case that a typical male fight-or-flight response is superior to a typical female **tend-and-befriend response**. There is likely an evolutionary benefit to both stress-related behavior patterns (Master et al., 2009; Taylor & Gonzaga, 2007; Taylor & Master, 2011). Sometimes differences are just differences and there's no need to advocate for one sex-related pattern as superior over another (although if they feel threatened by this information, white male rats are highly likely to fight for their position ... or run and hide in little holes in our cupboards). In this case it seems clear: Neither behavior pattern represents psychopathology ... and neither will always be the superior response to threat.

Despite new research and theoretical modifications linked to work of individuals like Gilligan and Taylor, behavior and beliefs outside the psychological laboratory remain strongly oriented toward male as normative. Old ways of thinking are hard to change.

Old Patterns: Can Men Understand Women?

Men sometimes playfully perpetuate male as normative and female as deviant. At a recent public lecture John was presenting with a panel on the "Amazing Brain." Off and on during the panel discussion there were observations and comments about differences between male and female brains. Toward the end of the evening, a man in the back raised his hand and asked: "I don't suppose anyone can ever really answer this, uh, this age-old question, but how can you understand women?" His question was carefully intoned and worded in such a way that it was clear that he wasn't (a) complimenting women because of their sophisticated complexity or (b) speaking about his own shortcomings or inabilities to comprehend women. This comment was an articulation of the age-old belief—perpetuated primarily by men—that women are irrational and therefore are impossible for rational-logical-superior men to understand.

John responded to this man's question by stating:

> I'm not really going there, but I guess I'd say that to understand women you'd actually have to spend time with them, listen to them, and be interested in what they have to say.

We encourage you to watch and listen for additional subtle or direct examples of male as normative in your everyday experiences. Additional examples we've seen or that we've read about in the literature include:

- Males are overrepresented in politics, entertainment, and literature: Spend an evening counting the number of male versus female characters on television shows or in movies. The *Sesame Street* puppets provide a prime example.

- When specific vocations are all or mostly male, the average salary is higher. Welders and custodians are generally paid more than teachers. Go figure. Garbage collectors make more than child-care workers.

- When males have problems, efforts will be made to deny those problems, explain them as failures of the system, or reframe them as hidden strengths. We once had a man at a workshop explain that male suicide rates were 3 to 4 times higher than female suicide rates because "men know how to get the job done."

- When women or minorities have problems it will be interpreted as due to their inherent weakness or defectiveness. High rates of depression and anxiety in women are sometimes explained by their fragile constitution.

- When a women or person from a minority group gains power or recognition, groups of primarily white males will make extreme, inaccurate, and inflammatory statements about that individual's character, mental health, or legitimacy. During early parts of Barack Obama's presidency, he was compared to Hitler and accused of not being an U.S. citizen.

- If an entity has no stereotypically male or female features, it will be referred to as male until proven otherwise. How could Big Bird or Bugs Bunny have been construed as male?

- Traditional masculine adjectives can be used as compliments for males and females (i.e., she or he is so active, dominant, strong!); in contrast, traditional feminine adjectives can't be effectively used for complimenting both sexes and even have less positive valence for females. Try this one out by calling one of your guy friends soft, sensitive, or demure. Also, using these same terms on women isn't necessarily complimentary. As Kaschak (1992) noted, "Women are subject to censure not only for behaving too much like men, but for behaving too much like women" (p. 40).

- Women's activities are referred to as *women's* activities. Male activities are simply activities. Women's work, versus work. Women's ways of knowing, versus ways of knowing.

Cumulatively these examples illustrate the point that maleness has been and still is the primary normative definition of being human. This leads to a core tenet of feminist (and multicultural) therapy: When a culture treats certain members as exemplary, or normal, and other members as different from normal and therefore inferior, it takes a psychological toll (Sparks & Park, 2002). The blame for the problems this toll creates rests with the culture, not in the individual.

Consciousness-Raising Is Part of Healing and Change

Another key feminist principle is that consciousness-raising facilitates healing and growth. To change, clients must recognize the culturally inflicted damage they carry. They must stop blaming themselves for not being heterosexual, white, male, or for being the wrong kind of male, and begin seeing that the primary source of their problems is a patriarchal, and male-dominated culture.

Without consciousness-raising, women and men might continually try to change themselves to survive in patriarchal, sexist environments. Empirical research supports that this "taking of responsibility" will add stress and distress. Denial of sexism in an environment is linked to higher distress (Moradi & DeBlaere, 2010; Moradi & Funderburk, 2006; Rederstorff, 2010).

The Personal Is Political

Fundamental to feminist therapy is the familiar feminist claim that **the personal is political**. This statement underlines how personal problems are intertwined with an individual's social-political cultural setting (Enns, 2004). In other words, personal transformation facilitates social transformation and vice-versa (Funkerburk & Fukuyama, 2001). One measure of success in feminist therapy might be increased social interest and awareness—an optimistic desire to change the world for the better—an outcome with which Adlerians would certainly agree. As stated by Worell and Remer (2003):

Overall, our feminist psychological practice approach seeks a dual outcome: assisting women toward empowerment in their own lives and seeking change in whatever social power structures form the basis of many of their problems. (p. 18)

The personal is political is a concept that relies on consciousness-raising, on recognizing the connection between one's personal misery and the related political practices. This is why consciousness-raising groups discussed previously were so powerful. As women met together and spoke of their experiences and feelings, they began to recognize the political significance of their personal situations. From the personal is political perspective, the goal is change—change in the women, but more importantly, change in the structure and function of the politics (or power arrangements) within their environments.

THE PRACTICE OF FEMINIST THERAPY

Feminist therapy is primarily theory-driven and not necessarily linked to specific techniques or procedures. This is unusual in the current psychotherapy-as-procedure political environment. Although feminist therapists are comfortable using techniques from a broad range of therapy orientations (e.g., Adlerian, person-centered, existential, cognitive-behavioral), the work they do must flow from and be compatible with their underlying feminist philosophy; Enns (2004) described feminism as an "umbrella framework" for psychotherapy practice (p. 8).

Feminist therapy is technically eclectic; feminist therapists use strategies and techniques originating from other theoretical perspectives. However, the underlying goals of feminist therapy are not eclectic. They include:

- Helping clients see the patterns and social forces that have diminished their sense of power and control.

- Encouraging clients to reclaim power, authority, and direction in their lives.

- Allowing clients to experience this shared power in the therapy relationship.

- Honoring and facilitating female ways of being or feminist consciousness, including growth stemming from deep, intimate relationships.

Worell and colleagues (Worell & Chandler, 1996; Worell, Chandler, & Robinson, 1996; Worell & Johnson, 2003) articulated a systematically feminist approach to counseling and psychotherapy. Essential ingredients of their approach include: (a) empowerment; (b) an analysis of power; and (c) evocation of feminist consciousness. We weave Worell's essential feminist therapy ingredients into the following sections.

Informed Consent

Informed consent is more than a written document (see Putting it in Practice 10.2). It's an important part of your interactions with clients. Because they believe the therapy relationship is a partnership, feminist therapists engage in ongoing informed consent. They let clients know why they suggest certain activities, homework, or topic areas. They check in on the therapy relationship frequently to ensure that they respect client questions and wishes. Consider the following exchange:

C: It says in your paperwork that you're a feminist. I didn't know that when I made the appointment.

T: Yes, it's important for us to consider that part of my professional identity. Probably some other parts, too.

C: Well, I don't know if I would have come in if I'd known this.

T: Sounds like you're unsure about working with someone like me who says she's a feminist.

C: Yes, I am. And I only have six visits total with my managed care.

T: Yeah, I can see why this would feel bad. How about this? Let's explore what I mean in my paperwork, and let's explore what brought you in, and if you feel it would be better to work with someone else, I won't turn this session in to your company.

C: Wow, really? I mean, yes. I guess that would be okay. Thanks.

T: What happened inside you when you read that informed consent?

C: Well, I'm not comfortable with gays and I think women need to raise their children at home, and I know it isn't good for animal testing and all, but I like wearing make-up and I respect my husband, at least when he's sober. [Client gets a little emotional.]

T: You know, I can tell you've got a lot on your mind, both from what you filled out and the way you just said that. I want to assure you about a couple things and then hear more about what's troubling you. Would that be okay?

C: Yeah. Sorry. I'm pretty strung out.

T: That's okay. You've made a good choice to get help. I just want you to know that my counseling work is all about you, not all about me. I don't need to change you at all. I just want to help you change in the ways you think are best for you. We don't need to talk about gays. I don't have any hard and fast rules about the ways women should dress or raise kids or anything. I just believe women deserve a fair shake, on their own terms. But I don't push it. I mostly listen and reflect things back to you.

C: But I like men, and I think they deserve our support, working and all. My dad worked himself to death, basically. [Client gets teary again.]

T: So far, I don't think we really disagree in ways that will matter in our work together, but I'm sure open to talking about it some more. And I can see that your dad meant a lot to you. [Therapist makes two statements, giving her client the choice to respond to further concerns about the feminist orientation or to move into some of what is troubling her.]

C: He was my savior. That's why I got together with my husband. They seemed so much alike. Boy, was I wrong. That's why I need help. I need perspective or something. I guess I want to just

get on with talking about it. It's okay what you believe as long as you're not going to push it or judge me. I've got to talk about it, or I'm going to just up and leave him.

T: Okay. Seems really important to let you get some things talked through today. But anytime you feel worried about what I'm thinking, or if you feel like I'm pushing an agenda, will you tell me?

C: Yeah. I think so.

From this interaction, it's possible to see how a feminist therapist might work effectively with clients who may not envision becoming feminists themselves. For most people, feeling empowered and respected is a welcome experience. However, an honest, careful exchange is both necessary and in keeping with ethical practice.

Assessment Issues and Procedures

This section on feminist therapy assessment is longer and more detailed than assessment sections in other chapters. There's irony about this because feminists generally avoid traditional standardized assessment. However, consistent with feminist theory, feminists approach assessment in a therapeutic and constructive manner. In other words, assessment doesn't involve one person judging another person's well-being. Instead, assessment is a mutual exploration of what's happening in the client's intrapsychic world within a cultural context. As a consequence, because mutual assessment and exploration of both the client and the world she lives in is inherently therapeutic, feminist therapists employ fewer specific techniques. Client symptoms are viewed as communications about what's wrong in the client's world and when treated as such and explored in a safe environment, they tend to shrink (Enns, 2004).

Standardized Assessment
Feminist therapists are familiar with standard assessment procedures, but generally avoid using them. This is because assessment and diagnosis place problems within the psyche of individuals—even

PUTTING IT IN PRACTICE 10.2

Aspects of a Feminist Informed Consent

Mental health professionals work from different theoretical perspectives. They have different beliefs about what hurts, limits, or damages people and what it takes to heal or change. My own perspectives will influence the ways I will work with you.

As a feminist, I believe both women and men deserve equal chances for jobs, recreation, and other things that make life meaningful. I believe that gender matters a great deal and can sometimes get in the way of our development. I also believe our culture can make things tough on men or women because of how narrowly we've defined these terms. Often, people find that exploring gender issues makes a big difference in the ways they feel about themselves.

What does this mean in my work with you?

First, it's important for you to know I won't try to change your beliefs. I will respect our differences.

Second, we'll be partners in our work together. You're the expert on you, and I hope I can offer my education and experiences as you work on the issues bringing you to counseling.

Third, as we explore the distress you're feeling in your life, we may talk about social and cultural forces outside of yourself that are increasing your distress. We may also talk about how you've come to believe unhelpful messages given to you by our culture.

Fourth, because therapy is about you and your life, we'll focus on what you can do, what you can think or believe, and how you can act to help you feel better about yourself and your life situation. Sometimes this will involve changing the way you think or other things inside yourself. Other times it will involve changing your life situation or learning to deal with your life situation more assertively.

Fifth, the overarching goal of therapy is to empower you as a person.

when there is ample evidence to suggest the problem is initiated and maintained by deviant social, political, and patriarchal forces.

Feminists avoid labeling nonconforming thoughts and behaviors as deviant. Brown and Ballou (2002) describe the rationale for this:

> The decision to call nonconforming thoughts, values, and actions psychopathology does two things. First, it discounts she or he who is described as such. Second, it blocks our ability to look outside the individual to see forces, dynamics, and structure that influence the development of such thinking, values and actions. (p. xviii)

The goals of feminist therapy include *not* discounting clients and *not* being seduced into thinking that the whole of the problem resides within the entity that entered the office. However, that said, if standardized assessments are used, they're done so collaboratively, sensitively, and the results are interpreted carefully and within the crucible of context; women and persons from other cultures are all too familiar with assessment processes than can marginalize them and inappropriately label them as deviant.

Feminist assessment focuses on individual client distress. Exploring this distress with an eye to the toxic interpersonal, emotional, and spiritual triggers captures an essential element of feminist assessment.

Diagnosis

The *Diagnostic and Statistical Manual of Mental Disorders* (*DSM*) has a checkered history when it comes to sex, gender, and racial sensitivity (Caplan, 1995; Caplan & Cosgrove, 2004). This is one among many reasons feminists eschew the *DSM*. Soon to be in its fifth edition, over the years the *DSM* has included and does include many controversial and gender biased disorders (Ali, Caplan, & Fagnant, 2010; Cosgrove & Riddle, 2004; Kupers, Ross, Frances, & Widiger, 2005). As this textbook was being written, the Association for Women in Psychology posted concerns about *DSM-5* (see AWP: http://www.psychologytoday.com/blog/science-isnt-golden/201107/association-women-in-psychology-addresses-dsm-5-concerns). Although feminist therapists don't refuse to diagnose clients, they do so in an educational and collaborative manner that involves the client directly and interactively.

Power Analysis and Empowerment

The purpose of **power analysis** is to help clients assert or acquire power. As women acquire power, feminist therapists work with them to feel a sense of **empowerment**—as equals in interpersonal, work, and intimate relationships who can speak up for their rights (Worell & Remer, 2003). Brown (2010) describes four *power types* that can be analyzed and understood within feminist therapy. Subsequently, these areas become targets for feminist therapy interventions.

1. **Somatic power.** Somatic power is related to body image and comfort. When individuals are disempowered, it's often manifest through negative body image or feeling dissociated from their bodies. Healthy personal power with regard to the body involves feelings safety and security and acceptance of one's body as it is, rather than preoccupation with unattainable media-based body ideals.

2. **Intrapersonal/intrapsychic power.** When there are power shortages in this dimension, individuals frequently oriented toward other people's thoughts and feelings or are consumed with a focus on past events that cannot change. Many oppressed individuals are so focused on taking care of others that they're out of touch with what they feel and what they want. Healthy intrapersonal/intrapsychic power is linked to self-awareness, clarity of purpose, and attunement with one's emotions.

3. **Interpersonal/social-contextual power.** A power shortage in the interpersonal domain is common among oppressed peoples. Often this situation is associated with feelings of helplessness, hopelessness, or isolation. Individuals might feel invisible or irrelevant. Healthy interpersonal power is characterized by the ability to be assertive. In terms of Bandura's self-efficacy concept, healthy interpersonal power involves confidence in one's ability to help oneself and to make a difference in the world.

4. **Spiritual/existential power.** Power shortages in this domain involve feeling meaninglessness and disconnection. In contrast, healthy spiritual/existential power involves feeling free to embrace culturally preferred spiritual or religious rituals and practices.

Bases of Self-Esteem and Self-Efficacy

Many women continue to evaluate themselves based on the success of their mating and nurturing accomplishments. Although these are important life dimensions, completely basing one's self-esteem on mating and nurturing distracts from the opportunity to focus on one's own individual needs and development. To check for imbalance in these areas consider the impact of answering following questions:

- How desirable or attractive am I to potential sexual partners?

- How much status does my current romantic partner have?

- What do others think of how I look?

- Is my house clean enough?

- Are my offspring getting all the opportunities they expect?

- How many people am I able to nurture or take care of?

The feminist therapy perspective considers it healthy for females and others to balance mating and nurturing activities with activities outside the family. Success outside of family can increase self-esteem, but there may be costs associated with venturing out of stereotypical female behaviors. Jean Baker Miller (1986) wrote,

> Some women have managed to create other roles for themselves to contribute to their self-esteem. But a woman who has done so has violated a dominant system of values that says she is not worthy: indeed, it implies there must be something wrong with her for even wanting alternatives. (p. 45)

It would be nice to believe that things are significantly different since Miller wrote those words, but the clinical experience of many feminist therapists suggests otherwise (Brown, 2010; Wright, 2002).

Gender-Role Comfort, Development, and Satisfaction

Women and men often limited their personal development to conform to traditional definitions of what it means to be male or female. Females have traditionally been encouraged to seek a male and that male is supposed to provide income, identity, and be a stabilizing force for the family. In the traditional scenario, females are cast as helpmates (wives) who support their husband's needs, career, and ambitions. An offensive old Groucho Marx joke captures the status of a traditional wife:

> Behind every successful man is a woman, behind her is his wife.

Examining how clients' feel about their **gender role** is an important part of feminist assessment. Many women and men seek counseling when their storybook marriage or partnership takes a bad turn and it's clear that "happily ever after" isn't happening. The focus on gender-role satisfaction central to feminist-informed therapy can be helpful before, during, or after relationship break-ups. This is true for heterosexual and gay or lesbian relationships. Although the dynamics are unique to different relationship configurations, explicitly negotiating couple and family gender-related roles and expectations is critical.

Within heterosexual relationships women continue to bear a disproportionate burden of household and parenting responsibilities (Askari, Liss, Erchull, Staebell, & Axelson, 2010; Fisher, 2009). This may be a conscious and intentional choice for some couples, but a feminist assessment of gender role comfort is helpful for examining the intentionality of gender roles within romantic relationships.

Important questions within this domain include:

- How do you feel about the sharing of household workloads within your relationship?

- If you have children, are you satisfied with your role in parenting?

- Have you and your partner talked specifically about who makes more money and how you feel about your relative incomes?

- How do you and your partner decide the relative worth or value of what each of you contributes to your relationship and to your household?

In recent years several writers have addressed what has been termed a **male crisis** within the popular media (Hymowitz, 2011; Kimmel, 2010). This crisis is related to an apparent lack of career ambition in young men, partially measured by a significant drop of male enrollments in college. Most recently it's estimated that about 55% to 60% of enrolled college/university students are female. Although males have traditionally been socialized to assume a provider role in relationships and families, fewer men are taking on that role. Based on our own observations of university students seen in a campus-based career counseling clinic, a significant number of distressed females are balancing employment, school, and romantic relationships. These young women are doing the lion's share of household work, attending college, and bringing substantially more income into the relationship. In contrast, at least some of the males seem more interested in getting stoned and playing video games than they are in pursuing academic or vocational goals. Of course, these are trends and there are many exceptions to these general observations.

Females, Males, and Bodies

We considered titling this section "Women and Their Bodies" but a negative body image epidemic has hit young girls so hard that it would be blatantly neglectful to only focus on adult females. Furthermore, boys and men are experiencing greater body dissatisfaction than ever before (Blashill, 2010; Jonason, Krcmar, & Sohn, 2009). Clearly, the U.S. marketing media has pushed images of unattainable bodies onto the general public with such force that there have been dramatically negative consequences.

Honoring the body is an important element of feminist therapy and clients' attitudes toward their bodies is a core assessment domain. Eating disorders, obesity, sexual dysfunctions, self-mutilation, psychosomatic disorders, and other body-related distresses are more common among females than males (Preti et al., 2009; Touchette et al., 2011). Noncombat posttraumatic stress disorder is also more common in females; this disorder has important physical/somatic dimensions. Many females who come to counseling have a history of physical or sexual abuse or rape. They may or may not focus on this trauma, but such experiences are likely to affect their relationship with their bodies. Feminist therapists will often inquire about how clients feel about their bodies.

Feminist therapists are concerned with the physical experiences of all clients and have been centrally involved in the shift in psychology toward acknowledging the negative effects of psychological and physical trauma. About 20 years ago, influential psychiatrist Judith Herman (1992) highlighted the resistance of mainstream society to grapple with these negative outcomes:

> The study of psychological trauma must constantly contend with this tendency to discredit the victim or to render her invisible. Throughout the history of the field, dispute has raged over whether patients with posttraumatic conditions are entitled to care and respect or deserving of contempt, whether they are genuinely suffering or malingering, whether their histories are true or false, and, if false, whether imagined or maliciously fabricated. In spite of a vast literature documenting the phenomena of psychological trauma, debate still centers on the basic question of whether these phenomena are credible and real. (p. 8)

Herman's comments illustrate how important it is for feminist therapists to be alert to victim guilt among traumatized clients. It also notes the therapist's central role in validating clients' trauma experiences. Exploring trauma with clients is always simultaneously an assessment and therapy process.

By focusing on the reality of their clients' physical experiences, feminist therapists have paved the way for mind-body integration approaches to psychological trauma. In addition, some feminist therapists contend that physical and psychological trauma (aka: posttraumatic stress disorder) constitutes one of the most significant and important psychiatric diagnoses for females. There's no question that trauma inflicted on human beings by other human beings takes an enormous toll on individuals and on society. This is an example of why the personal *is* political, and why positive therapy outcomes include social, political, and legal reform.

Therapy Relationships

> A genuine feminist politics always brings us from bondage to freedom, from lovelessness to loving.

Mutual partnership is the foundation of love. A feminist practice is the only movement for social justice in our society which creates the conditions where mutuality can be nurtured. (hooks, 2000, p. 104)

Feminists place great emphasis on therapy relationships as a primary therapeutic factor. This relationship should be **mutually empathic** and **egalitarian**. Rader and Gilbert (2005) describe the components of an egalitarian feminist therapy relationship:

According to Gilbert (1980), an egalitarian relationship was achieved when the therapist: (a) viewed the client as his/her own expert, (b) informed the client of the therapy process and his/her role and rights in that process (e.g., a client's right to "shop around" for a therapist or to understand the potential risks of therapy), (c) used strategies that promoted the client's autonomy and power, (d) encouraged the expression of anger, and (e) modeled appropriate behaviors for the client. (Rader & Gilbert, 2005, p. 427)

Gilbert's (1980) fourth item, "encouraging expression of anger," is worth further examination. Feminist therapy encourages anger expression for at least four reasons:

1. Direct expression of anger has been traditionally discouraged for females in many cultures.

2. Anger is a vehicle for insight or consciousness-raising. Anger helps clients clarify their sense of mistreatment. It also helps them identify counseling goals.

3. Anger may occur within counseling and toward the counselor; feminist counselors welcome this anger and are prepared to explore its potential underlying insights.

4. Anger is an appropriate emotional response to oppression and abuse. To suppress this response is to inhibit clients from experiencing their full range of humanity.

For all these reasons and more, the anger expression is encouraged in the feminist therapist's office. Nurturing anger can facilitate **feminist consciousness**. Feminist consciousness involves becoming aware of balance and equality in roles and relationships.

The feminist therapy relationship is similar to the person-centered therapy (PCT) relationship. There is congruence, unconditional positive regard, and empathy. Although these factors are important, feminist therapy is even more relationship-based than PCT. Jordan (2010), speaking about the feminist-oriented relational-cultural therapy (RCT), contrasts PCT and RCT:

In his later years, Rogers noted that he felt his very being, his presence, was of great importance in the healing process. But even then Rogers did not take the next step RCT takes, which is to locate the healing in the therapeutic relationship itself. RCT might be characterized as "relationship-centered therapy" in contrast with Rogers's client–centered therapy. (Jordan, 2010, p. 16)

Reflecting this relationship focus, feminist therapy tends to be a more explicitly focused on relationship connection and mutuality than any other therapy approach, including person-centered therapy. Further, feminist therapists are more likely to employ self-disclosure as a therapeutic change strategy.

Self–Disclosure

Self-disclosure is used to facilitate therapy in several ways (Jordan, 2010; R. Sommers-Flanagan, 2012). First, therapists self-disclose to model openness and transparency. Second, self-disclosure is used to enhance relationship connection. As therapists and clients come to know one another, trust builds. Third, self-disclosure is used to share experiences and wisdom in a non-hierarchical manner. It's not that the therapist is the only one who has knowledge and life experiences, it's just that to hold back helpful knowledge and experience is anti-therapeutic. The client's knowledge and experience is equally valued. Fourth, self-disclosure can facilitate an egalitarian relationship. Again, the more this type of relationship is established, the more trust develops, and the more open clients can be about their challenging situations and traumatic experiences. Examples of self-disclosure are included in the case vignettes and case analysis.

There are limits on self-disclosure. The therapy office shouldn't become a place where therapists focus too much on their own pain. If you're interested in doing feminist therapy, supervision is a good place for you to learn how to balance your self-disclosure in ways that maximize its usefulness for clients.

Focusing on Sex and Sexuality

Sexuality is a topic where many men and women feel rigid about gender roles and ashamed or confused if they don't fit into the male-female cultural norms. Female sexuality is still less well-understood than male sexuality. In an article titled "Female Sexual Disorders: Psychiatric Aspects," the author stated directly, "Knowledge of female sexuality has consistently lagged behind our knowledge of male sexuality" (Segraves, 2002, p. 420).

Many people don't understand their own bodies well and might be unable to express their sexual needs in their intimate relationships or might fear their needs are abnormal or shameful. The female orgasm has been the subject of many books and much lively debate, from at least Sigmund Freud forward. Part of the women's movement in the 1960s focused on women's reclaiming their bodies, and this continues to be a focus in feminism today, as is analyzing the rigidity of attitudes about sexual orientation and the effect of homophobic attitudes on all people. Celia Kitzinger (2001) writes:

> The classic models of lifespan development, interpersonal attraction, relationship formation and dissolution, parenting, personality, stress and coping, and so on are based on an unacknowledged assumption of heterosexuality just as surely as they are based on sexist assumptions of masculinity and femininity. (p. 275)

In discussing relationships, sexuality, and intimacy, a feminist therapist provides an open and safe space for these topics to be explored at the client's pace, offering information and education without an agenda or rigid idea of what's normal or acceptable, but rather helping clients to determine these boundaries for themselves.

What About Men?

Feminist theory and science directly examines how society damages individuals who don't fit into gender stereotypes (e.g., from sissies and tomboys to transgendered people) but that's not all. Contemporary feminism also focuses on the price individuals pay when they fit too well! Many problems faced by men, such as homophobia, aggression, workaholism, and the inability to relate to women, children, or even their own emotions, are by-products of male socialization (Levant & Pollack, 1995). The painful costs of devaluing all things feminine and strict rules for being male are evidenced in William Pollack's (2000) book, *Real Boys' Voices*. Scotty, a 13-year-old boy from a small town in the Northeast, said,

> Boys are supposed to shut up and take it, to keep it all in. It's harder for them to release or vent without feeling girly. And that can drive them to shoot themselves. (p. ix)

As feminists began exposing gender role fallacies during the 1960s and 1970s, they also began revealing the damage to men by the narrow definitions of masculinity enforced in our culture. The men's movement grew from these efforts. A limited list of influential and enlightening men's movement books includes:

- *The Myth of Male Power* by Warren Farrell (1993)
- *I Don't Want To Talk About It: Overcoming the Secret Legacy of Male Depression* by Terrence Real (1998)
- *The Macho Paradox: Why Some Men Hurt Women and How All Men Can Help* by Jackson Katz (2006) [Katz is also creator of the movie *Tough Guise: Violence, Media and the Crisis in Masculinity* (1999).]
- *Guyland* by Michael Kimmell (2010)

The challenge for feminists and men's movement advocates is to engage males who are trapped tightly in male stereotypes that give them privilege, but limit their full development. Pollack's **boy code** is one way in which an effort has been made to increase awareness of the ways that contemporary gender-based stereotypes adversely affect males (see Putting it in Practice 10.3).

Feminist Therapy in Action: Brief Vignettes

As you read the following vignettes look for therapy interactions that you believe are distinctly feminist. In particular, watch for mutuality, self-disclosure, empowerment, and valuing of feminine consciousness.

Vignette I: Laura Brown

Laura Brown

In this vignette we review highlights of an unscripted demonstration videotape featuring Laura S. Brown, PhD, working in her third session with a client named Ellen (L. Brown, 1994). The client-therapist interactions below are paraphrased rather than verbatim. Ellen is a 34-year-old client mandated to engage in counseling because of a drug problem.

Early in the session, Ellen explains that she went to a Narcotics Anonymous (NA) meeting in Baltimore, and Dr. Brown lifts her eyebrows, saying "Baltimore?" in a surprised tone. Ellen acknowledges that it is quite a distance from her home, but she doesn't want to be seen by anyone who might know her locally. This leads to a gentle inquiry: "Ellen, what will people see if they see the real Ellen?"

Ellen defends herself against this question, talking for a while about clothes, jewelry, and the desire she believes everyone shares to stay hidden. Dr. Brown stays on the theme, asking about what dark secrets Ellen fears that people might see, and

Ellen talks about her drug use and her feelings that this is her own business, not something people need to know about or judge her on. She makes the claim that it really hasn't interfered with her life, but catches herself, just as Dr. Brown says, with warmth, "Wait a minute. What's wrong with this picture?"

Ellen admits that her drug use did cause a slight problem, in that she lost her job and has to go to counseling, but she denies most of the problem. Rather than going after the denial, Dr. Brown comments gently:

Dr. Brown: How things look is very important to you, and it is very hard for you to keep it up. It's very tiring.

Ellen: Yes, I work hard at how I look. And I'm not saying it isn't tiring.

Dr. Brown: Let yourself notice the tiredness. Don't talk about it. Just notice your body and how tired it is in there. Feel how hard it is to keep that pretty picture in place.

Ellen complies, with Dr. Brown's guiding encouragement. She relaxes her body and is quiet, while Dr. Brown encourages her to keep relaxing. Ellen actually lets herself tear up a little bit. She's able to talk about how hard she tries and how much she wishes her father would be proud of her. She spontaneously explores her father's gender messages—either be a lawyer like him or a wife and mother. Ellen explains that she can't do either. She faces how alone that makes her feel. Dr. Brown asks a strategic question: "Ellen, when did you get yourself to be at peace that you're father will never, ever say he's proud of you, no matter what you do?" Ellen admits that though her father will never say that, she isn't at peace about it and at 34 is still letting that wish drive her life. Together, for a short time, Dr. Brown and Ellen explore how alone she is and how no one has ever really taken care of her much. At this point, Dr. Brown tells Ellen she would like to revisit something Ellen mentioned last session—the fact that when Ellen was in college, someone she knew broke into her apartment and raped her.

PUTTING IT IN PRACTICE 10.3

The Boy Code

In the 1990s, Harvard professor William Pollack conducted a series of qualitative interviews with boys to determine what they viewed as the rules by which boys are required to live. He summarized their responses as the ***boy code***. The boy code includes the following rules:

- Stand on your own two feet.
- Separate from your mother and all things female ASAP.
- Never show any feelings—except anger.
- Stay on top, in control, and in the limelight.
- Remember, sex is a conquest.
- Bullying and teasing is normal boy behavior.
- Never give in, never apologize, and never really listen to anyone else (these are signs of weakness).
- Don't show any fear of violence.
- Never "rat" or "nark" on another boy. (Pollack, 2000)

Pollack's boy code is often viewed as an unhealthy contributor to violence and distress in young males. In an effort to achieve gender balance, we searched for an existing ***girl code***, but found none. Consequently, we conducted an informal survey with our students and obtained the following gender-based rules for girls. After checking them out, think about whether you've got something new to add to either list.

- Always look pretty.
- Always be clean and smell good.
- Be as thin as you can be.
- Want to be a mother.
- Want to take care of other people and the family home.
- Be more interested in the needs of others than your own.
- Be sexy, but not too sexy.
- Defer to your man—especially in public.
- Always be nice and polite—if not, you'll be a bitch.
- You need a man to be complete.
- Don't compete with men or boys.

Ellen: Yeah, I don't think there's that much to talk about. It was college. I was trying things out, you know. Freedom. Being an adult. Lots of sex and stuff. I was giving it away for free anyway, so I didn't think there was much to do. I told my brother later. He said I should tell the police and see a psychologist, but I didn't. I mean I sort of chose that life. I thought, hey, if guys can sow their wild oats, so can I. So I was pretty out there. I tried it all. No inhibitions. I guess the drugs aided that. I can say that back then, I really was a drug addict.

Dr. Brown: So, you felt like, I can do this. It's my choice, and if it hurts or feels bad, it's my own fault?

Ellen: Yeah, I chose it. That's how I feel about the rape, I guess. I don't know.

Dr. Brown: Ellen, what's your body saying as you say, "I don't know"?

Ellen: It's tired...I didn't stand up for my own body. It's a little sad. But I can't go back now and change it.

Dr. Brown: No, but we can explore how that experience might be affecting things now—how being an adult, sexual woman is for you now. What do you wish would have happened?

Ellen tearfully admits her wish that someone might have helped her, been there for her. She condemns herself as well, claiming that she should have handled it, wishing she had fought her assailant but noting that her drug-induced state made that unlikely. She ends with a sort of wistful statement: "I wish someone would have been there, but there wasn't anyone. So I dealt with it."

As the session ends, Dr. Brown asks Ellen to consider doing two things during the week: going to one more NA meeting and using her art, either in writing or painting, to explore the question: What does Ellen want? Ellen agrees, saying that she has neglected her painting. Smiling, Ellen also says that the painting will have to be a Monet, because she only has impressions, but no clarity. Dr. Brown counters with support and the observation that even a Monet, from the right position, is clear. Ellen acts surprised and pleased.

At the conclusion of the recording, Dr. Brown reflects on the session. Her goals for Ellen were to help the relationship develop and encourage Ellen to listen to her emotional self, which Dr. Brown explains to be especially important with women who have used substances to numb emotions after traumatic experiences. She also notes her intention to gently begin exploring gender issues and how Ellen constructs herself as an adult woman. In Ellen's case, as in many, it's important for the client to know that she will not be abandoned, judged, or overpowered as she begins to explore her pain and seek ways to make changes (adapted from Brown, 1994).

Vignette II: Relational–Cultural Therapy

Relational-cultural therapy (RCT) is a feminist-oriented therapy developed by Jean Baker Miller, Judith Jordan, and other collaborators at the Stone Center (Jordan, 2010). RCT founders were trained in psychoanalysis and so the orientation is toward depth psychotherapy that closely examines relationship connections, disruptions, and growth potential from mutually empathic intimate relationships. Core concepts of RCT include (from Jordan, 2010):

1. People grow through and toward relationship throughout the life span.

2. Movement toward mutuality rather than separation characterizes mature functioning.

3. Relationship differentiation and elaboration characterize growth.

4. Mutual empathy and mutual empowerment are at the core of growth-fostering relationships.

5. Authenticity is necessary for real engagement and full participation in growth-fostering relationship.

6. In growth-fostering relationships, all people contribute and grow or benefit. Development is not a one-way street.

7. One of the goals of development from a relational perspective is the development of increased relational competence and capacities over the life span. (p. 24)

Mutual empathy is a central tool in RCT work. Using modern brain research as a foundation, Jordan describes how empathic relationships can change clients:

> Empathy is not just a means to better understand the client; in mutually empathic exchanges, the isolation of the client is altered. The client feels less alone, more joined with the therapist. It is likely that in these moments of empathy and resonance, there is active brain resonance between therapist and client (Schore, 1994), which can alter the landscape and functioning of the brain. Thus, those areas of the brain that register isolation and exclusion fire less and those areas that indicate empathic responsiveness begin to activate.

Jordan (2010) describes a case in which she worked with a woman named Barbara, a "well-educated white woman who had seen six therapists before she began treatment with" Jordan (p. 53). Barbara's previous therapy experiences had been negative. She had been labeled with various psychiatric diagnoses was in the hospital due to a suicide attempt when Jordan began RCT with her.

The therapy was characterized by open exchanges in both directions. Barbara made her evaluation of Jordan clear: "She [Jordan] was not much better than the other clinicians she had seen" (p. 53). Jordan worked intermittently through long silences to both resonate with Barbara's fears and express what she could provide:

> I did not press her to give up her fears, acknowledged it had been a hard road, and told her that while I could not guarantee that I would understand her any better than the others, I was committed to trying. But I also suggested she had no real reason to trust me.

A turning point in therapy appeared to occur when Barbara came to a session following a fresh self-mutilation incident (she had scratched her arm until it bled). Barbara became provocative. She asked if she might be "fired" as a client. She asked if perhaps Jordan would be embarrassed or worried that she was seeing a client who had blood dripping from her arm. Jordan (2010) describes her response:

> I hesitated and agreed that the thought had crossed my mind (what her colleagues might think), but that I also could see she was in real pain and needed to be able to communicate that to me. She looked at first triumphant (at my admission of personal concern about my "reputation") but then genuinely relieved (perhaps that I had spoken a piece of truth about myself that she knew anyway). We then had a truly collaborative conversation about how she might be able to really let me know her conversation about her pain and whether she could trust my response. (p. 54)

You can see from these descriptions that RCT is an approach that involves deep and authentic interpersonal exchanges. There are rough patches (challenges and disconnections), but as therapists stay with empathy, honest self-disclosure, and focus on therapy process, positive changes can happen.

Jordan reported that after over 2 years of challenging therapy, the process settled down. In the end, Barbara made remarkable process (immensely improving her job status, beginning to date a gentle and kind woman, and moving beyond her self-destructive behaviors). In ending, Jordan quotes Barbara:

> Isn't it ironic that when you showed yourself as most fallible and vulnerable, I had the most trust in you? You didn't always get it right . . . and often it took awhile for you to get it at all, but you almost always came back, trying and clearly imperfect. That made you feel safe to me. (p. 55)

RCT is about authenticity. Be sure to compare this style with the more professional and clinical approaches discussed elsewhere in this text. Which style would you prefer?

CASE ANALYSIS AND TREATMENT PLANNING

In an interesting twist we're featuring a case with a male therapist and male client in the feminist chapter. This is intentional and designed to illustrate how working within a feminist model can work for boys and men. In particular, this case focuses on a 16-year-old male's struggle with emotional expression. John SF is the therapist and the case is told in a storytelling format.

Josh was a white, 16-year-old sophomore in high school. He had never met his biological father and lived in a middle-class neighborhood with his mother and three younger sisters. His mother was suffering from bipolar disorder. Josh's main loves were consistent with his gender identity. They included basketball, cars, girls, and sarcasm. He very much disliked school.

Josh and I had been meeting for therapy for years. At the beginning of one of our sessions Josh handed me a packet of photos.

"Hey, what's this about?" I asked.

He responded with a half-mumble about some recent awards ceremony. I thought I discerned a little pride in that mumble. I looked through the pictures while he told me about each one. There was one in particular that he gently lifted from my hands. It was a picture of him in a line-up with five other people. He carefully pointed out that he was standing next to the Lieutenant Governor of Oregon. I teased him because there were no pictures of him and the *actual* governor.

"What's the deal?" I asked. "Wouldn't the Guv pose with you?" Josh rolled his eyes and signaled for me to move on to the next photo.

The Problem List and Problem Formulation

Unlike CBT, feminist therapy doesn't involve collaboratively generating a concrete problem list and then proceeding to develop problem formulations—as if these problems resided in the client. Instead, because problems and problem-formulation are inseparable, we can't talk about the problems without also talking about cultural factors creating and contributing to the problems.

If problems are listed and discussed as problems, they're likely discussed as situational challenges. In Josh's case, his mother had brought him to therapy due to anger problems. Anger continued to be a regular focus in Josh's therapy. Like many 16-year-old boys immersed in the dominant U.S. culture, Josh's emotional life was highly constricted. He was living

by Pollack's boy code (2000) and unable or unwilling to risk feeling anything other than anger and irritation. From the feminist worldview, this wasn't Josh's problem; it was a problem that his culture insisted on keeping him in an emotional straitjacket.

Josh's problem and problem formulation list looked something like the following:

1. Learning to deal more effectively with sadness, grief, and anger within the context of a repressive emotional environment.

2. Coming to an understanding that his beliefs and views of emotional expression were not in his best interest, but instead, foisted upon him by toxic cultural attitudes about how boys and men should experience and express emotion.

3. Developing trust and confidence in himself—despite not having a father figure or a mother who could provide him and his sisters with a safe and stable home environment.

4. Learning to talk about what he really feels inside and pursue his life passions whatever they might be instead of reflexively pursuing culturally "manly" activities.

5. Expanding Josh's limited emotional vocabulary through facilitating his feminist consciousness.

Interventions

Feminist therapists are technically eclectic and use a wide range of interventions imbedded in an egalitarian relationship characterized by mutuality. In Josh's case, the interventions included:

1. Encouraging Josh to speak freely and openly about his life experiences.

2. Empathic listening with intermittent focusing on more tender emotions, depending on how much of this Josh was willing or able to tolerate.

3. Therapist self-disclosure and modeling.

As Josh and I continued to look at photos together, I responded with interest and enthusiasm. Because connection is a meaningful part of therapy, I didn't rush him to move on to our therapy agenda. I shifted back and forth between saying, "Cool" or "What's going on there?" to making sarcastic wisecracks like "Now why exactly did the government actually let you into the capital building?" This adolescent sarcasm was a way of using his communication style to express interest and affection indirectly, mirroring his humor and style. After seeing most of the photos I asked, "Who's the young woman standing in the line next to you?" I could tell from his response that I had asked a good question.

"Oh, yeah, her. Her name is Sharice; her mentor was getting the same award as my mentor. I danced with her. She's a good dancer."

And so we talked for a while about dancing and what it was like for him to feel attracted to her. We were ten minutes into therapy and both of us had completely ignored the fact that we hadn't been able to see each other for five weeks. Finally, I decided to break the avoidance pattern. I asked "So . . . how are you doing with all that's been going on?"

He looked toward me, glancing downward.

"I'm doing okay, I guess."

Because this was a young man who had been socialized to keep his emotions tightly wrapped, I gently probed a little more.

"I understand it's been pretty wild times?"

He looked up, eyes fixed on some invisible spot on the ceiling. I recognized this strategy. It's an old trick that I learned from a previous client. She had bragged about learning it from her father. She said one sure-fire way to avoid crying in public is to look up at the ceiling. Apparently the upward gaze constricts the tear ducts and so tears simply cannot flow.

He looked back down and said, "I've been pretty busy. My mom's been in the hospital for about a month now."

"I heard she had a pretty hard time."

He grunted and then, slowly, in a quiet growly voice, the words, "Let-me-tell-you-about-it" seeped out from behind his teeth. I recognized that this is not a statement indicating he wants to tell me about what happened. Instead, it's an expression about him witnessing a powerful event. And it's an expression that tells me, in no uncertain terms, that

I was not there, that I was not a witness, that he knows all about it . . . and I don't. Silence follows. I cautiously probed a bit more by sharing more of what I knew.

"When I talked with your mom yesterday, she told me that she got pretty caught up in some housing project." This statement lit a fire in Josh and he plunged into the story.

"You won't believe what she did. It was so f*ing stupid. Some punk developer is gonna build three houses. Three houses at the end of our street. This is *no big deal*. She just f*ing freaked out. She chained herself up to a tractor to stop them from building a house. Then she called the f*ing senator and road department and I don't know who in hell else she called and she was totally nuts. So I told her she had a choice. I told her that she could go back home or I'd call the police and have her committed. She wasn't taking care of my sisters. She was being a s*** for a mom. So I just gave her a choice."

I nodded and said, "What a great idea you had. You must be practicing to be a parent. That's the kind of choice parents give their kids."

His voice grew louder as he continued: "I gave her the choice five times. Five f*ing times! She bought a Mercedes and a Volvo over the phone. She's gonna s*** bricks when she gets the bills. So I called the cops. And the woman asked me what to do. I'm f***ing 16 years old and they f*ing ask me what to do. I didn't know what to say. We were on the phone forever. I told 'em to come get her. They finally sent some really big cops over to take her away."

"Then what happened?"

"My mom was still acting nuts and my sisters were crying. So I just picked them up and held them and they took her away. We sat and they cried and we snuggled for a while. And then I drove us home. I don't have my license, but I can drive. My mom is still pissed at me about that, but I don't give a s***!"

Now, I have an image of Josh in my mind. I see an awkward and 16-year-old boy "snuggling" his sobbing sisters while the cops take their raging mother away. The girls were 9 and 6 and 4 years old. In my mental version of this scene, they're taking up his considerable lap. These are the same sisters he complained about and harassed on a regular basis.

Talking with teenage boys about emotional issues is tricky business. Too much empathy and they retreat. No empathy and you're teaching the wrong lesson. Throughout Josh's storytelling, I used gentle sarcasm, empathy, and sometimes careful emotional exploration, like, "What was that like for you to really be there for your sisters?" But I knew if I asked too much about feelings or forced him to go too deep too fast, I would no longer be cool and our relationship would be harmed or over.

I knew that Josh needed to know that it's okay, even a positive thing, for boys and men to feel and express their more tender feelings.

Much of the session focused on empathy for Josh's anger. Josh ranted and I listened. He was immensely angry and disappointed and hurt about his mother's behavior.

About halfway through our session, I asked Josh a question that I use with boys; it's a question designed to let us talk about feelings and sadness in a way that's more safe and distant.

"So Josh," I said, "When was the last time you cried?"

The question caught him by surprise. After a short pause he spoke with extreme deliberation, "I... don't... cry... I... just... get... pissed."

There's something very efficient about the way Josh expressed this masculine emotional principle. I was reminded of a phrase I memorized after years of playing Monopoly. The phrase is printed on a small card that says, "Go to jail. Go directly to jail. Do not pass Go. Do not collect $200." While sitting with Josh, I offered a new version of this phrase, "Go directly to anger. Do not experience sadness. Do not let yourself cry." Josh responded by offering me further education about emotions.

"Crying doesn't do any good. It doesn't change anything. It's just stupid."

"I know, I know" I said. "The whole idea of crying sounds pretty stupid to you. It's not like crying will change your mom and make her better."

"Nothing will ever change her."

I renewed my pursuit of when he last cried. He insisted that was so long ago that he can't really recall, but we both know that several years ago he had sat on my couch and sobbed himself to sleep. Instead of going back there, I asked him what might make him cry now. Would he cry if his girlfriend broke up with him... if he lost his favorite CD... if one of his sisters got cancer... if he didn't get a chance to graduate from high school? Josh fended off my questions about tears by repeating his resolve to get "pissed" about everything that might make him feel sad. But the question about one of his sister's getting cancer stumped him. He admitted, "Yeah, I might cry about that..." while quickly adding, "...but I'd do it alone!"

I responded, "Right. Absolutely. I'd never expect you to cry in front of somebody. There might be some things worth crying about... even though it wouldn't change things... but you'd want to do the crying alone."

We talked a bit indirectly and intellectually about sadness and tears, trying to model that we can talk about it—once removed—and if he cried someday, it would be perfectly okay, there would be no need to feel ashamed.

Toward the end of the session, I decided to lighten things up by teasing Josh about his social insensitivity. I said, "I can't believe that we've talked this whole hour and you never asked me a single thing about myself."

Josh grinned. He knew therapy was all about him and not about me. He probably knew I was playing some sort of therapy game with him. He was a good sport and played along.

"Okay. So what am I supposed to ask?"

I acted chagrinned, saying, "After all those questions I asked you, at least you should ask me when I last cried."

"Okay. God you don't know when to drop things. Okay. So when did you cry?"

I leaned forward and said, "I think it was yesterday."

And then I looked into his wide-open eyes and said, "Yeah. As a therapist, I hear some really hard stories and even though it doesn't change anything, sometimes it feels better to let my sadness out."

It was time for the session to end. We both stood and I said, "I know we have to stop talking for today, but of course we can talk more about this or anything else when we meet next time."

Outcomes Measurement

Feminists generally don't use outcomes assessments (Santos de Barona & Dutton, 1997). As discussed earlier, assessment potentially labels clients and adds to pressure and expectations to behave in particular ways. In Josh's story, his progress was mainly monitored through verbal and narrative updates. However, it might have been reasonable to have him respond to a few measures of feminist therapy process and outcome. These measures focus on the degree to which the therapist is collaborative and shares power.

- The Working Alliance Inventory (Horvath & Greenberg, 1986; Horvath & Greenberg, 1989)

- Client Therapy With Women Scale (Worell et al., 1996)

Additionally, RCT researchers have developed a measure called the Relational Health Indices (Liang et al., 2002; Liang, Tracy, Kenny, Brogan, & Gatha, 2010). This is a 37-item questionnaire that has been used with men. It measures three dimensions of growth-fostering relationships: engagement, authenticity, and empowerment/zest. It might be useful to have Josh complete this questionnaire regularly to both as a means of evaluating his relationships and as a structured way to help him talk about relationship issues.

Feminist therapies sometimes have therapists complete questionnaires about their behaviors during therapy. This can be useful in determining how closely therapists are following a feminist therapy model. For example, as I worked with Josh I could have repeatedly completed the Feminist Self-Disclosure Inventory (Simi & Mahalik, 1997) to monitor whether and how I was using self-disclosure as a therapy technique.

Finally, more traditional assessments could be used to monitor progress with Josh as long as this was done so in a manner that empowered him, rather than causing him to feel put upon for having to engage in assessment tasks. A more traditional assessment might include the Youth Outcomes Questionnaire-Self-Report (Y-OQ-SR; Ridge, Warren, Burlingame, Wells, & Tumblin, 2009; Wells, Burlingame, Lambert, Hoag, & Hope, 1996). Additionally, although it would take time to help him come to the point of seeing it as useful, Josh might benefit from regularly completing questionnaires focusing on emotional awareness and expression.

CULTURAL AND GENDER CONSIDERATIONS

Professional cynics might argue that feminist therapy has been limited to special populations or to just one special population—discontented white women with feminist leanings. Historically, there was some amount of truth to this complaint. In 1992 Brown and Brodsky published an article titled *The Future of Feminist Therapy* (1992). They stated,

> Currently, feminist therapy theory is neither diverse nor complex in the reality it reflects. It has been deficient from the start in its inclusiveness of the lives and realities of women of color, poor or working class women, non–North American women, women over sixty-five, or women with disabilities. (p. 52)

However, as discussed throughout this chapter, feminism has transformed itself and is now sensitive to oppression as experienced by all marginalized and minority populations. Acknowledging historical shortcomings, feminist therapists and writers have worked and are working to continually expand their awareness and educate future generations about the relevance of feminism to their lives by challenging the idea that feminism only applies to discontented middle-class white women. Feminists have been among the first and most vocal of those advocating for diverse and multicultural perspectives in the practice of counseling and psychotherapy. For example, years before other professional conferences had signers for the deaf, feminist conferences made a point of having signers and of meeting only in fully accessible conference centers.

At the core of feminist thinking is the notion that subjugation of any segment of the human species based on race, ethnicity, religious beliefs, sex, disability, or sexual orientation is wrong (Barrett et al., 2005; Espín, 1997; Gilligan, 2003). Therefore, feminist theory is applicable to other populations suffering from externally imposed limits, stereotypes, abuse, and exploitation.

Despite feminist therapy's laudable stance toward all oppressed populations, the naturally activist orientation of feminist therapists can produce tension between feminists and diverse groups. For example, within different spiritual or religious traditions women's roles are frequently narrow and punishments to women stepping outside their roles can be severe. Although feminist therapists will advocate and work toward consciousness and change in these situations, adherents to particular religious or cultural norms are unlikely to welcome feminist critique on their values. This is where the potential for conflict is highest and where feminists might be viewed as imposing their values on other cultural groups, rather than accepting the cultural group's values.

EVIDENCE-BASED STATUS

Whether feminist therapy measures up to the treatment outcomes standards of modernist empirical science is easily answered. Feminist therapy does not measure up. However, similar to person-centered and existential perspectives, feminist therapists aren't interested in measuring up to this standard. Why would they want to measure up to a standard they view as a narrow-minded means through which individuals seeking feminist therapy can be further controlled and marginalized?

Despite this general negative attitude towards rigid approaches to therapy outcomes research, there is empirical research attesting to feminist

therapy goals, accomplishment, and effectiveness. Several examples are summarized:

Simi and Mahalik (1997) found evidence that feminist therapists tend to behave differently than other therapists in several ways. In their study of 143 female therapists, feminist therapists were more likely to: (a) create an egalitarian relationship in therapy; (b) encourage their clients to select a positive role model during therapy; and (c) inform clients of their sexual orientation.

Several other studies using a variety of measures support Simi and Mahalik's (1997) findings that feminist therapists offer a distinct therapy consistent with feminist theoretical principles (Chandler, Worell, Johnson, Blount, & Lusk, 1999; Worell & Chandler, 1996; Worell et al., 1996; Worell & Remer, 2003). Overall, it appears that feminist therapists provide a distinctive product characterized by power sharing, an egalitarian relationship, self-disclosure, client empowerment, and support for feminist goals.

Worell and Johnson (2003) summarized the existing feminist therapy research and provided this optimistic conclusion:

> These preliminary studies on measuring process and outcomes in feminist therapy are suggestive and encouraging. They suggest that feminist therapy, when articulated in a structured and clearly defined model, is a unique and measurable form of intervention that provides positive outcomes for women in personal distress. (p. 327)

Overall, as with other less symptom-oriented therapies, it's difficult to compare feminist treatment outcomes with contemporary cognitive and behavioral therapies.

CONCLUDING COMMENTS

Perhaps more than any other chapter in this text, feminist theory and therapy tends to get students and readers a bit riled up. Sometimes there's strong opposition to these ideas and other times students decide they want to begin self-identifying as feminists. Either of these responses is fine. More importantly than a sense of agreement or disagreement, we hope you can consider the question: Could you become a feminist therapist? In one last overview, Worell and Remer (2003) provide eight tenets of feminist psychology. Consider whether these statements fit for you:

1. We advocate inclusiveness. We acknowledge that the social impact of gender is experienced unequally and unfairly for women with diverse personal and social identities, including ethnicity and culture, sexual and affectional orientation, socioeconomic status, nationality, age, and physical characteristics.

2. We advocate equality. We recognize that the politics of gender are reflected in lower social status and unequal access to valued resources for a majority of women in most societies.

3. We seek new knowledge. We value and advocate increased understanding about the diversity of women's experience as it is framed by multiple personal and social identities.

4. We attend to context. Women's lives are embedded in the social, economic, and political contexts of their lives and should not be studied in isolation.

5. We acknowledge values. Personal and social values enter into all human enterprises; education, science, practice, and social advocacy are never value-free.

6. We advocate change. We are committed to action to accomplish social, economic, and political change toward establishing equal justice for all persons.

7. We attend to process. Decision-making processes that affect personal and group outcomes should be consensual and consistent with feminist principles of mutual respect and honoring all voices.

8. We expand psychological practice. We recognize that feminist principles can be applied to all professional activities in which we engage: theory building, prevention, counseling and therapy, assessment, pedagogy, curriculum development, research, supervision, leadership, and professional training (p. 18).

QUESTIONS FOR REFLECTION

Now that you've made it through this chapter, try on the feminist label again. What's it like to say, "I'm a feminist therapist" this time? What are your gut reactions now? What goes through your mind? Are you closer or further from embracing a feminist therapist label?

CHAPTER SUMMARY

Feminist theory and therapy is part of a grassroots historical effort to bring sexual inequities into awareness and resolve them through egalitarian and nonhierarchical solutions. The feminist movement in the United States is generally divided into three stages: (1) First wave feminism—characterized by striving for universal suffrage and property rights; (2) second wave feminism—characterized by an effort to obtain equal rights for women; and (3) third wave feminism—characterized by worldwide and multicultural efforts to dismantle oppressive and damaging patriarchic systems.

Many factors contributed to the development and implementation of feminist therapy. As women became more established within academic and scientific communities they produced numerous groundbreaking publications. Additionally, women's consciousness-raising groups helped move women to take action together to improve their situations.

Three primary feminist theoretical principles were defined and discussed. These included: (1) sex and gender powerfully affect identity; (2) deviance comes from dysfunctional culture; and

(3) consciousness-raising is a part of healing and change.

The practice of feminist therapy is not associated with a particular set of techniques or procedures. Instead, feminist therapists seek to integrate feminist philosophical principles into counseling and psychotherapy. This process involves informed consent, nonstandardized assessment of a variety of feminist-related issues, development of a therapeutic relationship, self-disclosure, empowerment, and development of feminist consciousness. Additionally, feminist therapists focus on sex, sexuality, body image issues, self-esteem, gender role comfort, and men's issues.

Feminist therapy is very sensitive to women's issues and has become progressively more oriented toward addressing multicultural issues and GLBT issues. The evidence base for feminist therapy is very limited. There is some evidence that feminist therapists are more focused on therapy process, relationship development, self-disclosure, and empowerment than other therapies. Additionally, a few research studies suggest there are positive outcomes.

FEMINIST KEY TERMS

Boy code

Consciousness-raising groups

Developmental sex divergences

Disorders of sexual development

Egalitarian

Empowerment

Ethic of caring

Feminist consciousness

Feminism

Fight or flight phenomenon

First wave feminism

Gender

Gender role

Girl code

Informed consent

Interpersonal/social-contextual power

Intersex conditions

Intrapersonal/intrapsychic power

Iron rule

Kinder, Kuche, Kirche as Scientific Law

Male as normative

Male crisis

Mutually empathic

Patriarchy

Power analysis

Relational-cultural therapy

Second wave feminism

Self-disclosure

Sex

Somatic power

Spiritual/existential power

Subversive

Tend and befriend response

The personal is political

Third wave feminism

Women and madness

RECOMMENDED READINGS AND RESOURCES

The following resources may help you deepen your understanding of feminist theory and therapy.

FEMINIST–RELATED THERAPY JOURNALS

Gender and Psychoanalysis

Men and Masculinities

Psychology of Men and Masculinity

Psychology Women Quarterly

Sex Roles

Women and Therapy

READINGS ON FEMINIST THEORY AND THERAPY

Brown, L. S. (2010). *Feminist therapy*. Washington, DC: American Psychological Association.

Chesler, P. (1972). *Women and madness*. New York, NY: Doubleday.

Collins, P. H. (2009). *Black feminist thought*. New York, NY: Routledge.

Enns, C. Z. (2004). *Feminist theories and feminist psychotherapies: Origins, themes, and diversity* (2nd ed.). New York, NY: Haworth Press.

Freidan, B. (1963). *The feminine mystique*. New York, NY: Norton.

Gilligan, C. (1982). *In a different voice*. Cambridge, MA: Harvard University Press.

Herman, J. (1997). *Trauma and recovery*. New York, NY: Perseus Books.

hooks, b. (2000). *Feminism is for everybody: Passionate politics*. Cambridge, MA: South End Press.

Horney, K. (1967). *Feminine psychology*. New York, NY: Norton.

Hrdy, S. B. (1999). *Mother nature*. New York, NY: Pantheon Books.

Katz, J. (2006). *The macho paradox: Why some men hurt women and how all men can help*. Naperville, IL: Sourcebooks.

Miller, J. B. (Ed.). (1973). *Psychoanalysis and women*. New York, NY: Brunner/Mazel.

Mitchell, J. (1976). *Psychoanalysis and feminism: Freud, Reich, Laing, and women*. New York, NY: Random House.

Tavris, C. (1998). *The mismeasure of woman*. New York, NY: Smith, Peter.

Thompson, C. (1971). *On women*. New York, NY: New American Library.

Worell, J. R., & Remer, P. (2003). *Feminist perspectives in therapy: Empowering diverse women* (2nd ed.). New York, NY: John Wiley & Sons.

TRAINING ORGANIZATIONS AND WEBSITES

Association for Women in Psychology (AWP; www.theworks.baka.com/awp)

Jean Baker Miller Training Institute (www.jbmti.org)

National Organization for Men Against Sexism (NOMAS; www.nomas.org)

National Organization for Women (NOW; www.now.org)

VIDEOS/DVDS

Ballou, M., & LaRoche, M. (2009). *Feminist counseling and cultural therapy*. North Amherst, MA: Microtraining Associates.

Brown, L. (2007). *Feminist therapy* [DVD]. Washington, DC: American Psychological Association.

Brown, L. (2009). *Feminist therapy over time* [DVD]. Washington, DC: American Psychological Association.

Jhally, S. (2007). *Dreamworlds 3* [Videotape]. Northampton, MA: Media Education Foundation.

Katz, J. (1999). *Tough guise*. [Videotape]. Northampton, MA: Media Education Foundation.

Kilbourne, J. (2000). *Killing us softly III* [Videotape]. Northampton, MA: Media Education Foundation.

GOING FARTHER AND DEEPER

Additional feminist counseling and psychotherapy resources are available at johnsommersflanagan.com.

CHAPTER 11

Constructive Theory and Therapy

We are what we think. All that we are arises with our thoughts. With our thoughts, we make the world.

—Buddha (quoted in Boldt, 1999, p. 91)

THIS CHAPTER

- Reviews key figures, historical, and philosophical factors contributing to the development and evolution of constructive psychotherapies
- Outlines and describes constructive theories of counseling and psychotherapy
- Describes and discusses principles and strategies associated with narrative and solution-focused practice, including
  - Assessment issues and procedures
  - Specific therapy techniques
- Provides short vignettes to demonstrate constructive approaches in action
- Illustrates how treatment planning, outcomes assessment, and gender and cultural issues can be integrated into a constructive therapy approach
- Reviews the empirical status of various narrative, solution-focused, and other constructive therapies
- Offers resources for further study

Without question, the best way to begin a chapter on constructive theory and therapy is with a story.

Once upon a time a man and a woman met in the forest. Both being academic philosophers well-steeped in epistemology, they approached each another warily. The woman spoke first, asking, "Can you see me?"

The man responded quickly: "I don't know," he said. "I have a plethora of neurons firing in my occipital lobe and, yes, I perceive an image of a woman and I can see your mouth was moving precisely as I was experiencing auditory input. Therefore, although I'm not completely certain you exist out there in reality—and I'm not completely certain there even is a reality—I can say without a doubt that you exist ... at least within the physiology of my mind."

Silence followed.

Then, the man spoke again,

"Can you hear me?" he asked.

This time the woman responded immediately. "I'm not completely certain about the nature of hearing and the auditory process, but I can say that in this lived moment of my experience I'm in a conversation with you and because my knowledge and my reality is based on interactive discourse, whether you really exist or not is less important than the fact that I find myself, in this moment, discovering more about myself, the nature of the world, and my knowledge of all things."

There are two main branches of constructive theory. These branches are similar in that both perspectives hold firmly to the postmodern idea that knowledge and reality is subjective. **Constructivists**, as represented by the man in the forest, believe knowledge and reality are constructed within individuals. In contrast, social constructionists, as represented by the woman in the forest, believe knowledge and reality are constructed through discourse or conversation. Constructivists focus on what's happening within the minds or brains of individuals; **social constructionists** focus on what's happening between people as they join together to create realities. Guterman (2006) described these two perspectives:

> Although both constructivism and social constructionism endorse a subjectivist view of knowledge, the former emphasizes individuals' biological and cognitive processes, whereas the latter places knowledge in the domain of social interchange. (p. 13)

In this chapter, we de-emphasize distinctions between constructivist and social constructionist perspectives. Mostly, we lump them together as constructive theories and therapies and emphasize the fascinating intervention strategies developed within these paradigms. This might be upsetting to staunch constructivists or radical social constructionists, but we take this risk with full confidence in our personal safety. That's because most constructive types are nonviolent thinkers who very much like talking and writing. Consequently, within our socially or individually constructed realities we've concluded that we're in no danger of harm from disgruntled constructive theorists or therapists.

KEY FIGURES AND HISTORICAL CONTEXT

Constructive theories and therapies help clients reconstruct or restory their lives in more adaptive and satisfying ways. This emphasis requires that therapy interactions focus primarily on the present and future. To explore constructive theories is to dive more deeply into the abyss of "as if" as introduced to philosophers (and Alfred Adler) in the early twentieth century by Hans Vaihinger (1911).

Postmodern Philosophy

Postmodern philosophy emphasizes that objectivity and reality are individually or socially constructed. These constructive ideas are philosophically and psychologically compelling, especially within our contemporary multivariate, multidimensional, and multicultural society. As a consequence of this philosophical position, we humans can no longer stake any claim to objectivity. Everything is perspective, and perspective is everything. Hierarchical structures of expert and nonexpert are challenged. Each of us views reality through our own particular lenses or created social discourse. The prominent social psychologist and social constructionist Kenneth Gergen (2009) explains:

> At the outset, constructionist ideas alert us to the absence of foundations (rational, empirical, ethical, or otherwise) for any position that one advocates. All articulated positions emerge from social process, and even the attempt to elaborate foundations must ultimately beg the question of how its elaborations are to be warranted. This scarcely suggests that we should abandon the positions we occupy. Rather, it is to become aware that we live within traditions that may or may not be adequate to the contingencies of today. Reflection, curiosity, and doubt must all be encouraged. (p. 99)

With reflection, curiosity, and doubt as our guides, we now turn to a look at the roots of constructive psychotherapy.

The Roots of Constructive Psychotherapy

Constructive approaches to counseling and psychotherapy also have roots in traditional talk therapy. As an example, Steven de Shazer, a co-originator of solution-focused therapy, used a phrase from Sigmund Freud (*Words were originally magic*) as a title for one of his solution-focused books (de Shazer, 1994). In the 1915 writings from which de Shazer was quoting, Freud wrote,

> Nothing takes place in a psycho-analytic treatment but an exchange of words....

The patient talks.... The doctor listens.... Words were originally magic and to this day words have retained much of their ancient magical power. By words one person can make another blissfully happy or drive him to despair.... Words provoke affects and are in general the means of mutual influence among men. (Freud, 1961, p. 17)

As Freud notes, the magical power of words began long before psychoanalysis. Ancient healers, storytellers, and religious evangelists knew the power of words. Regardless of your particular religious or spiritual beliefs, it's difficult to argue over the word and story power included in the I Ching, the Bible, the Koran, the Talmud, the sayings of Confucius, the Book of Mormon, and other religious documents.

Early philosophers who contributed to constructive theory and therapy include Immanuel Kant and Hans Vaihinger. Kant's view that knowledge of reality can only be approximated and Vaihinger's conception of many individual fictional realities both are at the root of contemporary constructive theory. Constructive thought is in opposition to modernism or objectivism. Both constructivism and social constructionism hold that individuals actively construct reality based on either their own perceptual experiences or jointly held social agreements. Both these perspectives make reality quite flexible. In contrast, objectivism holds that individuals know reality by passively receiving sensory information directly from the environment (aka: the real world).

George Kelly, Personal Construct Theory, and Preposterous Interpretations

With the publication of *The Psychology of Personal Constructs*, George Kelly (1955) developed the first unarguably constructive approach to psychotherapy. He wrote,

Life provides man with no scientific footholds on reality, suggests to him no narrative plots, offers no rhythmic metaphor to confirm the moving resonance of a human theme. If he chooses to write tragedy, then tragedy it will be; if comedy, then that is what will come of it; and if burlesque, he, the sole reader, must learn to laugh at his

misanthropic caricatures of the only person he knows—himself. (Kelly, 1969, p. 24)

Kelly described many foundational constructive psychological concepts. Although Vaihinger and other philosophers influenced him, his theoretical work is based primarily on clinical observation. For example, early in his transformation from Freudian analysis to personal constructs, Kelly began "deliberately" offering clients *preposterous interpretations*. His only criteria were that the interpretative statements (a) integrate his clients' current perspective and (b) have ramifications "for approaching the future in a different way" (Kelly, 1969, p. 52). Somewhat to his surprise, Kelly discovered that his preposterous interpretations often worked very well in moving clients toward more positive future behavior and emotions.

Milton Erickson, Strategic Hypnotherapy, and Solution-Based Approaches

Milton Erickson

Stephen de Shazer and others trace the modern origin of solution-focused constructive thinking to the late, great hypnotherapist Milton Erickson (de Shazer, 1985; Haley, 1973; O'Hanlon, 1988; O'Hanlon & Bertolino, 1998). Erickson is also considered the innovative inspiration for the strategic therapy approach with individuals and families (I. Goldenberg & H. Goldenberg, 2008). In his therapeutic work, Erickson made no effort to correct "causative underlying maladjustments" lurking in his clients' unconscious, self, past, or environment (Haley, 1967, p. 393). Instead, his focus was on how to deconstruct and reconstruct the skills and strengths his clients brought with them to therapy. The following case, adapted from Rossi (1980) and later summarized in O'Hanlon and Bertolino (1999), illustrates Erickson's strength-based approach.

A 70-year-old woman named Ma met with Erickson. She was unable to read despite many years of sincere effort. She had resolved to learn how to read at age 16 but had subsequently become frightened and blanked out whenever someone tried to teach her. Erickson promised her that she would be reading and writing within three weeks.

Erickson's approach to teaching Ma to read was innovative. He told her that she wouldn't have to learn anything that she didn't already know. The core of his message was that she already had within her all of the skills and strengths needed to learn to read and write.

He asked her to pick up a pencil in any old way she wanted. Then, he had her make some marks with the pencil on paper, just scribbling, like any baby might do. Progressively, he had her make straight lines at various angles, donut holes, donut halves, and two sides of a gabled roof. As a way to decrease her anxiety about writing, Erickson did not have the woman learn to copy letters but instead had her draw objects that she had been familiar with during her lifetime. He had her practice making these familiar marks on paper between sessions.

During their next meeting, Erickson explained to Ma that the only difference between a pile of lumber and a house was that the house was put together in a particular way. Ma agreed but didn't see the relevance between building a house from lumber and turning pencil marks on a page into letters. Then, Erickson helped Ma make a series of 26 new marks, based on the marks she had previously produced. Of course, these marks were the 26 letters of the English alphabet.

Erickson's work with Ma continued along the same lines. He coaxed her into naming the different letters and words she produced. After all, just as farm animals needed names, so did the marks she produced on a piece of paper. Eventually, he had her write a sentence: "Get going Ma and put some grub on the table." This was a statement she had frequently heard from her late husband, which helped Ma realize that reading was just like talking. In the end, without causing Ma any anxiety whatsoever, Erickson taught her to read and write in less than three weeks.

Erickson was a powerful and creative individual whose work is still highly regarded (Cade, 2009;

Lankton & Frischholz, 2009; Patterson, 2010; Zeig, 2010). He made many contributions to what we know about psychotherapy today. He is best known for brief hypnotherapeutic techniques and innovative approaches to working with individual cases. One of his most significant contributions to therapy is the intervention referred to as utilization (Erickson, 1954).

Utilization is both an intervention and a theoretical concept. Erickson believed it was crucial for clients to utilize whatever strengths they brought with them to therapy. These strengths included their humor, work experiences, language style, personal resources, and nonverbal behaviors. As with Ma, Erickson incorporated or utilized the personal qualities his clients possessed into their therapeutic work.

Erickson's legacy is characterized by three of his personal attributes. We believe these qualities continue to shine through and shape the contemporary practice of many constructive therapies and therapists. Erickson was many things, but in particular he was:

- Optimistic (and confident)
- Clever (and intelligent)
- Indirect (and collaborative)

Erickson was so positive and creative with clients that, before long, often without even realizing what had happened, clients would experience a doubling or trebling of their previously unnoticed and underutilized personal strengths and resources. As we see later, he was a masterful listener and had a knack for framing or constructing solutions that his clients could instantly "get."

QUESTIONS FOR REFLECTION

Consider the following questions: How much of Erickson's personality is reflected in the development and evolving nature of constructive theory and therapy? Have you noticed how the personalities of other major theorists (e.g., Freud, Adler, Rogers, Beck) shaped how their therapies are practiced? How might feminist and multicultural life experiences shape theory?

The Palo Alto Projects and Brief Therapy in Italy

In 1952 Gregory Bateson began the Double-Bind Communications Project (DBCP) with Jay Haley, John Weakland, and Donald Jackson (as consultant) in Palo Alto, California. This project focused on communication patterns in schizophrenic families. Shortly after this project started, Haley and Weakland became interested in communication patterns that occur between hypnotherapist and client. With Bateson's encouragement, Haley and Weakland began attending some of Milton Erickson's hypnosis workshops and visited him regularly in Phoenix.

In 1958 Jackson established the Mental Research Institute (MRI) along with Virginia Satir and Paul Watzlawick, also in Palo Alto. This project and the DBCP both focused on the power of verbal and nonverbal communication in influencing human behavior. The project boundaries were somewhat blurred because Jackson was heavily involved in both. Together, the projects resulted in more than 200 professional publications, including numerous books (Bateson, Jackson, Haley, & Weakland, 1963; Watzlawick, Beavin, & Jackson, 1967; J. Weakland, 1962).

In 1968 the Brief Therapy Center was established at MRI. By then the DBCP had ended and Haley and Weakland had joined MRI. Around the same time, four Italian psychiatrists led by Mara Selvini-Palazzoli broke away from their psychoanalytically trained colleagues and formed the Milan Center for the Study of the Family. Their goal was to work more specifically with family systems using briefer therapy models. The Milan group was strongly influenced by the Palo Alto group and, in particular, by the publication *Pragmatics of Human Communication* (Watzlawick et al., 1967). Watzlawick became the main consultant for the Milan group.

Haley and Cloe Madanes (who was trained at MRI) later married and developed the strategic approach to family and individual therapy (Madanes & Haley, 1977). The essence of strategic therapy is to devise a unique strategy for each particular client or family problem. There are numerous strategic therapy techniques, but the most relevant to our discussion is positive relabeling or reframing.

In one famous case, Haley informed a woman whose husband had recently chased her around the house with an ax that her husband "was simply trying to get close to her" (I. Goldenberg & H. Goldenberg, 2008, p. 280). Obviously Haley's **positive relabeling** in that case was a bit over the top, but strategic therapy approaches were boldly positive. Similarly, in her work at the Milan Center, Selvini-Palazzoli and her group (Selvini-Palazzoli, Boscolo, Cecchin, & Prata, 1974) developed an active-directive family therapy technique called **positive connotation**, in which negative symptoms or behaviors are recast in a positive light (e.g., "Your child is setting fires in order to get your attention and some emotional warmth in his life").

QUESTIONS FOR REFLECTION

Some writers have strongly criticized the extremely positive reframing approaches that Haley and Selvini-Palazzoli popularized. What are your thoughts on this issue? How do you think provocatively positive reframes might affect clients?

Efran and Fauber (1995) offer the following criticism of overly positive therapy interventions based on "verbal magic":

In our view, some workers have stretched the meaning of such terms as reframing and positive connotation ... to the breaking point. They underestimate the solidity of a constructed reality and assume that because something is language dependent, it is insubstantial and can be easily modified by relabeling problems willy-nilly. They feel free to portray faults as virtues, failures as successes, and selfishness as altruism. Some therapists will say almost anything for strategic effect. Critics have attacked such ad hoc conceptualizations as superficial and manipulative—an uncomfortable melding of the roles of therapist and con artist.... We tend to agree. (p. 291)

Clearly, a significant danger associated with constructive approaches is the minimization or denial of what Efran & Fauber (1995) refer to as the solidity of constructed reality.

Discovering Solutions and Narratives

The work of Kelly, Erickson, Bateson, MRI, the Milan Group, and Haley and Madanes are directly related to contemporary constructive theory and therapy. Within the constructive paradigm, this chapter focuses primarily on two distinct therapeutic movements and approaches: solution-focused and narrative therapies.

Solution-Focused Brief Therapy

Steve de Shazer and Insoo Kim Berg cofounded the Brief Family Therapy Center (BFTC) in Milwaukee in 1978 and developed **solution-focused brief therapy** (SFBT). Their approach emphasized that clients don't need to know anything about why or how their problem originated. Even further, therapists also don't need to know anything about how clients' problems developed—and they need to know very little about the problem itself. Instead, solution-focused brief therapy primarily (and often exclusively) focuses on helping clients generate solutions (de Shazer et al., 2007). de Shazer refers to standard therapy interventions as **"formula tasks"** and **"skeleton keys"** (de Shazer, 1985, p. 119). In the following, he describes the similarity of his approach to that of the Milan group:

[The Milan group's] prescription (which follows a formula) and our "formula tasks" (each of which are standardized) suggest something about the nature of therapeutic intervention and change which has not been clearly described before: Interventions can initiate change without the therapist's first understanding, in any detail, what has been going on. (de Shazer, 1985, p. 119)

Also, de Shazer was inspired by Ludwig Wittgenstein's (1968) concepts of language games as interpersonal determinants of reality. Berg and de Shazer (1993) articulate this linguistic development:

As the client and therapist talk more and more about the solution they want to construct together, they come to believe in the truth or

reality of what they are talking about. This is the way language works, naturally. (p. 6)

Not long after solution-focused brief therapy began growing in popularity, William O'Hanlon and Michele Weiner-Davis developed **solution-oriented therapy** (O'Hanlon, 1988). The solution-oriented approach is derived from three main theoretical-practical precursors: (1) Milton Erickson's work; (2) strategic intervention and problem-solving techniques developed at MRI; and (3) de Shazer and Berg's solution-focused brief therapy. O'Hanlon (1998) describes the evolution of his approach:

In the early 1980's I began a correspondence with Steve de Shazer.... [H]e and some colleagues had begun what came to be called the Brief Family Therapy Center.... De Shazer and I shared a common view that mainstream therapies that saw clients as pathological and resistant were all wrong. People were naturally cooperative if approached in the right way and treated as resourceful and competent. De Shazer's work began to take shape and has turned into "solution-focused therapy." ... My work took shape and I began to call it "solution-oriented therapy." ... Because the two were often confused and I have some major differences with the Milwaukee approach, I began to speak of my approach as "possibility therapy." (p. 139)

The differences between SFBT and **possibility therapy** are small but important. As compared to SFBT, O'Hanlon's approach is described as,

- Having more focus on acknowledging and validating clients' emotions and experience.
- Somewhat less directive and less formulaic.
- More collaborative.
- More open to considering political, gender, and historical factors as important in problem development.

O'Hanlon also believes that therapists must take responsibility for pursuing issues that clients don't bring up—especially if the issues lead to violent, dangerous, or painful life outcomes. In contrast, de Shazer (Hoyt, 1994) has gone on record to say that therapists should avoid reading "between the lines" and instead simply stick with what the client is saying is the problem and whatever is working (e.g., "[if] he says he doesn't drink too much and it's not a problem. Leave it alone. Take it seriously"; pp. 29–30).

Narrative Therapy

Michael White of Australia and David Epston of New Zealand met in 1981 at an Australian–New Zealander family therapy conference and subsequently developed a therapeutic approach based on *narrative metaphor* (I. Goldenberg & H. Goldenberg, 2008). The personal narrative metaphor is the story that defines and organizes each individual's life and relationship with the world. As we live and accumulate experiences, we each develop a personal story or narrative that gives our lives meaning and continuity. Much like a well-written story, our personal narrative includes an organized plot, characters, points of tension and climax, and a beginning, middle, and end.

White was strongly influenced by Michel Foucault (1965), a French intellectual and social critic. Foucault accused dominant culture of oppressively maintaining power and control over minority groups by eliminating alternative historical perspectives. Eventually, the dominant culture turns its historical stories into objective truth, and alternative ways of being are pathologized. White's application of Foucault's thinking to the therapy process allows individuals who have oppressed themselves through personal narratives to deconstruct and reconstruct their life stories into more complete, more adaptive, and personally meaningful storylines (M. White & Epston, 1990). **Narrative therapy** as formulated by White and Epston also helps individuals break free from internalized social, cultural, and political oppression and rewrite their life stories from a perspective of personal freedom.

David Epston introduced narrative metaphor concepts to White (I. Goldenberg & H. Goldenberg, 2007). He also has pioneered the use of letters to clients as an extension of therapy (Epston, 1994). In collaboration with Stephan Madigan of Canada, Epston cofounded the **Anti-anorexia/Anti-bulimia League**, an organization that turns so-called eating disordered patients into empowered community and political activists. According to Madigan, narrative approaches spring from diverse sources, including Foucault, Bateson, feminism, anthropology, geography, and postmodernism (Carlson & Kjos, 2000; Madigan, 2011). These approaches also carry the distinct flavor of George Kelly's (1955) psychology of personal constructs.

THEORETICAL PRINCIPLES

Constructive therapies are approaches that begin with the recognition that humans are meaning makers who construct, not simply uncover, their psychological realities. They are based on "the construction that we are constructive."

—Michael F. Hoyt, *The Handbook of Constructive Therapies* (1998, p. 3)

A powerful conceptualization of constructive therapy comes from Michael White (1993), who described therapists as not just "taking history," but "making history." Certainly, in their own particular and sometimes peculiar way, constructive theorists and therapists are currently making history in counseling and psychotherapy.

Postmodernism

The most basic position that postmodernists hold is antirealism (aka: subjectivism). Postmodernists firmly believe there is no such thing as objective fact. This position is, of course, at once illogical, subjective, nonlinear, and essentially unprovable, but from the postmodernist's perspective, such is the inherent nature of all things. de Shazer articulates the subjective or antirealist nature of client symptoms when he writes, "There are no wet beds, no voices without people, no depressions. There is only *talk* about wet beds, *talk* about voices without people, and *talk* about depression" (de Shazer, 1993, p. 93).

Let's take a moment to deconstruct postmodernism. As a term, *postmodernism* derives from art and literature. It originally referred to a movement or perspective that was in opposition to or in reaction against modern art or literature. Of course, this means that to define postmodernism adequately, we must first define modernism. Technically, modernism is associated with the scientific, objective, and deterministic paradigm of an external reality. In some ways, however, defining modernism is like trying to catch a snowflake because all things modern melt away very quickly with the passage of time. It's possible to define the modern art and modern science period and style, but when doing so, we're struck that using the word *modern* in that context is a misnomer. Modern art is no longer "modern" art in the sense that it is no longer contemporary but instead representative of a static period in time. And most likely, postmodernism, too will come to represent a period of time and a way of thinking that emphasizes the profound subjectivity of reality.

If you're feeling confused, that's exactly the point. Milton Erickson sometimes based his therapeutic interventions on what he referred to as the **confusion technique** (M. H. Erickson, 1964). In an effort to produce positive change, he would speak to clients in ways that were circular, nonlinear, and confusing.

Once confusion set in, client responsiveness to hearing and accepting alternative ways of thinking were increased. As discussed in Chapter 8, Albert Ellis helped clients deconstruct irrational beliefs through vigorous disputation—a forceful approach, based on modernist, rational thinking. In contrast, like Erickson, constructive therapists help clients deconstruct and reconstruct specific beliefs as well as personal narratives through a careful and subtle use of words and language. This theoretical perspective encourages cognitive activity that involves what Gergen (2009a; 2009b; 2011) described earlier—reflection, curiosity, and doubt.

QUESTIONS FOR REFLECTION

Think about what it's like to experience confusion. What might be the purpose of Erickson's confusion tactics? When you're confused about something do you reach out and grab onto the first thing that makes sense? Could that work as a therapy strategy?

Language and Languaging

Constructive therapists focus on how language builds, maintains, and changes each individual's worldview (H. Anderson, 2007; H. Anderson & Burney, 2004; Lipchik, 2002). As Hoyt (1998, p. 4) stated, "Language and languaging are the ways we make meaning and exchange information." Language determines reality. Efran and Fauber (1995) described,

> Language is where people live.... It allows people to have names, to "know" who they are, and to carve separable things out of the interconnected flux that they take to be the universe. One can manage to play baseball without a shortstop, but not without the words and symbols that differentiate first base from home plate. Without language, it would not be possible for a person to engage in self-conscious thought, to keep an appointment book, or to have problems. (p. 279)

Given their focus on language, constructive therapists are open to an entire domain of therapy interventions including relabeling, reframing, solution-focused questioning, restorying, and problem externalization (Guterman, 2006; Murphy, 2008). We review these approaches in the Practice of Constructive Psychotherapies section.

Change Is Constant and Inevitable

Solution-focused and narrative therapists believe change is constant and therefore change is inevitable. Change happens every day, both in the domain of internal human perception (what you see, hear, etc.) and the domain of social discourse.

From the constructive perspective, because change is inevitable, therapists can help guide the change in positive directions. Perhaps even more importantly, constructive theorists believe that only a small change is required to change so-called big problems (de Shazer et al., 2007).

Problems Are Co-Created

Constructive theory holds that you can change the past from the present. This is because problems are either creations (constructivist) or co-creations (social constructionist). The client—as creator/author/architect—can take apart the problem (deconstruct it) and then reassemble it differently.

As described in more detail later, therapy conversations are opportunities to reconstruct, restory, or accommodate experiences from the past. You may recall the concept of introjection or "swallowing whole" from Chapter 6 (Gestalt therapy). In constructive therapy, particularly its narrative therapy format, the therapist helps clients cough up their old life stories and chew them up in a new and different way before trying to swallow and digest them again.

This process is supported by recent brain research. Memories are electro-chemically stored in the brain, typically in the hippocampal region. When memories are accessed, they're pulled out of storage and into active memory; they may even be re-experienced in some ways. Then, when the memories are placed back in long-term storage, they're reconsolidated. Neuroscientists claim this reconsolidation process is open and involves **re-remembering** (Quirk & Mueller, 2008; Rüegg, 2009). As a consequence, every remembering is an opportunity to re-remember things differently. Of course, as humans we often re-remember things differently (depending on mood, who we're with, time of day, etc.), which fits with the idea of change being constant. In the case of trauma, when memories are very troublesome, constructive therapies take advantage of this re-remembering process to shift the storyline toward more positive and controllable outcomes.

Therapy Is a Collaborative, Cooperative, Co-Constructive Conversation

Constructive therapists seek to establish a collaborative relationship with clients. Guterman (2006) noted: "Borrowing from the field of anthropology, some social constructionists have described their role as a participant-observer" (p. 15). This idea implies an interconnection between client and therapist and leads to a process wherein therapists "act with" their clients collaboratively rather than "acting on" their clients as an outside modernist influencer.

This collaborative formulation of therapist-client relationships has led to constructive therapists denouncing the concept of resistance. If you recall, much of the old modernist psychoanalytic model was based on the therapist as an authority who interpreted reality to clients and then helped clients work through their resistance to the psychoanalytic reality. In contrast, constructive therapists view resistance as natural and as the responsibility of the therapist—and not the fault of the client. For example, O'Hanlon and Weiner-Davis (1989) wrote:

> [C]lients do not always follow therapists' suggestions ... this is not viewed as resistance. When this happens, clients are simply educating therapists as to the most productive and fitting method of helping them change. (pp. 21–22)

Moving responsibility for cooperation and resistance from clients to therapists is a major contribution of constructive theory. It's not surprising that many involuntary clients are relieved when an appointed therapist focuses on strengths and possibilities, rather than trying to break down denial and get them to admit to owning the problem. The gentle, collaborative, and positive approach that constructive therapists advocate may be why many therapists and agencies that work with involuntary or mandated clients find constructive approaches so useful (Rosenberg, 2000; Tohn & Oshlag, 1996).

Therapy Focuses on Strengths and Solutions

With the preceding emphasis on collaboration and cooperation and co-construction of new stories, you might think constructive therapists strive for an absolutely equal sharing of power in their relationship with clients. After all, egalitarianism is a basic constructive theoretical position. Even further, the client is respected and viewed as her own best expert. Not long ago, a student in one of our theories classes queried us about this egalitarian theoretical position. As we lectured on solution-focused methods for leading clients toward solutions, she exclaimed, "But just a few minutes ago you said constructive theory embraces equality between therapist and client and views the client as the best expert on her own reality. I thought that meant constructive therapists don't lead their clients?"

Well, the truth is that although constructive therapists respect and accept their client's perspectives, they also direct and lead clients in a preplanned direction—toward personal strengths and positive problem-solving abilities. As Weakland (1993) stated, "Just as one cannot not communicate, one cannot not influence" (p. 143). Weiner-Davis (1993) asked, "Since we cannot avoid leading, the question becomes, 'Where shall we lead our clients?'" (p. 156).

The answer to this question is simple: Constructive therapists direct clients toward (a) solutions, (b) exceptions to their problem-centered viewpoint, (c) optimism and self-efficacy, and (d) new versions of personal stories that promote greater psychological health (Monk, 1997; Winslade & Monk, 2007). In this way, constructive theory and therapy are clearly laden with the values of Erickson's utilization concept.

Theory of Psychopathology

Constructive theory doesn't support or use traditional psychopathology models. Diagnosing clients is viewed as an unhelpful procedure. Client symptoms such as anxiety and depression are not objective entities but part of an individual's personal emotional experience cast within an overall personal life narrative. Instead of using diagnostic categories, constructive therapists meet clients where they are, emphasizing unique strengths that each client brings to therapy.

On the other hand, constructive therapists are practical and in touch with contemporary needs for diagnostic assessment and categorization (Guterman, 2006). As most of us recognize, diagnosis and labeling constitute a means of professional communication, and this form of communication is used—while simultaneously being questioned. Consequently, solution-focused, possibility, and narrative approaches are routinely applied to the treatment of many different traditional problems. These applications include alcoholic narratives, grief therapy, eating disorders, domestic violence, dissociative disorders, and more (Connie & Metcalf, 2009; Hoyt, 1998; Metcalf, 2008; Monk, Winslade, Crocket, & Epston, 1997).

Broadly speaking, there are two main determinants of client problems, regardless of whether the client is an individual, couple, or family:

The client has gotten stuck using ineffective solutions. This view, derived from Erickson's work and the Mental Research Institute approach, emphasizes that individuals become stuck repeating maladaptive behavior patterns even though they possess many personal strengths and resources. For the most part, clients become stuck because they construct their experiences, using language and other meaning-making procedures, in a manner leading to stuckness. Constructive therapists examine client symptoms, problems, and psychopathology for the sole purpose of deconstruction. As noted previously, many solution-focused therapists almost completely ignore client statements about problems and reorient therapy conversations toward solutions.

The client believes in an unhealthy, pathology-based self-, couple, or family narrative. Narrative therapists believe that human problems develop when clients write themselves into their self-narratives as inadequate, problem-plagued losers. Clients often show up in therapy because they have constructed a narrative in which the dominant theme of "personal problem" is obscuring a nondominant theme of "personal strength and resourcefulness."

Deconstructing and reconstructing of the client's personal narrative is the road to improvement.

THE PRACTICE OF CONSTRUCTIVE PSYCHOTHERAPIES

Constructive therapy is collaborative. This may be the biggest reason why constructive therapists don't emphasize psychoeducation or role induction procedures. Instead of formally introducing clients to the therapy process, the constructive therapist continuously collaborates with clients to identify goals, strategies, and the overall therapy direction. (See Putting it in Practice 11.1: Informed Consent From the Constructive Perspective)

Assessment Issues and Procedures

Constructive therapy approaches use minimal formal assessment procedures. In keeping with

PUTTING IT IN PRACTICE 11.1

Informed Consent From the Constructive Perspective

I'm looking forward to working with you in counseling. This next section describes a little bit about my theoretical orientation and my ways of working with people. Questions are always welcome!

There are many words used to describe the kind of work I do, but some people call it constructivist. This means that I believe people construct many aspects of their lives, and when things aren't going well, it's possible to change the way things are constructed. Each of us has our own reality, and our own beliefs about things. Sometimes, problems can be changed or pushed back by working on the way we see things and experience them.

As we work together, I will be excited to hear your life story and help you notice the way you tell your story. I will help you turn your attention to your successes and your strengths. We will explore how to build on these successes and strengths. We will also work to get a grip on those pesky problems that creep into our lives, and experiment with ways to see them differently.

I believe words can be magic. Just talking together, paying attention to the words we use, can bring about change. We don't need to go over every detail of your past, and we won't necessarily need to meet for very long. Sometimes my clients only need a few sessions to make the changes they want to make.

In my work with people who are fighting back problems in their lives, I am curious and optimistic. Each individual has a unique reality that I am always excited to learn about. Believe it or not, we can tinker with your reality in ways that can make your life seem new, better, and more in your own control. . . .

de Shazer's (1985) emphasis on keys to solution and White and Epston's (1990) emphasis on client narratives, the primary therapy focus is either on identifying and implementing solutions or on deconstructing problem narratives and constructing more satisfying narratives (White, 2007; White & Denborough, 2011). Narrative therapists spend a bit more time assessing and exploring client problems than solution-focused brief therapists, but, overall, too much time spent discussing problems might only strengthen, build, and further deepen the client's problem-focused worldview. The main therapy goal is to help clients move past their problem focus and develop solution- and strength-focused worldviews and adaptive personal narratives.

Even though solution-focused brief therapists want clients to shift from problem talk to solution talk, it's still important to begin therapy by allowing clients to tell their stories. If therapists ignore the client's problem, rapport can be damaged. The general rule for solution-focused brief therapists at the beginning of therapy is to follow the client's lead. This rule flows from Erickson's indirect hypnotic approach with clients, in which therapists begin by pacing the client and later take the lead and make indirect and direct suggestions (Haley, 1967). Insoo Kim Berg also articulated this philosophy when she wrote about leading from behind (Berg & Miller, 1992).

The primary therapist tool in solution-focused and narrative therapy is questioning. However, excessive questioning can be problematic. To help address potential negative outcomes associated with using too many questions, Monk (1997) describes a role induction statement in narrative therapy with a young client:

> A therapy of questions can easily make the client feel like the subject of an interrogation. To avoid the power imbalance that might follow from this kind of conversation, I sought permission from Peter to ask him some more questions, saying that if I asked too many questions, he could either not answer them or tell me he was "questioned out." (p. 9)

As we explore constructive assessment strategies, keep in mind the possibility that clients could get **questioned out**.

Opening the Session

Discovering the client's problem view is the primary initial focus for constructive therapists. The solution-focused brief therapist usually begins therapy with a query like, "What brings you here?" This standard opening allows clients to discuss their conceptualization of the problem and take the lead in the ensuing therapeutic conversation.

In keeping with their optimistic orientation, solution-based therapists ask questions that stimulate clients to begin moving up a positive path. The following opening questions fit with a solution-focused/narrative model:

- What could happen during our time today that will make your visit with me worthwhile?
- If this session goes very well, what will we accomplish together?
- How did you decide to come to counseling?

Usually, these questions prompt clients to identify specific goals they want from treatment. Identifying or constructing reasonable goals is an important assessment component of solution-based therapies.

Narrative therapists generally want to know more about the original construction of the problem; this involves gathering information about how the problem first started and how it initially affected the client's view of herself (Monk, 1997). Early narrative-based assessment questions include:

- How will your life go forward if [the problem] continues into the future?
- How will your life go forward if [the problem] gets smaller or goes away completely?

A key concept to keep in mind when constructing assessment questions from the narrative perspective is to work on externalizing the problem from the person or the family. This is accomplished by consistently referring to the problem as a separate entity and not something intrinsic to the individual. We discuss externalizing questions as a specific therapy technique later in this chapter.

Scaling Questions

Solution-focused therapists use **scaling questions** as a means of assessment and treatment (Murphy, 2008). Scaling questions ask clients to rate problems, progress, or any therapy-related issue on a 1 to 10 scale. Typically, 1 is considered the lowest or worst possible rating and 10 the highest or best possible rating. Scaling questions are used in a variety of creative ways.

Following a qualitative examination of scaling questions in therapy, Strong, Pyle, and Sutherland (2009) described how scaling questions operate in terms of constructive theory:

> Asking a how a client will move from a 6 on a scale to a 7 requires a linguistic ladder of sorts to be constructed and serve both client and counselor in constructing still-to-be articulated solutions. (p. 182)

The following therapy excerpt illustrates how a solution-focused therapist might use scaling questions in practice to (1) obtain an initial rating of the size of the client's problem from the client's perspective, (2) monitor client progress, (3) identify intermediate therapy goals, and (4) make specific plans for improvement.

(1) Therapist: Tell me, on a scale from 1 to 10, with 1 representing feeling completely and totally depressed and 10 representing feeling the best a person can possibly feel, how would you rate your feelings today?

Client: I'm about the same as last week

(2) Therapist: Last week you gave yourself a rating of 3. What rating would you give yourself today?

Client: Hmm. I guess I think I'm still at about a 3.

(3) Therapist: So if you're still at a 3 right now, exactly what would need to be different to bump your rating up to a 4?

Client: I don't know. Maybe if I could get up in the morning without feeling so damn tired. Or if I could make it through the workday without thinking about how stupid and meaningless my job is.

(3) Therapist: So if you weren't tired in the morning that would make it a 4? Or would you need to have both those changes happen, both waking up refreshed and thinking that your job is meaningful?

Client: Either waking up feeling good or feeling better about my job would make it a 4. Both of those would make it a 5 or maybe even a 6.

(4) Therapist: Let's look at your job first. What exactly do you need to do to make it feel just a little more meaningful? What would make your job meaningful enough to bump your daily rating up to a 4 for tomorrow?

Percentage Questions

Percentage questions are similar to scaling questions; they give therapists a simple method for measuring exactly what change would look like. Typical percentage questions include: "How would your life be different if you were 1% less depressed?" "How about if you were 10% less depressed?" and "How about if you were 100% less depressed?"

Assessing Client Motivation

Solution-focused therapists frequently categorize clients in terms of three motivational levels (Murphy, 2008):

1. **Customers for change**: These clients are eager to work in therapy and ready to make changes.

2. **Complainants**: These clients are interested in therapy because of the insistence or interest of a significant other.

3. **Visitors to treatment**: These are typically mandated clients who aren't interested in change and show up only because they have to.

Ideally, therapists can indirectly convince clients who are complainants or visitors to become customers for change (de Shazer, 1988).

To assess motivation and obtain a commitment for change, at the end of the first session, a narrative therapist might ask:

> Are you more interested in finding a way to move beyond that depression that's got a hold on you and your life, or are you more interested in accepting that your depressed state is permanent and therefore you just need ways of coping with depression?

Of course, the motivated and committed client will voice a greater interest in the former option as opposed to the latter.

The Credulous Approach to Assessment

In his usual common-sense manner, Kelly pioneered the **credulous approach to assessment**. He summarizes this approach by stating, "If you don't know what is wrong with a person, ask him [sic]; he may tell you" (1955, p. 322). Kelly's approach—and every approach associated with constructive therapy—emphasizes that clients are the best expert on their own lives and should be treated as such.

Is Formal Assessment Really Required for a Constructive Therapist?

The radical solution-focused view of assessment holds that traditional assessment is unnecessary. de Shazer (1985) articulates this position:

> For an intervention to successfully fit, it is not necessary to have detailed knowledge of the complaint. It is not necessary even to be able to construct with any rigor how the trouble is maintained in order to prompt solution.... All that is necessary is that the person involved in a troublesome situation does something different, even if that behavior is seemingly irrational, certainly irrelevant, obviously bizarre, or humorous. (p. 7)

Despite his irreverent position regarding assessment of client problems, de Shazer has a straightforward but complex method for evaluating client complaints and quickly providing potential solutions. His approach doesn't involve traditional or formal assessment, but it does offer therapists a menu of potential formula solutions linked to client complaints. de Shazer's system is summarized in Putting it in Practice 11.2.

Specific Therapy Techniques

In this section we include specific therapy techniques derived from solution-focused brief therapy, solution-oriented therapy (or possibility therapy), and narrative therapy. We make theoretical distinctions regarding each technique when possible, but practically speaking, constructive therapies use many overlapping technical procedures.

The Pretreatment Change Question

Solution-focused therapists cite research that indicates clients often begin improving between the time they call for an appointment and the first session (Beyebach, Morejon, Palenzuela, & Rodriguez-Arias, 1996). To help clients focus on how they're already using their strengths and resources effectively, a version of the following question can be asked at the beginning of the first session:

> What changes have you noticed that have happened or started to happen since you called to make the appointment for this session. (de Shazer & Dolan, 2007, p. 5)

Solution-focused brief therapists report that a large percentage of clients have begun making changes prior to their first session (Weiner-Davis, de Shazer, & Gingerich, 1987).

Unique Account and Redescription Questions

As a specific therapy tool, White (1988) developed **unique account and redescription questions**. We refer to these questions as "How did you manage that?" questions. Such questions constitute the mainstay of many narrative and solution-based approaches. They're phrased in many different ways and accompanied by genuine interest, and used whenever clients say anything that might be construed as progress. Narrative therapists typically refer to these glimmers of hope as a **unique**

PUTTING IT IN PRACTICE 11.2

De Shazer's Complaint–Solution Assessment System

In his complaint-solution assessment system, de Shazer (1985) identified 12 typical complaints that he viewed as doors leading to various solutions. This complaint-solution system is summarized below:

Client complaint	Formula solution prescription
The client complains about a *sequence of behavior*: "When I'm depressed, I can't get myself out of bed in the morning."	Assign a specific task: "On the days when you do get out of bed in the morning, what's the first thing you do? Go ahead and do that each morning."
The client complains about the *meanings ascribed to a situation*: "My wife won't stop nagging me about getting a better job. She thinks I'm a lazy good-for-nothing husband."	Use reframing: "It's clear your wife loves you very much and is concerned about your happiness."
The client complains about the *frequency of a problem behavior or experience*: "I'm always worrying about everything—my husband's health, my daughter's marriage, our financial situation."	Assign a specific task: "You're worrying is important. I'd like you to schedule a half hour every day to just focus on worrying. What time would work best for you?"
The client complains about the *physical location where the problem occurs*: "I only drink when I'm out with my buddies on Friday's after work."	Suggest a new location: "Where could you and your buddies go after work and not drink?"
The client complains that *the problem is involuntary*: "I can't stop myself from pulling out hair from my eyebrows."	Prescribe the symptom, ask for exceptions to the rule, or suggest a new location: "I notice you still have plenty of eyebrow hairs left; would you get to work on that this week?" or "What's happening during those times when you don't pull out your eyebrow hairs?" or "Where are you when you don't pull out your eyebrow hairs?"
The client complains about *significant others involved in the problem*: "And then my wife totally sabotages my diet by baking all these cakes and cookies."	Ask when guilt will be resolved or what difference it will make to them: "When will your wife be free from guilt over contributing to your weight problem?" or "What difference will it make to your wife if you choose not to eat her cakes and cookies?"

Client complaint	Formula solution prescription
The client complains about *who or what is to blame* for the problem: "This whole situation is my brother's fault. He is totally insensitive and selfish."	Ask when guilt will be resolved: "When is it likely for your brother's guilt in this matter to be resolved?"
The client complains about *an environmental factor or situation* such as job, economic status, living space, etc.: "My job sucks. My boss rides me constantly and I don't like any of my coworkers."	Suggest a new location: "You could either quit your job or spend time with your boss and coworkers at some place where you might actually enjoy them."
The client complains about *a physiological state or feeling*: "I weigh about 190 pounds and have tried everything to lose weight. I'd like to weigh 125 to 130 pounds."	Use symptom prescription: "The first thing you need to do is go home and start eating. When you get up to 220 pounds, come back and I can help you" (adapted from Haley, 1973, pp.115–119).
The client complains about *the past*: "My parents were abusive and critical of me when I was young. They favored my sister."	Talk about a past success: "You were able to graduate from high school with high honors."
The client complains about *likely future situations that are catastrophic or dire*: "I know I'm gonna flunk my history test."	Talk about a past success or focus on new expectations: "How did you pass your last one?" or "What would you have to do to get a D on your exam?"
The client has *excessively idealistic or utopian expectations*: "I know I'll be able to get a job this summer, no problem."	Focus on new expectations or focus on a minimal change: "What if it was hard to get a job this summer? How would you cope with that?" or "Tell me what it would look like if you just put 10% more effort into getting a job."

Source: Adapted from de Shazer (1985).

outcome or sparkling moment (Monk et al., 1997; White & Epston, 1990). Examples include:

- How did you beat the fear and go out shopping?

- How did you manage to get yourself out of bed and come to this appointment despite the depression?

- You just stopped drinking last week cold turkey! How did you accomplish that?

- What were you telling yourself when you were feeling a little better last month?

From the narrative perspective, the client's personal narrative can never match the depth and richness of the client's lived experiences.

Unfortunately, what usually gets dismissed or pruned away from the client's story are the moments of strength, the instant of courage in the face of adversity, and experiences of positive decision making. Consequently, it's crucial for therapists not only to highlight these sparkling moments but also to help the client articulate and repeat their occurrences using words, images, and even movements. The key is to acknowledge, not ignore, these positive, lived moments. Monk (1997) compares the therapist's nurturance for sparkling moments to the process of building a fire:

These sparkling moments, or new developments in relation to the problem-saturated story, need to be historicized so that they do not hang lifeless and disconnected. I like to describe this stage of the narrative interview as similar to the task of building a fire. To keep the first flickering flame alive, you place tiny twigs very carefully and strategically over the flame. If the twig is too large, the flame could be suffocated. If there is only one twig, it will quickly be spent and the flame will be extinguished. The fire needs to be gently nurtured by the placing of twigs in such a way that oxygen can feed the flames. Larger sticks are then placed on the fire, and soon the fire has a life of its own. (pp. 16–17)

Monk's analogy is an excellent warning. Therapists need to pay attention to sparkling moments but not to jump in too enthusiastically when they first emerge. If therapists are too excited about client progress, clients may quickly retreat back to their safe and unsatisfactory life stories.

In a qualitative study of unique outcomes imbedded in stories of abuse, Draucker (2003) summarized her findings:

Six types of unique outcomes stories were identified in the women's narratives (rebellion, breaking free, resurgence, refuge, determination, confidant) and three types in the men's narratives (reawakening, buddy and normal guy, champion). Findings suggest that unique outcomes stories are common in narratives otherwise focused on abuse. (p. 7)

Helping clients uncover the sparkling moments or unique and positive twists on their challenging life experiences is at the heart of narrative therapy. Although Draucker (2003) observed substantial male-female differences in her study, it's important for therapists practicing narratively to be open to whatever general or specific positive and unique outcomes their clients generate.

Externalizing Conversations

Virtually everyone recognizes the tendency for clients (and other humans) to blame either themselves or others when things go awry. Blaming is a natural, but often unhelpful human phenomenon.

Many clients come to therapy in distress because the narratives or stories they tell themselves about themselves are saturated with problems for which they are responsible. **Externalizing conversations** are designed to help clients, couples, and families push their problems outside the intrapsychic realm. Ramey, Tarulli, Frijters, and Fisher (2009) define externalizing succinctly:

Externalizing involves using language to position problems and other aspects of people's lives outside of themselves in an effort to separate people from dominant, problem saturated stories. (p. 263)

Through problem externalization, clients can dissociate from the problem, look at it from a greater distance, and develop strategies for eliminating it. Examples of externalizing questions include:

- How long have you been working against this marijuana problem?

- What exactly are you doing when you're free from that fog of depression?

- Who are you with when you feel lighter and happier and like you've thrown off the weight of that depression?

- How might you tell your anxiety thank you and good bye? (Adapted from J. Sommers-Flanagan & R. Sommers-Flanagan, 2009, p. 92)

When individual clients, couples, or families engage in therapeutic externalizing conversations, they usually experience relief. This may be because often, clients come to counseling worrying that the therapist's all-seeing and all-knowing eye will pierce their defenses and hold them 100% responsible for their problems.

QUESTIONS FOR REFLECTION

Can you imagine using externalizing questions with clients? Consider how you might initiate an externalizing conversation with: (1) A client who comes in complaining of "biological" depression, or (2) a parent and teenager who come in to work on the teen's pattern of delinquent behavior.

Externalizing conversations take away clients' sense of accountability and reduce defensiveness, thereby allowing client and therapist to work collaboratively against the problems.

Carl Rogers With a Twist

O'Hanlon (1998) credits Carl Rogers with teaching him the importance of showing empathy and compassion for clients. He also describes a unique technique for showing empathy and compassion while at the same time helping clients move beyond their negative or traumatic feelings from the past. Examples of this technique, **Carl Rogers With a Twist**, include:

Client: I feel like cutting myself.

Therapist: You've felt like cutting yourself (O'Hanlon & Bertolino, 1998, p. 47).

[In this example the therapist is validating the client but shifting to past tense.]

Client: I have flashbacks all the time.

Therapist: So you have flashbacks a lot of the time.

[In this example the therapist transforms the client's verbal disclosure from a global to a partial perception.]

Client: I'm a bad person because I was sexually abused.

Therapist: So you've really gotten the idea that you are bad because you were sexually abused.

[In this last example the therapist shifts the client's words from factual to perceptual.]

O'Hanlon's Carl Rogers with a twist technique is an excellent example of a subtle, indirect, linguistically based strategy for shifting client perspectives. It's also a good example of solution-oriented therapists actively directing clients toward the positive.

Relabeling and Reframing

From the constructive perspective, **relabeling and reframing** are core therapy tools. For example, clients are customers for change (not clients), and therapy is a conversation (not counseling or an interview). In fact, some therapists aren't therapists at all; they're referred to as coaches and consultants. Constructive therapists systematically relabel and reframe any part of therapy necessary to gain access to clients and engage them in social discourse.

In our experience, we've seen therapy-reluctant teens quickly become cooperative when we relabel the therapy process. For example, teens who boldly claim, "I think therapy is stupid" and "You can't make me talk in here" suddenly calm down and talk openly when we respond to their complaints with,

> Yeah, okay, so let's not do therapy today. How about if we have a consultation meeting instead? I won't be your therapist today; I'll just be your consultant. (See J. Sommers-Flanagan & R. Sommers-Flanagan, 2007)

Language use is a foundation for reframing or, in Haley's (1976) terms, positive relabeling. In his solution-focused book on working with adolescents, Selekman (1993) recommended using a **forced-teaming** reframe with an adolescent who was referred by a probation officer. He suggested that he and the client team together to surprise and prove to the probation officer that the boy can avoid trouble and be successful. This approach captures the boy's attention, intriguing him and motivating him to work harder with the counselor.

Similarly, many parents resist using positive reinforcement approaches with their children because they view such strategies as bribery. In our work with difficult adolescents, it has been helpful when parents redefine rewards as positive incentives rather than bribery; this helps parents become more open to using positive approaches to influencing their children (J. Sommers-Flanagan & R. Sommers-Flanagan, 2007).

Presuppositional Questions

In and of itself, goal setting is a powerful force for change. Surprisingly, it wasn't until 1970 that goal setting was conceptualized as a direct way to modify individual and group behavior (Ryan, 1970). Locke and Latham (2002, 2007) and others have demonstrated that individuals perform better when they have specific, difficult goals.

Constructive therapists use **presuppositional questions** to co-create therapeutic and life goals with clients (DeJong & Berg, 2002). These questions presuppose that a positive change has already been made and then ask for specific descriptions of these changes. O'Hanlon and Bertolino (1998) illustrate a presuppositional question using an approach they refer to as *videotalk:*

> Let's say that a few weeks, months, or more time has elapsed and your problem has been resolved. If you and I were to watch a videotape of your life in the future, what would you be doing on that tape that would show that things were better? (p. 90)

There are many creative versions of presupposition questions using language ranging from crystal balls to letters (or postcards) from the future (White & Epston, 1990). The main point is to construct a question that helps clients hear, feel, and picture themselves functioning in the future without problems. Some therapists believe that the longer clients can focus on positive, problem-free, goal-attained futures within a session, the greater likelihood they have of making the solution-focused future happen.

The Miracle Question

The miracle question is by far the most well-known solution-focused therapy technique (Hurn, 2003; Nau & Shilts, 2000; Santa Rita, 1998; Strong & Pyle, 2009). de Shazer's (1988) original version of the miracle question is:

> Suppose you were to go home tonight, and while you were asleep, a miracle happened and this problem was solved. How will you know the miracle happened? What will be different? (p. 5)

The miracle question is simply another presuppositional question that helps clients focus on a positive future. When clients respond to the question, it's important for counselors to obtain clear, concrete, and behaviorally specific descriptions of what would be different. In some ways, this question helps clients develop and hopefully maintain a positive future vision. The question also builds rapport with clients; when therapists validate and

nurture each answer the client provides, the therapy alliance is deepened.

The miracle question is a flexible intervention that can be modified for use with various populations. For example, Bertolino (1999) suggested an alternative wording when using the miracle question with young clients:

> Suppose that when you went home tonight and went to sleep, something strange happened to you and your life changed for the better. You may or may not know what actually happened, but you knew that your problem had gone away. What will be different? (p. 75)

In the preceding example Bertolino used word *strange* instead of *miracle*. He also suggested that therapists working with youth might use the word *weird* or an alternative word the client has previously used in therapy. He advised therapists to modify their language style when working with young clients.

Tohn and Oshlag (1996) described a slightly different version of the miracle question for use with mandated clients:

> **Suppose** that tonight, after our session, you go home and fall asleep, and while you are sleeping a miracle happens. The miracle is that **the problems that brought you here today** are solved, but you don't know that the miracle has happened because you are asleep. When you wake up in the morning, what will be some of the first things you will **notice** that will be different that will tell you this miracle has happened? (pp. 170–171, bold in original)

Tohn and Oslag explained that beginning with the word suppose is crucial because it leads clients toward pretending that the miracle has already happened, rather than speculating on whether it will or will not happen. They also noted that saying "the problems that brought you here" focuses the question on the reality of the situation. In contrast, they claimed that when therapists use "your problem is solved," clients are likely to respond with a more grandiose disappearance of the problem. Finally, they used the word *notice* toward the end of the intervention to help clients respond using a wide range of sensory experiences.

Formula Tasks

In addition to the formula **pretreatment change question** discussed previously, there are other solution-based formula tasks (de Shazer, 1985; de Shazer, 1984; de Shazer & Molnar, 1984). de Shazer originally developed the formula task concept, but following his lead others have created additional formula tasks. As Reiter (2007) noted, positive expectancy is a significant component in successful formula tasks:

> By expecting that change/difference will occur for the client, based on the way that it makes most sense for the client, the therapist is sending a message to the client(s) that a new more useful mode of operation is not only possible, but will occur sometime in the near future.

The **first session formula task** is designed to help clients shift from a focus on the past and negative expectations to a present-future focus and positive expectations. This task is based on the assumption that, in general, there are many positive qualities already existing within most people who come for treatment.

> Between now and next time we meet, we [I] would like you to observe, so that you can describe to us [me] next time, what happens in your [pick one: family, life, marriage, relationship] that you want to continue to have happen. (de Shazer, 1984, p. 15)

Reiter (2007) described how the first-session formula task works:

> This formula task is designed to shift clients' lenses from that of a problem-focused orientation to a solution-focused orientation. Instead of doing the typical thing that the client has been doing (i.e., focusing on when things are not going well), the client now is doing something different and focusing on times of strength and resources. (p. 31)

Selekman (1993) reported that when he uses the first-session formula task, clients he works with usually return to their second session with two or three specific descriptions of positive interactions they would like to have continue.

Reiter also described another of de Shazer's popular formula tasks, the **write-read-burn task**:

> This intervention involved spending at least one hour, but no more than one-and-a-half hours per day, on odd-numbered days, writing down good and bad memories (of a boyfriend). On even-numbered days, the client was to read the previous day's notes and then burn them. After this first case, this task was generically used for clients who had complaints dealing with obsessive thoughts or depressive thoughts.

As you can see this task has a bit of a Milton Erickson feel to it. It includes some paradox and the likelihood is that clients will insightfully decide they've had quite enough of writing, reading, and burning in a relatively short time period.

Exception Questions

Exception questions are also a commonly employed solution-based intervention (DeJong & Berg, 2002; Murphy, 2008). In keeping with the theoretical position that only small changes are needed to instigate larger changes, exception questions seek minor evidence that the client's problem is not always huge and overbearing. Bertolino (1999) provides several examples of exception questions with teenage clients:

- It seems that when this problem is happening, things are pretty difficult. When does the problem seem less noticeable to you? What is everyone doing when it's less noticeable?

- When does the problem appear to happen less?

- What is your son/daughter doing when he/she is not in trouble?

- Tell me what it's like when the problem is a little less dominating.

Exception questions are designed to build hope and to identify small behavioral patterns or sequences when the problem is either occurring less or not occurring at all. Constructive therapists use exception sequences to build a case for preexisting client strengths and resources. These sequences can be helpful in building up or feeding the client's adaptive storyline in contrast to the problem-saturated storyline.

The Do Something Different Task
The **do something different task** is a direct but nonspecific intervention that's especially well-suited for disrupting repeating and dissatisfying behavior sequences. For example, if a parent comes to therapy complaining about her son's recurrent tantrums, the therapist might tell the parent to do something totally different the next time a tantrum occurs (J. Sommers-Flanagan & R. Sommers-Flanagan, 2011).

As is the case with very direct but nonspecific interventions, the therapist cannot know in advance what different behavior the client may select. This unknown and unknowable component of the intervention fuels both creativity and danger. It releases clients from entrenched behavior patterns but may also implicitly give them permission to act out inappropriately or even violently. In one case reported by de Shazer (1985), the father of a young boy with a pattern of lying came up with the idea of rubbing his son's face in actual bullshit whenever a lie was suspected. Fortunately, the boy's mother wouldn't allow such an intervention, so the father chose a less violent option of buying a can of "bullshit repellent" from a local novelty shop and spraying his son with it on the next occasion of a lie. Although de Shazer reports success in this case, it clearly illustrates that clients are very capable of coming up with bad and even abusive ideas for "doing something different" when left completely on their own.

Letter Writing
To deepen the therapy process and further stimulate alternative storylines, Epston (1994; White & Epston, 1990) pioneered the use of **letter writing** as a narrative therapeutic technique. Epston uses and recommends several letter formats. Next, we describe some of these formats and provide brief examples. For more detailed examples, you should consult White and Epston's (1990) *Narrative Means to Therapeutic Ends* as well as other more recent letter writing publications (S. Alexander, Shilts, Liscio, & Rambo, 2008; H. Davidson & Birmingham, 2001; Keeling & Bermudez, 2006; Rombach, 2003).

In the **summary letter**, narrative therapists write to clients immediately following a therapeutic conversation. Summary letters typically are written from the therapist's perspective but highlight sparkling moments and use the client's words to produce a more strength- and hope-based storyline.

Letters of invitation are typically written to family members who are reluctant to attend therapy sessions. These letters highlight the individual's important status in the family, focusing on positive reasons for attending a session, rather than on negative consequences of nonattendance. The following **letter of invitation**, written by Mary Underwood and David Epston, illustrates a narrative strategy of telling a storyline with more than one possible outcome and then allowing the client to choose her direction (White & Epston, 1990, pp. 89–90). In our opinion, this particular letter is quite risky.

Dear Jane,
I'm writing because we didn't get to meet each other last Wednesday at 5 p.m.
My name is Mary. I've worked at Leslie Centre for four years. I have a daughter just a little younger than you.
When your mother phoned to say your family wouldn't be coming in, she said you were feeling badly with acne that had flared up. I can understand how you felt—I sometimes get a rash on my face and neck myself.
It's hard writing to you when I don't even know what you look like. If you send me a photo, I'll send you one.
Well it's pretty clear that things are going wrong in your family. Growing up is very hard these days—I'm sure it's harder than it used to be. It sounds like you're failing to get to school sometimes and failing to get on with your life. That would sure make anyone feel miserable.
When I meet with your mother and father next time, I would think that you'll probably have another attack of acne—and I know what it's like

to face people when you're not at your best—I do it quite often.

So I'll understand if you don't feel up to coming and facing into your future.

But, on the other hand, I'd feel really badly talking behind your back with your mother and father.

I've been thinking of this dilemma quite a bit and I've come up with some ideas. I wonder what you think about them:

1. Could you get a friend to represent you at the session—a bit like a lawyer—who could come in your place and speak for you?

2. If that's not a good idea, what about you let your mother or father choose a friend of theirs to represent you?

3. If that's not a good idea, what about you go on "stand by" at the telephone while your parents are here? Then I can call you if I get the impression that your parents have forgotten what it's like to be your age. I can ask for a few ideas about how it feels for you.

Sounds like you've got your parents pretty worried about you.

If you really want to show your parents this letter it doesn't really matter. But I'd prefer you didn't.

I'm planning to meet with your mother and father on Wednesday, April 3rd, at 5:30 p.m. I suppose you might come or you might not or you might try one of those other ideas. It's up to you, I guess.

Well, bye for now,
Yours sincerely,
Mary

Redundancy letters articulate observations and client reports of overlapping or enmeshed family roles. For example, a daughter in a family system may be overly identified with her mother and therefore enacting a parental role with younger siblings. Along with the observation of this family dynamic, the redundancy letter outlines the client's impulse, using her own words, to move forward and establish a more unique identity of her own. Redundancy letters are often accompanied

by a discharge letter; in a discharge letter one family member formally discharges another family member from performing a redundant duty (e.g., the mother and therapist work together to write a kind and compassionate letter to the daughter releasing her from parental duties).

At the end of therapy, **letters of prediction** are written to help clients continue strength-based storylines into the future. Epston asks clients permission to make predictions for the future and then mails the letters—usually with a "private and confidential" label and an instruction "not to be viewed until [6 months after the final session]" (White & Epston, 1990, p. 94). He cites two reasons for using prediction letters. First, he notes that the letters serve as a 6-month follow-up or review that is both interesting and potentially helpful (White & Epston, 1990, p. 94). Second, he suspects that most clients will not wait 6 months to open the letter and that it therefore serves as a possible positive prophesy.

Both Epston and White discuss writing many other types of letters, letters that spring from the issues and concerns expressed to them during sessions. Some of these additional letter variations include letters of reference, counter-referral letters, and letters for special occasions. White, in particular, includes several examples of what he refers to as brief letters designed to strengthen the positive therapeutic narrative. An example follows in which White maps a client's personal influence in her own life:

Dear Molly,
Anorexia nervosa had claimed 99% of your life. You only held 1% of your own territory. You have said that you now hold 25% of your own territory. This means that you have reclaimed 24% of yourself from anorexia nervosa, and you achieved this over the last eight months. And yet, you despair for all those lost years, for the two-thirds of your life under its influence.

Tell me, if you were to pick up another 24% over the next eight months, and then 24% over the next eight months and so on, how long would it take you to reach 200% and be experiencing double value in your life? And should you keep on in this way, how old would you be at the point when you have regained all the time that was lost? And what will it mean that your life is accelerating right at the time that others are slowing down in their lives?

Just curious,

M.W. (White & Epston, 1990, p. 116)

White's letter is a good example of problem externalization using scaling information for feedback, a linguistic flexibility intervention, and personal influence mapping.

Clearly, writing letters to clients has great potential for influencing clients. In our work with young clients we have experimented with in-session note-passing. We've noticed that clients are often surprised and touched at receiving a written communiqué from a concerned and interested therapist (J. Sommers-Flanagan & Sommers-Flanagan, 2007). White (1995) estimated that a single letter may have a potency equivalent to four to five therapy sessions.

Reflecting Teams or Therapeutic Breaks

The contemporary concept of a reflecting team stems from Norwegian psychiatrist Tom Andersen's approach to family therapy (1987, 1991, 1995). Following his lead, many therapists have integrated **reflecting teams** or therapeutic breaks into individual, couple, and family therapy (Cox, Bañez, Hawley, & Mostade, 2003; de Barbaro et al., 2008; de Oliveira, 2003; Fishel, Buchs, McSheffrey, & Murphy, 2001). This approach, which emphasizes multiple perspectives or realities, is highly consistent with constructive thinking.

To reflect is to step back and create space to assist with problem solving (West, Watts, Trepal, Wester, & Lewis, 2001). West, Watts, Trepal, Wester, and Lewis provide an everyday example:

Have you ever been confronted with a decision, then requested the evening to sleep on it and awoke the next morning with a clearer direction?

Andersen's (1987) reflective team is a feedback procedure that's much different from the traditional one-way mirror in family therapy training. In the one-way mirror paradigm, a supervisor and

fellow students sit behind a one-way mirror and observe family therapy sessions. Sometimes the supervisor communicates with the therapist about appropriate therapeutic interventions via a bug-in-the-ear device. Overall, the standard procedure emphasizes supervisory input and a rich discussion of "the case" either midway during the session or immediately afterward.

Consistent with postmodern constructive thinking, Andersen's reflecting team breaks down hierarchical boundaries of traditional one-way mirror supervision by introducing a two-way mirror reflecting team. Originally, his reflecting team procedures consisted of the following:

1. During an impasse when the therapist is unsure how to proceed, or at a preplanned time, a reflecting team meeting is initiated.

2. The therapy session stops as the therapist and family turn to the mirror and the lights and sound system are reversed.

3. The therapist and family watch and listen as the reflecting team spontaneously provide tentative hypotheses about the family's problem issues.

4. During the reflecting team meeting, care is taken to talk about the family in a respectful, nonpathologizing manner.

5. When the reflecting team meeting ends, the lights and sound system are again reversed and family members and therapist have a conversation about the reflecting team's conversation.

Reflecting teams seek to honor the family, while at the same time providing fresh new perspectives. This procedure helps the family feel important, listened to, and accepted. After using the reflecting team approach for a number of years, Andersen (1995) described some of his discoveries:

When we finally began to use this mode we were surprised at how easy it was to talk without using nasty or hurtful words. Later it became evident that how we talk depends on the context in which we talk. If we choose to speak about the family without them present, we easily speak "professionally," in a detached manner. If we choose to speak about them in their presence, we naturally use everyday language and speak in a friendly manner. (p. 16)

The reflecting team approach as articulated by Andersen is a gentle and collaborative experience. He emphasizes that the reflecting team speak with uncertainty, with inclusive both-and language ("*both* this could be true *and* this other thing could be true, too"), and without negative connotations (Andersen, 1991, p. 61).

Andersen's (2007) approach is in contrast to the more provocative and sometimes confusing or double-binding approaches derived from Erickson's work, the MRI group, and even the preceding White and Epston narrative letters. For example, de Shazer (1985) reported using the following feedback intervention with a couple whose drug use was, in the eyes of the woman, adversely affecting their marriage.

> You've got a problem.
> It seems to us, Ralph, that your marital problems are being exacerbated by the drugs, or fogged over by the drugs, or perhaps even created by the drugs. Perhaps you need to stop the drugs, just to see what is going on. But, on the other hand, we agree with you Jane, that if you two were to stop the drugs, then there might be nothing there. And, you might not have time to create anything before the marriage broke up. In short, we don't know what the fuck you are going to do.
> I suggest you think about what I just said, and decide what actions you are going to take . . . first. (p. 52)

de Shazer reported that the clients cut down on their drug use immediately after the intervention. Within weeks, both clients stopped using drugs and managed to stay married and to develop healthier common interests.

QUESTIONS FOR REFLECTION

As you contrast Andersen's and de Shazer's styles, what major differences do you notice? Which approach are you more comfortable with and why?

Constructive Therapy in Action: Brief Vignettes

As you may sense from this chapter, solution-focused therapy emphasizes a collaborative relationship, but also includes active use of a variety of specific techniques. Most of these techniques involve questioning. In contrast, narrative therapy is less technically focused and more oriented toward an attitude and a deeper relationship, although when narrative therapists use interventions, they also tend to use questions which are often very similar in content to the questions that solution-focused therapists use.

Vignette I: A Resistant (Reluctant) Teenager

This is a brief case excerpt of Brent Richardson illustrating several solution-focused therapy techniques. Richardson is the author of *Working With Challenging Youth: Lessons Learned Along the Way* (Richardson, 2001). The case is taken from a recent journal article (J. Sommers-Flanagan et al., 2011).

The case involves a father and his teenage son (Brian). As they begin therapy, they're in conflict and are struggling to communicate. Richardson uses solution-focused techniques to increase positive feelings and to get the father and son working together more productively.

Dad: I can't get a word in edgewise. There's no respect. He's always interrupting me.

Brian: Me?! He never lets me finish a sentence. My opinion doesn't matter.

BGR: I can see both of you are really frustrated with times in the past that you haven't felt heard. [Carl Rogers with a twist.] How long have the two of you been fighting against this interruption habit? [Externalizing question.]

Dad: I would say about 2 years now.

BGR: Interesting, so does that sound about right to you Brian—that this interrupting habit has been winning much of the time over the past 2 years? [Continuing to externalize the problem.]

Brian: Yeah, that's about right.

BGR: So, it sounds like that for most of your life Brian, you and your dad have gotten along better. Tell me about a time when you felt like you and your dad were on the same page. [Exception-oriented question.]

Brian: I remember when he coached me in Little League baseball. We got along then.

BGR: Brian, I notice that your body language seemed to relax as you remembered those times. Mr. Jones, tell me about a recent time in which you and Brian were relating in a way that felt better to you. [Exception-oriented question.]

Dad: Well, there aren't many.

BGR: That's okay. Take your time and pick one.

Dad: (Pause). After the baseball game the other night, we were driving home and Brian asked me about hitting the ball to the opposite field. I felt like he really listened.

BGR: I can tell that felt good. BGR continues: This question is for both of you. Tonight, when the two of you are really listening to one another, what is that going to look like? How are you going to make that happen? [Presuppositional question.] (J. Sommers-Flanagan et al., 2011, p.74)

One foundational idea behind solution-focused therapy is that whatever you spend time doing and thinking tends to stay the center of your focus, and thus, to grow in strength and salience. In this case Richardson relentlessly and skillfully gets both father and son to focus on positive interactions they had and continue to have.

Vignette II: Leila and the Tiger

This vignette is a case story presented by a psychiatrist, Glen Simblett, in *Narrative Therapy in Practice: The Archaeology of Hope* (1997). We selected this case because it focuses on making therapeutic connection across a multicultural divide.

As with some storytelling or narrative approaches, we won't do much interpretation of the story. We leave it to you to come to your own learning and conclusions.

Leila was Maori [a New Zealand native]. Twenty-four years old. A woman. A patient. She stood in my office and handed me a drawing. Neither of us sat down. I was puzzled. This was meant to be a routine outpatient follow-up to Leila's recent discharge from a psychiatric unit. Pictures are not normally a part of that. Ten minutes earlier, I had been uncertain if she was even going to keep the appointment. We had only met a couple times. The last time had been particularly difficult and unpleasant. She had been so troubled by hallucinatory voices commanding her to hurt herself and her family that I had coerced her into accepting admission to the hospital for further assessment and treatment. I had later heard that while there she had stopped talking, eating, and drinking. Her physical health had deteriorated rapidly. Against the advice of her doctors, she had stopped treatment and persuaded her family to discharge her from the hospital to see a tohunga [a Maori healer]. Some incredulity had been expressed about that by the white mental health workers. They asked if potatoes in her shoes were going to stop a depressive psychosis or schizophrenia.

I was about to find out.

The drawing was an incomplete profile of the head of a tiger.

"It's a tiger," I said lamely.

She waited silently. There had been some words written beside the tiger. I could still see the erasure marks.

"Was something written there?"

Leila nodded—the slightest tilt of her head. "There was a story to go with it. I changed my mind about writing it."

I knew that I was holding something significant in my hands but did not have the faintest idea how to respond. I was outside my psychiatric training. Outside the country I was born in. Outside my culture. I knew enough to register that, but not enough to know how to proceed.

I clutched at straws.

"I really like this picture, but I don't know what it means," I said.

"Do you want to hear the story?"

We still hovered uncertainly. I noticed that she was nearer the door than I was, and the door was still open. She avoided my gaze.

"Yes, I would like to."

Leila took a deep breath. "This is a tiger. A tiger has nine lives. This tiger only has five lives left. Do you want to know what happened to the other lives?"

I did, but I didn't. Part of me knew what was coming next, and I didn't want to hear it.

"Yes I do," I lied.

"It lost its first life in the family it was born in because of their abuse and punishment. It lost its second life to drugs and alcohol. She lost her third life in a marriage where there was no room for her hopes and ideas." She paused, for the first time catching my gaze with culturally surprising boldness. "She lost her last life when she was admitted to a psychiatric unit."

Another pause.

"She hasn't got many lives left now," Leila added.

She waited silently. Patiently. It was not an accusation. Just a statement. The way it was for her.

Where do you go from here? You begin again, maybe. I invited her to sit down. We closed the door and we talked. We tried to understand each other's point of view. We tried not to blame.

I still find it hard to understand why she gave me another chance like that, why she did not just give up on yet another Pakeha [white] doctor who did not understand. I often wonder if I would have been so generous if the roles had been reversed. The tiger drawing still hangs on the wall of my office. It acts as a gentle caution and constant reminder to me of the dangers of dominant discourse. (Simblett, 1997, pp. 121–122)

Simblett's experience with Leila and his exposure to White and Epston's narrative approach transformed the way he practices psychiatry. He now reads referral letters from other physicians aloud to his patients and asks for their comments. He also formulates client problems differently. For example, rather than viewing clients with anorexia symptoms as having family relationship problems and internal psychological problems, he provides them information about the Auckland Anti-Anorexia/Anti-Bulimia Leagues to help empower them to fight against anorexia. The story of Leila and the tiger is about Simblett's personal experience, but it may have relevance to you as you listen to client stories.

CASE ANALYSIS AND TREATMENT PLANNING

The following case example is excerpted from Tammie Ronen's book, *Cognitive-Constructivist Psychotherapy With Children and Adolescents* (Ronen, 2003). We selected this case because it illustrates how constructive approaches can be integrated with more traditional cognitive approaches, and because, as Michael Mahoney noted in the book's foreword, "Tammie is one of most creative child therapists in the world" (p. vii).

This is the case of a 12-year-old girl named Sharon. Sharon was a bedwetter. She had a diagnosis of primary nocturnal enuresis (p. 162).

Ronen employed a diverse approach to assessment. In addition to a standard interview wherein she evaluated the specific enuresis antecedents, behaviors, and consequences, she had Sharon lead the family in a family sculpture activity and then had Sharon draw her family as a group of animals. The results helped in the development of a problem and strengths list.

Problem-Strengths-Goals List

Constructive approaches focus on strengths and goals. Although Sharon had a specific problem, it can be transformed into a positive goal. For example, her problem of wetting her bed once a night about 5 to 6 nights a week, can be transformed into:

> Sharon is working toward having a dry bed every night.

Similarly, the problem of reduced social contact can be reworded to reflect what she wants to accomplish, instead of focusing on the problem using problem language:

Sharon is increasing her confidence and will soon be able to go on overnight social outings.

In keeping with a constructive model, Sharon's strengths included:

- Sharon has good relationships with her parents and a close family.

- Sharon is a good student and reports having many friends.

- Sharon is motivated and was cooperative during the initial session.

Problem and Strengths Formulation

The initial interview revealed that Sharon and her parents had tried many different strategies to address the bedwetting. She had play therapy for 2 years at age 6. She used the bell-and-pad device at age 10. After trying the bell-and-pad, she tried medications. None of these interventions were successful.

Ronen formulated the bedwetting problem as having two main contributing factors. These included (a) Sharon appeared to have poor self-control and (b) the parents seemed overprotective of Sharon. Ronen reflected on the problem formulation:

> I could not give a full explanation as to the cause of enuresis, but I could see how the parents were ineffective in handling it. I noted that Sharon was a nice, intelligent girl; yet she had been overly dependent on her parents when it came to her previous attempts to cease her bedwetting. For example, it was the parents who had ensured she took her medication every night, because "she tended to forget." While using the bell-and-pad technique, the parents set up the equipment every night and came to awaken her when the alarm rang, because "she couldn't hear anything while sleeping." In addition, Sharon construed herself as a bedwetting girl who couldn't control her behavior. This particular narrative of her not having control over bedwetting incidents that just seemed to happen was also a target of treatment.

The treatment goals included: (a) have Sharon take more responsibility for the bedwetting; (b) have Sharon learn self-control strategies.

Interventions

Ronen employed at least five different interventions:

1. She asked the parents to require Sharon take care of the wet laundry, wash it, and make the bed when there was a bedwetting incident.

2. Explore and understand Sharon's "meaning making" of the bedwetting experience.

3. Shift Sharon's ideas about the bedwetting to within her control through Socratic questioning and paradoxical examples.

4. Homework monitoring of bedwetting and internal sensations.

5. Psychoeducation and demonstrations of how the brain controls bladder functioning.

Therapist: What do you think, why do you wet your bed at night?

Sharon: I don't feel anything when I'm asleep. It's not my fault. It's not up to me.

T: Let's check this out. How many times do you fall out of your bed at night?

S: Never.

T: How come?

S: Because I don't move when I sleep.

T: Really? Let's check it out: Please find a nice position in which you'll feel comfortable. Now, I want you to stay in the same position and not move at all.

We continued talking and after 2 minutes Sharon started fidgeting from side to side.

T: You see, Sharon, after 2 minutes you already moved. Why?

S: It hurts. I can't stay in the same position all day long.

T: You know, the same thing happens at night. You feel uncomfortable, and for that reason you move from one side to the other.

S: Well, then, I guess that when I get close to the edge of the bed I just turn to the other side. (p. 168)

Ronen also provided psychoeducation. She taught her about how drinking fills up the bladder and how the bladder's pressure of filling up sends the message to the brain to eventually open up the valve and let the bladder drain out. She wrote:

It was important for me to help Sharon realize that it was she who conceptualized herself as of being enuretic, and she was responsible for the meaning she put into her own behavior. We looked at books with illustrations of the human body and of the bladder, and we discussed the brain and its role:

Therapist: Could you stand up please?
Sharon: Sure (standing up).
T: How did you do that?
S: What do you mean?
T: What made you stand up? From what you already learned about the brain.
S: Oh, yes, the brain commanded me to stand up. (p. 169)

After six weeks of therapy, Sharon's bedwetting had reduced to only one to two times weekly. Although she had considerable success, she still tended to minimize her control over the bedwetting. An additional intervention was applied. Ronen had her keep a nightly chart predicting whether she would have bedwetting incident. As Sharon's confidence in her ability to control her enuresis increased, so did her success at staying dry.

After Sharon had three consecutive dry weeks her therapy frequency was reduced to one session every three weeks. These sessions focused on relapse prevention, especially helping Sharon from slipping back into an "I have no control over this" narrative when she had regressions.

Ronen described Sharon's status at the end of treatment:

After three months of being dry, the follow-up stage was terminated. Sharon stayed dry even when she went to sleep late, drank before going to sleep, or forgot to empty herself before going to bed. The charts emphasized the change in her wetting behavior and showed that Sharon was dry and did not regress. Follow-up by telephone revealed that Sharon stayed dry. (p. 173)

Outcomes Assessment

In Sharon's case outcomes assessment included ongoing parent reports as well as charts that Sharon completed, tracking her enuresis. Typically, both narrative and solution-focused approaches are open to using a variety of traditional and creative self-report outcomes assessment instruments.

CULTURAL AND GENDER CONSIDERATIONS

Oh sun, moon, stars, our other relatives peering at us from the inside of god's house walk with us as we climb into the next century naked but for the stories we have of each other. Keep us from giving up in this land of nightmares which is also the land of miracles.
We sing our song which we've been promised has no beginning or end.

—Joy Harjo (from *Reconciliation—A Prayer*)

In theory, constructive therapies are deeply multicultural and gender sensitive. Constructive theory emphasizes respect for the individual; respect for personal language, languaging, and narrative; and respect for each individual's construction of reality. There is also a strong focus on problem externalization; this method of formulating problems fits well with feminist and multicultural perspectives emphasizing the role of outside social factors in causing or contributing to client problems. However, in practice, constructive therapies may not always live up to their theoretical ideals.

Overall, multicultural sensitivity among constructive therapies seems to fall along a continuum. On the far left of the continuum lies narrative therapy, the most multiculturally oriented of all constructive approaches. This approach has been

PUTTING IT IN PRACTICE 11.3

Therapy Is Research and Research Is Therapy: The Evolution of a Strategic Constructivist

This commentary is written by Giorgio Nardone.

I was still a young epistemologist with a planned academic career, when I first arrived at MRI to study at the so-called Palo Alto School of Thinking. This experience made me shift from the pure philosophy of science to psychotherapy. So from then onward, I began to dedicate my studies and works to human problems and their possible solutions. Moreover, Paul Watzlawick and John Weakland were the encouraging and stimulating supervisors of my first research project on phobic-obsessive disorders treatment, still today my most popular topic.

Thanks to this successful project, many colleagues approached me to ask for training, as well as a lot of patients ask for therapy for the so-called untreatable phobias or obsessions. All this pushed me to work more and more, both in therapy and in research. This is the way in which, every time a research project finishes another takes off, in a sort of virtual spiral.

I still have in my mind the encouraging image of John saying no while nodding yes. Paul is for me much more than a master colleague, and a friend; we have shared till now 15 years of working together, three co-authored books, and more than 100 workshops and conferences, held all around the world.

Thanks both to their initial help and the further work together with my collaborator, I have successfully tried to evolve the MRI traditional brief strategic therapy beyond its limits, particularly through long-term empirical-experimental research. I set up specific protocols of the treatments for phobic-obsessive pathologies as well as for eating disorders, which revealed elevated results both in terms of efficacy (87% solved cases) and efficiency (mean duration of therapy seven sessions) in their application on more than 500 cases during 10 years of work at the Strategic Therapy Center in Arezzo.

My current objectives rely mostly on the fact that I am constantly faced by the challenge of devising effective strategies for the solution of further complicated pathologies. I actually do not place my trust in any strong theory but only in operative knowledge, because even the best theory, if rigid, becomes a deterministic trap. If the work is driven by the goal to be reached, this helps to keep our mind elastic and free and our strategies concrete and effective. From my point of view, therapy is research and research is therapy. We can really get to how a problem works only by means of its solution.

used successfully with traumatized children and adults from low-income countries (Vromans & Schweitzer, 2011). The approach is inherently sensitive to human diversity perhaps because White and Epston were influenced by their work with aboriginal tribal populations in Australia and New Zealand as well as theoretical origins associated with Foucault's philosophical positions.

O'Hanlon's possibility therapy (previously solution-oriented therapy) also values and honors human diversity. However, his approaches are somewhat more formulaic and therefore could be practiced in ways reflecting a less-than-ideal multicultural orientation and gender sensitivity.

At the other end of the continuum lies solution-focused brief therapy. With its emphasis on brevity, formulaic interventions, and disinterest in each individual's unique problem, solution-focused brief therapy has the greatest potential among constructive approaches of being multiculturally insensitive. However, it should be emphasized that this approach is not inherently insensitive and that it has attracted a strong international appeal.

As with many theoretical perspectives, cultural and gender sensitivity seems more connected with individual practitioners than the theory itself. Although constructive therapists emphasize respecting clients, traditional constructive emphases on confusion, provocation, and cleverness may cause constructive approaches to be sometimes perceived as paradoxically disrespectful. For example, de Shazer's previously described client feedback of: "we don't know what the fuck you are going to do" could easily be viewed as disrespectful. Similarly, in the letter writing example from Mary Underwood and David Epston, a number of double binding and minimizing statements were written to a young female client, including: "When I meet with your mother and father next time, I would think that you'll probably have another attack of acne" and "If you really want to show your parents this letter it doesn't really matter. But I'd prefer you didn't."

Based on our review of constructive therapy approaches, we think it's appropriate to caution therapists experimenting with these strategies against becoming too cavalier or clever.

Although most constructive therapists are focused and respectful professionals, we occasionally read examples of therapy interventions that, to be blunt, appear insensitive and possibly unprofessional. Of course, this is a warning to be heeded by therapists associated with all theoretical orientations. But, after re-reading several examples in this chapter we felt this was a good place to emphasize the importance of living up to highest standards of professional sensitivity.

EVIDENCE-BASED STATUS

The two different constructive approaches to therapy reviewed in this chapter (solution-based and narrative) take two distinctly different approaches to outcomes research.

Solution-Focused Therapy Research

It should come as no surprise that solution-focused therapists are enthusiastic supporters of solution-focused therapy (SFT). They typically point to a variety of data indicating that their therapy approach is at least equivalent to traditional therapies. In some ways, their claims are consistent with their theoretical perspective of persistently focusing on the positive. For example over the years they've offered these claims:

- SFTs are brief (de Shazer, 1991). Using this reasoning in combination with numerous case reports, testimonials, client surveys, and a single, uncontrolled outcome study conducted at the BFTC, SF therapists stake their claim to therapeutic effectiveness (DeJong & Hopwood, 1996; McKeel, 1996).

- There is a "large body of research" indicating brief therapy is effective (Koss & Shiang, 1994). Actually, we're not sure where this "large body" of pre-1994 research resides.

- Research has already convincingly shown that all therapy approaches are essentially equivalent and therefore solution-focused approaches are equally effective (Duncan, Hubble, Miller, & Coleman, 1998). This is a reasonable general argument, but SFT approaches, in particular, weren't included in this convincing research base.

Despite these early claims, in a 1996 review published in the *Handbook of Solution-Focused Brief Therapy* it was concluded that no definitive empirical research existed:

> Not only does no single collection of studies exist, but for the most part there simply are no research studies to report! In fact, in spite of having been around for ten years, no well-controlled, scientifically sound outcome studies on solution-focused therapy have ever been conducted or published in any peer-reviewed professional journal. (Miller et al., 1996, p. 2)

More recently, Smock (2009) has made a statement similar to the enthusiastic claims from the 1990s.

> To date there are numerous studies, several reviews of the research, and a few meta-analyses completed that showcase SFT's effectiveness. (pp. 147–148)

Smock's statement is technically correct. In the past 15 years (since Miller et al., 1996 noted "no well-controlled, scientifically sound outcome studies on solution-focused therapy"), there have been many more publications focusing on SFT outcomes. These studies include case reports, single subject designs, and pilot studies (Bell, Skinner, & Fisher, 2009; Conoley et al., 2003; Hosany, Wellman, & Lowe, 2007; Kvarme et al., 2010). There has also been the beginning of more well-controlled research (Knekt et al., 2008). However, it's important to look more closely at some of the most systematic SFT reviews to determine exactly what is being used to "showcase" effectiveness:

Gingerich and Eisengart (2000) conducted a literature review of outcomes studies on SFT (aka SFBT). They identified 15 studies, only five of which they considered relatively well-controlled. They summarized their findings by stating:

> Since none of the five studies met all of the stringent criteria for efficacy studies, and all five studied different populations (that is, there were no replications by independent investigators), we cannot conclude that SFBT has been shown to be efficacious. We do, however, believe that these five studies provide initial support for the efficacy of SFBT. (Gingerich & Eisengart, 2004, p. 493)

Gingerich and Eisengart's conclusions were mostly reasonable. However, there were significant shortcomings inherent in the studies included in the group of five "well-controlled" studies. For example, Gingerich and Eisengart (2004) included a one-session SFT intervention for depressed college students compared to a one-session interpersonal psychotherapy intervention for depression ($n = 40$). Although the authors' claimed this study was well-controlled and compared SFT with another well-established treatment, the other treatment also was delivered in a one-session format—which is not how IPT was designed to be delivered. As a consequence, this study was really more of a testament that providing "depressed" college students with one session of counseling may be helpful (although it may also only be as helpful as a placebo intervention).

A second review of SFT efficacy/effectiveness was reported by a Dutch research group. Their abstract read as follows:

> A meta-analysis of 21 studies including 1421 clients was conducted to achieve quantitative evidence for the efficacy of solution-focused brief therapy (SFBT). The results show a positive and small to medium effect of SFBT ($d = .37$). The strongest effects were found in more recent studies. The effect of SFBT is larger for clients in residential settings than for clients treated in non-residential settings. Also, SFBT is more effective for clients with behavior problems than for clients with marital problems, psychiatric problems or other problems. Although SFBT does not have a larger effect, it does have a positive effect in less time and satisfies the client's need for autonomy. Therefore, it is reasonable to consider this form of therapy when it is tuned to the client and his problem. (p. 81)

The third recent review of empirical research was a meta-analysis of 22 SFT studies (J. S. Kim, 2008). Kim reported that the only subset of the 22 studies to show statistical significance were 12 studies focusing on "internalizing" disorders (e.g., depression, anxiety, low self-esteem). Kim reported an effect size of $d = .26$ for these 12 studies. This indicates a small but positive effect of SFT over control groups within these studies. Kim also noted that these studies are more representative of effectiveness research rather than efficacy research.

Overall, the empirical evidence attesting to SFT's efficacy remains relatively weak and evidence attesting to its effectiveness is small.

Perhaps the most balanced conclusion regarding SFT efficacy research was articulated by Corcoran and Pillai (2009):

> The most striking finding is that very little research has still been conducted on solution-focused therapy. That only ten studies met the basic criteria of having two groups with which to compare treatment response is remarkably low. . . . Overall, this study indicates that the effects of solution-focused therapy are equivocal and more rigorously designed research needs to establish its effectiveness. Therefore, practitioners should understand there is not a strong evidence basis for solution-focused therapy at this point in time. (pp. 240–241)

Narrative Therapy Research

In recent years empirical research has accumulated attesting to the efficacy of several different narrative approaches. Summary reviews follow.

A meta-analytic review of **narrative exposure therapy** (NET) for traumatized adults indicated that a brief manualized treatment (4 to 10 sessions) produced positive outcomes in six small studies ($n = 9$ to $n = 111$). These studies included traumatized Romanian adults, Sudanese refugees, Rwandan and Somali refugees, and Rwandan orphans (Vromans & Schweitzer, 2011). Reported effect sizes ranged from $d = 0.71$ to 3.15 (we should note here that we're not sure how an effect size of 3.15 was attained).

Similarly positive results were reported for three studies using NET for children (aka: KIDNET).

These studies were very small ($n = 6$ to 16) and not amenable to meta-analysis. Overall, the conclusions were that KIDNET is a promising treatment for children exposed to trauma (Vromans & Schweitzer, 2011). There also has been research indicating that narrative therapy with Latino youth may be effective (Malgady, 2010; Malgady & Costantino, 2003).

There are at least two major reviews of the efficacy of personal construct therapy. Personal construct therapy is a form of narrative therapy developed by Robert Neimeyer and based on Kelly's (1955) work.

Holland and colleagues (Holland, Neimeyer, Currier, & Berman, 2007) conducted a meta-analysis on 22 personal construct therapy research studies. They reported a small, but positive effect size of $d = 0.38$. In contrast, Metcalfe and colleagues (Metcalfe, Winter, & Viney, 2007) reported a meta-analysis of 20 studies showing that personal construct theory had an effect size of $d = 0.55$ when compared to no treatment, but no differential effectiveness when compared with alternative treatments. Overall, outcomes data suggest that personal construct therapy may have small positive treatment effects.

CONCLUDING COMMENTS

There's probably no single existing theoretical orientation containing the breadth of diversity associated with constructive theory. On the one hand, solution-based approaches emphasize formulaic, brief, and surface-oriented techniques designed to produce relatively small changes. These small changes are then viewed as having a potential ripple effect in producing bigger and more profound changes over time. It's not surprising that solution-based approaches are sometimes criticized for ignoring client problems and denying the significance of human emotional pain and suffering.

On the other hand, narrative approaches use language to produce profound, transformative client changes. Although there's some overlap in technique, in contrast to solution-based therapists, narrative therapists aren't in a hurry to fix clients and send them out the door in a minimum amount of time and with a minimum of human intimacy. Instead, narrative therapists spend more time listening to the depths of clients' personal stories, searching for tiny sparkling moments in the rubble of difficult lives. Narrative therapists join with clients in attacking maladaptive personal narratives. This joining is not merely surface or superficial.

CHAPTER SUMMARY

Postmodern philosophy is the foundation for constructive theory and therapies. In contrast to modern-objectivist philosophy, postmodern philosophy emphasizes that everything is subjective and reality is a construction. There are two main constructive perspectives: (1) constructivism; and (2) social constructionist.

The roots of constructive theory and therapy are also linked with the work of George Kelly, Milton Erickson, and Gregory Bateson and the Palo Alto projects. Kelly discovered that his clients would improve when he used preposterous interpretations. Erickson was a strategic hypnotherapist who could construct new realities and options for clients. Bateson led a team that focused extensively on language in human interaction. From these beginnings narrative therapy and solution-focused therapy were developed.

The primary theoretical principles underlying constructive approaches include: (a) postmodernism; (b) language and languaging; (c) change is constant and inevitable; (d) problems are co-created; (e) therapy is a collaborative, cooperative, co-constructive conversation; and (f) therapy focuses on strengths and solutions. There are two main ways that constructive therapists think of psychopathology. These include the development and maintenance of negative and maladaptive personal narratives and getting stuck using unhelpful solutions.

Constructive therapists generally don't employ pathology-focused formal assessment procedures. Instead, narrative therapists encourage clients to tell their personal and problem-saturated stories and solution-focused therapists ask questions to simultaneously initiate an assessment and treatment process.

Solution-focused and narrative therapists use overlapping techniques to help clients change. Some of the main techniques include: (a) scaling questions; (b) the pretreatment change question; (c) unique account and redescription questions; (d) focusing on unique outcomes or sparkling moments; (e) externalizing conversations; (f) Carl Rogers with a twist; (g) relabeling and reframing; (h) the miracle question; (i) formula tasks, and (j) exception questions.

Narrative therapies tend to be very gender and culturally sensitive. In contrast, because solution-focused therapists have little interest in client problems, they may come across as less sensitive. However, clients who don't want to talk about their problems may find solution-focused approaches very desirable.

Evidence supporting both narrative and solution-focused approaches is accumulating. Currently there are a small number of small studies suggesting that narrative exposure therapy is efficacious. There are also several studies indicating solution-focused therapies are effective with some clinical populations. Additional research is needed to support the efficacy of both these constructive approaches.

CONSTRUCTIVE THERAPY KEY TERMS

Anti-anorexia/anti-bulimia league

Carl Rogers with a twist

Complainants

Confusion technique

Constructivist

Credulous approach to assessment

Customers for change

Do something different task

Exception questions

Externalizing conversations

First session formula task

Forced teaming

Formula tasks

Letter of invitation

Letter writing

Letters of prediction

Narrative exposure therapy (NET)

Narrative therapy

Percentage questions

Positive relabeling or positive connotation

Postmodern philosophy

Presuppositional questions

Pretreatment change question

Questioned out

Redundancy letters

Reflecting teams

Relabeling and reframing

Re-remembering

Scaling questions

Skeleton keys

Social constructionist

Solution-focused brief therapy (SFBT)

Solution-oriented therapy (aka: possibility therapy)

Summary letter

The miracle question

Unique account and redescription questions

Unique outcomes or sparkling moments

Utilization

Visitors to treatment

Write-read-burn task

RECOMMENDED READINGS AND RESOURCES

The following resources are available to help deepen your understanding of constructive theory and practice.

CONSTRUCTIVE JOURNALS

Constructivism in the Human Sciences
Journal of Constructivist Psychology

Journal of Strategic and Systemic Therapies

READINGS ON NARRATIVE AND SOLUTION-FOCUSED APPROACHES

Berg, I. K., & Miller, S. D. (1992). *Working with the problem drinker: A solution-focused approach*. New York, NY: Norton.

Bertolino, B. (1999). *Therapy with troubled teenagers: Rewriting young lives in progress*. New York, NY: John Wiley & Sons.

de Shazer, S. (1984). The death of resistance. *Family Process, 23*(1), 11–17.

de Shazer, S. (1985). *Keys to solution in brief therapy*. New York, NY: Norton.

de Shazer, S., Dolan, Y., Korman, H., McCollum, E., Trepper, T., & Berg, I. K. (2007). *More than miracles:*

The state of the art of solution-focused brief therapy. New York, NY: Haworth Press.

DeJong, P., & Berg, I. K. (2002). *Interviewing for solutions* (2nd ed.). Belmont, CA: Brooks/Cole.

Erickson, M. H. (1964). The confusion technique in hypnosis. *American Journal of Clinical Hypnosis, 6,* 183–207.

Foucault, M. (1965). *Madness and civilization: A history of insanity in the age of reason*. New York, NY: Random House.

Gergen, K. J. (2009a). *An invitation to social construction* (2nd ed.). Thousand Oaks, CA: Sage.

Guterman, J. T. (2006). *Mastering the art of solution-focused counseling*. Alexandria, VA: American Counseling Association.

Hoyt, M. F. (2002). How I embody a narrative constructive approach. *Journal of Constructivist Psychology, 15*(4), 279–289.

Madigan, S. (2011). *Narrative therapy*. Washington, DC: American Psychological Association.

Metcalf, L. (2008). *Counseling toward solutions: A practical solution-focused program for working with students, teachers, and parents* (2nd ed.). San Francisco, CA: Jossey-Bass.

Miller, S. D., Hubble, M. A., & Duncan, B. L. (1996). *Handbook of solution-focused brief therapy*. San Francisco, CA: Jossey-Bass.

Murphy, J. J. (2008). *Solution-focused counseling in middle and high schools*. Alexandria, VA: American Counseling Association.

Neimeyer, R. A., & Mahoney, M. (Eds.). (1995). *Constructivism in psychotherapy*. Washington, DC: American Psychological Association.

O'Hanlon, W. H., & Weiner-Davis, M. (1989). *In search of solutions: A new direction in psychotherapy*. New York, NY: Norton.

White, M., & Denborough, D. (2011). *Narrative practice: Continuing the conversations*. New York, NY: Norton.

White, M., & Epston, D. (1990). *Narrative means to therapeutic ends*. New York, NY: Norton.

Winslade, J. M., & Monk, G. D. (2007). *Narrative counseling in schools: Powerful & brief* (2nd ed.). Thousand Oaks, CA: Corwin Press.

TRAINING ORGANIZATIONS AND WEBSITES

Institute for Solution-Focused Therapy (www.solution focused.net/home.html)

The Institute of Narrative Therapy (www.theinsti tuteofnarrativetherapy.com/)

Milton Erickson Foundation (www.erickson-foun dation.org/)

Narrative Approaches.com (www.narrativeapproaches .com)

Solution-Focused Brief Therapy Association (SFBTA; http://www.sfbta.org/)

VIDEOS/DVDs

Angus, L. (2007). *Narrative therapy* [DVD]. Washington, DC: American Psychological Association.

Carlson, J., & Kjos, D. (2000). *Narrative therapy with Stephen Madigan* [Videotape]. Boston: Allyn & Bacon.

Madigan, S. (2010). *Narrative therapy over time* [DVD]. Washington, DC: American Psychological Association.

Sklar, G. (2006). *Solution-focused brief counseling*. North Amherst, MA: Microtraining Associates.

Winslade, J., & Monk, G. (2010). *Narrative therapy: A process for a post modern world*. North Amherst, MA: Microtraining Associates.

GOING FARTHER AND DEEPER

Additional constructive counseling and psychotherapy resources are available at johnsommersflanagan.com.

CHAPTER 12

Family Systems Theory and Therapy

By KIRSTEN W. MURRAY, JOHN SOMMERS-FLANAGAN,
and RITA SOMMERS-FLANAGAN

THIS CHAPTER

- Reviews key figures and historical and other factors linked to the development and evolution of family systems theory
- Outlines and describes theoretical principles underlying family systems therapy practice
- Describes and discusses principles and techniques associated with traditional family systems approaches, including intergenerational family therapy, structural family therapy, strategic family therapy, and humanistic-experiential family therapy
- Provides an overview of recent developments in family systems theory and practice
- Illustrates how treatment planning, outcomes assessment, and gender and cultural issues can be integrated into a family systems therapy approach
- Reviews the empirical status of various family systems therapy approaches
- Offer resources for further study

In the film *Annie Hall* (1977), there's a joke about a patient who goes to a psychiatrist. He complains to the psychiatrist that his brother "... thinks he's a chicken." Then, when the psychiatrist recommends to the patient that perhaps he should send his brother for treatment, the patient tells the psychiatrist, "... but I need the eggs!"

As concerning as it is to have a brother laying eggs and clucking like a chicken, it turns out that his behavior serves a purpose for the family. Ultimately a sibling who thinks he's a chicken becomes the predictable norm for the family. This egg-laying brother not only provides food for the family, but ultimately provides other things too: There's no time to worry about Dad's drinking because his son thinks he's a chicken; Mom is too busy taking care of her chicken/son to address strife in her marriage; because his brother is so busy clucking around the house, no one puts energy into addressing Tommy's falling grades. Welcome to a systemic lens of the world.

Family systems approaches depart from the idea of treating individuals in isolation. Instead, systemic approaches recognize that symptoms occur and are supported in relational contexts. For counseling to be most effective, one's primary system, usually the family, is the treatment focus.

There are many distinct approaches for working with families. This chapter exposes you to what a family systems approach is all about and highlights distinguishing features of particular family systems theories and approaches.

When working with families, it's important to let go of the notion that the problem is central to an individual; instead, problems are viewed as created and maintained by and for the family. As demonstrated in the opening paragraph, our symptoms (believing to be a chicken) are often maintained to meet the needs of our families (providing eggs).

As difficult as symptoms become, it's not lost on family therapists that all symptoms are purposeful.

While other theoretical models (e.g., psychoanalytic and Adlerian) consider the family when formulating treatments, the idea that problems are central to the family and therefore the family must be treated remains radical and new by many standards. This purely systemic perspective began in the early 1950s and has since been expanded on by family therapy pioneers from multiple perspectives.

QUESTIONS FOR REFLECTION

According to family systems theory, every family member's behavior serves a function. What problem behaviors occurred in your own family? Can you consider what function those behaviors played for your family? This isn't to blame anyone. When family systems therapy works well—everyone changes.

HISTORICAL CONTEXT AND HIGHLIGHTS

Family dynamics were originally discovered by the first family. No doubt, the first couple had conflicts. Then, when children came along, conflicts became more complex, and voilà, the inner workings and relationships within the family emerged as something to talk about. And talking sometimes made things even more complex. Then the community around the family noticed and other people stepped in and tried to help. These other people probably included resident community experts such as clergy, doctors, lawyers, and even neighbors or friends who had no idea what they were getting themselves into.

Adler's Contributions: Child Guidance Clinics in Vienna

As you might guess from your careful reading of Chapter 3, Alfred Adler (1927) was probably the first modern theorist to focus on family dynamics. His Individual Psychology was systems-based; he emphasized family constellations as a means of understanding individuals. However, no matter how important family dynamics were to Adler, the individual was the primary focus in treatment. Referring to this tendency to think like a family therapist while working with individuals, Blume (2006) wrote:

> Family therapy with one person has a long and proud history. (p. 5)

Adler established more than 30 **child guidance clinics** in and around Vienna following World War I. Among other activities, Adler offered family therapy demonstrations at these clinics where he was observed by parents, teachers, and community members. Adlerian-oriented child guidance clinics spread to the United States, but were eliminated from Vienna in the mid-1930s by the Nazi regime.

Following Adler, child guidance clinics and then marriage and family clinics became more popular throughout the United States (I. Goldenberg & H. Goldenberg, 2008). These clinics focused on helping families handle child-rearing responsibilities, infidelity, divorce, financial conflicts, and sexual problems. Up through the 1930s and into the 1940s most work with families involved working with children and/or parents separately.

Nathan Ackerman in New York

Nathan Ackerman is generally considered the first modern family therapist. His intellectual openness combined with direct experiences working with children and parents in an Adlerian-style clinic apparently inspired him to experiment with new ways of working with families. For example, in the following quotation from a 1948 article, he contrasts his view of including fathers as part of the psychotherapy process with more conventional therapy:

> Conventional child guidance procedure tends to condense treatment of the child's environment to therapy of the mother. The fundamental closeness of child to mother is a recognized factor. Nevertheless, this is one example of oversimplification which sometimes leads to failure in treatment. If the therapy of the environment is to be child-oriented, the primary need is an intimate

knowledge of the relationship between the parents, and the relationship of each parent to the child. The father's personality, as well as the mother's must be understood, and the emotional interaction between these two persons must be dealt with. Often, the father must receive treatment as well as the mother, if adequate results are to be achieved. (Ackerman & Neubauer, 1948, p. 86).

Similarly, mothers' support groups were routinely a part of the work at his New York clinic. In a 1959 publication, he discussed an example of the strong, emotionally charged material generated from these group experiences. (Note that this excerpt precedes the women's consciousness-raising groups that contributed so significantly to feminist therapy movements discussed in Chapter 10; the content captures the convergence of group therapy, feminist psychology, and family dynamics that was happening during the 1950s):

> The mother had an outburst of anger at the therapist when she discovered in group therapy sessions for mothers that women could enjoy sex and even experience orgasm. She felt bitter that her husband had withheld this information from her all these years. Until now she believed that men had a corner on sex and that women submitted purely out of a sense of duty. She was hurt and angry at her husband, but blew up at her female therapist. (Ackerman & Lakos, 1959, p. 62)

Ackerman's work is a nice illustration, but certainly not the only one, of how many different streams of thought, clinical experiences, and social movements were simmering together in the crucible that would eventually produce family therapy. In the next section we look at various events related to the evolution of family therapy.

A Timeline of Family Therapy History

The following timeline includes a series of highlights designed to help you glimpse the many threads contributing to the tapestry of modern family therapy.

1910s

- Richmond (1917) published *Social Diagnosis*. An early social worker, she advocated for including fathers in welfare interviews and the family in treatment; she paid particular attention to emotional bonding and cohesion.

1920s

- Adler established more than 30 child guidance clinics in Vienna; Adlerian-oriented clinics were also established in the United States.
- The Marriage Consultation Center in New York opened its doors in 1929, thanks to the work of Abraham and Hannah Stone.

1930s

- Ackerman (1938) published The Unity of the Family in the *Archives of Pediatrics*.
- Rogers (1939) published *Clinical Treatment of the Problem Child*, in which he acknowledged the impossibility of having lasting effects on children's problems without involving parents.

1940s

- The American Association of Marriage Counselors is formed in 1941 (later to become the American Association for Marriage and Family Therapy in 1978).
- Bowen began clinical work in 1946 at the Menninger Clinic, treating schizophrenic children. His work led to rich theory development emphasizing family member differentiation and triangles.
- Levy (1943) and Fromm-Reichmann (1948) began attending to the mother's role and parenting style when treating schizophrenic children.
- Whitaker began conducting biannual conferences in 1946 where colleagues met to discuss and observe one another's work with families.

- Bowlby (1949) began using family interviews as a secondary form of treatment to complement his individual approach.

1950s

- In his *Field Theory* manuscript (1951), Lewin established that groups are more than the sum of their parts.

- Don Jackson (1954) began documenting patterns of shifting disturbance among family members: when treatment was successful with one family member, symptoms would arise in another.

- Bateson, Haley, Weakland, and Jackson focused on schizophrenic communication among family members, publishing *Toward a Theory of Schizophrenia* (1956).

- Lidz, Cornelison, Fleck, and Terry (1957) began attending to the role fathers and marital relationships play in schizophrenic families.

- Whitaker (1958) developed an experiential approach for working with families at the Atlanta Psychiatric Clinic.

- Jackson and Weakland (1959) first published the notion that symptoms preserve homeostasis among family members, emphasizing that problems occur in contexts.

1960s

- Satir (1964), a contributing member of the Palo Alto Group published *Conjoint Family Therapy*.

- Minuchin began his career, focusing on family patterns and structures with urban poor families. He was named the director of the Philadelphia Child Guidance Clinic in 1965.

- In 1967 Selvini-Palazzoli and colleagues form the Institute for Family Studies in Milan.

The 1970s and 1980s are referred to as **the golden age of family therapy**, when treatments, centers, theoretical concepts, and core publications flourished (Nichols & Schwarts, 2007, p. 27). This time period was characterized by the excitement and optimism that new and radical ideas bring. While inspiration was gathered from these innovative and creative therapists, the originality of their concepts began dissipating over the years, and the energy they generated in the 1970s and 1980s leveled off. While there continue to be many followers of original family therapy models, new energy is infiltrating the field via critiques and developments from evidence-based, feminist, multicultural, and postmodern perspectives. Regardless of approach, the roots of family therapy lie in fundamental systemic concepts.

THEORETICAL DEVELOPMENTS AND PRINCIPLES

Surprisingly enough, the stimulus to attend to family systems rather than individuals in isolation came from outside the counseling and psychotherapy world.

Cybernetics

At the Josiah Macy Foundation conferences held over the years 1946 to 1953, a multidisciplinary group of science, mathematics, and engineering professionals gathered to discuss mathematics, computer systems, and communication engineering. Conference participant goals were to examine these machine-like systems, evaluate their efficiency and stability, and decipher how systems communicated and used feedback loops to achieve regulation. This shift in thinking towards systems represented the birth of **cybernetics** (Wiener, 1948).

Gregory Bateson (1972) later used his anthropological roots to shift cybernetics from engineering and mathematics to the social sciences. He focused on human communication, viewing families as cybernetic systems. Because families can achieve self-regulation and stability through their norms, Bateson began examining family communication patterns associated with psychopathology. In particular, with his Mental Research Institute

(MRI) colleagues, Bateson (1956) looked at families that had a child diagnosed with schizophrenia. Bateson observed patterns between mothers and their children characteristic of a *double-bind* scenario. The hallmark of double-bind communication is the feeling of being trapped in a no-win situation. Double-binds involve contradictory messages, and may sound something like this:

Mother: (Appears agitated and disappointed about something.)

Child: "Mom, are you okay?"

Mother: "I'm fine," she answers in a short and irritated tone.

Child: (Turns away from his mother to continue playing his game.)

Mother: "Well, won't you talk to me? Can't you see that I've had a hard day?"

Child: (Pursuing further and standing, reaches to give her a hug).

Mother: "Never mind, I'm fine, please just go play."

As illustrated in the preceding exchange, no matter how he responds, the boy is in a lose-lose, or double-bind situation. If the boy carries on without his mother, he fails her. When he pursues her, he disappoints her. After observing many families, the MRI group reported that schizophrenic families were characterized by double-bind communications. As a result, a **double-bind theory** was developed to explain schizophrenic symptoms (Bateson, Jackson, Haley, & Weakland, 1956). Bateson et al. gave an example describing the nature of the double bind in their original article:

> In the Eastern religion, Zen Buddhism, the goal is to achieve Enlightenment. The Zen Master attempts to bring about enlightenment in his pupil in various ways. One of the things he does is to hold a stick over the pupil's head and say fiercely, "If you say this stick is real, I will strike you with it. If you say this stick is not real, I will strike you with it. If you don't say anything, I will strike you with it." We feel that the schizophrenic finds himself continually in the same situation as the pupil, but

he achieves something like disorientation rather than enlightenment. (pp. 175–176)

Although the theory itself was refuted, attending to double-bind communication set into motion the importance of studying and modifying interactional patterns present in families (Cullin, 2006; Stark & von der Haar, 1977).

Many studies related to schizophrenia and family systems began surfacing at this time. For example, Levy (1943) theorized about **overprotective mothers** and Fromm-Reichmann (1948) discussed dominating, rejecting, and insecure **schizophrenogenic mothers**. Jay Haley (a member of the MRI research team) was quoted as saying, "We discovered that schizophrenics had mothers!" (Napier & Whitaker, 1978, p. 48).

Given the sociopolitical status of women at the time, it's no surprise that mothers were first in line to get blamed for family problems and children's mental disturbances (although Bateson et al., 1956, made it clear that the double-bind communicator was not necessarily the mother—it could be a father or a sibling). Somewhat later, however, researchers apparently *discovered the existence of fathers* and began examining fathers' roles in family interactions (Lidz et al., 1957). As family interaction patterns and contexts were recognized as major contributors to mental health, attending to systems and treating families gained prevalence. Systems formulations were evolving.

General Systems Theory

Unlike cybernetics—a model derived from strict, rule-bound, closed systems with mechanical structures—**general systems theory** considers nuances of human actors within systems. Developed by biologist Ludwig von Bertalanffy (1950), general systems theory asserts that human systems function more like organisms and less like machines (this was clearly a step in the right direction).

Human systems aren't closed; they're open and have fluid boundaries that accept and give influence. This is in stark comparison to cybernetic mechanical and rule-bound systems. Living systems don't function in closed loops where "A" always leads to "B" and eventually "C." General systems theory recognizes that all parts of a system can impact the others, leaving room for many possible outcomes.

Consider a couple with a new baby. Adding this tiny player to a two-person system changes family dynamics. The couple's family responsibilities shift toward providing and caring for their child. From changing diapers, to night-time feedings, to navigating a new sleeping schedule, the couple is powerfully influenced. Further, there are many possible responses to this new family addition. The couple may maintain an egalitarian relationship and divide tasks, they may take on very specific provider or caretaker roles, or their culture may include godparents and extended family in caretaking responsibilities. Potential outcomes in response to a systemic change are theoretically infinite; living systems can discover various means to multiple ends.

General systems theory not only accounts for many possibilities, but also explains the many systems and **subsystems** layered around and within the family. Subsystems are smaller, self-sustaining parts of a larger system. Many subsystems make up an individual: from cells, to tissues, to organs such as the heart, to the circulatory system, to the individual as a whole; we are all layers of subsystems that contribute to larger systemic functioning. Families contain subsystems (the parent subsystem and sibling subsystem are some examples) and simultaneously function as a part of a larger system themselves. From the family, to the neighborhood, to the school system, to the community, to the county, to the nation, to the world, there are points of influence from various subsystems that impact the family and vice versa.

Urie Bronfenbrenner (1979) developed **ecological systems theory** to organize, explain, and differentiate systemic forces that influence children's development. In his system there are six factors or levels of influence. These include:

1. The child (or individual): The child is an entity that's affected and influenced by the other five forces or factors.

2. The *microsystem*: This is the setting where the child lives. The microsystem includes parents, siblings, classmates at school, and others with whom the child has regular contact.

3. The *mesosystem*: This is the interaction between the micro- and exosystems. An example would be the interaction between the child's family and his or her school administration.

4. The *exosystem*: This includes entities or systems outside the microsystem with which that the individual or microsystem interacts. Examples include parents' employers, extended family, the school board, and mass media.

5. The *macrosystem*: This refers to culture, laws, politics, socioeconomics of a region or country.

6. The *chronosystem*: This refers to changes occurring in the other five domains over time. For example, children develop increasing cognitive skills, families experience divorce, instability, and restabilize, schools change administrations, and laws, cultural values, and socioeconomics change with time.

Because subsystems contribute to the makeup and external contexts of the family, their influence on the family is constant and significant. Let's refer again to the couple with a new baby. Imagine now that their child has been has been diagnosed with Down syndrome. This diagnosis impacts the child's internal functioning and ripples out to the family (microsystem) as they seek support from the medical community, their neighborhood, church, extended family, and community (exosystem). On yet another level, now imagine the parents are a lesbian couple. How they interact with and are affected by the macrosystemic factors of political climate, religious groups and attitudes, as well as the exosystem (their neighborhood, friends, and families of origin), will affect their interactions and support for their child.

With emphasis on contexts, multiple outcomes, and the power of systems functioning as a whole and openly interacting with other systems, general systems theory shows that systems are more than the sum of their parts. This shift in systemic epistemology laid the groundwork for second order cybernetics.

Second-Order Cybernetics

In the original cybernetics movement (now termed **first-order cybernetics**), observers of a system were immune to its influence. With the development of quantum physics, postmodern philosophies, and constructive epistemologies (see Chapter 11), questions arose regarding experts as outside observers with no influence on the family system. A shift occurred. No longer was the family counselor an expert-observer; now family counselors were participant-observers.

At first contact, family therapists enter or join the family system. They go from being external to internal. This happens very quickly and can catch therapists by surprise. For example, Dr. X is sitting in her office doing paperwork. Her telephone rings. She answers:

Dr. X: Hello. This is Dr. X's family counseling clinic.

Father: Uh. Yeah. Hello. My name is Robert and my wife told me to call for a family therapy appointment.

Dr. X: Okay. I have appointments available next Tuesday and next Thursday after 3 p.m.

Father: Hmm. Now I'm not so sure. I didn't realize you would be a woman. Are there any men who work in your office?

Dr. X: Actually no, there's just me. I'm a licensed family counselor.

Father: Damn. I guess I'd better take that 3 p.m. time. My wife will be pissed if I don't get this done.

Although this example may seem extreme, it's not. Family dynamics nearly always emerge or spill into initial telephone contacts. From the moment the father hears Dr. X's voice, Dr. X is in the family system. She's no longer a dispassionate expert-observer. This is a **second-order cybernetics** rule: When therapists work with families, they immediately become an influence, if only by their presence.

Those embracing a **second-order cybernetic** philosophy assert that counselors are nonexperts whose role is to co-construct meanings and solutions with the family. New interactions evolve in partnership (I. Goldenberg & H. Goldenberg, 2008).

Each phase in systems evolution has been grounded in the core principle of attending to the system instead of the individual. The goal of family therapy is to shift the focus from the individual to family contexts and interpersonal relationships. These are the sites where symptoms are created and maintained.

The critical underpinnings of any systemic counseling theory are grounded in the cybernetic and general system theories. These concepts include, but are not limited to: circular causality, the identified patient, first- and second-order change, the ability to attend to process, and homeostasis. We now explore these crucial elements that guide a family counselor's conceptualization and intervention strategies when working with families.

Where Is the Problem and Where Is the Solution?

Similar to feminist, constructive, and multicultural perspectives, family systems theory places "the problem" outside the individual. If we look at this through ecological systems theory, feminist and multicultural theorists point to macrosystems (e.g., culture) as the source of the problem and intervention target. Constructive theorists will look at both micro- and macrosystems. In contrast, family systems theorists and therapists focus more exclusively on the microsystem of family as both the source of the problem and the location where the intervention should occur.

If you're coming from a perspective dominated by Western culture, this might contradict your values of independence and personal responsibility. Family counselors, however, are often known for seeing everything through their family lens. So, to begin the leap into a systemic approach, we must let go of the idea that symptoms are contained and maintained within the individual and view problems and symptoms as belonging to the whole family system.

Circular Causality

To successfully embrace an entire family as a client, one must first embrace the notion of **circular causality**: Everyone, in one way or another, contributes to the process that maintains problems and successes. Most of us are accustomed to engaging in a more linear thinking style. Linear thought is clear, logical, and seeks answers in a direct-causation manner. For an example, let's consider the Stevens family. The father in the family is struggling with an alcohol addiction. Linear thinking would be:

$$A\ (\text{Dad}) + B\ (\text{Alcohol abuse})$$
$$= C\ (\text{Unhappy Family})$$

Given this conceptualization, if Dad stops drinking, the Stevens family will be happy. The solution is clear and simple. It examines Dad in isolation. Circular thinking, however, asks us to take contexts and other players into consideration.

When expanding our scope beyond Dad's specific drinking behavior, we discover he has a family ... and his family has dynamics. We notice the following:

- Mom regularly berates Dad.

- This berating escalates when the 17-year-old son misbehaves.

- Dad doesn't intervene with his son's misbehavior, instead he laughs.

As you can see, Dad's alcohol-related behavior is now nestled comfortably within a multidimensional family system—which makes things decidedly more complex and circular. You can see that the family becomes lost in a pattern where behaviors are influenced by and support alcohol use. An equation for circular thinking might resemble something like this, where there's no clear beginning or end point, only a process that is maintained between two (or more) variables (see Figure 12.1):

FIGURE 12.1   Simple Circular Causality

Transitioning into circular thinking is difficult. When a family comes to see you, they'll likely have what family counselors refer to as an **identified patient**, or IP. In the case of the family described above, Dad would likely be the IP. Often, phrases like, "if she or he would just change, things would be better for our family" are used to describe the IP. As a helping professional, you can often learn who the IP is when the family calls for an appointment; it's usually obvious. Having an IP provides safety and comfort for the family, as it keeps the problem localized to one person. When the IP holds the problem in its entirety, the rest of the family can avoid examining their own problem behaviors as well as any responsibility for the IP's problem.

Reconceptualizing Clients

When the family walks in, almost everyone wants to talk about the IP. This makes getting family members to shift to a family systems lens a significant challenge.

Helping a family see the circular causality present in their family system begins when the counselor shifts the focus away from the IP and has family members look at themselves and their various relationships within the family. Asking all family members to examine their own contributions to the family problem is threatening. Family members will feel vulnerable and defensive. Anderson and Stewart (1983) described this process:

> While all therapists encounter resistance, the resistance experienced by family therapists is particularly challenging. Since most families present with one symptomatic member, other family members may fail to see the relevance of involving the whole family, or fear that requests for such family involvement amount to the therapist's blaming them for their problem member's difficulties. (p. 2)

To avoid family sessions that target the IP, the counselor must make it clear that family therapy constitutes a new way of looking at the situation and that the client is the whole family. If you practice family therapy, there will be many tempting moments to collude with family members and view the IP as the "true client." When this happens, you're just doing individual counseling with the rest of the family members sitting in the room. To engage the entire family in change, you must help all family members recognize and grapple with their roles and contributions to the problem. As a family counselor, your focus will be on relational interactions.

The next task involves achieving family buy-in for the same perspective; in short, seeing themselves in their entirety as the client. Remember, the IP has carried the family's load of problems—sometimes for a very long time. And the family has invested substantial energy in maintaining this member as "the keeper of the problems."

Shifting a family's perspective from linear to circular requires patience and finesse. In the Stevens family example, alcohol abuse is the symptom that brings the family to counseling. What follows is a family therapy dialogue with the Stevens family. The goal is for the family to see how symptoms situate themselves in relational contexts so they can view the problem in a more circular fashion:

Counselor: After talking with you on the phone, Mom, I gathered that one concern bringing you to family counseling is your husband's drinking.

Mom: That's correct. I really want to be here to support him in getting better. Our family just can't keep going like this.

Dad: [Crosses arms, sits back in his chair, and glares at his wife.] I told you, I'd come here with you, but I'm done being yelled at and blamed for everything. I don't want this to turn into another lecture.

Counselor: [Addressing Dad.]. So, it seems like this topic has ran its course between the two of you before. I wonder, Dad, if you had to describe the difficulties present in your family, what would they be?

Dad: Well for one, she's in my business all the time. Poking around, asking questions about where I am? Did I do this? Did I forget that? She's always looking over my shoulder and yelling at me if I did something wrong. I can't stand it. She's the same way with Scotty. For God's sake, our son is nearly an adult, and she can't let him do a damn thing on his own. And she is always wanting me to discipline him.

Son: [Fidgets, looking uncomfortable in his seat.]

Counselor: [Addressing the son.] How would you sum up what's happening in your family?

Son: They just fight all the time. Well, not all the time. But they're either fighting or not paying attention to each other. I wish they would just divorce and get it over with already. I'm sick of it.

Counselor: So, when your parents fight, what do you do?

Mom: Oh, he's a good kid, usually. He's graduating with honors. Really, he's not who we need to worry about. I just hate that he sees his Dad drunk. His Dad is a horrible example, and never corrects Scotty when he acts up. Thank God Scotty is doing the best he can without a good father.

Counselor: So Scotty, what do you do when your parents fight?

Scotty: Just zone out, basically. I hang in my room, text with friends, leave the house, do my own thing. Just try to ignore them.

Counselor: From what I'm learning, it seems like you escape what's happening in your family by closing yourself in your room. Your Dad might be escaping what's happening in your family by drinking. And your Mom is alone.

Counselor: [Looking toward Mom.] I'm wondering if you feel alone in your family? Like you're not sure how to connect with your husband and son anymore. It seems like you're working very hard to stay connected, but maybe in a pretty directive way.

Mom: When are we going to talk about his drinking. That's why we're here.

Counselor: Well, I asked you to come in for family counseling. And while Dad's drinking is certainly an issue, there may be more problems happening under the surface. So, what I'm trying to do now, is get a better idea of what's happening with the *whole* family. I think this is the best way to get a clearer picture of the three problems you've all mentioned so far: Dad's drinking, Scotty's isolation and occasional acting out, and the strain on you and your husband's relationship. So, while you see the problem as Dad's drinking, we can expand the problem to include everyone's perspective.

Mom: Yes, but if he stopped drinking, he'd spend more time with Scotty, I would stop nagging, and things would be better.

Counselor: I see what you mean. Let's focus on all three things at once: the drinking, the isolation, and the nagging. My hope is that we can come up with a shared idea of what the problem facing your family is. The word that keeps coming to mind for me is loneliness. Everyone sounds lonely. Mom tries to connect by being bossy. It doesn't work. Dad, feeling angry and disconnected, drinks. Angry and hurt about the drinking, Mom becomes more directive and bossy. Scotty, hearing his parents fight, escapes from home. Even though you're all under the same roof, everyone sounds pretty alone. And it seems that the more lonely you feel, the more you try to escape the problem by drinking, arguing, or isolating.

As you can see, the counselor was trying to shift how the family talks about the problem, expanding the issue from Dad's drinking to their relational contexts. The counselor shifted the focus away from Dad (the IP), and began co-constructing a new language for the problem, gaining input from all of the family members. Making this shift is difficult for Mom; she's very invested in addressing Dad's drinking. In cases like this, the counselor must be both assertive and empathic, managing the ebb and flow of building a relationship with Mom while also challenging her to embrace a new way of thinking. The counselor subtly and less subtly expands the problem to highlight family members' roles and contributions to the problem. When shifting away from alcohol abuse and looking at deeper isolation patterns, the counselor sets the groundwork for second-order change.

First- and Second-Order Change

Systemic perspectives recognize two types of change: change that addresses symptoms and change that addresses patterns. Making changes to symptoms themselves is **first-order change**. This involves making surface behavioral changes while ignoring underlying family system dynamics. For the Stevens family, first-order change would involve Dad attending AA and getting sober, while the family maintains their interactional patterns that result in isolation. The symptom itself can be addressed but system patterns often hold strong. First-order changes are sometimes referred to as shallow, as the behavior itself can be changed, but it's often difficult to maintain a new behavior (not drinking) in the light of unchanging systemic patterns (marital berating and isolation). The first-order change of becoming sober without addressing family patterns places Mr. Stevenson at greater risk for relapse, as maintaining a new behavior in an unchanged system is often difficult.

In contrast, **second-order change** involves changing deeper interactional patterns in the family. For the Stevens family, the interactional patterns would remain the same no matter what symptoms brought the family to counseling (isolation and loneliness are central themes whether or not the family chose to focus on Dad's drinking, Mom's nagging, or Scotty's disengagement). Because symptoms are indicators of underlying family patterns, second-order change is the ultimate goal. Thus, family counselors aim to look beyond the family's symptoms and into the relational patterns that maintain them. When conceptualizing the Stevens family, a counselor may wonder:

- What's happening in the family that maintains Dad's drinking?

- What purpose does Dad's drinking serve for the family?

These questions focus on the family as a whole and aim at understanding interaction patterns that support the symptom. The questions don't center on what causes symptoms. From a family systems perspective, there's no clear beginning or "root cause," but rather a circular pattern where the behavior of one family member influences and sustains the behavior of another. As noted by Nichols and Schwarts (2007),

> The essence of family therapy is to see patterns of connection where others see only isolated events. (p. 7)

By looking more deeply at family process and not getting lost in problem content that emerges in a session, counselors can identify family patterns more efficiently and can predict family behaviors regardless of content that surfaces within a session.

Homeostasis

The ability to predict family interactional patterns is grounded in the concept of **homeostasis**. Families, by their very nature, strive for homeostasis, or a sense of balance and equilibrium that's consistent and predictable. Achieving homeostatic balance creates safety and familiarity for families. An important note on homeostasis: the patterns that are familiar to a family, even if uncomfortable, are safer than new and unknown patterns. Recall the saying, "Better the devil you know, than the devil you don't." This readily applies to families in homeostasis: there's more security in embracing well-known family patterns, no matter how unhealthy and disruptive, than embracing new, unfamiliar patterns.

Families are incredibly invested in maintaining homeostasis. They'll repeatedly return to what's familiar. When entering counseling, families are asked to surrender their old ways—their homeostasis. This, as you can imagine, is a source of great anxiety, as any change will stimulate disequilibrium. Once in flux, systems must be allowed time to accommodate. Times of change are often followed by times of rest, allowing the family to adapt to interactional changes that have occurred.

Attending to Interaction Patterns

Attending to a family's interaction patterns is vital, whether referencing circular causality, establishing the family as the client, creating second-order change, or remaining mindful of homeostasis. The bottom line is the same for each concept: addressing family members' relationships is the heart of family counseling. So, what exactly do family therapists attend to? Here's a short list of interactional patterns from family systems theories: subsystems, boundaries, coalitions, alliances, triangles, hierarchies, roles, and rules.

Subsystems

Recall our discussion about general systems theory and subsystems. Systems inherently organize themselves into smaller groups; in a family, these groups can be organized around gender, age, interests, beliefs, relationship status, and many other identifiers. Sibling and parental units are the most common example of family subsystems.

Family therapists attend to subsystems when seeking to understand where family symptoms are most prevalent. The goal is not to find causal factors, but to look into the relationships central to maintaining the symptom. In the case of the Stevens family, this may lead us to the parental subsystem. When counseling this family, one may begin to tease out the nuances of the marital relationship that set the stage for maintaining the couple's isolation.

Boundaries

Imagine a family as a Venn diagram, with circles around every person, every subsystem, and even the family itself. Although these lines are invisible, these boundaries are in the counselor's mind's eye when deciphering where one individual or subsystem ends and another begins. **Boundaries** are an ever-present force when working with families. Boundaries, in their healthiest form, protect and enhance systemic functioning. The ultimate goal of a family system is to intentionally open and close boundaries; the family's boundaries are considered clear when they intentionally open their boundaries to accept new influence and then close their boundaries to allow the system to adjust to the recent influence.

When boundaries are either too rigid or diffuse, troublesome consequences often result.

Rigid boundaries appear exactly as they sound: thick, cemented, and difficult to penetrate. A family with rigid boundaries won't accept influence and attempts to keep the same impenetrable boundaries across time and contexts. Imagine a family with a 14-year-old daughter who is beginning to form friendships outside the home. She's engaging in new behaviors: going to movies with friends and attending school dances. The parental subsystem sets a summer curfew of 9:30 p.m., enforcing a mutually agreeable boundary between their daughter and subsystems outside the family.

Five years later, when their 19-year-old daughter returns home after her first year of college, her parents stick to the 9:30 p.m. curfew. The parents' refusal to change boundaries given new contexts is an overly rigid boundary. Difficulty in the parent-child relationship is likely to ensue.

Diffuse boundaries exist at the other extreme and are characteristically loose, open, and perhaps absent. Diffuse boundaries can be common between a troubled parental subsystem and the child subsystem. Consider a couple that has a 9-year-old daughter and is also having marital difficulties (the Davis family). The couple's troubles persist and they cope by leading parallel lives, rarely communicating to each other directly; they find family connection with their child. Over time, Dad becomes more absent and Mom turns to her daughter to "vent" about her disappointing marriage. The daughter is then elevated to a "pseudo-companion" and essentially becomes mom's personal counselor. In this case, the boundary between Mom and daughter has become diffuse. Mom talks to her daughter about sex, abuse, and drug use in ways unusual (and perhaps unhealthy) for a parent-child subsystem. These diffuse boundaries can also set the stage for other interactional patterns warranting attention: triangulation, alliances, and coalitions.

Alliance, Coalition, and Triangulation

Imagine, for a moment, that you're alone in a conflict: No one sees the world as you, there's no one to encourage and empathize with you, and most of all, there's no one to affirm that you're right. This state is so uncomfortable that you may actively seek *alliances* to ease your distress.

Forming alliances is a natural means for gaining connection and support. Alliances occur when family members position themselves in support of one another. One alliance type seen in families is the **coalition**; this occurs when two family members side together against a third.

For example, in the Davis family, as Dad drifts away and the boundary between mother and daughter becomes increasingly diffuse, the stage is set for a coalition. Mom could begin confiding in her child about the disappointment she feels over Dad's absence and her anger about him not only ignoring her, but the daughter as well. To comfort her Mom, the daughter speaks of her disappointment in her father. The relationship between mother and daughter is strengthened as a result of binding together against Dad.

Another fascinating shift in family structures during conflict is **triangulation**. Although sometimes confused with coalitions because it also involves three people and is used as a means to provide comfort, the aim of a triangulation is different. Triangulation is being used when a dyad in conflict *pulls in* a third party. The third party holds the focus to relieve relationship distress. This enables the dyad to ignore their own struggle and come together as they place energy into the third party. Consider a couple that has been married 13 years and are parents to Maria, a 12-year-old girl. After discovering an intimate e-mail exchange between his wife and a co-worker, the father approaches his wife with concern about his daughter's choice of friends. Instead of focusing on their relationship concerns, the couple colludes to regain a sense of connection by coming together "for their daughter's sake." Typically, the dyad pulls in a more vulnerable or less powerful family member. For example, a child having academic problems or a recently divorced sibling; it's easier to hold the focus on someone lower in the family's hierarchy. If a family therapist suspects that presenting issues involve triangulation, they might ask "If Maria weren't the problem, what would the problem be?"

Rules and Roles

Just as its Maria's job to be the "problem child" for her family, there are many other roles in need of filling. Some systems theories go into great depth describing various **family roles**. For example, when exploring family roles, renowned family therapist Salvador Minuchin would often ask families:

- Who's the sheriff in this family?
- Who's the lawyer?
- Who's the social worker?

As family members develop expectations for one another (i.e., for homeostasis—remember, systems are predictable), roles become more prevalent. Family roles are limitless. Examples can include: breadwinner, caretaker, disciplinarian, cook, jester, problem solver, protector, logical one, reactive one, needy one. And to make it more interesting, family members can hold more than one role. Family counselors examine roles to help identify family norms. When uncovering family consistencies and patterns, roles are only one piece of the puzzle.

Family rules, like roles, provide predictability for families. Rules set expectations for behavior and can be spoken or unspoken. *Overt rules* are spoken and direct. Examples of overt rules include openly communicated curfews, bed times, and household chores. *Covert rules*, on the other hand, are unspoken, but well-established family rules; these rules often are very powerful partly because they're not openly discussed or questioned, but rather, quietly followed. Covert rules might include:

- Don't talk about Mom's drinking
- When you really want something, ask Grandma first
- When you're sad, keep it to yourself
- Don't talk about bills until payday
- Never speak to anyone directly
- Hug every family member when you say goodbye
- Never directly express approval or affection

When beginning work with families, counselors enter the family system's well-established patterns.

To form a clear picture of a family, counselors must view them from several perspectives; using lenses to examine rules, roles, alignments, coalitions, triangulations, boundaries, and subsystems is an excellent start. Even when a fairly clear family picture is established, it's hard to know what to do next. This is where theory translates into practice.

FAMILY SYSTEMS THERAPY IN PRACTICE

Family therapists practice in many different ways. Some family therapists employ traditional theoretical models in their work with families. You can look back at any of the preceding chapters and find practitioners who use specific theories to guide their family therapy work. There are psychodynamic family therapists, Adlerian family therapists, behavioral family therapists, and more.

As we look into family therapy practice in this chapter, we explore four distinct family systems approaches. Although these approaches have some traditional theoretical roots (e.g., psychoanalytic or humanistic-existential), they were birthed and grew directly out of family therapy research and practice. These family systems approaches include:

1. Murray Bowen's Intergenerational Family Therapy
2. Salvador Minuchin's Structural Family Therapy
3. Jay Haley's Strategic Family Therapy
4. Virginia Satir and Carl Whitaker's Humanistic and Experiential Family Therapy

These approaches share a systems perspective, but employ distinct ways of joining and working with families (see Putting it in Practice 12.1 to see a sample informed consent for family therapy).

Intergenerational Family Therapy

Developed by Murray Bowen, **intergenerational family therapy** has psychodynamic foundations, focusing largely on a family's history and patterns

PUTTING IT IN PRACTICE 12.1

Informed Consent From the Family Systems Perspective

The following is an excerpt of a sample informed consent from a family systems perspective. As you read it, pretend you're sitting in the counselor's waiting room, about to go in for your first session with your family.

I'm very glad to see the entire family here, ready to begin counseling together. Family counseling takes a great deal of commitment from the whole family; just your presence here is a sign of the love and support you have for one another.

In the beginning, it can sometimes be difficult to understand why *everyone* has to come to counseling when it seems that only one, or maybe a few of you, are having difficulties. One thing you'll notice in family counseling is that I never believe a problem is only about one person. Instead of focusing on one person, I'll be looking at your family relationships. We'll work together to understand where your family is stuck in old patterns of relating. This is important because the patterns your family has created together is what causes people to have problems. When the family starts to grow and change, everyone will get better because you will create healthier patterns in your family. This doesn't mean that anyone in particular is to blame for problems in your family. It does mean that everyone can consider making changes that could contribute to healthier family patterns.

So, what will we do in counseling to help your family grow?

- Everyone will share their ideas of what the problem is and how they see the family. Together we'll make a drawing called a genogram that maps out your relationships and important family events. This will help all of us understand your family in new ways.

- We'll focus on how you communicate and react to one another "in the moment" and create new ways of communicating to help you speak directly to one another with genuiness and empathy. Often, I will help you express your feelings to one another to help you establish a stronger connection.

- Sometimes, I may coach you to try new things in a session, like move from one seat to another, or try other new behaviors.

Learning to relate to one another in new ways can be scary and risky. There are times I'll ask you to express yourself and take risks with your family that seem unusual. My hope for counseling is that you'll try some of these new things with me and later try them out at home.

Last of all, I want to welcome your whole family to counseling. I'm glad you care enough about each other to come together to create some new and healthier family patterns.

established across generations. Bowen was the first to articulate key family theoretical concepts including triangulation, emotional cutoff, enmeshment, differentiation of self, and the use of genograms. An intergenerational approach sees differentiation—the successful establishment of a calm, observant, and logical self in the face of familial turmoil—as its overarching goal. Once family members attain differentiation, they're emotionally and intellectually self-sufficient and able to resist the unconscious grasp of their family of origin's rules and roles (Bowen, 1978).

QUESTIONS FOR REFLECTION

After reading the Informed Consent description of family therapy in Putting it in Practice 12.1, what do you think family counseling might be like? What are your impressions of the counselor? How would members of your family respond to this approach?

Role of the Therapist
The counselor or therapist serves as an investigator and later as a coach, looking into the past to identify a family's interactional patterns and then directing them toward differentiation. The therapist's role is consistent with psychodynamic theory; the counselor remains objective, detached, and explicitly unaffected by the family. A primary objective is to maintain a safe distance when working with a family to avoid enmeshment. In this way the therapist maintains and models successful differentiation.

Key Concepts
Intergenerational family systems therapists investigate a family's intergenerational family style. As therapists assess levels of **differentiation** present in the family, they look for indicators of triangulation, emotional cutoff, and enmeshment. Emotional cutoffs and enmeshments are viewed as polar positions on the differential continuum (see Figure 12.2).

Successful differentiation is marked by gaining intellectual and emotional distinction or independence from one's family. Becoming **emotionally cut off** involves either physical or emotional distance. **Enmeshment**, on the other hand, is characterized by incredibly diffuse boundaries. It can be difficult to tell where one family member ends and another begins. When exploring family relationships on the differentiation continuum, the task is to help family members understand their current functioning and move toward optimal differentiation.

Intergenerational family systems therapy has a strong individualist value system. As a consequence, families within cultural groups with collectivist orientations (e.g. Latino, Asian) may appear highly enmeshed. In contrast, if the therapist is operating from a collectivist orientation, families from the dominant U.S. culture all may appear emotionally cut off. This is a good example of how powerful therapist perspective is in determining whether a given family (or individual) appears functional or dysfunctional (pathological).

Facilitating Change
The main goal is to help family members achieve individuation while remaining connected. In the evaluation interview, therapists gather historical information about the presenting problem(s) and family members' perceptions of what creates and sustains the problem(s). This process often involves using a genogram.

The genogram is a primary tool for teaching family members about relationship dynamics in their system. Similar to a family tree, the genogram includes all family members and uses symbols to note gender, age, alliances, coalitions, triangles, enmeshments, cutoffs, addictions, and mental health concerns. Additionally, events such as births, deaths, marriages, separations, and divorces are included.

At a minimum, genograms extend back three generations. By seeing family patterns across generations, patterns of triangulation, enmeshment, and

Emotionally Cutoff   *Differentiation*   *Enmeshment*

FIGURE 12.2 The Differential Continuum

cutoff become clearer. Patterns from previous generations act as clues to current family functioning. When constructing and looking at a genogram, family members can reflect on their family from a different perspective. Families can stand back and take on roles as objective researchers, seeing ingrained family patterns across generations. Throughout the process, the family can be shown new ways to think about family relationships, while supporting emergence of an emotionally regulated and differentiated family structure.

Constructing a Genogram

To construct a successful **genogram**, therapists must first join with a family and create a sense of safety. Genogram work can involve vulnerability and risk for families. Genogram construction can include significant disclosures about family events and relationships. The process can reveal both family structure and illuminate meaning the family places on particular events, situations, and relationships.

Taking a curious stance can allow therapists to flow in conversation with the family while supporting a deeper and richer understanding. Common symbols are used when constructing genograms (see Figure 12.3). When family structure and interaction patterns are represented using these symbols, family themes become clearer. (See Putting it in Practice 12.2 for the Griswold family description, and Figure 12.4 for the beginning of their genogram.)

Structural Family Therapy

Salvador Minuchin

Although Bowen's intergenerational approach examines family structure, it primarily attends to differentiation across and within generations. In contrast, the structural family therapy approach places more emphasis on homeostasis, subsystems, boundaries, and coalitions as they relate to a family's organization and current functioning.

Structural family therapy was developed by Salvador Minuchin (1974). At the Philadelphia Child Guidance Clinic in the 1970s Minuchin worked with poor and ethnically diverse families. His theory's trademark is its focus on changing the organizational structure of families. The goal of structural family therapy remains the same today: create a path for new behavior through organizational changes to a family's dysfunctional structure (Minuchin, 1974).

Role of the Counselor

To change family structure, structural family therapists take a directive role in leading families toward change. Structural family therapists engage families and develop a relationship characterized by increased kinship and trust. The relationship between therapist and family is essential to this approach; the therapist makes personal adjustments to foster a meaningful connection and adapt to a unique family's style of relating.

Key Concepts

Family behavior is a function of its structure. Key concepts of this approach are built around this central idea and so the primary objective is to change family structure to better nurture the growth of its members.

Structural family therapists focus on family boundaries in order to understand and change family structure. This allows therapists to understand rigid and diffuse relational styles within the family. In structural family work, you attend to boundaries around individual family members, but also examine how boundaries are defined between subsystems, urging the development of clear and intentional boundary making.

An ideal structure consists of a parental unit in clear leadership with clear boundaries over the child subsystem. When a family maintains boundaries that are too rigid or diffuse, the result is a structure that supports coalitions, overinvolvement, scapegoating, and conflict.

Facilitating Change

The big (and challenging) question is: How can you help a family develop clear boundaries and maintain a fair hierarchical structure, while also eliminating

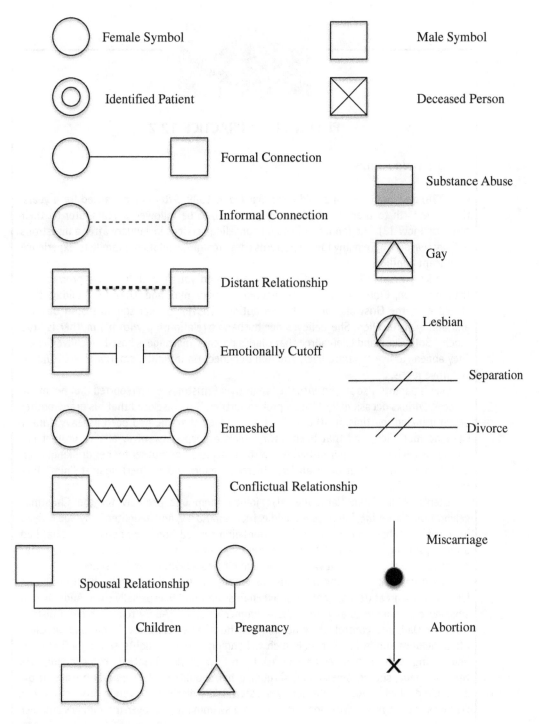

FIGURE 12.3 Common Genogram Symbols
Adapted from McGoldrick, Gerson, & Shellenberger, 2005.

PUTTING IT IN PRACTICE 12.2

The Griswold Family

Clark (38) and Ellen (36) Griswold were married in 1989. After being married for 4 years, they gave birth to their daughter Audry (now 16), to be followed 3 years later by their son Russ (now 13). The family requested counseling services in January after a disastrous holiday season where many family patterns came to light, leading the family to experience significant conflict.

Clark's parents, Clark Sr. and Nora, were married young, and depended primarily on their only son, Clark, to achieve connection in their marriage. Over the holiday, they stayed with the Griswold family. Nora's doting behavior on her son was both obvious and annoying to Ellen. She believes her husband's relationship with his mother is "too much." Both Clark and Ellen agree that Clark's parents' marriage is based on convenience. They appear to live separate lives, and don't connect on intimate, emotional, spiritual, or cognitive levels.

Ellen's parents also stayed with the family over Christmas. Ellen reported that her mom, Frances, "drinks occasionally." When probed further, Russ disclosed that his grandmother began drinking martinis at 10 a.m. Clark also added that she had been a heavy drinker since he met Ellen, and that Ellen always feels a deep sense of loyalty to protect her mother, especially when her father, Art, verbally attacks her mother for her drinking. Ellen added that it has often been an "us" (herself, sister, and mother) against "him" (her father) scenario.

Ellen's older sister, Catherine, also joined them unexpectedly for the Christmas celebration. Catherine, her husband Eddie, their son Rocky, and daughter Ruby Sue arrived in an old Winnebago on Christmas Eve, after being evicted from their house. Eddie has had difficulty finding work, and Catherine, currently pregnant, works two jobs while caring for her other two children. Ellen worries that Eddie takes advantage of her sister.

When you ask about the relationships within the immediate family, both Clark and Ellen report a great deal of conflict between Russ and Audry, especially since Audry began smoking pot more regularly after their summer vacation. Audry reports feeling distant from her Dad, and controlled by her mother. Russ feels very close to his Dad, as Clark often includes him in family rituals such as hanging Christmas lights, sharing a first beer, and flirting with women. When you ask Ellen how Clark's flirtatious behavior impacts their marriage, she becomes quiet, shrugging her shoulders. Clark quickly brushes it off as no big deal while Audry rolls her eyes. Later, Audry discloses to you in private that her Dad was caught naked with someone else in a swimming pool over the family's summer vacation.

After reading this information about the Griswold family, review Figures 12.3 and 12.4, respond to the following questions:

- Given what you know about the family, how would you continue constructing their genogram? What are you left curious about?
- What themes in the family need further cultivating?
- How would you approach the family to gather further information?
- What events or relationships would you want to have represented on the genogram, even though there are no standard symbols given?
- Considering the information you've gathered so far, what will be some of your treatment goals?

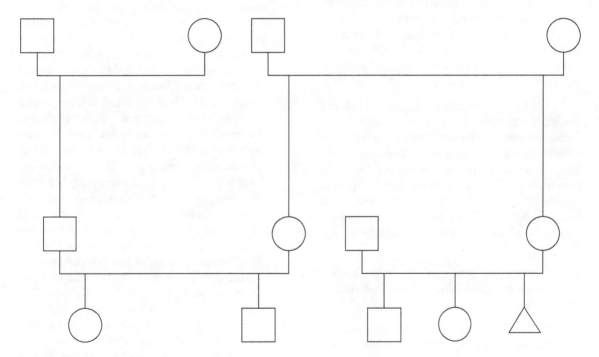

FIGURE 12.4   Griswold Family Genogram Shell

coalitions and attending to homeostasis? A structural approach breaks the actions for accomplishing these tasks into clear steps.

1. The therapist joins the family. Often this involves making and effort to "fit in" with the family by highlighting similarities and embracing similar affective styles and mannerisms. This joining,

often referred to as **mimesis** in structural circles, sets the foundation for a trustworthy and open relationship.

2. While joining with the family, the therapist simultaneously begins conceptualizing the family's structure, attending to (a) who is in the **scapegoated** role of identified patient; (b) who

holds the most power in the family; (c) what coalitions are in place; and (d) where the sources of conflict reside. To keep track of these relational structures, the counselor relies on a relational shorthand structural therapists refer to as **family mapping**. Using symbols, the immediate family structure is highlighted, mapping out boundaries, conflict, coalitions, and scapegoating.

3. In addition to family mapping, therapists gain further insight by evoking **family enactments**. Enactments occur when the family conflict is brought into the here-and-now to witness the conflict play out during a session. This allows the dysfunctional structure of the family to be seen, rather than merely described. During an enactment, therapists are charged with focusing on what's happening with every family member while expanding their view of the problem beyond the identified patient.

4. Once the family organization is understood and the source of their dysfunction unraveled, the therapist intervenes through re-structuring. Ever mindful of the delicate balance between stability and change, interventions are used with an awareness of when to push the family to open their boundaries and accept influence and when to encourage the family to close their boundaries so they can successfully adapt to recent changes.

5. Three techniques are used to help families change their structure: (a) unbalancing, (b) intensifying, and (c) reframing.

   a. **Unbalancing** occurs when the therapist intentionally aligns with a family member whose power needs elevating in the family hierarchy. If a family's structure includes a father and child in a coalition against the mother, the counselor would unbalance the coalition by aligning with the mother and empowering her within the system. Unbalancing supports the emergence of a new structure where the father and child's coalition becomes less stable and room is made for a new family structure to emerge.

   b. **Intensifying** further encourages new structuring. This involves encouraging strong emotional expression of family members in the here-and-now to enhance motivation for change. As emotions heighten, internal pressure for system change builds and the therapist can introduce change more easily. Intensifying increases a family's discomfort so that the distress involved with change becomes less than the pain involved with remaining the same.

   c. **Reframing** is relied on throughout the counseling process and is probably one of the most widely used family therapy techniques. Reframing is a restatement of the family's problem from another perspective. The problem is often softened so that its purpose is more easily understood and a greater sense of empathy among family members is fostered. Imagine a family whose daughter is getting married; over the course of the planning, the mother of the bride becomes increasingly hurt as she's left out of decision-making. The mother, resolving to be a contributing force when it comes to the wedding, begins to take over planning. A reframe of the mother's behavior could sound like: "It seems as if Mom is afraid of being pushed out of her daughter's life. Maybe, asserting herself over these wedding plans is her way of reminding the family that she loves her daughter and wants to remain close with her." Keep in mind that reframes don't excuse behavior, and don't endorse behavior, but only serve as an entry point to address the core structural issue more effectively. In this case, reframing Mom's behavior about the wedding sheds light on the re-negotiation of boundaries that need to take place between mother and daughter.

When fostering change from a structural perspective, the objective is clear: change the family structure and symptoms will relinquish their hold. Structural family therapy is considered moderately directive, but our next focus, strategic family therapy, has an even stronger counselor-as-expert perspective.

Strategic Family Therapy

Strategic family therapy grew out of work from the Mental Research Institute in Palo Alto, California. Jay Haley, a prominent name in both constructive therapy and strategic family therapy believed insight wasn't needed for change (Haley, 1976). Instead, he believed families can change by simply following a counselor's suggested strategies.

Role of the Counselor

The strategic approach to helping families relies heavily on the counselor. Directive strategies are the gateway for client change. Strategic counselors embrace an expert role and use this role to convince families to follow directives. These directives are determined (sometimes in consultation with reflecting teams observing the session) by questioning the solutions families have been using.

Key Concepts

The assumption is that families are using ineffective and unhelpful problem-solving strategies. Consequently, strategic therapists focus on how families are trying to solve their own problems. Strategic therapists maintain that the real problem involves one of three inadequate solutions:

1. Needing to act, but failing to do so.

2. Needing to stop acting, but failing to stop acting.

3. Solving a problem at a level that is ineffective. (Nichols & Schwarts, 2007)

Strategic interventions come down to addressing one of these problems. Once the problem is identified, therapists facilitate change by interrupting these failing solution patterns.

Facilitating Change

To facilitate change from a strategic perspective, counselors interrupt old, ineffective solution patterns. Because this approach doesn't require insight, there's no need to bring nonworking solutions to family awareness or to process its impact. Rather, counselors often rely on giving paradoxical directives, advising families to do the opposite of what they need (Bitter, 2009). Using paradox is designed to break family patterns that keep problems active.

Common paradoxical interventions include **prescribing the symptom**, **creating ordeals**, and **positioning**. When prescribing the symptom, the counselor may say something like:

> I know you say you're depressed, but I'm not sure you're quite depressed enough. For the next week, really commit to your depression; make it obvious and allow it to really get in your way.

An *ordeal* is used to interrupt family patterns by distracting them and upping the ante, so to speak. This involves the counselor creating an ordeal that overshadows the current problem with another problem or task for the family to focus on.

When using *positioning*, counselors endeavor to appear hopeless in the face of the family's problem. They suggest that things are much worse than the family first thought.

As discussed in previous chapters, paradoxical strategies remain controversial and have drawn ethical questions since their inception. Consistent with Miller and Rollnick (2002), we don't recommend using paradox with clients in the ways articulated by the strategic family therapy school.

When approaching families strategically, counselors wield substantial power for creating change. While some theories embrace this expert counselor role, others believe that the motivation for change and growth can be found within the family itself (Miller & Rollnick, 2002).

Humanistic and Experiential Models

Virginia Satir and Carl Whitaker are two primary voices behind the humanistic and experiential movement in family counseling. Although each developed a distinct approach, they share common factors.

The relationship between the counselor and the family is central to experiential and humanistic family counseling. Experiential and humanistic family counselors remain in the here-and-now with the family during the therapy process. Slowing the process down and attending to communication styles and metaphors during a session sets an attentive and emotionally attuned tone. Above all else, when working from this framework, families are encouraged to explore, discover, and make new changes in the moment (Satir, 1983; Whitaker, 1981). Change isn't intellectually discussed or assigned as homework, it's spontaneously created and experienced in the here-and-now.

Role of the Counselor

Counselors remain attuned to themselves throughout the counseling process. They actively engage families and use themselves to facilitate change. Counselors also self-disclose, model personal congruence, and authentically engage the family. Intuition often serves as the spark to ignite family change. As counselors allow their **congruent** and spontaneous selves to emerge, the stage is set for families to let go of stagnant patterns and become open to new experiences. To use themselves effectively, experiential and humanistic counselors remain committed to their own personal growth. The counselor's continued engagement in their own growth and discovery is central to their capacity to facilitate growth in others. In this spirit, experiential and humanistic counselors grow and benefit from therapeutic encounters alongside the families they help.

The use of a co-therapy team is a recommended practice. Working in tandem with another counselor not only allows for two sets of eyes and ears, but also places the relationship between counselors front and center for families. This relationship can be used to model authenticity, connectedness, freedom of expression, communication, and conflict management. *The family crucible* (Napier & Whitaker, 1978) provides an illuminating example of a co-therapy relationship and the process of counseling one family over time using **symbolic experiential family therapy**.

Key Concepts

Humanistic and experiential counselors depathologize clients. Rather than seeking a diagnosis or label to define family dysfunction, experiential counselors

shift the meaning of symptoms. They also view families as stuck in their unique growth process. Growth is embraced as an inherent drive within all families and individuals. To become "unstuck" counselors help families value one another equally, openly articulate feelings, accept differences, and take risks to remain flexible and move into the unknown. Counselors seek to break down rigid structures and processes.

The **human validation process model** was developed by Virginia Satir and focused on modifying communication stances to help families move beyond their inflexible roles and rules. The way individuals communicate indicates one of five stances:

1. Placating
2. Blaming
3. Super-reasonable
4. Irrelevant
5. Congruent

Communication stances were seen as windows into a family's patterns. Satir was able to "level" family members artfully and see through their ineffective and protective communication stances and draw out more congruent messages.

When families use congruent communication, they have more flexibility to express and reach their potential, and are able to achieve a greater sense of connection. A **congruent** communication stance is characterized by authentic, direct, sensitive, and clear communication. Congruent communicators share their inner experience while valuing themselves and others.

The **placating** position is self-deprecating and places others above oneself. When taking a **blaming** position, little thought or concern is given to others and an air of self-importance flows from the communicator. **Super-reasonable** communicators see the world through a lens of coolness and logic. They sometimes use this style to excuse themselves and others from needing to work on uncontrollable factors. **Irrelevant** communicators are sometimes the family clown or distractor. This person puts his or her energy into shifting the focus away from the self, others, or other relevant factors (see Putting it in Practice 12.3 for an activity to help you deepen

PUTTING IT IN PRACTICE 12.3

Getting in Touch With Satir's Communication Stances

Virginia Satir

The following scenario illustrates Satir's communication stances. Imagine yourself as a single mother waiting up late to greet your adolescent daughter when she arrives home 1 hour after curfew. When she walks through the door, your response is:

> Placating: "I'm so glad you're home. I've been waiting up to see if you need anything. Did you have a good time?"

> Blaming: "You've ruined my night. I was supposed enjoy my night off from work, not sitting here worrying about you. This is ridiculous. You have no concern or respect for me and I'm sick of it."

Super-reasonable: "We really need to check your cell phone. It must not be working."

Irrelevant: "Hey. Wanna watch a movie?"

Now, try practicing these styles of communicating when responding to the following family predicaments, giving voice to the placating, blaming, super-reasonable, and irrelevant stances:

> You're the oldest son, age 15, in a family of five. You just learned your parents are planning to divorce. Your response is _____.

> You and your partner have been together 29 years. Your partner recently informed you that he/she has been diagnosed with lung cancer. Your response is _____.

> You're a grandfather living with your daughter, her husband, and their three children. You find pot and condoms in your 3-year-old grandson's school bag. Your response is _____.

After constructing a variety of responses to the given scenarios, consider the inner processes of the family member you have taken on in your role. What underlying dynamics might lead to each response you thought of? What would a congruent response sound like? Accessing unspoken responses and becoming attuned to emotions is the heart of an experiential counselor's conceptualization process. Once attuned to these inner workings, counselors then rely on intuition to construct here-and-now experiences that foster change.

your understanding of and empathy for Satir's communication stances).

Facilitating Change

Within humanistic/experiential frames, experience produces change (Keith & Whitaker, 1981). The primary goal is to create an experience with the family that allows for freedom of expression and new interaction patterns. To foster risk taking, the counselor must establish solid rapport with the family. Congruent interactions with family members foster trust. Demonstrating "realness," being genuinely expressive, and sending level messages are building blocks for rapport.

Drawing on the ability to remain attuned in the moment, the counselor recognizes unspoken, rigid, and readily accepted processes and structures that limit family growth. Once aware of these covert themes, counselors promote experiences that break down barriers with open, upfront, and expressive here-and-now communication. Potential techniques are limited only to the counselor's imagination. Techniques can be fun, spontaneous, and responsive to the family's needs at that moment in time, but they must always be aligned with a process that fosters openness, acceptance, and connectedness.

Family sculpting is a classic example of an experiential technique. In this intervention, the family becomes moldable and is asked to become mannequin-like so the counselor or a family member can position family members in physical statures representing their relationships. This nonverbal technique allows for what remains unspoken to be communicated clearly.

To depict a placating and blaming relationship, for example, a counselor might position the family member in a blaming role on top of a chair or table towering sternly over the placating family member who is on his or her knees. Experiences like these can evoke meaningful emotion and foster new patterns of family communication. Throughout the process, the counselor encourages family members to own their feelings and share them openly. These exaggerated experiences help family members to decide to change. The counselor's role is to provide an environment where experimentation and change are possible.

CONTEMPORARY FAMILY THERAPY DEVELOPMENTS

The experiential, structural, strategic, and intergenerational approaches described previously constitute foundational perspectives in the family systems movement. Elements of these approaches often remain at the core of more recent family therapy developments. Next we examine a range of more contemporary approaches, beginning with functional family therapy.

Functional Family Therapy

Functional family therapy (FFT) arrived on the family systems scene based on the work of James Alexander and Bruce Parsons (J. Alexander & Parsons, 1982; Onedera, 2006). FFT is an integration of behavioral and systemic approaches, with particular focus on the purpose (or function) of family member behavior. Through the FFT lens, behaviors create and define our interpersonal relationships, generating and maintaining intimacy and other important relationship dimensions.

When a family seeks therapy, the therapist helps make the specific functional qualities of family member behaviors more explicit. The goal is to help family members change risky and damaging behavior, while working to address or fulfill the behavior's original intent through alternative means.

Consistent with its behavioral roots, FFT has developed a strong evidence base and is widely used to serve families with disadvantaged and at-risk youth. Researchers have focused especially on adolescents across cultures and ethnicities struggling with violence, drug abuse, and other criminal behaviors; a number of small treatment outcomes research studies support FFT efficacy in reducing repeated criminal behaviors (Alexander & Parsons, 1973; Barton, Alexander, Waldron, Turner, & Washburn, 1985; Sexton & Alexander, 2002; Waldron, Slesnick, Brody, Turner, & Peterson, 2001).

Role of the Counselor

FFT therapists employ interventions supported by empirical research. Elements of the **curious researcher** emerge as the counselor approaches families with an investigative stance in an effort to understand and describe functions of specific behaviors. The therapist seeks to answer the question: What is the interpersonal payoff of the identified behavior of concern?

Consider a family arriving at a court-ordered appointment as a result of their son's recent violent behavior. An FFT clinician might begin by musing about core functions of the son's behavior and how it serves the family. For example,

- Is this the son's way of maintaining a connection with Dad, albeit a tumultuous one?

- Do Mom and Dad use the son's behavior to maintain their roles as disciplinarian and consoler?

While remaining curious about behavioral functions, the counselor simultaneously works to create a nonblaming environment and fosters relationships attentive to interpersonal needs.

Key Concepts
All behavior is purposeful and serves to create either distance or intimacy in family relationships. A goal of FFT is to help families understand their behaviors in these terms, rather than labeling behavior as good or bad. The systemic concept of circular causality is central, as the family is encouraged to see the problem beyond the identified patient and consider the IP's behavior to be serving a family purpose.

The family is encouraged to recognize everyone's contribution to problem maintenance. After understanding the behavior's purpose for the family, the next goal is behavior change. However, an important differentiation must be made here: this model seeks only to change behavior—not the function the behavior serves. Thus, therapists seek to help families fulfill the behavioral purpose in less risky and more relationally responsive ways.

Facilitating Change
Following analysis and discussion of family member behaviors, therapists implement change techniques. Relabeling, similar to the reframing technique discussed earlier, is used to explain family member's behavior in a sympathetic way, revealing positive underlying behavioral motives.

Consider a family that brings their daughter, Jill, for counseling. With all family members present, it becomes clear that Jill's recent drug use is capturing her mom's attention and allowing her mom to increase the intimacy in her relationship with Jill's father. Relabeling Jill's behavior and defining it in circular terms could sound something like this:

> Could it be that Mom's intense focus on Jill's behavior is a way of joining forces with you, Dad? Maybe her focus on Jill is really an attempt to get closer to you. Jill, you're making quite the sacrifice to help your parent's marriage.

Relabeling helps family members restructure cognitions around the problem and can lead to softer affective responses that are more sensitive to the family's interpersonal needs. After a greater understanding is reached about everyone's role in the problem and more empathy is fostered among family members to eliminate blaming, therapists help the family change their overt behaviors using, you guessed it, behavioral interventions. The ultimate aim of these interventions is to help the family remain true to the initial intent of their behaviors, but find other means to achieve the same function. For Jill's family, this could mean that instead of seeking her mother's attention with drug use, she could begin playing on her high school basketball team (or any other more positive behaviors) and receive her mom's attention when playing in games, thereby building intimacy in their relationship.

Multisystemic Family Therapy

Like FFT, **multisystemic family therapy** (MSFT) was developed to address issues in families with troubled children and adolescents. The multisystemic model was developed by Scott Henggeler (Henggeler & Bordin, 1990; Henggeler & Lee, 2003; Henggeler, Schoenwald, Borduin, Rowland, & Cunningham, 1998; Henggeler, Schoenwald, Borduin, Rowland, & Cunningham, 2009) and integrates cognitive-behavioral and systemic approaches. The model embraces a systemic intervention model that goes beyond the family and takes additional systems into consideration. For example, moving treatment into systems outside the family (e.g., schools, community centers) is an alternative to meeting in a consulting office with a family. In addition to extending outward, the model also moves inward, attending to systems within individuals; client development is also a focus of assessment and treatment. Cognitive-behavioral interventions are used to facilitate change.

MSFT has significant empirical support. Outcome studies show that MSFT successfully engages families in treatment, has positive effects on family functioning, decreases aggression with peers, and reduces recidivism rates with youth in the legal system (Henggeler, Pickrel, Brondino, & Crouch, 1996; Henggeler, Clingempeel, Brondino, & Pickrel, 2002; Henggeler, Melton, & Smith, 1992). Extensive training through the Multisystemic Therapy Institute is necessary to become a multisystemic family therapist (see: www.mstservices.com).

Narrative Family Therapy

In contrast to behaviorally based models that share an objective, modernist perspective, **narrative family therapy** was created from the postmodern epistemological movement and therefore holds that reality is socially constructed. Developed by Michael White and David Epston (1990; see Chapter 11), narrative approaches are based on a foundation of assumptions; namely, that the world exists of multiple viewpoints and realities and that realities gain strength and staying power when we give them meaning with our language in the contexts of our relationships (Gergen, 2009a). Similar to the description in Chapter 11, narrative family therapy helps families re-author their life stories.

Using a narrative approach, counselors take on an empathic and collaborative role, expressing curiosity about the family's dominant story that, in most cases, has left a family hopeless, out of options, and stuck. After gaining this perspective, counselors guide the family through a process of deconstructing the family story—questioning meanings and storylines and externalizing problems. When creating an alternate story, counselors look for exceptions in the dominant problem-saturated narrative,

asking questions that help the family describe times when negative parts of the story were less encompassing, or when "the problem" didn't get the better of them.

New family narratives include more balance and reflection on strengths, perseverance through challenge and stress, and sparkling moments or unique outcomes. In this approach, the problem isn't, in fact, the problem. The problem instead lies in the power given to dominant stories that limit and weaken families. Through exposure to alternate realities guided by a counselor's curiosity and urging of thick and rich descriptions, new possibilities come to light as clients establish fresh perspectives on the problem.

Feminist Family Therapy

Just as the narrative approach challenges dominant stories to expose new perspectives, **feminist family therapy** seeks to raise awareness of prevailing patriarchal themes, sexism, heterosexism, racism, and many other isms. Feminist family therapy grew out of critiques of systems theory, questioning concepts of circular causality (particularly in cases of relationship violence), confronting the necessity of the clinician's neutral stance (especially when the need to advocate for less powerful family member arises), and challenging early family systems views that blamed and demonized mothers (Dankoski & Deacon, 2000; Enns, 1988; Simola, 1992).

There isn't a single feminist approach to working with families. In fact, because there are many variations of feminism, there are many feminist approaches. However there are central beliefs that guide feminist family therapy approaches. These include:

- Recognizing patriarchy as a well-established and limiting social factor.

- Attending to and shifting power differentials and hierarchies that sustain oppression.

- Recognizing the personal as political and taking action to intervene at systemic levels beyond the family (challenging limiting factors upheld in the workplace, school systems, governing forces, etc.).

- Embracing the idea that families of all shapes and kinds need support.

- Attending to the implications of gender and gender roles. (Bitter, 2009)

Feminist family therapists also engage families in therapeutic relationships that are both phenomenological and egalitarian, while maintaining a therapeutic alliance built on client consent and collaboration. Feminist family therapists work with families to create flexible roles, level power structures, and establish a family environment that's respectful, nurturing, and caring.

QUESTIONS FOR REFLECTION

When engaging the informed consent process with a family, how will you handle confidentiality? How will this be different than handling confidentiality in an individual session? Be sure to discuss these questions with classmates and with your instructor.

CASE ANALYSIS AND TREATMENT PLANNING

The following is an excerpt from an experiential and humanistic family therapy session. The Jackson family has been court-ordered to counseling after their 17-year-old son (Jake) was arrested on drug charges. The family consists of Jake's mom, dad, 14-year-old sister Anna, 10-year-old brother Luke, and 8-year-old sister Sarah. This is the family's third session and it was established that Mom and Dad both have a long history of methamphetamine use and production. Two years prior, the children were removed from their care and placed in state custody while Mom served a three-year prison sentence.

Counselor: I'm glad to see you all made it back this week. I know you all said it was important to do this for Jake, but I'm wondering if you might be getting something out of this time together, too?

Mom: I just want to be out of the damn system, get them off our backs.

Counselor: Yeah, that system has been a big part of your family for a while now. You're ready to move on. Wash your hands of them.

Mom: Yup.

Counselor: And, they're still hanging on.

Dad: They're going to be sticking their nose in our business forever.

Counselor: So, there are things, like child protection services and the legal system that just won't let go of this family. No matter how hard you try to move on, they don't let go.

Sarah: Yeah, we work really hard.

Counselor: I bet you do. I've seen you work very hard in here. You work so hard to comfort your mom. Whenever someone begins to feel angry with your mom, you cuddle right up next to her.

Mom: She's my baby girl.

Counselor: That's a big job, a lot of protecting to do, and you're so little, the baby even? I think you should carry this big shield. (Counselor hands Sarah a toy shield resembling a knight's armor.) While we're together I want you to use this shield to protect who needs protecting.

Anna: (Rolls her eyes.)

Counselor: What's up Anna?

Anna: Nothing.

Counselor: (Using a playful tone.) I saw your eyes go back in your head. Jake, what do you think Anna might be thinking?

Jake: That this is a bunch of bull****.

Counselor: (To Anna.) Is that about right?

Anna: Yeah.

Luke: (Giggles.)

Counselor: It seems like you guys have put up with a lot of bull**** lately. Piles and piles of bull****. Let's make a pile in here, of the unfair, stupid **** you've had to deal with. I'll start. (The counselor writes on a piece of paper *alone*, shows the family the word, crumples the piece of paper, and throws it in the middle of the room.)

Counselor: I think it's crap that you kids feel alone in the world, like everyone is against you.

Dad: What are you trying to say? That I'm not doing my job? You f***ing people have no idea.

Sarah: (Hides behind shield.)

Counselor: Sarah, do you need some protecting right now?

Dad: (Exhales loudly.)

Sarah: (Cuddles into her Mom, Mom puts her arm around Sarah, kissing her on the head.)

Counselor: (To Dad.) What's it like to see Sarah like this?

Dad: I hate it. I hate how she (Mom) babies her.

Counselor: It seems like Mom does the comforting in the family and you draw the hard line. It must be tough sometimes, playing the bad guy.

Dad: Well, somebody's got to do it.

Counselor: Would you say that it's bull**** that it always has to be you?

Dad: (Reluctantly.) Sure.

Counselor: (Hands Dad a piece of paper to add to the pile.)

Counselor: (To Sarah.) It looks like you might be feeling afraid.

Sarah: (Shakes her head.)

Counselor: Dad, what do you think Sarah might need right now, while she's cuddled into Mom, holding up her shield?

Dad: She wants her mom.

Counselor: I'm thinking you might be able to do something for her too. Why don't you move over to this couch and sit next to Sarah. Sarah, would that be okay?

Sarah: (Nods her head.)

Dad: (Moves next to Sarah, puts his arm around her.)

Counselor: So Jake, what would you add to the pile?

Jake: No one here used to give a s*** about me. I was never taken care of like Sarah is now.

Counselor: (Hands Jake paper and pen to add to the pile.) Talk to your mom about this. Tell her about your anger and your hurt.

Jake: Mom, you weren't there for me. I took care of these kids most of the time. I'm so sick of cleaning up your messes.

Mom: (Tears up, looks down.)

Counselor: Mom, let's let Dad sit with Sarah, so you can focus on Jake. Move over here so you can face him.

Mom: (Moves over, avoids looking at Jake.)

Counselor: It's even hard to look at him. You're feeling a lot of guilt. Tell Jake about your tears.

Mom: I'm just really sorry.

Jake: You being sorry don't take it away. It just doesn't fix everything.

Sarah: (Moves toward Mom, climbs into her lap.)

Counselor: Sarah, you're doing your job for the family so well. Working so hard to keep your Mom happy. (To Mom.) Is this a job you want Sarah to have?

Mom: Well, I like her hugs, but it's not her job to keep me happy.

Counselor: Sarah, I wonder if you could be brave and try something new for me. Let's let Mom feel what she needs to feel and talk to Jake. This is going to be a little scary, being so new. Who would you like to sit with while Mom and Jake tell each other about their hurt and sorrow?

Anna: (Opens her arms for Sarah. Sarah walks over and is held next to her. An authentic conversation between Mom and Jake continues while the counselor supports congruent communication in the moment.)

The Problem List

Experiential family counselors attend to problems emerging in the moment while working to facilitate an awareness of the deeper issues impacting a family. In this case, the first problem to emerge was the family's struggle with the legal system. Notice how the counselor both acknowledged this as a problem while also bringing the family into the moment and addressing the communication patterns and structural issues that were impeding the family's growth. Based on what was observed and addressed in the moment, the problem list includes (notice this doesn't include Jake's legal issues because that's a problem linked to his IP role):

- Sarah's rigid role to protect her mother.
- Mom and Dad's inflexible caretaker and disciplinarian roles.
- The parentification and later role dismissal of Jake.
- Dad and Anna's resistance/fear of the counseling process.
- The family's covert rule not to talk about past hurts, current fears, and anger regarding their drug use history and the children's removal from the home.
- Mom and Dad's marriage appears to be one of parallel lives with limited connection that relies on triangulation to shift their focus to the children, instead of focusing on their relationship.

Problem Formulation

To gain a deeper understanding of the family's problems, the counselor looks into the processes and structures keeping the family stuck. The Jackson family has been using a process characterized by not speaking directly to each other, not disclosing authentic reactions to one another (especially where past hurts are concerned), and triangulating outside systems like child protective services and legal authorities to foster family connectedness. Their structure, although able to shift in times of crisis (e.g., Jake taking on a parenting role when his parents were unavailable) is also quite rigid. Sarah is entrenched in her mother-placating role, Luke appears irrelevant at times, Dad takes on a blaming stance and Mom embraces placating. Thus, the family isn't a pleasant or supportive place for the members to exist. As the problem formulation

becomes clearer, the counselor creates experiences where the family can experiment with new, more authentic ways of being, including ways in which they might experience positive feelings and support from one another.

Interventions

In an experiential model, the counselor's interventions are active. Change doesn't occur through talk or insight. Change happens through action in the now. When facilitating change with the Jackson family, the counselor spontaneously creates experiences responsive to the family's moment-to-moment needs. When the counselor witnesses Sarah placating Mom, the counselor intervenes by emphasizing the role and giving Sarah a toy shield to shift it into a playful (and obvious) experience. As Sarah relies on Mom for comfort, the counselor intervenes by asking Dad to move near Sarah to provide comfort, creating flexibility in his disciplinarian role. Further, the counselor empathizes with the family's frustration about being in counseling and in the system.

Instead of allowing the family to collude to oppose counseling, the counselor connects and joins with their frustration and then directs the family to uncover other sources of "unfairness" using a spontaneous experience to create a metaphorical pile of bull**** in the counseling session. This experience freed the family to express frustrations about what was happening within the family. This experience ultimately led to the counselor encouraging Sarah to let go of a placating role and support Jake in congruent communication with his Mom.

Outcomes Measurement

There are many formal tests and rating scales for measuring family therapy efficacy or effectiveness. Additionally, less formal assessments, such as reconstructing a genogram to look for evidence of change or repeated family sculpting can also be used.

Family counselors with feminist and postmodern perspectives rarely use formal written assessments—especially assessments that identify pathology and systemic dysfunction (Bitter, 2009). Complex family systems have layers of complexity that don't readily lend themselves to quantitative research.

Family counselors tend to rely on self-report and direct observations to determine the family counseling effectiveness. When using self-report, counselors seek family member perspectives about family roles, rules, relationships, and satisfaction with family functioning. When relying on observation, counselors use their knowledge and perceptions, evaluating families from an "outsider" perspective.

The Family Adaptability and Cohesion Evaluation Scale (FACES) is a commonly used self-report instrument for assessing family members' satisfaction. This 20-item scale asks family members to rate their current and ideal family situation in terms of flexibility and connectedness (Olson, 2000). The closer the two scores are, the greater the satisfaction. This assessment could be utilized as a pre- and postintervention measure with the Jackson family (or other families).

The McMaster Clinical Rating Scale (Epstein, Baldwin, & Bishop, 1983) is another common family functioning assessment tool that evaluates six areas: (1) roles, (2) communication, (3) problem solving, (4) affective responsiveness, (5) affective involvement, and (6) behavioral control. Additional formal assessments that could be considered for the Jacksons or other families include:

- The Beavers Interactional Competence and Style (BICS)

- The Circumplex Clinical Rating Scale (CCRS)

- Global Assessment for Relational Functioning (GARF), an appendix of the *DSM-IV*

A final note: When selecting assessment procedures for measuring outcomes, you should be aware that there are well over 1,000 couple and family assessments available (I. Goldenberg & H. Goldenberg, 2008). No doubt many were constructed in alignment with a variety of theoretical concepts. When selecting an outcomes assessment, be sure to find one or more that share a similar lens to your theoretical orientation and are representative of what you intend to measure.

CULTURAL AND GENDER CONSIDERATIONS

The cultural and gender sensitivity of family therapy varies considerably across the different approaches reviewed in this chapter. Historically, as noted in this chapter, family therapy was no friend of women. Fortunately, with increasing consciousness aided by feminist psychology and counseling, most family therapy approaches no longer explicitly blame mothers for their children's psychopathology.

In terms of cultural sensitivity, Bowen's intergenerational approach, with its focus on individuation and pathologizing of emotional cutoff and enmeshment could be very insensitive to diversity issues. To be blunt, it's difficult to think of which cultural group, including members of the dominant culture, that Haley's strategic approach wouldn't offend.

On the other hand, Minuchin's structural family therapy was used respectfully with minority populations in and around Philadelphia and Satir strove for authenticity and empathy with all clients—although the interpersonal, here-and-now focus that she and Carl Whitaker employed might be uncomfortable for some cultural groups.

More contemporary approaches such as multisystemic family therapy and narrative therapy tend to be very multiculturally sensitive. Each of these approaches takes deliberate steps to work with families where they are, rather than insisting they fit a white, dominant cultural model. In contrast, functional family therapy has been exposed to a feminist critique for promoting traditional family roles, although Alexander provided a rebuttal for that critique (Alexander, Warburton, Waldron, & Mas, 1985; Avis, 1985) Additionally, Jose Szapocznik of the University of Miami (who has a Polish-Cuban ancestry), is the developer of **one-person family therapy** an approach that has been used to effectively treat drug-abusing and multiproblem minority youth (Szapocznik & Kurtines, 1989; Szapocznik, Lopez, Prado, Schwartz, & Pantin, 2006; Tolan, Szapocznik, & Sambrano, 2007).

Thus far, specific family therapy approaches to address the particular needs of GLBT clients is minimal. Most of the published work in this area comes from the *Feminist Family Therapy* journal (Halstead, 2003; Hernández, Rickard, & Giambruno, 2008; Malley & McCann, 2002). Clearly, more work and research in this area is needed.

Overall, when it comes to gender and cultural sensitivity the verdict is mixed. Although there are some relic approaches that need substantial modifications, most contemporary approaches appear multiculturally informed and gender sensitive. Hopefully new research and practice addressing gender and culture will grow in the future.

EVIDENCE-BASED STATUS

As might be expected, much of the family therapy research literature is fragmented and there's limited rigorous programmatic scientific research. There's the problem of having so many different family therapy models and the difficulty of separating research on family therapy versus research on family systems therapy. In other words, it's difficult to know whether positive outcomes are based on simply getting the whole family together in the same room for therapy or whether a systems-based rationale and intervention is a helpful factor.

The good news is that generally research on family therapy is positive. Shadish and Baldwin (2003) reported on 20 meta-analyses of couple and family research. They reported a combined (couple and family outcomes) overall effect size of $d = .65$ compared to no treatment controls. This is a moderately positive effect size, but the efficacy of couple therapy was slightly better than family therapy.

The following specific findings have been reported regarding various family therapy approaches.

- For adolescent drug abuse, family therapy in general and multisystemic family therapy in particular appears more efficacious than other treatment approaches (Henderson, Dakof, Greenbaum, & Liddle, 2010; Liddle et al., 2001; Liddle, Dakof, Turner, Henderson, & Greenbaum, 2008; Liddle, Rowe, Dakof, Henderson, & Greenbaum, 2009; R. J. Williams & Chang, 2000).

- Family treatments seem generally helpful with regard to improving schizophrenia treatment outcomes. In studies where family therapy was combined with medication, treatment relapse rates were reduced by about 50% (Barbato & D'Avanzo, 2000; Bressi, Manenti, Frongia, Porcellana, & Invernizzi, 2007).

- Several small-scale studies show that functional family therapy reduces recidivism and repeat offending (e.g., felonies, violent crime) among initial criminal offenders (Barton, Alexander, Waldron, Turner, & Warburton,1985; Gordon, Graves, & Arbuthnot, 1995; Sexton & Turner, 2010).

- Family therapy appears promising for assisting families who have children with health problems such as childhood obesity and asthma (Ng et al., 2008; Young, Northern, Lister, Drummond, & O'Brien, 2007).

- In one research study attachment-based family therapy was efficacious for treating adolescent suicide ideation (Diamond et al., 2010).

- Involving the family appears to enhance alcohol treatment (Edwards & Steinglass, 1995).

- The reports on family therapy outcomes for anorexia and bulimia nervosa are mixed. Individual treatment may be as effective or more effective for eating disorders (Ball & Mitchell, 2004; Lock, Couturier, & Agras, 2006; Schmidt et al., 2007)

- There's no controlled empirical research focusing on Bowen family systems therapy (Shadish, Ragsdale, Glaser, & Montgomery, 1995; Shadish & Baldwin, 2002; Stanton & Shadish, 1997).

- Research evaluating the efficacy of humanistic and strategic family therapy has not generated positive outcomes (Stanton & Shadish, 1997; Shadish et al., 1995; Shadish & Baldwin, 2002).

- Structural therapy has generated a few positive outcomes studies suggesting it may be effective for substance abuse, psychosomatic disorders, and conduct disorders (Shadish et al., 1995; Shadish & Baldwin, 2002; Stanton & Shadish, 1997).

Overall, family-based interventions show efficacy and effectiveness in treating an impressive array of disorders. Some of the evidence is quite clear (e.g., multisystemic family therapy appears to be the treatment of choice in many cases for minority clients with drug use problems). However, the question remains, what exactly is effective about family therapy? Although it's too soon to answer that question, general counseling and psychotherapy research suggests that a strong working alliance, the therapist's belief in the effectiveness of therapy, client confidence in the therapist, and client commitment to change are all indicators of successful family and individual therapy (Duncan, Miller, Wampold, & Hubbell, 2010).

CONCLUDING COMMENTS

If nothing else, this chapter should reinforce the notion that we don't exist in isolation. Instead, we exist in living, breathing systems with all of their intricate structures, deep-rooted patterns, and powerful relationships. Treatment at the systemic level must address these complexities and also engage families in ways that facilitate change. Regardless of the systemic model embraced, the driving conceptual forces in family counseling (homeostasis, rules and roles, the notion of the identified patient, boundaries, alliances, coalitions, and triangles) remain consistent over time and approach. Further, common factors in family therapy are what appear to garner the most research support. This involves facilitation of counseling relationship where an alliance with the family sets a foundation for accessing familial resources and generating

hope, which in turn, stimulates risk taking, new learning, and positive change in families.

CHAPTER SUMMARY

As an early systems theorist, Alfred Adler was one of the first modern therapists to consider the family as directly relevant to treatment of the individual. However, for many years following Adler very few researchers and practitioners focused on families and even fewer involved fathers in treatment. Several early explanations for child psychopathology openly blamed mothers for their children's problems.

As a derivative of cybernetics, general systems theory, and second-order cybernetics, family systems theory incorporated concepts from outside counseling and psychology in efforts to understand how families operated and how individuals affect other individuals within family systems. Based on these dynamics, family systems models emphasize that family member problems serve a purpose within the family system. Consequently, individual client problems are formulated as family problems and the family microsystem is the focus of treatment.

Family systems theory doesn't employ a linear model for understanding families. Instead, concepts such as circular causality, homeostasis, first- and second-order change, alliances, subsystems, triangulation, and coalitions became the language of family therapy. Many original thinkers and therapists became enamored with the power of family processes and applied their creative minds to the treatment of problems within family contexts.

This chapter mentions or covers 10 different family therapy approaches. The primary approaches reviewed include: (a) intergenerational family therapy; (b) structural family therapy; (c) strategic family therapy; (d) humanistic-experiential family therapy; (e) functional family therapy; (f) multisystemic family therapy; (g) narrative family therapy; and (h) feminist family therapy.

Although most family therapies are gender and culturally sensitive, intergenerational family therapy and strategic family therapy tend to be less sensitive to individual client and family dynamics. In particular, multisystemic family therapy, functional family therapy, structural family therapy, and one-person family therapy have been used extensively with minority populations. There is little research or publishing in the area of treating gay and lesbian families.

Overall, family-based interventions show both efficacy and effectiveness. Of course, this depends on the type of family therapy, the clinical population, and other factors. Of the specific family therapy approaches, multisystemic and functional family therapy have the strongest empirical support.

FAMILY SYSTEMS KEY TERMS

Alliances

Blaming

Boundaries

Child guidance clinics

Chronosystem

Circular causality

Coalition

Congruent

Creating ordeals

Curious researcher

Cybernetics

Differentiation

Diffuse boundaries

Double-bind theory

Ecological systems theory

Emotional cutoff

Enmeshment

Exosystem

Family enactments

Family mapping

Family roles

Family rules

Family sculpting

Feminist family therapy

First-order cybernetics

First-order change

Functional family therapy

General systems theory

Genogram

Homeostasis

Human validation process model

Identified patient (IP)

Intensifying

Intergenerational family therapy

Irrelevant

Macrosystem

Mesosystem

Microsystem

Mimesis

Multisystemic family therapy

Narrative family therapy

One-person family therapy

Overprotective mothers

Placating

Positioning

Prescribing the symptom

Reframing

Rigid boundaries

Scapegoating

Schizophrenogenic mothers

Second-order change

Second-order cybernetics

Strategic family therapy

Structural family therapy

Subsystems

Super-reasonable

Symbolic experiential family therapy

The golden age of family therapy

Triangulation

Unbalancing

RECOMMENDED READINGS AND RESOURCES

The following resources may help you explore family systems theory and therapy in greater depth.

FAMILY THERAPY JOURNALS

American Journal of Family Therapy
Family Process
Journal of Family Psychology
Journal of Family Psychotherapy
Journal of Feminist Family Therapy

Journal of Marital and Family Therapy
The Family Journal
The Family Therapy Networker
The International Journal of Family Therapy

READINGS ON FAMILY SYSTEMS THEORY AND THERAPY

Alexander, J., & Parsons, B. V. (1982). *Functional family therapy*. Monterey, CA: Brooks/Cole.

Bitter, J. R. (2009). *Theory and practice of family therapy and counseling*. Belmont, CA: Brooks/Cole.

Blume, T. W. (2006). *Becoming a family counselor: A bridge to family therapy theory and practice*. Hoboken, NJ: John Wiley & Sons.

Bowen, M. (1978). *Family therapy in clinical practice*. New York, NY: Aronson.

Goldenberg, I., & Goldenberg, H. (2008). *Family therapy: An overview* (7th ed.). Belmont, CA: Brooks/Cole.

Henggeler, S. W., & Bordin, E. S. (1990). *Family therapy and beyond: A multisystemic approach to treating the behavior problems of children and adolescents*. Pacific Grove, CA: Brooks/Cole.

Minuchin, S. (1974). *Families and family therapy*. Cambridge, MA: Harvard University Press.

Nichols, M. P., & Schwarts, R. C. (2007). *The essentials of family therapy* (3rd ed.). Boston, MA: Pearson.

Satir, V. M. (1983). *Conjoint family therapy* (3rd ed.). Palo Alto, CA: Science and Behavior Books.

Silverstein, L. B., & Goodrich, T. J. (Eds.). (2003). *Feminist family therapy: Empowerment in social context*. Washington, DC: American Psychological Association.

Szapocznik, J., & Kurtines, W. M. (1989). *Breakthroughs in family therapy with drug abusing and problem youth*. New York, NY: Springer.

TRAINING ORGANIZATIONS AND WEBSITES

Ackerman Institute for the Family (http://www.ackerman.org/#/)

The Minuchin Center for the Family (www.minuchincenter.org/)

The Multicultural Family Institute (www.multiculturalfamily.org/)

The Philadelphia Child and Family Therapy Training Center (www.philafamily.com/)

The Family Therapy Institute (www.familytherapyinstitute.com/)

VIDEOS/DVDs

Alexander, J. (2006). *Functional family therapy* [DVD]. Washington, DC: American Psychological Association.

Lebow, J. (2007). *Integrative family therapy* [DVD]. Washington, DC: American Psychological Association.

Madsen, B. (2011). *Collaborative helping for families in crisis* [DVD]. North Amherst, MA: Microtraining Associates

GOING FARTHER AND DEEPER

Additional family systems therapy resources are available at johnsommersflanagan.com.

CHAPTER 13

Developing Your Multicultural Orientation and Skills

You can't understand people until you've walked a mile in their moccasins.

—Seen on a sign in a café in Absarokee, Montana

THIS CHAPTER

- Reviews the key figures and historical factors contributing to the development and evolution of multicultural theory and therapy
- Outlines and describes core multicultural theoretical principles
- Describes and discusses principles and strategies associated with multicultural therapy practice, including
  - Multicultural competencies
  - Assessment issues
  - Acculturation
  - Individualist and collectivist orientations
  - Cultural adaptations
  - Spirituality
- Provides short vignettes to demonstrate multicultural therapy principles in action
- Illustrates how treatment planning, outcomes assessment, and gender and cultural issues can be integrated into a multicultural approach
- Reviews the empirical status of multicultural approaches and adaptations
- Offers resources for further study

Culture is like your shadow. It follows you everywhere. You can't escape it and often you're not aware of it. Culture is ubiquitous. Culture is a part of the fabric of every being.

In a perfect world this chapter's content would be seamlessly integrated into the other 13 chapters. But we don't live in a perfect world. Most theoretical approaches are beginning to embrace diversity, but there's not enough research and practice literature within each theoretical model to justify eliminating this chapter in favor of integrating the material into other chapters.

Another reasonable alternative would be to place this chapter at the beginning of the text as a means of orienting you to methods for addressing culture and diversity—no matter which theoretical perspective or techniques you use. We almost went that direction, but instead decided to maintain the historical position of multiculturalism as the fourth force in counseling and psychotherapy theory. The good news is that this chapter's content is flexible enough for instructors to use it as an initial orientation chapter or a closing chapter. Either way, the goal is of this chapter is to continue moving toward understanding and integrating multicultural and diversity awareness, knowledge, and skills into all counseling and psychotherapy approaches.

But now, we've had enough of this intellectualizing. To borrow a phrase from Gestalt therapy, we need to wake up and come to our multicultural senses. We hope this chapter helps in that continual re-awakening process.

A MULTICULTURAL PRELUDE

Given that all counseling and psychotherapy is multicultural, this chapter is different from the rest. This chapter is an orientation to multicultural counseling fundamentals. Some principles discussed here have been touched on in previous chapters. All of the principles here will touch you if you choose to practice counseling or psychotherapy.

Multicultural theory isn't a specific theory of psychotherapy. As Derald Wing Sue and others (J. Sommers-Flanagan, Hays, Gallardo, Poyrazli, Sue, & Sommers-Flanagan, 2009) emphasized in an APA symposium, it's impossible and impractical to have 12 "other theories" of psychotherapy and then a 13th multicultural theory. Instead, all counseling and psychotherapy theories and approaches must be or become multiculturally sensitive and accessible—or cease to exist. We can't expect culturally diverse clients to change to fit a dominant culture. Theoretical approaches must open themselves up and accommodate all clients.

In Chapter 11 we discussed how language shapes thought. The reverse is also true; thought shapes language. In addition, culture shapes language and language shapes culture. If there's one big lesson from multicultural psychology, it's that we live in a multidimensional world with multiple ways of seeing reality; for example, instead of a unitary Freudian psychic determinism, we have multideterminism. This brings us to the conclusion that we're not even talking about one big lesson—it can't ever be one big lesson; multiculturalism is the land of many lessons.

HISTORICAL AND CONTEMPORARY CONTEXT

Similar to feminist theory, multicultural theory didn't spring to life as a result of abstract speculation about the nature of humans and human need. It came into being—or was driven into being—by the painful recognition that the privileged white male worldview wasn't the only viable worldview on the planet. Such recognition included firsthand experience of the damaging application of this narrow worldview to the psychological functioning and needs of diverse peoples.

Historical Examples of Cultural Oppression

There are many appalling historic examples of minority oppression that predate Western civilization. But for our purposes, the most relevant historical examples come from the recent past in the United States.

In some of our worst scenarios, white upper-class males made sweeping statements about other, less dominant cultures. Further, they made sweeping indictments about the so-called abnormal functioning or limited intellectual and functional potential of persons of color and women. When viewed from a multicultural perspective, these judgments are remarkably racist. At the time, however, sometimes they were sometimes framed as multiculturally sensitive. Take, for example, the following statement from the highly regarded *Southern Literary Messenger* in 1843. This statement claims that the white race suffers terribly from slavery, while African Americans thrive as slaves:

> We are not friendly to slavery. We lament and deplore it as the greatest evil that could be inflicted on our country. We lament it not for the sake of the black race but of the white. The former, who are slaves, are not only far happier in a state of slavery than of freedom, but we believe the happiest class on this continent. (Quoted in Kutchins & Kirk, 1997, p. 204)

This example of considering slavery as a benefit to African Americans might be more stunning if it were simply an isolated example of multicultural insensitivity and racism. Unfortunately, there are many other examples where dominant white American-European physicians, psychologists, counselors, and social workers displayed profound insensitivity toward diverse cultures. A few powerful examples are included in Putting it in Practice 13.1.

For one group to claim that another group is benefiting from systematic oppression is not an unusual argument. In her powerful book *For Your Own Good*, Alice Miller (1984) points out this same dynamic from the perspective of children who are hit, kicked, slapped, and physically abused all for the sake of helping them develop properly. Similar arguments have been made by various religious groups seeking to save individuals from their homosexual behaviors (L. White, 1994).

The dominant culture is both intentionally and inadvertently oppressive. Gushue and Constantine (2007) commented on the naive **color blind phenomenon** that exists within professional mental health settings:

> Unlike more overt forms of racism, the color-blind perspective does not necessarily make explicit claims about White superiority. Rather, color-blind attitudes reflect the seemingly benign position that race should not and does not matter. Included in this stance, however, is a denial that racism continues to benefit White individuals. (Gushue & Constantine, 2007, p. 323)

Unconscious or unintentional racism or sexism is another reason why studying counseling and psychotherapy in context (and out of context) is so important. Context and culture affect everything.

QUESTIONS FOR REFLECTION

Does the dominant U.S. culture:

- Seek to understand the perspective of non-dominant groups by asking them for their opinion—and then listening to their answers?
- Step into the alternative culture to deepen mutual understanding and respect?
- Consider the possibility that nondominant group members might fear reprisal for speaking openly?

The Recent History of Multicultural Competency and Practice Guidelines

The multicultural movement in psychology and counseling was made possible in part by shifting awareness with the U.S. populace and political changes within the U.S. government. For example, passage of the Civil Rights Act of 1964 led to substantial changes in educational, housing, and employment access for many minority groups. The act bolstered the confidence of people of color and empowered them to organize themselves (Arredondo & Perez, 2006). Within psychology, the Association of Black Psychologists was formed in 1968, followed by the Asian American Psychological Association, the National Hispanic Psychological Association (now known as the National Latina/o Psychological Association), and the Society of Indian Psychologists. Together, these groups combined to form the Council of National Psychological Associations for the Advancement of Ethnic Minority Interests (CNPAAEMI; see Arredondo & Perez, 2006).

The development of guidelines for training counselors and psychologists was stimulated by a number of events and people. In particular, there was a group of "multicultural advocates and allies" who, being members of both the American Counseling Association and the American Psychological Association and holding leadership positions pushed for progress in addressing multicultural competencies (Arredondo & Perez, 2006, p. 1).

Patricia Arredondo, who has been active as a multicultural leader and reformer in both ACA and APA, described several critical historical events leading to formal adoption of multicultural guidelines (Arredondo & Perez, 2006).

- In 1981, Allen Ivey, president of APA Division 17, Counseling Psychology, commissioned a report from the Professional Standards Committee, headed by Derald Wing Sue, to address cross-cultural issues. The first multicultural competencies document, listing 10 competencies, was published as "Position Paper: Cross-Cultural Counseling Competencies" (Sue et al., 1982).

- In 1991, Thomas Parham, president of the Association of Multicultural Counseling and

PUTTING IT IN PRACTICE 13.1

Historical Examples of Multicultural Insensitivity

In 1851 physician S. A. Cartwright claimed discovery of two mental diseases peculiar to Africans. The first, ***drapetomania***, caused slaves to have uncontrollable urges to run away from their masters. The cure? Whipping the devil out of them. The second disease, ***dysaethesia***, affected mind and body, causing disobedience and disrespect. The cure? Extra hard labor, causing blood to finally reach the brain and give liberty to the mind (Szasz, 1970).

Among his many conclusions about women's inferiority, Freud claimed women had underdeveloped superegos:

> they show less sense of justice than men, that they are less ready to submit to the great necessities of life, that they are more often influenced in their judgments by feelings of affection or hostility—all these would be amply accounted for by the modification in the formation of their superego which we have already inferred. (Freud, 1948, pp. 196–197)

Unfortunately, from Freud's perspective, there's no cure for being born a woman.

Baca and Cervantes (1984) quote Lewis Terman (1916), author of the Stanford-Binet Intelligence Scale, as having written:

> A low level of intelligence is very, very common among Spanish-Indians and Mexican families of the Southwest and also among Negroes. Their dullness seems to be racial . . . [and] . . . there will be discovered enormously significant racial differences in general intelligence, differences which cannot be wiped out by any scheme of mental culture.

> Children of this group should be segregated into special classes and be given instruction which is concrete and practical. They cannot master abstractions but they often can be made efficient workers, able to look out for themselves. There is no possibility at the present in convincing society that they should not be allowed to reproduce, although from a eugenic point of view they constitute a grave problem because of their unusually prolific breeding. (p. 147)

As these examples amply illustrate, human tolerance for differences is often limited and those in power or in the majority usually define differences as inferiorities or mental disorders. This is especially true if these differences irritate or frighten those in power because, as Thomas Szasz (1970) noted, categorizations of mental illness is a subjective process:

> Which kinds of social deviance are regarded as mental illnesses? The answer is, those that entail personal conduct not conforming to psychiatrically defined and enforced rules of mental health. (p. xxvi)

Development (AMCD), a division of ACA, commissioned the Professional Standards Committee to review and revise the 1982 cross-cultural competencies document. The AMCD committee produced 31 multicultural counseling competencies in the document "Multicultural Counseling Competencies and Standards: A Call to the Profession" (Sue, Arredondo, & McDavis, 1992). Two years earlier, APA published *Guidelines for Providers of Psychological Services to Ethnic, Linguistic, and Culturally Diverse Populations* (APA, 1990).

- To amplify the 1992 and 1993 multicultural counseling competencies, another AMCD Professional Standards Committee produced a document with 119 explanatory statements for the 31 competencies, which was published as "Operationalization of the Multicultural Counseling Competencies" (Arredondo et al., 1996). The Arredondo et al. publication also introduced the dimensions of personal identity model...highlighting the concept of multiple or collective identities and multiple contexts.

- Three competencies related to organizational change were added, bringing the AMCD competency list to 34. The result was the book *Multicultural Counseling Competencies: Individual and Organizational Development* (Sue et al., 1998).

- A task force composed of members of APA Divisions 17 and 45, co-chaired by Nadya Fouad and Patricia Arredondo, developed "Guidelines on Multicultural Education, Training, Research, Practice, and Organizational Change for Psychologists," the task force document, was unanimously approved by the APA Council of Representatives in August 2002 and published in the *American Psychologist* (APA, 2003). In a collateral action, in 2002, the ACA endorsed the 31 multicultural guidelines recommended by the AMCD in 1992 (Arredondo & Perez, 2006, p. 2).

Following organizational changes supporting people of color and ethnic minorities, national, state, and local professional organizations focusing on the interests and rights of other minority groups flourished. For example, in 1985, APA's Division 44 (the Society for the Psychological Study of Lesbian and Gay Issues) was founded. The APA also has many other divisions that focus on issues pertinent to minority groups including aging (Division 20), disabilities (Division 22), intellectual and developmental disabilities (Division 33), women (Division 35), religion (Division 36), and ethnic minorities (Division 45).

More recently action has been taken to help educate mental health professionals regarding how to work effectively with cultural groups outside the ethnic-racial domain. For example, the ACA's Association for Lesbian, Gay, Bisexual, and Transgender Issues in Counseling's (ALGBTIC) 2009 published Competencies for Counseling with Transgender Clients. The APA also has specific guidelines for psychological practice with (a) girls and women; (b) older adults; (c) lesbian, gay, and bisexual clients; and (d) persons with disabilities. You can access more detailed information and resources at the organizations' websites (ACA: http://www.counseling.org/; APA: http://www.apa.org/).

Multicultural Leaders: Many Cultures, Many Paths

As noted in the previous section, there have been and continue to be many contributors to the multicultural movement in counseling and psychology. These leaders come from diverse cultural backgrounds, including American Indian (or Native American or First Nations People); African American (or Black American); Arab American (or Middle Eastern), Asian American; Latino/a (or Hispanic), and more. Additionally, other minority groups including gay, lesbian, bisexual, and transgender (GLBT) people and individuals with disabilities are often part of the communal voice of multiculturalism.

Rather than providing a long list of names of prominent individuals here, we feature two to give you a taste of the multidimensional flavor of multicultural psychology and counseling.

Lillian Comas-Diaz

I inherited a healing lineage. My ancestors drank in the fountains of shamanism, Christian healing, spiritualism, gitano (Gypsy) wisdom, and Oricha beliefs. As a result, my dharma was to become a psychotherapist. Like many underprivileged Puerto Ricans of their generation, my parents migrated to the continental United States in search of work. Poor in their pockets, but rich in their hearts, they received their first born with acceptance and hope: I was born with a cleft palate. Longing to hear my voice, my father named me after his favorite singer—Lily Pons. My parents armed themselves with perseverance and prayed for a miracle. Physicians at the University of Illinois answered their prayers when they repaired my cleft palate in an experimental operation. A medical expert examined me 50 years later and declared my cleft palate repair "one of the best surgeries" she had seen. "Medicine did not have the correct technique at the time of your surgery" (Comas-Díaz, 2008). Almost in disbelief, the doctor dried her tears and declared my cleft palate operation a "divine intervention." (Comas-Diaz, 2010, p. 162)

Lillian Comas-Diaz recounted her dharmic path using words that some of us cannot understand. This is the essence of multiculturalism—because there are so many unique pathways in individual, family, and communal life, adhering to one rigid psychology for everyone is unacceptable.

Comas-Diaz is executive director of the *Transcultural Mental Health Institute* in Washington, DC. She's also a clinical professor of psychiatry at George Washington University School of Medicine. She has edited or co-edited several books, including: *Clinical Guidelines in Cross Cultural Mental Health* (Comas-Diaz & Griffith, 1988), *Women of Color: Integrating Ethnicity and Gender Identity in Psychotherapy* (Comas-Diaz, 1994), *Women Psychotherapists: Journeys in Healing* (2008), and *WomanSoul: The Inner Life of Women's Spirituality* (Rayburn & Comas-Díaz, 2008).

Derald Wing Sue

Many Whites, for example, fail to realize that, people of color from the moment of birth are subjected to multiple racial microaggression from the media, peers, neighbors, friends, teachers, and even in the educational process and/or curriculum itself. (Derald Wing Sue, 2010, p. 7)

Derald Wing Sue

Derald Wing Sue was born to a Chinese-American family in Portland, Oregon. Raised in a primarily white neighborhood, he reported being taunted and bullied due to his racial background.

Currently he is professor of psychology and education at Teacher's College, Columbia University. His work crosses the boundaries between the counseling and psychology disciplines and he is one of the most cited multicultural authors of all time. He and his brothers, Stanley Sue and David Sue (all of whom are trained in psychology) have been strong voices in multicultural theory and practice for 30-plus years. Derald Wing Sue and David Sue are coauthors of the renowned multicultural text, *Counseling the Culturally Different* (D. W. Sue & D. Sue, 2008). Derald also has published many other books, including, *Microaggressions in Everyday Life: Race, Gender and Sexual Orientation* (2010) and *Microaggressions and Marginality* (2010).

THEORETICAL PRINCIPLES

Multicultural theory as applied to counseling and psychotherapy is a distinct discipline or focus. Consequently, it's important to review and define key terminology.

Key Terminology

The following conceptual terms provide a foundation for understanding multicultural theoretical principles.

Culture

Defining **culture** is a task with political overtones. Christopher (1996) stated,

Culture permeates our lives much more thoroughly or pervasively than we tend to consider. Because of Western culture's individualistic orientation, we tend to think of the individual first and of culture second.... What this tendency to give primacy to the self overlooks is the manner in which culture precedes us. (p. 17)

Using the influential anthropologist Geertz's (1973) definition of culture as webs of significance that give coherence and meaning to our lives, Christopher states, "Our social practices, institutions, family structures, and daily life make sense and 'hang together' because of these webs of significance" (p. 17). Further, he points out that culture shapes us and tells us both what should be considered a good life and what should be considered deviant (Christopher, 2001; Christopher & Bickhard, 2007).

Alternatively, Wade Nobles (2006), an African American scholar, defined culture as:

[T]he vast structure of behaviors, ideas, attitudes, values, habits, beliefs, customs, language, rituals, ceremonies, and practices peculiar to a particular group of people which provides them with a general design for living and patterns for interpreting reality. (p. 71)

Moving forward it's important to remember that culture permeates our lives, it precedes us (we are born into it), and it constitutes a general design for living and pattern for interpreting reality (see Putting it in Practice 13.2).

In our work with young people, we've claimed that children belong to a different culture than adults (J. Sommers-Flanagan & Sommers-Flanagan, 2007). This concept illustrates the constantly changing nature of culture; even though you were a member of a group once, you don't necessarily know what it means to be a member now. Parents and young people can easily attest to enormous group and cultural pressures on young people—pressures that adults may or may not fully understand. Failing to look, speak, act, and dress within defined youth-cultural bounds can be a source of painful harassment. Counselors working with young people

can find the application of multicultural counseling principles helpful.

Multiculturalism

Multiculturalism is a relatively new term that carries political baggage. It's broadly defined as the valuing of diverse perspectives. Multiculturalists believe all cultures have positive and enriching value. A multiculturalist agenda involves the appreciation and promotion of cultural diversity. For better or worse, attempting to accommodate more than one culture is a political act and therefore generates controversy, opposition, and sometimes violence.

The cultures represented in the term multicultural are often dependent on the speaker. Many argue that the worst discrimination and abuse has occurred across racial divides. Others argue that history provides many horrifying examples of religious discrimination. Gender, disability, sexual orientation, and class also represent cultures within the meaning of multicultural. Citizens of the United States tend to resist the idea of class as a source of cultural discrimination, but as columnist Ellen Goodman (2003) writes,

Through thick and thin, boom and bust, we tenaciously hold on to the belief that we are, fundamentally, a classless society. This self-image survives even though we have the most unequal distribution of wealth in the Western world. It survives even though 1 percent of us owns 40 percent of the wealth. And even though there's less income mobility between generations in our country than in any other but South Africa and Great Britain. (p. 4)

We believe the term multicultural should indeed include class as well as other categories with distinct values and patterns of living. Although there are problems with the term and struggles within the dominant culture for both definition and sincere expression, the idea of multiculturalism is profound and will be pivotal in coming decades.

Multicultural Counseling

Given controversies and ambiguities in defining both culture and multiculturalism, you might guess

PUTTING IT IN PRACTICE 13.2

Dimensions That Vary Across Cultures

Culture permeates our lives and affects our beliefs and practices on many subtle dimensions. The following list includes several of these dimensions. We challenge you to articulate the practices or beliefs of your own culture on each of these. Then, either through direct observation or through readings, explore how other cultures vary on these dimensions. Add and share with your classmates additional dimensions you discover.

- Eye contact
- Conception of time and timeliness
- Signs of respect
- Language
- Spirituality and religion
- Kinship systems
- Directness in communication style
- Collectivist versus individual orientation
- Aging
- Dress
- Gender roles
- Definitions of the good life
- Educational practices
- Family definitions and duties

that defining multicultural counseling would also be challenging. D. W. Sue and D. Sue offer a definition of **multicultural counseling:**

> Multicultural counseling and therapy can be defined as both a helping role and a process that uses modalities and defines goals consistent with the life experiences and cultural values of clients, recognizes client identities to include individual, group, and universal dimensions, advocates the use of universal and culture-specific strategies and roles in the healing process, and balances the importance of individualism and collectivism in the assessment, diagnosis, and treatment of client and client systems. (2008, p. 42)

In addition to progress made by the American Psychological Association and the American Counseling Association discussed previously, the American Psychiatric Association's *DSM* now has (since

1994) sections titled "Specific Culture and Gender Features" for each psychiatric diagnosis. Although this is progress, some authors have questioned the legitimacy and sincerity of token references to multicultural issues (Fernandez, 2001).

> What does it name? Often, it seems to be used mindlessly as a mild concession to the many differences around us. While the term seems to challenge established attitudes, it has often been used to depoliticize any effective resistance to those attitudes. (p. iv)

When authentically applied to mental health conditions, multicultural perspectives elevate and centralize culture as a factor in defining psychological functioning, psychological distress, and psychological well-being (Alarcón et al., 2009; Canino & Alegría, 2008; Paniagua, 2010). There can be no consideration of psychiatric diagnosis without including an extensive examination of culture.

Multicultural Principles

The following basic multicultural principles form the foundation of multicultural theory and practice.

Principle I: Cultural Membership Is Linked to Disadvantage and Privilege

In a now-classic paper titled "White privilege: Unpacking the invisible knapsack," Peggy McIntosh (1998) articulated the invisible nature of privileges accorded to the dominant culture. She pointed out that in the United States, middle- and upper-class white people carry (in their invisible knapsack) readily available unearned assets. One effect of membership in the dominant culture is unconsciousness or obliviousness to cultural advantages or **white privilege**. Often, students from dominant cultures have trouble talking about their cultural values and practices because, to them, these values seem universal rather than culturally determined. (see Putting it in Practice 13.3).

One obvious problem facing multicultural theorists and practitioners is that "[w]e are all of us as individuals already mixed ethnically and culturally; our roots are historically constructed out of subtly mediated cultural strands" (Fernandez, 2001, p. ix). We share attributes and beliefs with many groups, and the salience of our membership varies for each of us and across the life span. Being from Montana seemed unremarkable to us until we lived in upstate New York, Belize City, and the United Kingdom. In those contexts, our Montana identities took on a more defined and shifting set of attributes. Regardless of how many cultures we're part of, each one shapes us whether or not we recognize it. Consistent with constructive theory, multiculturalism suggests that we construct our worldviews based on our cultural experiences and memberships, and consciously or not, we are privileged or disadvantaged by these memberships as well.

As is true with the definition of multicultural, there's controversy within multicultural counseling about which groups to include under the umbrella of diversity (D. W. Sue & D. Sue, 2008). In one sense, all counseling is multicultural in that the counselor and the client are always from different families and have different life experiences, possibly different sexes, different socioeconomic experiences, and so on. Most multicultural thinkers acknowledge these differences but believe that to call all counseling multicultural misses the point of the power of culture in our lives. D. W. Sue and D. Sue, Hays (2008), and others adhere to an inclusive model of diversity that includes race, religion, sex, disability, and socioeconomic class. In contrast, some authors argue that broadening the definition of diversity weakens the power of certain cultural domains, most notably race (Helms, 1994).

In the late 1980s a panel Rita organized with four women of color addressed this issue in a psychology of women class. When asked, each claimed that her experience of racial prejudice was far greater and more damaging than the experience of sexism as a woman. For them, race trumped sex in terms of cultural definition, power, and oppression. In more recent panels and classroom discussions we've noticed students making stronger arguments for class distinctions in the United States carrying even more negative judgments than sex or race.

PUTTING IT IN PRACTICE 13.3

Exploring Examples of White Privilege

Prochaska and Norcross (2010) describe three examples of white privilege from the 2008 presidential election:

1. White privilege is when you can get pregnant at age 17 and everyone is quick to insist that your life and that of your family is a personal matter, and that no one has a right to judge you or your parents, even as Black and Latino families with similar challenges are regularly typified as irresponsible and pathological.

2. White privilege is when you are a gun enthusiast and do not make people immediately scared of you.

3. White privilege is when you can develop a painkiller addiction, having obtained your drug of choice illegally, go on to beat that addiction, and everyone praises you for being so strong, while being an ethnic minority who did the same thing is routinely labeled a drug addict who probably winds up in jail. (p. 408)

Can you identify additional examples of white privilege in your life or in the lives of others?

QUESTIONS FOR REFLECTION

With what group of others do you most closely identify? Those from your home town? Those of your same sex? Religion? Race? Income level? IQ level? Who do you feel most relaxed with? Most known? How do you think your particular identity might influence your counseling approach?

Principle II: We Make Distinctions Between Groups of People Based on Race, Religion, Sex, Sexual Orientation, Ethnicity, Physical and Mental Disabilities, and Socioeconomic Status

Implicit in multicultural theory is the notion of group differences. If you met a young woman who grew up in an Amish community in Pennsylvania, you'd probably assume you're different from her in many ways. If you met five of her friends and relatives, you might assume they have many commonly held beliefs, experiences, and ways of being. As you well know, humans make meaning by noticing similarities and differences around them. Our brains are always sorting out the salient attributes of a given set of stimuli. If something has four legs and a flat surface, we call it a table. When we use this same strategy with "types" of people, difficulties immediately arise. Which are the appropriate attributes to use when grouping people into cultures or subcultures? As noted earlier, no human has exactly the same life experiences and so members of a given group often seem more different than alike. We can learn all about a given group and still meet many members who violate the group norms. One great problem in applying cultural/racial knowledge is the tendency for practitioners to assume everyone from a particular group (e.g., Asian, Native American,

GLBT) holds the same cultural values (Sue & Zane, 2009).

The human tendency to make distinctions between individuals and groups based on differences can lead to stereotyping. A **stereotype** is a standardized and oversimplified mental picture or idea about members of a group.

Principle III: A Multiculturalist Stance Can Foster Greater Understanding Between Cultural Groups and Facilitate Egalitarian Treatment of All Humans

D. W. Sue et al. (1999) wrote,

> Multiculturalism is not only about understanding different perspectives and worldviews but also about social justice. As such it is not value neutral. Multiculturalism stands against beliefs and behaviors that oppress other groups and deny them equal access and opportunity. (p. 1064)

Multicultural advocates have worked vigorously to decrease stereotyping, discrimination, and increase social justice. But this is difficult work, fraught with strong emotional responses. In a recent qualitative study focusing on what white trainees fear about racial dialogues, the following five themes were identified (D. W. Sue, Rivera, Capodilupo, Lin, & Torino, 2010):

1. Denial of whiteness or white privilege.

2. Endorsement of colorblindness.

3. Fear of appearing racist.

4. Feelings of having no right to dialogue on race.

5. Reactions of anxiety, helplessness, and feeling misunderstood. (pp. 209–210)

These and other research results and multicultural education experiences show how challenging it is for humans to live in culturally inclusive ways. The values and beliefs we were raised with or have found true don't easily move aside so we can examine and accept other's values and beliefs as valid. Although great progress has been made on this third multicultural principle, there's much more work to be done (L. Smith, Constantine, Graham,

& Dize, 2008; T. B. Smith, Constantine, Dunn, Dinehart, & Montoya, 2006).

Sue et al. (2010) offered the following recommendations for continued progress in facilitating valuable multicultural and intercultural discussions:

- Instructor/facilitator validation of participant feelings and emotional reactions.

- Facilitation of open discussions.

- Instructor/facilitator role modeling of openness and honesty, as well as reflections on their own biases and weaknesses. (pp. 210–211)

In addition, it was noted that instructor passivity was a negative or unhelpful strategy when facilitating multicultural discussions.

Theory of Psychopathology

Like feminist theory, multicultural theory relies primarily on social forces to understand suffering and psychopathology. Multicultural practitioners are extremely cautious in using standardized assessment instruments and diagnoses (Mezzich et al., 2008; Paniagua, 2010). Multicultural therapists also don't quickly impose pathological labels on troubling behaviors but instead seek to understand the meaning of the behaviors from within the cultural context of each individual or family.

Within different cultures, the names of disorders, beliefs about causation, and types of symptoms vary greatly. In fact, human distress may not be seen primarily through a psychological lens. It may be viewed religiously or philosophically instead. This has led some to argue for the development of indigenous psychologies (Ho, 1998). From the University of Hong Kong, David Ho wrote,

> In particular, much of Western psychology may be irrelevant or inapplicable in Asia. Western ideological presuppositions, such as individualism, are alien to the Asian ethos. Thus, a reliance on Western psychology can only lead to an incomplete, even distorted, understanding of Asia or of Asians. Moreover, the wholesale importation of Western psychology into Asia represents a form

of cultural imperialism that perpetuates the colonialization of the mind. To an alarming degree, Asians are now confronted by stereotypes about themselves generated not only by Western researchers but also by Asian researchers relying on imported, mainly American, psychology. (p. 89)

A clinical example from cognitive-behavioral therapy (CBT) illustrates how imported Western ideas of psychopathology may not fit Asian clients. One common target for CBT interventions involves modifying negative self-statements. While this treatment target makes sense from the Western perspective, members of Asian cultures often view these internal self-statements as valuable and motivating (Craske, 2010; Hwang & Wood, 2007). Consequently, modifying or eliminating negative self-statements would make little sense to many Chinese, Japanese, or other Asian clients.

THE PRACTICE OF MULTICULTURALLY SENSITIVE THERAPY

Practicing multicultural therapy is linked to multicultural competence. However, as we begin exploring multicultural competency in greater depth, keep in mind that no one achieves multicultural competence. That would be akin to learning to speak every language in the world. Multicultural competency is a process, not an outcome. As professionals, we continually work on our competencies. Put another way, we like to think of therapists practicing with "multicultural humility," which opens us up to lifelong learning about and appreciation of cultural diversity (J. Sommers-Flanagan & R. Sommers-Flanagan, 2011; see Putting it in Practice 13.4).

PUTTING IT IN PRACTICE 13.4

Aspects of Informed Consent That Includes the Multicultural Perspective

I'm looking forward to working with you in counseling.... This next section describes a little bit about an important part of my orientation and my ways of working with people. Questions are always welcome!

I believe people are who they are as a result of many life experiences, choices, and circumstances. Each person is a unique blend of culture, genetics, and choice. Your cultural group, your race, your sex and sexual orientation, your spiritual or religious beliefs, your skills and abilities, and your struggles or limits are all important to who you are. I might not know very much about some of these aspects of you, but I will do my best to learn and understand. I will do my best to respect you and our differences. When possible, I will do some research and reading to better understand your culture or life experiences if they're new to me.

I believe all humans grow up with some fears and prejudices and I'm no exception. If you notice me being insensitive or if I say something that reveals ignorance, I sincerely hope you'll tell me. I'm a lifelong learner, and will appreciate your help in understanding your unique experiences, beliefs, and aspirations.

The Multicultural Competencies

Multicultural competencies as defined by the Association for Multicultural Counseling and Development (AMCD) are organized into three broad categories:

1. Counselor Awareness of [his/her] Own Cultural Values and Biases
2. Counselor Awareness of Client's Worldview
3. Culturally Appropriate Intervention Strategies

Within each of these categories there are three subheadings: (1) beliefs and attitudes; (2) knowledge; and (3) skills. The three-part mantra of multicultural competencies blends the headings and subheadings into *awareness, knowledge, and skills* (D. W. Sue & Torino, 2005).

- *Awareness* refers to counselors being aware of their own cultural heritage, biases, and reactions to other cultural groups.

- *Knowledge* refers to counselors gathering knowledge about other cultural perspectives in an effort to more deeply understand and appreciate those perspectives.

- *Skills* refers to counselors using specific skills that have been shown to be useful or effective in working with specific cultural groups.

The AMCD competency guidelines are at: http://www.counseling.org/Resources/ Competencies/Multcultural_Competencies.pdf

The American Psychological Association published their *Guidelines on Multicultural Education, Training, Research, Practice, and Organizational Change for Psychologists* in 2002. This APA document identifies six guidelines focusing on:

1. Self-awareness of biased attitudes and beliefs.
2. Multicultural sensitivity/responsiveness.
3. Multiculturalism in psychological education.
4. Culturally sensitive research.
5. Culturally appropriate clinical skills.
6. Culturally informed organizational change processes.

The complete APA guidelines are available at: http://www.apa.org/pi/oema/resources/policy/ multicultural-guidelines.aspx

The multicultural competencies of awareness, knowledge, and skills are woven into the following sections.

Assessment Issues and Procedures

Multicultural assessment begins with sorting out your existing and potential biases. Developing self-awareness and adding cultural knowledge can prepare you to implement culturally specific assessment strategies. Let's start that process with an in-text reflection activity.

Consider the following scenarios slowly, frequently pausing for reflection. Or, if you prefer, speed read through them now and come back to them later when you have time to think seriously about your reactions.

- Imagine you have an opportunity to work with a gay client...or a lesbian client...or a transgender client...or your client tells you she or he is bisexual. As you imagine these scenarios, what are your first reactions, both emotional and cognitive? What are your biases? What stereotypes come to mind? Reflect on where your general ideas about these unique individuals came from. Did your ideas come from your family, the media, friends, religion, or other sources?

- Now imagine you have an opportunity to work with a client who has a disability. Perhaps it's a brain injury acquired later in life...or a lifelong disability such as hearing impairment or cerebral palsy. Again, let yourself track your reactions, biases, stereotypes, and how you acquired your general ideas about these unique people.

- Repeat this process, as needed, for every minority group you can think of. Then find a trusted friend, classmate, colleague, relative, or therapist to talk with about your full range of responses.

The burden of accepting and valuing all people can feel immense. You may initially feel overwhelmed by this activity. Or, you may believe you've worked through all your personal biases. Either way, time can help. We once had a Muslim student who shared with us that it made her feel physically ill when class lecture content and discussions focused on gay and lesbian people. Several years later, she shared her progress. It required the difficult personal reflection and exploration of many issues, but she was able to open up her worldview and see all prospective clients, including gay and lesbian people, in an affirming manner.

Diagnosis

The first problem with multicultural assessment is diagnosis. As noted earlier, there are horrifying historical examples of insensitivity to diverse individuals, families, and communities.

In 1994, the *DSM-IV* introduced a new, albeit short, section on "Specific Culture, Age, and Gender Features." This section was associated with some, but not all *DSM* diagnoses. Additionally, the *DSM-IV-TR* also has a new glossary of 25 "**Culture Bound Syndromes**." Two examples of culture bound syndromes from the *DSM-IV-TR* (2000) include:

- **Amok**: This Malaysian disorder is characterized by wild, homicidal aggression. It's typically found among males who were previously quiet and withdrawn. Precipitating factors can include sleep deprivation, stress, alcohol, and extreme heat.

- **Windigo**: This disorder occurs among Algonquin Indians. Usually this disorder affects male hunters who become anxious and agitated, fearing they have been bewitched and will become a cannibal.

Hays (2008) described the irony inherent in this special *DSM* glossary.

[The] Glossary of Culture-Bound Syndromes... provides descriptions of 25 such syndromes. The separation of this section into an appendix tends to reinforce the idea that culture is relevant only to members of minority groups, when in fact no psychiatric disorder can be understood

apart from the culture in which it occurs.... For example, the symptoms of recurrent depression in a European American woman are no less linked to cultural influences than the symptoms of nervios [another *DSM* culture-bound syndrome] in a Latina client. (p. 156)

In this description Hays provides us with a great example of the invisibility of culture to those immersed in it.

Testing

Psychological and intellectual assessment has been used in biased and prejudicial ways with ethnic minorities and women. Although appropriate training in psychological assessment is always essential, lack of such training when using testing instruments with minority populations is ethically egregious. There is a knowledge base and ethical codes to guide your use of assessment materials (see APA and ACA ethical codes).

To provide culturally competent assessment, therapists should use a culture-specific service delivery, possibly including test administration in the client's native language; evaluate the client as a cultural being prior to testing; observe for culture-specific syndromes; select culture-specific tests; and critically examine the standardization procedures and norms used in testing procedures (Dana, 1993, 1996).

Clinical Interviewing as a Collaborative Assessment Process

Counselors and psychotherapists should always engage in collaborative assessment processes when working with diverse and minority clients. In her book, *Addressing cultural complexities in practice: Assessment, diagnosis, and therapy*, Hays (2008) described a detailed and multicultural assessment process. In some cases she emphasized the need to include family members or interpreters as a part of the assessment. She also recommended obtaining a client timeline and information linked to her **ADDRESSING** acronym. This acronym helps therapists gather a range of information related to multiple dimensions of client identity (see Table 13.1 for the ADDRESSING acronym).

Table 13.1 ADDRESSING Client Multiple Identities

Hays uses the following model to obtain comprehensive information about the many dimensions of her client's identities (see Hays, 2008). This approach helps therapists recognize the wide range of cultural and personal dimensions affecting client identity.

A	Age and generational influences
D	Developmental disabilities
D	Disabilities acquired later in life
R	Religion and spiritual orientation
E	Ethnic and racial identity
S	Socioeconomic status
S	Sexual orientation
I	Indigenous heritage
N	National origin
G	Gender

There are many culture-related issues, including (a) language, (b) norms and mores against speaking negatively about one's family, and (c) privacy issues related to religion, that can make it difficult for therapists to obtain reliable and valid information from clients. As you find yourselves working with minority and diverse clients it's wise to seek consultation and supervision on a regular basis.

Attend to the Therapeutic Relationship With Humility

Trappist monk Thomas Merton (1974) wrote about his deep regrets for the ways religious missionaries have contributed to cultural genocide. He asked the thought provoking question, "What would the world be like if different cultures had encountered each other with questions instead of answers? What if the questions went something like these?"

- What can you tell me about yourselves?

- What would you like to know about us?

- What can you teach me about the Creator?

Merton's ideas about how to approach other cultures speak to therapist awareness issues and are a good reminder of valuing the perspectives of those who are different from us. This doesn't mean therapists should turn to diverse and minority clients for

their personal education; it does mean we should have an attitude of valuing what we can learn from diverse perspectives. Without that attitude, multicultural clients will likely leave therapy prematurely. In fact, early research indicated that about 50% of ethnic diverse clients dropped out of treatment after only one therapy session (S. Sue, 1977).

Talking About Differences

The basic rule in conducting therapy with diverse and minority clients is to be open to talking about your obvious differences, but to not always initiate a conversation about those differences early in a session. Therapists who make a practice of always bringing up cultural differences (e.g., "I noticed you're an African American person and I want to let you know that I'll do my best to respect your cultural perspective") run the risk of forcing clients to deal with diversity issues even when they don't want to. It's good standard practice to include multiculturally sensitive language in your informed consent and to include office décor that communicates multicultural sensitivity (see Putting it in Practice 13.4: A Multiculturally Sensitive Informed Consent). This might involve:

- Intentional efforts to be fully accessible to people with disabilities.

- Gay, lesbian, bisexual, and transgender sensitive materials in the office and waiting room.

- Art or knickknacks that show interest and respect for a variety of cultures.

Rather than talking about specific cultural differences between you and your clients at the beginning of therapy, a more general statement about how you handle diverse perspectives can be helpful. For example, multiculturally sensitive counselors might say something like,

> In my work, I've come to believe that culture is very important in our lives. By culture, I mean things like race, religion, sex and sexual orientation, and other things we think of as identifying features. You and I are probably different in some ways, and alike in some ways.

When we bump into the ways we are different, I hope we can talk about them if they matter to you. I'll try to be open to your perspective. If you think I'm missing the boat, I hope you'll let me know.

It's important to avoid burdening clients with educational needs. For example, we had a gay student in our mental health counseling program who eventually became weary of answering student and faculty queries about gay and lesbian culture. He cleverly gave us the hint by purchasing three books he believed to be useful and donating them to the clinic library. Then, when asked a question, he refused to answer unless the person asking had shown interest by at least skimming through his donated books.

When the Therapist Has Minority Status

If you're a member of a minority culture and are training to be a mental health professional in the dominant culture, you face unique challenges. One counselor we know who was born and raised in Malawi has worked out a very gracious introduction that includes acknowledging her accent and cultural differences in a way that helps clients feel more comfortable in the first session. During the informed consent portion of the first interview, she says something like:

> I imagine you might be a little surprised to find a counselor like me here in Montana. I grew up in Malawi, Africa, and my education is both from there and from here in the United States. Sometimes, people find my accent a little hard at first, so I you to feel comfortable asking me to repeat myself. I mean, really. Can you imagine doing counseling if we can't understand each other?

Using her obvious accent, this counselor wisely opens the door to important questions clients may have when encountering therapists from different cultures: "Can this person really understand me enough to help?"

Similar issues may arise for gay and lesbian therapists or therapists with visible or invisible disabilities. In each case it's important to consult—especially with professional mentors who have been through similar situations—about how to deal with

the issues in ways that facilitate positive interactions with clients.

Avoiding Generalizations and Stereotyping

One counselor we knew was seeing a Chinese American woman for the first time. He asked about her family and her Asian heritage shortly after she complained that everyone seemed to treat her like a child. She responded energetically with,

> I know you think Chinese women act quiet, like black-eyed Barbie dolls, but not me. It's not about being Chinese at all. It's about my coworkers and my stupid husband. I have something to say once in a while, and I say it. But they get all bent out of shape.

Multicultural counseling is like qualitative research; *you may not generalize*. This is because skin color, ethnicity, sexual orientation, disabilities, and other client characteristics all exist within unique individuals, groups, and communities. Just as you would never generalize your findings from eight clients in a phenomenological-qualitative study, you shouldn't use your knowledge of the preceding categories and generalize to the person or people in your office.

S. Sue and Zane (2009) commented on how, when it comes to multicultural knowledge, a little bit *does not* go a long ways (and often a large amount of knowledge won't take you very far either):

> Perhaps the most difficult issue confronting the mental health field is the role of culture and cultural techniques in psychotherapy. We believe that cultural knowledge and techniques generated by this knowledge are frequently applied in inappropriate ways. The problem is especially apparent when therapists and others act on insufficient knowledge or overgeneralize what they have learned about culturally dissimilar groups. (p. 5)

One concept that can help us understand why cultural knowledge and techniques that are supposed to work with specific cultural groups often don't work is *acculturation*.

Understand Acculturation

Acculturation (or *ethnocultural orientation*) refers to "a process of giving up one's traditional cultural values and behaviors while taking on the values and behaviors of the dominant social structure" (Atkinson et al., 1995). Garrett and Pichette (2000) identified five cultural orientations within American Indian populations (Herring, 1996; LaFromboise, Trimble, & Mohatt, 1990):

1. *Traditional*. The individual thinks in the native tongue and practices traditional tribal customs and tribal worship methods.

2. *Marginal*. The individual is not fully connected with traditional Indian culture or mainstream society. Both languages may be spoken.

3. *Bicultural*. The individual is relatively comfortable and conversant in both sets of cultural values.

4. *Assimilated*. The individual is oriented toward the mainstream social culture and has little interest in traditional tribal practices.

5. *Pan-traditional*. The individual has been exposed to and perhaps adopted mainstream values but has made an intentional effort to return to traditional values.

Individual and group or community acculturation can strongly influence client openness to counseling or psychotherapy. For example, a recent study on attitudes towards professional counseling among Asian American students published in the *Asian American Journal of Psychology* concluded:

the results indicate that acculturation status, loss-of-face concerns, and conceptions of mental illness appear to be significant moderators of Asian American college students' attitudes toward mental health, mental health professionals, and help-seeking. (Leong, Kim, & Gupta, 2011)

This study illustrates why two Asian American college students who appear nearly identical—at least to the multiculturally oblivious—might hold widely differing attitudes toward seeking mental health counseling.

Acculturation is directly related to **the melting pot**. This concept implies that, over time, cultures should melt down, adding their own flavor and color to the "American soup," while losing their distinguishing features in the process. Many believe this was a thinly disguised way of asserting that minority groups should shed their inferior ways of being and in a generation or two become "white" (Axelson, 1999).

More recent ways for describing how cultures live side by side, mixing and marrying, include the salad or stew metaphor. Cultures remain identifiable, each uniquely contributing to the whole. Of course, no metaphor is perfect, at the societal level nor at the individual level. Cultural identity and even racial identity, at the individual level, can be unique mixtures and expressions. Take, for example, the famous golfer Tiger Woods, who is African-Indonesian-white American, or Thomas Jefferson's descendants from his wife's half-sister and slave, Sally Hemings, who was half-African, half-white. One branch of her lineage developed a black identity, and the other developed a white identity.

Multicultural counselors realize that cultural identity isn't static and that racial identity and affiliation cannot be assumed by glancing at skin color or eye shapes. However, culturally sensitive counselors also realize that client behavior can be greatly influenced by being a minority within a dominant culture. Family functioning and identity also can be challenged and severely stressed when second-generation members assume values and practices of the dominant culture (Ferrer-Wreder, Palchuk, Poyrazli, Small, & Domitrovich, 2008; Poyrazli, 2009).

Practicing multicultural counseling involves following your clients' multicultural lead. This requires sensitivity and flexibility. For instance, consider the case of Jake, a young man from the Crow Indian Reservation in Montana. Jake was a busy physician who was having trouble relating to his son. His counselor asked about tribal affiliation, and Jake stated he was 75% Crow but that he "wasn't traditional." Jake claimed that being Crow was unrelated to his difficulties. A careful inquiry into what Jake meant by these statements revealed deeply conflicted feelings Jake had about the many cultures (Crow, medical professional, and father) to which he belonged and the pressures he experienced because of this.

Even when clients insist their cultural background isn't relevant to counseling, multiculturally aware mental health practitioners keep an open mind. It isn't necessary to insist on working directly with cultural material or conflicts, but awareness of potential cultural issues is informative.

Be Aware of Individualist Versus Collectivist Orientations

A common dialectic in the multicultural literature is the individualist versus collectivist worldview. **Individualist** cultures, like the dominant U.S. culture, place enormous value on individual's personal liberty and self-interest. Autonomy is regarded as a virtue and personality is viewed as separate from family and culture.

In **collectivist** cultures, values and norms are shared. The self and the personality are defined in terms of group memberships, and the group needs and values are more central than those of the individual. Collectivists tend to evaluate themselves based on attaining group goals, whereas individualists orient toward individual responsibility and personal goals (Fouad & Arredondo, 2007; Pedersen, Draguns, Lonner, & Trimble, 2008).

Although individualism still dominates, theorists within Western culture point to problems with this orientation. In 1975 Robert Hogan wrote,

> A central theme in Western European history for about 800 years has been the decline of the medieval synthesis or, alternatively, the emergence of individualism. Two hundred years ago individualism was a moral and religious ideal capable of legitimizing revolutions and inspiriting sober and thoughtful minds. Sometimes in the last century, however, social thinkers began to regard individualism in more ambivalent terms, even in some cases as a possible indicator of social decay. (p. 533)

If you have an individualist perspective, you may find it difficult to see or understand problems with such a perspective. However, in the interest of personal growth, we offer another comment critical of individualism.

> The defining mark of contemporary American culture is the celebrated idea of liberty without limits. Freedom is cost in purely individualistic terms, there being no notion of, nor respect for, the common good. The individual is entitled to do exactly as he pleases, short of the most blatant and egregious violation of another person's rights. There is endless talk of the rights of the individual, but nary a word spoken of any concomitant responsibilities. Right and wrong are relative, having no discernible objective reference or content. That which burdens the individual is seen as unfair, and anything that restricts choices is condemned. This is the heart and soul of the new freedom. It is also the heart and soul of our psychological and social disorders. (Donohue, 1990, p. 221)

Just as therapists with individualist values may have trouble understanding clients with collectivist values, clients with collectivist values may not see the need to focus on themselves with individual interventions. They may not value setting personal goals. They could see a critique of family members as a critique of them. To get a sense of a collectivist perspective, consider this quotation from the ancient Hindu holy text, the *Bhagavad Gita*, as quoted by Michael Brannigan (2000):

> The man who has given up all desire
> and moves without wanting anything
> Who says neither mine nor I
> wins peace. (p. 44)

Bicultural clients and clients who are second-generation U.S. citizens may struggle with how to juggle newly discovered individualist desires while honoring their family's wishes and/or original cultural practices. For example, Native American college students may be attending college because of their own personal ambitions or they may be attending to bring honor to their family or tribe. Or perhaps one day they're in touch with their personal academic goals and the next day they're more in touch with their familial or tribal academic goals. Trying to balance and sort out these divergent values can cause clients personal and familial distress.

Make Cultural Adaptations

Multicultural counselors practice humility by knowing their limits and seeking consultation, supervision, and additional training when needed and also as a proactive measure. Hays (2008) recommended consulting with experts in specific cultural or diversity issues. In the following excerpt, she described how a white therapist named Kate used a consultant in her work with a Muslim couple (Mouna and Majid):

> The consultant also called Kate's attention to the assumption embedded in Kate's statement that she did not want Mouna and Majid to assume that she agreed with the U.S. government's actions. The consultant told Kate that although it was likely (considering the couple's more recent immigration, Majid's strong Muslim identity, and the current political climate) that the couple disagreed with U.S. policies, it was also possible that they did not. The consultant explained that although more recently immigrated Arabs and Muslims tend to be less satisfied with U.S. foreign policy, up until the 1980s the majority of Arab Americans were Republican and tended toward assimilation into the dominant culture.... The consultant reminded Kate that there can be just as much diversity in the way Arab and Muslim people see the world and themselves as there is between ethnic and religious cultures. She encouraged Kate to continue her reading and look for community events at which she might meet a wide variety of Arab and Muslim people. (p. 164)

Consultation can be crucial. As a therapist you can't be expected to know how to work effectively with every minority group on the planet. For most U.S. counselors and psychotherapists, working directly with a Muslim couple from Tunisia would require special preparation.

In addition to consultation, there are other **cultural adaptations** associated with positive treatment outcomes (Griner & Smith, 2006). In a meta-analysis of 76 studies, Griner and Smith (2006) listed 10 cultural adaptations that may be linked to positive outcomes. These variables include:

1. Explicit incorporation of cultural content/values into the intervention.
2. Racial/**ethnic matching** of client and therapist.
3. Provision of services in clients' native language if other than English.
4. An explicit cultural or multicultural paradigm of the agency or clinic.
5. Consultation with individuals familiar with the client's culture.
6. Outreach efforts to recruit underserved clientele.
7. Provision of extra services designed to enhance client retention, such as child care during sessions.
8. Oral reading of materials to clients with limited English language literacy.
9. Cultural sensitivity training for professional staff.
10. Provision of referrals to external agencies for additional services.

Of these variables, **language matching**, when needed, appears most important to enhancing positive outcomes (Griner & Smith, 2006).

Learn Multicultural Therapy Skills

S. Sue (1998) identified three specific skills that he considers indicative of cross-cultural therapeutic competency. These skills include:

1. *Scientific mindedness*. Therapists who use scientific mindedness form hypotheses about their clients rather than coming to firm and premature conclusions. These therapists also develop creative ways to test their initial hypotheses about minority clients and then act on the basis of the data they obtain and not their prejudices or prejudgments.

2. *Dynamic sizing*. Therapists with this skill know when to generalize and be inclusive and when to individualize and be exclusive. This means knowing when to apply general knowledge about a culture to an individual and when to focus more on the individual than the culture.

3. *Culture-specific expertise*. This involves acquiring knowledge about one's own culture and about the client's culture. It also involves the application of that knowledge in a culturally sensitive, nonstereotyping, and effective manner.

Invite Spirituality Back In

In cultures other than Western European, the title of this section would be ludicrous. **Spirituality** wouldn't be invited back in because it would never have left. For most indigenous people and for most people born and raised in Asia, Africa, or Latin America,

> Spirituality is a life force that undergirds our existence in the universe. (Sue et al., 1999, p. 1064)

In contrast, those reared and educated in the logical positivist psychology domain may find being open to the spiritual domain more challenging. For multicultural therapists, being open to and inviting in spirituality isn't optional. Sue and colleagues (D. W. Sue, Bingham, Porche-Burke, & Vasquez, 1999) noted:

> [A] psychology based solely on the separation of science and spirituality and that uses primarily the segmented and reductionistic tenets of the natural sciences is one that may not be shared by three quarters of the world nor by the emerging culturally diverse groups in the United States. (p. 1065)

From Thomas Moore (1994), in his best-selling book, *Care of the Soul*, we hear,

> In the modern world, we separate religion and psychology, spiritual practice and therapy. There is considerable interest in healing this split, but if it is going to be bridged, our very idea of what we are doing in our psychology has to be radically

re-imagined. Psychology and spirituality need to be seen as one. (p. xv)

If spirituality and psychology are reunited, serious implications for therapists and therapy follow. A psychotherapy that focuses on caring not only for the client's psychological symptoms but also for his or her soul and spirit is a very different psychotherapy. Of course, this chapter isn't the place to learn how to integrate spirituality into counseling; it's just a good place to start thinking about how to be open to a wide range of religious viewpoints.

Karasu (1999) contends that counseling and psychotherapy stemming from the traditional—psychoanalytic, behavioral, and humanistic—approaches leave clients spiritually bereft. He states that even if

> psychological conflicts are relatively resolved, deficits filled, and defects corrected, ultimately patients still experience posttherapeutic dysphoria, a loss of meaning or sense of emptiness, a nonluminous hollow. These diverse strategies have shed limited light and left patients bereft, because in the process of treatment (if not the psychopathology itself) the person's soul has been neglected and spiritual connections severed. (p. 144)

For many clients and therapists there is more to life than behavior change and more to their symptoms than cognitive restructuring might address. Although secular humanists such as Carl Rogers sometimes approach human relationships in a manner that seems intrinsically spiritual or divine, even his approach can be seen as missing something essential that many people seek. See Putting it in Practice 13.5 for one simple example of a spiritually oriented therapy technique.

QUESTIONS FOR REFLECTION

Is it possible to integrate religious and spiritual concepts into counseling while still honoring the approaches we've studied in this book? How would you answer the question, where is the soul and where is the spirit in modern counseling and psychotherapy?

PUTTING IT IN PRACTICE 13.5

This homework assignment is from the book *Favorite Counseling and Therapy Homework Assignments* (Breggin, 2001, pp. 58–59). We believe it provides a good fit for the spiritual themes in this chapter.

A Dangerous Assignment

Based on the therapy principle, "Do unto others as you would have others do unto you," I rarely assign homework to my clients. . . .

There is, however, one exception: a homework assignment that I guarantee will improve my clients' lives and the lives of almost everyone they touch. If only as an experiment for a week or two, I suggest that they try being nice to everyone they meet. I explain, "Before we get together again, try being courteous and kind to everyone you deal with, even people you find unworthy or aggravating."

Some religions speak of greeting the God within each person we meet; the Quakers talk about addressing "that of God," which is in other people with respect and even reverence. Naturally, like most of us, my clients are tempted to dismiss "being nice" as utopian, unmanly, embarrassing, and even dangerous. Rarely does anyone gratefully declare, "That's a great idea, Peter. An application of universal truths to my personal life. I can't wait to put it into action."

Multicultural Therapy in Action: Brief Vignettes

The following two case vignettes illustrate applications of multicultural counseling and psychotherapy principles. However, keep in mind that applying these principles isn't a standardized process and these two examples are only examples and not norms.

Vignette I: Anger Management

Taylor Wind Runner, a Job Corps student studying the electrical trade, was referred for therapy due to anger management problems. He was a 20-year-old male with a Salish tribal affiliation. His scores on the educational achievement test were very high and he was doing well in all areas at the Job Corps center where he was a student. However, he was required to see a mental health counselor because of repeated incidents of abusive language toward other students.

Taylor was open and honest about his problem.

Taylor: Yeah, people here are stupid and they piss me off. It's not all my fault though. You wouldn't believe the stupid things people say here.

Counselor: Actually, I've heard lots of stories about lots of people saying stupid things here. It's amazing. I'd like to hear your stories of what people are saying if you're willing to tell me.

Taylor: It's mostly stupid racist stuff.

Counselor: I'm very sorry to hear that. I can imagine that would feel very bad, but I can't exactly know what it feels like. You can give me an example if you'd like, but you don't have to.

Taylor: I don't mind.

Counselor: What sorts of things are they saying?

Taylor: Like one guy came up to me yesterday and asked me: "Why do Indians eat dogs." And he thought he was funny. I just started yelling and I threatened him and then I got in trouble.

Counselor: So this guy comes up to you and he thinks he's being funny, but he's being rude and racist.

Taylor: Yeah. I don't think I should have to put up with that here.

Counselor: You're absolutely right. We've got rules here about no racist talk. That's completely unacceptable.

Taylor: Well nothing ever happens to these guys . . . so I take care of it myself.

Counselor: I've heard about you saying some pretty nasty things back sometimes. I guess it's like basketball . . . one guy does something dirty, a cheap shot, then they always catch the guy who's trying to get even and call a foul on him.

Taylor: That's exactly how it is. The other guy starts it and I get caught. It's totally not fair.

Counselor: You're right about that too. Now it's just a matter of us figuring out how to deal with it.

Taylor: Yeah I know. I've been told we can do some dormitory education or mediation or I can file a complaint, but no way am I doing any of that shit. That will just make things worse.

Counselor: Okay. I hear you. It sounds like you know some of the options, but you don't want any part of that.

Taylor: That's right.

Counselor: So, if you're okay with this, you and I can work together and we can figure out what else you can do . . . in the moment . . . to handle this without getting quite so pissed and without getting in trouble. But I want you to know that I agree with you. It's not your fault. We should be able to do something to get these guys to stop saying racist crap. You shouldn't have to deal with it.

Taylor: Yeah, but I always have to deal with it. You can't just make somebody shut up. You know, I've tried and it just doesn't work. People just keep on yapping.

Taylor and his counselor were able to form an alliance and work together to help Taylor develop skills for dealing with racism. After considerable discussion, Taylor came to the conclusion that students who make "Stupid racial jokes" are "Ignorant." He and his counselor explored that together and then talked about how to "Educate" people who were ignorant. In the past Taylor had tried this by using verbally abusive and threatening language. Both Taylor and the counselor agreed that approach wasn't working and Taylor came up with the idea of using each racial slur as an opportunity to educate people. Because Taylor was very intelligent, they were able to reframe the problem as an intellectual challenge . . . with the question being: How could Taylor educate other students who were clearly uneducated about Indian people? The discussion led to further sessions and Taylor was empowered to use his brains to work with the counselor to develop programs at the Job Corps on valuing all cultures and all races. In the end, Taylor felt heard, empowered, contributed to cultural education at Job Corps, and graduated.

In this case the counselor listened and empathized with Taylor's situation, but also went further than typical nondirective listening to openly validate Taylor's anger. This is important because it communicated to Taylor that the counselor was on his side on the racism issue and Taylor's anger wasn't identified as strictly "his" problem. Then, although Taylor decided to make changes in how he approached the situation, they worked together on a social problem Taylor was facing and not a "Taylor problem" that others were facing. Finally, the counselor followed Taylor's lead, empowering him to "educate" other students in ways that Taylor found personally and culturally meaningful. The counselor avoided taking over the issue and following his own agenda—instead he was respectful of Taylor's agenda.

Vignette II: What's Good About You?

In collaboration with our colleague Dudley Dana, PhD, we developed an informal self-esteem assessment and intervention activity called "***What's good about you?***" To initiate the activity, the therapist obtains client consent or assent and then says, "I'm going to ask you the same question 10 times. The only rule is that you can't use the same answer twice. So, I'll ask you the same question 10 times, but you have to give me 10 different answers."

The question to be asked is, of course, "What's good about you?" Most young clients immersed in the dominant culture enjoy the activity and it provides material for discussion. This activity is described in greater detail elsewhere (J. Sommers-Flanagan & R. Sommers-Flanagan, 2007).

One day when John was working with an Asian American teen, he decided to initiate the *What's good about you?* activity.

JSF: Okay. Are you ready for the question?

Client: Yes. I'm ready.

JSF: What's good about you?

Client: (Silence of about 5 seconds.) "I don't want to do this."

JSF: Oh yeah, that's totally fine. We don't have to do anything in particular in here.

Client: I'm just not comfortable with that. I don't want to do this. I don't talk like that about myself.

JSF: Right. I'm very sorry. I guess this was a pretty dumb idea. I really didn't intend to make you uncomfortable.

Client: You know this is the kind of thing my parents want me to do all the time. They want me to focus on the positive and think happy things and all that crap.

JSF: It's not really something you want to do.

Client: And it's not what Asian people do either. My grandmother is totally humble. I don't want to brag about myself. I'd rather be like her.

JSF: Even though your parents want this sort of thing, it doesn't fit with your culture, and you like your grandmother's way of being better anyway.

Client: It's like my friends. My parents want me to be more like my friends. They want me to live the happy American life. Sometimes I want to be more like my friends too, but it doesn't fit for me. I'm more serious and intense and all that.

JSF: And so there are lots of different thoughts and feelings you're having. You don't really want to be the way your parents want you to be . . . it doesn't really fit for you. You feel attracted to being more humble like your grandma and your Asian culture. But then there's a little feeling of wanting to be a bit more like your friends, too.

Client: Yeah. It's all a pretty big mess in here, huh?

This case illustrates several points in working with diverse clients.

- John tries to use an individualist technique with a client who has collectivist values (a poor idea to start with).
- Rather than pressing forward with an activity that causes the client cultural discomfort, the process is stopped.
- John apologizes and expresses interest in the client's perspective.
- As many multicultural writers suggest, the client has multiple identities. He's Asian and he's American. He's a teenager pushing away from his parents' influence, but has found his grandmother's humility very appealing.

In this case the key is to stay open to exploring the client's multiple identities of self and of being part of a collective. He has a variety of mixed feelings and likely needs support as he engages in a bicultural-adolescent identity development process.

CASE ANALYSIS AND TREATMENT PLANNING

Shonda was a 19-year-old American Indian athlete whose father was half-Latino. She came to college on a full-ride basketball scholarship. In high school Shonda was a local legend, leading her team to three state titles. She was the pride of her Blackfeet tribe and her small town.

College was a different story. Almost on arrival, she got involved with a young man from another tribe and began partying. Her grades slipped; she missed practices or arrived late. Although still occasionally spectacular on the court, she was becoming progressively more inconsistent. Her coach finally contacted Dr. N., a counselor in town known to work successfully with both athletes and with American Indian families. Shonda's coach insisted that she try counseling; he made the call himself, even offering to accompany Shonda to the first session. Over the telephone he told Dr. N. that Shonda seemed down, unresponsive to guidance, and irritable. When she engaged and asserted herself on the court, it wasn't unusual for her to blow up and get into a shoving match with a teammate. Shonda's coach was also very worried about her alcohol use.

Comment: Shonda embodies a number of cultures. She identifies herself as American Indian, but her father's heritage includes being half-Latino, and Shonda spoke a little Spanish as well as a little Blackfeet. Besides these racial-ethnic identities, Shonda has a strong identity as an athlete. Athletes, as a cultural group, don't easily admit weakness and don't easily seek counseling (Maniar, Curry, Sommers-Flanagan, & Walsh, 2001). Dr. N., having worked with reluctant athletes before, is well aware of this attribute.

Shonda arrived for her first session alone. She immediately told Dr. N. that she didn't want to come but that she'd rather come herself than have her coach drag her in. After the usual informed consent discussions and after Dr. N. told Shonda what the coach had said, she asked, "But I'm interested in what brings *you* in to see me, Shonda. From your perspective."

Shonda responded with an attempt at humor: "My feet brought me, I guess."

Dr. N. laughed and smiled and finally said, "Good answer. Sometimes I ask questions in a weird way. I guess my feet brought me here today, too. I'm guessing from what you said before that your feet just *barely* brought you here today."

Shonda smiled, apparently pleased that Dr. N. liked her joke.

Comment: Dr. N. knew that many American Indians enjoy laughter and joking. Rather than interpreting Shonda's joke as sarcastic hostility or feeling put off by the joke, she felt included and trusted with a bit of humor.

Encouraged, Dr. N. decided that it was time to get a few cultural cards on the table. She asked, with genuine interest, "I know you played ball for Benton. Are you a member of the Blackfeet tribe?"

Shonda nodded, averting her gaze, but smiling. "Yeah. My mom's from there, and all my folks. But I have cousins who are white and cousins who are very dark. Strange, huh? And my boyfriend's only half, so if we had kids, they wouldn't even meet the quota."

Comment: Shonda's response to Dr. N's entry into the cultural arena produced a variety of cultural and personal information and illustrates how a brief disclosure presents a huge range of alternatives to the multicultural counselor. Consider these options:

- Shonda's mentioning of the blood quota may be a test for Dr. N. because blood quota is not a well-known issue outside Indian country. How should Dr. N. respond? Should she ignore the blood quota issue? Should she act more informed or less informed than she actually is?

- Shonda shares her multiracial identity. Should Dr. N. pursue this area in order to gather more specific information about Shonda's racial identity?

- When Shonda mention's having "kids" with her boyfriend it might indicate a pregnancy, hope of a pregnancy, and all that becoming pregnant means symbolically and literally. Should Dr. N. directly ask about whether Shonda is pregnant or thinking about getting pregnant?

- American Indian girls and young women often get overt messages about achievement and covert messages about getting pregnant and having babies. Should Dr. N. explore these issues?

- Overall, Shonda's initial response is relatively open and therefore gives Dr. N. hope for a connection. Shonda's averted gaze also may indicate a sign of respect. Should Dr. N. notice this openness and appreciate it?

Dr. N. nodded sympathetically. Her mind was filled with the preceding options. Dr. N. knew that she and Shonda didn't have enough of a relationship to ask directly about underlying issues—yet. So she resolved to continue listening very carefully and to stay with the central content of what Shonda was saying instead of trying to interpret deeper possibilities.

"Wow. That blood quota controversy is really something. I've been following the news on it a little bit. What do you think about it?"

"It sucks. You know I learned more about it at college than I knew before about how it was genocide, really. A planned way to make sure there were no Indians at all after a while."

"Yeah, it's pretty awful. Lots of those policies seem to hurt Indians more than being helpful. And some of the policies are so complicated that you have to come to college to learn more about them. How did you learn about it in class?"

"I'm taking a Native American studies class. I like it. But English sucks and so does my math class."

"Yeah," Dr. N. smiled. "It must be quite an adjustment, coming away to college, taking classes you don't like and keeping up your basketball, all at the same time."

"Nah. My cousin Sidney is here. He introduced me to Derrick. It's been pretty fun. But the coach. He's the one having a problem. I can play ball, if he'll just get off my case."

The Problem (and Strengths) List

Like feminist therapy, from the multicultural perspective problems aren't "in" individuals. Shonda doesn't "own" the problems. The problems exist and are a challenge for Shonda to contend with. They include:

- Understanding and managing her multiple identities and how they influence her in positive and less positive ways.

- Dealing with the adjustment to college; this adjustment is historically a big challenge for Native students who feel pressure to represent themselves, their tribes, and their families.

- Related to her college adjustment, Shonda is engaging in a range of behaviors (e.g., alcohol use) that may be self-destructive; however, it's important to view her alcohol use within a cultural context.

Shonda also has a range of strengths that might help her in dealing with her challenging and stressful situation. These include, but are certainly not limited to:

- Excellent athletic (basketball) skills.

- Excellent sense of humor and use of humor.

- A strong family connection.

- A strong tribal connection.

Problem Formulation

To this point Dr. N. has been working at connection and to help Shonda become comfortable in the room. Shonda is responsive, but as soon as Dr. N. mentions "adjustment" and "basketball," Shonda disagrees, asserting that the adjustment is no problem and that her coach is her problem. At this point Dr. N. could directly ask about what the coach does that's a problem, but instead she uses a person-centered reflection because she wants Shonda to see that she won't force a viewpoint that Shonda doesn't agree with.

"So you've been having fun and the adjustment hasn't been too hard and it sounds like you still want to play ball. It's just the coaching and practice that aren't going well?"

Shonda looked around the office, not immediately responding to Dr. N. She yawned. Then she offered an engaging smile and asked, "How many times do I need to come in here?"

Comment: It's hard to say whether Dr. N.'s paraphrase fell flat or whether it made Shonda consider the implications of a longer-term relationship because it was accurate. Either way, what's important is for Dr. N. to acknowledge openly that engaging in therapy is her choice.

"I don't know. I don't even know if you need to come here. I'm interested in what you think. Most people I see tell me counseling is helpful. But it's not right for everybody. How about we talk about counseling and whether it might be helpful for you before we make any decisions either way about how many times you should come, or even if you need to come at all. Is that okay with you?"

Comment: Dr. N. is staying open to the possibility that Shonda may not engage in counseling, while at the same time trying to evaluate her expectations about counseling before any firm decisions are made.

Shonda paused, looking down. Dr. N. sat quietly. Finally, Shonda said, "I don't know. I don't even know if I can stick around here very long. College isn't what I thought it would be."

Comment: Shonda indirectly answered the question by opening up a new area of discussion. It's not unusual for Indian clients to be subtle and indirect in their verbal responses.

Dr. N. glanced at Shonda and looked downward herself for a few seconds before cautiously asking, "What is it about college that's making it hard to want to stick around?"

Shonda fidgeted in the silence that followed. Dr. N. reminded herself to breathe and to wait patiently. Shonda was deciding what to say and what not to say, and it was important for that process to be respected. Finally, she said, "It's really stupid. College is okay. It just feels weird. I've been on the res 18 years. I know everybody and everybody knows me. It's home. This isn't home. It's that simple. I like my cousin and I like Derrick, but God I miss my mom and my family back home."

Comment: Therapy has now started. It would be inappropriate for Dr. N. to go back to her question about Shonda's expectations for counseling. Now is a time to gently and somewhat indirectly explore Shonda's feelings. In other words, Dr. N. should avoid using stock questions like, "How do you feel about that?"

"When you put it that way," Dr. N. began, "I get an image of you with a big, weird, and sorta bad feeling inside. What about being on the reservation would help make the weird feelings get better?"

"I'd be around my family. I'd know everybody on the res and everybody would know me. There's no strangers there. Around here, aside from my cousin and Derrick, everybody is a stranger. Especially my God-damn coach. Man he's strange."

Comment: In clinical and diagnostic terms, Dr. N. might categorize Shonda's description of her experience at college as indicative of separation anxiety. If Dr. N. was behaviorally oriented, she might systematically evaluate Shonda's anxiety symptoms and then educate her about options for anxiety reduction. In psychodynamic terms, Shonda might be seen as recapitulating her dilemma in the counseling session. The issue is, "Shall I stay here where I feel uncomfortable and anxious, or shall I go away to some place where I'm comfortable and not anxious?"

The problem formulation that makes the most sense at this point includes anxiety and adjustment. Shonda is adjusting to college and it's not going the way she expected. She's adjusting to her basketball coach. She's missing home. It would be easy for Dr. N. to begin pushing information onto Shonda— "Hey, most Indian people who leave the reservation feel incredibly homesick" or "Yeah, you know your coach is weird, but really he cares a lot about your well-being." The problem with pushing information is that it's not effective and it's not therapy.

Interventions

As the session progressed, Dr. N. engaged Shonda in a brief brainstorming activity focusing on what might make being at college "feel better" if she decided to stay. During the activity, Dr. N. used humor on occasion (at one point asking Shonda about the possibility of having her family come live in her dorm room). Overall, the session proceeded smoothly, and toward the end Dr. N. asked Shonda if she would come for three more sessions just to sort out whether to stay in college or go home. Shonda agreed, and they scheduled an appointment.

Dr. N. didn't assign Shonda homework to complete between sessions. Shonda had indicated she didn't like her math and English classes and so homework wouldn't likely be welcomed. Instead, because the therapy connection was fragile, Dr. N. did some homework herself. She went online and to find out more information about the reservation where Shonda grew up.

Shonda showed up 15 minutes late for her second session. Neither she nor Dr. N. commented on the lateness. Among some American Indians there is a concept referred to as Indian time. In essence, this concept emphasizes the fact that things happen when they happen. Although Shonda's lateness might reflect Indian time, it also might reflect her ambivalence about therapy. However, interpreting lateness is a bad idea early in therapy with an Indian client [This is also a good example of scientific mindedness; Dr. N. is aware of the hypotheses about Shonda's lateness, but doesn't come to any conclusions.] The therapist needs to relax the time-bound orientation associated with the dominant white culture. Dr. N. also chose to open the session with two gifts, one metaphorical and the other edible.

After greeting and as soon as they sat down, Dr. N. opened with, "Hey, Shonda. I picked up a chocolate chip cookie for you from the bakery down the street. They're pretty good." Dr. N. handed a small bakery bag to Shonda and pulled an identical bag for herself out of her purse. "I figured with all that basketball practice you have that you probably get pretty hungry."

"Thanks," Shonda replied. "I love chocolate chip cookies."

"You know, after our talk last time I thought I should find out a little more about what life is like up on your reservation, so I got on the Internet and found a couple of websites that had some information."

"Really? I didn't know my res had a website. What'd you find out?"

"Well, of course there was some info about the Indian Health Services. And I found a little café or bar or something that had a website."

"Yeah. That musta been the Brown Horse Bar and Grill. That's where the drunks hang out."

"Right. Okay, so I've got a quiz for you. The Indian Health Services website had a staff directory, and since you said you know everyone on the res, I thought I'd throw a couple names out and see if you recognize them."

Comment: Socializing and gift giving are very important in most Indian cultures. Dr. N. wants her therapy office to be a comfortable place for Shonda, so she's making clear efforts to connect with her and understand her cultural experiences. Typically, if Shonda was on the reservation and feeling distress, she might go talk with an aunt or grandmother and some sort of food might be included in the interaction. In the ensuing conversation, Shonda proves that she knows just about everybody who works at Tribal Health. After about 8 to 10 minutes of munching cookies and checking on Shonda's knowledge of the Tribal Health staff, Dr. N. moves toward a more serious topic.

"So, Shonda, last time we talked about how it feels pretty weird for you to be here, away from the res. Have you had any thoughts or reactions to our conversation from last time?"

"Well yeah," Shonda began, "I kept thinking about the one thing you said about having my family come live in my dorm room. It just sorta made me feel good. I thought about what it would be like having my mom in my dorm room making me fry bread and waking me up in the morning."

"That sounds like a nice scene. Do you think she'd come down and do the same for me?"

Shonda giggled. "You know, I bet she would. And you'd love her fry bread. Everybody loves her fry bread. You know, that's probably why I know everybody on the res, 'cause every one of them's had my mom's fry bread."

"How often have you been talking to your mom?" Dr. N. asked.

"About twice a week. Just enough to make me miss her crazy like."

"Well, I guess the best thing to say about that is that it totally sucks," Dr. N. offered.

The multiculturally sensitive interventions in this session included:

- Gentle brainstorming of what will help Shonda be more comfortable at college.

- Humor designed to connect.

- Providing food and eating together.

- Socializing in a way to connect with Shonda's culture and her strengths and familiarity with the reservation.

- Empathy for her missing home.

- Overall, Dr. N. is trying to get Shonda to adjust to being with her and in counseling and this adjustment may generalize to her being at college.

Final Comment: From a traditional psychodynamic, person-centered, or behavioral therapy perspective, the preceding interactions may not seem much like therapy. However, this case is provided to illustrate a culturally sensitive therapy approach.

As therapy proceeded, Dr. N. continued to work with Shonda using a culture-sensitive frame. She also helped Shonda begin to notice and then change the ways in which she was coping with her homesickness or separation anxiety. Sometimes through humor and sometimes through more serious but indirect communication, Dr. N. guided Shonda to the creation of a home away from home. This involved joining the campus Native American Club, learning some calming and soothing techniques to use instead of alcohol, and developing a support system both on and off campus. As it turns out, Shonda's relationship with Derrick continued, and Dr. N. and Shonda were able to talk directly about using birth control rather than risking a pregnancy that would almost certainly land her back on the reservation. Shonda was able to see that returning to the reservation was always an option for her, but that if she decided to return, she would prefer doing so intentionally and on her own terms.

Outcomes Measurement

Asking what would be an appropriate set of outcome measures for Shonda is a challenge. There are, of course, standardized measures of adjustment.

There are also symptom checklists that might be appropriate. However, in this case, we believe the only appropriate outcome measures would be measures that Dr. N. can playfully employ and explore with Shonda. As long as Dr. N. uses a culturally sensitive approach, doesn't take the results too seriously, and employs process and outcomes measurement collaboratively, it would be possible to use virtually any brief outcome measures.

QUESTIONS FOR REFLECTION

What are your thoughts and reactions to the therapy approach Dr. N. used in this case? How do you suppose Dr. N. introduced herself? Do you think Dr. N. insisted that Shonda call her Dr. N. or that she used her first name?

CULTURAL AND GENDER CONSIDERATIONS

Multicultural counseling is designed to be culturally and gender sensitive. In Shonda's case, Dr. N. is an interesting combination of directive and nondirective. She's directive in that she actively explores Shonda's culture, changes her own behavior to connect with Shonda, and asks Shonda challenging questions. However, she's also very nondirective in that she never tells Shonda what she should do or how she should live her life. This combination of directiveness and nondirective respect for Shonda's perspective is multiculturally sensitive.

In the dichotomous world of sexuality, Shonda currently would identify herself as a heterosexual. Nevertheless, many of the issues with which she has and will attend to in her life have to do with unfair discrimination that marginalizes her as a person and as a tribal member . . . and this naturally connects her with other minority groups, such as GLBT people. Interestingly, there's an approach to working with GLBT clients called **affirmative therapy**; this approach includes ideas that can be helpful for working with non-GLBT clients (see Putting it in Practice 13.6 for a story about a young therapist who discovers affirmative psychotherapy).

PUTTING IT IN PRACTICE 13.6

Becoming an Affirmative Therapist for LGBT Clients

This commentary is authored by Nick Heck, M.A. As this book was going to press, Nick was a doctoral student in clinical psychology at the University of Montana.

To complete a final assignment for my first graduate-level interviewing course, I reviewed a book (Fox, 2006) that described affirmative psychotherapy with bisexual clients. I kept careful notes as I read each chapter and it soon became clear that I had no idea what any of the book's contributors meant when they used the term affirmative psychotherapy. I thought to myself, "How can I become a psychologist who practices affirmative psychotherapy with lesbian, gay, bisexual, and transgender (LGBT) clients when I have no idea what affirmative psychotherapy is?" I needed a definition so I continued to read and search PsychINFO for answers.

Before I share more of my experiences, ask yourself, "What is affirmative psycho-therapy?" and "What does it mean to be an affirmative therapist or counselor for LGBT clients?" You might be thinking, "Is affirmative psychotherapy is a brand of psychotherapy similar to cognitive-behavioral therapy (CBT) or functional analytic psychotherapy?" That was my assumption, and I knew there had to be interventions specific to this new brand of psychotherapy. Where was the affirmative psychotherapy equivalent to CBT's seven-column thought record for identifying and correcting maladaptive thinking patterns? Where was the affirmative psychotherapy intervention manual? When I read the *Handbook of Counseling and Psychotherapy with Lesbian, Gay, Bisexual and Transgender Clients* (Bieschke, Perez, & DeBord, 2007) I was sure one of the chapters would outline interventions specific to affirmative psychotherapy. That chapter was nowhere to be found.

When I began practicum, everything I thought I knew about psychotherapy went out the window. For example, I had a preconceived notion that after I finished my first intake interview (during which I would administer a semi-structured interview), my supervisor would say, "Your client has [insert disorder X here]. You should read [insert treatment manual for disorder X here]." You may laugh at my naïveté, but that's the impression I had of psychotherapy when I finished my undergraduate studies. I quickly realized that psychotherapy involved more than routinized administration of specific therapeutic interventions. Before I could even think about successfully implementing specific interventions, I would have to learn how to develop a therapeutic relationship with my clients.

To develop relationships with LGBT clients, I had to unlearn some "bad habits" that develop as a result of living in a heterosexist society that embraces a dichotomous view of gender. I could no longer make implicit or explicit assumptions about sexual orientation or gender identity. It took time to become comfortable asking a client who has a child, "Is there a second parent in your child's life?" The first time I asked this question, the client simply responded by saying "Yes." I didn't know what to say next; I mean I could have said, "Is this second parent a man or a woman?" but that would have been awkward and invalidating of transgender people.

Later in my second year I co-facilitated a therapy group for transgender clients. In planning to co-facilitate this group, I met regularly with my supervisor to discuss readings related to group therapy and therapy with transgender individuals. Initially, I approached supervision with the same simplistic views that I had when I started seeing clients individually. I envisioned meetings with my supervisor where we would discuss specific readings, but I also thought we would be reviewing treatment manuals to identify specific interventions that might be helpful for working with transgender clients within a group therapy framework.

When speaking about my development (as a therapist in training) at our clinic "graduation," my supervisor shared how she had initially been "apprehensive" in allowing me to co-facilitate a therapy group for transgender clients, because I wouldn't stop talking about empirically supported treatments. Clearly, she recognized that no such treatment existed. And so she helped us become validating, supportive, and affirmative group therapists. As my co-facilitator and I became more confident in our abilities and group cohesion increased, we were eventually able to integrate a greater number of interventions consistent with experiential-process group therapy, as described by Yalom and Leszcz (2005). Supervision, in addition to ongoing reading and self-reflection, challenged and changed my views of gender and helped further my development as an affirmative therapist.

In addition to my group work and supervision experiences, I frequently read (and reread) books and journal articles related to affirmative psychotherapy with LGBT clients. In addition, professional associations have published reports related to counseling and psychotherapy with LGBT clients. Some of these include the American Psychological Association's *Guidelines for Psychotherapy with Lesbian, Gay, and Bisexual Clients* (APA, 2000) and the American Counseling Association's *Competencies for Counseling with Transgender Clients* (ACA, 2009). I also joined APA's Division 44 (Society for the Psychological Study of Lesbian, Gay, Bisexual, and Transgender Issues), which offers a Listserv that disseminates LGBT practice, research, and policy information.

Not long ago, a request came across the Listserv asking when the term "gay affirming" emerged and for the original definition and description of LGBT affirmative psychotherapy. Senior LGBT scholars replied and directed the member toward a special edition of the *Journal of Homosexuality* that contained the seminal article on affirmative psychotherapy. For those of you interested, you should read Alan Malyon's 1982 article titled, "Psychotherapeutic implications of internalized homophobia in gay men." I truly wish someone had directed me to this article earlier in my career and I hope it will help you begin (or continue) your journey toward becoming a LGBT affirmative therapist.

EVIDENCE-BASED STATUS

The rational foundation for establishing multicultural or culturally sensitive therapy approaches is unarguable. Taking each client's individual cultural background into consideration is the rational and logical thing to do.

In contrast, the empirical foundation for multicultural therapy is more controversial (G.C.N. Hall, 2001). Problems associated with empirical validation of culturally sensitive treatments are legion. It's hard to imagine how researchers could collect data to support multicultural treatment efficacy. Think about cases involving American Indians, Laotian refugees, Asian Americans, or Latino immigrants. How could researchers accurately measure the concerns of all these clients as they enter treatment? In many cases, the client's conception of the problem may be dramatically different from a traditional Western diagnostic label. Further, can you imagine using a manualized treatment approach with a young Latino immigrant suffering from susto? (**Susto** can occur when a frightening incident causes a person's soul to leave his or her body. The result is depression and physical malady. The customary treatment in Mexico and Central America includes ritual healings in which the person's soul is called back to the body.) Even if a manualized treatment were acceptable, could researchers find the right standardized questionnaires to determine treatment efficacy? As with Shonda, although questionnaires might be employed, they should be used collaboratively, for exploratory purposes, and not taken too seriously.

Treatment Outcomes Research

Perhaps due to the preceding challenges, there hasn't been much therapy outcomes research with ethnic-minority clients. In a review of the status of ethnic minorities in treatment outcomes studies, Sue and Zane (2009) reported:

> Since 1986, about 10,000 participants have been included in RCTs evaluating the efficacy of treatments for certain disorders. For nearly half of these participants (N = 4,991), no information on race or ethnicity was given. For another 7% of

participants (N = 656), studies only reported the general designation "non-white." For the remaining 47% of participants (N = 4,335), very few minorities were included; not a single study analyzed the efficacy of the treatment by ethnicity or race. (p. 331)

Given the lack of research in this area, a more practical and answerable question is this: What therapy situations and therapist skills produce positive outcomes among culturally diverse populations?

Ethnic Matching

Research on **ethnic matching** is equivocal. In some cases ethnic matching seems to have salutatory effects on outcomes, but in other cases it seems unimportant (S. Sue, Fujino, Takeuchi, & Zane, 1991). In their meta-analysis of 76 studies on culturally adapted therapies, Griner and Smith (2006) found an inverse relationship between ethnic matching and positive outcomes.

Sue and colleagues also evaluated the relationship of ethnic-specific services on treatment outcomes (Takeuchi, Sue, & Yeh, 1995). **Ethnic-specific services** are defined as treatments that try to respond to the cultural needs of clients (e.g., culturally sensitive greetings are used, Chinese clients are offered tea as well as coffee). Overall, research showed that ethnic clients stay in treatment longer when offered ethnic-specific services. Additional research indicated that clients benefit from a cognitive match, in which the therapist and client use similar ways of identifying goals and resolving problems and have similar degrees of acculturation (S. Sue, 1998).

Cultural Adaptation and Multicultural Training

Research on cultural adaptation as a strategy for improving treatment outcomes is positive. Based on a meta-analysis of 76 studies, Griner and Smith (2006) reported:

- Overall, the effect size from 76 studies was $d = .45$ (a positive effect of moderate magnitude).

- Diverse clients who were less acculturated benefited more from cultural adaptations.

- In particular, older Latino/a clients who were less acculturated had very positive outcomes.

- Although general multicultural adaptation was good, specific multicultural adaptation had more positive outcomes.

- Although ethnic matching showed no positive effects (and were generally associated with more negative outcomes) language matching produced outcomes twice that of nonlanguage matching.

- Interventions provided in same race groups were approximately four times more effective than interventions provided in mixed race groups.

The effects of multicultural training on therapy outcome are similarly positive. Therapists with greater multicultural competence report higher self-efficacy, and treatment outcomes are generally better (Constantine et al., 2008). Smith and colleagues (2006) also reported that multicultural education is linked to more positive educational outcomes.

Overall, the research consistently points to the conclusion that culture, multicultural education and training, and multicultural competence do matter.

QUESTIONS FOR REFLECTION

Outcome research with multicultural populations is lacking. As a budding researcher and practitioner, how would you address this issue? If you decided to do your thesis or dissertation on this topic, how would you proceed?

CONCLUDING COMMENTS

Conceptually, multicultural theory is simple. What could be simpler than a theoretical stance pointing out that culture is central in human development and human perception? However, as D.W. Sue et al. (1999) stated unequivocally, multicultural theory isn't value neutral. In fact, the theory itself entails a belief in social justice. Harvard philosopher John Rawls (1971) proposed that social justice could be achieved only if we chose our social policies from behind a veil of ignorance so that we could not know where or who we might be in the society

for which we were making the rules. We might be white, black, poor, rich, prematurely disabled, male, female, old, young, and so on. If we had absolutely no way of knowing where we would step into life, what would we consider the best social policy?

Many argue that even Rawls gets it wrong because his system insinuates that humans achieving a consensus will then fail to take into account minority views (Tjeltveit, 1999). And, of course, such a veil is impossible. We can only approximate understanding the experiences of other people, and we can never rid ourselves of our own cultural identities. The best we can hope for is a rich understanding of ourselves as members of our cultural communities and a constantly evolving appreciation and understanding of other cultures, other values, and other people.

CHAPTER SUMMARY

Culture is ubiquitous, therefore, all approaches to counseling and psychotherapy must address cultural issues. This chapter focused on how counselors and psychotherapists can become multiculturally oriented and sensitive.

Throughout the world and in the United States there's a long history of cultural oppression. In many cases when people are different they're labeled deviant. Some of the more horrific recent examples include slavery and other forms of racial oppression.

The passing of the Civil Rights Act in 1964 opened up greater opportunities for cultural minorities. Subsequently, groups with racial and cultural interests were formed (e.g., the Association for Black Psychologists). More recently, additional growth and development in multicultural thinking has resulted in more organizations in support of gender issues, including publication of the *Guidelines for Psychotherapy with Lesbian, Gay, and Bisexual Clients* (APA, 2000) and the ACA's *Competencies for Counseling with Transgender Clients* (ACA, 2009). There are now many multicultural and diversity leaders within counseling and psychology.

Multicultural theory has three underlying principles. These include: (1) cultural membership is linked to disadvantage and privilege; (2) we make distinctions between groups of people based on race, religion, sex, sexual orientation, ethnicity, physical and mental disabilities, and socioeconomic status; and (3) a multiculturalist stance can foster greater understanding between cultural groups and facilitate egalitarian treatment of all humans. Flowing from these principles, like feminist theory, a multicultural perspective doesn't locate psychopathology within the individual. Instead, psychopathology is viewed as caused by oppressive social forces.

Multiculturally sensitive therapy practice is guided by the multicultural competencies. The competencies are summarized as requiring: (a) cultural awareness (including an emphasis on the therapist's self-awareness; (b) cultural knowledge; and (c) culturally specific skills.

As noted, there's a long history of dominant population groups oppressing minority groups. As a consequence, all assessment and diagnosis procedures should be used carefully, collaboratively, and in a culturally sensitive manner with minority populations. Multiculturally sensitive therapists should also: (a) understand acculturation; (b) be aware of individualist versus collectivist orientations; (c) make cultural adaptations (especially language-matching when indicated); (d) learn multicultural therapy skills; and (e) be open to spirituality.

Evaluating the efficacy and effectiveness of multicultural approaches is challenging. Historically, counseling and psychotherapy researchers have not conducted many efficacy or effectiveness studies focusing on cultural, gender, or disability variables. Gathering more research data on these important variables is a challenge for the future.

MULTICULTURAL KEY TERMS

Acculturation (aka ethnocultural orientation)

ADDRESSING

Affirmative therapy

Amok

Assimilated

Bicultural

Collectivist

Color blind phenomenon

Cultural adaptation

Cultural awareness

Cultural knowledge

Culture

Culture bound syndromes

Culture-specific expertise

Drapetomania

Dynamic sizing

Dysaesthesia

Ethnic matching

Ethnic-specific services

Individualist

Language matching

Marginal

Multicultural competencies

Multicultural counseling

Multiculturalism

Pan-traditional

Scientific mindedness

Spirituality

Stereotype

Susto

The melting pot

Traditional

What's good about you?

White privilege

Windigo

RECOMMENDED READINGS AND RESOURCES

The following resources may help you explore multicultural theory and therapy in greater depth.

MULTICULTURAL JOURNALS

Cultural Diversity and Ethnic Minority Psychology
Journal of Cross Cultural Psychology
Journal of Gay and Lesbian Psychotherapy

Journal of Gay and Lesbian Mental Health
Journal of Multicultural Counseling

READINGS ON MULTICULTURAL THEORY AND THERAPY

Adler, L. L., & Mukherji, B. R. (1995). *Spirit versus scalpel: Traditional healing and modern psychotherapy*. Westport, CT: Bergin & Garvey.

Arredondo, P., & Perez, P. (2006). Historical perspectives on the multicultural guidelines and contemporary applications. *Professional Psychology: Research and Practice, 37*(1), 1–5.

Paniagua, F. (2001). *Diagnosis in a multicultural context: A casebook for mental health professionals*. London, England: Sage.

Pedersen, P. B., Draguns, J. G., Lonner, W. J., & Trimble, J. E. (2008). *Counseling across cultures* (6th ed.). Thousand Oaks, CA: Sage.

Smith, T. B., Constantine, M. G., Dunn, T. W., Dinehart, J. M., & Montoya, J. A. (2006). Multicultural education in the mental health professions: A meta-analytic review. *Journal of Counseling Psychology, 53*(1), 132–145.

Sparks, E. E., & Park, A. H. (Eds.). (2002). *The integration of feminism and multiculturalism: Ethical dilemmas at the border*. Washington, DC: American Psychological Association.

Sue, D. W., & Sue, D. (2008). *Counseling the culturally diverse: Theory and practice* (4th ed.). Hoboken, NJ: John Wiley & Sons.

Sue, S. (1999). Science, ethnicity, and bias: Where have we gone wrong? *American Psychologist, 54*, 1070–1077.

Vontress, C. E., Johnson, J. A., & Epp, L. R. (1999). *Cross-cultural counseling: A casebook*. Alexandria, VA: American Counseling Association.

TRAINING ORGANIZATIONS AND WEBSITES

Association for Multicultural Counseling and Development (AMCD; www.amcdaca.org/amcd/default.cfm)

Society for the Study of Ethnic Minority Issues (www.division45.org/)

VIDEOS/DVDs

Comas-Diaz, L. (1994). *Ethnocultural psychotherapy* [Videotape]. Washington, DC: American Psychological Association.

Harris, J. (2006). *Multicultural counseling and psychotherapy* [DVD]. North Amherst, MA: Microtraining Associates.

Vasquez, M.J.T. (2010). *Multicultural therapy over time* [DVD]. Washington, DC: American Psychological Association.

GOING FARTHER AND DEEPER

Additional multicultural counseling and psychotherapy resources are available at johnsommersflanagan .com.

CHAPTER 14

Integrative and Evidence-Based New Generation Therapies

THIS CHAPTER

- Reviews the key figures and historical factors contributing to the development and evolution of eclectic and integrationist therapy approaches
- Outlines and describes models of theoretical integration
- Describes, discusses, and articulates the evidence-based status of modern eclectic and integrationist therapy approaches, including
  - Multimodal therapy
  - Eye-movement desensitization reprocessing (EMDR)
  - Emotion-focused therapy (EFT)
  - Dialectical behavior therapy (DBT)
  - Interpersonal psychotherapy (IPT)
  - Acceptance and commitment therapy (ACT)
  - The transtheoretical model
- Offers resources for further study

The future is always connected to the past... through a road we call the present. This chapter briefly examines motivations, patterns, and conceptual organizations from the past. This look at the past will bring us to the present emphasis in counseling and psychotherapy on eclectic or integrational approaches and we will examine five new generation psychotherapy systems and an overarching change model. Each of these systems is multitheoretical, practical, empirically based... and represents a piece of the counseling and psychotherapy future.

ONE THEORY OR MANY?

It should be obvious at this point in this text that within the helping professions, we can't agree about much. There are typically as many disagreements as there are agreements over how to best work with clients—even among very intelligent and skilled people. This continual disagreement leads us to wonder: Why is there such vast theoretical and practical diversity in counseling and psychotherapy approaches? After all, some authors have reported more than 450 different counseling and psychotherapy theories and approaches (Corsini & Wedding, 2000).

We have two main explanations for the vast theoretical and practical diversity in counseling and psychotherapy: individuality/cultural specificity and human conflict.

Individuality/Cultural Specificity

Adler captured this concept well by using *Individual Psychology* as the name for his particular brand of psychological theory and therapy. Adler emphasized that every child born into a family creates a new and different family.

The fact that every perspective is unique is a fascinating part of the psychology of individual differences. We're like snowflakes; even identical twins experience the world differently. As a consequence, how could we expect uniformity in counseling and psychotherapy theory and practice? Although many theorists, like Sullivan (1953) and Glasser (1998), emphasized universality, there's no way to completely reconcile universality with individuality. Integrational and eclectic approaches to therapy allow therapists to address each client as a unique being.

As feminists and multiculturalists emphasize, sex, race, ethnicity, social class, sexual orientation, religion, and many other factors distinguish individuals from one another. These gender and multiculturally specific factors constitute additional variables that counseling and psychotherapy theories must address.

Imagine the ways you might explain the potential benefits of psychotherapy to a Wyoming cattle rancher. Then imagine doing the same for Laotian refugees or American Indians. Considering these divergent perspectives gives us a glimpse of why having a single psychological system to explain everything might break down. Values imbedded within different cultural and subcultural perspectives will always influence whether contemporary therapy is viewed as a valuable service, witchcraft, hocus-pocus, a waste of time, a growth opportunity, or a choice of the desperate. Integrational and

eclectic therapy approaches have a better chance of addressing the range of cultural backgrounds values, and needs in the real world.

Human Conflict

Thus far in this book, we've reviewed 12 relatively distinct theoretical approaches to counseling and psychotherapy. Adherents to the various theoretical perspectives frequently debate and criticize one another. Practitioners have strong feelings of loyalty to one's perspectives and equally strong doubt about others.

Our friends in the conflict management field are quick to point out that conflict shouldn't be avoided because it can lead to positive transformations. Certainly, when it comes to the history, evolution, and diversity of counseling and psychotherapy, human conflict has been a good thing. Consider the following:

- In 1896 Freud was ostracized by his colleagues for suggesting that sexual abuse was at the roots of hysteria. Freud later recanted his seduction hypothesis, but in the process he invented a remarkable theory of human personality and psychotherapy.

- In 1911 Adler had the audacity to suggest that women's penis envy had social roots—including systematic discrimination. For that insight, Sigmund Freud and his psychoanalytic cronies sent Adler packing from the Vienna Psychoanalytic Society. Fortunately for everyone, Adler never recanted his view.

- In 1913 Jung and Freud finalized their theoretical divorce. Jung individuated from Freud and continued developing his unique approach to understanding the human psyche. Just think about the richness of theory we would have lost had Jung suppressed his unique thoughts about symbol, archetype, and the collective unconscious.

- In the late 1920s Adler dismissed Frankl from his study group. One would have hoped that Adler, so empathic toward the oppressed and working-class citizens, wouldn't have squelched alternative viewpoints, but history and humans often disappoint. Frankl emerged like a phoenix after World War II championing *meaning* as central in psychotherapy and human development.

- In the 1920s and 1930s Karen Horney wrote forcefully about the neglected feminine perspective in psychoanalysis. Instead of submitting to proper authority, she voiced her views and entered into conflict with her colleagues.

- When, in 1936, he was rebuffed by Freud, Fritz Perls didn't slip away into obscurity. Instead, he emerged with the attitude, "I'll show you—you can't do this to me" and became remarkably influential (F. Perls, 1969b, p. 57).

- In the 1950s and 1960s there were great discussions and debates between Carl Rogers and B. F. Skinner. These clashes of divergent perspectives stimulated many ensuing debates and publications.

- In the late 1960s and continuing into the present, feminist therapists have reshaped theories and techniques that would have otherwise continued to reinforce a male-as-normative status quo in psychotherapy.

- In the 1970s staunch behaviorists, including Joseph Wolpe, threatened to exile cognitivists such as Beck, Goldfried, Meichenbaum, and Mahoney from behavior therapy. This brush with exile proved fruitful as a new journal, *Cognitive Therapy and Research*, was born.

- As we see later in this chapter, in the 1990s Francine Shapiro's Eye Movement Desensitization Reprocessing (EMDR), received sharp criticism. Fortunately, instead of shying away from empirical scrutiny, Shapiro continued to work toward evaluating and validating her treatment approach.

There have been many other examples of productive conflict in counseling and psychotherapy theory and practice. These conflicts have undoubtedly contributed to the depth and breadth of theories and approaches available today. We take solace in the fact that Adler, Jung, Frankl, Horney, Perls, Mahoney, Meichenbaum, Shapiro, and many others did not go quietly into the night or lose their voices. Instead, the history of psychotherapeutic theory is peppered with examples of how rejection serves as a great motivator. We hope the outcomes of these conflicts will cause you to think positively about future arguments you'll be having with your classmates, professors, and eventual colleagues.

QUESTIONS FOR REFLECTION

Is conflict inevitable? Would we have attained the theoretical diversity and sophistication we now have in counseling and psychotherapy without intense arguments, debates, division, and conflict?

PSYCHOTHERAPY INTEGRATION: HISTORICAL AND THEORETICAL TRENDS

Overall, there are four major options open to ethical, theory-based counseling and psychotherapy:

1. Ideological purity
2. Theoretical integration
3. Focus on common factors
4. Technical eclecticism

It's no wonder that when dealing with so many theoretical and therapeutic alternatives, theorists, therapists, and researchers have scattered into different groups, seeking the security of an overarching explanation to hang on to. Perhaps what we all long for is a set of principles to tell us exactly what to say and do with every client. This is a good rationale for picking a single theory and learning how to apply it very well.

Ideological Purity

Historically, most therapists were ideological purists. There's great advantage in studying and learning one theoretical approach to therapy and applying it ethically and competently. **Ideological purity** emphasizes depth over breadth. It's appealing in a practical sense; it allows you to become a master of one approach, rather than a mediocre jack-of-all-trades. It can ease the ambiguity inherent in practicing therapy.

However, when taken to an extreme, ideological purity can turn into dogmatism. As Freud's behaviors illustrated, one can have a damaging lack of openness toward alternative ways of thinking and practicing. The underlying message of the ideological dogmatist is this: I've found my theoretical orientation. I live by its tenets and treat it as sacred and unalterably true . . . for everyone.

Even in today's diverse world, many professionals are ideological purists—they practice one form of therapy and practice it well. Judith Beck's description of why she's a cognitive therapist (see Chapter 8) is an excellent example of ideological purity (but not dogmatism).

Theoretical Integration

Theoretical integration involves combining of two or more theoretical approaches to maximize therapeutic effectiveness. Historically, most theoretical integrations involved integrating psychoanalytic and behavior therapies.

In 1950 Dollard and Miller published *Personality and Psychotherapy: An Analysis in Terms of Learning, Thinking, and Culture*. This book was an impressive effort at integrating psychoanalytic and behavioral principles. Dollard and Miller were ahead of their time; their work actually preceded the development of specific, applied behavior therapy techniques.

During the ensuing 20 to 25 years, only a few select theorists discussed theoretical integration (Alexander, 1963; London, 1964). The next major effort at integration was Wachtel's (1977) publication of *Psychoanalysis and Behavior Therapy: Toward an Integration*.

Contemporary theoretical integration efforts don't focus exclusively on integrating behavioral and psychoanalytic approaches. Instead, as described later, theorist-therapist-researchers are integrating two or more nonpsychoanalytic approaches in an effort to facilitate treatment process and outcome.

Common Factors

In Chapter 1 we discussed recent developments in the **common factors** approach to counseling and psychotherapy. Early writings on common factors began to appear in the literature in the 1930s (Rosenzweig, 1936). Somewhat later, Alexander and French (1946) articulated their concept of **corrective emotional experience**. This concept is potentially inclusive of alternative theoretical perspectives:

> In all forms of . . . psychotherapy, the basic therapeutic principle is the same: To re-expose the patient, under more favorable circumstances, to emotional situations which he could not handle in the past. The patient, in order to be helped, must undergo a corrective emotional experience suitable to repair the traumatic influence of previous experiences. (p. 66)

Over the years many others have conceptualized and articulated common therapy principles or factors. Central among these principles is Rogers's *certain type of relationship* as discussed in Chapter 6. Currently, many theorists integrate Rogers's concepts of unconditional positive regard, congruence, and accurate empathy into their therapeutic approaches.

QUESTIONS FOR REFLECTION

Can you recast Alexander and French's corrective emotional experience in other theoretical language? For example, could you describe Mary Cover Jones's work with Little Peter as a corrective emotional experience?

Jerome Frank (1961, 1973; J. D. Frank & J. B. Frank, 1991) developed a comprehensive common factors model of psychotherapy. He stated:

> All psychotherapeutic methods are elaborations and variations of age-old procedures of psychological healing. These include confession, atonement and absolutions, encouragement, positive and negative reinforcements, modeling, and promulgation of a particular set of values. These methods become embedded in theories as to the causes and cures of various conditions which often become highly elaborated. (Frank, 1985, pp. 49–50)

Frank's common factors model was developed from his study of historical and intercultural sources (1961). It includes several components that continue to be relevant to practicing therapists.

The Demoralization Hypothesis

Frank emphasized that not only are there common factors or components of effective therapy, but people who come for therapy are also experiencing a common form of distress. He refers to this common distress as **the demoralization hypothesis**:

> Demoralization occurs when, because of lack of certain skills or confusion of goals, an individual becomes persistently unable to master situations which both the individual and others expect him or her to handle or when the individual experiences continued distress which he or she cannot adequately explain or alleviate. Demoralization may be summed up as a feeling of subjective incompetence, coupled with distress. (Frank, 1985, p. 56)

There's evidence supporting the existence of demoralization among many therapy clients (J. D. Frank & J. B. Frank, 1996). Frank identifies several demoralization symptoms, such as low self-esteem, anxiety, sadness, and hopelessness. These are often the initial target of most therapies.

Shared Therapeutic Components

Frank defined the following shared components of effective therapy.

- *An emotionally charged, confiding relationship with a helping person.* This component has been articulated by many theorists and is supported by empirical research (Duncan, Miller, Wampold, & Hubble, 2010; Elliott & Zucconi, 2006; J. C. Norcross & Lambert, 2011).

- *A healing setting.* A healing setting includes two functional parts. First, the setting elevates the therapist's prestige as a healer or helper. Second, the setting provides a sense of safety.

- *A rationale, conceptual scheme, or myth.* Clients need a plausible explanation for their symptoms and for the treatment approach to be used.

- *A ritual.* Clients (and therapists) need a process or ritual they both believe will bring about a cure or improved functioning.

Frank used the terms *myth* and *ritual* to convey universal aspects of all psychotherapeutic approaches across cultures. The content of specific myths and rituals doesn't necessarily have healing properties. Instead, myths and rituals function specifically to combat demoralization:

> All therapeutic myths and rituals, irrespective of differences in specific content, have in common functions that combat demoralization by strengthening the therapeutic relationship, inspiring expectations of help, providing new learning experiences, arousing the patient emotionally, enhancing the sense of mastery or self-efficacy, and affording opportunities for rehearsal and practice. (Frank, 1985, p. 61)

QUESTIONS FOR REFLECTION

Turn to Chapter 1 and review Lambert's common therapeutic factors based on his analysis of empirical outcomes research. How do Lambert's common factors match up with Frank's formulations?

Technical Eclecticism

In opposition to ideological purism, some professionals, like the boss described in Putting it in Practice 14.1, avoid singular theoretical commitments. These therapists choose one technique for one client and another for a different client and even two theoretically divergent techniques for a single client without much concern for overall theoretical compatibility. Their selection of a particular therapy technique is usually based on one of three factors: (1) empirical research, (2) what's practical for the situation, or (3) clinical intuition. In common parlance, this has been referred to as an eclectic orientation. In a more disparaging description, one of our supervisors used to call it "flying by the seat of your pants."

Eclecticism has been lauded and criticized over the years. Theoretical orientation studies nearly always show that an eclectic or integrative orientation is most common for every category of mental health therapist (clinical and counseling psychologists, counselors, social workers, and psychiatrists; Bechtoldt, Norcross, Wyckoff, Pokrywa, & Campbell, 2001; Norcross, Karg, & Prochaska, 1997).

This finding is somewhat surprising to those trained when choosing a single theoretical orientation was common. Back then, being eclectic was considered bad form. For example, in 1970 Eysenck referred to eclecticism as a "mish-mash of theories, a hugger-mugger of procedures, a gallimaufry of therapies" (p. 145). Of course, it's ironic that Eysenck said this because in his infamous 1952 psychotherapy efficacy review he identified 7,293 cases treated by eclectic means with a 64% "cure" or recovery rate. Perhaps what's most interesting in Eysenck's original review is that eclectic psychotherapy treatment was evaluated nearly 10 times as often as were other approaches, suggesting this "hugger-mugger of procedures" was remarkably common long before it was overtly fashionable.

Good and Bad Eclecticism

More recently, there has been a distinction made between "bad" (seat-of-the-pants) eclecticism and "good" (empirical and/or planful) eclecticism. Similar to Eysenck's criticisms, Lazarus, Beutler, and

Norcross (1992) commented on therapy approaches blended together in "an arbitrary, subjective, if not capricious manner" (p. 11). When one chooses therapy techniques in a whimsical, unreasoned, or impulsive manner, it's called **syncretism** (Lazarus et al., 1992, p. 12). As one of our colleagues who thinks he's funny says, "Sometimes counselors mix up the words eclectic and electric—they think they can just do whatever turns them on" (Richardson, personal communication, November 2002). In contrast, **technical eclecticism** is positively defined as "[s]electing what appears to be best in various doctrines, methods, or styles" (Lazarus et al., 1992, p. 11).

Surprisingly, behavioral theory and therapy may be the most flexible of all theoretical orientations. Behaviorists contend they practice therapy based on scientific research and observable processes. Their interest isn't in a static theory, but in what has been tested in the laboratory and demonstrated as effective in the real world. This makes behaviorists naturally eclectic. Consequently, it's not surprising that initial movements toward technical eclecticism came from the behavioral camp.

The Who-How-Whom Question

In 1969 Gordon Paul posed the following question to his behavioral colleagues: "What treatment, by whom, is most effective for this individual with that specific problem, under which set of circumstances, and how does it come about?" (Paul, 1969, p. 44). This question, sometimes referred to as **the who-how-whom question**, provides a solid rationale for technical eclecticism. It's consistent with matching specific therapy approaches with specific clients (and specific problems)—a goal that's openly endorsed by eclectic therapists. This approach is also consistent in principle with the medical model and the proliferation of psychiatric diagnosis and empirically supported treatment procedures. A main purpose of the *Diagnostic and Statistical Manual of Mental Disorders* (*DSM*) is to identify specific mental disorders entities that are best ameliorated through the application of specific (often pharmacological) treatments.

Eclectic approaches to therapy have been popular for at least four decades. Despite Eysenck's

PUTTING IT IN PRACTICE 14.1

Eclecticism Requires Expertise in Multiple Domains

A colleague of ours who worked as a rehabilitation counselor told us that in her first job interview, she was asked if she had a single theoretical orientation or if she was eclectic. The expected answer was eclectic. She later discovered new boss believed adherence to a single theory was a sign of intellectual weakness and applied laziness. He insisted that his counselors display person-centered attributes, be comfortable with cognitive-behavioral strategies, be aware of and sensitive to feminist and multicultural theory, and be well versed in many career and human development theories and assessment strategies. He also insisted on a well-articulated treatment rationale and encouraged counselors to pay attention to what worked and why. This wasn't an office for the theoretically faint of heart. In this setting, eclectic meant "you'd better know quite a bit about quite a lot and pay attention to what works."

admonitions, approximately 50% of clinical psychologists identified themselves as eclectic in 1970 (Garfield & Kurtz, 1975). About 5 years later, 64% of clinical psychologists claimed to be eclectic (Garfield & Kurtz, 1977). More recent surveys conducted with a broader range of mental health professionals indicate that between 30% and 70% of all professionals label themselves eclectic (Bechtoldt et al., 2001; Norcross et al., 1997).

THE PRACTICE OF ECLECTIC AND NEW GENERATION INTEGRATIVE THERAPIES

This section provides an overview of Arnold Lazarus's technical eclecticism, five exciting contemporary counseling and psychotherapy approaches, and an overarching model for understanding change. As a group, we refer to the five newer, integrative approaches as **new generation therapies**. The two behaviorally oriented of these therapies, DBT and ACT, have been described as

third wave (Hayes, 2004), but, following Spiegler and Guevremont (2010), it seems best to describe these as generational approaches. Each of these approaches combines two or more theories, has empirical support, and is garnering a large following of mental health professionals.

Multimodal Therapy: The Technical Eclecticism of Arnold Lazarus

As an example of an old-style eclecticism that many practitioners still find useful, we start our look at specific eclectic and integrative approaches with a review of the technical eclecticism of Arnold Lazarus (2006, 2008). Lazarus has been a prolific and controversial clinician and writer for more than 50 years. He coined the term *technical eclecticism* in 1967, noting the following:

> To attempt a theoretical rapprochement is as futile as trying to picture the edge of the universe. But to read through the vast amount of literature on psychotherapy, *in search of techniques*, can be

clinically enriching and therapeutically rewarding. (Lazarus, 1967, p. 416)

Currently, his position on theoretical integration remains essentially the same. He's not interested in blending theories; as a self-identified behaviorist, he's only interested in practical application of approaches that are helpful to his clients.

Lazarus also has an opinion about why technical eclecticism is preferable to theoretical purity. In 1971, he claimed,

> [T]he most essential ingredients for an effective psychotherapist are *flexibility* and *versatility*. This implies an ability to play many roles and to use many techniques in order to fit the therapy to the needs and idiosyncrasies of each patient. By contrast, therapists with pet theories or specially favored techniques usually manage, in their own minds at least, to fit their patients' problems within the confines of their particular brand of treatment. (p. 33)

Multimodal therapists apply specific techniques and adopt different interpersonal styles to help clients obtain their goals. Multimodal therapists focus on: assessment, technical applications, and therapist interpersonal style.

Assessment

Lazarus described the underlying assumption for his assessment system:

> The multimodal orientation (A. A. Lazarus, 1997) is predicated on the assumption that most psychological problems are multifaceted, multidetermined, and multilayered, and that comprehensive therapy calls for a careful assessment of seven parameters or "modalities." (Lazarus, 2000, p.93)

The seven modalities are listed and described in Table 14.1. At the end of each description there's a question suggested by Lazarus to guide the clinician's thinking about the category (Lazarus, 2008). Lazarus used the acronym **BASIC I.D.** to represent the seven parameters of human functioning.

Assessment and diagnosis involve a thorough evaluation of the BASIC I.D. Subsequently, treatment focuses on alleviating problems occurring within these seven domains.

Technical Applications

Multimodal therapists will use any therapy technique that seems appropriate based on empirical research or a logical or practical rationale. Sometimes multimodal therapists also use their intuition when determining what therapy approach to use (Lazarus, 1997).

Multimodal therapy requires skill in a wide variety of therapeutic interventions. For example, in the glossary of his 1989 book, Lazarus listed 39 principal techniques. Learning these techniques, which range from focusing to behavior rehearsal, is a challenge inherent in being a multimodal therapist.

Therapist Style

Because every client is different, therapists change their style based on each new client. Lazarus (1971) states: "a flexible therapist has no fixed pattern of approaching new patients. He usually perceives what his patient needs and then tries to fit the role" (p. 50). For example, Lazarus criticizes person-centered therapists for not shifting their interpersonal styles based on different client traits: "These person-centered counselors do not ask if individual differences may warrant a confrontational style for some, or point to an austere business-like atmosphere for others . . . or when a sphinx-like guru might be made to order" (Lazarus, 1993, pp. 404–405).

Lazarus refers to shifting a therapeutic style as becoming an **authentic chameleon**. Some interpersonal variables therapists should consider varying depending on clients' needs, preferences, or expectations include:

- Level of formality or informality.

- Amount of personal disclosure.

- How much or how often a new topic of conversation is initiated.

- Level of directiveness.

Table 14.1 The BASIC I.D.

Area of functioning	Description
Behavior	This category includes observable and measurable behaviors. Therapists gather information about (a) frequent actions, (b) habits, and (c) frequent behavioral reactions. Examples: smoking, regular aerobic exercise (or lack thereof), hair pulling, nail biting, yelling. Question: What behaviors does the client want to increase or decrease?
Affective responses	This category includes emotions and moods. Therapists gather information about emotions that clients find problematic or helpful. Examples: anger, sadness, anxiety, guilt. Question: What affective reactions are proving disturbing?
Sensations	This category includes taste, touch, smell, vision, and hearing. Therapists are interested in the client's pleasant or unpleasant sensations. Examples: pain, dizziness, palpitations, depersonalization. Question: What are the client's precise sensory pains and pleasures?
Imagery	This category includes mental pictures or visualization. Therapists ask clients about the images they see and experience during stress or distress and during functional or dysfunctional moments. Examples: helpful or success images that occur before and during a stressful event and unhelpful, disturbing, or failure images. Question: What intrusive images need to be replaced by positive visualizations?
Cognition	This category includes nonvisual cognitions. Therapists gather information about what clients think or say to themselves when functioning well and when functioning poorly. Examples: personal values, rational and irrational thoughts, cognitive distortions, maladaptive automatic thoughts. Question: What dysfunctional beliefs and faulty cognitions are in need of restructuring?
Interpersonal relationships	This category includes all human interactions. Therapists gather information about the nature, quality, and quantity of satisfying and dissatisfying interpersonal relationships. Examples: friendships, romantic relationships, primary family relationships, family of origin relationships, and work relationships. Question: Who are the significant others and what essential processes are at play vis-à-vis his or her interpersonal network?
Drugs and biology	This category includes all physical or biological areas, including substance use. Therapists gather information about the client's eating, sleeping, and activity levels as well as medications and drug use. Examples: physical exam information, amount of alcohol and drug use. Question: What are the important facts about the client's drug use (recreational or prescribed) and his or her general medical-biological well-being?

Source: Questions are from Lazarus (2000, pp. 93–94).

- Level of supportiveness.
- Level of reflectiveness. (Lazarus, 1993)

One method for determining what interpersonal style to adopt with new clients is to obtain specific assessment data prior to the initial meeting. Lazarus recommends using the *Multimodal Life History Inventory*, which includes questions pertaining to therapy expectations (A. A. Lazarus & C. N. Lazarus, 1991). If a client writes, "I hope therapy is like a mirror so I can start understanding myself better," a more person-centered approach may be desirable.

QUESTIONS FOR REFLECTION

What interpersonal style variables might you vary depending on the client you're seeing? How will you decide how to approach a given client? What factors will you consider when deciding your interpersonal approach?

Determining the best therapeutic style is often a judgment call you have to make on the spot. Lazarus (1993) shares a story in which he sensed that a particular client (a 39-year-old woman) would respond well to humor and sarcasm:

> When she first entered my office, she looked me up and down and asked, "Why do you have graves outside your office?" In perfect Rogerian style I said, "I have graves outside my office?" "Look out the window dummy!" she replied. I went to my office window and looked out. Two new flower beds had been installed alongside the front walk on the grass. It was early spring and the shoots had yet to emerge from the soil. "Well, since you ask," I said, "I have just buried one of my clinical failures in the one grave and the other is earmarked for you ... if you turn out to be an uncooperative client." The twinkle in her eye told me that my response was an appropriate one. (p. 406)

Although Lazarus's humor apparently worked, if used with the wrong client at the wrong time (you can imagine the situation), Lazarus's joke might have had a less favorable impact. Using humor and sarcasm and acting like an authentic chameleon in therapy can be risky. However, learning to modify your style with clients is a skill that may well be worth cultivating—with reasonable caution.

Eye Movement Desensitization and Reprocessing

Eye Movement Desensitization and Reprocessing (EMDR) is an evidence-based treatment for trauma in adults and children. It was developed by Francine Shapiro (1989); it has an interesting history and unique treatment protocol.

EMDR Development

Shapiro discovered EMDR while exploring her own personal trauma experience and disturbing memories. In 1979, while working on her doctorate in English literature at New York University, she was diagnosed with cancer. Rather than continuing with her doctoral work in English literature, she left New York to study clinical psychology.

Francine Shapiro

Years later, in 1987, as Shapiro was walking through a park, she felt distress stemming from past memories. After focusing on these memories for a few minutes she noticed that her disturbing thoughts were gone. When she brought them back into her mind, she found these thoughts had lost much of their disturbing quality. She then tried to recreate what she had just experienced and discovered that her eyes were moving back and forth (horizontally) very rapidly. Later, she found that when she intentionally focused on a trauma-related memory and simultaneously moved her eyes back and forth, the memory became less distressing in what appeared to be a desensitization process. As she continued exploring eye movements and desensitization, she recognized that the eye movements alone weren't adequate for therapeutic benefits and so she added additional dimensions to her treatment protocol.

Initially, Shapiro labeled her treatment approach Eye Movement Desensitization (EMD; Shapiro, 1989). There was an emphasis on bilateral eye movements as a means for trauma desensitization. However, she later renamed her approach EMDR, primarily to capture the more complex information processing that she believed was related to its efficacy (Shapiro, 1995). Although other writers have classified EMDR as a behavior therapy and an exposure therapy, Shapiro considers EMDR an integrative treatment (and we agree). It includes principles from the following theoretical perspectives:

- *Psychodynamic.* There's a focus on past traumatic events.

- *Behavioral.* Consistent with exposure therapy, there's a focus on present fear/anxiety and specific stimuli.

- *Cognitive*. Clients are asked to identify negative and positive beliefs about the self; there is also utilization or activation of an information-processing model.

- *Person-centered*. EMDR therapists often follow the client's lead rather than always dictating the course or direction of therapy.

- *Physiological or body-centered*. There's a focus on physical-affective links associated with trauma experiences.

In the early years of its development and application, EMDR was viewed as controversial, with some academics and professionals highly critical of EMDR. This may have been because of Shapiro's early claims that EMDR could have a positive effect in a single session. Interestingly, Prochaska and Norcross (2003) speculated that gender bias from the male-dominated professions of psychology and psychiatry may have contributed to negative critiques of Shapiro's work. Whatever the reasons, even the mention of EMDR within some circles would stimulate unprofessional derisive reactions. Some authors even went so far as to classify it as a "power therapy" (which, by the way, is an insult in psychotherapy-speak; Figley, 1997). The following quotation captures the disrespectful tone sometimes employed by EMDR critics:

> The most widely known and studied of the Power Therapies is EMDR. This technique involves the waving of fingers in front of a patient's face, or alternative maneuvers such as finger snapping, to alter neural connections between affect, cognition and memory. Although the face validity of this technique is questionable and its theoretical explanation approaches the limits of neurobabble... EMDR has been taught to over 23,000 clinicians worldwide in the short span of eight years. Training in EMDR now requires a "Level II" workshop for certification in the eye movement method... despite several studies finding that eye movements add nothing to treatment outcome. (Rosen, Lohr, McNally, & Herbert, 2000, pp. 134–135)

In response to her critics, Shapiro has consistently provided clarifying information and pointed to empirical research supporting EMDR as a valid treatment approach. Below is a sample of Shapiro's effort to clarify misconceptions associated with EMDR:

> Contrary to a common misconception, EMDR, as it is currently practiced, is not a simple, by-the-book procedure dominated by the use of repeated eye movements (despite its name), but rather an integrated form of therapy incorporating aspects of many traditional psychological orientations... and one that makes use of a variety of bilateral stimuli besides eye movements. The inaugural study... did indeed stress directed eye movements as the primary component of the therapy. This incorrect and unfortunate interpretation of the method can be explained by the author's concentration on the concrete actions in which she was engaging during therapy, rather than on the attendant complexity of the methodology actually employed and the underlying processes thought to be engendered by it. (F. Shapiro, 1999, p. 37)

Although some writers continue to discount or minimize EMDR as a clinical procedure (Lohr, 2011; Lohr, Olatunji, Parker, & DeMaio, 2005), research evidence supporting EMDR efficacy is quite substantial. We've obtained EMDR training ourselves and found that it's a rather sophisticated and structured approach that has a strong cognitive treatment component. We've also found it quite helpful in addressing and reducing troubling trauma symptoms in adults and adolescents.

EMDR Protocol
The standard EMDR protocol includes eight basic phases. These phases are very briefly described below:

1. *History*: Assessment of client readiness and initial treatment planning.

2. *Preparation*: Making sure clients have skills for coping with stress that might be generated from the treatment process.

3. *Assessment*: A target memory is identified. A current negative belief about the self-linked to the target memory is identified and rated, along with a hoped for positive belief. Associated emotional and physical characteristics are articulated.

4. *Desensitization*: Bilateral stimulation (eye-movements, tapping, or audio stimulation) ensues. Therapist explains and initiates this process, but then follows the clients' experiencing.

5. *Installation*: Bilateral stimulation is repeated linking the positive belief to the memory.

6. *Body scan*: There is a review of clients' physical/body sensations. Negative sensations are processed through bilateral stimulation.

7. *Closure*: The client is asked to keep a journal of experiences during the upcoming week and is reminded of the self-calming strategies used in Stage 2.

8. *Reevaluation*: When clients return for the next session a reevaluation of status and progress is conducted.

Detailed information regarding EMDR practice can be obtained from Shapiro's many works in the area (Shapiro, 1989, 1995, 2001, 2002). Additionally, EMDR training is available worldwide (see www.emdr.com).

The Evidence Base for EMDR

APA's Division 12 lists EMDR as a well-established treatment for noncombat PTSD. EMDR is also endorsed or listed as an empirically supported treatment by the American Psychiatric Association, the Department of Veterans Affairs and Department of Defense, the California Evidence-Based Clearinghouse for Child Welfare, and several other organizations.

Highlights of recent research include the following:

- Davidson and Parker (2001) reported a meta-analysis of 34 studies. The results indicated that EMDR has a significantly positive effect compared with no treatment and an equivalent

effect compared with alternative treatments. They noted that the eye-movements themselves showed no additive effects over the desensitization process without eye-movements.

- In a meta-analysis of EMDR versus exposure therapy versus relaxation training, EMDR and relaxation training were reported as producing equivalent results. Although EMDR and exposure treatment were equal in terms of attrition, worsening of symptoms, and reduction of numbing and hyperarousal symptoms, exposure therapy was faster at reducing avoidance symptoms, produced larger reductions in avoidance and trauma reexperiencing, and resulted in resolution of PTSD diagnosis at a higher rate (Taylor et al., 2003).

- A French review of EMDR versus CBT for a range of problems found that EMDR and CBT were equal with regard to PTSD outcomes, but CBT was superior for treating phobias and panic disorder (Bériault & Larivée, 2005).

- In seven direct comparisons between EMDR and trauma-focused CBT (TF-CBT) the two treatment procedures were determined equally efficacious (Seidler & Wagner, 2006).

- In a single study comparing 88 adults with trauma who were randomly assigned to EMDR versus fluoxetine (Prozac) versus pill placebo conditions, the researchers found EMDR was more efficacious than the medication. They concluded that EMDR produced: "substantial and sustained reduction of PTSD and depression in most victims of adult-onset trauma" (van der Kolk et al., 2007, p. 37).

- In a meta-analysis of seven studies that focused on EMDR for children who had experienced trauma, an effect size (versus no treatment) of $d = .56$ (moderate effects) was reported. EMDR was also slightly superior to CBT, $d = .25$ (small effect size; Rodenburg, Benjamin, de Roos, Meijer, & Stams, 2009).

Despite these rather substantial and positive empirical reports, criticism of EMDR continues, albeit less intensely (Lohr, 2011; Lohr et al., 2005). For example, Lohr (2011) recently wrote:

> [R]esearch demonstrated that the modest efficacy of eye movement desensitization and reprocessing (EMDR) was unrelated to the eye movement procedure . . . and the reprocessing procedure. (p. 101)

Although scrutiny of all therapeutic procedures is necessary, lingering criticism and questioning of the validity of EMDR seems excessive given the breadth and depth of its empirical support. We've experienced this ourselves at workshops; also a reviewer of the first edition of this text indicated she or he would not use the text because EMDR was included as a reasonable treatment approach. Our conclusion about this is to say that, of course, EMDR is not always efficacious and is not a panacea . . . but that research supports its efficacy for trauma treatment in particular. There is also accumulating evidence suggesting it may be effective in the treatment of other mental health problems.

As with many treatments, it has been difficult to definitively pinpoint why EMDR works. Some contend it's simply an alternative imaginal desensitization protocol. The eye-movements and other bilateral stimulation procedures may or may not add to the other portions of the treatment. There is a strong cognitive component focusing on client trauma-related beliefs. Positive expectations and a positive focus are also present. The process may (or may not) be dependent upon memory consolidation and reconsolidation.

Shapiro has developed a theoretical explanation focusing on information processing (Adaptive Information Processing). She believes that trauma produces disturbing information that must be cognitively or neurologically processed. The overwhelming quantity and/or quality of the information causes information processing to be disconnected from more adaptive ideas or information that ordinarily might be integrated into the negative event or events. The application of EMDR may help clients reconnect trauma memories with more adaptive memories and beliefs. Shapiro's explanation is speculative and additional research is needed to further address underlying mechanisms associated with EMDR efficacy.

In recent years EMDR treatment has expanded into problem areas other than PTSD. On the EMDR Institute website (emdr.com) research supporting EMDR as a treatment for phobia, panic, and somatoform disorders is listed and summarized. Additionally, EMDR treatment protocols are available for other problems, including, but not limited to: anxiety, grief and loss, pain, and performance enhancement (Shapiro, 2001, 2002). Additionally, it should be noted that many EMDR practitioners offer pro bono services to trauma victims through the EMDR Humanitarian Assistance Programs (see emdrhap.org). EMDR has been offered to many victims of natural and human-caused trauma in the Balkans, Bosnia, Haiti, Indonesia, Japan, Northern Ireland, Oklahoma City, New York City, San Salvador, and many other locales (see Putting it in Practice 14.2 for a story of two therapists who combine EMDR and DBT to address the needs of a traumatized population).

Interpersonal Psychotherapy

Interpersonal psychotherapy (IPT) is a short-term and focal approach to treating depression. It emerged quickly and established itself as an efficacious therapy for depression. IPT was developed in the 1970s by the late Gerald Klerman of Harvard University and a group of associates from Yale University. It was empirically validated in the 1980s.

IPT Development

Interpersonal psychotherapy has its roots in the interpersonal psychiatry of Harry Stack Sullivan and the attachment theories of John Bowlby and Mary Ainsworth (Ainsworth, 1969; Bowlby, 1977; Sullivan, 1953). It also employs cognitive and behavioral interventions. It's particularly unique in that it was designed, not as a general psychotherapeutic approach, but as a specific treatment for depression.

PUTTING IT IN PRACTICE 14.2

Two Counselors Integrate Two Integrational Theories—Together

This commentary was co-written by Laura M. Schmuldt, PhD, and Troyann I. Gentile, PhD, both from Lindsey Wilson College in Columbia, Kentucky.

Selecting a theory of counseling is an endeavor that makes most graduate students cringe. It has been compared to enrolling in medical school only to learn that you're expected to develop your own theory of surgery: overwhelming and frankly, frightening. Many students find themselves surprised by the self-exploration required in the process.

We are two counselor educators who believe that development of theory demands self-reflection and exploration of research—but these experiences cannot exist in a vacuum. Our theoretical development (and it's always a work in progress!) was enhanced and finessed through our conversations—often informal and meandering—and our shared commitment to a very unique project. Our story will be described exclusively in the words of "us" and "we" and "our"; for although we each bring individual values, ideas, and knowledge to the equation, we've found our professional collaboration is inseparable from our work within a very specific set of circumstances.

Through amazing chance and circumstance, we became involved in a project working with the adult survivors of the Romanian orphanages. The collective histories of these individuals, now a cohort of more than 170,000, ranging in age from 18 to 34, are notoriously well-documented.

In 1989, shortly after the "fall" of communism in Romania, tragic images of undernourished children, tied to steel cribs, rhythmically banging their heads against the walls, locked in dimly lit rooms and supervised by custodial staff, attracted international attention. Though conditions have improved overall, a generation of "lost children"—adult survivors of the orphanages—remains. Having been taught nothing about money, work ethic, how to find a job or a place to live, paying bills, manners or even simple hygiene, many cannot fend for themselves and become jobless and homeless on the streets with other adult survivors. These individuals often turn to begging for and stealing food, drug addiction, and worst of all, are vulnerable and subject to underground prostitution and human trafficking.

At this point in the story, you may be wondering: What could possibly be offered to individuals from such dreadful circumstances? This question helped our theoretical foundation evolve. We reasoned that such individuals grew up in the ultimate "invalidating environment," a term coined by Marsha Linehan, creator of Dialectical Behavior Therapy (DBT). An invalidating environment is one that consistently communicates to a person that his or her interpretation of reality is somehow flawed, incorrect, and inaccurate.

As such, it's a challenge for such individuals to trust their own sense of the world and their ability to meet and negotiate challenges (self-invalidation). A sentence from Linehan's work resonated with us: "Given what you've been through, this behavior makes sense." We've grown to believe that validation is perhaps the most important mediator of human relationships. At a minimum, we reasoned, these survivors needed to learn a set of skills—skills for accurately interpreting events and responding to them in a way that won't ultimately create more suffering. In other words, when deeply painful emotions are present, the mind seeks relief. Relief can come about in ways that work in the short-term, but fail in the long term (e.g., drugs, reckless sexual behavior, overeating, over-spending). We continually noticed that mindfulness—quieting the mind and focusing simply on what we were experiencing in the moment—was critical in our interpretation of the adults' behavior and our judgments about the complexities of this unfamiliar culture. As such, DBT became our tool for not simply approaching this population, but for also addressing our personal feelings of burnout (counselors need validation, just like clients).

But what about the very real symptoms of posttraumatic stress disorder (PTSD) experienced by literally every adult survivor we encountered? To grow up in the Romanian orphanages meant experiencing negligence and abuse of an unspeakable, even ghastly, degree. Again, we turned to theory and were intrigued by the clinical efficacy of Eye-Movement Desensitization and Reprocessing (EMDR). We discovered a means of reducing the power of traumatic memories while simultaneously prompting clients to rapidly connect the painful memory to memories that are holistic, resilient, and hopeful. Additionally, EMDR allowed processing of trauma without necessarily describing and discussing the trauma in intricate detail. This aspect of treatment is critically important in that these clients often lack language for describing their experiences.

Our project is in many ways "under construction"—and we believe that this is analogous to the development of one's personal theory of counseling or psychotherapy. We advise you, as we've strived to do, to establish a network of colleagues who thrive on learning about the process of human change and challenge you to grow as a clinician. Through this collaboration we've had opportunities to come together with each other's theoretical paradigms and create inspiration. Further, we encourage you to develop skills as generalists and specialists. Most importantly, perhaps, we challenge you, on a daily basis, to find hope in whatever dire circumstances and clinical difficulties you encounter.

Klerman and colleagues describe the approach in contrast to psychodynamic approaches:

Both interpersonal and psychodynamic approaches are concerned with the whole life span, and both consider early experience and persistent personality patterns important. In understanding human transactions, however, the psychodynamic therapist is concerned with object relations while the interpersonal therapist focuses on interpersonal relations. The psychodynamic therapist listens for the patient's intrapsychic wishes and conflicts; the interpersonal therapist listens for the patient's role expectations and disputes. (Klerman, Weissman, Rounsaville, & Chevron, 1984, p. 18)

Interpersonal psychotherapy is a rarity. It quickly established itself as an effective treatment for depression in adults principally due to positive outcomes achieved in one large scale RCT (Elkin et al., 1989). It focuses on diagnosing and treating the various interpersonal problems associated with depression. These include grief, role disputes, role transitions, and interpersonal deficits. Because it focuses on real interpersonal relationships instead of internalized object relations, it's a step removed from a psychoanalytic treatment, but rooted in and guided by psychodynamic principles (Klerman, Weissman, Rounsaville, & Chevron, 1995; Moreau, Mufson, Weissman, & Klerman, 1991; Weissman, Markowitz, & Klerman, 2000)

Characteristics and Protocol

IPT has the following characteristics:

- It's time-limited.
- It focuses on one or two interpersonal problem areas.
- It focuses on current, rather than past, interpersonal relationships.
- It has an interpersonal, rather than intrapsychic, emphasis.
- It addresses cognitive-behavioral issues but emphasizes these factors only in terms of how they affect important social relationships.
- It recognizes, but does not focus on, personality variables.
- It's based on a medical model in which the client is viewed as having clinical depression, a specific medical disorder for which a specific treatment is most appropriate.

Weissman et al. (2000) describe the underlying conceptual foundation of IPT:

> The idea underlying IPT is simple: psychiatric syndromes such as depression, however multidetermined their causes, usually occur in a social and interpersonal context. A marriage breaks up; a friendship dissolves; children leave home; a job is lost; a loved one dies; a person moves, is promoted, or retires. (p. xi)

IPT focuses on helping clients (a) recognize the relationship between depressive symptoms and interpersonal problems and (b) find ways to deal more effectively with interpersonal problems, thereby alleviating depressive symptoms.

IPT includes three treatment phases. In the first three sessions, a diagnostic evaluation and psychiatric history are conducted and a framework for treatment is established. An interpersonal inventory is also obtained. This inventory reviews the client's current social functioning and interpersonal relationships. It also examines any relationship changes that may have occurred near the time when the depressive symptoms increased.

Consistent with the medical model, during this first phase of treatment the client is assigned the sick role. This strategy may seem foreign to those of us trained in providing psychosocial treatments. Assignment of the sick role includes the giving of a diagnosis (clinical depression) and carries with it two implications: (1) clients may be relieved of overwhelming social obligations, and (2) clients are expected to work in treatment to recover their full functioning. Also during the first phase of treatment, clients are evaluated for possible simultaneous antidepressant medication treatment, educated about the nature of depression, and offered an interpersonal formulation.

The interpersonal formulation involves linking the client's depressive symptoms to one of four possible specific interpersonal situations:

1. *Grief.* Complicated bereavement following the death of a loved one.
2. *Interpersonal role dispute.* Conflicts in an important social relationship (spouse, family member, coworker, or close friend).
3. *Role transition.* A change in life status, including the beginning or end of a relationship, retirement, graduation, medical diagnosis, and so on.
4. *Interpersonal deficit.* When a client lacks social skills that contribute to relationship problems.

During the middle (second) phase of treatment, the therapist applies strategies to address interpersonal problems, as articulated in the interpersonal formulation. IPT strategies are reviewed and described in the interpersonal treatment manual (see Klerman et al., 1984; Weissman et al., 2000). IPT sessions typically begin with the query, "How have things been since we last met?" (Weissman et al., 2000, p. 21). The purpose of this question is to help clients focus on recent interpersonal events and recent mood. The therapist's job is to link these two issues and help clients make plans to address the interpersonal problems fueling their depressive symptoms.

The final treatment phase focuses on recognition and consolidation of treatment gains. Additionally, strategies for facing and coping with future depressive episodes are reviewed.

The Evidence Base for IPT

IPT for depression in adults was initially evaluated in the National Institute of Mental Health (NIMH) Treatment of Depression Collaborative Research Program (Elkin et al., 1989). This study randomly assigned 239 patients with depressive symptoms to an antidepressant medication (imipramine), cognitive therapy, or IPT. This study was tightly controlled and coordinated across three sites. All three treatments outperformed the placebo condition (which included a placebo pill and supportive meetings). Based on Beck Depression Inventory scores, 70% of the IPT patients recovered, as compared to 69% for imipramine, 65% for cognitive therapy, and 51% for placebo. Subsequent studies have shown IPT as efficacious for perinatal depression, women with depressive and PTSD symptoms, and other depressive disorders (Grote et al., 2009; Talbot et al., 2011).

IPT has also been shown to effectively treat depressive symptoms in adolescents (Mufson, Dorta, Moreau, & Weissman, 2004). In one school-based mental health study, IPT for adolescents (IPT-A) significantly reduced depressive symptoms and improved overall functioning as compared with treatment as usual (Mufson et al., 2004). It has also been successfully implemented as a prevention intervention with youth at risk for depression (Young, Mufson, & Davies, 2006; Young, Mufson, & Gallop, 2010).

IPT also shows promise in treating eating disorders. Although it was slower in producing results than cognitive or behavioral treatment, in the long run, IPT produced better outcomes than behavior therapy (Fairburn, 1993; Fairburn, Jones, Peveler, & Hope, 1993).

Interestingly, although most research doesn't demonstrate that antidepressant medications combined with psychotherapy improves outcomes, IPT plus antidepressants have consistently increased positive outcomes (Klerman & Weissman, 1991; M. D. Miller et al., 1998; M. D. Miller et al., 2001). This may be because IPT explicitly embraces the medical model and yet addresses interpersonal symptoms that don't respond well to medication treatments.

Emotion-Focused Therapy

Emotion-focused therapy (formerly process-experiential therapy) was discussed previously in Chapter 5 and illustrated in a case in Chapter 6. EFT has roots in person-centered theory and uses the Gestalt empty chair technique as a means of focusing in on and deepening emotional experiencing and expression (Greenberg, Rice, & Elliott, 1993). EFT is broadly classified as an empirically supported neo-humanistic therapy approach.

EFT Development

Leslie Greenberg

EFT was developed by Leslie Greenberg. Greenberg originally trained as a mechanical and industrial engineer, but was dissatisfied and decided to leave Johannesburg, South Africa and came to York University to obtain his doctorate in counseling psychology. There, he studied with Laura Rice who had trained with Carl Rogers at the Chicago Counseling Center. Subsequently, Greenberg obtained training in Gestalt therapy and also in family therapy at MRI. EFT is a blend of person-centered therapy and Gestalt technique, but Greenberg and his colleagues emphasize that EFT has a person-centered foundation and should fall more into the domain of person-centered therapy than Gestalt therapy (R. Elliott, personal communication, July 15, 2011). Greenberg also was involved in the development of emotion-focused couple therapy (L. S. Greenberg & Johnson, 1988; Johnson & Greenberg, 1985).

Over the past 25-plus years Greenberg and his colleagues have focused on ways in which anxiety, depression, and other disorders include a range of processing blocks or difficulties within the cognitive-affective domain (Elliott & Greenberg, 2002; L. Greenberg, 2006; Paivio & Greenberg, 1995). They provided a succinct general description of EFT rationale and process:

> Markers of unfinished business or lingering negative feelings toward a significant other commonly occur in therapy, and there is agreement across orientations that unresolved anger and sadness are among the generating conditions of anxiety, depression, and a variety of interpersonal problems.... Drawing on Gestalt therapy techniques,... an intervention for resolving such unfinished emotional issues has been devised.... Empty-chair dialogue intervention (ECH), in which the client engages in an imaginary dialogue with the significant other, is designed to access restricted feelings allowing them to run their course and be restructured in the safety of the therapy environment. The process of resolving unfinished business using ECH has been rigorously modeled,... and the model has been empirically verified.... Resolution consists of changed perceptions of self and other so that clients shift from viewing themselves as weak and victimized to a stance of greater self-empowerment and either view the significant other with greater understanding or hold them accountable for harm. (Paivio & Greenberg, 1995, p. 419)

Narrative components of EFT also have been discussed. When clients experience a facilitated empty chair dialogue from a person-centered perspective, they can shift existing personal narratives. Narrative therapists refer to these shifts as unique outcomes or sparkling moments and these experiences—reflected back to clients via person-centered methodology—can open up the possibility

and elaboration of new meaning. Essentially, clients begin to see themselves and others differently. This process was described in an article examining narrative change within an EFT case:

> Thus, unique outcomes—or, as we prefer, innovative moments (or i-moments)—can be defined as all occurrences (thought, acted, and imagined) that are different from the problematic self-narrative and are, in this sense, a representation of client self-change. They are openings to the elaboration of new meanings, challenging the hegemonic role of problematic self-narratives in clients' lives. (Gonçalves et al., 2009, p. 269)

In a successful EFT case, Gonçalves et al. measured these i-moments (aka unique outcomes or sparkling moments) using the Innovative Moments Coding System (IMCS; Goncalves, Matos, & Santos, 2009; Gonçalves, Mendes, Ribeiro, Angus, & Greenberg, 2010). They concluded that a reconceptualization of self and other was essential in producing change in counseling or psychotherapy.

Characteristics and Protocol

An EFT process emphasizes the formation of a relationship based on Rogers's core conditions and then, from the trusting relationship foundation, seeks to explore and resolve the client's cognitive-affective unfinished business. This treatment is much more active than traditional person-centered therapy and relies heavily on the Gestalt empty chair technique to help clients experience and address their emotional issues.

As Goldman and Greenberg (1997) stated, resolution of affective problems is based on the following person-centered theoretical principles:

> Clients are consistently encouraged to identify and symbolize internal experience and bodily felt referents in order to create new meaning. Therapy is seen as facilitating conscious choice and reasoned action based on increased access to and awareness of inner experience and feeling. (pp. 402–403)

After the client-therapist relationship is adequately established (usually this takes at least two sessions), emotion-focused therapists take an active and directive role in helping clients identify areas where they're suffering from unresolved emotions (aka: unfinished business). The therapist provides continuous process facilitation and at "all times, ... tries to make psychological *contact* with and convey a *genuine* understanding of the client's internal experience" (Goldman & Greenberg, 1997, p. 403).

The assessment and case formulation process in EFT involves simultaneously experiencing of and observing for global and specific indicators of affective problem markers. Usually when these markers are identified, they lead directly to a particular form or style of intervention—reflective listening, emotional validation, empty chair dialogue. The affective markers, therapeutic tasks, and desired resolution states for EFT are summarized in Table 14.2.

Within the context of a focused, active, and directive therapeutic style with a special emphasis on empty-chair dialogue and two-chair enactment, EFT remains focused on therapist-client process. The goal of EFT is to help "clients to explore and re-integrate previously disallowed or muted self-information" (Goldman & Greenberg, 1997, p. 409).

Close observations of EFT process has also led to new hypotheses about emotional functioning and emotional transformation. Greenberg and colleagues (2008) stated:

> Empirical evidence also is mounting in support of the importance of transforming emotions by changing one emotion with another emotion, ... and this suggests that a maladaptive emotion state can be effectively transformed by undoing it with the presence of another, more adaptive emotion. (p. 186)

Table 14.2 Affective Markers, Therapeutic Tasks, and Desired Resolution States in Process Experiential Therapy

Affective marker	Therapeutic task	Desired resolution state
The client expresses a problematic reaction through puzzlement about appropriate emotional and behavioral responses to a specific situation.	The therapist uses reflection of content, feeling, and walking within to help the client's primary feelings systematically unfold.	The client obtains a new view of self-in-the-world functioning.
The client has an absent or unclear felt sense of his or her experience.	The therapist uses an experiential focusing technique to help the client obtain a clearer sense of his or her felt experience.	The client is able to symbolize a felt sense and productively process an experience.
The client experiences a self-evaluative split: One aspect of the self is critical toward another aspect of self.	The therapist gently prompts the client toward using a two-chair dialogue.	The client experiences self-acceptance and integration of previously split components of the self.
There is a self-interruptive split in which a part of the client interrupts or constricts an emotional experience.	The therapist gently prompts the client toward using a two-chair enactment.	The client is able to experience self-expression and empowerment.
A lingering unresolved feeling toward a significant other or unfinished business emerges.	The therapist gently prompts the client toward dialoguing with a significant other using an empty-chair technique.	The client is able to either forgive the other or hold the other accountable. The self is affirmed or separated from the other.
The client experiences a heightened sense of vulnerability, shame, or insecurity.	The therapist empathically affirms the client.	The client experiences self-affirmation and feels understood and stronger.

Source: Adapted from Goldman and Greenberg (1997).

EFT: The Evidence Base

Research on EFT continues to accumulate. Highlights of recent and historical research findings include:

- EFT has empirical support for treating depression (Ellison, Greenberg, Goldman, & Angus, 2009; R. N. Goldman, Greenberg, & Angus, 2006; Watson, Gordon, Stermac, Kalogerakos, & Steckley, 2003). It's listed on the Division 12 website as probably efficacious or moderately supported by empirical research.

- EFT also is listed as empirically supported for couple counseling and there's research suggesting its utility as a group therapy modality for reducing recidivism among individuals incarcerated for intimate partner violence (Pascual-Leone, Bierman, Arnold, & Stasiak, 2011).

- EFT has been found superior to psychoeducation in resolving old conflicts (unfinished business) and facilitating forgiveness (L. J. Greenberg, Warwar, & Malcolm, 2008; Malcom & Greenberg, 2000).

Overall, EFT is a promising approach especially for clients who have depressive symptoms linked to unresolved interpersonal relationships. Because EFT can also produce negative outcomes, therapists who are comfortable working with intense emotions and are interested in this therapy modality should seek additional training and supervision.

Dialectical Behavior Therapy

Dialectical behavior therapy (DBT) is one of the most popular new generation behavior therapies. Although it has historically and primarily been applied in the treatment of Borderline Personality Disorder (BPD), more recently it has been applied to other problem areas and clinical populations.

DBT Development

Marsha Linehan and her colleagues at the University of Washington Suicidal Behaviors Research Clinic developed dialectical behavior therapy (DBT) as a specific treatment for women who were exhibiting parasuicidal behavior and suffering from borderline personality disorder (BPD; M. Linehan, 1993a, 1993b). Parasuicidal behavior includes all intentional self-injurious behavior, some of which is characterized by suicidal intent and some of which is not. DBT is an integrative treatment approach in that it blends cognitive-behavioral and Eastern meditation practices with elements of psychodynamic, person-centered, Gestalt, strategic, and paradoxical approaches (Heard & Linehan, 1994).

Marsha Linehan

DBT is a comprehensive approach directed toward a difficult clinical population. Typically, therapists who work with clients who engage in repeated suicidal and self-destructive behaviors and who regularly experience emotional dysregulation, quickly become discouraged, cynical, and burned out. This often led therapists to criticize their clients, sometimes disparagingly referring to them as "borderlines." In contrast, DBT maintains a positive perspective and the model weaves in support for therapists to cope with this difficult client population.

Characteristics and Protocol

DBT is based on a biosocial theoretical model of BPD. The primary deficit associated with BPD is emotional dysregulation. BPD clients are viewed as being biologically predisposed to emotional dysregulation. Linehan believes "individuals with BPD have emotional responses to environmental stimuli that occur more quickly, are more intense, and have a slower return to baseline than the responses of non-BPD individuals" (Linehan & Schmidt, 1995, p. 562).

On the social side, BPD clients are viewed as being within an environment that provides a poor fit for emotionally dysregulated behavior. Over time, this social environment often becomes "chronically and pervasively" emotionally invalidating—BPD clients consistently receive communications indicating that their emotional and behavioral responses are "incorrect, faulty, inappropriate."

DBT is also founded on **dialectical philosophy** and integrates Buddhist concepts of acceptance. Dialectical philosophy emphasizes that reality includes opposing forces that are constantly shifting and changing. The three-stage process through which change occurs is referred to as the dialectic. As applied to a suicidal client, the dialectic transformation occurs in the following stages:

- *First.* An initial proposition, "Life has meaning and positive possibilities," is experienced.

- *Second.* The initial proposition is negated through a contradictory experience: "Life has no relevance, meaning, or positive possibilities."

- *Third.* The contradiction is resolved through the negation of the negation: "Life can be both inherently meaningful and completely irrelevant."

Through DBT, the client is encouraged to grapple with both sides of this contradiction. The result is greater acceptance of transitory meaning and irrelevance in life and improved emotional regulation skills.

DBT also embraces another dialectic. Clients and their emotional condition are completely embraced and accepted (as in Eastern philosophy and person-centered theory). At the same time, the client is engaged in a purposeful change process to help with emotional dysregulation and environmental invalidation (Linehan, 1993a). Essentially, the therapist is communicating: "I accept you as you are, and I am helping you to change." This statement is considered an example of a **radical acceptance** therapy stance.

DBT practice is comprehensive and includes five functions delivered in various modalities. The functions include:

1. Enhancing skills and capabilities.

2. Improving client motivation.

3. Generalizing skills and capabilities from therapy to outside therapy.

4. Improving the therapist's capabilities and motivation to treat BPD patients.

5. Structuring the client's environment to support and validate the client's and therapist's capabilities. (Linehan, 1993a)

To address these functions, the therapist and client engage in the following: (a) clients commit to 12 months of psychoeducational skills training in a group format; (b) clients work individually with a therapist to increase motivation, address skill acquisition and application barriers, and generalize specific skills to the real world; (c) therapists also commit to participating in a weekly professional consultation group for technical assistance and emotional support; (d) family sessions or consultations with the client's personal environment are conducted to facilitate client emotional validation and skill development.

As you can see, DBT is not a therapy for the meek. It requires that both therapist and client make considerable commitments to training and ongoing skill development (see Putting it in Practice 14.3 for a DBT therapist's story of developing an interest in and acquiring DBT training).

DBT: The Evidence Base

DBT for BPD is evidence based. Division 12 lists it as having strong empirical support. Programmatic research shows positive outcomes after two years (Koons et al., 2001; M. M. Linehan et al., 2006; van den Bosch, Verheul, Schippers, & van den Brink, 2002).

DBT is especially popular because it provides a means through which therapists can work effectively with a very challenging treatment population. In recent years it's also been formulated as a preventative strategy for challenging, but subthreshold, adolescents at risk for developing BPD (A. L. Miller, Rathus, & Linehan, 2007). Miller, Rathus, and Linehan described the application of

PUTTING IT IN PRACTICE 14.3

On Becoming a "DBT Therapist"

K. Michelle Hunnicutt Hollenbaugh, Ph.D., Texas A&M University, Corpus Christi

When I originally began attending local Dialectical Behavior Therapy (DBT) trainings while working in a community mental health center, I never expected it to become an area of specialization. My supervisor was running DBT skills training groups, and believed it was important for all her supervisees to attend the trainings. Basically, I had to go to the trainings.

At first I was dubious. However, as I attended weekly trainings for the next year, two things happened:

1. I found myself using DBT skills in my own life on a daily basis. This included mindfulness meditation and working to accept frustrating situations as reality—to reduce personal suffering.

2. I realized I was no longer afraid to work with clients others labeled *difficult*. In treatment team meetings, while other clinicians were reluctant to accept new clients with the dreaded Borderline Personality Disorder (BPD), I was not. This was very empowering. It fueled my interest and further pursuit of DBT training. Then, I began running a DBT skills training group. And I started implementing as many aspects of DBT therapy as possible into my work with clients.

DBT is a complex therapy. Many facets are involved, training is a big commitment, and so I ran into barriers. Behavioral Tech (the organization founded by Marsha Linehan for DBT training) only offers the intensive 10-day DBT training to whole treatment teams; without financial support from the mental health center to form and fund a full team, I was unable to attend this training. And so instead, I continued to attend and offer local trainings and worked with other local therapists in a consultation team to continue our DBT growth and development. When honing my behavioral reinforcement skills, I practiced in consultation team meetings, with my clients, but also with family members and friends.

There was never a specific time when I said, "Now, I'm a DBT therapist." For me, it has been a process happening over time and having a DBT therapist title didn't occur to me until others began referring to me as such.

The journey to becoming a DBT therapist is difficult. I floundered at times; there were skills group sessions that fell apart before my eyes and clients that dropped out and never returned. But I continue to work to develop my skills and improve. I'm certain I'll face barriers and failures in the future.

You don't need to specialize in BPD to learn and use DBT. Although the majority of published research is on its use with BPD, DBT skills training is helpful for a variety of diagnoses and settings.

There are several helpful basic assumptions in DBT:

- Clients are doing the best they can.
- Clients want to improve.
- Clients need to do better, try harder, and be more motivated to change.
- Clients may not have caused all of their problems, but they have to solve them anyway.
- The lives of suicidal, borderline individuals are unbearable as they are currently being lived.
- Clients must learn new behaviors in all relevant contexts.
- Clients cannot fail therapy.
- Therapists treating BPD need support. (from Linehan, 1993a, pp. 106–108)

Notice that these are assumptions. What we believe shapes what we do and DBT is a state of mind. To be a DBT therapist, you must believe your client is doing the best she can. You must also believe she can do better. You must believe that your client's life is unbearable as it's currently being lived and that your client cannot fail therapy. Above all, DBT therapists must incorporate a dialectical worldview—a view that's flexible and free from absolutes. This returns to the concept of accepting reality and a mantra often used in DBT—"everything is as it is; and everything is as it should be."

DBT as a prevention strategy for adolescents who display suicidal behaviors:

DBT has been found effective for older adolescents and adults diagnosed with BPD, in large part because it explicitly targets the internal and external risk factors for suicidal behavior and [nonsuicidal self-injurious behavior]. Of those self-referring teens referred to our outpatient program, . . . 37% meet at least three Axis II diagnostic criteria for BPD (e.g., angry outbursts, confusion about self, and impulsive behaviors), and 26% meet full criteria. . . . We believe that this treatment is beneficial to those with subthreshold BPD . . . as we consider DBT a prophalaxis against developing the more

ingrained, refractory set of behavioral problems seen in BPD. (p. 1)

Overall, DBT is a well-established treatment for BPD with potential for effectiveness in treating additional conditions such as substance abuse, violent offenders, and elderly clients with depression and personality disorders.

Acceptance and Commitment Therapy

ACT is another new generation behavior therapy with a strong emphasis on the Buddhist (or person-centered) concept of acceptance. It has become increasingly popular in recent years. **Acceptance and commitment therapy** is abbreviated as

ACT, which is pronounced as a word and not as a set of initials. The ACT developers identify their approach as integrational:

> Is ACT a behavior therapy, a cognitive-behavioral therapy, a type of clinical behavior analysis, a contextual therapy, or a humanistic/existential/ Gestalt therapy? It is all of these.... We do not view the distinctions between these streams of thought to be important to the ACT work, and relish the fact that it spans several seemingly distinct traditions. (Hayes, Strosahl, & Wilson, 1999, p. 79)

ACT Development
In essence, ACT is a radical behavior therapy that takes the novel position of rejecting existing diagnostic and medical models. ACT developers believe the assumptions of healthy normality (and abnormality as a disease) are flawed. The disease, disorder, or psychopathology model is viewed as incorrect and unhelpful (Hayes et al., 1999). They wrote:

> Considering how much attention has been afforded the medical model within psychology and psychiatry, it is a bit shocking to note how little progress has been made in establishing syndromes as disease entities.... The "comorbidity" rates in the current diagnostic system are so high as to challenge the basic credibility of the nosology.... Even if clients can be given a label such as panic disorder with agoraphobia, or obsessive-compulsive disorder, many of the issues within therapy will still have to do with other problems: jobs, children, relationships, sexual identity, careers, anger, sadness, drinking problems, or the meaning of life. (Hayes et al., 1999, p. 5)

The main point emphasized by Hayes and his colleagues is that clinical researchers have been seeking support for an invalid model. They offer an alternative or supplemental view:

> ACT supplements the traditional view by bringing a different assumption to the study of psychological distress. It is based on the assumption of destructive normality: The idea that

ordinary human psychological processes can themselves lead to extremely destructive and dysfunctional results and can amplify or exacerbate unusual pathological processes. (Hayes et al., 1999, p. 6)

Characteristics and Protocol
In a nutshell, ACT therapists contend that therapists shouldn't consider negative cognitions as unhealthy or deviant. They believe doing so can actually make clients worse. This position is similar to therapists advocating behavioral activation therapy for depression instead of CBT. Here's how the reasoning goes:

- In CBT, clients are viewed as having negative cognitions that contribute to a depressive or anxious state.

- CBT expects clients to dispute or restructure their cognitions to eliminate them and doing so is thought to improve well-being and mental health.

- CBT contends that if these cognitions can't be managed it's a bad or dysfunctional thing.

- In contrast, ACT says all thoughts are normal and natural and not deviant.

- ACT practitioners coach clients to use mindfulness approaches to accept their thoughts—instead of trying to fight their thoughts off—because the thoughts aren't bad things anyway.

- ACT also emphasizes values-based committed action—which is viewed as healthy in and of itself.

- ACT practitioners and researchers contend that pathologizing normal negative thoughts can worsen depression, anxiety, and other mental health conditions.

ACT is based on **relational frames theory (RFA)**. Hayes and others contend that RFA is extremely complex and difficult to digest easily. He attributes the fact that it took nearly 20 years for the first ACT book to be published as evidence of its complexity (Fletcher & Hayes, 2005).

In his book, *ACT Made Simple* (2009), Russ Harris described ACT:

> At its core, ACT is a behavioral therapy: it's about taking action. But it's not about just any old action. First, it's about values-guided action. There's a big existential component to this mode: What do you want to stand for in life? What really matters, deep in your heart? What do you want to be remembered for at your funeral? . . . Second, it's about mindful action: action that you take consciously, with full awareness—open to your experience and fully engaged in whatever you're doing. (p. 8)

ACT integrates mindfulness into clinical practice. That's why ACT begins with the word *acceptance*. It also emphasizes values-based committed action—which is where the word commitment comes from. Finally, it emphasizes action in the direction of values-based commitments . . . which is why the authors want us to say ACT all as one word, to emphasize action.

ACT: The Evidence Base

Research on ACT is in the early stages, but many new publications are appearing. ACT is included on the Division 12 list as a probably efficacious treatment for depression (Forman, Herbert, Moitra, Yeomans, & Geller, 2007). ACT researchers have conducted several head-to-head therapy outcomes studies with traditional CBT treatments and reported relatively positive outcomes (Forman et al., 2007; Juarascio, Forman, & Herbert, 2010; Twohig et al., 2010).

ACT represents an exciting new direction in counseling and psychotherapy. In many ways, it's a kinder and gentler approach to change. Early research suggests that it may be as effective or more effective than traditional therapy approaches.

The Transtheoretical Change Model

In the late 1970s James Prochaska began looking at theories of psychotherapy in a new way. While reviewing traditional psychotherapy systems, he discovered most theories emphasize personality and psychopathology, both of which orient therapists toward why people don't change rather than why people do change (Prochaska, 1979). Consequently, he and his colleagues began their groundbreaking work on developing a new theory of therapy—a transtheoretical model focusing on how people change (Prochaska, 1995; Prochaska & DiClemente, 1982; Prochaska, DiClemente, & Norcross, 1993).

The **transtheoretical model** is a higher-order integrational theory of psychotherapy, emphasizing both common factors and theoretical integration. We review the model here because it can be helpful as an overarching way to understand counseling and psychotherapy theories. The model seeks to:

- Respect the fundamental diversity and essential unity of therapy systems.
- Emphasize empiricism.
- Account for how people change inside and outside of therapy.
- Address physical and mental health problems.
- Encourage therapists to be innovators and not simply borrowers from various systems.

When the transtheoretical model was developed, counseling and psychotherapy were ripe for creative, integrative ideas. In the 1970s, eclecticism was very popular, but it was also associated with soft thinking, fragmentation, and superficiality, as described earlier in this chapter (Eysenck, 1970).

Prochaska (1995) considers his development of the transtheoretical model to be a product of increasing divergence in the field. Based on Guilford's (1956) model of intelligence he notes that periods of divergence need to be followed by higher levels of convergent thinking. Consequently, because therapy approaches had become so fragmented in the 1970s, the time was right for greater rapprochement or convergence in counseling.

The transtheoretical model focuses on three different dimensions of change:

1. Change processes
2. Stages of change
3. Levels of change

Change Processes

Beginning with research focused on addictive behaviors, Prochaska and colleagues identified common **change processes** occurring across divergent theoretical orientations. They identified 10 primary change processes (Prochaska, 1995; Prochaska & Norcross, 2003). These processes, along with their likely theoretical roots, are listed in Table 14.3.

Stages of Change

Some clients come to therapy ready to change for the better. Other clients end up in therapy with little or no motivation for change. Recognizing these basic differences, as well as more subtle change levels, Prochaska identified six **stages of change**:

1. *Precontemplation.* During this stage, the individual has little or no interest in changing his behavior.

2. *Contemplation.* During this stage, the individual is aware that a problem exists, but she has not yet made a clear commitment to making a personal change.

3. *Preparation.* During preparation, there may be some intention and effort made toward change. For example, a sedentary individual may go out and buy running shoes or join a fitness club. There may be occasional ventures forth into action, but mostly these individuals are so deep into contemplation that they're beginning some

minimal action toward change but are not yet into the action stage.

4. *Action.* During action, people are plunging into the change process. These are the clients whom most therapists love to see because their motivation is so high that they quickly engage in the therapy process and often make considerable and immediate progress. Prochaska (1995) defines this stage as the "successful alteration of a problem behavior for a period from 1 day to 6 months."

5. *Maintenance.* During maintenance, people continue with their action and deepen their commitment toward permanent change. There is continual work or action toward relapse prevention. This stage continues from 6 months to infinity, but relapse often occurs at some point during maintenance. For example, many alcohol- or drug-addicted individuals reach the maintenance stage only to experience relapse. Then, they generally cycle back through the stages of change again in an effort to obtain mastery over their problem. This recycling tendency is apparent in many nonclients as many individuals repeatedly make the same New Year's resolutions (for 5 or more years) until finally maintaining their goal for over 6 months (Norcross & Vangarelli, 1989).

6. *Termination.* During termination, people have 100% confidence (or self-efficacy) that they will

Table 14.3   Common Change Processes and Theoretical Origins

Consciousness-raising	Processes of personal insight and awareness that stem from feedback and education	Psychodynamic theory Feminist theory
Dramatic relief	Catharsis and expressive procedures	Gestalt theory
Self-re-evaluation	An examination of self, self-schema, and other variables	Cognitive therapy, construcivist, and Adlerian
Environmental re-evaluation	Information processing with an environmental focus	Cognitive and constructivist theory
Self-liberation	A focus on personal freedom	Existential and choice theory
Social-liberation	A focus on freedom from social oppression	Feminist, existential, and constructivist
Counterconditioning	New learning that overcomes old learning	Behavioral
Stimulus control	Management of environmental stimuli	Behavioral
Reinforcement management	Management of environmental contingencies	Behavioral
Helping relationship	The healing potential of a helping relationship	Person-centered

not engage in the problem behavior again. They also report having no urges to engage in the problem behavior again. Prochaska uses a 5-year criterion of symptom liberation, plus 100% confidence, for classification into this stage. In a study of recovering alcoholics and smokers, 17% and 16% of former drinkers and smokers were classified as being in the termination stage of change (Snow, Prochaska, & Rossi, 1992).

Levels of Change

Prochaska identified five different **levels of change**:

1. Symptom/situational problems
2. Maladaptive cognitions
3. Current interpersonal conflicts
4. Family-systems conflicts
5. Intrapersonal conflicts

Based on the transtheoretical model, change efforts are initially directed toward the symptom-situation level because most clients come to therapy seeking relief from a particular distressing symptom or situation. However, as Prochaska points out, rarely does therapy proceed in a simple and straightforward manner that focuses solely on symptom elimination (Prochaska, 1995). Instead, as clients participate in therapy for longer periods, they delve deeper into cognitive, interpersonal, familial, and intrapsychic issues.

One advantage of the transtheoretical model is its emphasis on the interactive and integrative nature of therapeutic processes, stages, and levels. For example, when clients are in the precontemplative stage, it's likely they will resist action-oriented therapy interventions. Alternatively, when clients are in the contemplative or preparation stages, they may be ready to experience a sudden and dramatic relief, followed by regression or relapse. It's best to focus on symptom and situational issues with clients in these early stages of change, as they're unlikely to be motivated to explore deeper, more personal issues (i.e., interpersonal, familial, or intrapsychic conflicts).

PUTTING IT IN PRACTICE 14.4

A Concluding Image: Group Therapy With Some Exceptionally Difficult Clients

There are indeed many ways to practice counseling and psychotherapy. There are also many ways to end a book. Because this is a textbook, we're tempted to end it with a logical and rational analysis of future trends in counseling and psychotherapy. However, because humans have difficulty predicting tomorrow's weather, we chose a different, more irreverent ending for this book. Instead of embracing the rational and logical conclusion, we leave you with a fantasy.

After reading and writing about so many great therapy minds, one of us (you can guess which one) had the following daydream: Imagine many of the historical and contemporary therapy masters gathered together in one location. They form a circle and begin a discussion. Old friends and rivals are reunited. Freud appears and shakes hands with Jean Miller Baker, who has brought quite a number of impressive-looking women with her. Fritz Perls tries to kiss some of their hands. Adler brings his wife. Carl Rogers signs a book for Prochaska. New friends are made, old rivalries rejuvenated. Insoo Kim Berg smiles quietly off to one side. Jung notes to himself that she must be an introvert. What might happen in this circumstance? What might happen in *"An Encounter Group for the Major Players"*?

After some initial mingling, the group process begins:

Rogers: I wonder where we might want to start.

Raissa Adler: Here's where I'm starting. I'm not taking the minutes for this meeting. I did that back in 1912 for the Free Psychoanalytic Society, so I've put in my time. It's someone else's turn, and I nominate a male, any male. Women have been taking notes in meetings for so long it's ridiculous. The problem with women's psyches has more to do with oppression than repression.

Feminists: [Including Jean Baker Miller, Judith Jordan, Espín, Lillian Comas-Diaz, and Laura Brown—all of whom, embracing the subversion concept, snuck into the group.] You go woman! We're with you.

Freud: That's it. Say whatever comes to mind.

Ellis: If you want to think that taking notes is oppression, that's up to you, but as far as I can tell, you're oppressing yourself with a bunch of damn crazy, irrational thinking.

Beck: You know Al, we've been through this before, but what I think you mean is that Raissa's thinking that taking notes is oppression could be maladaptive, but not irrational.

Glasser: Raissa can choose to take notes or choose not to take notes. She can also choose to think she's oppressed or choose not to think she's oppressed. Personally, Raissa, I recommend that you read my book, *Choice Theory*. I want you to read it, and I think it will help you, but of course, whether you read it or not, that's completely your choice.

F. Perls: Be here now, Raissa. Act out those feelings. Be the pen. Talk to the paper.

L. Perls: Fritz, she can be the pen without your assistance. If by chance she finds herself, that's beautiful.

Ellis: She won't find a goddamn thing in this group of love-slobs without a flashlight.

Skinner: Uh. Albert. I've been wanting to mention to you that if you could just keep quiet when people in here say inappropriate things, we might have a chance at extinguishing that particular behavior.

Ellis: Well, Burris, did you have an irrational thought that someone might actually care about your opinion before you engaged in that speaking behavior, or was it just a function of its consequences?

V. Satir: Albert, if you could just get up on that chair and talk down to Burris, I think you could get in touch with your placating style.

Skinner (Whispering to Ellis): Seriously man. Just ignore her. I'm talking about a complete extinction schedule. Just like I'm ignoring you—except for when you sit quietly and listen to me like you're doing now.

Rollo May: Freedom and dignity are the essence of being. There's far too much freedom, with very little dignity in this room.

I. K. Berg: If a miracle happened and we all got out of this group without anyone getting murdered, what would that look like?

A. Adler: My God, I just remembered an earlier memory. No wonder I felt so inferior.

Freud: I hate that word. I just want to be recognized for my contributions. It would make my mother proud.

Rogers: It's like if only I can make my mother happy. And getting recognized, being remembered, that's one big way you can have that experience.

Ellis: Siggy, my man. Let me just say this. That crap about being recognized and making your mother proud is the most f—ing ridiculous thing I've ever heard in my life. What's the big deal if everybody forgets you? What's the terrible, awful, very bad thing that will happen? I mean, think logically about this. You'll be dead and it won't make a white rat's ass difference if people remember you or not.

Feminists: That's right. I can't believe we're agreeing with Albert Ellis. White males can afford to play with such big ideas. Immortality. Do you have a clue about the legacy you've actually left? There have been decades of girls and women with destroyed self-esteems. Do you recognize that they litter your road to "greatness"?

Mahoney: I can see Freud as great and I can see feminism as great. Even this lived moment in our genetic epistemology exudes the potential for greatness. We are not a passive repository of sensory experience, but instead, we're co-constructing this reality right now.

Prochaska: This entire group seems to me to be in precontemplation.

D. W. Sue: Yeah, well, I might consider change if we could construct in a minority voice or two? Most of what I've heard thus far is the construction of a very narrow, white reality. Culture is primary, and we need to include color if we're to meet the needs of everyone, including Raissa, who happens to have a strong Russian ethnocultural identity.

Raissa Adler: [Slowly stands and walks over and embraces D. W. Sue.]

Rogers: What I'm seeing and what I'm hearing, if I'm getting this right, is affection and appreciation. Two people who have, now and again, felt marginalized are able to connect more deeply with each other right now than with anyone else.

M. White: Actually, Carl, I think I'd just call this a sparkling moment.

CONCLUDING COMMENTS

In every human domain, we have more information than we can possibly sort out and use effectively. Wisdom consists of knowing both *what* to know and *how* to use what you know. A careful analysis and synthesis of the material in this book will go a long ways toward helping you begin your journey as a mental health professional.

Studying counseling and psychotherapy theory and practice is challenging. It can be tempting to walk away from the intellectual work and just try to be helpful to people in distress. We're glad you've grappled with the ideas in this book and made it this far. We hope you'll continue thinking hard about theories long into the future.

In the end, we challenge you to look beyond the face value of these theories. We encourage you to treat them as more than narrow historical artifacts—the musings of narcissistic or slightly addled forefathers and mothers. If you can view these theories as a product of time, place, deep contemplation, and a sincere desire to understand and alleviate human suffering, you'll be better served.

At the very least, ethical mental health professionals should be able to do three things: First, they should be able to articulate their own theories of why humans develop mental distress and what helps bring relief and healing. Second, they should be able to compare and contrast their theories with those in this book. Finally, they should be able to explain their choices of techniques in the context of both theory and evidence-based outcomes. Good luck with that.

CHAPTER SUMMARY

For the past century, theorists and practitioners have argued over whether we're better served by one grand theory that accounts for everything or many patchwork approaches designed to meet the idiosyncratic needs of each individual client. No doubt, this argument will continue for another century or two.

There are two good explanations for why there are so many different approaches to counseling and psychotherapy. First, therapy approaches need to deal with individuality and cultural specificity. Second, over time, human conflict has greatly affected the proliferation of different theories.

There are four main ways of practicing counseling and psychotherapy. These include: (1) theoretical purity; (2) theoretical integration; (3) common factors; and (4) technical eclecticism. There are advantages and disadvantages associated with each of these approaches.

In recent years there has been much more focus on integrating theoretical concepts and developing hybrid therapy approaches. Lazarus's technical eclecticism model was an early example of selecting strategies associated with different approaches to address unique client needs. More recently, five different "new generation" therapies have come to the forefront as integrational and evidence-based approaches. These include: (1) EMDR; (2) IPT; (3) EFT; (4) DBT; and (5) ACT. Each of these approaches was summarized in this chapter as well as an overarching theory of change, the transtheoretical change model.

INTEGRATIVE KEY TERMS

Action

Acceptance and commitment therapy (ACT)

Authentic chameleon

BASIC I.D.

Change processes

Common factors

Contemplative

Corrective emotional experience

Demoralization hypothesis

Dialectical behavior therapy (DBT)

Dialectical philosophy

Emotional dysregulation

Emotion-focused therapy (EFT)

Eye movement desensitization reprocessing (EMDR)

Ideological purity

Interpersonal psychotherapy (IPT)

Levels of change

Maintenance

Multimodal therapy

New generation therapies

Precontemplative

Preparation

Radical acceptance

Relational frames theory

Stages of change

Syncretism

Technical eclecticism

Termination

The who-how-whom question

Theoretical integration

Transtheoretical model

RECOMMENDED READINGS AND RESOURCES

The following readings and resources may help you in furthering your understanding of the integrative theories of counseling and psychotherapy.

INTEGRATIVE JOURNALS

Evidence-Based Mental Health
Integrative Psychiatry

Journal of Psychotherapy Integration

READINGS ON INTEGRATIVE APPROACHES

Ahn, H.-N., & Wampold, B. E. (2001). Where oh where are the specific ingredients? A meta-analysis of component studies in counseling and psychotherapy. *Journal of Counseling Psychology, 48*(3), 251–257.

Brooks-Harris, J. (2008). *Integrative multitheoretical psychotherapy*. Boston, MA: Houghton-Mifflin.

Frank, J. D., & Frank, J. B. (1991). *Persuasion and healing* (3rd ed.). Baltimore: Johns Hopkins University Press.

Greenberg, L. S. (2011). *Emotion-focused therapy*. Washington, DC: American Psychological Association.

Kabat-Zinn, J. (1994). *Wherever you go there you are*. New York, NY: Hyperion.

Klerman, G.L.E., & Weissman, M. M. (Eds.). (1993). *New applications of interpersonal psychotherapy*. Washington, DC: American Psychiatric Association.

Lazarus, A. A. (2006). *Brief but comprehensive psychotherapy: The multimodal way*. New York, NY: Springer.

Linehan, M. M. (1993). *Cognitive behavioral therapy of borderline personality disorder*. New York, NY: Guilford Press.

Linehan, M. M. (1993). *Skills training manual for treating borderline personality disorder*. New York, NY: Guilford Press.

Miller, A. L., Rathus, J. H., & Linehan, M. M. (2007). *Dialectical behavior therapy with suicidal adolescents*. New York, NY: Guilford Press.

Prochaska, J. O., DiClemente, C. C., & Norcross, J. C. (1993). In search of how people change. *American Psychologist, 47*, 1102–1114.

Shapiro, F. (2001). *Eye Movement Desensitization and Reprocessing: Basic principles, protocols, and procedures* (2nd ed.). New York, NY: Guilford Press.

TRAINING ORGANIZATIONS AND WEBSITES

Society for the Exploration of Psychotherapy Integration (SEPI; www.cyberpsych.org/sepi/)

The EMDR Institute (www.emdr.com)

Dialectical Behavior Therapy Association (DBTA; www.pesi.com/dbta/)

Behavioral Tech LLC (behavioraltech.org/index.cfm)

Institute for Interpersonal Psychotherapy (www.ipt-institute.com/)

VIDEOS/DVDs

Greenberg, L. S. (1994). *Process-experiential psychotherapy* [Videotape]. Washington, DC: American Psychological Association.

Lazarus, A. A. (1994). *Multimodal therapy* [Videotape]. Washington, DC: American Psychological Association.

Norcross, J. C. (1994). *Prescriptive eclectic therapy* [Videotape]. Washington, DC: American Psychological Association.

Shapiro, F. (1998). *EMDR (eye movement desensitization reprocessing) for trauma* [Videotape]. Washington, DC: American Psychological Association.

GOING FARTHER AND DEEPER

Additional eclectic and integrative counseling and psychotherapy resources are available at johnsommers flanagan.com.

References

Abbass, A., & Driessen, E. (2010). The efficacy of short-term psychodynamic psychotherapy for depression: A summary of recent findings. *Acta Psychiatrica Scandinavica, 121*(5), 398–398.

Ackerman, N. (1938). The unity of the family. *Archives of Pediatrics 55*, 51–62.

Ackerman, N. W., & Lakos, M. H. (1959). *The treatment of a child and family*. Oxford, England: Prentice-Hall.

Ackerman, N. W., & Neubauer, P. B. (1948). *Failures in the psychotherapy of children*. New York, NY: Grune & Stratton.

Adler, A. (1898). *Gesundheitsbuch fur die schneidergewerbe [Healthbook for the tailors' trade]*. Berlin: C. Heymanns.

Adler, A. (1927). *Understanding human nature*. Garden City, NY: Garden City.

Adler, A. (1931). *What life should mean to you*. Oxford, England: Little, Brown.

Adler, A. (1935). Introduction. *International Journal of Individual Psychology, 1*(1), 5–8.

Adler, A. (1937). Position in the family constellation influence life-style. *International Journal of Individual Psychology, 3*(3), 211–227.

Adler, A. (1958). *What life should mean to you*. New York, NY: Capricorn.

Adler, A. (1964). *Problems of neurosis: A book of case histories*. New York, NY: Harper Torchbooks.

Adler, A. (1964). *Social interest: A challenge to mankind* (J. Linton & R. Vaughan, Trans.). New York, NY: Capricorn.

Adler, A. (1983). *The practice and theory of individual psychology*. (P. Radin, Trans.). Totowa, NJ: Littlefield, Adams.

Adler, R. (1982). Minutes of the society for free psychoanalytic research: September 1912 to January 1913. *Individual Psychology: Journal of Adlerian Theory, Research & Practice, 38*(1), 22–27.

Agras, W. S., Schneider, J. A., Arnow, B., Raeburn, S. D., & Telch, C. F. (1989). Cognitive-behavioral and response-prevention treatments for bulimia nervosa. *Journal of Consulting & Clinical Psychology, 57*, 215–221.

Ainsworth, M. D. (1969). Object relations, dependency, and attachment: A theoretical review of the infant-mother relationship. *Child Development, 40*(4), 969–1025.

Ainsworth, M. D., & Bell, S. M. (1970). Attachment, exploration, and separation: Illustrated by the behavior of one-year-olds in a strange situation. *Child Development, 41*, 49–67.

Alarcón, R. D., Becker, A. E., Lewis-Fernández, R., Like, R. C., Desai, P., Foulks, E., et al. (2009). Issues for DSM-V: The role of culture in psychiatric diagnosis. *Journal of Nervous and Mental Disease, 197*(8), 559–560.

Alberti, R. E., & Emmons, M. L. (1970). *Your perfect right: A guide to assertive behavior*. San Luis Obispo, CA: Impact.

Alberti, R., & Emmons, M. (2008). *Your perfect right* (9th ed.). San Luis Obispo, CA: Impact.

Alexander, F. (1963). The dynamics of psychotherapy in light of learning theory. *American Journal of Psychiatry, 120*, 440–448.

Alexander, F., & French, T. M. (1946). *Psychoanalytic psychotherapy*. New York, NY: Ronald.

Alexander, J., & Parsons, B. V. (1982). *Functional family therapy*. Monterey, CA: Brooks/Cole.

Alexander, J. F., & Parsons, B. V. (1973). Short-term behavioral intervention with delinquent families: Impact on family process and recidivism. *Journal of Abnormal Psychology, 81*, 219–225.

Alexander, J. F., Warburton, J., Waldron, H., & Mas, C. H. (1985). The misuse of functional family therapy: A non-sexist rejoinder. *Journal of Marital and Family Therapy, 11*(2), 139–144.

Alexander, S., Shilts, L., Liscio, M., & Rambo, A. (2008). Return to sender: Letter writing to bring hope to both client and team. *Journal of Systemic Therapies, 27*(1), 59–66.

Ali, A., Caplan, P. J., & Fagnant, R. (2010). *Gender stereotypes in diagnostic criteria*. New York, NY: Springer Science + Business Media.

Amendt-Lyon, N. (2008). Gender differences in Gestalt therapy. *Gestalt Review, 12*(2), 106–121.

American Counseling Association. (2005). *The American Counseling Association Code of ethics*. Alexandria, VA: American Counseling Association.

American Psychiatric Association. (2000). *Diagnostic and statistical manual of mental disorders* (IV-TR ed.). Washington, DC: Author.

American Psychological Association. (1990). *Guidelines for providers of psychological services to ethnic, linguistic, and culturally diverse populations*. Washington, DC: Author.

American Psychological Association. (2000). Guidelines for psychotherapy with lesbian, gay, and bisexual clients. *American Psychologist, 55*, 1440–1451.

American Psychological Association. (2002). Ethical principles of psychologists and code of conduct. *American Psychologist, 57*, 1060–1073.

American Psychological Association. (2003). Guidelines for multicultural education, training, research, practice, and organizational change for psychologists. *American Psychologist, 58*, 377–402.

Andersen, T. (1987). The reflecting team: Dialogue and metadialogue in clinical work. *Family Process, 26*, 415–426.

Andersen, T. (1991). *The reflecting team: Dialogues and dialogues about dialogues*. New York, NY: Norton.

Andersen, T. (1995). Reflecting processes: Acts of informing and forming: You can borrow my eyes, but you must not take them away from me! In S. Friedman (Ed.), *The reflecting team in action: Collaborative practices in psychotherapy* (pp. 11–37). New York, NY: Guilford Press.

Andersen, T. (2007). Reflecting talks may have many versions: Here is mine. *International Journal of Psychotherapy, 11*(2), 27–44.

Anderson, C. M., & Stewart, S. (1983). *Mastering resistance: A practical guide to family therapy*. New York: Guilford Press.

Anderson, E. M., & Lambert, M. J. (1995). Short-term dynamically oriented psychotherapy: A review and meta-analysis. *Clinical Psychology Review, 15*, 503–514.

Anderson, H. (2007). A postmodern umbrella: Language and knowledge as relational and generative, and inherently transforming. In H. Anderson & D. Gehart (Eds.), *Collaborative therapy: Relationships and conversations that make a difference* (pp. 7–19). New York, NY: Routledge/Taylor & Francis.

Anderson, H., & Burney, J. P. (2004). A postmodern collaborative approach: A family's reflections on "in-the-room" and "on-the-challenge course" therapy.

It's all language. In T. Strong & D. Paré (Eds.), *Furthering talk: Advances in the discursive therapies* (pp. 87–108). New York, NY: Kluwer Academic/Plenum.

Anderson, S. K., & Handelsman, M. M. (2010). *Ethics for psychotherapists and counselors: A proactive approach*. Malden, MA: Wiley-Blackwell.

Anestis, M. D., Anestis, J. C., & Lilienfeld, S. O. (2011). When it comes to evaluating psychodynamic therapy, the devil is in the details. *American Psychologist, 66*(2), 149–151.

Ansbacher, H. L., & Ansbacher, R. R. (Eds.). (1956). *The individual psychology of Alfred Adler*. New York, NY: Harper.

Arredondo, P., & Perez, P. (2006). Historical perspectives on the multicultural guidelines and contemporary applications. *Professional Psychology: Research and Practice, 37*(1), 1–5.

Arredondo, P., Toporek, R., Brown, S., Jones, J., Locke, D. C., Sanchez, J., & Stadler, H. (1996). *Operationalization of the multicultural counseling competencies*. Alexandria, VA: Association for Multicultural Counseling and Development.

Asay, T. P., & Lambert, M. J. (1999). The empirical case for the common factors in therapy: Quantitative findings. In M. A. Hubble, B. L. Duncan, & S. D. Miller (Eds.), *The heart and soul of change* (pp. 33–56). Washington, DC: American Psychological Assocation.

Askari, S. F., Liss, M., Erchull, M. J., Staebell, S. E., & Axelson, S. J. (2010). Men want equality, but women don't expect it: Young adults' expectations for participation in household and child care chores. *Psychology of Women Quarterly, 34*(2), 243–252.

Association of Lesbian, Gay, Bisexual, and Transgender Issues in Counseling. (2009). *Competencies for counseling with transgender clients*. Alexandria, VA: Author.

Atkinson, D. R., & Lowe, S. M. (1995). The role of ethnicity, cultural knowledge, and conventional techniques in counseling and psychotherapy. In J. G. Ponterotto, J. M. Casas, L. A. Suzuki, & C. M. Alexander (Eds.), *Handbook of multicultural counseling* (pp. 387–414). Thousand Oaks, CA: Sage.

Atkinson, D. R., Lowe, S. M., & Mathews, L. (1995). Asian-American acculturation, gender and willingness to seek counseling. *Journal of Multicultural Counseling and Development, 23*, 130–138.

Atkinson, D. R., Maruyama, M., & Matsui, S. (1978). The effects of counselor race and counseling approach on Asian Americans' perceptions of counselor credibility. *Journal of Counseling Psychology, 25*, 76–83.

Avis, J. M. (1985). The politics of functional family therapy: A feminist critique. *Journal of Marital and Family Therapy, 11*(2), 127–138.

Axelson, J. A. (1999). *Counseling and development in a multicultural society* (3rd ed.). Belmont, CA: Wadsworth.

Baca, L., & Cervantes, H. T. (1984). *The bilingual special education interface.* St. Louis, MO: Times Mirror/Mosby College.

Bachman, J. G., & O'Malley, P. M. (1977). Self-esteem in young men: A longitudinal analysis of the impact of educational and occupational attainment. *Journal of Personality and Social Psychology, 35*(6), 365–380.

Badenoch, B. (2008). *Being a brain-wise therapist: A practical guide to interpersonal neurobiology.* New York, NY: Norton.

Baker, T. B., McFall, R. M., & Shoham, V. (2008). Current status and future prospects of clinical psychology: Toward a scientifically principled approach to mental and behavioral health care. *Psychological Science in the Public Interest, 9*(2), 67–103.

Balint, E. (1950). Changing therapeutic aims and techniques in psychoanalysis. *International Journal of Psychoanalytic Psychology, 31,* 117–124.

Balint, M., Ornstein, P. H., & Balint, E. (1972). *Focal psychotherapy.* Philadelphia, PA: Lippincott.

Ball, J., & Mitchell, P. (2004). A randomized controlled study of cognitive behavior therapy and behavioral family therapy for anorexia nervosa patients. *Eating Disorders: The Journal of Treatment & Prevention, 12*(4), 303–314.

Ballou, M. B. (1984). Thoughts on reality therapy from a feminist. *Journal of Reality Therapy, 4*(1), 28–32.

Ballou, M., & Brown, L. S. (Eds.). (2002). *Rethinking mental health and disorder: Feminist perspectives.* New York: Guilford.

Bandura, A. (1965). Vicarious processes; A case of no-trial learning. In L. Berkowitz (Ed.), *Advances in experimental social psychology* (Vol. 2, pp. 49–91). New York, NY: Academic Press.

Bandura, A. (1971). Psychotherapy based on modeling procedures. In A. E. Bergin & S. L. Garfield (Eds.), *Handbook of psychotherapy and behavior change: An empirical analysis* (pp. 653–708). New York, NY: John Wiley & Sons.

Bandura, A. (1977). Self-efficacy: Toward a unifying theory of behavioral change. *Psychological Review, 84,* 191–215.

Bandura, A. (1978). The self system in reciprocal determinism. *American Psychologist, 33,* 344–358.

Bandura, A., & Adams, N. E. (1977). Analysis of self-efficacy theory of behavioral change. *Cognitive Therapy and Research, 1,* 287–310.

Bandura, A., Blanchard, E. B., & Ritter, B. (1969). Relative efficacy of desensitization and modeling approaches for inducing behavioral affective, and attitudinal changes. *Journal of Personality and Social Psychology, 13,* 173–199.

Bandura, A., Ross, D., & Ross, S. A. (1963). Imitation of film-mediated aggressive models. *Journal of Abnormal & Social Psychology, 66,* 3–11.

Bandura, A., & Walters, R. H. (1963). *Social learning and personality development.* New York, NY: Holt, Rinehart, and Winston.

Bankart, C. P. (1997). *Talking cures: A history of Western and Eastern psychotherapies.* Pacific Grove, CA: Brooks/Cole.

Barbato, A., & D'Avanzo, B. (2000). Family interventions in schizophrenia and related disorders: A critical review of clinical trials. *Acta Psychiatrica Scandinavica, 102*(2), 81–97.

Barber, J. P., Connolly, M. B., Crits-Christoph, P., Gladis, L., & Siqueland, L. (2009). Alliance predicts patients' outcome beyond in-treatment change in symptoms. *Personality Disorders: Theory, Research, and Treatment, S*(1), 80–89.

Barber, J. P., Gallop, R., Crits-Christoph, P., Barrett, M. S., Klostermann, S., McCarthy, K. S., et al. (2008). The role of the alliance and techniques in predicting outcome of supportive-expressive dynamic therapy for cocaine dependence. *Psychoanalytic Psychology, 25*(3), 461–482.

Barlow, H., & Craske, M. G. (2000). *Mastery of your anxiety and panic.* New York, NY: Graywind.

Barnett, J. E., Lazarus, A. A., Vasquez, M.J.T., Johnson, W. B., & Moorehead-Slaughter, O. (2007). Boundary issues and multiple relationships: Fantasy and reality. *Professional Psychology: Research and Practice, 38*(4), 401–410.

Barrett, S. E., Chin, J. L., Comas-Diaz, L., Espin, O., Greene, B., & McGoldrick, M. (2005). Multicultural feminist therapy: Theory in context. *Women & Therapy, 28*(3–4), 27–61.

Barrett-Lennard, G. T. (1981). The empathy cycle: Refinement of a nuclear concept. *Journal of Counseling Psychology, 28,* 91–100.

Barton, C., Alexander, J. F., Waldron, H., Turner, C. W., & Warburton, J. (1985). Generalizing treatment effects of functional family therapy: Three replications. *American Journal of Family Therapy, 13*(3), 16–26.

Bateson, G. (1972). *Steps to an ecology of mind*. New York, NY: Dutton.

Bateson, G., Jackson, D. D., Haley, J., & Weakland, J. (1956). Toward a theory of schizophrenia. *Behavioral Science, 1*, 251–264.

Bateson, G., Jackson, D. D., Haley, J., & Weakland, J. H. (1963). A note on the double bind: 1962. *Family Process, 2*(1), 154–161.

Battista, J., & Almond, R. (1973). The development of meaning in life. *Psychiatry: Journal for the Study of Interpersonal Processes, 36*(4), 409–427.

Baumeister, R. F., & Leary, M. R. (1995). The need to belong: Desire for interpersonal attachments as a fundamental human motivation. *Psychological Bulletin, 117*(3), 497–529.

Baumgardner, P., & Perls, F. (1975). *Legacy from Fritz*. Oxford, England: Science & Behavior.

Baumrind, D., Larzelere, R. E., & Cowan, P. A. (2002). Ordinary physical punishment: Is it harmful? Comment on Gershoff (2002). *Psychological Bulletin, 128*(4), 580–589.

Beauchamp, T. L., & Childress, J. F. (2001). *Principles of biomedical ethics*. New York, NY: Oxford University Press.

Beauvoir, S. D. (1952). *The second sex*. New York, NY: Knopf.

Bechtoldt, H., Norcross, J. C., Wyckoff, L. A., Pokrywa, M. L., & Campbell, L. F. (2001). Theoretical orientations and employment settings of clinical and counseling psychologists: A comparative study. *The Clinical Psychologist, 54*, 3–6.

Beck, A. T. (1961). A systematic investigation of depression. *Comprehensive Psychiatry, 2*, 163–170.

Beck, A. T. (1963). Thinking and depression. *Archives of General Psychiatry, 9*, 324–333.

Beck, A. T. (1970). The core problem in depression: The cognitive triad. In J. Masserman (Ed.), *Depression: Theories and therapies* (pp. 47–55). New York, NY: Grune & Stratton.

Beck, A. T. (1976). *Cognitive therapy and the emotional disorders*. Oxford, England: International Universities Press.

Beck, A. T., Emery, G., & Greenberg, R. L. (1985). *Anxiety disorders and phobias: A cognitive perspective*. New York, NY: Basic Books.

Beck, A. T., Epstein, N., Brown, G., & Steer, R. (1988). An inventory for measuring clinical anxiety: Psychometric properties. *Journal of Consulting & Clinical Psychology, 56*, 893–897.

Beck, A. T., Rush, A., Shaw, B., & Emery, G. (1979). *Cognitive therapy of depression*. New York, NY: Guilford Press.

Beck, A. T., Ward, C. H., Mendelson, M., Mock, J., & Erbaugh, J. (1961). An inventory for measuring depression. *Archives of General Psychiatry, 4*, 561–571.

Beck, H. P., Levinson, S., & Irons, G. (2009). Finding little Albert: A journey to John B. Watson's infant laboratory. *American Psychologist, 64*(7), 605–614.

Beck, J. S. (1995). *Cognitive therapy: Basics and beyond*. New York, NY: Guilford Press.

Beck, J. S. (2005). *Cognitive therapy for challenging problems: What to do when the basics don't work*. New York, NY: Guilford Press.

Begley, S. (2007). *Train your mind, change your brain*. New York, NY: Ballantine Books.

Beitman, B. D. (1987). *The structure of individual psychotherapy*. New York, NY: Guilford Press.

Bell, A. C., & D'Zurilla, T. J. (2009). Problem-solving therapy for depression: A meta-analysis. *Clinical Psychology Review, 29*(4), 348–353.

Bell, R. J., Skinner, C. H., & Fisher, L. A. (2009). Decreasing putting yips in accomplished golfers via solution-focused guided imagery: A single-subject research design. *Journal of Applied Sport Psychology, 21*(1), 1–14.

Benjamin, J. (1990). An outline of intersubjectivity: The development of recognition. *Psychoanalytic Psychology, 7*, 33–46.

Benson, H. (1976). *The relaxation response*. New York, NY: Avon Books.

Berg, I. K., & de Shazer, S. (1993). Making numbers talk: Language in therapy. In S. Friedman (Ed.), *The new language of change: Constructive collaboration in psychotherapy* (pp. 5–24). New York, NY: Guilford Press.

Bériault, M., & Larivée, S. (2005). Guérir avec l'EMDR: Preuves et controverses. French review of EMDR efficacy: Evidences and controversies. *Revue De Psychoeducation, 34*(2), 355–396.

Bernstein, D. A., & Borkovec, T. D. (1973). *Progressive relaxation training: A manual for the helping professions*. Champaign, IL: Research Press.

Bertolino, B. (1999). *Therapy with troubled teenagers: Rewriting young lives in progress*. New York, NY: John Wiley & Sons.

Beutler, L. E. (2009). Making science matter in clinical practice: Redefining psychotherapy. *Clinical Psychology: Science and Practice, 16*(3), 301–317.

Beutler, L. E. (2011). Prescriptive matching and systematic treatment selection. In J. C. Norcross, G. R.

VandenBos & D. K. Freedheim (Eds.), *History of psychotherapy: Continuity and change* (2nd ed., pp. 402–407). Washington, DC: American Psychological Association.

Beutler, L. E., Harwood, T. M., Bertoni, M., & Thomann, J. (2006). Systematic treatment selection and prescriptive therapy. In G. Stricker & J. Gold (Eds.), *A casebook of psychotherapy integration* (pp. 29–41). Washington, DC: American Psychological Association.

Beutler, L. E., Moleiro, C., & Talebi, H. (2002). How practitioners can systematically use empirical evidence in treatment selection. *Journal of Clinical Psychology. Special Issue: Reprioritizing the Role of Science in a Realistic Version of the Scientist-Practitioner Model, 58*(10), 1199–1212.

Bieschke, K. J., Perez, R. M., & DeBord, K. A. (2007). *Handbook of counseling and psychotherapy with lesbian, gay, bisexual, and transgender clients* (2nd ed.). Washington, DC: American Psychological Association.

Binder, J. L. (2004). *Key competencies in brief dynamic psychotherapy: Clinical practice beyond the manual*. New York: Guilford.

Binswanger, L. (1933). *Ueber ideenflucht. Flight of ideas*. Oxford, England: Orell Fuessli.

Binswanger, L. (1963). *Being-in-the-world: Selected papers of Ludwig Binswanger*. New York, NY: Basic Books.

Bitter, J. R. (2009). *Theory and practice of family therapy and counseling*. Belmont, CA: Brooks/Cole.

Bitter, J. R., Christensen, O. C., Hawes, C., & Nicoll, W. G. (1998). Adlerian brief therapy with individuals, couples, and families. *Directions in clinical and counseling psychology* (pp. 95–111). New York, NY: Hatherleigh.

Blackhart, G. C., Eckel, L. A., & Tice, D. M. (2007). Salivary cortisol in response to acute social rejection and acceptance by peers. *Biological Psychology, 75*(3), 267–276.

Blashill, A. J. (2010). Elements of male body image: Prediction of depression, eating pathology and social sensitivity among gay men. *Body Image, 7*(4), 310–316.

Blom, R. (2006). *The handbook of Gestalt play therapy: Practical guidelines for child therapists*. London, England: Kingsley.

Blow, A. J., & Sprenkle, D. H. (2001). Common factors across theories of marriage and family therapy: A modified Delphi study. *Journal of Marital and Family Therapy, 27*, 385–402.

Blume, T. W. (2006). *Becoming a family counselor: A bridge to family therapy theory and practice*. Hoboken, NJ: John Wiley & Sons.

Boesky, D. (1990). The psychoanalytic process and its components. *Psychoanalytic Quarterly, 59*, 550–584.

Bohart, A. C. (1995). The person-centered psychotherapies. In A. S. Gurman & S. B. Messer (Eds.), *Essential psychotherapies* (pp. 85–127). New York, NY: Guilford Press.

Bohart, A. C., Elliott, R., Greenberg, L. S., & Watson, J. C. (2002). Empathy. In J. C. Norcross (Ed.), *Psychotherapy relationships that work: Therapist contributions and responsiveness to patients* (pp. 89–108). New York, NY: Oxford University Press.

Bohart, A. C., & Greenberg, L. S. (1997). *Empathy reconsidered*. Washington, DC: American Psychological Association.

Boisvert, C. M., & Faust, D. (2003). Leading researchers' consensus on psychotherapy research findings: Implications for the teaching and conduct of psychotherapy. *Professional Psychology: Research & Practice, 34*, 508–513.

Boldt, L. G. (1999). *Zen and the art of making a living*. New York: Penguin Putnam.

Bordin, E. S. (1979). The generalizability of the psychoanalytic concept of the working alliance. *Psychotherapy: Theory, Research & Practice, 16*(3), 252–260.

Boss, M. (1963). *Psychoanalysis and daseinsanalysis*. Oxford, England: Basic Books.

Bottome, P. (1936). Limits to a human being—if any. *International Journal of Individual Psychology, 2*(4), 37–48.

Bowen, M. (1978). *Family therapy in clinical practice*. New York, NY: Aronson.

Bowers, K. S., & Meichenbaum, D. (1984). *The unconscious reconsidered*. New York, NY: John Wiley & Sons.

Bowlby, J. (1977). The making and breaking of affectional bonds: II. Some principles of psychotherapy. *British Journal of Psychiatry, 130*, 421–431.

Bowlby, J. (1978). Attachment theory and its therapeutic implications. *Adolescent Psychiatry, 6*, 5–33.

Bowlby, J. (1988a). Developmental psychiatry comes of age. *American Journal of Psychiatry, 145*(1), 1–10.

Bowlby, J. (1988b). *A secure base: Parent-child attachment and healthy human development*. New York, NY: Basic Books.

Bowlby, J. P. (1949). The study and reduction of group tensions in the family. *Human Relations, 2*, 123–138.

Bowman, C. E., & Nevis, E. C. (2005). *The history and development of Gestalt therapy*. Thousand Oaks, CA: Sage.

Braith, J. A., McCullough, J. P., & Bush, J. P. (1988). Relaxation-induced anxiety in a subclinical sample of chronically anxious subjects. *Journal of Behavior Therapy and Experimental Psychiatry, 19*(3), 193–198.

Brannigan, M. C. (2000). *Striking a balance: A primer in traditional Asian values*. New York, NY: Seven Bridges Press.

Breggin, P. R. (1991). *Toxic psychiatry: Why therapy, empathy and love must replace the drugs, electroshock and biochemical theories of the "new psychiatry."* New York: St. Martins.

Breggin, P. R. (2001). A dangerous assignment. In H. G. Rosenthal (Ed.), *Favorite counseling and therapy homework assignments* (pp. 58–59). Washington, DC: Accelerated Development.

Brenner, C. (1973). *An elementary textbook of psychoanalysis* (Rev. ed.). Madison, CT: International Universities Press.

Bressi, C., Manenti, S., Frongia, P., Porcellana, M., & Invernizzi, G. (2007). Systemic family therapy in schizophrenia: A randomized clinical trial of effectiveness. *Psychotherapy and Psychosomatics, 77*(1), 43–49.

Breuer, J., & Freud, S. (1895). *Studies on hysteria* (Standard Edition ed.). London: Hogarth Press.

Bridson, K. (2010). *Stunned: The new generation of women having babies, getting angry, and creating a mothers' movement*. Deerfield Beach, FL: HCI.

Brockmon, C. (2004). The fish is in the water and the water is in the fish: A perspective on the context of gay and lesbian relationships for gestalt therapists. *Gestalt Review, 8*(2), 161–177.

Bronfenbrenner, U. (1979). *The ecology of human development*. Cambridge, MA: Harvard University Press.

Broverman, I. K., Broverman, D. M., Clarkson, F. E., Rosenkrantz, P. S., & Vogel, S. R. (1970). Sex-role stereotypes and clinical judgment of mental health. *Journal of Consulting and Clinical Psychology, 34*, 1–7.

Brown, L. (Director). (1994). *Feminist therapy*. [Video/DVD] Washington, DC: American Psychological Association.

Brown, L. S. (1994). *Subversive dialogues: Theory in feminist therapy*. New York, NY: Basic Books.

Brown, L. S. (2010). *Feminist therapy*. Washington, DC: American Psychological Association.

Brown, L., & Ballou, M. (1990). *Diversity and complexity in feminist therapy*. New York, NY: Guilford Press.

Brown, L. S., & Brodsky, A. M. (1992). The future of feminist therapy. *Psychotherapy, 29*, 51–57.

Brown, T., & Swenson, S. (2005). Identifying basic needs: The contextual needs assessment. *International Journal of Reality Therapy, 24*(2), 7–10.

Browne, E. G. (1921). *Arabian medicine*. New York, NY: Macmillan.

Bruch, H. (1981). Teaching and learning of psychotherapy. *Canadian Journal of Psychiatry, 26*, 86–92.

Bry, A. (1973). *Inside psychotherapy*. New York, NY: Signet.

Buber, M. (1970). *I and thou*. New York, NY: Scribner.

Bugental, J.F.T. (1987). *The art of the psychotherapist*. New York, NY: Norton.

Bugental, J.F.T. (1999). *Psychotherapy isn't what you think: Bringing the psychotherapeutic engagement into the living moment*. Phoenix, AZ: Zeig, Tucker.

Bugental, J.F.T. (2000). Outcomes of an existential-humanistic psychotherapy: A tribute to Rollo May. *The Humanistic Psychologist, 28*(1–3), 251–259.

Burdenski, T. K., Jr. (2010). What does the future hold for choice theory and reality therapy from a newcomer's perspective? *International Journal of Choice Theory and Reality Therapy, 29*(2), 13–16.

Burdenski, T. K., Jr. & Faulkner, B. (2010). Empowering college students to satisfy their basic needs: Implications for primary, secondary, and post-secondary educators. *International Journal of Choice Theory and Reality Therapy, 30*(1), 73–97.

Burdenski, T. K., Jr. Faulkner, B., Britzman, M. J., Casstevens, W. J., Cisse, G. S., Crowell, J. L., et al. (2009). The impact of the Glasser scholars project on participants' teaching and research initiatives: Part 1. *International Journal of Reality Therapy, 29*, 43–49.

Burke, J. F. (1989). *Contemporary approaches to psychotherapy and counseling: The self-regulation model*. Pacific Grove, CA: Brooks/Cole.

Burns, D. (1989). *The feeling good handbook*. New York, NY: Morrow.

Burns, D., & Spangler, D. L. (2000). Does psychotherapy homework lead to improvements in depression in cognitive–behavioral therapy or does improvement lead to increased homework compliance? *Journal of Consulting and Clinical Psychology, 68*(1), 46–56.

Burns, M. K., Vance, D., Szadokierski, I., & Stockwell, C. (2006). Student needs survey: A psychometrically sound measure of the five basic needs. *International Journal of Reality Therapy, 25*, 4–8.

Bush, J. W. (2002). *Epictetus, the fundamentals*. Retrieved October 12, 2011: http://www.anxietyinsights.info/read/page/jwb_epictetus_fundamentals.htm.

Byrd, K. R., Patterson, C. L., & Turchik, J. A. (2010). Working alliance as a mediator of client attachment dimensions and psychotherapy outcome. *Psychotherapy: Theory, Research, Practice, Training, 47*(4), 631–636.

Cade, B. (2009). Monty python-focused therapy. In E. Connie & L. Metcalf (Eds.), *The art of solution focused therapy* (pp. 111–124). New York, NY: Springer.

Cain, D. J. (2010). *Person-centered psychotherapies*. Washington, DC: American Psychological Association.

Campbell, D. T., Stanley, J. C., & Gage, N. L. (1963). *Experimental and quasi-experimental designs for research*. Boston, MA: Houghton Mifflin.

Canino, G., & Alegría, M. (2008). Psychiatric diagnosis—Is it universal or relative to culture? *Journal of Child Psychology and Psychiatry, 49*(3), 237–250.

Caplan, P. J. (1995). *They say you're crazy: How the world's most powerful psychiatrists decide who's normal*. Reading, MA: Addison-Wesley/Addison Wesley Longman.

Caplan, P. J., & Cosgrove, L. (Eds.). (2004). *Bias in psychiatric diagnosis*. Lanham, MD: Aronson.

Carkuff, R. R. (1987). *The art of helping* (6th ed.). Amherst, MA: Human Resource Development Press.

Carlson, J., & Glasser, W. (2004). Adler and Glasser: A demonstration and dialogue. *The Journal of Individual Psychology, 60,* 308–324.

Carlson, J., & Kjos, D. (Directors). (2000). *Narrative therapy with Stephen Madigan*. [Video/DVD] Boston, MA: Allyn & Bacon.

Carlson, J., & Kjos, D. (Directors). (2000). *Person centered therapy with Dr. Natalie Rogers*. [Video/DVD] Boston, MA: Allyn & Bacon.

Carlson, J., Watts, R. E., & Maniacci, M. (2006). *Adlerian therapy: Theory and practice*. Washington, DC: American Psychological Association.

Carton, J. S., & Nowicki, S., Jr. (1998). Should behavior therapists stop using reinforcement? A reexamination of the undermining effect of reinforcement on intrinsic motivation. *Behavior Therapy, 29,* 65–86.

Cassidy, J., & Shaver, P. R. (2008). *Handbook of attachment: Theory, research, and clinical applications* (2nd ed.). New York, NY: Guilford Press.

Castonguay, L. G., Boswell, J. F., Constantino, M. J., Goldfried, M. R., & Hill, C. E. (2010). Training implications of harmful effects of psychological treatments. *American Psychologist, 65*(1), 34–49.

Chambless, D. L., Baker, M. J., Baucom, D. H., Beutler, L. E., Calhoun, K. S., Crits-Christoph, P., et al. (1998). Update on empirically validated therapies, II. *The Clinical Psychologist, 51,* 3–16.

Chambless, D. L., Caputo, G., Bright, P., & Gallagher, R. (1984). Assessment of fear in agoraphobia: The Body Sensations Questionnaire and the Agoraphobia Cognitions Questionnaire. *Journal of Consulting & Clinical Psychology, 52,* 1090–1097.

Chambless, D. L., Caputo, G., Gracely, S., Jasin, E., & Williams, C. (1985). Assessment of fear in agoraphobics: The Mobility Inventory for Agoraphobia. *Behaviour Research and Therapy, 23,* 35–44.

Chambless, D. L., Crits-Christoph, P., Wampold, B. E., Norcross, J. C., Lambert, M. J., Bohart, A. C., et al. (2006). What should be validated? In J. C. Norcross, L. E. Beutler, & R. F. Levant (Eds.), *Evidence-based practices in mental health: Debate and dialogue on the fundamental questions* (pp. 191–256). Washington, DC: American Psychological Association.

Chambless, D. L., & Hollon, S. D. (1998). Defining empirically supported therapies. *Journal of Consulting & Clinical Psychology, 66*(1), 7–18.

Chandler, R., Worell, J., Johnson, D., Blount, A., & Lusk, M. (1999). Measuring long-term outcomes of feminist counseling and psychotherapy. *Annual Convention of the American Psychological Association*, Boston, MA.

Chang, E. C., D'Zurilla, T. J., & Sanna, L. J. (Eds.). (2004). *Social problem solving: Theory, research, and training*. Washington, DC: American Psychological Association.

Chen, Z., Williams, K. D., Fitness, J., & Newton, N. C. (2008). When hurt will not heal: Exploring the capacity to relive social and physical pain. *Psychological Science, 19*(8), 789–795.

Chesler, P. (1972). *Women and madness*. New York, NY: Doubleday.

Chima, I. M., & Nnodum, B. (2008). Efficacy of reality therapy and cognitive coping behaviour training in handling adjustment problems of empty-nester retirees. *The Nigerian Journal of Guidance & Counselling, 13*(1), 190–200.

Christakis, N. A. (2011). Holism. In *Edge: World Question Center*, p. 6. Retrieved July 2, 2011 from http://www.edge.org/q2011/q11_6.html

Christopher, J. C. (1996). Counseling's inescapable moral visions. *Journal of Counseling & Development, 75,* 17–25.

Christopher, J. C. (1999). Situating psychological well-being: Exploring the cultural roots of its theory and research. *Journal of Counseling & Development, 77,* 141–152.

Christopher, J. C. (2001). Culture and psychotherapy: Toward a hermeneutic approach. *Psychotherapy: Theory, Research, Practice, Training, 38*(2), 115–128.

Christopher, J. C., & Bickhard, M. H. (2007). Culture, self and identity: Interactivist contributions to a metatheory for cultural psychology. *Culture & Psychology, 13*(3), 259–295.

Clark, A. J. (2002). *Early recollections: Theory and practice in counseling and psychotherapy*. New York, NY: Brunner-Routledge.

Clark, A. J. (2007). *Empathy in counseling and psychotherapy: Perspectives and practices*. Mahwah, NJ: Erlbaum.

Clark, A. J. (2010a). Empathy and sympathy: Therapeutic distinctions in counseling. *Journal of Mental Health Counseling, 32*(2), 95–101.

Clark, A. J. (2010b). Empathy: An integral model in the counseling process. *Journal of Counseling & Development, 88,* 348–356.

Clark, D. A., Beck, A. T., & Alford, B. A. (1999). *Scientific foundation of cognitive theory and therapy of depression.* New York, NY: John Wiley & Sons.

Clarkin, J. F., Levy, K. N., Lenzenweger, M. F., & Kernberg, O. F. (2004). The personality disorders institute/borderline personality disorder research foundation randomized control trial for borderline personality disorder: Rationale, methods, and patient characteristics. *Journal of Personality Disorders, 18*(1), 52–72.

Clarkson, P. (1997). Variations on I and thou. *Gestalt Review, 1,* 56–70.

Clarkson, P. (2003). *The therapeutic relationship* (2nd ed.). Philadelphia, PA: Whurr.

Cohen, J. (1977). *Statistical power analysis for the behavioral sciences* (Rev. ed.). Hillsdale, NJ, England: Erlbaum.

Collins, P. H. (2009). *Black feminist thought: Knowledge, consciousness, and the politics of empowerment.* New York, NY: Routledge.

Comas-Díaz, L. (Director). (1994). *Ethnocultural psychotherapy.* [Video/DVD] Washington, DC: American Psychological Association.

Comas-Díaz, L. (2008). Latino psychospitituality. In K. J. Schneider (Ed.), *Existential-integrative psychotherapy: Guideposts to the core of practice* (pp. 100–109). New York, NY: Routledge/Taylor & Francis.

Comas-Díaz, L. (2010). On being a Latina healer: Voice, consciousness, and identity. *Psychotherapy: Theory, Research, Practice, Training, 47*(2), 162–168.

Comas-Díaz, L., & Griffith, E.E.H. (Eds.). (1988). *Clinical guidelines in cross-cultural mental health.* Oxford, England: John Wiley & Sons.

Connie, E., & Metcalf, L. (Eds.). (2009). *The art of solution focused therapy.* New York, NY: Springer.

Conoley, C. W., Graham, J. M., Neu, T., Craig, M. C., O'Pry, A., Cardin, S. A., et al. (2003). Solution-focused family therapy with three aggressive and oppositional-acting children: An N=1 empirical study. *Family Process, 42*(3), 361–374.

Constantine, M. G., Fuertes, J. N., Roysircar, G., & Kindaichi, M. M. (2008). Multicultural competence: Clinical practice, training and supervision, and research. In W. B. Walsh (Ed.), *Biennial review of counseling psychology: Volume 1* (pp. 97–127). New York, NY: Routledge/Taylor & Francis.

Corcoran, J., & Pillai, V. (2009). A review of the research on solution-focused therapy. *British Journal of Social Work, 39*(2), 234–242.

Cormier, S., Nurius, P. S., & Osborn, C. J. (2009). *Interviewing and change strategies for helpers: Fundamental skills and cognitive-behavioral interventions* (6th ed.). Monterey, CA: Brooks/Cole.

Corsini, R. (1998). Turning the tables on the client: Making the client the counselor. In H. G. Rosenthal (Ed.), *Favorite counseling techniques: 51 therapists share their most creative strategies* (pp. 54–57). Washington, DC: Accelerated Development.

Corsini, R., & Wedding, D. (Eds.). (2000). *Current psychotherapies* (6th ed.). Itasca, IL: Peacock.

Cosgrove, L., & Riddle, B. (2004). Gender bias and sex distribution of mental disorders in the *DSM-IV-TR.* In P. J. Caplan & L. Cosgrove (Eds.), Bias in psychiatric diagnosis (pp. 127–140). Lanham, MD: Aronson.

Cox, J. A., Bañez, L., Hawley, L. D., & Mostade, J. (2003). Use of the reflecting team process in the training of group workers. *Journal for Specialists in Group Work, 28*(2), 89–105.

Craig, R. J. (2005). The clinical process of interviewing. In R. J. Craig (Ed.), *Clinical and diagnostic interviewing* (2nd. ed., pp. 21–41). Lanham, MD: Aronson.

Crandall, J. E. (1975). A scale for social interest. *Journal of Individual Psychology, 31*(2), 187–195.

Crandall, J. E. (1977). Further validation of the social interest scale: Peer ratings and interpersonal attraction. *Journal of Clinical Psychology, 33*(1), 140–142.

Craske, M. G. (1999). *Anxiety disorders: Psychological approaches to theory and treatment.* Boulder, CO: Westview Press.

Craske, M. G. (2010). *Cognitive–behavioral therapy.* Washington, DC: American Psychological Association.

Crits-Christoph, P., Gibbons, M.B.C., & Hearon, B. (2006). Does the alliance cause good outcome? Recommendations for future research on the alliance. *Psychotherapy: Theory, Research, 43,* 280–285.

Croll, M. (1992). The individualist roots of reality therapy: A textual analysis of Emerson's "self-reliance" and Glasser's reality therapy. *Journal of Reality Therapy, 11,* 22–26.

Crumbaugh, J. C. (1968). Cross-validation of purpose-in-life test based on Frankl's concepts. *Journal of Individual Psychology, 24*(1), 74–81.

Crumbaugh, J. C. (1977). The seeking of noetic goals test (SONG): A complementary scale to the purpose in life test (PIL). *Journal of Clinical Psychology, 33*(3), 900–907.

Crumbaugh, J. C., & Henrion, R. (1988). The PIL test: Administration, interpretations theory and critique. *International Forum for Logotherapy, 11*(2), 76–88.

Cuijpers, P., van Straten, A., & Warmerdam, L. (2007a). Behavioral activation treatments of depression: A meta-analysis. *Clinical Psychology Review, 27*(3), 318–326.

Cuijpers, P., van Straten, A., & Warmerdam, L. (2007b). Problem solving therapies for depression: A meta-analysis. *European Psychiatry, 22*(1), 9–15.

Cull, M. (2002). Treatment of intersex needs open discussion. *BMJ: British Medical Journal, 324*(7342), 919–919.

Cullin, J. (2006). Double bind: Much more than just a step "toward a theory of schizophrenia." *ANZJFT Australian and New Zealand Journal of Family Therapy, 27*(3), 135–142.

Daldrup, R. J., Beutler, L. E., Engle, D., & Greenberg, L. S. (1988). *Focused expressive psychotherapy: Freeing the overcontrolled patient*. New York, NY: Guilford Press.

Dana, R. H. (1993). *Multicultural assessment perspectives for professional psychology*. Boston, MA: Allyn & Bacon.

Dana, R. H. (1996). Culturally competent assessment practice in the United States. *Journal of Personality Assessment, 66*, 472–487.

Dankoski, M. E., & Deacon, S. A. (2000). Using a feminist lens in contextual therapy. *Family Process, 39*(1), 51–67.

Davey, G.C.L. (2006). Cognitive mechanisms in fear acquisition and maintenance. In M. G. Craske, D. Hermans, & D. Vansteenwegen (Eds.), *Fear and learning: From basic processes to clinical implications* (pp. 99–116). Washington, DC: American Psychological Association.

Davidson, F. (Producer & Director). (1995). *On old age : A conversation with Joan Erikson at 90*. [Motion Picture] USA: Davidson Films, 668 Marsh Street, San Luis Obispo CA 93401.

Davidson, H., & Birmingham, C. L. (2001). Letter writing as a therapeutic tool. *Eating and Weight Disorders, 6*(1), 40–44.

Davidson, P. R., & Parker, K.C.H. (2001). Eye movement desensitization and reprocessing (EMDR): A meta-analysis. *Journal of Consulting and Clinical Psychology, 69*(2), 305–316.

Davies, S. C., Jones, K. M., & Rafoth, M. A. (2010). Effects of a self-monitoring intervention on children with traumatic brain injury. *Journal of Applied School Psychology, 26*(4), 308–326.

Dawes, R. M. (1994). *House of cards: Psychology and psychotherapy built on myth*. New York, NY: Free Press.

de Barbaro, B., Drozdzowicz, L., Janusz, B., Gdowska, K., Dembinska, E., Kolbik, I., et al. (2008). Multi-couple reflecting team: Preliminary report. *Journal of Marital and Family Therapy, 34*(3), 287–297.

de Becker, G. (1997). *The gift of fear*. New York: Dell.

DeCarvalho, R. J. (1996). Rollo R. May (1909–1994): A biographical sketch. *Journal of Humanistic Psychology, 36*(2), 8–16.

Deci, E. L. (1971). Effects of externally mediated rewards on intrinsic motivation. *Journal of Personality and Social Psychology, 18*, 105–115.

Deci, E. L., Koestner, R., & Ryan, R. M. (2001). Extrinsic rewards and intrinsic motivation in education: Reconsidered once again. *Review of Educational Research, 71*(1), 1–27.

DeJong, P., & Hopwood, L. E. (1996). Outcome research on treatment conducted at the brief family therapy center, 1992–1993. In S. D. Miller, M. A. Hubble, & B. L. Duncan (Eds.), *Handbook of solution-focused brief therapy* (pp. 272–298). San Francisco, CA: Jossey-Bass.

Dell'Osso, B., Priori, A., & Altamura, A. C. (2011). Efficacy and safety of transcranial direct current stimulation in major depression. *Biological Psychiatry, 69*(8), 23–24.

de Maat, S., de Jonghe, F., Schoevers, R., & Dekker, J. (2009). The effectiveness of long-term psychoanalytic therapy: A systematic review of empirical studies. *Harvard Review of Psychiatry, 17*, 1–23.

de Oliveira, A.S.B. (2003). An "appropriated unusual" reflecting team: Inviting parents to be on the team. *Journal of Family Psychotherapy, 14*(2), 85–88.

de Shazer, S. (1984). The death of resistance. *Family Process, 23*(1), 11–17.

de Shazer, S. (1985). *Keys to solution in brief therapy*. New York, NY: Norton.

de Shazer, S. (1988). *Clues: Investigating solutions in brief therapy*. New York, NY: Norton.

de Shazer, S. (1991). *Putting differences to work*. New York, NY: Norton.

de Shazer, S. (1993). Creative misunderstanding: There is no escape from language. In S. G. Gilligan & R. Price (Eds.), *Therapeutic conversations* (pp. 81–90). New York, NY: Norton.

de Shazer, S. (1994). *Words were originally magic*. New York, NY: Norton.

de Shazer, S., Dolan, Y., Korman, H., McCollum, E., Trepper, T., & Berg, I. K. (2007). *More than miracles: The state of the art of solution-focused brief therapy*. New York, NY: Haworth Press.

de Shazer, S., & Molnar, A. (1984). Four useful interventions in brief family therapy. *Journal of Marital & Family Therapy, 10*(3), 297–304.

Dewey, J. (1920). *Reconstruction in philosophy*. New York: Henry Holt.

Diamond, G. S., Wintersteen, M. B., Brown, G. K., Diamond, G. M., Gallop, R., Shelef, K., et al. (2010). Attachment-based family therapy for adolescents with suicidal ideation: A randomized controlled trial. *Journal of the American Academy of Child & Adolescent Psychiatry, 49*(2), 122–131.

DiIorio, C., Dudley, W. N., Wang, D. T., Wasserman, J., Eichler, M., Belcher, L., et al. (2001). Measurement of parenting self-efficacy and outcome expectancy related to discussions about sex. *Journal of Nursing Measurement, 9*(2), 135–149.

Dinkmeyer, D. C., Dinkmeyer, D. C., Jr., & Sperry, L. (1987). *Adlerian counseling and psychotherapy* (2nd ed.). Columbus, OH: Merrill.

Dinkmeyer, D., & Dreikurs, R. (1963). *Encouraging children to learn: The encouragement process*. Oxford, England: Prentice Hall.

Dobson, D., & Dobson, K. S. (2009). *Evidence-based practice of cognitive-behavioral therapy*. New York, NY: Guilford Press.

Dodge, K. A. (1980). Social cognition and children's aggressive behavior. *Child Development, 51*, 162–170.

Dodge, K. A., & Frame, C. L. (1982). Social cognitive biases and deficits in aggressive boys. *Child Development, 53*, 620–635.

Dodge, K. A., & Somberg, D. R. (1987). Hostile attributional biases among aggressive boys are exacerbated under conditions of threat to the self. *Child Development, 58*, 213–224.

Dollard, J., & Miller, N. E. (1950). *Personality and psychotherapy: An analysis in terms of learning, thinking, and culture*. New York, NY: McGraw-Hill.

Donohue, W. A. (1990). *The new freedom: Individualism and collectivism in the social lives of Americans*. New Brunswick, NJ: Transaction.

Draucker, C. B. (2003). Unique outcomes of women and men who were abused. *Perspectives in Psychiatric Care, 39*(1), 7–16.

Dreikurs, R. (1948). *The challenge of parenthood*. Oxford, England: Duell, Sloan & Pearce.

Dreikurs, R. (1950). *Fundamentals of Adlerian psychology*. New York, NY: Greenberg.

Dreikurs, R. (1969). *Psychodynamics, psychotherapy, and counseling*. Chicago, IL: Alfred Adler Institute.

Dreikurs, R., & Mosak, H. H. (1966). The tasks of life I: Adler's three tasks. *Individual Psychology, 4*, 18–22.

Dreikurs, R., & Mosak, H. H. (1967). The tasks of life: II: The fourth life task. *Individual Psychology, 4*, 51–55.

Drossel, C., Rummel, C., & Fisher, J. E. (2009). Assessment and cognitive behavior therapy: Functional analysis as key process. In W. T. O'Donohue & J. E. Fisher (Eds.), *General principles and empirically supported techniques of cognitive behavior therapy* (pp. 15–41). Hoboken, NJ: John Wiley & Sons.

Dryden, W. (1989). Albert Ellis: An efficient and passionate life. *Journal of Counseling and Development, 67*, 539–546.

Duan, C., Rose, T. B., & Kraatz, R. A. (2002). Empathy. In G. S. Tryon (Ed.), *Counseling based on process research: Applying what we know* (pp. 197–231). Boston, MA: Allyn & Bacon.

Dubelle, S. (1997, September). Part two: Excerpts from an interview with Heinz Ansbacher, Ph.D. *The Quarterly: Publication of the Adlerian Psychology Association of British Columbia*, pp. 5–7.

Duncan, B. L., Miller, S. D., & Sparks, J. A. (2004). *The heroic client: A revolutionary way to improve effectiveness through client-directed, outcome-informed therapy* (Rev. ed.). San Francisco, CA: Jossey-Bass.

Duncan, B. L., Miller, S. D., Wampold, B. E., & Hubble, M. A. (Eds.). (2010). *The heart and soul of change: Delivering what works in therapy* (2nd ed.). Washington, DC: American Psychological Association.

D'Zurilla, T. J., & Goldfried, M. R. (1971). Problem solving and behavior modification. *Journal of Abnormal Psychology, 78*(1), 107–126.

D'Zurilla, T. J., & Nezu, A. M. (2010). *Problem-solving therapy*. New York, NY: Guilford Press.

Eagle, M. (2003). Clinical implications of attachment theory. *Psychoanalytic Inquiry, 23*, 27–53.

Edwards, M. E., & Steinglass, P. (1995). Family therapy treatment outcomes for alcoholism. *Journal of Marital and Family Therapy. Special Issue: The Effectiveness of Marital and Family Therapy, 21*(4), 475–509.

Efran, J. S., & Fauber, R. L. (1995). Radical constructivism: Questions and answers. In R. A. Neimeyer & M. Mahoney (Eds.), *Constructivism in psychotherapy* (pp. 275–304). Washington, DC: American Psychological Association.

Elkin, I. E., Shea, T., Watkins, J. T., Imber, S. D., Stotsky, S. M., Collins, J. F., et al. (1989). National Institute of Mental Health treatment of depression collaborative research program: General effectiveness of treatment. *Archives of General Psychiatry, 46*, 974–982.

Ellenberger, H. F. (1970). *The discovery of the unconscious: The history and evolution of dynamic psychiatry.* New York, NY: Basic Books.

Elliott, R., Bohart, A. C., Watson, J. C., & Greenberg, L. S. (2011). Empathy. *Psychotherapy, 48*(1), 43–49.

Elliott, R., & Greenberg, L. S. (2002). *Process–experiential psychotherapy.* Washington, DC: American Psychological Association.

Elliott, R., & Greenberg, L. S. (2007). The essence of process-experiential/emotion-focused therapy. *American Journal of Psychotherapy, 61*(3), 241–254.

Elliot, R., Greenberg, L. S., & Lietaer, G. (2002). Research on experiential psychotherapies. In M. Lambert (Ed.), *Handbook of psychotherapy and behavior change* (5th ed.). New York, NY: John Wiley & Sons.

Elliott, R., Watson, J. C., Goldman, R. N., & Greenberg, L. S. (2004). *Process-experiential theory made simple.* Washington, DC: American Psychological Association.

Elliott, R., & Zucconi, A. (2006). Doing research on the effectiveness of psychotherapy and psychotherapy training: A person-centered/experiential perspective. *Person-Centered and Experiential Psychotherapies, 5*, 81–100.

Elliott-Boyle, D. (1985). A conceptual analysis of codes of ethics. *Journal of Mass Media Ethics, 1*, 22–26.

Ellis, A. (1962). *Reason and emotion in psychotherapy.* New York, NY: Lyle Stuart.

Ellis, A. (1970). Tribute to Alfred Adler. *Journal of Individual Psychology, 26*, 11–12.

Ellis, A. (1987). The evolution of rational-emotive therapy (RET) and cognitive behavior therapy (CBT). In J. K. Zeig (Ed.), *The evolution of psychotherapy* (pp. 107–132). New York, NY: Brunner/Mazel.

Ellis, A. (1999a). *How to make yourself happy and remarkably less disturbable.* San Luis Obispo, CA: Impact.

Ellis, A. (1999b). Vigorous disputing of irrational beliefs in rational-emotive behavior therapy (REBT). In H. G. Rosenthal (Ed.), *Favorite counseling and therapy techniques* (pp. 76–77). Washington, DC: Accelerated Development.

Ellis, A., & Dryden, W. (1997). *The practice of rational-emotive therapy* (Rev. ed.). New York, NY: Springer.

Ellis, A., & Grieger, R. (1977). *Handbook of rational-emotive therapy.* New York, NY: Springer.

Ellison, J. A., Greenberg, L. S., Goldman, R. N., & Angus, L. (2009). Maintenance of gains following experiential therapies for depression. *Journal of Consulting and Clinical Psychology, 77*(1), 103–112.

Emmelkamp, P.M.G. (1994). Behavior therapy with adults. In A. E. Bergin & S. L. Garfield (Eds.), *Handbook of psychotherapy and behavior change.* (pp. 379–427). New York, NY: John Wiley & Sons.

Emmelkamp, P.M.G., Bruynzeel, M., Drost, L., & van der Mast, C. A. P. (2001). Virtual reality treatment in acrophobia: A comparison with exposure in vivo. *Cyber Psychology and Behavior, 4*, 335–339.

Emmelkamp, P.M.G., Krijn, M., Hulsbosch, L., de Vries, S., Schuemie, M. J., & van der Mast, C.A.P. (2001). Virtual reality treatment versus exposure in vivo: A comparative evaluation in acrophobia. *Behaviour Research and Therapy, 39*, 184–194.

Engle, D., & Holiman, M. (2002). A case illustration of resistance from a Gestalt-experimental perspective. *Journal of Clinical Psychology, 58*(2), 151–156.

Enns, C. Z. (1988). Dilemmas of power and equality in marital and family counseling: Proposals for a feminist perspective. *Journal of Counseling and Development, 67*, 242–248.

Enns, C. Z. (2004). *Feminist theories and feminist psychotherapies: Origins, themes, and diversity* (2nd ed.). New York, NY: Haworth Press.

Epp, A. M., & Dobson, K. S. (2010). *The evidence base for cognitive-behavioral therapy.* New York, NY: Guilford Press.

Epstein, N. B., Baldwin, L. M., & Bishop, D. S. (1983). The McMaster family assessment device. *Journal of Marital and Family Therapy, 9*, 171–186.

Epston, D. (1994). Extending the conversation. *The Family Networker, 18*(6), 30–37, 62–63.

Erickson, M. H. (1954). Special techniques of brief hypnotherapy. *Journal of Clinical and Experimental Hypnosis, 2*, 109–129.

Erickson, M. H. (1964). The confusion technique in hypnosis. *American Journal of Clinical Hypnosis, 6*, 183–207.

Erickson, S. K., Lilienfeld, S. O., & Vitacco, M. J. (2007). Failing the burden of proof: The science and ethics of projective tests in custody evaluations. *Family Court Review, 45*(2), 185–192.

Erikson, E. H. (1963). *Childhood & society* (2nd ed.). New York, NY: Norton.

Espín, O. M. (1993). Feminist therapy: Not for White women only. *The Counseling Psychologist, 21*(1), 103–108.

Espín, O. M. (1997). *Latina realities: Essays on healing, migration, and sexuality.* Boulder, CO: Westview Press.

Esterson, A. (1998). Jeffrey Masson and Freud's seduction theory: A new fable based on old myths. *History of the Human Sciences, 11*(1), 1–21.

Esterson, A. (2001). The mythologizing of psychoanalytic history: Deception and self-deception in Freud's accounts of the seduction theory episode. *History of Psychiatry, 12,* 329–352.

Estes, W. (1944). An experimental study of punishment. *Psychological Monographs, 57* (Whole No. 263).

Eysenck, H. J. (1952). The effects of psychotherapy: An evaluation. *Journal of Consulting Psychology, 16,* 319–324.

Eysenck, H. J. (1959). Learning theory and behaviour therapy. *Journal of Mental Science, 105,* 61–75.

Eysenck, H. J. (Ed.). (1960). *Behaviour therapy and the neuroses.* New York, NY: Pergamon.

Eysenck, H. J. (Ed.). (1964). *Experiments in behavior therapy.* New York, NY: Pergamon.

Eysenck, H. J. (1970). A mish-mash of theories. *International Journal of Psychiatry, 9,* 140–146.

Fabian, J. M. (2006). A literature review of the utility of selected violence and sexual violence risk assessment instruments. *Journal of Psychiatry & Law, 34*(3), 307–350.

Fairbairn, W. R. (1952). *Psychoanalytic studies of the personality.* Oxford, England: Routledge & Kegan Paul.

Fairburn, C. G. (1993). Interpersonal psychotherapy for bulimia nervosa. In G. L. Klerman & M. M. Weissman (Eds.), *New applications of interpersonal psychotherapy* (pp. 353–378). Washington, DC: American Psychiatric Association.

Fairburn, C. G., Jones, R., Peveler, R. C., & Hope, R. A. (1993). Psychotherapy and bulimia nervosa: Longer-term effects of interpersonal psychotherapy, behavior therapy, and cognitive behavior therapy. *Archives of General Psychiatry, 50*(6), 419–428.

Farmer, R. F., & Nelson-Gray, R. O. (2005). *The history of behavior therapy.* Washington, DC: American Psychological Association.

Farrell, W. (1993). *The myth of male power: Why men are the disposable sex.* New York: Berkley Books.

Fenichel, O. (1945). *The psychoanalytic theory of neurosis.* New York, NY: Norton.

Ferenczi, S. (1920). The further development of an active therapy in psychoanalysis. In J. Rickman (Ed.), *Further contributions to the theory and techniques of psychoanalysis* (pp. 47–81). London, England: Hogarth Press.

Ferenczi, S. (1950). *The selected papers of Sandor Ferenczi.* New York, NY: Basic Books.

Fernandez, R. (2001). *Imagining literacy.* Austin: University of Texas Press.

Ferrer-Wreder, L., Palchuk, A., Poyrazli, S., Small, M. L., & Domitrovich, C. E. (2008). Identity and adolescent adjustment. *Identity: An International Journal of Theory and Research, 8*(2), 95–105.

Ferster, C. B. (1973). A functional analysis of depression. *American Psychologist, 28*(10), 857–870.

Field, T. (2009). *Progressive muscle relaxation.* Washington, DC: American Psychological Association.

Figley, C. (1997). The active ingredients of the power therapies. *The Power Therapies: A Conference for the Integrative and Innovative use of EMDR, TFT, EFT, Advanced NLP, and TIR.* Lakewood, CO.

Finn, S. E. (2009). The many faces of empathy in experiential, person-centered, collaborative assessment. *Journal of Personality Assessment, 91*(1), 20–23.

Fiore, M. C., Jaen, C. R., Baker, T. B., Bailey, W. C., Benowitz, N., Curry, S. J., et al. (2008). *Treating tobacco use and dependence: 2008 update.* Rockville, MD: U.S. Department of Health and Human Services, U.S. Public Health Service.

First, M. B., Spitzer, R. L., Gibbon, M., & Williams, J.B.W. (1997). *User's guide for the structured clinical interview for DSM-IV axis I disorders: Clinician version.* Washington, DC: American Psychiatric Press.

Fish, R. C., & Mozdzierz, G. J. (1991). Validation of the Sulliman scale of social interest with psychotherapy outpatients. *Individual Psychology: Journal of Adlerian Theory, Research & Practice. Special Issue: Social Interest, 47*(1), 150–158.

Fishel, A. K., Buchs, T., McSheffrey, C., & Murphy, C. (2001). Adding written reflections to the reflecting team. *Journal of Family Psychotherapy, 12*(3), 81–88.

Fisher, J. (2009). The unpaid workload: Gender discrimination in conceptualisation and its impact on maternal wellbeing. In P. S. Chandra, et al. (Eds.), *Contemporary topics in women's mental health: Global perspectives in a changing society* (pp. 525–538). Hoboken, NJ: John Wiley & Sons.

Fishman, D. B., & Franks, C. M. (1997). The conceptual evolution of behavior therapy. In P. L. Wachtel & S. B. Messer (Eds.), *Theories of psychotherapy: Origins and evolution* (pp. 131–180). Washington, DC: American Psychological Association.

Fletcher, L., & Hayes, S. C. (2005). Relational frame theory, acceptance and commitment therapy, and a functional analytic definition of mindfulness. *Journal of Rational-Emotive & Cognitive Behavior Therapy, 23*(4), 315–336.

Forcehimes, A. A., & Tonigan, J. S. (2008). Self-efficacy as a factor in abstinence from alcohol/other drug abuse: A meta-analysis. *Alcoholism Treatment Quarterly, 26,* 480–489.

Forman, E. M., Herbert, J. D., Moitra, E., Yeomans, P. D., & Geller, P. A. (2007). A randomized controlled effectiveness trial of acceptance and commitment therapy and cognitive therapy for anxiety and depression. *Behavior Modification, 31*(6), 772–799.

Forsyth, J. P., Fusé, T., & Acheson, D. T. (2009). Interoceptive exposure for panic disorder. In W. T. O'Donohue & J. E. Fisher (Eds.), *General principles and empirically supported techniques of cognitive behavior therapy* (pp. 394–406). Hoboken, NJ: John Wiley & Sons.

Fouad, N. A., & Arredondo, P. (2007). *Becoming culturally oriented: Practical advice for psychologists and educators.* Washington, DC: American Psychological Association.

Foucault, M. (1965). *Madness and civilization: A history of insanity in the age of reason.* New York, NY: Random House.

Fox, R. C. (2006). *Affirmative psychotherapy with bisexual women and bisexual men.* Binghamton, NY: Haworth Press.

Frank, J. D. (1961). *Persuasion and healing: A comparative study of psychotherapy.* Oxford, England: Johns Hopkins University Press.

Frank, J. D. (1973). *Persuasion and healing: A comparative study of psychotherapy.* (Rev. ed.). Baltimore, MD: Johns Hopkins University Press.

Frank, J. D. (1985). Further thoughts on the anti-demoralization hypothesis of psychotherapeutic effectiveness. *Integrative Psychiatry, 3*(1), 17–20.

Frank, J. D., & Frank, J. B. (1996). Demoralization and unexplained illness in two cohorts of American soldiers overseas. *Journal of Nervous and Mental Disease, 184*(7), 445–446.

Frank, J. D., & Frank, J. B. (1991). *Persuasion and healing: A comparative study of psychotherapy* (3rd ed.). Baltimore, MD: Johns Hopkins University Press.

Frankl, V. (1963). *Man's search for meaning.* Boston, MA: Beacon.

Frankl, V. (1967). *Psychotherapy and existentialism: Selected papers on logotherapy.* New York, NY: Clarion.

Frankl, V. E. (1959). The spiritual dimension in existential analysis and logotherapy. *Journal of Individual Psychology, 15*, 157–165.

Franklin, A. J., Boyd-Franklin, N., & Kelly, S. (2006). *Racism and invisibility: Race-related stress, emotional abuse and psychological trauma for people of color.* Binghamton, NY, US: Haworth Maltreatment and Trauma Press/ The Haworth Press.

Franklin, M. E., DeRubeis, R. J., & Westen, D. I. (2006). Are efficacious laboratory-validated treatments readily transportable to clinical practice? In J. C. Norcross, L. E. Beutler & R. F. Levant (Eds.), (pp. 375–402). Washington, DC: American Psychological Association.

Franklin, M. E., & Foa, E. (1998). Cognitive-behavioral treatment of obsessive compulsive disorder. In P. E. Nathan & J. M. Gorman (Eds.), *A guide to treatments that work* (pp. 339–357). Oxford, England: Oxford University Press.

Franklin, M. E., Ledley, D. A., & Foa, E. B. (2009). Response prevention. In W. T. O'Donohue & J. E. Fisher (Eds.), *General principles and empirically supported techniques of cognitive behavior therapy* (pp. 543–549). Hoboken, NJ: John Wiley & Sons.

Franks, C. M., & Barbrack, C. R. (1983). Behavior therapy with adults: An integrative perspective. In M. Hersen, A. E. Kazdin, & A. S. Bellack (Eds.), *The clinical psychology handbook* (pp. 507–523). New York, NY: Pergamon.

Freeman, A., Pretzer, J., Fleming, B., & Simon, K. M. (2004). *Clinical applications of cognitive therapy* (2nd ed.). New York, NY: Kluwer Academic/Plenum.

French, T. M. (1958). *The integrations of behavior.* Chicago, IL: University of Chicago Press.

Freud, S. (1896). *The aetiology of hysteria* (The Standard Edition ed.). London: Hogarth Press.

Freud, S. (1909). Analysis of a phobia in a five-year-old boy. In J. Strachey (Ed.), *Standard edition of the complete psychological works of Sigmund Freud* (Vol. 10, pp. 3-149). London, England: Hogarth Press.

Freud, S. (1923). *Group psychology and the analysis of the ego.* In J. Strachey (Ed.), *Standard edition of the complete psychological works of Sigmund Freud.* (J. Strachey Trans.). (pp. 97–108). London: Hogarth Press.

Freud, S. (1948). Some psychical consequences of the anatomical distinction between the sexes. In J. Strachey (Ed.), *The standard edition of the complete works of Sigmund Freud* (J. Strachey Trans.). (pp. 186–197). London: Hogarth.

Freud, S. (1957). The future prospects of psycho-analytic therapy. In J. Strachey (Ed.), *The standard edition of the complete works of Sigmund Freud* (J. Strachey Trans.). (Vol. 11, pp. 139–152). London, England: Hogarth Press.

Freud, S. (1958). On the beginning of treatment: Further recommendations on the technique of psychoanalysis. In J. Strachey (Ed.), *Standard edition of the complete psychological works of Sigmund Freud.* (J. Strachey Trans.). (pp. 122–144). London, England: Hogarth Press.

Freud, S. (1963). *Introductory lectures on psycho-analysis*. (J. Strachey Trans.). London: Hogarth Press.

Freud, S. (1964). *New introductory lectures on psychoanalysis*. (J. Strachey Trans.). London, England: Hogarth Press.

Freud, S. (1966). The dynamics of transference. In J. Strachey (Ed.), *Standard edition of the complete psychological works of Sigmund Freud*. (J. Strachey Trans.). (pp. 97–108). London: Hogarth Press.

Fromm-Reichmann, F. (1948). Notes on the development of treatment of schizophrenic by psychoanalytic psychotherapy. *Psychiatry, 11*, 263–274.

Fry, P. S. (2000). Religious involvement, spirituality and personal meaning for life: Existential predictors of psychological wellbeing in community-residing and institutional care elders. *Aging & Mental Health, 4*(4), 375–387.

Fry, P. S. (2001). The unique contribution of key existential factors to the prediction of psychological well-being of older adults following spousal loss. *The Gerontologist, 41*(1), 69–81.

Funkerburk, J. R., & Fukuyama, M. A. (2001). Feminism, multiculturalism, and spirituality: Convergent and divergent forces in psychotherapy. *Women & Therapy, 24*(3/4), 1–18.

Gardner, W. L., Pickett, C. L., Jefferis, V., & Knowles, M. (2005). On the outside looking in: Loneliness and social monitoring. *Personality and Social Psychology Bulletin, 31*(11), 1549–1560.

Garfield, S. L., & Kurtz, R. (1975). Clinical psychologists: A survey of selected attitudes and views. *The Clinical Psychologist, 28*, 4–7.

Garfield, S. L., & Kurtz, R. (1977). A study of eclectic views. *Journal of Consulting & Clinical Psychology, 45*, 78–83.

Garrett, M. T., & Pichette, E. F. (2000). Red as an apple: Native American acculturation and counseling with or without reservation. *Journal of Counseling & Development, 78*(1), 3–13.

Gaston, L. (1990). The concept of the alliance and its role in psychotherapy: Theoretical and empirical considerations. *Psychotherapy: Theory, Research, 27*, 143–153.

Gaston, L. (1991). Reliability and criterion-related validity of the California Psychotherapy Alliance Scales—patient version. *Psychological Assessment, 3*(1), 68–74.

Gay, P. (1988). Psychoanalysis in history. In W. M. Runyan (Ed.), *Psychology and historical interpretation*. (pp. 107–120). New York, NY: Oxford University Press.

Gedo, J. E. (1979). *Beyond interpretation*. New York, NY: International Universities Press.

Geertz, C. (1973). *The interpretation of cultures*. New York: Basic Books.

Geller, J. D. (2003). Self-disclosure in psychoanalytic-existential therapy. *Journal of Clinical Psychology. Special Issue: In Session: Self Disclosure, 59*(5), 541–554.

Gelso, C. J., & Hayes, J. A. (1998). *The psychotherapy relationship: Theory, research, and practice*. New York, NY: John Wiley & Sons.

Gendlin, E. T. (1981). *Focusing* (2nd ed.). New York, NY: Bantam.

Gendlin, E. T. (1996). *Focusing-oriented psychotherapy: A manual of the experiential method*. New York, NY: Guilford Press.

Gere, J., & MacDonald, G. (2010). An update of the empirical case for the need to belong. *The Journal of Individual Psychology, 66*(1), 93–115.

Gergen, K. J. (2009a). *An invitation to social construction* (2nd ed.). Thousand Oaks, CA: Sage.

Gergen, K. J. (2009b). The problem of prejudice in plural worlds. *Journal of Theoretical and Philosophical Psychology, 29*(2), 97–101.

Gergen, K. J. (2011). The self as social construction. *Psychological Studies, 56*(1), 108–116.

Gershoff, E. T. (2002). Corporal punishment by parents and associated child behaviors and experiences: A meta-analytic and theoretical review. *Psychological Bulletin, 128*(4), 539–579.

Gershoff, E. T., & Bitensky, S. H. (2007). The case against corporal punishment of children: Converging evidence from social science research and international human rights law and implications for U.S. public policy. *Psychology, Public Policy, and Law, 13*(4), 231–272.

Gfroerer, K. P., Kern, R. M., & Curlette, W. L. (2004). Research support for individual psychology's parenting model. *The Journal of Individual Psychology, 60*(4), 379–388.

Ghent, E. (1989). Credo: The dialectics of one-person and two-person psychologies. *Contemporary Psychoanalysis, 25*, 169–209.

Ghezzi, P. M., Wilson, G. R., Tarbox, R.S.F., & MacAleese, K. R. (2009). Guidelines for developing and managing a token economy. In W. T. O'Donohue & J. E. Fisher (Eds.), *General principles and empirically supported techniques of cognitive behavior therapy* (pp. 663–668). Hoboken, NJ: John Wiley & Sons.

Gilbert, L. A. (1980). Feminist therapy. In A. M. Brodsky & R. T. Hare-Mustin (Eds.), *Women and psychotherapy* (pp. 245–266). New York: Guilford.

Gilbert, L. A., & Scher, M. (1999). *Gender and sex in counseling and psychotherapy*. Boston. MA: Allyn & Bacon.

Gilliam, A. (2004). The efficacy of William Glasser's reality/choice theory with domestic violence perpetrators: A treatment outcome study. ProQuest Information & Learning). *Dissertation Abstracts International: Section B: The Sciences and Engineering, 65* (1-B) (Electronic; Print).

Gilligan, C. (1982). *In a different voice: Psychological theory and women's development.* Cambridge, MA: Harvard University Press.

Gilligan, C. (2003). Hearing the difference: Theorizing connection. *Anuario De Psicologia, 34*(2), 155–161.

Gilligan, C., & Attanucci, J. (1988). Two moral orientations: Gender differences and similarities. *Merrill-Palmer Quarterly: Journal of Developmental Psychology, 34*(3), 223–237.

Gingerich, W. J., & Eisengart, S. (2000). Solution-focused brief therapy: A review of the outcome research. *Family Process, 39*(4), 477–498.

Glasser, W. (1965). *Reality therapy: A new approach to psychiatry.* New York, NY: Harper & Row.

Glasser, W. (1998). *Choice theory: A new psychology of personal freedom.* New York, NY: HarperCollins.

Glasser, W. (2000). *Reality therapy in action.* New York, NY: HarperCollins.

Glasser, W. (2002). *Unhappy teenagers: A way for parents and teachers to reach them.* New York, NY: HarperCollins.

Glasser, W. (2003). *Warning: Psychiatry can be hazardous to your mental health.* New York, NY: HarperCollins.

Glasser, W. (2010). My vision for the international journal of choice theory and reality therapy. *International Journal of Choice Theory and Reality Therapy, 29*(2), 12.

Glover, E. (1959). Critical notice. *British Journal of Medical Psychology, 32*, 68–74.

Glynn, S. M. (1990). Token economy approaches for psychiatric patients: Progress and pitfalls over 25 years. *Behavior Modification Special Issue: Recent Developments in the Behavioral Treatment of Chronic Psychiatric Illness, 14*(4), 383–407.

Goddard, A., Murray, C. D., & Simpson, J. (2008). Informed consent and psychotherapy: An interpretative phenomenological analysis of therapists' views. *Psychology and Psychotherapy: Theory, Research and Practice, 81*(2), 177–191.

Goldenberg, I., & Goldenberg, H. (2008). *Family therapy: An overview* (7th ed.). Belmont, CA: Brooks/Cole.

Goldfried, M. R., & Davison, G. C. (1976). *Clinical behavior therapy.* New York, NY: Holt, Rinehart and Winston.

Goldfried, M. R., & Davison, G. C. (1994). *Clinical behavior therapy* (Exp. ed.). Oxford, England: John Wiley & Sons.

Goldman, R., & Greenberg, L. S. (1997). Case formulation in process-experiential therapy. In T. D. Eells (Ed.), *Handbook of psychotherapy case formulation* (pp. 402–429). New York, NY: Guilford Press.

Goldman, R. N., Greenberg, L. S., & Angus, L. (2006). The effects of adding emotion-focused interventions to the client-centered relationship conditions in the treatment of depression. *Psychotherapy Research, 16*(5), 536–546.

Goldstein, K. (1939). *The organism: A holistic approach to biology derived from pathological data in man.* Salt Lake City, UT: American Book.

Gonçalves, M. M., Matos, M., & Santos, A. (2009). Narrative therapy and the nature of "innovative moments" in the construction of change. *Journal of Constructivist Psychology, 22*(1), 1–23.

Gonçalves, M. M., Mendes, I., Ribeiro, A. P., Angus, L. E., & Greenberg, L. S. (2010). Innovative moments and change in emotion-focused therapy: The case of Lisa. *Journal of Constructivist Psychology, 23*(4), 267–294.

Goodman, E. (2003, January 12). Bush takes sides with the powerful. *The Missoulian*, p. 4.

Gordon, D. A., Graves, K., & Arbuthnot, J. (1995). The effect of functional family therapy for delinquents on adult criminal behavior. *Criminal Justice and Behavior, 22*(1), 60–73.

Gortner, E. T., Gollan, J. K., Dobson, K. S., & Jacobson, N. S. (1998). Cognitive–behavioral treatment for depression: Relapse prevention. *Journal of Consulting and Clinical Psychology, 66*(2), 377–384.

Gottlieb, M. C., & Younggren, J. N. (2009a). Is there a slippery slope? Considerations regarding multiple relationships and risk management. *Professional Psychology: Research and Practice, 40*(6), 564–571.

Gould, W. B. (1993). *Viktor E. Frankl: Life with meaning.* Pacific Grove, CA: Brooks/Cole.

Graham, S. R., & Liddle, B. J. (2009). Multiple relationships encountered by lesbian and bisexual psychotherapists: How close is too close? *Professional Psychology: Research and Practice, 40*(1), 15–21.

Greenberg, L. (2006). Emotion-focused therapy: A synopsis. *Journal of Contemporary Psychotherapy, 36*(2), 87–93.

Greenberg, L. J., Warwar, S. H., & Malcolm, W. M. (2008). Differential effects of emotion-focused therapy and psychoeducation in facilitating forgiveness and letting go of emotional injuries. *Journal of Counseling Psychology, 55*(2), 185–196.

Greenberg, L. S. (2011). *Emotion-focused therapy.* Washington, DC: American Psychological Association.

Greenberg, L. S., Elliott, R., & Lietaer, G. (1994). Research on experiential psychotherapy. In A. E. Bergin & S. L. Garfield (Eds.), *Handbook of psychotherapy and behavior change* (4th ed.). New York, NY: John Wiley & Sons.

Greenberg, L. S., & Foerster, F. S. (1996). Task analysis exemplified: The process of resolving unfinished business. *Journal of Consulting & Clinical Psychology, 64*(3), 439–446.

Greenberg, L. S., & Johnson, S. M. (1988). *Emotionally focused therapy for couples.* New York, NY: Guilford Press.

Greenberg, L. S., & Malcolm, W. (2002). Resolving unfinished business: Relating process to outcome. *Journal of Consulting & Clinical Psychology, 70*(2), 406–416.

Greenberg, L. S., Rice, L. N., & Elliot, R. (1993). *Facilitating emotional change: The moment-by-moment process.* New York: Guilford.

Greenberg, L. S., & Watson, J. (1998). Experiential therapy of depression: Differential effects of client-centered relationship conditions and process experiential interventions. *Psychotherapy Research, 8*(2), 210–224.

Greenberg, L. S., Watson, J. C., Elliot, R., & Bohart, A. C. (2001). Empathy. *Psychotherapy: Theory, Research, Practice, Training, 38*(4), 380–384.

Greenberger, D., & Padesky, C. A. (1995). *Mind over mood: Change how you feel by changing the way you think.* New York, NY: Guilford Press.

Greever, K. B., Tseng, M. S., & Friedland, B. U. (1973). Development of the social interest index. *Journal of Consulting and Clinical Psychology, 41*(3), 454–458.

Greever, K. B., Tseng, M. S., & Friedland, B. U. (1974). Measuring change in social interest in community college freshmen. *Individual Psychologist, 11*(1), 4–6.

Griner, D., & Smith, T. B. (2006). Culturally adapted mental health intervention: A meta-analytic review. *Psychotherapy: Theory, Research, 43*(4), 531–548.

Grisham, J. R., Brown, T. A., & Campbell, L. A. (2004). *The anxiety disorders interview schedule for DSM-IV (ADIS-IV).* Hoboken, NJ: John Wiley & Sons.

Grote, N. K., Swartz, H. A., Geibel, S. L., Zuckoff, A., Houck, P. R., & Frank, E. (2009). A randomized controlled trial of culturally relevant, brief interpersonal psychotherapy for perinatal depression. *Psychiatric Services, 60*(3), 313–321.

Groth-Marnat, G. (2009). *Handbook of psychological assessment* (5th ed.). Hoboken, NJ: John Wiley & Sons.

Guilford, J. (1956). The structure of intellect. *Psychological Bulletin, 53*, 267–293.

Gushue, G. V., & Constantine, M. G. (2007). Color-blind racial attitudes and white racial identity attitudes in psychology trainees. *Professional Psychology: Research and Practice, 38*(3), 321–328.

Guterman, J. T. (2006). *Mastering the art of solution-focused counseling.* Alexandria, VA: American Counseling Association.

Guthrie, R. V. (2004). *Even the rat was white: A historical view of psychology* (2nd ed.). Upper Saddle River, NJ: Pearson.

Haley, J. (Ed.). (1967). *Advanced techniques of hypnosis and therapy: Selected papers of Milton H. Erickson, M.D.* New York, NY: Grune & Stratton.

Haley, J. (1973). *Uncommon therapy: The psychiatric techniques of Milton H. Erickson.* New York, NY: Norton.

Haley, J. (1976). *Problem solving therapy.* San Francisco. CA: Jossey-Bass.

Haley, J. (1977). A quiz for young therapists. *Psychotherapy, 14*(2), 165–168.

Hall, C. S., & Lindzey, G. (1970). *Theories of personality* (2nd ed.). New York, NY: John Wiley & Sons.

Hall, G.C.N. (2001). Psychotherapy research with ethnic minorities: Empirical ethical, and conceptual issues. *Journal of Consulting & Clinical Psychology, 69*, 502–510.

Hall, R. E., & Rowan, G. T. (2003). Identity development across the lifespan: Alternative model for biracial Americans. *Psychology and Education: An Interdisciplinary Journal, 40*(2), 3–12.

Halstead, K. (2003). Over the rainbow: The lesbian family. In L. B. Silverstein & T. J. Goodrich (Eds.), *Feminist family therapy: Empowerment in social context* (pp. 39–50). Washington, DC: American Psychological Association.

Hamilton, J. W. (1995). Some comments on Kohut's "the two analyses of Mr. Z." *Psychoanalytic Psychology, 11*, 525–536.

Hannan, C., Lambert, M. J., Harmon, C., Nielsen, S. L., Smart, D. W., Shimokawa, K., et al. (2005). A lab test and algorithms for identifying clients at risk for treatment failure. *Journal of Clinical Psychology, 61*(2), 155–163.

Hardy, G., Cahill, J., & Barkham, M. (2007). *Active ingredients of the therapeutic relationship that promote client change: A research perspective.* New York, NY: Routledge/Taylor & Francis.

Harlow, H. K., Harlow, M. K., Dodsworth, R. O., & Arling, G. L. (1966). Maternal behavior of rhesus monkeys deprived of mothering and peer association in infancy. *Proceedings of the American Philosophical Society, 110,* 58–66.

Harlow, H. K., Harlow, M. K., & Suomi, S. J. (1971). From thought to therapy: Lessons from a private laboratory. *American Scientist, 659,* 538–549.

Harmon, S. C., Lambert, M. J., Smart, D. M., Hawkins, E., Nielsen, S. L., Slade, K., et al. (2007). Enhancing outcome for potential treatment failures: Therapist-client feedback and clinical support tools. *Psychotherapy Research, 17*(4), 379–392.

Harris, R. (2009). *ACT made simple: An easy-to-read primer on acceptance and commitment therapy.* Oakland, CA: New Harbinger.

Hartl, T. L., Zeiss, R. A., Marino, C. M., Regev, L. G., Leontis, C., & Zeiss, A. M. (2007). Clients' sexually inappropriate behaviors directed toward clinicians: Conceptualization and management. *Professional Psychology: Research and Practice, 38*(6), 674–681.

Hartmann, H. (1958). *Ego psychology and the problem of adaptation.* Madison, CT: International Universities Press.

Haun, J. J., & Truax, P. (2007). Cognitive behavior therapy for atypical generalized anxiety disorder (GAD): When functional assessment reveals social fears function, such as worry, in GAD. *Clinical Case Studies, 6*(3), 195–217.

Hayek, F. A. (1979). *Law, legislation, and liberty: The political order of a free people.* Chicago, IL: University of Chicago Press.

Hayes, S. C. (2002). Buddhism and acceptance and commitment therapy. *Cognitive & Behavioral Practice, 9*(1), 58–66.

Hayes, S. C. (2004). Acceptance and commitment therapy, relational frame theory, and the third wave of behavioral and cognitive therapies. *Behavior Therapy, 35,* 639–665.

Hayes, S. C., Strosahl, K. D., & Wilson, K. G. (1999). *Acceptance and commitment therapy: An experiential approach to behavior change.* New York, NY: Guilford Press.

Hays, P. A. (2008). *Addressing cultural complexities in practice: Assessment, diagnosis, and therapy* (2nd ed.). Washington, DC: American Psychological Association.

Heard, H. L., & Linehan, M. (1994). Dialectical behavior therapy: An integrative approach to the treatment of borderline personality disorder. *Journal of Psychotherapy Integration, 4,* 55–82.

Heide, F. J., & Borkovec, T. D. (1984). Relaxation-induced anxiety: Mechanisms and theoretical implications. *Behaviour Research and Therapy, 22,* 1–12.

Helms, J. E. (1994). How multiculturalism obscures racial factors in the therapy process. Comment on Ridley et al. (1994), Sadowski et al. (1994), Ottavi et al. (1994), and Thompson et al. (1994). *Journal of Counseling Psychology, 41,* 162–165.

Henderson, C. E., Dakof, G. A., Greenbaum, P. E., & Liddle, H. A. (2010). Effectiveness of multidimensional family therapy with higher severity substance-abusing adolescents: Report from two randomized controlled trials. *Journal of Consulting and Clinical Psychology, 78*(6), 885–897.

Henggeler, S. W., & Bordin, C. M. (1990). *Family therapy and beyond: A multisystemic approach to treating the behavior problems of children and adolescents.* Pacific Grove, CA: Brooks/Cole.

Henggeler, S. W., Clingempeel, W. G., Brondino, M. J., & Pickrel, S. G. (2002). Four-year follow-up of Multisystemic therapy with substance-abusing and substance-dependent juvenile offenders. *Journal of the American Academy of Child and Adolescent Psychiatry, 41*(7), 868–874.

Henggeler, S. W., & Lee, T. (2003). Multisystemic treatment of serious clinical problems. In A. E. Kazdin & J. Weisz (Eds.)., *Evidence-based psychotherapies for children and adolescents* (pp. 301–322). New York: Guilford Press.

Henggeler, S. W., Melton, G. B., & Smith, L. A. (1992). Family preservation using multisystemic therapy: An effective alternative to incarcerating serious juvenile offenders. *Journal of Consulting and Clinical Psychology, 60*(6), 953–961.

Henggeler, S. W., Pickrel, S. G., Brondino, M. J., & Crouch, J. L. (1996). Eliminating (almost) treatment dropout of substance abusing or dependent delinquents through home-based multisystemic therapy. *American Journal of Psychiatry, 153,* 427–428.

Henggeler, S. W., Schoenwald, S. K., Borduin, C. M., Rowland, M. D., & Cunningham, P. B. (1998). *Multisystemic treatment of antisocial behavior in children and adolescents.* New York, NY: Guilford Press.

Henggeler, S. W., Schoenwald, S. K., Borduin, C. M., Rowland, M. D., & Cunningham, P. B. (2009). *Multisystemic therapy for antisocial behavior in children and adolescents* (2nd ed.). New York, NY: Guilford Press.

Hepburn, R. (1965). Questions about the meaning of life. *Religious Studies, 1,* 125–140.

Herlihy, B., Corey, G., Bludworth, J., Borders, L. D., Cain, H., Caldwell, L. D., et al. (2006). *Boundary issues in counseling: Multiple roles and responsibilities* (2nd ed.). Alexandria, VA: American Counseling Association.

Herman, J. L. (1992). *Trauma and recovery: The aftermath of violence—from domestic abuse to political terror.* New York, NY: Basic Books.

Hernández, P., Rickard, J., & Giambruno, P. (2008). Transformative family therapy with a lesbian couple: A case study. *Journal of Feminist Family Therapy: An International Forum, 20*(4), 281–298.

Herring, R. D. (1996). Synergetic counseling and Native American Indian students. *Journal of Counseling & Development, 74*, 542–547.

Hettema, J., Steele, J., & Miller, W. R. (2005). Motivational interviewing. *Annual Review of Clinical Psychology, 1*, 91–111.

Hill, C. E. (2009). *Helping skills: Facilitating, exploration, insight, and action* (3rd ed.). Washington, DC: American Psychological Association.

Hill, K. A. (1987). Meta-analysis of paradoxical interventions. *Psychotherapy, 24*, 266–270.

Ho, D. Y. F. (1998). Indigenous psychologies. *Journal of Cross-Cultural Psychology, 29*(1), 88–103.

Hodge, D. R., & Limb, G. E. (2009). Establishing the preliminary validity of spiritual eco-maps with Native Americans. *Clinical Social Work Journal, 37*(4), 320–331.

Hoffman, E. (1994). *The drive for self: Alfred Adler and the founding of individual psychology.* Reading, MA: Addison-Wesley.

Hoffman, L., Stewart, S., Warren, D., & Meek, L. (2009). Toward a sustainable myth of self: An existential response to the postmodern condition. *Journal of Humanistic Psychology, 49*(2), 135–173.

Hogan, R. (1975). Theoretical egocentrism and the problem of compliance. *American Psychologist, 30*, 533–540.

Holland, J. M., Neimeyer, R. A., Currier, J. M., & Berman, J. S. (2007). The efficacy of personal construct therapy: A comprehensive review. *Journal of Clinical Psychology, 63*(1), 93–107.

Holtzheimer, P. E., & Mayberg, H. S. (2010). Deep brain stimulation for treatment-resistant depression. *American Journal of Psychiatry, 167*(12), 1437–1444.

hooks, b. (2000). *Feminism is for everybody: Passionate politics.* London: Pluto Press.

Hopko, D. R., Armento, M. E. A., Cantu, M. S., Chambers, L. L., & Lejuez, C. W. (2003). The use of daily diaries to assess the relations among mood state, overt behavior, and reward value of activities. *Behaviour Research and Therapy, 41*(10), 1137–1148.

Horner, A. J. (1998). *Working with the core relationship problem in psychotherapy: A handbook for clinicians.* San Francisco, CA: Jossey-Bass.

Horney, K. (1950). *Neurosis and human growth: The struggle toward self-realization.* New York, NY: Norton.

Horney, K. (1967). *Feminine psychology.* New York: Norton.

Horowitz, L. M., Rosenberg, S. E., Baer, B. A., Ureño, G., & Villaseñor, V. S. (1988). Inventory of interpersonal problems: Psychometric properties and clinical applications. *Journal of Consulting and Clinical Psychology, 56*(6), 885–892.

Horowitz, M. J., Marmar, C., Krupnick, J., Wilner, N., Kaltreider, N., & Wallerstein, R. (1984). *Personality styles and brief psychotherapy.* New York, NY: Basic Books.

Horvath, A. O., & Greenberg, L. S. (1986). *The development of the working alliance inventory.* New York, NY: Guilford Press.

Horvath, A. O., & Greenberg, L. S. (1989). Development and validation of the working alliance inventory. *Journal of Counseling Psychology, 36*(2), 223–233.

Hosany, Z., Wellman, N., & Lowe, T. (2007). Fostering a culture of engagement: A pilot study of the outcomes of training mental health nurses working in two UK acute admission units in brief solution-focused therapy techniques. *Journal of Psychiatric and Mental Health Nursing, 14*(7), 688–695.

Hoyt, M. F. (1994). On the importance of keeping it simple and taking the patient seriously: A conversation with Steve de Shazer and John Weakland. In M. F. Hoyt (Ed.), *Constructive therapies* (pp. 11–40). New York, NY: Guilford Press.

Hoyt, M. F. (Ed.). (1998). *The handbook of constructive therapies: Innovative approaches from leading practitioners.* San Francisco, CA: Jossey-Bass/Pfeiffer.

Hoyt, M. F. (2000). Cognitive-behavioural treatment of post-traumatic stress disorder from a narrative constructivist perspective: A conversation with Donald Meichenbaum. In M. Scott & S. Palmer (Eds.), *Trauma and post-traumatic stress disorder* (pp. 49–69). London, England: Cassell.

Hrdy, S. B. (1999). *Mother nature.* New York, NY: Pantheon Books.

Hubble, M. A., Duncan, B. L., & Miller, S. D. (Eds.). (1999). *The heart and soul of change.* Washington, DC: American Psychological Association.

Hud-Aleem, R., & Countryman, J. (2008). Biracial identity development and recommendations in therapy. *Psychiatry, 5*(11), 37–44.

Hughes, D. (1998). *Building the bonds of attachment: Awakening love in deeply troubled children.* Northvale, NJ: Aronson.

Hunter, P., & Kelso, E. N. (1985). Feminist behavior therapy. *Behavior Therapist, 8*(10), 201–204.

Hurn, R. (2003). Butterflies in possibility land: An example of the miracle question when counselling briefly. *Counselling Psychology Review, 18*(4), 17–27.

Hwang, W., & Wood, J. J. (2007). Being culturally sensitive is not the same as being culturally competent. *Pragmatic Case Studies in Psychotherapy, 3*, 44–50.

Hycner, R. (1990). The I–Thou relationship and gestalt therapy. *Gestalt Journal, 13*(1), 41–54.

Hycner, R., & Jacobs, L. (Eds.). (2009). *Relational approaches in Gestalt therapy.* Cambridge, MA: Gestalt-Press Book.

Hycner, R. H. (1985). Dialogical gestalt therapy: An initial proposal. *Gestalt Journal, 8*(1), 23–49.

Hyde, J. S. (2005). The gender similarities hypothesis. *American Psychologist, 60*(6), 581–592.

Hymowitz, K. (2011). *Manning up: How the rise of women has turned men into boys.* New York, NY: Basic Books.

Iaculo, G., & Frew, J. E. (2004). Relational support in the gay coming-out process. *Gestalt Review, 8*(2), 178–203.

Ilgen, M., & Moos, R. (2005). Deterioration following alcohol-use disorder treatment in project MATCH. *Journal of Studies on Alcohol, 66*(4), 517–525.

Ivey, A. E., D'Andrea, M., Ivey, M. B., & Simek-Morgan, L. (2002). *Theories of counseling and psychotherapy: A multicultural perspective* (5th ed.). Boston: Allyn & Bacon.

Jackson, D. D. (1954). Suicide. *Scientific American, 191*, 88–96.

Jackson, D. D., & Weakland, J. H. (1959). Schizophrenic symptoms and family interaction. *Archives of General Psychiatry, 1*, 618–621.

Jacobs, L. (1992). Insights from psychoanalytic self-psychology and intersubjectivity theory for gestalt therapists. *Gestalt Journal, 15*(2), 25–60.

Jacobs, L. (2001). Pathways to a relational worldview. In M. R. Goldfried (Ed.), *How therapists change: Personal and professional reflections* (pp. 271–287). Washington, DC: American Psychological Association.

Jacobs, L. (2009). Attunement and optimal responsiveness. In R. Hycner, & L. Jacobs (Eds.), *Relational approaches in Gestalt therapy* (pp. 131–169). Cambridge, MA: GestaltPress Book.

Jacobson, E. (1924). The technic of progressive relaxation. *Journal of Nervous & Mental Disease, 60*(6), 568–578.

Jacobson, E. (1938). *Progressive relaxation.* Chicago, IL: University of Chicago Press.

Jacobson, E. (1978). *You must relax.* (5th ed.). New York, NY: McGraw-Hill.

Jacobson, N. S., Dobson, K. S., Truax, P. A., Addis, M. E., Koerner, K., Gollan, J. K., et al. (1996). A component analysis of cognitive-behavioral treatment for depression. *Journal of Consulting and Clinical Psychology, 64*(2), 295–304.

Jacobson, N. S., Martell, C. R., & Dimidjian, S. (2001). Behavioral activation treatment for depression: Returning to contextual roots. *Clinical Psychology: Science and Practice, 8*(3), 255–270.

James, W. (1992). *William James, writings 1878-1899.* New York: Library of America.

Janet, P. (1901). *Fixed ideas.* New York, NY: Putnam.

Jenkins, A. H. (1997). The empathic context in psychotherapy with people of color. In A. C. Bohart & L. S. Greenberg (Eds.), *Empathy reconsidered: New directions in psychology* (pp. 321–342). Washington, DC: American Psychological Association.

Johnson, S. (2010). Emotionally focused couple therapy: It's all about emotion and connection. In M. Kerman (Ed.), *Clinical pearls of insight: 21 leading therapists offer their key insights* (pp. 133–143). New York: Norton.

Johnson, S. M., & Greenberg, L. S. (1985). Differential effects of experiential and problem-solving interventions in resolving marital conflict. *Journal of Consulting and Clinical Psychology, 53*(2), 175–184.

Jonason, P. K., Krcmar, M., & Sohn, S. (2009). Male body image: The role of muscle magazine exposure, body mass index, and social comparison in men's body satisfaction. *Social Behavior and Personality, 37*(5), 627–630.

Jones, E. E. (1953). *Sigmund Freud: Life and Work (Vol 1: The Young Freud 1856–1900).* London: Hogarth Press.

Jones, M. C. (1924a). The elimination of children's fear. *Journal of Experimental Psychology, 8*, 382–390.

Jones, M. C. (1924b). A laboratory study of fear: The case of Peter. *Ped. Sem, 31*, 308–316.

Jordan, J. V. (2010). *Relational–cultural therapy.* Washington, DC: American Psychological Association.

Jordan, J. V., Walker, M., & Hartling, L. M. (Eds.). (2004). *The complexity of connection: Writings from the Stone Center's Jean Baker Miller Training Institute.* New York, NY: Guilford Press.

Joyce, P., & Sills, C. (2010). *Skills in Gestalt counseling and psychotherapy* (2nd ed.). London, England: Sage.

Juarascio, A. S., Forman, E. M., & Herbert, J. D. (2010). Acceptance and commitment therapy versus cognitive therapy for the treatment of comorbid eating pathology. *Behavior Modification, 34*(2), 175–190.

Jung, C. G. (1953). *Two essays on analytical psychology* (Bollingen series 20). New York, NY: Pantheon Books.

Jusoh, A. J., Mahmud, Z., & Ishak, N. M. (2008). The patterns of reality therapy usage among Malaysian counselors. *International Journal of Reality Therapy, 28*(1), 5–14.

Kaplan, D. (2011, July). Changing distorted thinking. *Counseling Today, 54,* 36–38.

Karasu, T. B. (1999). Spiritual psychotherapy. *American Journal of Psychotherapy, 53,* 143–162.

Kaschak, E. (1992). *Engendered lives.* New York, NY: HarperCollins.

Katz, J. (2006). *The Macho Paradox: Why some men hurt women and how all men can help.* New York: Sourcebooks.

Kawahara, D. M., & Espín, O. M. (2007). Asian American women in therapy: Feminist reflections on growth and transformations. *Women & Therapy, 30*(3–4), 1–5.

Kazdin, A. E. (2007). Mediators and mechanisms of change in psychotherapy research. *Annual Review of Clinical Psychology, 3,* 1–27.

Kazdin, A. E. (2008). *The Kazdin method for parenting the defiant child: With no pills, no therapy, no contest of wills.* Boston, MA: Houghton Mifflin.

Kazdin, A. E. (2010). Problem-solving skills training and parent management training for oppositional defiant disorder and conduct disorder. In J. R. Weisz & A. E. Kazdin (Eds.), *Evidence-based psychotherapies for children and adolescents* (pp. 211–226). New York, NY: Guilford Press.

Kazdin, A. E., Siegel, T. C., & Bass, D. (1992). Cognitive problem-solving skills training and parent management training in the treatment of antisocial behavior in children. *Journal of Consulting and Clinical Psychology, 60*(5), 733–747.

Keeling, M. L., & Bermudez, M. (2006). Externalizing problems through art and writing: Experiences of process and helpfulness. *Journal of Marital and Family Therapy, 32*(4), 405–419.

Keillor, G. (Director). (2002, July 25, 2002). *The writer's almanac.* [Radio broadcast] Minneapolis: Minnesota Public Radio.

Keith, D. V., & Whitaker, C. A. (1982). Experiential-symbolic family therapy. In A. M. Horne & M. M. Ohlsen (Eds.), *Family counseling and therapy.* Itasca, IL: Peacock.

Kelly, F. D., & Main, F. O. (1978). Idiographic research in Adlerian psychology: Problems and solutions. *Journal of Individual Psychology, 34*(2), 221–231.

Kelly, G. A. (1955). *The psychology of personal constructs.* New York, NY: Norton.

Kelly, G. A. (1969). Ontological acceleration. In B. Maher (Ed.), *Clinical psychology and personality: The selected papers of George Kelly* (pp. 7–45). New York, NY: John Wiley & Sons.

Kendall, P. C. (Ed.). (2000). *Child and adolescent therapy: Cognitive-behavioral procedures* (2nd ed.). New York, NY: Guilford Press.

Kendall, P. C., Comer, J. S., Marker, C. D., Creed, T. A., Puliafico, A. C., Hughes, A. A., et al. (2009). In-session exposure tasks and therapeutic alliance across the treatment of childhood anxiety disorders. *Journal of Consulting and Clinical Psychology, 77*(3), 517–525.

Keshen, A. (2006). A new look at existential psychotherapy. *American Journal of Psychotherapy, 60*(3), 285–298.

Kim, J. (2007). A reality therapy group counseling program as an Internet addiction recovery method for college students in Korea. *International Journal of Reality Therapy, 26*(2), 3–9.

Kim, J. S. (2008). Examining the effectiveness of solution-focused brief therapy: A meta-analysis. *Research on Social Work Practice, 18*(2), 107–116.

Kim, K. I., & Hwang, M. G. (2001). The effects of internal control and achievement motivation in group counseling based on reality therapy. *International Journal of Reality Therapy, 20*(3), 11-17.

Kimmel, M. (2010). *Guyland: The perilous world where boys become men.* New York, NY: Harper.

Kirschenbaum, H., & Henderson, V. L. (Eds.). (1989). *Carl Rogers: Dialogues.* Boston, MA: Houghton Mifflin.

Kissane, D. W., Bloch, S., Smith, G. C., Miach, P., Clarke, D. M., Ikin, J., et al. (2003). Cognitive-existential group psychotherapy for women with primary breast cancer: A randomized controlled trial. *Psycho-Oncology, 12*(6), 532–546.

Kitzinger, C. (2001). Sexualities. In R. K. Unger (Ed.), *Handbook of the psychology of women and gender* (pp. 272–285). New York, NY: John Wiley & Sons.

Kivlighan, D. M., Jr. (2002). Transference, interpretation, and insight: A research-practice model. In G. S. Tryon (Ed.), *Counseling based on process research: Applying what we know* (pp. 166–196). Boston, MA: Allyn & Bacon.

Klerman, G. L., & Weissman, M. M. (1991). Interpersonal psychotherapy: Research program and future prospects. In L. E. Beutler & M. Crago (Eds.), *Psychotherapy research: An international review of programmatic studies* (pp. 33–40). Washington, DC: American Psychological Association.

Klerman, G. L., Weissman, M. M., Rounsaville, B. J., & Chevron, E. S. (1984). *Interpersonal psychotherapy of depression.* New York, NY: Basic Books.

Klerman, G. L., Weissman, M. M., Rounsaville, B., & Chevron, E. S. (1995). Interpersonal psychotherapy for depression. *Journal of Psychotherapy Practice & Research, 4*(4), 342–351.

Knekt, P., Lindfors, O., Härkänen, T., Välikoski, M., Virtala, E., Laaksonen, M. A., et al. (2008). Randomized trial on the effectiveness of long- and short-term psychodynamic psychotherapy and solution-focused therapy on psychiatric symptoms during a 3-year follow-up. *Psychological Medicine: A Journal of Research in Psychiatry and the Allied Sciences, 38*(5), 689–703.

Koffka, K. (1935). *Principles of Gestalt psychology.* Oxford, England: Harcourt, Brace.

Kohn, A. (2005). *Unconditional parenting: Moving from rewards and punishments to love and reason.* New York, NY: Atria.

Kohut, H. H. (1959). Introspection, empathy, and psychoanalysis. *Journal of American Psycholanalysis Association, 7,* 459–483.

Kohut, H. H. (1971). *The analysis of self.* New York, NY: International Universities Press.

Kohut, H. H. (1977). *Restoration of the self.* New York, NY: International Universities Press.

Kohut, H. H. (1984). *How does analysis cure?* Chicago, IL: University of Chicago Press.

Kondas, D. (2008). Existential explosion and gestalt therapy for gay male survivors of domestic violence. *Gestalt Review, 12,* 58–74.

Koons, C. R., Robins, C. J., Tweed, J. L., Lynch, T. R., Gonzalez, A. M., Morse, J. Q., et al. (2001). Efficacy of dialectical behavior therapy in women veterans with borderline personality disorder. *Behavior Therapy, 32*(2), 371–390.

Korchin, S. J. (1976). *Modern clinical psychology: Principles of intervention in the clinic and community.* New York: Basic Books.

Kottler, J. A., & Brown, R. W. (1996). *Introduction to therapeutic counseling.* Pacific Grove, CA: Brooks/Cole.

Kottler, J. A., & Brown, R. W. (2008). *Introduction to therapeutic counseling* (8th ed.). Pacific Grove, CA: Brooks/Cole.

Kovacs, M. (1992). *Childrens depression inventory.* Toronto, Ontario: Multi-Health Systems.

Krijn, M., Emmelkamp, P. M. G., Ólafsson, R. P., Bouwman, M., van Gerwen, L. J., Spinhoven, P., et al. (2007). Fear of flying treatment methods: Virtual reality exposure vs. cognitive behavioral therapy. *Aviation, Space, and Environmental Medicine, 78*(2), 121–128.

Krumboltz, J. D. (1965). Behavioral counseling: Rationale and research. *Personnel and Guidance Journal, 44,* 383–387.

Kupers, T. A., Ross, R., Frances, A., & Widiger, T. A. (2005). Issue 2: Is there gender bias in the *DSM-IV?* In R. P. Halgin (Ed.), *Taking sides: Abnormal psychology.* (pp. 14–40). New York, NY: McGraw-Hill.

Kutchins, H., & Kirk, S. A. (1997). *Making us crazy.* New York: The Free Press.

Kvarme, L. G., Helseth, S., Sørum, R., Luth-Hansen, V., Haugland, S., & Natvig, G. K. (2010). The effect of a solution-focused approach to improve self-efficacy in socially withdrawn school children: A non-randomized controlled trial. *International Journal of Nursing Studies, 47*(11), 1389–1396.

Lacan, J. (1988). *The seminar of Jacques Lacan, Book I.* (J. Forrester Trans.). Cambridge: Cambridge University Press.

Lafferty, P., Beutler, L. E., & Crago, M. (1989). Differences between more and less effective psychotherapists: A study of select therapist variables. *Journal of Consulting and Clinical Psychology, 57*(1), 76–80.

LaFromboise, T. D., Trimble, J. E., & Mohatt, G. V. (1990). Counseling intervention and American Indian tradition: An integrative approach. *The Counseling Psychologist, 18,* 628–654.

Lambert, M. (2007). Presidential address: What we have learned from a decade of research aimed at improving psychotherapy outcome in routine care. *Psychotherapy Research, 17*(1), 1–14.

Lambert, M. J. (1992). Implications of outcome research for psychotherapy integration. In J. C. Norcross & M. R. Goldstein (Eds.), *Handbook of psychotherapy integration* (pp. 94–129). New York, NY: Basic Books.

Lambert, M. J. (2010a). "Yes, it is time for clinicians to routinely monitor treatment outcome." In B. L. Duncan, S. D. Miller, B. E. Wampold, & M. A. Hubble (Eds.), *The heart and soul of change: Delivering what works in therapy* (2nd ed., pp. 239–266). Washington, DC: American Psychological Association.

Lambert, M. J. (2010b). *Prevention of treatment failure: The use of measuring, monitoring, and feedback in clinical practice.* Washington, DC: American Psychological Association.

Lambert, M. J., & Erekson, D. M. (2008). Positive psychology and the humanistic tradition. *Journal of Psychotherapy Integration, 18*(2), 222–232.

Lambert, M. J., & Lambert, M. J. (2010). *Predicting negative treatment outcome: Methods and estimates of accuracy*. Washington, DC: American Psychological Association.

Landreth, G. L. (2002). *Play therapy: The art of the relationship* (2nd ed.). New York, NY: Brunner-Routledge.

Lankton, S., & Frischholz, E. (2009). Editorial: The first decade in review. *American Journal of Clinical Hypnosis, 51*(4), 317–330.

Lau, M. A., Bishop, S. R., Segal, Z. V., Buis, T., Anderson, N. D., Carlson, L., et al. (2006). The Toronto Mindfulness Scale: Development and validation. *Journal of Clinical Psychology, 62*(12), 1445–1467.

Lazarus, A. A. (1958). New methods in psychotherapy: A case study. *South African Medical Journal, 32*, 660–664.

Lazarus, A. A. (1967). In support of technical eclecticism. *Psychological Reports, 21*, 415–416.

Lazarus, A. A. (1971). *Behavior therapy and beyond*. New York, NY: McGraw-Hill.

Lazarus, A. A. (1973). *Clinical behavior therapy*. New York: Brunner/Mazel.

Lazarus, A. A. (1989). *The practice of multimodal therapy: Systematic, comprehensive, and effective psychotherapy*. Baltimore, MD: Johns Hopkins University Press.

Lazarus, A. A. (1991). A plague on little Hans and little Albert. *Psychotherapy: Theory, Research, Practice, Training, 28*(3), 444–447.

Lazarus, A. A. (1993). Tailoring the therapeutic relationship, or being an authentic chameleon. *Psychotherapy, 30*, 404–407.

Lazarus, A. A. (1997). *Brief but comprehensive psychotherapy: The multimodal way*. New York, NY: Springer.

Lazarus, A. A. (2000). Multimodal replenishment. *Professional Psychology: Research & Practice, 31*(1), 93–94.

Lazarus, A. A. (2006). *Brief but comprehensive psychotherapy: The multimodal way*. New York, NY: Springer.

Lazarus, A. A. (2008). Technical eclecticism and multimodal therapy. In J. L. Lebow (Ed.), *Twenty-first century psychotherapies* (pp. 424–452). Hoboken, NJ: John Wiley & Sons.

Lazarus, A. A., Beutler, L. E., & Norcross, J. C. (1992). The future of technical eclecticism. *Psychotherapy: Theory, Research, Practice, Training. Special Issue: The Future of Psychotherapy, 29*(1), 11–20.

Lazarus, A. A., & Lazarus, C. N. (1991). *Multimodal life history inventory*. Champaign, IL: Research Press.

Leahy, R. L. (2003). *Cognitive therapy techniques: A practitioner's guide*. New York, NY: Guilford Press.

Leahy, R. L. (Ed.). (2004). *Contemporary cognitive therapy: Theory, research, and practice*. New York, NY: Guilford Press.

Leak, G. K. (2006). An empirical assessment of the relationship between social interest and spirituality. *The Journal of Individual Psychology, 62*(1), 59–69.

Leak, G. K., & Leak, K. C. (2006). Adlerian social interest and positive psychology: A conceptual and empirical integration. *The Journal of Individual Psychology, 62*(3), 207–223.

Leber, P. (1991). Is there an alternative to the randomized controlled trial? *Psychopharmacology Bulletin, 27*, 3–8.

Ledley, D. R., Marx, B. P., & Heimberg, R. G. (2010). *Making cognitive-behavioral therapy work: Clinical process for new practitioners* (2nd ed.). New York, NY: Guilford Press.

Lee, K., Noda, Y., Nakano, Y., Ogawa, S., Kinoshita, Y., Funayama, T., et al. (2006). Interoceptive hypersensitivity and interoceptive exposure in patients with panic disorder: Specificity and effectiveness. *BMC Psychiatry, 6*, 1–9

Lejuez, C. W., Hopko, D. R., Acierno, R., Daughters, S. B., & Pagoto, S. L. (2011). Ten year revision of the brief behavioral activation treatment for depression: Revised treatment manual. *Behavior Modification, 35*(2), 111–161.

Lejuez, C. W., Hopko, D. R., LePage, J. P., Hopko, S. D., & McNeil, D. W. (2001). A brief behavioral activation treatment for depression. *Cognitive and Behavioral Practice, 8*(2), 164–175.

Leong, F. T. L., Kim, H. H. W., & Gupta, A. (2011). Attitudes toward professional counseling among Asian-American college students: Acculturation, conceptions of mental illness, and loss of face. *Asian American Journal of Psychology, 2*(2), 140–153.

Levant, R. F., & Pollack, W. S. (1995). *A new psychology of men*. New York, NY: Basic Books.

Levy, D. M. (1943). *Maternal overprotection*. New York, NY: Columbia University Press.

Levy, S. T. (1984). *Principles of interpretation*. New York, NY: Aronson.

Lewin, K. (1951). *Field theory in social science: Selected theoretical papers* (edited by Dorwin Cartwright.). Oxford, England: Harpers.

Lewinsohn, P. M. (1974). *A behavioral approach to depression*. Oxford, England: John Wiley & Sons.

Lewinsohn, P. M., & Libet, J. (1972). Pleasant events, activity schedules, and depressions. *Journal of Abnormal Psychology, 79*(3), 291–295.

Lewinsohn, P. M., Steinmetz, J. L., Antonuccio, D., & Teri, L. (1984). Group therapy for depression: The coping with depression course. *International Journal of Mental Health, 13*(3–4), 8–33.

Lewis, T., Amini, F., & Lannon, R. (2001). *A general theory of love*. New York: Vintage.

Ley, R. (1988). Panic attacks during relaxation and relaxation-induced anxiety: A hyperventilation interpretation. *Journal of Behavior Therapy and Experimental Psychiatry, 19*(4), 253–259.

Liang, B., Tracy, A. J., Kenny, M. E., Brogan, D., & Gatha, R. (2010). The relational health indices for youth: An examination of reliability and validity aspects. *Measurement and Evaluation in Counseling and Development, 42*(4), 255–274.

Liang, B., Tracy, A., Taylor, C. A., Williams, L. M., Jordan, J. V., & Miller, J. B. (2002). The relational health indices: A study of women's relationships. *Psychology of Women Quarterly, 26*(1), 25–35.

Lichtenthal, W. G., Nilsson, M., Zhang, B., Trice, E. D., Kissane, D. W., Breitbart, W., et al. (2009). Do rates of mental disorders and existential distress among advanced stage cancer patients increase as death approaches? *Psycho-Oncology, 18*(1), 50–61.

Liddle, H. A., Dakof, G. A., Parker, K., Diamond, G. S., Barrett, K., & Tejeda, M. (2001). Multidimensional family therapy for adolescent drug abuse: Results of a randomized clinical trial. *The American Journal of Drug and Alcohol Abuse, 27*(4), 651–688.

Liddle, H. A., Dakof, G. A., Turner, R. M., Henderson, C. E., & Greenbaum, P. E. (2008). Treating adolescent drug abuse: A randomized trial comparing multidimensional family therapy and cognitive behavior therapy. *Addiction, 103*(10), 1660–1670.

Liddle, H. A., Rowe, C. L., Dakof, G. A., Henderson, C. E., & Greenbaum, P. E. (2009). Multidimensional family therapy for young adolescent substance abuse: Twelve-month outcomes of a randomized controlled trial. *Journal of Consulting and Clinical Psychology, 77*(1), 12–25.

Lidz, T., Cornelison, A., Fleck, S., & Terry, D. (1957). Intrafamilial environment of the schizophrenic patient I: The father. *Psychiatry, 20*, 329–342.

Lilienfeld, S. O. (2007). Psychological treatments that cause harm. *Perspectives on Psychological Science, 2*(1), 53–70.

Lilienfeld, S. O., Lynn, S. J., & Lohr, J. M. (2003). *Science and pseudoscience in clinical psychology*. New York, NY: Guilford Press.

Linehan, M. M. (1993a). *Cognitive behavioral therapy of borderline personality disorder*. New York, NY: Guilford Press.

Linehan, M. M. (1993b). *Skills training manual for treating borderline personality disorder*. New York, NY: Guilford Press.

Linehan, M. M. (2000). The empirical basis of dialectical behavior therapy: Development of new treatments versus evaluation of existing treatments. *Clinical Psychology: Science & Practice, 7*(1), 113–119.

Linehan, M. M., Comtois, K. A., Murray, A. M., Brown, M. Z., Gallop, R. J., Heard, H. L., et al. (2006). Two-year randomized controlled trial and follow-up of dialectical behavior therapy vs therapy by experts for suicidal behaviors and borderline personality disorder. *Archives of General Psychiatry, 63*(7), 757–766.

Linehan, M., & Schmidt, H. I. (1995). The dialectics of effective treatment of borderline personality disorder. In W. O'Donohue & L. Krasner (Eds.), *Theories of behavior therapy* (pp. 553–584). Washington, DC: American Psychological Association.

Linnenberg, D. M. (2006). Thoughts on reality therapy from a pro-feminist perspective. *International Journal of Reality Therapy, 26*, 23–26.

Lipchik, E. (2002). *Beyond technique in solution-focused therapy: Working with emotions and the therapeutic relationship*. New York, NY: Guilford Press.

Littell, J. H. (2010). Evidence-based practice: Evidence or orthodoxy? In B. L. Duncan, S. D. Miller, B. E. Wampold, & M. A. Hubble (Eds.), *The heart and soul of change: Delivering what works in therapy*. (2nd ed., pp. 167–198). Washington, DC: American Psychological Association.

Liu, H., Ting, Y., & Cheng, J. (2010). The effects of a reality therapy group guidance program for underachieving elementary students in regard to their Mandarin learning attitudes and achievements. *Bulletin of Educational Psychology, 42*(1), 53–76.

Lobb, M. S. (2009). The therapeutic relationship in gestalt therapy. In R. Hycner & L. Jacobs (Eds.), *Relational approaches in Gestalt therapy* (pp. 111–129). Cambridge, MA: GestaltPress Book.

Lobb, M. S., & Lichtenberg, P. (2005). *Classical Gestalt therapy theory*. Thousand Oaks, CA: Sage.

Lock, J., Couturier, J., & Agras, W. S. (2006). Comparison of long-term outcomes in adolescents with anorexia nervosa treated with family therapy. *Journal of the*

American Academy of Child & Adolescent Psychiatry, 45(6), 666–672.

Logsdon-Conradsen, S. (2002). Using mindfulness meditation to promote holistic health in individuals with HIV/AIDS. *Cognitive and Behavioral Practice, 9,* 67–72.

Lohr, J. M. (2011). What is (and what is not) the meaning of evidence-based psychosocial intervention? *Clinical Psychology: Science and Practice, 18*(2), 100–104.

Lohr, J. M., Olatunji, B. O., Parker, L., & DeMaio, C. (2005). Experimental analysis of specific treatment factors: Efficacy and practice implications. *Journal of Clinical Psychology, 61*(7), 819–834.

London, P. (1964). *The modes and morals of psychotherapy.* New York, NY: Holt, Rinehart, and Winston.

Luborsky, L. (1984). *Principles of psychoanalytic psychotherapy: A manual for supportive-expressive treatment.* New York, NY: Basic Books.

Luborsky, L. (1985). A verification of Freud's grandest clinical hypothesis: The transference. *Clinical Psychology Review, 5,* 231–246.

Luborsky, L. B., Barrett, M. S., Antonuccio, D. O., Shoenberger, D., & Stricker, G. (2006). *What else materially influences what is represented and published as evidence?.* Washington, DC: American Psychological Association.

Luborsky, L., Diguer, L., Seligman, D. A., Rosenthal, R., Krause, E. D., Johnson, S., et al. (1999). The researcher's own therapy allegiances: A "wild card" in comparisons of treatment efficacy. *Clinical Psychology: Science & Practice, 6*(1), 95–106.

Luborsky, L., Singer, B., & Luborsky, L. (1975). Comparative studies of psychotherapies: Is it true that "everybody has won so all shall have prizes?" *Archives of General Psychiatry, 32,* 995–1008.

Luria, A. (1961). *The role of speech in the regulation of normal and abnormal behavior.* New York, NY: Liveright.

Maag, J. W. (2001). Rewarded by punishment: Reflections on the disuse of positive reinforcement in the schools. *Exceptional Children, 67,* 173–186.

Madanes, C., & Haley, J. (1977). Dimensions of family therapy. *The Journal of Nervous and Mental Disease, 165,* 88–98.

Madigan, S. (2011). *Narrative therapy.* Washington, DC: American Psychological Association.

Mahler, M., Pine, F., & Bergman, A. (1975). *The psychological birth of the human infant: Symbiosis and individuation.* New York, NY: Basic Books.

Mahoney, M. (1984). Psychoanalysis and behaviorism: The yin and yang of determinism. In H. Arkowitz & S. B. Messer (Eds.), *Psychoanalysis and behavior therapy:*

Is integration possible? (pp. 303–325). New York, NY: Plenum.

Mahoney, M. (1985). Psychotherapy and human change processes. In M. Mahoney & A. Freeman (Eds.), *Cognition and psychotherapy* (pp. 3–48). New York: Plenum.

Mahoney, M. (1991). *Human change processes.* New York, NY: Basic Books.

Malcom, W. M., & Greenberg, L. S. (2000). Forgiveness as a process of change in individual psychotherapy. In M. E. McCullough, K. I. Pargament, & C. E. Thoresen (Eds.), *Forgiveness: Theory, research, and practice* (pp. 179–202). New York, NY: Guilford Press.

Malgady, R. G. (2010). Treating Hispanic children and adolescents using narrative therapy. In J. R. Weisz & A. E. Kazdin (Eds.), *Evidence-based psychotherapies for children and adolescents* (2nd ed., pp. 391–400). New York, NY: Guilford Press.

Malgady, R. G., & Costantino, G. (2003). Narrative therapy for Hispanic children and adolescents. In A. E. Kazdin & J. R. Weisz (Eds.), *Evidence-based psychotherapies for children and adolescents* (pp. 425–435). New York, NY: Guilford Press.

Malley, M., & McCann, D. (2002). Family therapy with lesbian and gay clients. In A. Coyle & C. Kitzinger (Eds.), *Lesbian and gay psychology: New perspectives* (pp. 198–218). Malden, MA: Blackwell.

Malouff, J. M., Thorsteinsson, E. B., & Schutte, N. S. (2007). The efficacy of problem solving therapy in reducing mental and physical health problems: A meta-analysis. *Clinical Psychology Review, 27*(1), 46–57.

Malyon, A. K. (1982). Psychotherapeutic implications of internalized homophobia in gay men. *Journal of Homosexuality. Special Issue: Homosexuality & Psychotherapy, 7,* 59–69. doi: 10.1300/J082v07n02_08

Manaster, G. J., & Corsini, R. J. (1982). *Individual psychology: Theory and practice.* Itasca, IL: F. E. Peacock.

Maniar, S. D., Curry, L. A., Sommers-Flanagan, J., & Walsh, J. A. (2001). Student athlete preferences in seeking help when confronted with sport performance problems. *Sport Psychologist, 15*(2), 205–223.

Mann, W. E. (1973). *Orgone, Reich and eros: Wilhelm Reich's theory of life energy.* Oxford, England: Simon & Schuster.

March, J. S., Franklin, M., Nelson, A., & Foa, E. (2001). Cognitive-behavioral psychotherapy for pediatric obsessive-compulsive disorder. *Journal of Clinical Child Psychology, 30,* 8–18.

Marlatt, G. A., & Witkiewitz, K. (2010). Update on harm-reduction policy and intervention research. *Annual Review of Clinical Psychology, 6,* 591–606.

Marriott, M., & Kellett, S. (2009). Evaluating a cognitive analytic therapy service; practice-based outcomes and comparisons with person-centred and cognitive-behavioural therapies. *Psychology and Psychotherapy: Theory, Research and Practice, 82*(1), 57–72.

Martell, C. R. (2008). Lesbian, gay, and bisexual women and men. In M. A. Whisman (Ed.), *Adapting cognitive therapy for depression: Managing complexity and comorbidity* (pp. 373–393). New York, NY: Guilford Press.

Mascaro, N., & Rosen, D. H. (2005). Existential meaning's role in the enhancement of hope and prevention of depressive symptoms. *Journal of Personality, 73*(4), 985–1014.

Mascaro, N., & Rosen, D. H. (2006). The role of existential meaning as a buffer against stress. *Journal of Humanistic Psychology, 46*(2), 168–190.

Mascaro, N., & Rosen, D. H. (2008). Assessment of existential meaning and its longitudinal relations with depressive symptoms. *Journal of Social and Clinical Psychology, 27*(6), 576–599.

Mascaro, N., Rosen, D. H., & Morey, L. C. (2004). The development, construct validity, and clinical utility of the spiritual meaning scale. *Personality and Individual Differences, 37*(4), 845–860.

Masson, J. M. (1984). *The assault on truth: Freud's suppression of the seduction theory.* New York: Farrar, Straus and Giroux.

Master, S. L., Amodio, D. M., Stanton, A. L., Yee, C. M., Hilmert, C. J., & Taylor, S. E. (2009). Neurobiological correlates of coping through emotional approach. *Brain, Behavior, and Immunity, 23*(1), 27–35.

Matson, J. L., & Boisjoli, J. A. (2009). The token economy for children with intellectual disability and/or autism: A review. *Research in Developmental Disabilities, 30*(2), 240–248.

May, R. (1953). *Man's search for himself.* Oxford, England: Norton.

May, R. (1962). Introduction. *Existential psychoanalysis* (H. E. Barnes Trans.). (pp. 1–17). Chicago, IL: Regnery.

May, R. (1969). *Love and will.* New York, NY: Norton.

May, R. (1975). *The courage to create.* Oxford, England: Norton.

May, R. (1977). *The meaning of anxiety* (Rev. ed.). New York, NY: Norton.

May, R. (1981). *Freedom and destiny.* New York, NY: Norton.

May, R. (1982). The problem of evil: An open letter to Carl Rogers. *Journal of Humanistic Psychology, 22*(3), 10–21.

May, R. (1983). *The discovery of being: Writings in existential psychology.* New York, NY: Norton.

May, R., Angel, E., & Ellenberger, H. F. (Eds.). (1958). *Existence: A new dimension in psychiatry and psychology.* New York, NY: Basic Books.

Mays, V. M. (1988). Even the rat was white and male: Teaching the psychology of black women. In P. A. Bronstein & K. Quina (Eds.), *Teaching a psychology of people: Resources for gender and sociocultural awareness* (pp. 142–146). Washington, DC: American Psychological Association.

McCartney, J. (1966). Overt transference. *Journal of Sex Research, 2*, 227–237.

McCleary, R. A., & Lazarus, R. S. (1949). Autonomic discrimination without awareness. *Journal of Personality, 18*, 171–179.

McGoldrick, M., Gerson, R., & Shellenberger, S. (2005). *Genograms: Assessment and intervention* (3rd ed.). New York, NY: Norton.

McIntosh, P. (1998). White privilege: Unpacking the invisible knapsack. In M. McGoldrick (Ed.), *Re-visioning family therapy: Race, gender and culture in clinical practice* (pp. 147–152). New York, NY: Guilford Press.

McIntosh, V. V. W., Carter, F. A., Bulik, C. M., Frampton, C. M. A., & Joyce, P. R. (2011). Five-year outcome of cognitive behavioral therapy and exposure with response prevention for bulimia nervosa. *Psychological Medicine: A Journal of Research in Psychiatry and the Allied Sciences, 41*(5), 1061–1071.

McKay, D. (2011). Methods and mechanisms in the efficacy of psychodynamic psychotherapy. *American Psychologist, 66*(2), 147–148.

McKeel, A. J. (1996). A clinician's guide to research on soluton-focused brief therapy. In S. D. Miller, M. A. Hubble, & B. L. Duncan (Eds.), *Handbook of solution-focused brief therapy* (pp. 251–271). San Francisco, CA: Jossey-Bass.

McMillin, R. (1986). *Handbook of cognitive therapy techniques.* New York, NY: Norton.

McNeil, D. W., Sorrell, J. T., Vowles, K. E., & Billmeyer, T. W. (2002). Social phobia. In M. Hersen (Ed.), *Clinical behavior therapy: Adults and children* (pp. 90–105). New York, NY: John Wiley & Sons.

Meichenbaum, D. (1969). The effects of instructions and reinforcement on thinking and language behaviors of schizophrenics. *Behaviour Research and Therapy, 7*, 101–114.

Meichenbaum, D. (1977). *Cognitive behavior modification: An integrative approach.* New York, NY: Plenum.

Meichenbaum, D. (1985). *Stress inoculation training*. New York, NY: Pergamon Press.

Meichenbaum, D. (1992). Evolution of cognitive behavior therapy: Origins, tenets, and clinical examples. In J. K. Zeig (Ed.), *The evolution of psychotherapy: The second conference.* (pp. 114–128). New York, NY: Brunner/Mazel.

Meichenbaum, D. (1996). Stress inoculation training for coping with stressors. *The Clinical Psychologist, 49,* 4–7.

Meichenbaum, D. (2003). Cognitive-behavior therapy: Folktales and the unexpurgated history. *Cognitive Therapy and Research, 27*(1), 125–129.

Meichenbaum, D., & Cameron, R. (1974). The clinical potential of modifying what clients say to themselves. *Psychotherapy, 11,* 103–117.

Meichenbaum, D., & Goodman, J. (1971). Training impulsive children to talk to themselves. *Journal of Abnormal Psychology, 77,* 115–126.

Meier, S. T., & Davis, S. (2008). *The elements of counseling* (6th ed.). Pacific Grove, CA: Wadsworth.

Meissner, W. W. (2007). Therapeutic alliance: Theme and variations. *Psychoanalytic Psychology, 24*(2), 231–254.

Melnick, J., & Nevis, S. M. (1998). *Diagnosing in the here and now: A Gestalt therapy approach.* New York, NY: Guilford Press.

Merton, T. (1974). *A Thomas Merton reader.* New York: Doubleday.

Metcalf, L. (2008). *Counseling toward solutions: A practical solution-focused program for working with students, teachers, and parents* (2nd ed.). San Francisco, CA: Jossey-Bass.

Metcalfe, C., Winter, D., & Viney, L. (2007). The effectiveness of personal construct psychotherapy in clinical practice: A systematic review and meta-analysis. *Psychotherapy Research, 17*(4), 431–442.

Meyer, T. J., Miller, M. L., Metzger, R. L., & Borkovec, T. D. (1990). Development and validation of the Penn State worry questionnaire. *Behaviour Research & Therapy, 28*(6), 487–495.

Mezzich, J. E., Kirmayer, L. J., Kleinman, A., Fabrega, H., Parron, D. L., Good, B. J., et al. (2008). The place of culture in *DSM-IV*. In J. E. Mezzich & G. Caracci (Eds.), *Cultural formulation: A reader for psychiatric diagnosis* (pp. 167–181). Lanham, MD: Aronson.

Mickel, E., & Sanders, P. (2003). Utilizing CLSI and BNSA to improve outcomes: Perceptions of the relationship between the basic needs and learning styles. *International Journal of Reality Therapy, 22*(2), 44–47.

Miller, A. (1984). *For your own good: Hidden cruelty in child-rearing and the roots of violence* (2nd ed.). New York, NY: Farrar, Straus, Giroux.

Miller, A. L., Rathus, J. H., & Linehan, M. M. (2007). *Dialectical behavior therapy with suicidal adolescents.* New York, NY: Guilford Press.

Miller, J. B. (Ed.). (1973). *Psychoanalysis and women.* New York: Brunner/Mazel.

Miller, J. B. (1976). *Toward a new psychology of women.* Boston, MA: Beacon.

Miller, J. H. (2010). Evidence-based practice and the future of counseling: The debate revisited. *Counselling Psychology Quarterly, 23*(4), 425–428.

Miller, M. D., Cornes, C., Frank, E., Ehrenpreis, L., Silberman, R., Schlernitzauer, M. A., et al. (2001). Interpersonal psychotherapy for late-life depression: Past, present, and future. *Journal of Psychotherapy Practice & Research, 10*(4), 231–238.

Miller, M. D., Wolfson, L., Frank, E., Cornes, C., Silberman, R., Ehrenpreis, L., et al. (1998). Using interpersonal psychotherapy (IPT) in a combined psychotherapy/medication research protocol with depressed elders: A descriptive report with case vignettes. *Journal of Psychotherapy Practice & Research, 7*(1), 47–55.

Miller, P. (1983). *Theories of developmental psychology.* San Francisco, CA: Freeman.

Miller, P. (2010). *Theories of developmental psychology.* (5th ed.). New York: Worth.

Miller, W. R. (1978). Behavioral treatment of problem drinkers: A comparative outcome study of three controlled drinking therapies. *Journal of Consulting & Clinical Psychology, 46*(1), 74–86.

Miller, W. R., & Rollnick, S. (2002). *Motivational interviewing: Preparing people for change* (2nd ed.). New York, NY: Guilford Press.

Miller, W. R., & Taylor, C. A. (1980). Relative effectiveness of bibliotherapy, individual and group self-control training in the treatment of problem drinkers. *Addictive Behaviors, 5*(1), 13–24.

Minuchin, S. (1974). *Families and family therapy.* Cambridge, MA: Harvard University Press.

Mitchell, S. A. (1988). *Relational concepts in psychoanalysis: An integration.* Cambridge, MA: Harvard University Press.

Mohr, D. C. (1995). Negative outcome in psychotherapy: A critical review. *Clinical Psychology: Science and Practice, 2*(1), 1–27.

Monk, G. (1997). How narrative therapy works. In G. Monk, J. Winslade, K. Crocket & D. Epston (Eds.), *Narrative therapy in practice: The archaeology of hope* (pp. 3–31). San Francisco, CA: Jossey-Bass.

Monk, G., Winslade, J., Crocket, K., & Epston, D. (Eds.). (1997). *Narrative therapy in practice: The archaeology of hope.* San Francisco, CA: Jossey-Bass.

Moore, T. (1994). *Care of the soul.* New York, NY: Perennial.

Moos, R. H. (2005). Iatrogenic effects of psychosocial interventions for substance use disorders: Prevalence, predictors, prevention. *Addiction, 100*(5), 595–604.

Moradi, B., & DeBlaere, C. (2010). *Women's experiences of sexist discrimination: Review of research and directions for centralizing race, ethnicity, and culture.* New York, NY: Springer.

Moradi, B., & Funderburk, J. R. (2006). Roles of perceived sexist events and perceived social support in the mental health of women seeking counseling. *Journal of Counseling Psychology, 53*(4), 464–473.

Moreau, D., Mufson, L., Weissman, M. M., & Klerman, G. L. (1991). Interpersonal psychotherapy for adolescent depression: Description of modification and preliminary application. *Journal of the American Academy of Child & Adolescent Psychiatry, 30*(4), 642–651.

Morgan, R. (1970). *Sisterhood is powerful.* New York: Vintage.

Morin, C. M., Bootzin, R. R., Buysse, D. J., Edinger, J. D., Espie, C. A., & Lichstein, K. L. (2006). Psychological and behavioral treatment of insomnia: Update of the recent evidence (1998–2004). *SLEEP, 29*(11), 1398–1414

Mosak, H. H. (1972). Life style assessment: A demonstration focused on family constellation. *Journal of Individual Psychology, 28*(2), 232–247.

Mosak, H. H. (1985). Interrupting a depression: The pushbutton technique. *Individual Psychology, 41,* 210–214.

Mosak, H. H. (1987). Guilt, guilt feelings, regret and repentance. *Individual Psychology, 43,* 288–295.

Mosak, H. H. (1989). Adlerian psychotherapy. In R. Corsini & D. Wedding (Eds.), *Current psychotherapies* (4th ed., pp. 65–116). Itasca, IL: Peacock.

Mosak, H. H. (1995). Adlerian psychotherapy. In R. Corsini & D. Wedding (Eds.), *Current psychotherapies.* (5th ed., pp. 51–94). Itasca, IL: Peacock.

Mosak, H. H., & Dreikurs, R. (1967). The life tasks III: The fifth life task. *Individual Psychology, 5,* 16–22.

Mosak, H. H., & Kopp, R. R. (1973). The early recollections of Adler, Freud, and Jung. *Journal of Individual Psychology, 29,* 157–166.

Mosak, H. H., & Maniacci, M. P. (1999). *A primer of Adlerian psychology: The analytic-behavioral-cognitive psychology of Alfred Adler.* Philadelphia, PA: Taylor & Francis.

Mosig, Y. D. (2006). Conceptions of the self in Western and Eastern psychology. *Journal of Theoretical and Philosophical Psychology, 26,* 39–50.

Mowrer, O. H. (1947). On the dual nature of learning: A reinterpretation of "conditioning" and "problem-solving." *Harvard Education Review, 17,* 102–148.

Mozdzierz, G. J., Greenblatt, R. L., & Murphy, T. J. (1986). Social interest: The validity of two scales. *Individual Psychology: Journal of Adlerian Theory, Research & Practice, 42*(1), 35–43.

Mozdzierz, G. J., Greenblatt, R. L., & Murphy, T. J. (1988). Further validation of the Sulliman scale of social interest and the social interest scale. *Individual Psychology: Journal of Adlerian Theory, Research & Practice, 44*(1), 30–34.

Mozdzierz, G. J., Greenblatt, R. L., & Murphy, T. J. (2007). The measurement and clinical use of social interest: Validation of the Sulliman scale of social interest on a sample of hospitalized substance abuse patients. *The Journal of Individual Psychology, 63*(2), 225–234.

Mozdzierz, G. J., & Semyck, R. W. (1980). Relationship between alcoholics' social interest and attitude toward success and failure. *Journal of Individual Psychology, 36*(1), 61–65.

Mufson, L., Dorta, K. P., Moreau, D., & Weissman, M. M. (2004). *Interpersonal psychotherapy for depressed adolescents* (2nd ed.). New York, NY: Guilford Press.

Mufson, L., Dorta, K. P., Wickramaratne, P., Nomura, Y., Olfson, M., & Weissman, M. M. (2004). A randomized effectiveness trial of interpersonal psychotherapy for depressed adolescents. *Archives of General Psychiatry, 61*(6), 577–584.

Murphy, J. J. (2008). *Solution-focused counseling in middle and high schools.* Alexandria, VA: American Counseling.

Myers, I. B. (1955). *Gifts differing: Understanding personality types.* Palo Alto, CA: Davies-Black.

Nanda, J. (2009). Mindfulness: A lived experience of existential-phenomenological themes. *Existential Analysis, 20*(1), 147–162.

Nanda, J. (2010). Embodied integration: Reflections on mindfulness based cognitive therapy (MBCT) and a case for mindfulness based existential therapy (MBET). A single case illustration. *Existential Analysis, 21*(2), 331–350.

Napier, A. Y., & Whitaker, C. A. (1978). *The family crucible.* New York, NY: Harper & Row.

Naranjo, C. (1970). Present-centeredness: Technique, prescription, and ideal. In J. Fagan & I. L. Shepherd

(Eds.), *What is Gestalt therapy?* (pp. 63–97). New York, NY: Science and Behavior Books.

Nau, D. S., & Shilts, L. (2000). When to use the miracle question: Clues from a qualitative study of four SFBT practitioners. *Journal of Systemic Therapies, 19*(1), 129–135.

Nezu, A. M., & Nezu, C. M. (2010). Problem-solving therapy for relapse prevention in depression. In C. S. Richards & M. G. Perri (Eds.), *Relapse prevention for depression* (pp. 99–130). Washington, DC: American Psychological Association.

Nezu, A. M., Nezu, C. M., Jain, D., Xanthopoulos, M. S., Cos, T. A., Friedman, J., et al. (2007). Social problem solving and noncardiac chest pain. *Psychosomatic Medicine, 69*(9), 944–951.

Ng, S. M., Li, A. M., Lou, V.W.Q., Tso, I. F., Wan, P.Y.P., & Chan, D.F.Y. (2008). Incorporating family therapy into asthma group intervention: A randomized waitlist-controlled trial. *Family Process: Special Issue on Families and Asthma, 47*(1), 115–130.

Nichols, M. P., & Schwarts, R. C. (2007). *The essentials of family therapy* (3rd ed.). Boston, MA: Pearson.

Nobles, W. (2006). *Seeking the Saku: Foundational writings for an African psychology.* Third World Press. Chicago, Illinois.

Norcross, J. C., Beutler, L. E., & Levant, R. F. (Eds.). (2006). *Evidence-based practices in mental health: Debate and dialogue on the fundamental questions.* Washington, DC: American Psychological Association.

Norcross, J. C., Karg, R. S., & Prochaska, J. O. (1997). Clinical psychologists in the 1990s. *TheClinical Psychologist, 50,* 4–9.

Norcross, J. C., & Lambert, M. J. (2011). Psychotherapy relationships that work II. *Psychotherapy, 48*(1), 4–8.

Norcross, J. C., & Vangarelli, D. J. (1989). The resolution solution: Longitudinal examination of new year's change attempts. *Journal of Substance Abuse, 1,* 127–134.

Novaco, R. W. (1979). The cognitive regulation of anger. In P. C. Kendall & S. D. Hollon (Eds.), *Cognitive behavioral interventions: Theory, research, and procedures* (pp. 241–285). New York, NY: Academic Press.

Nutt, R. L. (2005). *Feminist and contextual work.* Hoboken, NJ: John Wiley & Sons.

O'Brien, W. H., & Carhart, V. (2011). Functional analysis in behavioral medicine. *European Journal of Psychological Assessment, 27,* 4–16.

Oaklander, V. (1978). *Windows to our children.* Moab, UT: Real People Press.

Oaklander, V. (1997). The therapeutic process with children and adolescents. *Gestalt Review, 1*(4), 292–317.

Oaklander, V. (2001). Gestalt play therapy. *International Journal of Play Therapy, 10*(2), 45–55.

Oaklander, V. (2006). *Hidden treasure: A map of the child's inner self.* London, England: Karnac Books.

O'Hanlon, B. (1988). Solution-oriented therapy: A megatrend in psychotherapy. In J. K. Zeig & S. R. Lankton (Eds.), *Developing Ericksonian therapy: State of the art* (pp. 93–111). Philadelphia, PA: Brunner/Mazel.

O'Hanlon, W. H. (1998). Possibility therapy: An inclusive, collaborative, solution-based model of psychotherapy. In M. F. Hoyt (Ed.), *The handbook of constructive therapies* (pp. 137–158). San Francisco, CA: Jossey-Bass.

O'Hanlon, W. H., & Bertolino, B. (1998). *Even from a broken web: Brief, respectful, solution-oriented therapy for sexual abuse and trauma.* New York, NY: John Wiley & Sons.

O'Hanlon, W. H., & Weiner-Davis, M. (1989). *In search of solutions: A new direction in psychotherapy.* New York, NY: Norton.

Oliver, M. (1992). *New and selected poems.* Boston: Beacon Press.

Olson, D. H. (2000). Circumplex model of marital and family systems. *Journal of Family Therapy, 22,* 144–167.

Onedera, J. D. (2006). Functional family therapy: An interview with Dr. James Alexander. *The Family Journal, 14*(3), 306–311.

Onedera, J. D., & Greenwalt, B. C. (2007). Choice theory: An interview with Dr. William Glasser. *The Family Journal, 15*(1), 79–86.

Orgler, H. (1963). *Alfred Adler: The man and his work.* New York, NY: Mentor Books.

Ost, L., Alm, T., Brandberg, M., & Breitholz, E. (2001). One vs. five sessions of exposure and five sessions of cognitive therapy in the treatment of claustrophobia. *Behaviour Research and Therapy, 39,* 167–183.

Overholser, J. C. (2006). Panacea or placebo: The historical quest for medications to treat depression. *Journal of Contemporary Psychotherapy, 36*(4), 183–190.

Page, R. C., Weiss, J. F., & Lietaer, G. (2002). *Humanistic group psychotherapy.* Washington, DC: American Psychological Association.

Paivio, S. C., & Greenberg, L. S. (1995). Resolving "unfinished business": Efficacy of experiential therapy using empty-chair dialogue. *Journal of Consulting & Clinical Psychology, 63*(3), 419–425.

Pan, J., Wong, D.F.K., Chan, C. L. W., & Joubert, L. (2008). Meaning of life as a protective factor of positive affect in acculturation: A resilience framework and a cross-cultural comparison. *International Journal of Intercultural Relations, 32*(6), 505–514.

Pan, J., Wong, D.F.K., Joubert, L., & Chan, C. L. W. (2008). The protective function of meaning of life on life satisfaction among Chinese students in Australia and Hong Kong: A cross-cultural comparative study. *Journal of American College Health, 57*(2), 221–231.

Paniagua, F. A. (2010). Assessment and diagnosis in a cultural context. In M. M. Leach & J. D. Aten (Eds.), *Culture and the therapeutic process* (pp. 65–98). New York, NY: Routledge/Taylor & Francis.

Parlett, M., & Lee, R. G. (2005). *Contemporary Gestalt therapy: Field theory*. Thousand Oaks, CA: Sage.

Pascual-Leone, A., Bierman, R., Arnold, R., & Stasiak, E. (2011). Emotion-focused therapy for incarcerated offenders of intimate partner violence: A 3-year outcome using a new whole-sample matching method. *Psychotherapy Research, 21*(3), 331–347.

Parloff, M. B., Waskow, I. E., & Wolfe, B. E. (1978). Research on therapist variables in relation to process and outcome. In S. L. Garfield & A. E. Bergin (Eds.), *Handbook of psychotherapy and behavior change: An empirical analysis* (pp. 233–282). New York, NY: John Wiley & Sons.

Patterson, C. H. (1973). *Theories of counseling and psychotherapy*. New York: Harper & Row.

Patterson, D. R. (2010). *Clinical hypnosis for pain control*. Washington, DC: American Psychological Association.

Paul, G. L. (1969). Behavior modification research: Design and tactics. In C. M. Franks (Ed.), *Behavior therapy: Appraisal and status* (pp. 29–62). New York, NY: McGraw-Hill.

Paul, R. A. (1991). Freud's anthropology: A reading of the "cultural books." In J. Neu (Ed.), *The Cambridge companion to Freud* (pp. 267–286). New York, NY: Cambridge University Press.

Pavlov, I. P. (1906). The scientific investigation of the psychical faculties or processes in the higher animals. *Science, 24*, 613–619.

Pavlov, I. P. (1927). *Conditioned reflexes* (G. V. Anrep Trans.). London: Oxford University Press.

Peck, M. S. (1978). *The road less traveled*. New York, NY: Simon & Schuster.

Pedersen, P. B., Draguns, J. G., Lonner, W. J., & Trimble, J. E. (2008). *Counseling across cultures* (6th ed.). Thousand Oaks, CA: Sage.

Peluso, P. R., Peluso, J. P., Buckner, J. P., Kern, R. M., & Curlette, W. (2009). Measuring lifestyle and attachment: An empirical investigation linking individual psychology and attachment theory. *Journal of Counseling & Development, 87*(4), 394–403.

Penedo, F. J., Traeger, L., Dahn, J., Molton, I., Gonzalez, J. S., Schneiderman, N., et al. (2007). Cognitive behavioral stress management intervention improves quality of life in Spanish monolingual Hispanic men treated for localized prostate cancer: Results of a randomized controlled trial. *International Journal of Behavioral Medicine, 14*(3), 164–172.

Pennebaker, J. W., Zech, E., & Rimé, B. (2001). *Disclosing and sharing emotion: Psychological, social, and health consequences*. Washington, DC: American Psychological Association.

Perls, F. (1969a). *Gestalt therapy verbatim*. Moab, UT: Real People Press.

Perls, F. (1969b). *In and out the garbage pail*. Moab, UT: Real People Press.

Perls, F., Hefferline, R. F., & Goodman, P. (1951). *Gestalt therapy*. New York, NY: Bantam Books.

Perls, F. S. (1945). *Ego, hunger and aggression: A revision of Freud's theory and method* (2nd ed.). Oxford, England: Knox.

Perls, F. S. (1970). Four lectures. In J. Fagan & I. L. Shepherd (Eds.), *What is Gestalt therapy?* (pp. 11–49). New York, NY: Science and Behavior Books.

Perls, L. (1990). A talk for the 25th anniversary. *Gestalt Journal, 13*(2), 15–22.

Persons, J. B. (1989). *Cognitive therapy in practice: A case formulation approach*. New York, NY: Norton.

Persons, J. B. (2008). *The case formulation approach to cognitive-behavior therapy*. New York, NY: Guilford Press.

Persons, J. B., & Tompkins, M. A. (1997). Cognitive-behavioral case formulation. In T. D. Eells (Ed.), *Handbook of psychotherapy case formulation* (pp. 314–339). New York, NY: Guilford.

Petersen, S. (2005). Reality therapy and individual or Adlerian psychology: A comparison. *International Journal of Reality Therapy, 24*(2), 11–14.

Petroff, E. A. (1986). *Medieval women's visionary literature*. New York, NY: Oxford University Press.

Philippot, P., & Segal, Z. (2009). Mindfulness based psychological interventions: Developing emotional awareness for better being. *Journal of Consciousness Studies. Special Issue: Ten Years of Viewing From Within: The Legacy of F. J. Varela, 16*(10–12), 285–306.

Pickett, C. L., Gardner, W. L., & Knowles, M. (2004). Getting a cue: The need to belong and enhanced sensitivity to social cues. *Personality and Social Psychology Bulletin, 30*(9), 1095–1107.

Pierce, C. M. (1978). Entitlement dysfunctions. *Australian and New Zealand Journal of Psychiatry, 12*(4), 215–219.

Pina, A. A., Silverman, W. K., Fuentes, R. M., Kurtines, W. M., & Weems, C. F. (2003). Exposure-based cognitive-behavioral treatment for phobic and anxiety disorders: Treatment effects and maintenance for Hispanic/Latino relative to European-American youths. *Journal of the American Academy of Child & Adolescent Psychiatry, 42*(10), 1179–1187.

Pine, F. (1990). *Drive, ego, object, and self: A synthesis for clinical work*. New York, NY: Basic Books.

Pipes, R. B., & Davenport, D. S. (1999). *Introduction to psychotherapy: Common clinical wisdom*. Englewood Cliffs, NJ: Prentice Hall.

Pollack, W. S. (2000). *Real boys' voices*. New York, NY: Penguin Books.

Pollet, T. V., Dijkstra, P., Barelds, D. P. H., & Buunk, A. P. (2010). Birth order and the dominance aspect of extraversion: Are firstborns more extraverted, in the sense of being dominant, than laterborns? *Journal of Research in Personality, 44*(6), 742–745.

Polster, E. (1966). A contemporary psychotherapy. *Psychotherapy: Theory, Research & Practice, 3*(1), 1–6.

Polster, E., & Polster, M. (1973). *Gestalt therapy integrated: Contours of theory and practice*. New York, NY: Brunner/Mazel.

Polster, M. (1991). *Eve's daughters: The forbidden heroism of women*. San Francisco, CA: Jossey-Bass.

Pomerantz, A. M., & Handelsman, M. M. (2004). Informed consent revisited: An updated written question format. *Professional Psychology: Research and Practice, 35*(2), 201–205.

Pope, K. S. (1988). How clients are harmed by sexual contact with mental health professionals. *Journal of Counseling & Development, 67*, 222–226.

Pope, K. S., & Vasquez, M. J. T. (2007). *Ethics in psychotherapy and counseling: A practical guide* (3rd ed.). San Francisco, CA: Jossey-Bass.

Poston, W. C. (1990). The biracial identity development model: A needed addition. *Journal of Counseling & Development, 69*(2), 152–155.

Powers, M. B., & Emmelkamp, P.M.G. (2008). Virtual reality exposure therapy for anxiety disorders: A meta-analysis. *Journal of Anxiety Disorders, 22*(3), 561–569.

Powers, M. B., Zum Vörde Sive Vörding, Maarten B., & Emmelkamp, P. M. G. (2009). Acceptance and commitment therapy: A meta-analytic review. *Psychotherapy and Psychosomatics, 78*(2), 73–80.

Powlishta, K. K., Sen, M. G., Serbin, L. A., Poulin-Dubois, D., & Eichstedt, J. A. (2001). From infancy through middle childhood: The role of cognitive and social factors in becoming gendered. In R. K. Unger (Ed.), *Handbook of the psychology of women and gender* (pp. 116–132). New York, NY: John Wiley & Sons.

Poyrazli, S. (2009). Considerations when interviewing immigrants. In J. Sommers-Flanagan & R. Sommers-Flanagan (Eds.), *Clinical interviewing* (4th ed., pp. 418–419). Hoboken, NJ: John Wiley & Sons.

Preti, A., de Girolamo, G., Vilagut, G., Alonso, J., de Graaf, R., Bruffaerts, R., et al. (2009). The epidemiology of eating disorders in six European countries: Results of the ESEMeD-WMH project. *Journal of Psychiatric Research, 43*(14), 1125–1132.

Prochaska, J. O. (1979). *Systems of psychotherapy: A transtheoretical analysis*. Chicago, IL: Dorsey.

Prochaska, J. O. (1995). An eclectic and integrative approach: Transtheoretical therapy. In A. S. Gurman & S. B. Messer (Eds.), *Essential psychotherapies* (pp. 403–440). New York, NY: Guilford Press.

Prochaska, J. O., & DiClemente, C. C. (1982). Transtheoretical therapy: Toward a more integrative model of change. *Psychotherapy, 19*, 276–278.

Prochaska, J. O., DiClemente, C. C., & Norcross, J. C. (1993). In search of how people change. *American Psychologist, 47*, 1102–1114.

Prochaska, J. O., & Norcross, J. C. (2003). *Systems of psychotherapy: A transtheoretical analysis* (5th ed.). Pacific Grove, CA: Brooks/Cole.

Prochaska, J. O., & Norcross, J. C. (2010). *Systems of psychotherapy: A transtheoretical approach*. Belmont, CA: Brooks/Cole.

Quinn, S. (1987). *A mind of her own: The life of Karen Horney*. New York, NY: Summit Books.

Quirk, G. J., & Mueller, D. (2008). Neural mechanisms of extinction learning and retrieval. *Neuropsychopharmacology, 33*(1), 56–72.

Rachman, S. (1965). Aversion therapy: Chemical or electrical? *Behaviour Research and Therapy, 2*, 289–300.

Rachman, S. (Ed.). (1997). *The best of behaviour research and therapy*. New York, NY: Pergamon.

Rader, J., & Gilbert, L. A. (2005). The egalitarian relationship in feminist therapy. *Psychology of Women Quarterly, 29*(4), 427–435.

Rakovshik, S. G., & McManus, F. (2010). Establishing evidence-based training in cognitive behavioral therapy: A review of current empirical findings and theoretical guidance. *Clinical Psychology Review, 30*(5), 496–516.

Ramey, H. L., Tarulli, D., Frijters, J. C., & Fisher, L. (2009). A sequential analysis of externalizing in narrative therapy with children. *Contemporary Family Therapy: An International Journal, 31*(4), 262–279.

Rapaport, D. (1951). *Organization and pathology of thought.* New York, NY: Columbia University Press.

Raskin, N. J. (1992, August). *Not necessary, perhaps sufficient, definitely facilitative.* Paper presented at the annual meeting of the American Psychological Association, Washington, DC.

Raskin, N. J., & Rogers, C. R. (1989). Person-centered therapy. In R. Corsini & D. Wedding (Eds.), *Current psychotherapies* (pp. 154–194). Itasca, IL: Peacock.

Rasmussen, K. G. (2011). Some considerations in choosing electroconvulsive therapy versus transcranial magnetic stimulation for depression. *Journal of ECT, 27*(1), 51–54.

Rayburn, C. A., & Comas-Díaz, L. (Eds.). (2008). *Woman soul: The inner life of women's spirituality.* Westport, CT: Praeger/Greenwood.

Real, T. (1998). *I don't want to talk about it: Overcoming the secret legacy of male depression.* New York, NY: Scribner.

Rederstorff, J. C. (2010). Feminist identity's contribution to well-being among black and white college students. (ProQuest Information & Learning). *Dissertation Abstracts International: Section B: The Sciences and Engineering, 70* (Electronic; Print).

Redsand, A. (2007). *Viktor Frankl: A life worth living.* New York, NY: Clarion.

Reich, W. (1975). *Early writings: I.* (P. Schmitz, Trans.). Oxford, England: Farrar, Straus & Giroux.

Reich, W., Higgins, M. B., Raphael, C. M., Schmitz, P., & Tompkins, J. (1988). *Passion of youth: An autobiography, 1897–1922.* New York, NY: Farrar, Straus & Giroux.

Reis, E. (2007). Divergence or disorder? The politics of naming intersex. *Perspectives in Biology and Medicine, 50*(4), 535–543.

Reis, E. (2009). *Bodies in doubt: An American history of intersex.* Baltimore, MD: Johns Hopkins University Press.

Reiter, M. D. (2007). The use of expectation in solution-focused formula tasks. *Journal of Family Psychotherapy, 18*(1), 27–37.

Reitman, D., Murphy, M. A., Hupp, S. D. A., & O'Callaghan, P. M. (2004). Behavior change and perceptions of change: Evaluating the effectiveness of a token economy. *Child & Family Behavior Therapy, 26*(2), 17–36.

Renik, O. (1993). Analytic interaction: Conceptualizing technique in light of the analyst's irreducible subjectivity. *Psychoanalytic Quarterly, 62,* 553–571.

Richardson, B. G. (2001). *Working with challenging youth: Lessons learned along the way.* Philadelphia: Brunner-Routledge.

Richmond, M. E. (1917). *Social diagnosis.* New York, NY: Sage.

Ridge, N. W., Warren, J. S., Burlingame, G. M., Wells, M. G., & Tumblin, K. M. (2009). Reliability and validity of the youth outcome questionnaire self-report. *Journal of Clinical Psychology, 65*(10), 1115–1126.

Ringstrom, P. A. (2001). Cultivating the improvisational in psychoanalytic treatment. *Psychoanalytic Dialogues, 11,* 727–754.

Robey, P. A. (2011). Reality therapy and choice theory: An interview with Robert Wubbolding. *The Family Journal, 19*(2), 231–237.

Rodenburg, R., Benjamin, A., de Roos, C., Meijer, A. M., & Stams, G. J. (2009). Efficacy of EMDR in children: A meta-analysis. *Clinical Psychology Review, 29*(7), 599–606.

Rogers, C. R. (1939). *The clinical treatment of the problem child.* Boston, MA: Houghton Mifflin.

Rogers, C. R. (1942a). *Counseling and psychotherapy.* Boston, MA: Houghton Mifflin.

Rogers, C. R. (1942b). The use of electrically recorded interviews in improving psychotherapeutic techniques. *American Journal of Orthopsychiatry, 12,* 429–434.

Rogers, C. R. (1951). *Client-centered therapy.* Boston, MA: Houghton Mifflin.

Rogers, C. R. (1957). The necessary and sufficient conditions of therapeutic personality change. *Journal of Consulting Psychology, 21,* 95–103.

Rogers, C. R. (1958). The characteristics of a helping relationship. *Personnel and Guidance Journal, 37,* 6–16.

Rogers, C. R. (1959). A theory of therapy, personality, and interpersonal relationships, as developed in the client-centered framework. In S. Koch (Ed.), *Psychology: A study of a science* (pp. 184–256). New York, NY: McGraw-Hill.

Rogers, C. R. (1960). The individual and the design of culture. *Conference on Evolutionary Theory and Human Progress,* 15–16.

Rogers, C. R. (1961). *On becoming a person.* Boston, MA: Houghton Mifflin.

Rogers, C. R. (Director). (1963). *Mrs. P.S.* [Video/DVD] Orlando, FL: American Academy of Psychotherapists.

Rogers, C. R. (Director). (1965). *Three approaches to psychotherapy.* [Video/DVD] Corona del Mar, CA: Psychological and Educational Films.

Rogers, C. R. (1967). Autobiography. In E. G. Boring & G. Lindzey (Eds.), *A history of psychology in autobiography* (pp. 341–384). New York, NY: Appleton.

Rogers, C. R. (1969). *Freedom to learn: A view of what education might become.* Columbus, OH: Charles E. Merrill.

Rogers, C. R. (1970). *Carl Rogers on encounter groups*. New York, NY: Harper & Row.

Rogers, C. R. (1975). Empathy: An unappreciated way of being. *Counseling Psychologist, 21*, 95–103.

Rogers, C. R. (1977). *Carl Rogers on personal power*. New York, NY: Delacorte Press.

Rogers, C. R. (1980). *A way of being*. Boston, MA: Houghton Mifflin.

Rogers, C. R., & Haigh, G. (1983). I walk softly through life. *Voices: The Art and Science of Psychotherapy, 18*, 6–14.

Rogers, N. (1996). *The creative connection*. New York: Science and Behavior Books.

Rollnick, S., & Miller, W. R. (1995). What is motivational interviewing? *Behavioural & Cognitive Psychotherapy, 23*(4), 325–334.

Rombach, M.A.M. (2003). An invitation to therapeutic letter writing. *Journal of Systemic Therapies, 22*(1), 15–32.

Ronen, T. (2003). *Cognitive-constructivist psychotherapy with children and adolescents*. New York, NY: Kluwer Academic/Plenum.

Rose-Inza, K., & Mi Gu, H. (2001). The effect of internal control and achievement motivation in group counseling based on reality therapy. *International Journal of Reality Therapy, 20*, 12–15.

Rosen, G. M., & Davison, G. C. (2003). Psychology should list empirically supported principles of change (ESPs) and not credential trademarked therapies or other treatment packages. *Behavior Modification. Special Issue: Empirically Supported Treatments, 27*(3), 300–312.

Rosen, G. M., Lohr, J. M., McNally, R. J., & Herbert, J. D. (2000). Power therapies, miraculous claims and the cures that fail. In M. J. Scott & S. Palmer (Eds.), *Trauma and post-traumatic stress disorder* (pp. 134–136). London, England: Cassell.

Rosenberg, B. (2000). Mandated clients and solution focused therapy: "It's not my miracle." *Journal of Systemic Therapies, 19*(1), 90–99.

Rosenfeld, E. (1978). An oral history of gestalt therapy: I. A conversation with Laura Perls. *Gestalt Journal, 1*, 8–31.

Rosengren, D. B. (2009). *Building motivational interviewing skills: A practitioner workbook*. New York, NY: Guilford Press.

Rosenthal, H. G. (Ed.). (1999). *Favorite counseling and therapy techniques*. Washington, DC: Accelerated Development.

Rosenzweig, S. (1936). Some implicit common factors in diverse methods in psychotherapy. *American Journal of Orthopsychiatry, 6*, 412–415.

Rowling, J. K. (1997). *Harry Potter and the sorcerer's stone*. New York, NY: Scholastic Press.

Roy v. Hartogs, 366 (New York 1975).

Rozsnafsky, J. (1974). The impact of Alfred Adler on three "free-will" therapies of the 1960's. *Journal of Individual Psychology, 30*, 65–80.

Rüegg, J. C. (2009). Traumagedächtnis und neurobiologie: Konsolidierung, rekonsolidierung, extinktion. Trauma memory and neurobiology: Consolidation, reconsolidation, extinction. *Trauma & Gewalt, 3*(1), 6–17.

Ruggiero, K. J., Morris, T. L., Hopko, D. R., & Lejuez, C. W. (2007). Application of behavioral activation treatment for depression to an adolescent with a history of child maltreatment. *Clinical Case Studies, 6*(1), 64–78.

Rutter, M. (1995). Clinical implications of attachment concepts: Retrospect and prospect. Journal of Child Psychology and Psychiatry, 36(4), 549–571.

Ruwaard, J., Broeksteeg, J., Schrieken, B., Emmelkamp, P., & Lange, A. (2010). Web-based therapist-assisted cognitive behavioral treatment of panic symptoms: A randomized controlled trial with a three-year follow-up. *Journal of Anxiety Disorders, 24*(4), 387–396.

Ryan, R. M., Lynch, M. F., Vansteenkiste, M., & Deci, E. L. (2011). Motivation and autonomy in counseling, psychotherapy, and behavior change: A look at theory and practice. *The Counseling Psychologist, 39*(2), 193–260.

Safran, J. D., Muran, J. C., & Eubanks-Carter, C. (2011). Repairing alliance ruptures. *Psychotherapy, 48*(1), 80–87.

Salois, E. M., Holkup, P. A., Tripp-Reimer, T., & Weinert, C. (2006). Research as spiritual covenant. *Western Journal of Nursing Research, 28*(5), 505–524.

Salomon, F. (2003). Maintaining a safe container. In J. Sommers-Flanagan & R. Sommers-Flanagan (Eds.), *Counseling and psychotherapy theories in context and practice* (p. 53). Hoboken, NJ: John Wiley & Sons.

Santa Rita, E. (1998). What do you do after asking the miracle question in solution-focused therapy? *Family Therapy, 25*(3), 189–195.

Santos de Barona, M., & Dutton, M. A. (1997). Feminist perspectives on assessment. In J. Worell & N. G. Johnson (Eds.), *Shaping the future of feminist psychology: Education, research, and practice* (pp. 37–56). Washington, DC: American Psychological Association.

Sapienza, B. G., & Bugental, J.F.T. (2000). Keeping our instruments finely tuned: An existential–humanistic perspective. *Professional Psychology: Research and Practice, 31*(4), 458–460.

Sartre, J. (1953). *Existential psychoanalysis* (H. E. Barnes, Trans.). Chicago, IL: Regnery.

Sartre, J. (1971). *Being and nothingness.* New York, NY: Bantam Books.

Satir, V. M. (1964). *Conjoint family therapy.* Palo Alto, CA: Science and Behavior Books.

Satir, V. M. (1983). *Conjoint family therapy* (3rd ed.). Palo Alto, CA: Science and Behavior Books.

Saul, L. (1973). *Psychodynamically-based psychotherapy.* New York, NY: Aronson.

Saunders, T., Driskell, J. E., Hall, J., & Salas, E. (1996). The effect of stress inoculation training on anxiety and performance. *Journal of Occupational Health Psychology, 1,* 170–186.

Schmidt, U., Lee, S., Beecham, J., Perkins, S., Treasure, J., Yi, I., et al. (2007). A randomized controlled trial of family therapy and cognitive behavior therapy guided self-care for adolescents with bulimia nervosa and related disorders. *American Journal of Psychiatry, 164*(4), 591–598.

Schneider, K. J. (2004). *Rediscovery of awe: Splendor, mystery, and the fluid center of life.* St. Paul, MN: Paragon House.

Schneider, K. J. (Ed.). (2008). *Existential-integrative psychotherapy: Guideposts to the core of practice.* New York, NY: Routledge/Taylor & Francis.

Schneider, K. J. (2010). An existential-integrative approach to experiential liberation. *The Humanistic Psychologist, 38*(1), 1–14.

Schneider, K. J., Galvin, J., & Serlin, I. (2009). Rollo May on existential psychotherapy. *Journal of Humanistic Psychology, 49*(4), 419–434.

Schneider, K. J., & Krug, O. T. (2010). *Existential–humanistic therapy.* Washington, DC: American Psychological Association.

Schneider, K. J., & May, R. (1995). *The psychology of existence: An integrative, clinical perspective.* New York, NY, England: McGraw-Hill.

Schofield, W. (1964). *Psychotherapy: The purchase of friendship.* Englewood Cliffs, NJ: Prentice-Hall.

Schore, A. N. (1994). *Affect regulation and the origin of the self: The neurobiology of emotional development.* Mahwah, NJ: Erlbaum.

Schulman, B. H. (1965). A comparison of Allport's and Adlerian concepts of life style. *Individual Psychology, 3,* 14–21.

Schulman, B. H. (1985). Cognitive therapy and the individual psychology of Alfred Adler. In M. Mahoney

& A. Freeman (Eds.), *Cognition and psychotherapy.* (pp. 243–258). New York: Plenum.

Schumacher, J. E., Milby, J. B., Wallace, D., Meehan, D., Kertesz, S., Vuchinich, R., et al. (2007). Meta-analysis of day treatment and contingency-management dismantling research: Birmingham homeless cocaine studies (1990–2006). *Journal of Consulting and Clinical Psychology, 75*(5), 823–828.

Schur, M. (1972). *Freud: Living and dying.* New York, NY: International Universities Press.

Schwartz, J. M., Gulliford, E. Z., Stier, J., & Thienemann, M. (2005). In S. G. Mijares & G. S. Khalsa (Eds.), *Mindful awareness and self-directed neuroplasticity: Integrating psychospiritual and biological approaches to mental health with a focus on obsessive-compulsive disorder.* New York, NY: Haworth Press.

Schwartz, J. M., Stoessel, P. W., Baxter, L. R., Martin, K. M., & Phelps, M. E. (1996). Systematic changes in cerebral glucose metabolic rate after successful behavior modification treatment of obsessive-compulsive disorder. *Archives of General Psychiatry, 53*(2), 109–113.

Segal, Z. V., Williams, J.M.G., & Teasdale, J. D. (2002). *Mindfulness-based cognitive therapy for depression: A new approach to preventing relapse.* New York, NY: Guilford Press.

Segraves, R. T. (2002). Female sexual disorders: Psychiatric aspects. *Canadian Journal of Psychiatry, 47*(5), 419–425.

Seidler, G. H., & Wagner, F. E. (2006). Comparing the efficacy of EMDR and trauma-focused cognitive-behavioral therapy in the treatment of PTSD: A meta-analytic study. *Psychological Medicine: A Journal of Research in Psychiatry and the Allied Sciences, 36*(11), 1515–1522.

Selekman, M. D. (1993). *Pathways to change: Brief therapy solutions with difficult adolescents.* New York, NY: Guilford Press.

Seligman, M.E.P. (1975). *Helplessness: On depression, develoment, and death.* San Francisco, CA: Freeman.

Selling, L. S. (1943). *Men against madness.* New York, NY: Garden City Books.

Selvini-Palazzoli, M., Boscolo, L., Cecchin, G., & Prata, G. (1974). The treatment of children through brief therapy of their parents. *Family Process, 13,* 429–442.

Serlin, I. (1999). An interview with Irvin Yalom. *Review of Existential Psychology and Psychiatry, 24*(1, 2, & 3), 142–146.

Sexton, T., & Turner, C. W. (2010). The effectiveness of functional family therapy for youth with behavioral problems in a community practice setting. *Journal of Family Psychology, 24*(3), 339–348.

Sexton, T. L., & Alexander, J. F. (2002). Functional family therapy: An empirically supported family-based intervention model for at-risk adolescents and their families. In T. Patterson (Ed.), *Comprehensive handbook of psychotherapy, Vol. II: Cognitive, behavioral, and functional approaches.* New York, NY: John Wiley & Sons.

Shadish, W. R., & Baldwin, S. A. (2002). Meta-analysis of MFT interventions. In D. H. Sprenkle (Ed.), *Effectiveness research in marriage and family therapy* (pp. 339–370). Alexandria, VA: American Association for Marriage and Family Therapy.

Shadish, W. R., Ragsdale, K., Glaser, R. R., & Montgomery, L. M. (1995). The efficacy and effectiveness of marital and family therapy: A perspective from meta-analysis. *Journal of Marital and Family Therapy. Special Issue: The Effectiveness of Marital and Family Therapy, 21*(4), 345–360.

Shah, I. (1966). *The exploits of the incomparable Mulla Nasrudin.* New York: Simon and Schuster.

Shapiro, F. (1989). Eye movement desensitization: A new treatment for post-traumatic stress disorder. *Journal of Behavior Therapy and Experimental Psychiatry, 20,* 211–217.

Shapiro, F. (1995). *Eye movement desensitization and reprocessing: Basic principles, protocols, and procedures.* New York, NY: Guilford Press.

Shapiro, F. (1999). Eye movement desensitization and reprocessing (EMDR) and the anxiety disorders: Clinical and research implications of an integrated psychotherapy treatment. *Journal of Anxiety Disorders, 13,* 35–67.

Shapiro, F. (2001). *Eye movement desensitization and reprocessing: Basic principles, protocols, and procedures* (2nd ed.). New York, NY: Guilford Press.

Shapiro, F. (2002). EMDR treatment: Overview and integration. In F. Shapiro (Ed.), *EMDR as an integrative psychotherapy approach: Experts of diverse orientations explore the paradigm prism* (pp. 27–55). New York: Guilford Press.

Sharaf, M. (1994). *Fury on earth: A biography of Wilhelm Reich.* New York, NY: Da Capo.

Shaw, B., & Beck, A. T. (1977). The treatment of depression with cognitive therapy. In A. Ellis & R. Grieger (Eds.), *Handbook of rational-emotive therapy* (pp. 309–326). New York, NY: Springer.

Shedler, J. (2010). The efficacy of psychodynamic psychotherapy. *American Psychologist, 65*(2), 98–109.

Shepard, M. (1972). *The love treatment.* New York, NY: Paperback Library.

Sherman, K. C. (2000). CT/RT in chronic pain management: Using choice Theory/Reality therapy as a cognitive-behavioral intervention for chronic pain management: A pilot study. *International Journal of Reality Therapy, 19*(2), 10–14.

Shoham-Salomon, V., & Rosenthal, R. (1987). Paradoxical interventions: A meta-analysis. *Journal of Consulting and Clinical Psychology, 55,* 22–28.

Shure, M. B. (1992). *I can problem solve: An interpersonal cognitive problem-solving program.* Champaign, IL: Research Press.

Sicher, L. (1935). A case of manic-depressive insanity. *International Journal of Individual Psychology, 1*(1), 40–56.

Sicher, L. (1991). A declaration of interdependence. *Individual Psychology, 47*(1), 10–16.

Siegel, D. J. (2007). Mindfulness training and neural integration: Differentiation of distinct streams of awareness and the cultivation of well-being. *Social Cognitive and Affective Neuroscience, 2*(4), 259–263.

Silverman, W. H. (1996). Cookbooks, manuals, and paint-by numbers: Psychotherapy in the 90's. *Psychotherapy, 33,* 207–215.

Simblett, G. J. (1997). Leila and the tiger: Narrative approaches to psychiatry. In G. Monk, J. Winslade, K. Crocket, & D. Epston (Eds.), *Narrative therapy in practice: The archaeology of hope* (pp. 121–157). San Francisco, CA: Jossey-Bass.

Simi, N. L., & Mahalik, J. R. (1997). Comparison of feminist versus psychoanalytic/dynamic and other therapists on self-disclosure. *Psychology of Women Quarterly, 21*(3), 465–483.

Simola, S. K. (1992). Differences among sexist, nonsexist and feminist family therapies. *Professional Psychology: Research and Practice, 23*(5), 397–403.

Skinner, B. F. (1938). *The behavior of organisms.* New York, NY: Appleton-Century-Crofts.

Skinner, B. F. (1948). *Walden two.* New York, NY: Macmillan.

Skinner, B. F. (1953). *Science and human behavior.* New York, NY: Macmillan.

Skinner, B. F. (1954). A new method for the experimental analysis of the behavior of psychotic patients. *Journal of Nervous and Mental Disease, 120,* 403–406.

Skinner, B. F. (1970). *Walden two* (Rev. ed.). London, England: Macmillan.

Skinner, B. F. (1971). *Beyond freedom and dignity.* New York, NY: Knopf.

Skinner, B. F. (1977). Why I am not a cognitive psychologist. *Behaviorism, 5,* 1–10.

Skinner, B. F., Solomon, H. C., & Lindsley, O. R. (1953). *Studies in behavior therapy: Status report I.* Unpublished report. Waltham, MA: Metropolitan State Hospital.

Smail, D. (1984). *Illusion & reality: The meaning of anxiety.* London, England: Constable.

Smith, B., Kenney, S. R., Sessoms, A. E., & Labrie, J. (2011). Assessing the efficacy of a choice theory-based alcohol harm reduction intervention on college students. *International Journal of Choice Theory and Reality Therapy, 30*(2), 52–60.

Smith, L., Constantine, M. G., Graham, S. V., & Dize, C. B. (2008). The territory ahead for multicultural competence: The "spinning" of racism. *Professional Psychology: Research and Practice, 39*(3), 337–345.

Smith, M. L., & Glass, G. V. (1977). Meta-analysis of psychotherapy outcome studies. *American Psychologist, 32*, 752–760.

Smith, M. L., Glass, G. V., & Miller, T. I. (1980). *The benefits of psychotherapy.* Baltimore, MD: Johns Hopkins University Press.

Smith, T. B., Constantine, M. G., Dunn, T. W., Dinehart, J. M., & Montoya, J. A. (2006). Multicultural education in the mental health professions: A meta-analytic review. *Journal of Counseling Psychology, 53*(1), 132–145.

Smuts, J. (1927). *Holism and evolution.* London: Macmillan.

Snow, M. G., Prochaska, J. O., & Rossi, J. S. (1992). Stages of change for smoking cessation among former problem drinkers. *Journal of Substance Abuse, 4*, 107–116.

Solomon, R. (1964). Punishment. *American Psychologist, 19*, 239–253.

Sommers-Flanagan, J. (2007). The development and evolution of person-centered expressive art therapy: A conversation with Natalie Rogers. *Journal of Counseling & Development, 85*(1), 120–125.

Sommers-Flanagan, J., Hays, P., Gallardo, M., Poyrazli, S., Sue, D. W., & Sommers-Flanagan, R. (2009, August). In J. Sommers-Flanagan (Chair), *The initial interview: Essential principles and techniques with diverse clients.* Symposium chair at the annual meeting of the American Psychological Association, Toronto, Ontario.

Sommers-Flanagan, J., & Heck, N. (2012). Counseling skills: Building the pillars of professional counseling. In K. MacCluskie & D. Perera (Eds.), *The counselor educator's survival guide* (pp. 149–166). New York, NY: Routledge.

Sommers-Flanagan, J., Richardson, B. G., & Sommers-Flanagan, R. (2011). A multi-theoretical, evidence-based approach for understanding and managing adolescent resistance to psychotherapy. *Journal of Contemporary Psychotherapy, 41*(2), 69–80.

Sommers-Flanagan, J., & Sommers-Flanagan, R. (2001). The three-step emotional change trick. In H. G. Kaduson & C. E. Schaefer (Eds.), *101 more favorite play therapy techniques* (pp. 439–444). New York: Jason Aronson.

Sommers-Flanagan, J., & Sommers-Flanagan, R. (Directors). (2004). *The challenge of counseling teens: Counselor behaviors that reduce resistance and facilitate connection.* [Video/DVD] North Amherst, MA: Microtraining Associates.

Sommers-Flanagan, J., & Sommers-Flanagan, R. (2007a). Our favorite tips for interviewing couples and families. *Psychiatric Clinics of North America, 30*(2), 275–281.

Sommers-Flanagan, J., & Sommers-Flanagan, R. (2007b). *Tough kids, cool counseling: User-friendly approaches with challenging youth* (2nd ed.). Alexandria, VA: American Counseling Association.

Sommers-Flanagan, J., & Sommers-Flanagan, R. (2009). *Clinical interviewing* (4th ed.). Hoboken, NJ: John Wiley & Sons.

Sommers-Flanagan, J., & Sommers-Flanagan, R. (2011). *How to listen so parents will talk and talk so parents will listen.* Hoboken, NJ: John Wiley & Sons.

Sommers-Flanagan, R. (2012). Boundaries, multiple roles, and the professional relationship. In. S. M. Knapp (Ed.), *APA handbook of ethics in psychology.* Washington, DC: American Psychological Association.

Sommers-Flanagan, R., Elliott, D., & Sommers-Flanagan, J. (1998). Exploring the edges: Boundaries and breaks. *Ethics & Behavior, 8*(1), 37–48.

Sommers-Flanagan, R., & Sommers-Flanagan, J. (2007). *Becoming an ethical helping professional: Cultural and philosophical foundations.* Hoboken, NJ: John Wiley & Sons.

Sommers-Flanagan, R., Sommers-Flanagan, J., & Welfel, E. R. (2009). The duty to protect and the ethical standards of professional organizations. In J. L. Werth, Jr., E. R. Welfel, & G. A. H. Benjamin (Eds.), *The duty to protect: Ethical, legal, and professional considerations for mental health professionals* (pp. 29–40). Washington, DC: American Psychological Association.

Sparks, E. E., & Park, A. H. (Eds.). (2002). *The integration of feminism and multiculturalism: Ethical dilemmas at the border.* Washington, DC: American Psychological Association.

Spence, J. A. (2009). Changes in perception of family environment and self-reported symptom status in adolescents whose parents participate in an Adlerian parent-training intervention (ProQuest Information & Learning). *Dissertation Abstracts International: Section B: The Sciences and Engineering, 69* (Electronic; Print).

Spiegler, M. D., & Guevremont, D. C. (2010). *Contemporary behavior therapy* (5th ed.). Belmont, CA: Wadsworth/Cengage Learning.

Spivack, G., Platt, J. J., & Shure, M. B. (1976). *The problem-solving approach to adjustment*. San Francisco, CA: Jossey-Bass.

St. Clair, M., & Wigren, J. (2004). *Object relations and self psychology: An introduction* (4th ed.). Belmont, CA: Brooks/Cole.

Staemmler, F. (2004). Dialogue and interpretation in Gestalt therapy: Making sense together. *International Gestalt Journal, 27*(2), 33–57.

Stanton, M. D., & Shadish, W. R. (1997). Outcome, attrition, and family–couples treatment for drug abuse: A meta-analysis and review of the controlled, comparative studies. *Psychological Bulletin, 122*(2), 170–191.

Stark, E., & von der Haar, H. (1977). On the double-bind hypothesis in schizophrenia research. *Psychologische Rundschau, 28*(1), 31–44.

Stern, D. N. (1985). *The interpersonal world of the infant*. New York, NY: Basic Books.

Sternberg, R. J., Roediger, H. L., & Halpern, D. F. (Eds.). (2007). *Critical thinking in psychology*. New York, NY: Cambridge University Press.

Stewart, S. H., & Watt, M. C. (2008). Introduction to the special issue on interoceptive exposure in the treatment of anxiety and related disorders: Novel applications and mechanisms of action. *Journal of Cognitive Psychotherapy, 22*(4), 291–302.

Stiles, W. B., Barkham, M., Mellor-Clark, J., & Connell, J. (2008). Effectiveness of cognitive-behavioural, person-centred, and psychodynamic therapies in UK primary-care routine practice: Replication in a larger sample. *Psychological Medicine: A Journal of Research in Psychiatry and the Allied Sciences, 38*(5), 677–688.

Story, T. J., & Craske, M. G. (2008). Responses to false physiological feedback in individuals with panic attacks and elevated anxiety sensitivity. *Behaviour Research and Therapy, 46*(9), 1001–1008.

Strong, T., & Pyle, N. R. (2009). Constructing a conversational "miracle": Examining the "miracle question" as it is used in therapeutic dialogue. *Journal of Constructivist Psychology, 22*(4), 328–353.

Strong, T., Pyle, N. R., & Sutherland, O. (2009). Scaling questions: Asking and answering them in counselling. *Counselling Psychology Quarterly, 22*(2), 171–185.

Sturmey, P. (2009). Behavioral activation is an evidence-based treatment for depression. *Behavior Modification, 33*(6), 818–829.

Sue, D., & Sue, D. W. (2008). *Foundations of counseling and psychotherapy: Evidence-based practices for a diverse society*. Hoboken, NJ: John Wiley & Sons.

Sue, D. W. (2010). *Microaggressions in everyday life: Race, gender, and sexual orientation*. Hoboken, NJ: John Wiley & Sons.

Sue, D. W. (2010). Microaggressions and marginality. Hoboken, NJ: John Wiley & Sons.

Sue, D. W., Arredondo, P., & McDavis, R. J. (1992). Multicultural counseling competencies and standards: A call to the profession. *Journal of Counseling & Development, 70*(4), 477–486.

Sue, D. W., Bernier, J. E., Durran, A., Feinberg, L., Pedersen, P., Smith, E. J., & Vasquez-Nuttall, E. (1982). Position paper: Cross-cultural counseling competencies. *The Counseling Psychologist, 10*, 45–52.

Sue, D. W., Bingham, R., Porche-Burke, L., & Vasquez, M.J.T. (1999). The diversification of psychology: A multicultural revolution. *American Psychologist, 54*, 1061–1069.

Sue, D. W., Carter, R. T., Casas, J. M., Fouad, N. A., Ivey, A. E., Jensen, M., et al. (1998). *Multicultural counseling competencies: Individual and organizational development*. Thousand Oaks, CA: Sage.

Sue, D. W., Rivera, D. P., Capodilupo, C. M., Lin, A. I., & Torino, G. C. (2010). Racial dialogues and white trainee fears: Implications for education and training. *Cultural Diversity and Ethnic Minority Psychology, 16*(2), 206–214.

Sue, D. W., & Sue, D. (2008). *Counseling the culturally diverse* (5th ed.). Hoboken, NJ: John Wiley & Sons.

Sue, D. W., & Torino, G. C. (2005). *Racial-cultural competence: Awareness, knowledge, and skills*. Hoboken, NJ: John Wiley & Sons.

Sue, S. (1977). Community mental health services to minority groups: Some optimism, some pessimism. *American Psychologist, 32*, 616–624.

Sue, S. (1998). In search of cultural competence in psychotherapy and counseling. *American Psychologist, 53*(4), 440–448.

Sue, S., Fujino, D., Takeuchi, D., & Zane, N. (1991). Community mental health services for ethnic minority groups: A test of the cultural responsiveness hypothesis. *Journal of Consulting & Clinical Psychology, 59*, 533–540.

Sue, S., & Zane, N. (2009). The role of culture and cultural techniques in psychotherapy: A critique and reformulation. *Asian American Journal of Psychology, S*(1), 3–14.

Sulliman, J. R. (1973). The development of a scale for the measurement of social interest (ProQuest Information & Learning). *Dissertation Abstracts International, 34* (6-B) (Electronic; Print).

Sullivan, H. S. (1953). *The interpersonal theory of psychiatry.* New York: Norton.

Sulloway, F. J., & Zweigenhaft, R. L. (2010). Birth order and risk taking in athletics: A meta-analysis and study of major league baseball. *Personality and Social Psychology Review, 14*(4), 402–416.

Sweeney, T. J. (2009). *Adlerian counseling and psychotherapy: A practitioner's approach* (5th ed.). New York, NY: Routledge/Taylor & Francis.

Szapocznik, J., Feaster, D. J., Mitrani, V. B., Prado, G., Smith, L., Robinson-Batista, C., et al. (2004). Structural ecosystems therapy for HIV-seropositive African American women: Effects on psychological distress, family hassles, and family support. *Journal of Consulting and Clinical Psychology, 72*(2), 288–303.

Szapocznik, J., & Kurtines, W. M. (1989). *Breakthroughs in family therapy with drug abusing and problem youth.* New York, NY: Springer.

Szapocznik, J., Lopez, B., Prado, G., Schwartz, S. J., & Pantin, H. (2006). Outpatient drug abuse treatment for Hispanic adolescents. *Drug and Alcohol Dependence, 84*(S1), S54–S63.

Szasz, T. S. (1970). *The manufacture of madness.* New York, NY: McGraw-Hill.

Takeuchi, D., Sue, S., & Yeh, M. (1995). Return rates and outcomes from ethnicity-specific mental health programs in Los Angeles. *American Journal of Public Health, 85*, 638–643.

Talbot, N. L., Chaudron, L. H., Ward, E. A., Duberstein, P. R., Conwell, Y., O'Hara, M. W., et al. (2011). A randomized effectiveness trial of interpersonal psychotherapy for depressed women with sexual abuse histories. *Psychiatric Services, 62*(4), 374–380.

Taylor, J. A. (1975). Early recollections as a projective technique: A review of some recent validation studies. *Journal of Individual Psychology, 31*(2), 213–218.

Taylor, S. (2002). *The tending instinct: Women, men and the biology of our relationships.* New York, NY: Henry Holt.

Taylor, S., Thordarson, D. S., Maxfield, L., Fedoroff, I. C., Lovell, K., & Ogrodniczuk, J. (2003). Comparative efficacy, speed, and adverse effects of three PTSD treatments: Exposure therapy, EMDR, and relaxation training. *Journal of Consulting and Clinical Psychology, 71*(2), 330–338.

Taylor, S. E., & Gonzaga, G. C. (2007). Affiliative responses to stress: A social neuroscience model. In E. Harmon-Jones & P. Winkielman (Eds.), *Social neuroscience: Integrating biological and psychological explanations of social behavior* (pp. 454–473). New York, NY: Guilford Press.

Taylor, S. E., Klein, L. C., Lewis, B. P., Gruenewald, T. L., Gurung, R. A. R., & Updegraff, J. A. (2000). Biobehavioral responses to stress in females: Tend-and-befriend, not fight-or-flight. *Psychological Review, 107*(3), 411–429.

Taylor, S. E., & Master, S. L. (2011). *Social responses to stress: The tend-and-befriend model.* New York, NY: Springer.

Terman, L. (1916). *The measurement of intelligence.* Boston, MA: Houghton Mifflin.

Thombs, B. D., Jewett, L. R., & Bassel, M. (2011). Is there room for criticism of studies of psychodynamic psychotherapy? *American Psychologist, 66*(2), 148–149.

Thorndike, E. L. (1911). *Animal intelligence.* New York, NY: Macmillan.

Thorndike, E. L. (1932). *The fundamentals of learning.* New York, NY: Teachers College, Columbia University.

Tillich, P. (1961). Existentialism and psychotherapy. *Review of Existential Psychology & Psychiatry, 1*, 8–16.

Tjeltveit, A. C. (1999). *Ethics and values in psychotherapy.* New York, NY: Routledge.

Tjeltveit, A. C. (2006). To what ends? Psychotherapy goals and outcomes, the good life, and the principle of beneficence. *Psychotherapy: Theory, Research, 43*(2), 186–200.

Tohn, S. L., & Oshlag, J. A. (1996). Solution-focused therapy with mandated clients: Cooperating with the uncooperative. In M. F. Hoyt (Ed.), *Handbook of solution-focused brief therapy* (pp. 152–183). San Francisco, CA: Jossey-Bass.

Tolan, P., Szapocznik, J., & Sambrano, S. (Eds.). (2007). *Preventing youth substance abuse: Science-based programs for children and adolescents.* Washington, DC: American Psychological Association.

Tolstoy, L. (1929). *My confession, my religion, the gospel in brief.* New York, NY: Scribner.

Tønnesvang, J., Sommer, U., Hammink, J., & Sonne, M. (2010). Gestalt therapy and cognitive therapy—Contrasts or complementarities? *Psychotherapy: Theory, Research, Practice, Training, 47*(4), 586–602.

Touchette, E., Henegar, A., Godart, N. T., Pryor, L., Falissard, B., Tremblay, R. E., et al. (2011). Subclinical eating disorders and their comorbidity with mood and anxiety disorders in adolescent girls. *Psychiatry Research, 185*(1–2), 185–192.

Truax, P. (2002). Behavioral case conceptualization for adults. In M. Hersen (Ed.), *Clinical behavior therapy: Adults and children* (pp. 3–36). New York: John Wiley & Sons.

Treatment for Adolescents With Depression Study (TADS) Team. (2004). Fluoxetine, cognitive-behavioral therapy, and their combination for adolescents with depression: Treatment for adolescents with depression study (TADS) randomized controlled trial. *JAMA: Journal of the American Medical Association, 292*(7), 807–820.

Turner, E. H., Matthews, A. M., Linardatos, E., Tell, R. A., & Rosenthal, R. (2008). Selective publication of antidepressant trials and its influence on apparent efficacy. *New England Journal of Medicine, 358*(3), 252–260.

Twohig, M. P., Hayes, S. C., Plumb, J. C., Pruitt, L. D., Collins, A. B., Hazlett-Stevens, H., et al. (2010). A randomized clinical trial of acceptance and commitment therapy versus progressive relaxation training for obsessive-compulsive disorder. *Journal of Consulting and Clinical Psychology, 78*(5), 705–716.

Unger, R. K. (Ed.). (2001). *Handbook of the psychology of women and gender*. New York, NY: John Wiley & Sons.

Vaihinger, H. (1911). *The psychology of "as if."* New York, NY: Harcourt, Brace and World.

van den Bosch, L. M. C., Verheul, R., Schippers, G. M., & van den Brink, W. (2002). Dialectical behavior therapy of borderline patients with and without substance use problems: Implementation and long-term effects. *Addictive Behaviors. Special Issue: Integration Substance Abuse Treatment and Prevention in the Community, 27*(6), 911–923.

van der Kolk, B. A., Spinazzola, J., Blaustein, M. E., Hopper, J. W., Hopper, E. K., Korn, D. L., et al. (2007). A randomized clinical trial of eye movement desensitization and reprocessing (EMDR), fluoxetine, and pill placebo in the treatment of posttraumatic stress disorder: Treatment effects and long-term maintenance. *Journal of Clinical Psychiatry, 68*(1), 37–46.

van der Pompe, G., Duivenvoorden, H. J., Antoni, M. H., & Visser, A. (1997). Effectiveness of a short-term group psychotherapy program on endocrine and immune function in breast cancer patients: An exploratory study. *Journal of Psychosomatic Research, 42*(5), 453–466.

van Deurzen, E. (1998). *Paradox and passion in psychotherapy: An existential approach to therapy and counselling.* Hoboken, NJ: John Wiley & Sons.

van Deurzen, E. (2010). *Everyday mysteries: A handbook of existential psychotherapy* (2nd ed.). New York, NY: Routledge/Taylor & Francis.

van Deurzen-Smith, E. (1997). *Everyday mysteries: Existential dimensions of psychotherapy.* London, England: Routledge.

van Deurzen-Smith, E. (1988). *Existential counselling in practice.* Thousand Oaks, CA: Sage Publications, Inc.

Villares, E., Brigman, G., & Peluso, P. R. (2008). Ready to learn: An evidence-based individual psychology linked curriculum for prekindergarten through first grade. *The Journal of Individual Psychology, 64*(4), 403–415.

Von Bertalanffy, L. (1950). An outline of general system theory. *British Journal for the Philosophy of Science, 1*, 134–165.

Vontress, C. E., Johnson, J. A., & Epp, L. R. (1999). *Cross-cultural counseling: A casebook.* Alexandria, VA: American Counseling Association.

Vromans, L. P., & Schweitzer, R. D. (2011). Narrative therapy for adults with major depressive disorder: Improved symptom and interpersonal outcomes. *Psychotherapy Research, 21*(1), 4–15.

Vygotsky, L. (1962). *Thought and language.* New York: John Wiley & Sons.

Wachtel, P. L. (1977). *Psychoanalysis and behavior therapy: Toward an integration.* New York, NY: Basic Books.

Wachtel, P. L. (2008). *Relational theory and the practice of psychotherapy.* New York, NY: Guilford Press.

Wachtel, P. L. (2010). One-person and two-person conceptions of attachment and their implications for psychoanalytic thought. *The International Journal of Psychoanalysis, 91*(3), 561–581.

Wagner-Moore, L. E. (2004). Gestalt therapy: Past, present, theory, and research. *Psychotherapy: Theory, Research, 41*(2), 180–189.

Waldron, H. B., Slesnick, N., Brody, J. L., Turner, C. W., & Peterson, T. R. (2001). Treatment outcomes for adolescent substance abuse at 4- and 7-month assessments. *Journal of Consulting and Clinical Psychology, 69*, 802–813.

Wallen, R. (1970). Gestalt therapy and Gestalt psychology. In J. Fagan & I. L. Shepherd (Eds.), *What is gestalt therapy?* (pp. 1–10). New York, NY: Science and Behavior Books.

Wallin, D. J. (2007). *Attachment in psychotherapy.* New York, NY: Guilford Press.

Waltz, J. (2003). Dialectical behavior therapy in the treatment of abusive behavior. *Journal of Aggression, Maltreatment & Trauma, 7*(1–2), 75–103.

Wampold, B. E. (2001). *The great psychotherapy debate: Models, methods, and findings.* Mahwah, NJ: Lawrence Erlbaum Associates.

Wampold, B. E. (2010). *The basics of psychotherapy: An introduction to theory and practice.* Washington, DC: American Psychological Association.

Wampold, B. E., Mondin, G. W., Moody, M., Stich, F., Benson, K., & Ahn, H. (1997). A meta-analysis of outcome studies comparing bona fide psychotherapies: Empiricially, "all must have prizes." *Psychological Bulletin, 122*(3), 203–215.

Warrington, J. (Ed.). (1956). *Aristotle's metaphysics.* New York: Dutton.

Watson, J. B. (1913). Psychology as a behaviorist views it. *Psychological Review, 20,* 158–177.

Watson, J. B. (1924). *Behaviorism.* Chicago, IL: University of Chicago Press.

Watson, J. B., & Rayner, R. (1920). Conditioned emotional reactions. *Journal of Experimental Psychology, 3,* 1–14.

Watson, J. C., Goldman, R. N., & Greenberg, L. S. (2007). Case studies in emotion-focused treatment of depression: A comparison of good and poor outcome. Washington, DC: American Psychological Association.

Watson, J. C., Goldman, R. N., & Greenberg, L. S. (2011). Humanistic and experiential theories of psychotherapy. In J. C. Norcross, G. R. VandenBos, & D. K. Freedheim (Eds.), *History of psychotherapy: Continuity and change* (2nd ed., pp. 141–172). Washington, DC: American Psychological Association.

Watson, J. C., Gordon, L. B., Stermac, L., Kalogerakos, F., & Steckley, P. (2003). Comparing the effectiveness of process-experiential with cognitive-behavioral psychotherapy in the treatment of depression. *Journal of Consulting and Clinical Psychology, 71*(4), 773–781.

Watts, R. E. (Ed.). (2003). *Adlerian, cognitive, and constructivist therapies: An integrative perspective.* New York: Springer.

Watts, R. E., & Eckstein, D. (2009). Individual psychology. In American Counseling Association (Ed.), *The ACA encyclopedia of counseling* (pp. 281–283). Alexandria, VA: American Counseling Association.

Watts, R. E., & Garza, Y. (2008). Using children's drawings to facilitate the acting "as if" technique. *The Journal of Individual Psychology, 64*(1), 113–118.

Watts, R. E., & Holden, J. M. (1994). Why continue to use "fictional finalism?" *Individual Psychology: Journal of Adlerian Theory, Research & Practice, 50*(2), 161–163.

Watts, R. E., & Peluso, P. R. (2005). Imaginary team members: A couples counseling perspective. *The Family Journal, 13*(3), 332–335.

Watts, R. E., Peluso, P. R., & Lewis, T. F. (2005). Psychological strategies. *The Journal of Individual Psychology, 61,* 380–387.

Watts, R. E., & Pietrzak, D. (2000a). Adlerian "encouragement" and the therapeutic process of solution-focused brief therapy. *Journal of Counseling & Development, 78,* 442–447.

Watzlawick, P., Beavin, J. H., & Jackson, D. D. (1967). *Pragmatics of human communication.* New York, NY: Norton.

Weakland, J. (1962). Family therapy as a research arena. *Family Process, 1*(1), 63–68.

Weakland, J. H. (1993). Conversation—but what kind? In S. G. Gilligan & R. Price (Eds.), *Therapeutic conversations* (pp. 136–145). New York, NY: Norton.

Webb, L., Lemberger, M., & Brigman, G. (2008). Student success skills: A review of a school counselor intervention influenced by individual psychology. *The Journal of Individual Psychology, 64,* 339–352.

Weber, D. A. (2003). A comparison of individual psychology and attachment theory. *The Journal of Individual Psychology, 59*(3), 246–262.

Weber, M., Colon, M., & Nelson, M. (2008). Pilot study of a cognitive-behavioral group intervention to prevent further weight gain in Hispanic individuals with schizophrenia. *Journal of the American Psychiatric Nurses Association, 13*(6), 353–359.

Weiner, I. B., & Bornstein, R. F. (2009). *Principles of psychotherapy: Promoting evidence-based psychodynamic practice* (3rd ed.). Hoboken, NJ: John Wiley & Sons.

Weiner-Davis, M. (1993). Pro-constructed realities. In S. G. Gilligan & R. Price (Eds.), *Therapeutic conversations* (pp. 149–157). New York, NY: Norton.

Weishaar, M. E. (1993). *Aaron T. Beck.* London, England: Sage.

Weissman, M. M., Markowitz, J. C., & Klerman, G. L. (2000). *Comprehensive guide to interpersonal psychotherapy.* New York, NY: Basic Books.

Weisz, J. R., Weiss, B., Alicke, M. D., & Klotz, M. L. (1987). Effectiveness of psychotherapy with children and adolescents: A meta-analysis for clinicians. *Journal of Consulting & Clinical Psychology, 55,* 542–549.

Weisz, J. R., Weiss, B., Han, S. S., Granger, D. A., & Morton, T. (1995). Effects of psychotherapy with children and adolescents revisited: A meta-analysis of treatment outcome studies. *Psychological Bulletin, 117,* 450–468.

Welfel, E. R. (2006). *Ethics in counseling and psychotherapy: Standards, research, and emerging issues* (3rd ed.). Belmont, CA: Thomson Brooks/Cole.

Wells, M. G., Burlingame, G. M., Lambert, M. J., Hoag, M. J., & Hope, C. A. (1996). Conceptualization and measurement of patient change during psychotherapy: Development of the outcome questionnaire and youth outcome questionnaire. *Psychotherapy: Theory, Research, 33*(2), 275–283.

West, J. D., Watts, R. E., Trepal, H. C., Wester, K. L., & Lewis, T. F. (2001). Opening space for client reflection: A postmodern consideration. *The Family Journal, 9*(4), 431–437.

Wheeler, G. (2005). Culture, self, and field: A Gestalt guide to the age of complexity. *Gestalt Review, 9*(1), 91–128.

Wheeler, G. (2006). New directions in Gestalt theory and practice: Psychology and psychotherapy in the age of complexity. *International Gestalt Journal, 29*(1), 9–41.

Wheeler, M. S., Kern, R. M., & Curlette, W. L. (1991). Life-style can be measured. *Individual Psychology: Journal of Adlerian Theory, Research & Practice, 47*(2), 229–240.

Whitaker, C. A. (1958). Psychotherapy with couples. *American Journal of Psychotherapy, 12,* 18–23.

Whitaker, C. S., & Malone, T. P. (1981). *The roots of psychotherapy.* New York, NY: Brunner/Mazel.

Whitaker, R. (2010). *Anatomy of an epidemic: Magic bullets, psychiatric drugs, and the astonishing rise of mental illness in America.* New York, NY: Crown Publishers/Random House.

White, L. (1994). *Stranger at the gate.* New York, NY: Simon & Schuster.

White, M. (1988). The process of questioning: A therapy of literary merit? *Dulwich Centre Newsletter,* 8–14.

White, M. (1993). Commentary: The histories of the present. In S. G. Gilligan & R. Price (Eds.), *Therapeutic conversations* (pp. 121–135). New York, NY: Norton.

White, M. (1995). *Re-authoring lives: Interviews and essays.* Adelaide, South Australia: Dulwich Centre.

White, M. (2007). *Maps of narrative practice.* New York, NY: Norton.

White, M., & Denborough, D. (2011). *Narrative practice: Continuing the conversations.* New York, NY: Norton.

White, M., & Epston, D. (1990). *Narrative means to therapeutic ends.* New York, NY: Norton.

Whitehouse, D. (1984). Adlerian antecedents to reality therapy and control theory. *Journal of Reality Therapy, 3,* 10–14.

Wickman, S. A., & Campbell, C. (2003). An analysis of how Carl Rogers enacted client-centered conversation with Gloria. *Journal of Counseling & Development, 81,* 178–184.

Wiener, N. (1948). Cybernetics. *Scientific American, 170*(5), 14–18.

Wilcocks, R. (1994). *Maelzel's chess player: Sigmund Freud and the rhetoric of deceit.* Lanham, MD, England: Rowman & Littlefield.

Williams, A. M., Diehl, N. S., & Mahoney, M. J. (2002). Mirror-time: Empirical findings and implications for a constructivist psychotherapeutic technique. *Journal of Constructivist Psychology, 15*(1), 21–39.

Williams, R. J., & Chang, S. Y. (2000). A comprehensive and comparative review of adolescent substance abuse treatment outcome. *Clinical Psychology: Science and Practice, 7*(2), 138–166.

Wilson, E. O. (1999). *Conscilience.* New York, NY: Random House.

Winnicott, D. W. (1965). *The maturational process and the facilitative environment.* New York, NY: International Universities Press.

Winnicott, D. W. (1975). *Through paediatrics to psychoanalysis: Collected papers.* Philadelphia, PA: Brunner/Mazel.

Winslade, J. M., & Monk, G. D. (2007). *Narrative counseling in schools: Powerful & brief* (2nd ed.). Thousand Oaks, CA: Corwin Press.

Wittgenstein, L. (1968). *Philosophical investigations* (3rd ed.). New York, NY: Macmillan.

Woldt, A. L., & Toman, S. M. (2005). *Gestalt therapy: History, theory, and practice.* Thousand Oaks, CA: Sage.

Wolfson, A. R. (1999). Cognitive behavior therapy: Is it working for women? *Behavior Therapist, 22,* 197–199.

Wolitzky, D. L., & Eagle, M. N. (1997). Psychoanalytic theories of psychotherapy. In P. L. Wachtel & S. B. Messer (Eds.), *Theories of psychotherapy: Origins and evolution* (pp. 39–96). Washington, DC: American Psychological Association.

Wolpe, J. (1948). *An approach to the problem of neurosis based on the conditioned response.* University of the Witwatersrand.

Wolpe, J. (1954). Reciprocal inhibition as the main basis of psychotherapeutic effects. *Proceedings of the South African Psychological Association No, 5,* 14.

Wolpe, J. (1958). *Psychotherapy by reciprocal inhibition.* Stanford, CA: Stanford University Press.

Wolpe, J. (1973). *The practice of behavior therapy* (2nd ed.). Elmsford, NY: Pergamon.

Wolpe, J. (1987). The promotion of scientific psychotherapy: A long voyage. In J. K. Zeig (Ed.), *The evolution of psychotherapy* (pp. 133–148). New York, NY: Brunner/Mazel.

Wolpe, J., & Plaud, J. J. (1997). Pavlov's contributions to behavior therapy: The obvious and the not so obvious. *American Psychologist, 52*(9), 966–972.

Wong, P.T.P. (2008a). Meaning management theory and death acceptance. In A. Tomer, G. T. Eliason, & P.T.P. Wong (Eds.), *Death attitudes: Existential & spiritual issues* (pp. 65–87). Mahwah, NJ: Lawrence Erlbaum.

Wong, P.T.P. (2008b). Transformation of grief through meaning: Meaning-centered counseling for bereavement. In A. Tomer, G. T. Eliason, & P.T.P. Wong (Eds.), *Death attitudes: Existential & spiritual issues* (pp. 375–396). Mahwah, NJ: Erlbaum.

Wood, J. M., Lilienfeld, S. O., Nezworski, M. T., Garb, H. N., Allen, K. H., & Wildermuth, J. L. (2010). Validity of Rorschach inkblot scores for discriminating psychopaths from nonpsychopaths in forensic populations: A meta-analysis. *Psychological Assessment, 22*(2), 336–349.

Wood, J. M., Nezworski, M. T., Lilienfeld, S. O., & Garbm, H. N. (2008). *The Rorschach inkblot test, fortune tellers, and cold reading*. Amherst, NY: Prometheus Books.

Woodside, M., Oberman, A. H., Cole, K. G., & Carruth, E. K. (2007). Learning to be a counselor: A pre-practicum point of view. *Counselor Education and Supervision, 47*(1), 14–28.

Worell, J., & Chandler, R. (1996). *Personal progress scale*. Unpublished manuscript.

Worell, J., Chandler, R., & Robinson, D. (1996). *Client therapy with women scale*. Unpublished manuscript.

Worell, J., & Johnson, D. (2003). Therapy with women: Feminist frameworks. In R. K. Unger (Ed.), *Handbook of the psychology of women and gender* (pp. 317–329). Hoboken, NJ: John Wiley & Sons.

Worell, J., & Remer, P. (2003). *Feminist perspectives in therapy: Empowering diverse women* (2nd ed.). Hoboken, NJ: John Wiley & Sons.

Wozniak, R. H. (Ed.). (1993). *Theoretical roots of early behaviourism: Functionalism, the critique of introspection, and the nature and evolution of consciousness*. London, England: Routledge/Thoemmes Press; Tokyo 156, Japan: Kinokuniya Co.

Wright, L. K. (2002). Book review: Letters to a young feminist. *Women & Therapy, 25*(1), 113–115.

Wubbolding, R. E. (1988). *Using reality therapy*. New York, NY: Harper & Row.

Wubbolding, R. E. (1991). Understanding reality therapy. New York: Harper & Row.

Wubbolding, R. E. (1999). Client inner self-evaluation: A necessary prelude to change. In H. G. Rosenthal (Ed.), *Favorite counseling and therapy techniques* (pp. 196–197). Washington, DC: Accelerated Development.

Wubbolding, R. E. (2000). *Reality therapy for the 21st century*. Muncie, IN: Accelerated Development.

Wubbolding, R. E. (2009). Applying reality therapy approaches in schools. In R. W. Christner, & R. B. Mennuti (Eds.), *School-based mental health: A practitioner's guide to comparative practices* (pp. 225–250). New York, NY: Routledge/Taylor & Francis.

Wubbolding, R. E. (2011). *Reality therapy*. Washington, DC: American Psychological Association.

Wubbolding, R. E., Al-Rashidi, B., Brickell, J., Kakitani, M., Kim, R. I., Lennon, B., et al. (1998). Multicultural awareness: Implications for reality therapy and choice theory. *International Journal of Reality Therapy, 17,* 4–6.

Wubbolding, R. E., & Brickell, J. (2000). Misconceptions about reality therapy. *International Journal of Reality Therapy, 19*(2), 64–65.

Wubbolding, R. E., Brickell, J., Imhof, L., Kim, R. I., Lojk, L., & Al-Rashidi, B. (2004). Reality therapy: A global perspective. *International Journal for the Advancement of Counselling, 26*(3), 219–228.

Wubbolding, R. E., Brickell, J., Loi, I., & Al-Rashidi, B. (2001). The why and how of self-evaluation. *International Journal of Reality Therapy, 21,* 36–37.

Wulfing, N. (2008). Anxiety in existential philosophy and the question of the paradox. *Existential Analysis, 19*(1), 73–80.

Yakushko, O., & Espín, O. M. (2010). *The experience of immigrant and refugee women: Psychological issues*. New York, NY: Springer.

Yalom, I. D. (1980). *Existential psychotherapy*. New York, NY: Basic Books.

Yalom, I. D. (1989). *Love's executioner*. New York, NY: Basic Books.

Yalom, I. D. (1992). *When Nietzsche wept*. New York, NY: HarperCollins.

Yalom, I. D. (1995). *Theory and practice of group psychotherapy*. New York, NY: Basic Books.

Yalom, I. D. (1999). *Momma and the meaning of life: Tales of psychotherapy*. New York, NY: Basic Books.

Yalom, I. D. (2002). *The gift of therapy*. New York, NY: HarperCollins.

Yalom, I. D. (2003). Existential psychotherapy and religious consolation: A short comment. *Tidsskrift for Norsk Psykologforening, 40*(11), 936–936.

Yalom, I. D., & Leszcz, M. (2005). *The theory and practice of group psychotherapy* (5th ed.). New York, NY: Basic Books.

Yontef, G. (1988). Assimilating diagnostic and psychoanalytic perspectives into gestalt therapy. *Gestalt Journal, 11*(1), 5–32.

Yontef, G. (2002). The relational attitude in Gestalt therapy theory and practice. *International Gestalt Journal, 25*, 15–35.

Yontef, G. (2005). The relational attitude in Gestalt therapy theory and practice. *Gestalt!, 9*(2).

Yontef, G. (2010). "From the radical center: The heart of Gestalt therapy" Erving and Miriam Polster, person and process. *Gestalt Review, 14*(1), 29–36.

Young, B. W., Medic, N., & Starkes, J. L. (2009). Effects of self-monitoring training logs on behaviors and beliefs of swimmers. *Journal of Applied Sport Psychology, 21*(4), 413–428.

Young, J. F., Mufson, L., & Davies, M. (2006). Efficacy of interpersonal psychotherapy-adolescent skills training: An indicated preventive intervention for depression. *Journal of Child Psychology and Psychiatry, 47*(12), 1254–1262.

Young, J. F., Mufson, L., & Gallop, R. (2010). Preventing depression: A randomized trial of interpersonal psychotherapy-adolescent skills training. *Depression and Anxiety, 27*(5), 426–433.

Young, K. M., Northern, J. J., Lister, K. M., Drummond, J. A., & O'Brien, W. H. (2007). A meta-analysis of family-behavioral weight-loss treatments for children. *Clinical Psychology Review, 27*(2), 240–249.

Zeig, J. (2010). An interview with Jeffrey K. Zeig. *Australian Journal of Clinical Hypnotherapy and Hypnosis, 31*, 10–30.

Zetzel, E. R. (1956). Current concepts of transference. *International Journal of Psychoanalysis, 37*, 369–376.

Zucker, K. J. (2001). Biological influences on psychosexual differentiation. In R. K. Unger (Ed.), *Handbook of the psychology of women and gender* (pp. 101–115). New York, NY: John Wiley & Sons.

Zwolinski, J. (2008). Biopsychosocial responses to social rejection in targets of relational aggression. *Biological Psychology, 79*(2), 260–267.

Photo Credits

About the Authors

Photo of John and Rita Sommers-Flanagan Page xvii

Todd Johnson, University of Montana

Chapter 2

Photo of Sigmund Freud Page 41

© Mary Evans Picture Library / Alamy

Photo of Anna Freud Page 51

© Mary Evans Picture Library / Alamy

Chapter 3

Photo of Alfred Adler Page 80

© Everett Collection Inc. / Alamy

Chapter 4

Photo of Viktor Frankl Page 123

Getty Images

Photo of Rollo May Page 124

Getty Images

Chapter 5

Photo of Carl Rogers Page 154

Courtesy of the Department of Special Collections, Davidson Library, University of California, Santa Barbara

Photo of Natalie Rogers Page 163

Fiona Chang

Chapter 7

Photo of John B. Watson Page 226

Courtesy of Furman University

Photo of Mary Cover Jones Page 227

© G. Paul Bishop

Photo of B. F. Skinner Page 228

© Everett Collection Inc. / Alamy

Chapter 8

Photo of Judith Beck Page 264

Photo Courtesy of Beck Institute for Cognitive Behavior Therapy

Photo of Albert Ellis Page 266

Courtesy of the Albert Ellis Institute

Photo of Aaron Beck Page 268

Photo Courtesy of Beck Institute for Cognitive Behavior Therapy

Chapter 9

Photo of William Glasser Page 301

Courtesy of the Willam Glasser Institute

Photo of Robert E. Wubbolding Page 314

Courtesy of the Center for Reality Therapy

Chapter 10

Photo of Karen Horney Page 337

Courtesy of Culver Pictures, Inc.

Photo of Laura Brown Page 355

Lynn Brown

Chapter 11

Photo of Milton Erickson Page 371

Courtesy of The Milton H. Erickson Foundation, Inc., www.erickson -foundation.org

Chapter 12

Photo of Salvador Minuchin Page 420

Courtesy of Salvador Minuchin

Photo of Virginia Satir Page 427

Used with permission of the Virginia Satir Global Network/www.satirglobal .org, All Rights Reserved.

Chapter 13

Photo of Derald Wing Sue Page 446

Courtesy of Derald Wing Sue

Chapter 14

Photo of Francine Shapiro Page 484

Courtesy of Francine Shapiro

Photo of Leslie Greenberg Page 491

Photo Courtesy of Leslie Greenberg

Photo of Marsha Linehan Page 494

Courtesy of Marsha Linehan

Name Index

Subject Index

About the Video Resource Center

Please visit www.wiley.com/go/videoresourcecenter to register and gain access to the videos for *Counseling and Psychotherapy Theories in Context and Practice: Skills, Strategies, and Techniques, Second Edition*. Your copy of this book contains an access code for the VRC. Please follow the directions for registration that are included with the access code.

If you purchased a used copy of this book, the access code included with this book will not work. However, you can buy access to the VRC at www.wiley.com/go/videoresourcecenter.

WHAT'S AVAILABLE AT THE VIDEO RESOURCE CENTER

The VRC features videos of 11 different therapy approaches in action, plus an introduction to the videos from the authors, John and Rita Sommers-Flanagan. The videos are not scripted and the diverse range of clients and therapists are not actors—they are real therapists and volunteer clients talking about real issues. The therapeutic approaches covered are:

- Psychoanalytic Approaches
- Adlerian Therapy
- Existential Therapy
- Person-Centered Therapy
- Gestalt Therapy
- Behavioral Therapy
- Cognitive-Behavioral Therapy
- Reality Therapy
- Feminist Therapy
- Solution-Focused Therapy
- Family Systems Therapy

CUSTOMER CARE

Thank you for purchasing for *Counseling and Psychotherapy Theories in Context and Practice: Skills, Strategies, and Techniques, Second Edition*. If you need any assistance with the VRC, please contact Wiley Customer Care at (877) 762-2974 or Wiley Product Technical Support at http://support.wiley.com.